THE OXFORD HANDBOOK OF

THE AMERICAN

MUSICAL

THE OXFORD HANDBOOK OF

THE AMERICAN MUSICAL

Edited by

RAYMOND KNAPP

MITCHELL MORRIS

STACY WOLF

OXFORD
UNIVERSITY PRESS

OXFORD
UNIVERSITY PRESS

Oxford University Press is a department of the University of Oxford.
It furthers the University's objective of excellence in research, scholarship,
and education by publishing worldwide.

Oxford   New York
Auckland   Cape Town   Dar es Salaam   Hong Kong   Karachi
Kuala Lumpur   Madrid   Melbourne   Mexico City   Nairobi
New Delhi   Shanghai   Taipei   Toronto

With offices in
Argentina   Austria   Brazil   Chile   Czech Republic   France   Greece
Guatemala   Hungary   Italy   Japan   Poland   Portugal   Singapore
South Korea   Switzerland   Thailand   Turkey   Ukraine   Vietnam

Oxford is a registered trade mark of Oxford University Press
in the UK and certain other countries.

Published in the United States of America by
Oxford University Press
198 Madison Avenue, New York, NY 10016

© Oxford University Press 2011

First issued as an Oxford University Press paperback, 2013.

Library of Congress Cataloging-in-Publication Data
The Oxford handbook of the American musical /
edited by Raymond Knapp, Mitchell Morris, Stacy Wolf.
p.   cm.
Includes bibliographical references and index.
ISBN 978-0-19-538594-6 (hardcover); 978-0-19-998736-8 (paperback)
1. Musicals—United States—History and criticism.   I. Knapp, Raymond.
II. Morris, Mitchell.   III. Wolf, Stacy Ellen.
ML1711.O95 2011
782.1'40973—dc22
2010049030

Printed in the United States of America
on acid-free paper

CONTENTS

PART III. MEDIA

PART IV. IDENTITIES

PART V. PERFORMANCE

Contributors

STEVEN ADLER, Professor of Theatre and Provost of Earl Warren College, University of California, San Diego

VIRGINIA ANDERSON, Assistant Professor of Theatre, Cal Poly, San Luis Obispo

GEOFFREY BLOCK, Distinguished Professor of Music History, University of Puget Sound

CHASE A. BRINGARDNER, Assistant Professor of Theatre, Auburn University

JENNIFER CHAPMAN, Assistant Professor Emeritus of Theatre, University of Wisconsin-Eau Claire

JOHN M. CLUM, Professor Emeritus of Theater Studies and English, Duke University

TODD DECKER, Assistant Professor of Music, Washington University in St. Louis

ZACHARY A. DORSEY, Visiting Assistant Professor of Performance and Communication Arts, St. Lawrence University

MICHELLE DVOSKIN, Assistant Professor of Theatre and Dance, Western Kentucky University

LIZA GENNARO, professional choreographer and Lecturer in Dance, Barnard College and Princeton University

BARBARA WALLACE GROSSMAN, Professor of Drama, Tufts University

RAYMOND KNAPP, Professor of Musicology, University of California, Los Angeles

PAUL R. LAIRD, Professor of Musicology, University of Kansas

JIM LOVENSHEIMER, Associate Professor of Musicology, Vanderbilt University

MITCHELL MORRIS, Associate Professor of Musicology, University of California, Los Angeles

GEORGE REDDICK, freelance writer, New York City

HOLLEY REPLOGLE-WONG, ACLS New Faculty Fellow in Music, University of California, Berkeley

THOMAS L. RIIS, Joseph and Rebecca Negler Endowed Professor of Music and Director of the American Music Research Center, University of Colorado, Boulder

DAVID SANJEK, Professor of Music and Director of the Salford Music Research Centre, University of Salford, UK

DAVID SAVRAN, Distinguished Professor of Theatre and Vera Mowry Roberts Chair in American Theatre, the Graduate Center, City University of New York

SUSAN SMITH, Senior Lecturer in Film Studies, University of Sunderland, UK

JESSICA STERNFELD, Assistant Professor of Music History, Chapman University

ROBYNN J. STILWELL, Associate Professor of Music in the Department of Performing Arts, Georgetown University

DOMINIC SYMONDS, Senior Lecturer in Drama, University of Portsmouth, UK

STACY WOLF, Professor of Theater and Director of the Princeton Atelier, Princeton University

TAMSEN WOLFF, Associate Professor of Drama, Princeton University

ELIZABETH L. WOLLMAN, Assistant Professor of Music, Baruch College, City University of New York

THE OXFORD HANDBOOK OF

THE AMERICAN MUSICAL

ABOUT THE COMPANION WEBSITE

....

www.oup.com/us/oham

Oxford has created a website to accompany *The Oxford Handbook of the American Musical*, which includes nearly two hundred audio, video, image, or text examples to illustrate or augment the discussions advanced in the text. To make this valuable resource easy to use, each example is keyed to its appropriate place in the text, and numbered sequentially within each of the essays that use this resource. For clarity, we've used the following notation (these particular indications would refer to examples 5-8 in the first essay):

🔊 Example 1.5 (Audio Example 1.5)

▶️ Example 1.6 (Video Example 1.6)

🖼️ Example 1.7 (Image Example 1.7)

📄 Example 1.8 (Text Example 1.8)

To access an example, simply click on the appropriate icon on the website. You must have a media player installed on your computer to hear the audio examples or view the video examples; a link on the website will direct you to a source for this program if it is not already installed.

Access with username Music2 and password Book4416.

INTRODUCTION

STACY WOLF

THE American musical is a paradox. On stage or screen, musicals at once hold a dominant and a contested place in the worlds of entertainment, art, and scholarship. Born from a mélange of performance forms that included opera and operetta, vaudeville and burlesque, minstrelsy and jazz, musicals have always sought to amuse more than instruct, and to make money more than make political change. In spite of their unapologetic commercialism, though, musicals have achieved supreme artistry and have influenced culture as much as if not more than any other art form in America, including avant-garde and high art on the one hand, and the full range of popular and commercial art on the other. Reflecting, refracting, and shaping U.S. culture since the early twentieth century, musicals converse with shifting dynamics of gender and sexuality, ethnicity and race, and the very question of what it means to be American and to be human. The musical explores identity, self-determination, and the American dream.

The form of the musical—the combination of music, dance, speech, and design—is paradoxical, too. By the middle of the twentieth century, spoken scenes in musicals were expected to conform to the style of nonmusical plays, with characters psychologized and realistically portrayed. When characters burst into song or dance, a different expressive mode took over, one that scholars like Richard Dyer have seen as utopian.[1] Even as artists aimed for "integration" among the musical's disparate parts, in emulation of Wagner's "total artwork," the pieces required different skills of creation, presentation, and interpretation. As Scott McMillin argues in *The Musical as Drama*, "When a musical is working well, I feel the crackle of difference…between the book and the numbers, between songs and dances, between dance and spoken dialogue."[2] In part because of its hybrid form and its commercial aspirations, the musical failed to register as a legitimate topic for scholarly study in either music or theater programs in universities until near the end of the twentieth century. Although audiences flocked to see *The Phantom of the Opera* on Broadway to the tune of 100 million people worldwide since its opening year on Broadway (1987), and the film of *The Sound of Music* (1965) held its place as the most popular movie musical of all time well into the twenty-first century, few college courses taught the history or criticism of musicals. And while young composers, lyricists, librettists, designers, and performers honed their craft and enrolled in professional training programs, they gained knowledge of the musical's history and theory through practice rather than through college classes that emphasized a scholarly approach to musicals.

Beginning in the 1990s, and gaining considerable momentum across the first decade of the new millennium, the study of American musicals on stage and on film has grown rapidly into a legitimate field. Many universities now offer surveys of musical theater or film history; or build a course focused on a composer, a subgenre, or a period in U.S. history; or include musicals in other courses, from American drama to popular culture to African American studies.[3] In departments of music and musicology, theater, film, media studies, and literature, more courses are taught each year about musicals or include the study of a musical play or film as an example of cultural or performance history. Increasingly, musical theater and musical film are seen as viable objects of scholarly inquiry.

Scholarship to support the study of musicals is gradually catching up to the enthusiastic reception of students, as more dissertations are written and books published on musicals each year. Where there were formerly only encyclopedic lists of musicals and their creators, coffee-table tomes, or hagiographies, there is now a growing field of academic studies of musicals. Some explicate and analyze a range of musicals; others trace a chronological history. Some authors stress context over analysis, locating musicals historically, and some books consider musicals from specific identity positions. Increasingly, studies focus on a single musical, often relying on archival research to unearth details about the production process. Finally, books take a biographical approach and center on a director, composer, choreographer, producer, performer, or another member of the creative team. (See bibliography.)

Even as scholarship has grown in diverse and wide-ranging ways, the teaching of musicals continues to be extremely challenging. This book grew out of our mutual passion for teaching musicals and our mutual frustration with available pedagogically oriented materials. When the three of us first met to talk about musicals, we complained—as most professors do—about the lack of a textbook for teaching musicals that adequately covered the wide range of possible approaches to the subject. Each of us had solved the problem in our own way, using a combination of texts and articles and our own expertise. From that start, we found common goals as instructors: first, to situate the musical historically; second, to locate the ideological work of the musical as "American"; and third, to practice a variety of methods and techniques to analyze musicals. Moreover, each of us was well aware of the strengths and weaknesses in our training, of the stubborn disciplinarity of each of our fields, and of the tendency to privilege one element of the musical over another based on our comfort level. We knew that a useful textbook for the study of the American musical needed more than our three voices to write it.

Although we designed this book as a teaching tool, we mean "teaching" in the broadest possible way for students, instructors, and the general reader. We intend this book not (necessarily) to be read cover to cover, nor (necessarily) assigned in order, but as a resource for instructors, students, and aficionados of the musical and as a complement to other studies currently available. As well, scholars expert in one area of the musical can use this book as a first resource in coming to terms with other aspects of the art form less familiar to them and as an additional resource for courses on related topics, such as Tin Pan Alley or Popular Song.

Any textbook defines its object of study by its choice of specific subjects, by its organization, and by its range. *The Oxford Handbook of the American Musical* consists of twenty-nine chapters written by scholars trained in music, musicology, ethnomusicology, theater, drama, dance studies, English, film, and media studies, among others. Rather than chart a clear and coherent narrative, or delineate distinct topics, we (the editors) asked each author to consider a "keyword" of the musical, to historicize the term, and to analyze it through several examples.[4] Even within these parameters for coherence and consistency, the essays gathered here are spectacularly eclectic, impressively wide-ranging, and appropriately unique, and we are profoundly grateful to our authors for the enthusiasm, knowledge, and insight they brought to their writing.

Each section of the book reopens the very question of how the study of the American musical might proceed, either by historiography (how one goes about writing a history of the musical); by history (how the events that took place construct a chronological narrative based on an unfolding process of transformation); by media (how distinctive are the formats in which the musical thrives); by identity (how creators' or audiences' social locations influence the form, and how the form has contributed to understanding and processes of identity formation); by the various elements of performance (how a musical is put together); and by the audience (how the commercialism of the musical organizes its production and its reception). This self-reflexive structure means that some essays mention the same musical in different analytical contexts, and some traverse the same historical moment from different interpretive perspectives. As a whole, then, the book is intentionally multifaceted and perhaps even contradictory. Without claiming comprehensiveness, the book considers the American musical prismatically.

Any book this complex—like the musical itself—has innumerable contributors beyond those headlined as editors and authors. The editors are extremely grateful for the abudant and varied support their scholarly communities have provided. On the institutional level, this included support, at UCLA, from the Office of Instructional Development, the Department of Musicology, and the Council on Research, along with a rich field of interactions among students and other faculty; we are especially grateful for insights that have found their way into this book from Juliana Gondek, Peter Kazaras, Elijah Wald, Sam Baltimore, Sarah Ellis, and Holley Replogle-Wong, and for Holley's exemplary work preparing and organizing materials for the book's Web site. At Princeton, we thank the Lewis Center for the Arts, especially Director Paul Muldoon; Director of the Program in Theater, Michael

Cadden; and Dean of the Faculty, David Dobkin. At Oxford University Press, we thank Senior Production Editor Joellyn Ausanka for guiding us through the copyediting and proofing stages of the book, Laura Mahoney and Linda Roppolo for their work designing the website and cover, Patterson Lamb for judicious copyediting, and Michael Philo Antonie for meticulous work on the page proofs. And most of all we thank Norm Hirschy, who has been unfailingly, even brilliantly helpful, at every step of the process.

NOTES

1. Richard Dyer, "Entertainment and Utopia," in *Genre: The Musical*, ed. Rick Altman (London: Routledge and Kegan Paul, 1981; originally published in *Movie* 2 [Spring 1977]: 2–13).

2. Scott McMillin, *The Musical as Drama: A Study of the Principles and Conventions behind Musical Shows from Kern to Sondheim* (Princeton, NJ: Princeton University Press, 2006), p. 2.

3. See Stacy Wolf, "In Defense of Pleasure: Musical Theatre History in the Liberal Arts [A Manifesto]," *Theatre Topics* 17.1 (March 2007): 51–60.

4. Frank Lentricchia and Thomas McLaughlin's important and influential book *Critical Terms for Literary Study* (Chicago: University of Chicago Press, 1990) was our inspiration for this book.

PART I

HISTORIOGRAPHY

CHAPTER 1

NARRATIVES AND VALUES

MITCHELL MORRIS

It warms my heart to know that you / Remember still the way you do.

Madame Alvarez, *Gigi*

Studies of the musical as a genre, as well as its precursors, spin-offs, and assorted cousins, typically shape themselves as accounts of change over time. To some extent, this is inherent in any popular genre of the arts: contemporaneity and fashionability are powerful values, and they gain their effectiveness only by contrast, explicit or implicit, with what came before them. The matrix of commercial necessities that enable the musical has therefore tended to foreground notions of "the new." As a sense of "tradition" has developed among artists and audiences, the notion of "the revival" has also become increasingly vivid. Attributes such as these indicate a general assumption that the historical location of a musical—not simply its place in the chronological sequence, but also the networks of affiliation and disaffiliation to other works in that sequence—is an important aspect of its framing. That location contributes to the set of expectations that we bring to the experience as audiences and artists (not only of revivals, but also of works that play on the forms and contents of the past). It also enables the construction of accounts of the musical as a genre that exists through time. We usually call such accounts "history." But what exactly do we mean when we call something "history"? And more specifically, what problems must we consider when we think about writing or reading the history of the musical? This chapter briefly explores these questions.

Making History

The oldest extant forms that record change through time are usually called "chronicles." The *Oxford English Dictionary* gives its first definition of this term as "a detailed and continuous register of events in order of time; a historical record, *esp.* one in which the facts are narrated without philosophic treatment, or any attempt at literary style."[1] This is not to say that the events registered are completely random—chronicles normally focus on relatively specific subject matter, whether it be lists of kings or presidents, meteorological or astronomical conditions, or performances of dramatic or musical works. What matters here is that chronicles are in some sense "pre-reflective," that is, they are primarily oriented toward listing events, not explaining them, and there is probably no overt reflection on the writer's selection of entries; the criterion for an event's inclusion in a chronicle is typically its membership in the class of events the chronicle aims to document. Chronicles exist from the earliest periods of written records and continue in various forms to the present day, no doubt because temporal ordering is typically central to the ways human life tends to be lived. All languages, after all, have ways of indicating past, present, and future.

History, by contrast, departs from the list of events in time by seeking various kinds of causal connections. That is, histories construct narratives of one sort or another; the events or series of events are linked in speech or writing to form a chain of causal relationships that may be roughly simultaneous (synchronic) and/or spread out over time (diachronic). The word "history" itself comes from the fifth century BCE Greek writer Herodotus of Halicarnassus, who called his account of the origins of the Greek and Persian wars an "inquiry" or *historía*.[2] History seeks to answer questions such as how or why events have occurred, how or why events are related.

Fundamental to the construction of a specifically historical narrative is reliance on forms of documentation: oral histories and folk tales or myths, eyewitness accounts of events, artifacts (typically the place where history begins to merge with archaeology), and written documents of many types. Such documents may be cited without question, especially in earlier historical accounts, but more often a historian spends considerable time reading the documents critically. In what context was a given document created, and what was it to be used for? Given the marked tendency of memories to undergo modification over time and the common human tendency to favor some interests above others, to what degree can a given document be trusted as an impartial account? When two or more documents disagree, how can they be evaluated, and how do we choose between the versions of an event that they offer? Historians characteristically aspire to factual accuracy, and critical assessment is a crucial part of a historian's task. A history is different from a fictional account precisely because it attempts to base its narrative on facts. But this then raises the question of defining the term "fact."

For the purposes of this discussion, a fact may be defined as a falsifiable propositional statement about an event, a person, an object, and so on. An example: "The original Broadway production of Rodgers and Hammerstein's *Oklahoma!* opened on March 31, 1943." This statement seems unassailable because there are so many bits of documentary evidence—newspaper reviews, paylists for musicians or stage crew, first-person recollections, and the other written materials accumulated around the production—that agree in supporting it. The process of falsification would depend on assembling supporting evidence—in this understanding of historical research, almost certainly documents of some sort—to support the new claim. The process of evaluating and deciding between these contradictory documents would be a central task for writing history.

So far this seems sensible, indeed unremarkable. But consider what is presupposed in the statement. The musical is specified as the work of a composer-lyricist team; other collaborators such as Agnes de Mille (choreographer), Lemuel Ayers (scenic designer), or Rouben Mamoulian (director) are left unmentioned. This choice is in keeping with our assumption that music and text are the stable components of a musical, and the other elements of the production more-or-less variable—assumptions that do not always correspond to the realities of productions. The "fact" in question concerns the musical's first public Broadway performance— a reasonable locus of our attention, but one that must leave out contingencies such as the show's out-of-town tryouts (it was called *Away We Go!* in its performances in New Haven and did not include what became the show's title song). Nothing in the statement is incorrect—though it matters that hypothetically the statement could indeed be proved false—but it inevitably represents a specific choice among the possible things that may be said.

Another way of putting this is that "facts" matter because they occupy a place in some larger ordering or narrative scheme. As described by the historian Lawrence Stone, narrative requires chronological organization (this does not necessarily exclude temporal shifts such as flashbacks or foreshadowings), the dominant presence of a particular story (though subsidiary stories may be folded into the primary one), description (though more abstract analysis may be interspersed within the description), human agents instead of abstract conditions, and particularities rather than generalities.[3] The requirements of narrative therefore exert pressure on a writer's selection of relevant facts. A vast number of things may be said about *Oklahoma!*, but any given narrative will require only a small percentage of these. In addition, our sense of what matters in a narrative typically depends on notions and commitments that exist prior to our work on that narrative. We never observe anything without some kind of conceptual scheme, implicit or explicit, that allows us to make sense of it—we have, in other words, theories. And it is a mistake to imagine that we can do without either facts or theories; it is a misperception to imagine that the two are fully separate. As musicologist Leo Treitler observes:

> "Facts" come into being only at the moment we assimilate them, for they are orderings of our perceptions, meant to give them coherence. There is therefore no distinct boundary between facts and theories, only lower order and higher order facts. Our traffic with facts is always "theory laden," as Hanson put it. You may

feel confident in your possession of a lower order fact—say the date of Mozart's
birth—and argue that it is incontestably true quite apart from your knowing it.
But that is because the signals are clear, unambiguous, and nonconflicting.[4]

If a fact, to the degree that it is a falsifiable statement that has resisted all challenges,
is held to be secure, it still must find a place in the larger network of facts that make
up the narrative as a whole. Though explanations require facts, facts by themselves
do not constitute explanations. And to consider how explanations work, we must
turn to the question of the language that makes up the explanation proper, which
requires a brief consideration of the more variable questions of rhetoric, before
proceeding to the specific historical inquiry in question.

The Emplotment Thickens

In an influential study of nineteenth-century historical writers, Hayden White
argues that historical explanations tended to operate according to three strategies:
formal argument, emplotment, and ideological implication.[5] If a chronicle is the
ordering of events in time, the "story" can be understood as a shaping or connecting
of the events of a chronicle through linguistic gestures of beginning, connecting, or
ending. But each story is meaningful because it has a particular kind of plot. White's
four principal plot types for historical narratives are Romance, Tragedy, Comedy,
and Satire (White, 7–11). The choice of plot—the emplotment—is not the result of
the facts on display in the chronicle; rather, the plot helps determine the selection of
facts out of the manifold of factual possibilities. Each mode of emplotment tends to
reinforce certain points of view; for example, a Romance will most likely emphasize
triumphs over adversity, a Comedy will favor reconciliations of the natural and
social worlds, a Tragedy will show a terrible (but exemplary) failure, and a Satire will
expose the inadequacies of all such views and expectations.

 Formal argument, which exists simultaneously with emplotment, seeks to create persuasive explanations by logical deduction and the postulation of general
principles that the cases at hand in the narrative are held to fulfill. Again, White
takes four styles of argumentation to be the prevailing modes of historical explanation: Formist, Organicist, Mechanistic, and Contextualist. The Formist approach
takes on the task of crafting explanations by cataloging the specificities (objects,
phenomena, agents, etc.) that create the unique characteristics of a particular historical field; the Organicist approach also works with such specificities but attempts
to interrelate them as parts of an overarching whole (this is almost certainly the
appropriate locus of the notion of the Zeitgeist, or "spirit of the times); the
Mechanistic strategy seeks to understand the specificities of a given historical field
as the results of some overarching set of causal laws; the Contextualist strategy sees
those same particulars as best explained by the set of contingent relationships that
obtain between those very particulars.[6] White's final explanatory quaternity, the

mode of ideological implication, offers the political formulations of Anarchism, Conservatism, Radicalism, and Liberalism.[7] These categories do not correspond to specific political groups or platforms but rather indicate a generalized set of attitudes toward such things as social change, or a stance toward the past and future.

The combination of emplotments, modes of argument, and ideological implications produce what White considers historiographical style. He believes that there are natural affiliations between modes. Thus, a Romantic mode of emplotment would combine readily with a Formist mode of argument and an Anarchist mode of ideological implication. By contrast, a Comic mode of emplotment would clash unprofitably with a Mechanistic mode of argument and be confounded utterly if further combined with a Liberal mode of ideological implication. But many historians—many of the most interesting historians—attempt fusions of various modes of explanation in their work.

As for how these modes of explanation can be discerned, White suggests a strong correlation between the kinds of figurative language favored in a narrative and the linked modes of explanation outlined above. Metaphor (relationships of resemblance), metonymy (relationships of contiguity), synecdoche (the equation of parts and wholes, especially in a figurative sense), and irony (the use of words to represent the opposite of their manifest meaning) are all commonly available in any writer's repertory; but Romance will tend to organize itself around metaphorical terms, Comedy will coalesce around the reductions of metonymy, Tragedy will favor the integrative functions of synecdoche, and Satire will show a persistent taste for irony.

Although the analytical categories tallied here may seem excessively schematic, they do serve as useful starting points for a rhetorical analysis of historical writing. But their very literary qualities may cause unease. Where have all the facts gone in this cluster of writerly techniques? What about "objectivity"?

The Way We (Actually) Were(n't)

The nineteenth-century German historian Leopold von Ranke has been endlessly cited for his declaration that the historian's task was to relate the past "as it actually was" (wie es eigentlich gewesen ist). Following in Ranke's wake, a strong tradition of historical writing, usually called "positivist history," operated under the claim that facts, as they present themselves to the imagination, can be understood without the conceptual apparatus of rhetoric and philosophical theory. The facts "speak for themselves."[8] A great deal of twentieth-century historiographical writing and reflection, however, has made the notion of "how it actually was" exceedingly problematic. Leaving aside the troublesome intercalation of fact and theory outlined above, even the empirical historical record—the kinds of chronicles that can be assembled—tends to demonstrate an unmanageable degree of diversity in many historical situations.

The most likely case is that in almost all historical moments things actually *were* a lot of different ways simultaneously. A historian's selection of facts, because it *must be* only a selection, is already a tacit claim about importance. If we choose to talk about musicals in 1972 by focusing on *Grease* instead of *Pippin*, we are affiliating ourselves with a particular set of narrative possibilities. If we attend to the circumstances of the production rather than the critical reception, we further narrow the scope of our narrative.

There is nothing wrong with these choices; no one can possibly discuss everything. Yet the notion of comprehensiveness, like the notion of absolute impartiality, exerts a beguiling fascination over scholars. And it remains fatally easy for respondents, critics, and reviewers to counter any narrative by protesting, "But what about X? What about Y?" Such criticisms are only productive if the objection carries with it a counterargument, itself open to correction or outright refutation. That is, the historical narratives that we work with as writers and readers—as opposed to chronicles, which can come closer to comprehensiveness (though not impartiality)— actually acquire full value only by being configured within a network of narratives; and this network of narratives is most effective when the various components offer opportunities for conflict as well as support. Historical narratives, like other forms of scholarship, are fundamentally dialogic.

And if the dialogic nature of historical narratives is central to their value, then Hayden White's analysis of historical rhetoric is especially helpful, for it allows us, after registering questions of "factual accuracy," to proceed to the larger claims that a particular narrative may be making about the objects of its study. In the case of the musical, of course, those objects are likely to fall under the rubric of what we usually call "works."

WORKING ON WORKS

The notion that music can take on forms that are more or less stable through time is not recent, of course. Even before the advent of musical notation, which can be taken to fix various aspects of music in at least semi-durable ways, it was possible for musical objects—songs, for instance—to achieve something that might be said to resemble the permanence we would predict of objects like statues or paintings. To the extent that the majority of Western music was, before about 1600, vocal rather than instrumental, music typically approached the condition of texts. Although they were in practice significantly variable, existing on a continuum from the idealized fixity of Scripture to the unrepeatable exuberance of an improvised epic, songs as composite entities (words plus music) could indeed have a long-term existence that arose from their relatively consistent repeatability. One of the interesting things that can be observed in Western music history is the gradual stabilization of musical scores, first in manuscript, then in print culture, then within print culture in particular an increasing tendency to fix aspects of performance (orna-ments, dynamics, tempo, articulation, timbre) that had earlier been left open to the oral traditions in which performers were trained. In fact, the musical, because of its complex location between the increasingly text-oriented practices of "classical music" and the improvisatory bent of "popular music," evinces contradictory pulls toward both poles at various moments in its history. But taken as a whole, the his-torical accounts of the musical have often tended to weigh in on the side of textual stability—seduced, perhaps, by the glamour and prestige associated with the notion of "the musical work."

By around 1800, Western music traditions were increasingly committed to what philosopher Lydia Goehr has called "the work-concept."[9] To offer a quick descrip-tion, a musical work is an open concept—that is, music classified as a work can actu-ally change with respect to its definition and practical experience under historical circumstances, intimately related with composing/performing/listening practices, without damaging its status as a work—that encourages us to posit an entity that exists "beyond" a score and its specific performances. This is a very big deal. For the purposes of this discussion, in particular, it presents a historical problem, since the kind of musical work Goehr has in mind is a sort of transcendental object only par-tially embedded in history. To some extent, this kind of music resembles the kind of art object that seems to have developed in Early Modern Europe in the visual arts: paintings whose manner of execution was at least as important as their object con-tent and whose functions were less devotion and decoration than a kind of proto-aesthetic contemplation. And the historiography of art shaped by writings such as Giorgio Vasari's *Lives of the Most Excellent Italian Painters, Sculptors, and Architects*, with its heroic accounts of Leonardo or Michelangelo, arguably presents the original template for later accounts of Artistic Greatness.

Certainly the passion for imagining Great Works by Great Artists (only capitals will do) was especially vivid in the writings of nineteenth-century critics of music and literature, creating notions of artistic potency allied with organic unity (and unitary authorship) that still shape the way many audience members come to value specific musicals. This is all the more important a set of ideas because the musical, almost always overtly collaborative, both challenges and acquiesces to the prestige of Greatness. To take a nineteenth-century comparison: Richard Wagner was an overtly Great Composer: one important measure of his Greatness was his terrifying determination to be a librettist-composer-producer-designer-conductor-director-critic, not some mere musician. His contemporaries W. S. Gilbert and Arthur Sullivan worked together to create operettas, amusing entertainments with an ambivalent attitude toward Greatness: their operettas were certainly works, but they eschewed the lofty, *religioso* tone that surrounded Wagner's operas. Both Wagner and Gilbert & Sullivan ended up with special societies devoted to their works, and strong, even domineering performing traditions. Wagner's high seriousness, his unitary Greatness, has over the years earned him vastly much more ink than Gilbert & Sullivan. And yet, *The Pirates of Penzance* seems to be at least as sturdy as *Parsifal* with respect to its place in the performed repertoire.

Also at stake in the creation of the work is the entangled notion of authorship. For the history of music, this required arguments that placed the composer (not the songwriter, note—and certainly not the performer) as the primary if not the sole progenitor of the work. This was a particularly fraught question for overtly collaborative genres such as opera, all the more because the metaphysical prestige of instrumental music became a core feature of nineteenth-century high culture; it became necessary to preserve the seriousness of opera by reducing the roles of figures such as the librettist, the choreographer, and the major singers. The model for this kind of argument is most eloquently expressed in the major thesis of Joseph Kerman's 1956 book *Opera as Drama*: "the dramatist is the composer."[10]

But to return to the work: an important practical result of the dominance of the work concept, and to the common understanding that works as such can engage with audiences far outside the contexts of their genesis and first performance, is that historians of the musical, like their counterparts in other areas of music or theater studies, continually sit on the horns of a dilemma. Shall we write a *history* of the musical, or a history of the *musical*? In what subtle combination of those terms? What role do our current reactions and responses have in the historical writing we propose to do? Literary critic Northrop Frye once offered a contrast between "ordinary history specializing in the names and dates of authors" versus one "largely concerned with conventions and genres,"[11] and in so doing he pointed at something of the same difficulty. And since our experience of a "work" is so frequently the impetus behind our quest for historical understanding, such that to exclude this response from the writing would be to misrepresent the real stakes of the historical work, how do we balance critical and historical imperatives?

PERIOD PIECE

Related to the problem of potential conflicts between critical and historical approaches is the vexed and vexing difficulty of making persuasive connections between the internal qualities of "works" and the cultural contexts within which they are generated and transmitted. In historical writing about the arts, the difficulty has often been solved by postulating "periods," segments of time and space that are to be regarded as in some way "of a piece." Theater historians may refer to "Restoration theater." Musicologists may talk about "Baroque opera." Art historians may discuss "Impressionism." Periods are in essence a collocation of nonce categories that by common scholarly consensus are treated as more or less stable over time. They may be defined by significant dates, characteristic genres, exemplary artistic figures or groups of figures, terms derived from historical sources, typical contexts of reception, conditions of production, and most important, "style" or "sensibility." More abstractly, they often operate by covertly persuading us that the cultural artifacts of a given period share some kind of underlying "unity."[12] Using

Hegel's influential term, they embody a Zeitgeist. Music scholars have long operated with a broad system of classifications such as Medieval, Renaissance, Baroque, Classical, Romantic, and Modern.[13] It is something of a permanent scandal that these terms match very poorly indeed with the same categories as they are manifested in the other arts. But they remain central to historical writing because they have essential practical (i.e., pedagogical) and disciplinary functions.

An activity closely bound up with periodization is the creation of a canon, a repertory of exemplary works that are treated as embodying the essential features of the historical sequence, and are regarded as especially worthy of study and emulation. Again, like periods, canons serve numerous practical and disciplinary functions, and some form of canon is probably unavoidable for scholarly exchange to take place. But it would be a mistake to regard canons as simply traditional, or handed down; canons are normally subject to intense contestation and revision, and the history of canon-making is an integral part of the history of the arts as surely as the history of artists, works, and audiences.

For the history of the musical, perhaps the most characteristic period label is the "Golden Age of the Broadway Musical." The terms that frame the period are already significant because they carry an inherent narrative. There was probably a lesser period before the Golden Age, and there is necessarily a lesser period after it. The archetypal narrative underwriting the Golden Age is the ancient organicist image of birth, flowering/maturity, and decline and fall: a cyclic plot that depends on notions of the seasons as much as it does on a description of the human life cycle. This three-stage archetype is challenged only by the archetype of the continuous progress to the present, often known as "the Whig interpretation of history," after the title of an influential book by English historian Herbert Butterfield.[14] (Bringing White's models of narrative into play, it is easy to see how the organicist archetype could be domesticated for use in Tragedy or Satire, and the Whig archetype could find congruence with Romance or Comedy.)

Moreover, the term "Golden Age," because it is so durably associated with stylistic features such as "the integrated musical," and because it carries a latent association with the intricate sociopolitical frameworks of the United States at the peak of its political and economic flourishing, can be taken to mount a complex argument by analogy about American society at the same time that it purports to restrict itself to matters of art and commerce. In effect, the history of the musical becomes at one level an allegory about the growth, prosperity, and possibly decline of American society. (Whether this be read as Tragedy or Satire presumably depends on your point of view at present.)

Could such notions be done away with entirely? There is no guarantee that rejecting the category of the Golden Age would make a huge difference in the ways that we are accustomed to valuing specific musicals, nor proof that its jettisoning would substantially alter the canon of exemplary works and artists that is gradually coalescing in the scholarly literature on the musical. A more interesting approach than simple rejection would be a close examination of the term and the uses made of it. For the real problem with critical terms comes from their reification; as they harden into unquestioned and unquestionable entities, they come to resemble unquestioned facts in and of themselves instead of tools by which we experiment with points of view.

IN OTHER WORDS

History is at its best an ongoing process of disputation. Like Honoré and Madame Alvarez in *Gigi*, we regale one another with different versions of the story and strive to persuade that our version is the better one, if only for the moment. Unlike Honoré and Mamita, however, our rules of scholarship compel us to pay attention to the corrections and refutations we offer one another. In that way, we aim at improving the effectiveness—the truth, if you will—of our accounts. If this matters to our scholarly scruples, it ought also to matter because of the difference it makes to the objects of our affection. As art critic Dave Hickey has pointed out, every time we speak or write about a particular "work," whether pro or contra, we increase its "value."[15] The value of an artwork is never intrinsic because works are occasions for relationships between people. Each musical bears the imprint of those who speak or write about it because in doing so they magnify it. And such sedimented affections, such accretions of value, are part of doing history, too.[16]

NOTES

1. www.oed.com. Accessed on October 30, 2010.

2. The earliest Chinese narrative history *Zuo Zhuan*, incidentally, is roughly contemporary with histories of Herodotus and Thucydides.

3. Lawrence Stone, "The Revival of Narrative: Reflections on a New Old History" (*Past & Present* [November 1979]: 3–24).

4. Leo Treitler, "The Present as History" (*Perspectives of New Music* 7.2 [Spring–Summer 1969]: 1–58), p. 25.

5. Hayden White, *Metahistory: The Historical Imagination in Nineteenth-Century Europe* (Baltimore: Johns Hopkins University Press, 1973), p. x. The following discussion depends on pp. 1–42.

6. White notes that Formist and Contextualist argumentation is overwhelmingly favored in professional historical writing (White 19–21). I would suggest that histories of the arts tend to be more inclined toward Organicist and Mechanistic modes than "regular" histories.

7. As is the case with the previous formulations, these four are not the only possible positions that may be occupied (White immediately lists Apocalypticism, Reactionism, and Fascism), but they are the dominant modes in the historical writing he considers.

8. Positivist history has been an exceedingly powerful current in both music and theater history. It's worth stressing that this position embodies a number of serious moral claims, such as

the value of neutrality as a kind of temporal relativism, and the writer's offer of potential freedom to the reader to make personal sense of the historical account.

9. Lydia Goehr, *The Imaginary Museum of Musical Works: An Essay in the Philosophy of Music* (Oxford: Oxford University Press, 1992).

10. Joseph Kerman, *Opera as Drama, New and Revised Edition* (Berkeley: University of California Press, 1988), p. xv.

11. Northrop Frye, "Literary History" (*New Literary History* 12.2 [Winter 1981]: 219–25).

12. As historian William Weber has pointed out, scholars characterized as "postmodern," though they might be considered opposed to Hegel's totalizing notions, are not necessarily free of the same postulates. See Weber, "Beyond Zeitgeist: Recent Work in Music History" (*Journal of Modern History* 66/2 [June 1994]: 321–25). For that matter, it is certain that to call something "postmodern," inasmuch as it requires a thing called "modern" to define itself, is to remain mired in a totalizing master narrative.

13. Theater history as a discipline has been much more unruly about its categories, which is surely an asset from the point of view of historians of the musical. Lack of consistency gives us greater room to maneuver.

14. Herbert Butterfield, *The Whig Interpretation of History* (London: G. Bell & Sons, 1931).

15. See, for instance, the discussion in Dave Hickey, "Buying the World" (*Daedalus* 131.4 [Fall, 2002]: 69–87).

16. Unsurprisingly, historiography has its own history. A useful introduction is Georg G. Iggers, *Historiography in the Twentieth Century: From Scientific Objectivity to the Postmodern Challenge. With a New Epilogue* (Middletown, CT: Wesleyan University, Press, 2005).

....

CHAPTER 2

TEXTS AND AUTHORS

....

JIM LOVENSHEIMER

A 2008 Vanderbilt University Opera Theater production was advertised on posters and flyers around campus as "Kurt Weill's *Street Scene*," which left some wondering what had become of Elmer Rice and Langston Hughes, authors of the book and lyrics, respectively. This is hardly an isolated event; composers routinely receive sole or primary credit for creating a musical. How many times have the phrases "Leonard Bernstein's *West Side Story*" (what would Jerome Robbins have said about that?) or "a Stephen Sondheim musical" been used to identify a work that in actuality was the result of a collaborative team, whose members share the responsibility for the musical's success or failure?

Giving privilege to the composer of a musical, or to any other single collaborator, is problematic in that, when the boundaries of collaboration are as messy as they often are in the creation of a musical, the role of any one contributor defies clear definition. When lyrics are drawn from a passage originally written by the author of the book, for instance, or when an entire production is conceived and staged by a choreographer-director whose work is never written down or recorded, who is the "author," and of what? And what, for that matter, is the "text" of a musical for which no single written version exists? The score, after all, contains little if any dialogue apart from song cues, and the book contains no music. As Stephen Banfield notes, "A musical exists in no definitive form, and a performance is created from no single source."[1] But this raises additional questions: if a performance draws from more than one text, does it in turn create a new cumulative text—what theater theoretician Kier Elam calls a "performance text"—and, if so, who counts as the author or authors of that text?[2] And just what constitutes that cumulative text? Certainly, a performance text must also include the contributions of performers in general and stars in particular; the latter are often thought of as having "created" their roles. Raymond Knapp has suggested that "a performer can create and inflect a character beyond what might be indicated through written words and/or music,"[3] and, as demonstrated later, many stars have been known to re-create, or improvise, from performance to performance, thus suggesting an ongoing authorship that thwarts any finalization of text whatsoever.

Defining the terms "texts" and "authors" with regard to the musical obviously presents multiple challenges, most of which are exacerbated by the genre's collaborative nature. Indeed, the multidisciplinary aspects of the musical make any single theoretical approach incomplete and ultimately unsatisfactory. Musicology, for instance, understandably tends to privilege the musical score over other elements. This approach, which recalls the advertisements for "Kurt Weill's *Street Scene*," is best demonstrated by Joseph P. Swain's *The Broadway Musical: A Critical and Musical Survey*, which in turn takes as its model Joseph Kerman's influential *Opera as Drama*.[4] Kerman argues that, at least in opera, the composer is the dramatist, an argument that when applied to the musical "leads all too easily to the premise that all musicals aspire to the condition of opera" (Banfield, 6). Theater historians and critics, who often still use the term "legitimate theater" for nonmusical plays and thus imply the illegitimacy of musicals, tend to ignore musical theater altogether, although the structuralist approach that dominates theater studies is also valuable for defining critical aspects of the musical, as we shall see. And whereas Roland Barthes introduces the useful term "informational polyphony" to refer to theater's "density of signs" in his essay "Introduction to the Structural Analysis of Narration," he does not go much further than suggesting that the "fundamental problems of semiology are present in the theatre."[5]

Nonetheless, while each of these disciplines offers at best a partial explanation of the musical's multivalent character, all three, when considered together, point toward a more comprehensive understanding of the terms "texts" and "authors" with regard to the musical. That a collaborative genre should require a collaborative critical approach is hardly surprising. As theater and cultural theorist David Savran notes about the musical,

> No form of Western theatre (with the possible exception of opera) uses as many different media to produce a totality that is always far more than the sum of its parts. As a result, analysis requires an implicit or explicit theorization of multiple (and often conflicting) systems of signification.[6]

Only when the seemingly disparate disciplines of literary theory, theater studies, and musicology are deployed to create a cooperative critical system is any headway made toward reaching a satisfactory definition, or definitions, of "texts" and "authors" for use in studying the musical.

TEXTS

For the purposes of this study, a general definition of "texts" can be borrowed, with accretions, from Bernhard Radloff's discussion of the term in the *Encyclopedia of Contemporary Literary Theory*: "a structure [script, musical score, body of dance, scenic design, etc.] composed of elements of signification [words, notes, choreography, etc.] by which the greater or lesser unity of those elements makes itself manifest."[7] Two other terms that sometimes substitute for "text" in practice are "work" and the aforementioned "performance text," which, although sometimes used interchangeably with "text," can also be usefully distinguished. Kier Elam introduces the term "performance text" as follows:

> Unlike the literary semiotician or the analyst of myth or the plastic arts, the researcher in theatre and drama is faced with two quite dissimilar—although immediately correlated—types of textual material: that produced *in* the theatre and that composed *for* the theatre. These two potential focuses of semiotic attention will be indicated as the theatrical or *performance* text and the written or *dramatic* text respectively. (3, emphasis original)

Elam's use of the term demonstrates the influence of the so-called Prague School of the 1930s and 1940s, a group of literary theorists who were among the first to explore the differing sign systems of written dramatic texts and performance contexts. Indeed, in 1940 the Czech theorist Jindřich Honzl made the succinct observation that "dramatic performance is a set of signs,"[8] opening the door to a subsequent distinction between individual dramatic texts—in the musical, the music, lyrics, spoken dialogue, and so on—and the totality, or "set," of their various signs in performance that, together, constitute the performance text, or "work." (Choreography, which technically is not a written text but which acts as a separate element that contributes to the performance text, is arguably one of the several dramatic texts.) Further, this set of signs/performance text/work, identifiable as an object, derives its meanings from the relationships of the individual texts that contribute to it. These relationships can be considered either sympathetic, as in what is often thought of as the integrated musical play model of Rodgers and Hammerstein, or conflicted, as in Scott McMillin's reading of the musical as the product of differences, or friction, between its elements.[9] Either way, the various dramatic texts of the musical do not necessarily relate to each other in any kind of hierarchical system, as the proponents of the composer-dominant approach might have it, but instead produce a somewhat egalitarian intertextuality. As Elam observes,

> Each text bears the other's traces, the performance assimilating those aspects of the written play [or score] which the performers choose to transcodify, and the dramatic text being "spoken" [or sung] at every point by the model performance—or [other] possible performances—that motivate it. (190–91)

This intertextuality can be rather slippery in the study of the musical, however, for the dramatic texts are often ephemeral, transitory, or changeable to a degree that can drastically alter the content and subsequent reception of the work.

The Rodgers and Hammerstein musical play was the dominant model for most musicals from 1943 until approximately 1970, and, as mentioned earlier, it is generally discussed in terms of its integration or unity of elements or texts. In his autobiography, Richard Rodgers defined this concept: "When a show works perfectly, it's because all the individual parts complement each other and fit together. No single element overshadows any other. In a great musical, the orchestrations sound the way the costumes look."[10] And for many years the Rodgers and Hammerstein Organization insisted that all productions of the team's works adhere strictly to the written script and score to ensure authorial intent and textual "completeness."

But this model becomes problematic when dealing with any musical, before or after the dominance of Rodgers and Hammerstein, that behaves differently from the model. Theater theoretician Bernard Beckerman notes, "So strong is the contemporary conception of unity that we hesitate to see quite disparate elements as constituting a single work. In thinking of a theatrical production, especially of a play, we assume a coherence of style and manner." But he subsequently (and for our purposes importantly) observes,

> When we regard the entire range of performances, whether of the popular circus or the more austere theatre, we encounter a rich mix of acts.... The distinctive American art of the musical theatre includes romantic narrative, songs, dances, and spectacular display.[11]

Beckerman's "rich mix" suggests what musical theater scholar Bruce Kirle, in *Unfinished Show Business*, saw as the key to reading the musical as an "open text," that is, a work that has no definitive form and "precludes the ultimate authority of the text."[12]

Kirle's preceding comment might be made even more precise by substituting "texts" for "text," since authority is found in neither a single element of the musical, as already suggested, nor in the collection of elements that constitutes the performance text. Again, Elam is useful. Recalling Barthes's "density of signs," Elam refers to the theater in general as "the systems of signs, or codes, which produce the performance" (27), adding,

> It is not, clearly, a single-levelled and homogeneous series of signs or signals that emerges, but rather a weave of radically differentiated modes of expression, each governed by its own selection and combination rules. (39)

Elam's observations recall theater theoretician Manfred Pfister's related observation:

> As a "performed" text, drama [and musicals], in contrast to purely literary texts, makes use not only of verbal, but also acoustic and visual codes. It is a "synaesthetic text." This important criterion provides the starting point for any semiotic analysis of drama.[13]

When the emphasis on various modes of expression in a musical is different in productions subsequent to the original, the performance text changes, sometimes profoundly, and this potential for alteration and new meanings leads Kirle to categorize the performance text, as well as the varied dramatic texts, as "open," or without ultimate authority. "Musicals wed text, performance, and reception," Kirle observes in his opening sentence, "to create meaning within specified historical contexts" (1). In other words, an "authoritative" performance text is impossible, for even if a musical were recreated as an exact replica of its original production, its performance text would be altered, or open, by virtue of a different historical context. And sometimes a revisionist production, coupled with a different social, cultural, or economic climate, can create a new work altogether. Terry Eagleton, writing of philosopher Hans-Georg Gadamer, explains,

> As the work passes from one cultural or historical context to another, new meanings may be culled from it which were perhaps never anticipated by its author or contemporary audience....All interpretation is situational, shaped and constrained by the historically relative criteria of a particular culture.[14]

For instance, the extremely successful revival of *Chicago* eliminates Bob Fosse's original spectacular production aesthetic and instead presents the show in a minimalist scenic environment. But it also takes on additional layers of meaning for audiences who have experienced the show business–driven trials of O. J. Simpson and the late Michael Jackson, events that long postdate the original production.

Kirle's argument for the musical as an open text recalls similar arguments in musicologist Richard Taruskin's *Text and Act*, in which he criticizes musicologists promoting the Early Music movement as misguidedly clinging to the idea

> of the reified *Werk*—the objectified musical work-thing to which fidelity is owed....Although easily distinguished from performance, which is ephemeral and contingent, the notion of "the (timeless) work," as it has been called...is not easily disengaged from that of the (permanent) text through which it is transmitted.[15]

He continues a few pages later with an observation that becomes an integral element of Kirle's defense of the pre–Rodgers and Hammerstein musical: "The whole trouble with Early Music as a 'movement' is the way it has uncritically accepted the post-Romantic work-concept and imposed it anachronistically on pre-Romantic repertories" (13). Kirle has a similar complaint:

> Formalistic histories have tended to regard nonintegrated, pre-Rodgers and Hammerstein musicals as unfinished or open texts and assumed their artistic inferiority while privileging the artistic aspirations of the post-Rodgers and Hammerstein texts as closed, autonomous, and artistically superior. (1)

Needless to say, Kirle does not uphold that implied superiority.

Authors

Kirle raises another important issue related to the texts of musicals that provides a transition to the equally thorny subject of authorship. After observing that the British producer Cameron Mackintosh "brags that his productions [of the same show] are interchangeable," Kirle complains that "interchangeable, duplicate productions seem more like mass-produced technology than theatre" (10). He goes on to contrast what he calls Mackintosh's "übermarionette school of musical theatre" with the individualized and often improvisatory nature of actors' performances in musical comedy. In the latter, Kirle suggests, the actors are "cocreators," which in turn implies the co-authorship alluded to earlier. In 1927, for example, Charles Winninger, as Captain Andy in *Show Boat*, acted out the remainder of a melodrama when roughnecks in the onstage audience interrupted the performance. "No one today is quite sure exactly what Winninger did or how long the specialty lasted," Kirle observes, because, while Winninger's specialty was part of the performance text, it was never part of the written dramatic text (38). Instead, the actor created it, differently, perhaps, from performance to performance. In a more recent example, Harvey Fierstein, during his tenure as a frumpy Baltimore housewife in *Hairspray*, improvised nightly with his co-star Dick Latessa, adding lines and bits of business that amused the audience as well as Latessa. Both of these "additions" might be seen as violations of the written texts, but most audiences enthusiastically accepted them as part of the performance text, as did the creators of the written texts. The contributions of the actors in these examples, separated as they are by seventy-five years, indicate how a completely ephemeral aspect of performance can confer co-authorship on the actor. That transference of authorship is not always approved by other authors, however: Kirle points out that soon after *Fiddler on the Roof* opened on Broadway, star Zero Mostel "started interpolating stage business and ad-libs," much to the chagrin of director Jerome Robbins and librettist Joseph Stein (34).

Even without improvisation, performance is a creative act. Further, because various external elements—different audiences, locations, contemporaneous events, and so on—often alter aspects of performance, no two performances are ever quite the same, even if they are intended to replicate previous performances. This in turn implies two related ideas: (1) because performance is fundamentally creative, it is at all times an integral part of the performance text, and (2) the performer is a co-author of that text.

These examples of co-creation demonstrate what Pfister refers to as "the sociology of authorship" (29). Pfister, who is writing about non–musical theater but whose observations apply with equal accuracy to the musical, notes:

> As far as dramatic texts are concerned, the sociology of authorship becomes even more complicated in view of the multiplicity of productive functions. That is, the author of the printed and literary text substratum is no more than one of the several "authors" of the multimedial, enacted text. (29)

The importance of this differentiation of authorship cannot be overestimated. How accurate is it, for instance, to refer to "Rodgers and Hammerstein's *Oklahoma!*" when one of the most memorable and discussed aspects of the original production was choreographer Agnes de Mille's uniquely balletic dances? Her work was, and continues to be, appreciated, but although she created an identifiable physical style for the work, she is rarely given *authorial* credit, perhaps in part because her dances were never part of a written text. Further, when Trevor Nunn directed his influential

1998 revival of the work at London's National Theatre, he replaced all of de Mille's dances as well as the original dance music while keeping the rest of the script and score, although not the orchestrations, virtually intact. De Mille's co-authorship of the work (and that of orchestrator Robert Russell Bennett) literally disappeared.

This disappearance of an author recalls Roland Barthes's important 1967 essay, "The Death of the Author." Seeking to reexamine and resituate the reader's role in the text, Barthes argues that "a text is made of multiple writings," further noting that "the reader is the space on which all the quotations that make up a writing are inscribed without any of them being lost; a text's unity lies not in its origins but in its destination."[16] This perspective links Barthes with other reception theorists, who shift the primary importance of a text from the author to the reader. Writing about an even earlier work—Jean-Paul Sartre's *What Is Literature?* (1948)—Terry Eagleton observes that "a work's reception is never just an 'external' fact about it, a contingent matter of book reviews and book shop sales [or, I would add, for the musical, out-of-town preview responses, newspaper reviews, and box-office sales]. It is a constitutive dimension of the work itself."[17] Thirty years later in *The Act of Reading*, Wolfgang Iser writes of the "strategies" and "codes" in texts that must be understood before the reader can construct meanings from those texts.[18] Similarly, the conventions of the musical must be understood and accepted by audiences ("readers") before any meaning can be created. When these conventions are replaced by a new set of codes, audiences, like readers of literary works, often have difficulty constructing meaning. (Here I am reminded of a confused woman overheard during the intermission of *Spring Awakening*, a 2006 musical that radically rethought the use of song, dance, and narrative in adapting Frank Wedekind's late nineteenth-century tale of adolescent sexuality: "I just don't understand it: it's not at all like *The Boy from Oz*.")

Following Barthes's essay by a year, Michel Foucault's "What Is an Author?" reconfigures the author-reader-text relation from a slightly more complex perspective. "A certain number of notions that are intended to replace the privileged position of the author," Foucault notes, "actually seem to preserve that privilege and suppress the real meaning of his disappearance."[19] He then proceeds to reassess the author within, and without, his or her texts, observing the following:

> [An] author's name is not simply an element in a discourse.... [I]t performs a certain role with regard to narrative discourse, assuring a classificatory function. Such a name permits one to group together a certain number of texts, define them, differentiate them from and contrast them to others. In addition, it establishes a relationship among the texts.... The author's name serves to characterize a certain mode of being of discourse. (147)

Foucault's observation that an authorial identity allows the grouping of texts—for our purposes, and despite their inaccuracies or incompleteness, "Rodgers and Hammerstein shows," "Sondheim musicals," or "Bob Fosse musicals," and so on—is important. He calls such authorial identities "founders of discursivity," and he observes that they are "unique in that they are not just the authors of their own works. They have produced something else: the possibilities and the rules for the formation of other texts" (154). For instance, how many shows after 1943 can be identified, in Foucault's sense, as "Rodgers and Hammerstein musicals" although that writing team had nothing to do with their creation? Creating a musical in the 1940s and 1950s that was not influenced by Rodgers and Hammerstein was virtually impossible: if a show did not follow the model, it recalled the model as something against which to react. And few reactions against the model lasted long on Broadway stages until the late 1960s (*Cabaret*, 1966; *Hair*, 1968) or the early 1970s (*Company*, 1970). In another application of Foucault's classification, however, we may note the number of musicals that, despite their being created by the same person, do *not* produce possibilities for other texts. Despite having written the scores to a number of Broadway hits, for instance, Elton John has yet to be recognized as the founder of a discourse within the musical. There is no such term as "an Elton John musical."

By the end of his essay, however, Foucault is prepared to acknowledge the disappearance, if not the death, of the author. In his penultimate paragraph, he observes the following:

> Although, since the eighteenth century, the author has played the role of the regulator of the fictive...still, given the historical modifications that are taking place, it does not seem necessary that the author-function remain constant in form, complexity, and even in existence. I think that, as our society changes, at the very moment when it is in the process of changing, the author-function will disappear, and in such a manner that fiction and its polysemic texts will once again function according to another mode, but still with a system of constraint— one which will no longer be the author, but which will have to be determined or, perhaps, experienced. (159–60)

Any new system of constraint, or understanding, that develops as a tool for critically responding to the musical will be based at least in part on the assumption that each audience member brings his or her own social and historical identity to the experience of any given show. Because of the open nature of a musical's text, both in terms of how it can be changed by its creators and/or interpreters and how it must of necessity be perceived differently according to the historical period in which it is experienced, its reception will always be a part of its meaning. This in turn implies that the audience, individually and collectively, will always play a role in its creation and re-creation.

Show Boat: A Case Study

The problems of definitively establishing text and author are perhaps best found in a number of much-revived and often rewritten "classic" musicals. To be sure, that designation is in itself problematic and often ironic, in that most such shows have undergone many changes since their first productions, so that the qualities that earn them "classic" status may have been long since excised in revivals. Nonetheless, older repertory shows provide particularly useful case studies for the problems considered above. Although any number of pre–Rodgers and Hammerstein musicals might serve in this regard, *Show Boat* is the outstanding example of a "classic" that has never been performed the same way in any two productions, a circumstance that brings the issue of its "text" to the forefront. Moreover, given that all productions—even the original—use songs not by Jerome Kern or Oscar Hammerstein II, the official composer and lyricist of the score, problems of authorship arise even beyond the issues raised earlier.

When *Show Boat* opened in 1927, it was generally agreed by critics and audiences to be a giant step forward for the American musical in terms of the genre at last becoming "serious." Although Hammerstein wrote a book that contained elements of musical comedy as well as of the operettas for which he was mostly known, he also allowed for spaces of actor co-authorship, such as Charles Winninger's comic business discussed earlier or Norma Terris's impersonations of contemporaneous entertainers. (Terris was Magnolia, the principal female character.) And, as Scott McMillin found in a previously overlooked early draft for *Show Boat*, Hammerstein and Kern, in fashioning the role of Joe specifically for Paul Robeson, created a second act scene that was to be a performance of interpolated spirituals.[20] Indeed, as Todd Decker has noted, the scene was called "A Paul Robeson Recital," thus acknowledging the centrality of the performer to the early concept of the work.[21] Nonetheless, the "text" of *Show Boat*, in 1927, was probably considered a fait accompli once the show opened. But the history of the show's revivals suggests that it was an open text almost from the beginning and demonstrates the difficulty of establishing any kind of textual authority for this or any other show.

Show Boat was first revived by Florenz Ziegfeld in 1932. Hoping to bolster his failing finances, Ziegfeld recruited many of the original cast members and replaced several with even bigger names. Paul Robeson, for instance, who turned down the original production but created a sensation as Joe in the later London production, was cast in the revival, although no attempt was made to reinstate the recital of spirituals. The production was as close to a replication of the original as possible. When it toured, however, it was increasingly truncated, first by cuts in the cast and finally in massive cuts to the show itself, which resulted in a ninety-minute version that played between features in movie palaces. According to Miles Kreuger, Hammerstein's assistant did the cutting.[22] While the 1936 film version closely followed the original stage version, the postwar 1946 revival brought changes indicative of a new era for the American musical.

The elements of operetta and musical comedy that had fused with great success in the original production at this point seemed dated in the wake of Hammerstein's own advancement of the form in *Oklahoma!* (1943) and *Carousel* (1945). When composer Jerome Kern died before the revival began rehearsals, Hammerstein took over the entire production. In a note for the cast album of the revival, Hammerstein made a telling comment: "Our present production had to be built to match the enhanced glamour of the public's memory of Ziegfeld's original production"

(Kreuger, 158). Hammerstein was reimagining the work to fit the *memory* of the audience's reception, and this resulted in major changes to the show's look. Kreuger notes,

> Because of Hammerstein's concern that the public in 1946 had come to expect a more decorative look [in musicals], there was a conscious effort to brighten the sets and costumes. In both color and form, the mounting was intentionally theatrical and artificial, thereby setting a trend for designing *Show Boat* on stage and screen that has lasted until today. (158)

Robert Russell Bennett updated the orchestrations, and while Hammerstein wrote in playbills that the script and score were largely "as they were when originally written in 1927," the cuts and changes were actually far more substantial than this comment suggests. The script was also trimmed of language that, in terms of race, was less acceptable in 1946 than it had been in 1927. The word "nigger," for instance, which occurred throughout the original script, was virtually eliminated. Finally, as a response to the impact of Agnes de Mille's influential use of dance in the first three Rodgers and Hammerstein musicals, much dance was added to the revival. Indeed, Kreuger refers to its "preoccupation with dance" (163). The changes that Hammerstein made to his earlier work, in general, were attempts to re-cast it in the mold of the Rodgers and Hammerstein musical play, a form that was codified only three years earlier. Even Hammerstein could not avoid being influenced by his own accomplishments.

Show Boat has experienced major overhauls with each new revival. The most recent Broadway production, directed by Harold Prince in 1994, contained a new second act sequence created by Prince and choreographer Susan Stroman. Prince also redistributed some of the musical numbers, most notably giving "Why Do I Love You," originally sung by Gaylord and Magnolia, to Parthy, played by Elaine Stritch. And just six years earlier, conductor John McGlinn, aided by numerous materials uncovered in a Secaucus, New Jersey, warehouse, recorded all the known music ever written for any production of the show. But while the result is a valuable collection of Kern and Hammerstein's efforts and reveals countless alterations made to the work throughout its history, those changes remain disconnected artifacts and argue against any "definitive" or authoritative versions. As Kreuger notes,

> Although the show's earliest alterations were made by Hammerstein himself as a method of keeping the work vital to a changing audience, the trend was begun to permit the show to follow whatever theatrical vogue might have been fashionable. Like an older building that has been "modernized" through the elimination of its distinctive architectural details, *Show Boat* has been left without its original form and with only diluted dramatic impact. (212)

Kreuger ends his consideration of the work with the hope that "perhaps the time has come to re-create *Show Boat* in the form that inspired *New York Telegram* critic Robert Garland to call it on opening night simply 'an American masterpiece'" (213).

The irony of Kreuger's wish is that, as we have observed, such a re-creation is impossible. And even if it were possible, would it be desirable? Apart from institutionalizing the work as a museum artifact, what would be the point of reverting to the 1927 version? Even if the original script and score could be replicated, the work would evoke vastly different responses from a post–civil rights movement, post–Rodgers and Hammerstein audience. These responses in turn would change the performance text, regardless of the dramatic texts that were used.

In 1927, the interpolation of musical numbers that were not created for the show into which they were inserted was still a common practice, and *Show Boat* contains several examples of this practice. Later versions of the show continued the practice and inserted other numbers, but two of the principal songs interpolated into the original production were Charles K. Harris's hit "After the Ball" and "Bill," a song by Kern and lyricist P. G. Wodehouse originally featured in the 1917 musical *Oh Lady! Lady!* (Sousa's "Washington Post" is also used to introduce the rehearsal scene in act 2 that contains "Bill.") The placement of the songs makes their use somewhat appropriate. In the second act, for instance, Julie rehearses "Bill" in the nightclub where she works, and, later in the act, Magnolia sings "After the Ball" at a New Year's Eve celebration, a deliberately nostalgic choice even in the onstage setting. But the presence of the songs, however appropriate their settings, presents a problem in terms of establishing authorship. Only Kern and Hammerstein get billing for having written the score, and while Wodehouse and Harris get credit for their contributions in the published score and in most programs, the musical text is nonetheless more collaborative than is generally known by most of the theatergoing public. The songs add period "authority" to the show even as they implicitly question the authority of the acknowledged composer and lyricist.

David Savran raises issues and questions appropriate to consider here:

> In the field of cultural production, problems of text and performance open up a number of crucially important questions for a history of popular-theatre forms: How can claims of authenticity obtain when original texts have disappeared as well as the performance styles and traditions that made the pieces work? If musicals are the most collaborative and conventionalized of theatrical forms, what is the value of a theory of authorship? Does it suffice to describe *Lady in the Dark* (1941) as a Kurt Weill musical? Or as a Kurt Weill-Ira Gershwin-Moss Hart-Gertrude Lawrence musical? Or does one need to mobilize a different model of cultural production? Perhaps one in which questions of authorship are displaced from the individual maker to a collective subject? Or to the history of conventions? Or to the class habitus of the producers? (214)

As we have seen, the disciplines of literary theory, theater theory and history, and musicology all inform the consideration of these and other questions that are unique to the musical. All of them share Savran's impulse toward considering the author of a musical as, to use his term, "a collective subject," although musicology is the slowest to embrace this idea. And all three of them have begun to deal with the issue of closed versus open texts, especially in terms of works for the stage. But the questions are still being discussed, and no definitive answers are as yet forthcoming.

In the end, while we may know who wrote the book, music, and lyrics for any given musical, the knowledge of who the author is (or authors are) might be slightly harder to discern, especially if, as members of the audience, we are part of the collective authorship. And figuring out what the text is has a great deal to do with when and how we experience any given performance. The difficulty of these issues is real, but they must be dealt with by anyone who cares about the musical. As the musical undergoes more and more serious critical interrogation, solutions to the problems posed in this essay might be forthcoming. But even if they are not, the problems make for challenging consideration.

NOTES

1. Stephen Banfield, *Sondheim's Broadway Musicals* (Ann Arbor: University of Michigan Press, 1993), p. 3.

2. Kier Elam, *The Semiotics of Theatre and Drama*, 2nd ed. (London: Routledge, 2002), p. 3.

3. Raymond Knapp, *The American Musical and the Formation of National Identity* (Princeton, NJ: Princeton University Press, 2005), p. 190.

4. Joseph P. Swain, *The Broadway Musical; A Critical and Musical Survey,* 2nd ed. (Lanham, MD: Scarecrow Press, 2002), and Joseph Kerman, *Opera as Drama,* rev. ed. (London: Faber and Faber, 1988).

5. Roland Barthes, "Introduction to the Structural Analysis of Narration," in *Image, Music, Text,* ed. and trans. Stephen Heath (New York: Hill and Wang, 1977, 261–67), p. 262.

6. David Savran, "Toward a Historiography of the Popular" (*Theatre Survey* 45.2 [November 2004]: 211–17), pp. 215–16.

7. Bernhard Radloff, "Text," in *Encyclopedia of Contemporary Literary Theory: Approaches, Scholars, Terms,* ed. Irena R. Makaryk (Toronto: University of Toronto Press, 1993, 639–41), p. 639.

8. Jindřich Honzl, "Dynamics in the Sign in the Theater," in *Semiotics of Art: Prague School Contributions,* ed. L. Matejka and K. Pomorsak (Cambridge, MA: MIT Press, 1976, 74–93), p. 74.

9. Scott McMillin, *The Musical as Drama: A Study of the Principles and Conventions behind Musical Shows from Kern to Sondheim* (Princeton, NJ: Princeton University Press, 2006).

10. Richard Rodgers, *Musical Stages: An Autobiography* (New York: Random House, 1975), p. 227.

11. Bernard Beckerman, *Theatrical Presentation: Performer, Audience, and Act* (London: Routledge, 1990), p. 90.

12. Bruce Kirle, *Unfinished Show Business: Broadway Musicals as Works-in-Process* (Carbondale: Southern Illinois University Press, 2005), p. 7.

13. Manfred Pfister, *The Theory and Analysis of Drama,* trans. John Halliday (Cambridge: Cambridge University Press, 1988), p. 7.

14. Terry Eagleton, *Literary Theory: An Introduction,* 2nd ed. (Minneapolis: University of Minnesota Press, 1996), pp. 61–62.

15. Richard Taruskin, *Text and Act: Essays on Music and Performance* (New York: Oxford University Press, 1995), pp. 10–11.

16. Roland Barthes, "The Death of the Author," in *Image, Music, Text,* ed. and trans. Stephen Heath (New York: Hill and Wang, 1977, 142–48), p. 148.

17. See Eagleton, 72, and Jean-Paul Sartre, *What Is Literature?* trans. Bernard Frechtman (London: Routledge, 2001).

18. Wolfgang Iser, *The Act of Reading: A Theory of Aesthetic Response* (Baltimore: Johns Hopkins University Press, 1980).

19. Michel Foucault, "What Is an Author?" in *Textual Strategies: Perspectives in Post-Structuralist Criticism*, ed. and trans. Josué V. Harari (Ithaca, NY: Cornell University Press, 1979, 141–60), p. 143.

20. Scott McMillin, "Paul Robeson, Will Vodery's 'Jubilee Singers,' and the Earliest Script of the Kern-Hammerstein *Show Boat*" (*Theatre Survey* 41 [2000]: 51–70), p. 66.

21. See Todd Decker, "'Do You Want to Hear a Mammy Song?' A Historiography of *Show Boat*" (*Contemporary Theatre Review* 19.1 [2009]: 8–21), pp. 20–21. Decker provides a more in-depth discussion of this interpolation in "Black/White Encounters on the American Stage and Screen (1924–2005)" (Ph.D. dissertation, University of Michigan, 2007), pp. 116–23.

22. Miles Kreuger, *Show Boat: The Story of a Classic American Musical* (New York: Da Capo Press, 1977), p. 108.

CHAPTER 3

MUSICAL STYLES AND SONG CONVENTIONS

PAUL R. LAIRD

THE musical theater demands that composers provide immediately accessible music in a variety of styles. Once a stage character reaches that magical moment when talking stops and singing begins, what she or he sings must be stylistically comprehensible to the audience. In a 1920s show, for example, two characters might be about to declare their love and the orchestra will begin a waltz. Or a secondary character might show the audience a new dance that corresponds to a song's name, opening with a spoken and sung verse before the chorus (or refrain) in a rapid duple meter with frequent syncopation. In a modern show, a dramatic moment might call for a rock style that will be declared by the drummer and electric guitar. Another song in the same show might be more contemplative, and the relaxed string accompaniment and brushes on the cymbals signal a traditional Broadway ballad.

Composers seeking appropriate music for the American musical theater since the late nineteenth century have used many styles. Although popular music has changed greatly over the years, some old musical styles have stayed current in the theater longer than one might expect. The waltz, for example, was passé as a couples dance by 1900 but remained significant as a theatrical song type throughout the twentieth century. This essay considers representative musical styles and types of songs that have appeared theatrically since the late nineteenth century. Some are primarily styles, such as jazz, which has been a profound influence on Broadway musicals and films since the 1920s, and ragtime, which denotes a style expressed in its purest form in rags. A number of composers, however, especially Irving Berlin, wrote songs in the 1910s and 1920s that used stylistic elements of ragtime while not being in the form of a rag. Similar distinctions could be made about blues and other musical styles. Also relevant are many dance types, such as the waltz and polka, which may carry dramatic associations, influence a composer's choice of meter, and shape melodic and rhythmic expectations.

In *The American Musical Theater* (1975), Lehman Engel provides a useful typology for songs in musicals.[1] Engel describes the importance of a show's opening musical number and the different approaches taken in this song type by various creators. He notes that the musical soliloquy, when a character lays bare inner feelings, is important to both opera and the musical. The ballad, usually a slower number with a memorable melody and often associated with love or another emotion, has been a staple for popular song composers. Engel coins the term "charm song," defined as "a song that embodies generally delicate, optimistic, and rhythmic music, and lyrics of light though not necessarily comedic subject matter" (87). He names "The Surrey with the Fringe on Top" from *Oklahoma!* as the archetypical charm song. The musical scene is a long segment "in which the words shifted back and forth between dialogue and lyric (sung) verse" (89). Engel traces its origins to grand opera and operetta, and shows the significant place it holds in a number of shows where the creators tell the audience much about characters and move the plot forward. Engel also describes the importance of comedic songs in musicals. A somewhat less convincing general category that Engel offers is the "rhythm song," which is "carried along, or propelled by, a musical beat which is most usually a regular one" (106). He also shows the importance of distributing the various song types across a show's musical program (109–22), and devotes an entire chapter to Broadway opera (132–54).

Broadway conventions also include other song types, such as the "I want" song and "eleven-o-clock number." The first takes place early in a show and discloses a main character's primary motivation, such as "Wouldn't It Be Loverly?" from *My Fair Lady* and "The Wizard and I" from *Wicked*. The so-called eleven-o-clock number goes back to a day when curtain times were later, and at about this hour a show included a number that heightened the energy level or dramatic interest in the second act. Examples include "Sit Down, You're Rocking the Boat" from *Guys and Dolls* and "You've Got to Be Carefully Taught" from *South Pacific*. Usually each act also ends with a strong number. Powerful act finales in recent shows include "Defying Gravity" in *Wicked* (Act 1) and "You Can't Stop the Beat" from *Hairspray* (Act 2), but it would be very difficult to generalize about musical style in finales.

The most typical popular song form used on Broadway is a verse followed by a chorus or refrain. A verse is often rendered in speech rhythms, often over a simple, chordal accompaniment, somewhat like operatic recitative. It is not commonly the verse that communicates stylistic information about the music. That comes in the chorus, which might range from a fast dance tempo to a slow ballad. It is also the chorus that a listener remembers; there are many famous songs for musical theater for which only the most rabid of fans know the verse. Typical forms of choruses appear below in the description of ballads.

RICHES FROM RAGS TO RAP: THE DEVELOPMENT
OF MUSICAL STYLES

The first popular musical style to emanate from African Americans and become a national craze was ragtime, popular from the early 1890s to about World War I. In a deliberate duple meter with syncopated melodies, rags by Scott Joplin and others influenced commercial songwriters to compose pieces, sometimes called rags, that imitated aspects of the style but did not carry all markers of the type. These songs usually had syncopated melodies, ragtime's most distinctive feature. Irving Berlin wrote a number of such songs, most famously "Alexander's Ragtime Band" (1911). Berlin wrote a Broadway score that included samples of his version of ragtime in *Watch Your Step* (1914). The first act finale was "The Syncopated Walk." Later musicals included ragtime references to help set a time and place. In *Show Boat* (1927), "Goodbye, My Lady Love" sounds like a rag, and there is also a reference to the style in the dance of "Shipoopi" from *The Music Man* (1957), a story that takes place just before World War I, making ragtime a useful stylistic signifier (⬤ Example 3.1).

An operetta score might include a variety of musical types, from the familiar strains of the waltz and march to contemporary popular music. *The Desert Song* (1926), for example, included numbers by Sigmund Romberg based on the genre's typical European roots, but also "It," which might have appeared in a contemporary musical comedy (⬤ Example 3.2). Despite this musical variety, however, the dominant stylistic expectation in an operetta was lyrical melodies composed for trained voices. The source for this style was opera, and many operetta performers had operatic training and might even have had a parallel career on the operatic stage. Emma Trentini, who sang with the Manhattan Opera Company, for example, appeared as the female lead in Victor Herbert's *Naughty Marietta* (1910) and other operettas. Herbert and other operetta composers wrote songs for stars like Trentini that featured a wide range, large leaps, delicate ornamentation, and other virtuoso touches. Famous examples of such writing include the "Italian Street Song" from *Naughty Marietta*, "Serenade" from *The Student Prince*, and "You Are Love" for *Show Boat*, a musical play that included touches from operetta models (⬤ Example 3.3). Even after the operetta declined in popularity in the 1930s, the style remained familiar; for example, Bernstein's *Candide* (1956), was described as an operetta and includes the operatic "Glitter and Be Gay."

Opera itself has also appeared on Broadway. This style includes virtuosic vocal writing for large voices and major segments of the show that are sung throughout. The most famous opera on Broadway was George Gershwin's *Porgy and Bess* (1935), with vocal demands on the major characters necessitating that the show be double or triple cast for Broadway runs with eight performances per week. Other operas that have appeared on Broadway include Marc Blitzstein's *Regina* (1949) and Gian Carlo Menotti's *The Consul* (1950) and *The Saint of Bleecker Street* (1954). It should be noted that the original version of Sondheim's *Sweeney Todd* (1979) and several megamusicals of the 1980s fit part of the genre's definition, being mostly sung and featuring large stage spectacle. Schoenberg and Boublil's *Les Misérables* (1985) and Andrew Lloyd Webber's *Phantom of the Opera* (1986) both include lengthy segments that are entirely sung and offer rich technical effects, and the latter includes true operatic scenes.

Jazz emerged as a popular musical style after World War I, and it was a major influence on musical theater. As a style, jazz has changed throughout its history, but the type that had the most influence on other music is swing of the 1930s. One can trace jazz influence on the musical theater before swing appeared, however. One of the first appearances of jazz gestures in a Broadway show was in *Shuffle Along* (1921), the first Broadway show conceived entirely by African Americans. Eubie Blake's score (lyrics by Noble Sissle) included rich syncopation and other jazz-like elements (probably with little improvisation). The point was made in the first song entitled "I'm Simply Full of Jazz," and other major songs included "Love Will Find a Way," "Bandana Days," "I'm Just Wild about Harry," and "Baltimore Buzz" (◉ Example 3.4). There was even a song in the second act called "Syncopation Stenos." After *Shuffle Along*, the sounds of jazz never left Broadway, but usually served as a novelty to add color to a score. A show that had a strong jazz feel was the African American *Hot Chocolates* (1929), with a score by Fats Waller and others, and with Louis Armstrong in the cast. George Gershwin brought jazz rhythms and blues intervals to the musical theater, but his music lacked the improvisation that most scholars believe a part of true jazz. His use of jazz rhythms appears in "Fascinating Rhythm" from *Lady, Be Good* (1924). A number of the composer's scores continued in this vein, including *Porgy and Bess*. During the swing era and later, typical Broadway orchestration resembled that of the big band (but also with strings), and orchestrators routinely used big band sounds. Later jazz styles, such as bop and free jazz, appeared less often on Broadway, but Leonard Bernstein made telling use of modern jazz sounds in *West Side Story*, especially in the song "Cool," reminiscent of music by the Modern Jazz Quartet (◉ Example 3.5). Jazz of earlier periods has appeared in several shows based on prominent musicians, including, for example, Fats Waller's songs in *Ain't Misbehavin'* (1978), Duke Ellington's tunes in *Sophisticated Ladies* (1981), and the music of Jelly Roll Morton in *Jelly's Last Jam* (1992).

Like jazz, the influence of blues in other areas of American concert music and musical theater has been more in use of the style's typical sounds than in its pure, improvisational form. Early blues figures, such as Ma Rainey and Bessie Smith, seldom if ever appeared on Broadway, although Smith was in the short-lived *Pansy* (1929). Far more important for the musical theater, and films as well, has been the appearance of the genre's distinctive melodic and harmonic gestures appearing in songs and instrumental numbers that are not in a typical blues form, like the famed 12-bar progression. Gershwin, for example, made routine use of blues melodic gestures in his melodies, such as the lowered third, fifth, and seventh degrees of the scale. One of his typical bluesy melodies is "Sam and Delilah" from *Girl Crazy* (1930), and a very famous example of a blues third in his output occurs in the closing gesture in *An American in Paris* (1928), which appeared as a ballet score in the 1951

MGM film by the same name (⬤ Example 3.6). Jerome Kern exemplified typical theatrical use of the blues in "Can't Help Lovin' Dat Man" from *Show Boat*. The song works well in the langorous tempo often associated with the genre and includes blues notes in the melody, but the typical harmonic gestures for the style occur only in the verse.[2] Blues had a huge influence on later popular styles that have appeared in musical theater, such as rhythm and blues and rock.

Folk music has been an occasional influence on musical theater and films, often appearing in shows where the plot or a particular character renders such music appropriate. Examples include the song "Edelweiss" from *The Sound of Music* (1959), a simple song that comes to represent Austria in that story, and "Next to Lovin' (I Like Fightin')" from *Shenandoah* (1975), among other tunes in that show, which involves a Virginia family during the American Civil War (⬤ Example 3.7). These songs both feature the diatonic, singable melodies one associates with most folk music. "Ol' Man River" from *Show Boat* (1927), with its moving melody and powerful lyrics that capture the Mississippi River's significance in the story, carries a potent folk essence (mingled with the nineteenth-century spiritual), but the demands on the baritone are unlike those of most folk songs. Country music, with a musical character that often resembles folk music, also appears in musical theater, with two good examples being "Shoeless Joe from Hannibal, Mo." (with the character of a hoedown) from *Damn Yankees* (1955) and much of the score of *Big River* (1985), by noted country musician Roger Miller (⬤ Example 3.8). English shows have included songs with folk characteristics as well, such as "Who Will Buy?" from *Oliver!* (1960) and "Deep into the Ground" from *Billy Elliot* (2005). *The Secret Garden* (1991), with music by Lucy Simon, takes place in the English countryside with several local characters, and its score is filled with references to English folk songs, especially the lowered seventh scale degree found in the modes that dominate folk music.

"Ol' Man River" from *Show Boat*, as noted above, sounds somewhat like a nineteenth-century African American spiritual, and Broadway composers also have occasionally alluded to the revival number, another type of inspirational song often found in religious music. Revival songs musically bear some resemblance to gospel music, and they have usually appeared in musicals for humorous, ironic effect, such as "Blow, Gabriel, Blow" from Cole Porter's *Anything Goes* (1934), Frank Loesser's "Sit Down, You're Rockin' the Boat" from *Guys and Dolls* (1950), and "Brotherhood of Man" from *How to Succeed in Business without Really Trying* (1961; ⬤ Example 3.9). Stephen Schwartz also included similar numbers in his score to *Godspell* (1971), such as "We Beseech Thee."

Various types of Latin music, especially dances, have made frequent appearances in the musical theater. While careful distinctions can be made between Latin music from different countries and traditions, the simple truth about its theatrical use—as in other Western music—is that many composers treat all influences from the Spanish- and Portuguese-speaking worlds as if from one source. Examples of this tendency include Frederick Loewe's composition of an Argentine tango for "The Rain in Spain" in *My Fair Lady* (1956) when textual references in the song clearly point to Iberia, and in *West Side Story* (1957), in which the Latin characters are Puerto Rican, but the composer Bernstein used mostly Afro-Cuban and Mexican dances (🎵 Example 3.10). References to Latin and Caribbean music appear as early as in Gershwin's "Land of the Gay Caballero" from *Girl Crazy* (1930) and memorably in Cole Porter's "Begin the Beguine" from *Jubilee* (1935), where the composer uses rhythms associated with this dance from French Martinique. In his score of compelling—if not always accurate—Latin references in *West Side Story*, Bernstein makes the region's driving and repetitious rhythms work to great advantage in "America" and the "Mambo," among other numbers. Latin influences have appeared as novelties in many musicals such as the song "Conga!" in Bernstein's *Wonderful Town* (1953) and "Spanish Rose" from Charles Strouse's *Bye Bye Birdie* (1960), where it carries the designation of a "tango." Other scores with rich influences from either Iberian or Latin sources are *Man of La Mancha* (1965) and *In the Heights* (2008).

Given the large numbers of Jews who participated in the American entertainment industry during the twentieth century, it is predictable that one finds Jewish influence on the musical theater.[3] As Jack Gottlieb has demonstrated, popular songs from the first half of the twentieth century frequently resemble Jewish liturgical modes.[4] Gottlieb, however, cites associations that would escape most musicians, let alone casual listeners. More obvious Jewish references appear in shows on Jewish topics, such as *Milk and Honey* (1961) with a score by Jerry Herman, and *Fiddler on the Roof* (1964) with music by Jerry Bock. Typical musical signifiers include the harmonic minor scale, melodic augmented second, imitations of cantorial singing (such as in "If I Were a Rich Man"), and klezmer's rapid dance rhythms (such as the wedding scene of *Fiddler*).

What might be referred to as the "classic" style of theatrical songs, often described as "Tin Pan Alley"—represented in the work of Berlin, the Gershwin brothers, Rodgers and Hart, Cole Porter, Rodgers and Hammerstein, and others—reigned supreme into the 1960s. Earlier musical styles from African American musicians such as spirituals, ragtime, jazz, and blues had been assimilated easily into the musical, but waves of African American influence after World War II, including rhythm and blues, rock-and-roll, gospel, and soul, entered the theater more slowly as songwriters continued to make use of earlier styles. Shows based mostly on rock and other popular styles did not appear until the late 1960s, and use of these styles was rare by older composers. Charles Strouse (born 1928) wrote two songs with some musical signifiers of 1950s rock-and-roll for *Bye Bye Birdie* (1960), to be sung by a character based on Elvis Presley, but "Honestly Sincere" and "One Last Kiss" were novelties in an otherwise traditional score. *Hair* (1967) was the first musical that could support the moniker "rock musical," with an amplified score by Galt MacDermot based primarily on a typical rock beat played by a common rock ensemble, with obvious bass lines and a prominent backbeat. The title tune, "Easy to Be Hard," and "Aquarius" were major hits (🎵 Example 3.11). Several more shows with similarly popular scores followed soon thereafter, including Stephen Schwartz's *Godspell* and *Jesus Christ Superstar* by Andrew Lloyd Webber and Tim Rice, both from 1971. Both scores demonstrate that "rock musicals" tended to include other styles, such as a counterpoint song inspired by Irving Berlin's music in *Godspell*

("All for the Best") and a campy 1930s soft-shoe in *Jesus Christ Superstar* ("King Herod's Song").

Schwartz's *Godspell* illustrates how popular styles appeared in scores by young composers starting around 1970.[5] Schwartz (b. 1948) understood rock, Motown, and the work of singer/songwriters such as Laura Nyro, James Taylor, Joni Mitchell, and Carole King. He agreed to write a new score for the existing show in March 1971, quickly composing a dozen songs in five weeks for a May Off Broadway opening. For each tune Schwartz chose a model and wrote a tune somewhat like that, usually focusing on a song's harmonic tendencies or accompanimental pattern. "Day by Day," for example, was inspired by Burt Bacharach's "What the World Needs Now," a waltz with many seventh chords. Schwartz wanted more energy later in the repetitious tune and switched to quadruple meter and a rock beat. The model for Schwartz's "Bless the Lord" was Laura Nyro's "Save the Country," especially the piano accompaniment, her use of bass notes that are not in the chord, and tempo changes. Schwartz's model for "All Good Gifts" was "Fire and Rain" by James Taylor, with a piano accompaniment not unlike certain tunes by Elton John. "Light of the World," the first act finale, was based on "Gemini Child" by the Mamas & the Papas, which had an accompanimental pattern in quarter notes of "boom – boom – chink," with a dissonant chord on the third beat. Of the four songs considered here, this sounds the most like rock.

Rhythm and blues, rock, gospel, and soul have filled scores in musical theater since about 1970, including those for *Don't Bother Me, I Can't Cope* (1972), *The Wiz* (1975), *Your Arms Too Short to Box with God* (1976), *Bring in 'da Noise, Bring in 'da Funk* (1996), and other shows. These primarily African American shows by Micki Grant, Charlie Smalls, Daryl Waters, and others demonstrated that audiences craved popular music in a theatrical context. Andrew Lloyd Webber showed his ability to write in popular styles from his earliest shows (such as *Jesus Christ Superstar*), and he continued to use these styles in his huge hits *Cats* (1981) and *Phantom of the Opera* (1986). In *Cats*, for example, the rock sound of "The Rum Tum Tugger" and funky, bump-and-grind music for "Macavity: The Mystery Cat" exist alongside music reminiscent of Puccini in "Growltiger's Last Stand" and the famous power ballad "Memory." Schwartz has continued his cultivation of popular styles in *Wicked* (2003), where the character Elphaba is a pop diva, singing in a style borrowing from rhythm and blues. Jonathan Larson's score for *Rent* (1996) is a catalog of various popular styles worked seamlessly into a strong story and rendered all the more powerful by Larson's keen sense of illustrating characters through lyrics. Another use of popular styles in the theater has been the "jukebox musical," where the catalog of one songwriter or popular music group becomes the basis for a score. Major jukebox musicals have included *Mamma Mia!* (based on songs by ABBA, 2001) and *Jersey Boys* (The Four Seasons, 2005).

Rap has appeared in musical theater, such as *In the Heights* (2008), a potent combination of various Latin styles and rap with music and lyrics by Lin-Manuel Miranda. Rap appears in such songs as "96,000" and the title song (◐ Example 3.12). Hollywood has used rap in musicals as well, such as in *Beat Street* (1984). But the principal of rhythmicized speech was not invented for rap, and one can find examples in earlier Broadway shows, and even earlier in the patter songs of Italian comic opera or Gilbert and Sullivan operettas from the nineteenth century, but certainly not with a rap accompaniment. Meredith Willson, for example, explored the possibility in *The Music Man* (1957) in such songs as "Trouble." Willson's light patter style for Harold Hill presented the character with the requisite verbal virtuosity for a musical con man. And Stephen Sondheim, who is particularly adept at reproducing pastiche versions of earlier styles, uses patter as one element of contrapuntal songs in *Company* ("Getting Married Today," 1970) and *Pacific Overtures* ("Please Hello," 1976).

Non-Western musical styles have made occasional appearances in the theater, most prominently in Sondheim's *Pacific Overtures* and in *The Lion King* (1997). The latter, based on the 1994 animated musical film by the same name with a score by Elton John and Tim Rice, as a stage musical includes new songs that make purposeful use of African sounds, such as "One by One" by Lebo M and "Shadowland" by Hans Zimmer, Lebo M, and Mark Mancina. Perhaps following the lead of *Pacific Overtures*'s use of Japanese instruments and theatrical styles, the African musical sensibility is enriched by a wide variety of percussion instruments. Combined with director Julie Taymor's imaginative production, *The Lion King* is profoundly different from standard Broadway fare. Stephen Schwartz made use of African and Latin models in his score to *Children of Eden* (1991) in the songs "Generations" and "The Naming," but world music has not made the same splash in the musical theater that it has in the popular music industry.

MARIAN WALTZES AND HAROLD MARCHES: SONG TYPES AND CONVENTIONS

The musical styles described above constitute major influences on musical theater, but what audiences have heard also has been determined by types of songs that carry their own stylistic expectations. Below is a selective list of these types more or less in chronological order of their appearance.

In the late nineteenth century, musical theater included frequent examples of sentimental popular songs, most famous in the earlier music of Stephen Collins Foster (1826–1864). These songs had lyrical, singable melodies with touches of chromaticism, and simple harmonies. Texts tended to address home, hearth, and nostalgia. A famous use of such a song on Broadway is "After the Ball" by Charles K. Harris, a huge hit that was interpolated in *A Trip to Chinatown* (1891) and then appeared in *Show Boat* (1927) to lend credence to an event from the 1890s. Broadway composers wrote such songs as well, a famous example being "Oh Promise Me" from *Robin Hood* (1891), with a score by Reginald De Koven. The song remained a favorite for wedding ceremonies well into the twentieth century.

Sentimental parlor songs appeared from Tin Pan Alley, the New York sheet music industry. Musical theater helped popularize these songs, and there were various types in the repertory. For the first few decades of the twentieth century George M. Cohan (1878–1942), the most successful writer and director of musical comedies, was also a major writer of hits for Tin Pan Alley. His songs included two-steps like "Give My Regards to Broadway" and waltzes such as "Mary." Cohan's strongly melodic songs clearly reflected the music of his time.

The waltz was old by this time, having developed in Austria in the late eighteenth century. Its triple meter was popular in sentimental songs, including "After the Ball." If not for the waltz's growing popularity in the theater, it might have died, but Franz Lehár wrote several in his score to the immensely popular operetta *The Merry Widow* (New York première, 1907), helping to make the waltz a dominant type of theatrical song for most of the twentieth century. There are many examples of fine waltzes in the operettas of Victor Herbert, Sigmund Romberg, and Rudolf Friml, and Richard Rodgers became one of the finest waltz composers of his time, as heard in such tunes as "Out of My Dreams" from *Oklahoma!* (1947) and "Ten Minutes Ago" from *Cinderella* (1957; ◆ Example 3.13). Sondheim's score to *A Little Night Music* (1973) is notable for its many waltzes, as well as other distinctive dance types.

The two-step became a popular dance before 1900. Among the most significant writers of two-steps was John Philip Sousa, whose marches provided dance music in social halls. Sousa also wrote for theater, and one of his marches heard on stage was "El Capitan," from the 1896 show by the same name. Marches became ubiquitous in the musical theater, heard frequently in 1920s operettas, especially in male chorus numbers like "Stouthearted Men" from Romberg's *The New Moon* (1928). Examples of marches from later shows are "Seventy-Six Trombones" and "The Wells Fargo Wagon" from Meredith Willson's *The Music Man* (1957) and "Motherhood" and "Before the Parade Passes by" from *Hello, Dolly!* (1963).

Musical theater composers also have made use of other European dances, building upon traditions established in European operetta. Johann Strauss, for example, in operettas such as *Die Fledermaus* (1874) included polkas in rapid duple meter as well as waltzes. Richard Rodgers wrote a polka for the famous scene featuring "Shall We Dance?" in *The King and I* (1951), and the song "The Lusty Month of May" from Lerner and Loewe's *Camelot* (1960) strongly resembles a polka (◆ Example 3.14). In *Candide* (1956), Leonard Bernstein referred to several European dances, including the polka in "We Are Women," the gavotte in "Life Is Happiness" and "The Venice Gavotte" (the same melody), the schottische in "Bon Voyage," and the barcarolle in "The King's Barcarolle." The score also includes waltzes and a tango.

Another song type that appeared fairly early in the twentieth century, and probably derived from Gilbert and Sullivan,[6] was the counterpoint, or combination song, explored by Irving Berlin in a number of his scores. Such a song includes two different melodies that can be combined, meaning that they are based upon the same harmonic scheme and do not clash when sounding together. Usually the tunes are sung separately and then combined as a third verse. Berlin first did this in *Watch Your Step* with the song "Play a Simple Melody," in which he contrasted a folk-like melody such as Stephen Foster might have written with a more modern, syncopated ditty.[7] Berlin's most famous examples of counterpoint songs appear in his later musicals: "You're Just in Love" from *Call Me Madam* (1950), and "An Old-Fashioned Wedding," which Berlin wrote for the 1966 revival of *Annie Get Your Gun* (⊘ Example 3.15). Other composers who have written such songs are Meredith Willson (who combined "Will I Ever Tell You?" and "Lida Rose" in *The Music Man*) and Stephen Schwartz (who has included such a song in most of his shows, including, for example "All for the Best" in *Godspell*, 1971, and "What Is This Feeling?" in *Wicked*, 2003).

The ballad as a song type goes back many years, but by the early twentieth century in American popular music it was usually a song with a verse and a chorus in a slower tempo that included the song's melody, usually presented in a 32-bar form with 8-measure phrases in a repetitive form such as AABA or ABAC. Ballads were love songs or contemplative solo numbers, such as "Why Do I Love You?" from *Show Boat* (1927) and "Embraceable You" from *Girl Crazy* (1930), both with verses in ABAC form (⊘ Example 3.16). "People Will Say We're in Love" from *Oklahoma!* (1943) is in AABA form, with a B section that is musically related to the A section.

A dance style from early in the twentieth century was the soft shoe, a tap dance performed with soft-soled shoes without metal taps. George Primrose popularized such steps in minstrel shows in the late nineteenth century,[8] and the soft shoe remained in the musical theater for decades. The musical style that developed to accompany such dances was a ballad-like song in quadruple meter with frequent dotted eighth-sixteenth note rhythms. One of the most famous such tunes appeared in the film *The Wizard of Oz* (1939) with the Scarecrow's "If I Only Had a Brain," soon reprised to fit the different needs of the Tin Man and Cowardly Lion. The soft-shoe has remained in the musical theater in numbers evoking earlier times, such as "Potiphar's Song" (marked in the score "'Twenties' style") from Andrew Lloyd Webber's *Joseph and the Amazing Technicolor Dreamcoat* (1968), the Wolf's "Hello Little Girl" in Sondheim's *Into the Woods* (1987), and the Wizard's "Wonderful" in *Wicked* (2003).

Lehman Engel's designation of the rhythm song involves pieces driven forward by a propulsive beat. There have been many such songs in musical theater based on popular music since the 1960s, but Engel here refers to what might be called the classical period of Broadway through about 1960. He names as examples of rhythm songs "Luck Be a Lady" from *Guys and Dolls* (1950) and "I'm Gonna Wash That Man Right Out of My Hair" from *South Pacific* (1949), and mentions as well such composite types as the rhythm-ballad in "Tonight" (a beguine) from *West Side Story* (1957). The kind of repetitive rhythms heard in these songs is reminiscent of dances.

Strongly propulsive rhythms have also played a major role on Broadway in tap dance numbers, a popular feature of many shows since the 1920s. For such a dance, metal taps are affixed to the soles of shoes, making the dancer's feet a novelty percussion instrument that frequently "plays" solo breaks within the orchestration.

The film *42nd Street* (1933) includes representative examples of tap dancing, especially by the star Ruby Keeler, from a time when many Broadway stars and choruses tapped their ways through faster dance numbers. Many of the early tap dancers were male, and among the stars who appeared on Broadway (and many film musicals as well) were Bill "Bojangles" Robinson, Fred Astaire, Gene Kelly, and the Nicholas Brothers. Examples of female stars known for their tap dancing include Marilyn Miller, Adele Astaire, Ginger Rogers, and Ann Miller. Although tap dancing became less common after World War II, it remained in shows making period references to the 1920s and 1930s, such as in the Broadway version of *42nd Street* (1980), *Crazy for You* (1992), and *The Drowsy Chaperone* (2006). *The Tap Dance Kid* (1983), *Jelly's Last Jam* (1992), and *Bring In 'da Noise, Bring in 'da Funk* (1996) were African American shows that made rich use of tap dancing. The African American tap dancer Savion Glover appeared in all three of these shows.

Musical theater composers have sometimes accessed lesser-known musical styles to serve a specific character or dramatic situation. A prominent example appears in Lerner and Loewe's *My Fair Lady* (1956), where the lower-class character Alfred P. Doolittle sings two songs based on the musical style typical of the English music halls, the British equivalent of American vaudeville: "With a Little Bit of Luck" and "Get Me to the Church on Time," rousing marches sung with texts that celebrate the interests of a working-class rogue. The subtle style of the French cabaret with its folksy melodies and common accordion accompaniment appear in various musicals, such as in "Those Canaan Days" from Lloyd Webber's *Joseph and the Amazing Technicolor Dreamcoat*, which uses a wide variety of musical types. Stephen Schwartz also used the French cabaret sound, associated closely with Edith Piaf, in his *The Baker's Wife* (1976), especially in the opening "Chanson."

Other song types common in musicals imply function rather than a specific musical style. Lehman Engel describes three such types. The musical scene is a segment of a show or film with nearly continuous singing and perhaps dialogue with underscoring, usually through contrasting musical styles, where the plot advances and the audience learns something about the characters. Examples of musical scenes include "Where's the Mate for Me?"/"Make Believe" from *Show Boat* (where the main love interests Magnolia and Gaylord meet), "If I Loved You" from *Carousel* (another meeting for the principal couple), the opening of Sondheim's *Sunday in the Park with George* (1984, where the audience meets all of the main characters and situations), and "Dancing through Life" from *Wicked* (where much of the plot is developed). The comedy song fulfills an important function in the musical. Engel distinguishes between short and long joke songs, the definitions of which depend upon how long it takes to develop each humorous moment. "Anything You Can Do" from *Annie Get Your Gun* (1946) is a short joke song, and "The True Love of My Life" from *Brigadoon* (1947) is an effective long joke song. Engel's charm song is a self-defining designation, an opportunity for a character to seduce the audience. The type often appears as an "I want" song, sung near the beginning of a show with a main character revealing his or her desires. Examples include "Something's Coming" from *West Side Story* and "Wouldn't It Be Loverly" from *My Fair Lady*.

Musical style is a powerful tool in conveying a show's dramatic sense. When working on *The Music Man*, composer, lyricist, and book writer Meredith Willson came up with a tune that worked both as a march and waltz, and he made use of the possibility when describing his main characters musically. Marian Paroo and Harold Hill are associated by singing the same melody, but he shows his masculinity and salesmanship by singing his march "Seventy-Six Trombones" (◉ Example 3.17). Marian's version is the more feminine waltz of "Goodnight, My Someone" (◉ Example 3.18). In the second act, after Hill has started to consider his feelings for Marian, they alternate between the two versions of the tune, and Hill confirms his love for Marian when he sings her version, a telling moment made possible by the differences in musical style between the march and waltz. When we fall in love we may not march or waltz, but we certainly expect a show's creators to impart some of the dramatic meaning in a show through their use of musical style.

NOTES

1. Lehmann Engel, *American Musical Theater* (New York: Macmillan, 1975), 77–131.

2. See Raymond Knapp, *The American Musical and the Formation of National Identity* (Princeton, NJ: Princeton University Press, 2005), 191–92.

3. For a useful study of Jews in the musical theater, see Andrea Most, *Making Americans: Jews and the Broadway Musical* (Cambridge, MA: Harvard University Press, 2004).

4. See Jack Gottlieb, *Funny, It Doesn't Sound Jewish: How Yiddish Songs and Synagogue Melodies Influenced Tin Pan Alley, Broadway, and Hollywood* (Albany: State University of New York in association with the Library of Congress, 2004).

5. Paul R Laird. Personal interview with Stephen Schwartz, New York, January 14, 2008.

6. Raymond Knapp, "'How great thy charm, thy sway how excellent!' Tracing Gilbert and Sullivan's Legacy in the American Musical," forthcoming in *The Cambridge Companion to Gilbert and Sullivan* (Cambridge: Cambridge University Press, 2009).

7. Laurence Bergeen, *As Thousands Cheer: The Life of Irving Berlin* (New York: Viking, 1990), 106–7.

8. See Mark Knowles, *Tap Roots: The Early History of Tap Dancing* (Jefferson, NC: McFarland, 2002), 108–9.

CHAPTER 4

EVOLUTION OF DANCE IN THE GOLDEN AGE OF THE AMERICAN "BOOK MUSICAL"

LIZA GENNARO

DURING the "Golden Age" of the American musical, generally identified as the period between 1943 and 1964, dance functioned as an essential narrative tool in musical theater production. Choreographers, partnering with writers, composers, and lyricists, developed a collaborative creative approach in which dance, music, and spoken narrative combined to produce the "book musical," an "integrated" form in which song and dance emerge seamlessly from spoken dialogue. Creating dances for a "book musical" requires a method different from that of concert venues, where the initial formative impulse of a dance develops solely from the mind of the choreographer. The musical theater choreographer's assignment is to negotiate and absorb the precepts defined by the time, place, and setting of the libretto, along with directorial choices regarding performance style and physical elements of the production, and to discover how those elements translate into dance. It is within the context of the "book musical"—and not in relation to so-called dansicals such as *Cats* (1982), *Contact* (2000), and *Movin' Out* (2002), which are more closely associated with the artistic process of the concert-venue choreographer—that I will discuss the evolution of dance in musicals.

From this perspective, the Golden Age began with Rodgers and Hammerstein's *Oklahoma!* (1943), choreography by Agnes de Mille, and ended with Bock and Harnick's *Fiddler on the Roof* (1964), directed and choreographed by Jerome Robbins. During these years, de Mille and Robbins set the standard for making dances in the "book musical," and while their methods were markedly different, they established a template that was adopted by future generations. In order to gauge the impact of de Mille's and Robbins's innovations, it is important to understand the function of dance in the musical theater prior to *Oklahoma!*

In the 1920s and '30s, dances in Broadway musicals served as fanciful interruptions to often-whimsical plots. Dance directors of the period were highly skilled professionals who created clever, amusing, and extravagant dance sequences capable of evoking immediate visceral audience response. One of the most notable and successful of the early twentieth-century dance directors was Ned Wayburn, who staged more than 600 revues and musical comedies on Broadway and who codified a system of choreography and maintained a popular chain of dancing schools that trained young hopefuls to dance in Broadway choruses.[1]

Wayburn's technique was rooted in American Delsarte, military drills, and the hierarchical systems of nineteenth-century ballet spectacles. His strategy for success was a methodically prescribed system for making dances that included six categories of musical theater dancing: Musical Comedy Technique, Toe Specialties, Exhibition Ballroom, Acrobatic Work, Tapping and Stepping, and Modern Americanized Ballet (Statyner, 8). In his book, *The Art of Stage Dancing*, he reveals an exact approach to making dances:

> The average routine consists of ten steps, one to bring you onto the stage, which is called a traveling step, eight steps to the dance proper, usually set to about 64 bars of music or the length of two choruses of a popular song; and an exit step, which is a special step designed to form a climax to the dance and provoke the applause as you go off the stage.[2]

Unpretentious and clear-thinking, Wayburn drilled his choruses on straightness of lines, body angle, and kick height, and aspired to an aesthetic of clean, glossy polish that smacked audiences into alertness. His brand of surefire dance entertainment dominated the Broadway scene in the 1920s where he and other dance directors (including George White, John Tiller, Bobby Connolly, Sammy Lee, and Albertina Rasch) enjoyed success.

It was important among this coterie of dance directors to develop individual signature styles. Rasch, one of the few women in the field, was a veteran of vaudeville, Broadway revues, and musicals. Born in Vienna in 1891, she trained at the Imperial Ballet School and performed with the Viennese Opera before traveling to America, where she enjoyed a successful career as a performer dancing at the New York Hippodrome and touring her act, a "traditional pointe specialty," in vaudeville (Reis 1983, 95). In the early 1920s Rasch joined the production staff of the Keith-Orpheum circuit, where she created the Albertina Rasch Dancers. Her lines of girls were unique in that they did not employ the tap and musical comedy dance vocabularies that were de rigueur during the period. Rather, Rasch created dances using classical *port de bras* and *pointe* technique, danced to American jazz. Her husband and musical director Dimitri Tiomkin reported that she "liked the idea of adapting the toe dancing technique of the ballet to the slangy rhythms of jazz. It appealed to her interest in novelties of choreography" (⏺ Example 4.1).[3]

Indeed, novelty was a hallmark of the period and one of the defining elements of the vaudeville, musical, and revue genres. Performers and dance directors, working tirelessly to invent performance acts that showcased unique talents and distinguished them from competitors, borrowed movement vocabularies from a wide range of dance styles. One of the most pillaged dance sources was African American vernacular dance, appropriated by white performers and absorbed into American performance culture.[4] In the twentieth century, legions of African American dance makers remained uncredited and poorly compensated for their creative contributions to the genre. However, despite the difficulties that plagued them in their attempts at recognition, they continued to create performance opportunities for themselves.

Throughout the 1910s, black musicals, which had enjoyed success in the first decade of the twentieth century with productions starring Bert Williams and George Walker, were absent from Broadway. During those years they quietly developed in theaters away from Broadway; and in 1921 the groundbreaking musical *Shuffle Along*, written by Noble Sissle and Eubie Blake and starring Aubrey Lyles and Flournoy Miller, opened at New York's 63rd Street Theatre.[5] The show was an enormous hit and introduced a new kind of dance to the musical theater, as noted by Marshall and Jean Stearns: "The most impressive innovation of *Shuffle Along* was the dancing of the sixteen girl chorus line...above all, musical comedy took on a new and rhythmic life, and chorus girls began learning to dance to jazz."[6]

As jazz entered the musical theater dance lexicon, so too did the earliest examples of American modern dance. A notable contributor to the evolution of musical theater dance in the 1920s was John Murray Anderson, who began his career as an exhibition ballroom dancer and produced the *Greenwich Village Follies*, which featured the "ballet ballads," narrative tales that combined song and dance into a cohesive whole.[7] Anderson demonstrated a sophisticated dance palette when, for his 1923 ballet ballad "The Garden of Kama," he featured a young dancer named Martha Graham, before her breakthrough as one of the greatest modern dancers of the twentieth century (Anderson, 81). In 1925 Anderson engaged Graham again, this time under the direction of Michio Ito.[8]

Anderson was among the first to demonstrate a taste for nonconventional casting, not only among his principal performers but also in his choruses, by deliberately choosing dancers and showgirls who were not "off the production line" but rather were individual "types" (Anderson, 62). Seymour Felix, another proponent of the individuated chorus, was among the earliest dance directors to consider the notion of integrated dance. In 1926 he bemoaned the standard chorus girl number packed with kicks and tricks that in his words "became a colorful but negative interruption to the action or comedy of the musical comedy book" and in 1928 proclaimed, "No longer are routines a matter of speed and noise...the cycle of acrobatics, 'hot' dancing, and stomping is over....Scrambled legs have become a bore. The important thing today is the so called 'book number.'"[9] It is remarkable that Felix spoke in terms of the "book number" as early as 1928; however, despite his protestations he—like other dance directors including Sammy Lee, who created the dances for Hammerstein and Kern's landmark musical *Show Boat* (1927)—did not cause a systemic overhaul in musical theater dance production.

While *Show Boat* is lauded in terms of musical theater writing, its dances have barely been considered. A 1928 review from the *American* offers some indication of them:

> Norma Terris (Magnolia) does a beautiful insinuating skirt dance with all the glorified girls as a background, Captain Andy does a humorous two-step with Parthy Ann, and Sammy White performs an extraordinary clog eccentric dance. Then, too, there are, in addition to these numbers, the extraordinary clogs, tap dances, waltzes and even can-can.[10]

The numbers were clearly craft-worthy and entertaining, but they employed standard musical theater dance vocabularies. While Hammerstein and Kern succeeded in creating a groundbreaking work in terms of integration of song and text, Lee created well-crafted dances that were unremarkable in terms of innovation.

George Balanchine is credited with reenvisioning dance in musicals and employing dance as an integral element essential to plot development, with his choreography for Rodgers and Hart's *On Your Toes* (1936). His ballet "Slaughter on Tenth Avenue," which starred Tamara Geva and Ray Bolger, was essential to the advancement of the musical play, which depended upon its storytelling capabilities (Example 4.2). Between 1936 and 1951, Balanchine choreographed over fifteen Broadway shows and introduced a highly sophisticated, classically based choreography to the genre. For Rodgers and Hart's *Boys from Syracuse* (1938) he created an *Adagio* for principal dancers George Church, Heidi Vossler, and Betty Bruce that represented the internal struggle of a man in love with two women. The women's sexuality was illustrated in their dance vocabularies; Vossler dancing *en pointe* represented "the delicacy of conjugal love" while Bruce in tap shoes represented a "steamier...carnal" attraction.[11] Photographs of the dance show complex intertwining of the three bodies reminiscent of Balanchine's 1928 ballet *Apollo* and demonstrate a high level of choreographic invention (see Figure 4.1). However, despite

(a)

(b)

Figure 4.1a and 4.1b Photographs from *Boys from Syracuse* and *Apollo*. George Balanchine's *Apollo*, created in 1928, pictured in revival here for New York City Ballet with Jacques d'Amboise, Melissa Hayden, Maria Tallchief, and Patricia Wilde (Martha Swope photographer, used by permission), demonstrates the complex intertwinings of bodies that Balanchine favored in his ballet choreography, which can also be seen in the photo of his choreography from *Boys from Syracuse* (1938), featuring George Church, Heidi Vossler, and Betty Bruce. These photographs demonstrate the high level of invention and craft typical of Balanchine in both his concert and Broadway choreographies. (Photographs reproduced with permission of the Jerome Robbins Dance Division, The New York Public Library for the Performing Arts, Astor, Lenox and Tilden Foundations)

his undisputed choreographic gifts, Balanchine in the 1930s was working in a genre that, in terms of dance, was subject to the prevalent dance styles of the period. While he was able to create moments of innovative dance, he was also required to employ acrobatics, novelty dance, tap (designed by a talented group of uncredited African American choreographers including Herbie Harper [*On Your Toes*] and Billy Pierce [*Babes in Arms*, 1937]).[12]

In his Broadway shows Balanchine adhered to a European aesthetic of glamour and exoticism evident in photographs of the *pas de trois* from *Boys from Syracuse*, which depicts his ballerinas in transparent harem pants and bare midriffs. Fantasy and parody were standard features of his integrated narrative ballets, as for example in "Honeymoon Ballet" from *I Married an Angel* (1938), which featured a corps de ballet, *en pointe*, dressed as airplanes with wings on their arms and aviator helmets, and "Peter's Journey" from *Babes in Arms* (1937) in which dancers portrayed mermaids *en pointe* in an underwater ballet (Hill, 2). His dances were unquestionably of high quality but did not cause radical alteration in the production of dance in musicals. That would not occur until 1943 with Agnes de Mille's dances for *Oklahoma!*

Hired based on the monumental success of her ballet *Rodeo* (1942) created for the *Ballet Russe de Monte Carlo*, de Mille, representing regular American folk with her dancing cowboys and prairie girls, brought an idealized image of the American West to the commercial theater, and with the support of Rodgers, Hammerstein, and director Rouben Mamoulian, created a set of dances that related directly to the time and setting of the libretto and enhanced character development. Unlike her previous Broadway experiences, Howard Deitz and Arthur Schwartz's *Flying Colors* (1932) and Harold Arlen and E. Y. Harburg's *Hooray for What* (1937), for *Oklahoma!* de Mille was given the opportunity to invent a movement lexicon that inhabited the entire show from beginning to end. Employing techniques she developed as a self-producing soloist in the 1920s and '30s, when she created and performed dance characterizations rendered in ballet and pantomime, and incorporating lessons learned from Martha Graham and Louis Horst, a composer and one of the primary architects of American modern dance, de Mille developed a system for expressing ideas through dance in the "book musical."

Based on Lynn Riggs's 1931 play *Green Grow the Lilacs*, *Oklahoma!* tells the story of three main characters: Laurey, a young plainswoman; Curly, a cowboy; and Jud, Laurey's farmhand and the play's villain. Laurey and Curly are in love; however, neither will admit to the attraction. Jud is attracted to Laurey, but she is terrified of him. The action of the play revolves around Laurey's decision to attend a box social with Jud, in part to spite Curly. As de Mille focused on the relationships between the three principal characters and Laurey's curiosity about the collection of sexually titillating postcards displayed on the walls of Jud's cabin, it was her conceit that Laurey secretly identified with the girls on the postcards and that she was as frightened of her own desires as she was of Jud.[13] She conceived the ballet "Laurey Makes Up Her Mind" as a dream exploring Laurey's attraction to both Curly and Jud, manifest in what becomes a nightmare exploring her repressed desires.

In the ballet, Laurey and Curly wed, but as Curly lifts Laurey's veil she sees to her horror that she has married Jud. Ignoring her pleas for help, the wedding guests and Curly fade into the distance. Laurey flees only to discover herself in a saloon where she is confronted and taunted by the Postcard Girls—garishly dressed saloon dancers. Employing early modern dance techniques of distortion, and Louis Horst's method of Introspection-Expression, de Mille distills the Postcard Girls' movement down to the merest suggestion of a Wild West saloon exhibition (⊙ Example 4.3).[14] The movements are rooted in the can-can and twentieth-century burlesque movement lexicons, both appropriate to the period, but rather than succumbing to pastiche, de Mille uses the vocabularies as a basis for movement innovation. Representing Laurey's innocent imaginings of wanton women, the Postcard Girls perform in slow motion. Their faces are hard and frozen and they roll their shoulders as if trying to escape an ill-fitting blouse. Drooping like rag dolls when lifted by the men, they appear flaccid and impotent. Devoid of energy, humanity, and sexuality, they move mechanically through their deconstructed can-can. By engaging in a modernistic deconstruction of the archetypal dance hall girl, de Mille rebuilt the construct as an extension of Laurey's psyche.

The ballet is one example of de Mille's highly sophisticated, multilayered system for creating dances in the musical theater and demonstrates her ability to employ modernist methods of movement innovation in a manner that Broadway audiences could absorb. Trusting in the potential of dance to serve as a conduit for emotions and ideas, de Mille created multilayered constructs in the musical theater that were grounded in the time, place, and characters of the libretto. Rife with social and political implications, de Mille's dances expanded the parameters of the libretto and disrupted the Broadway casting blueprint by knocking the iconic chorus girl, a patriarchal fabrication of female beauty and allure, off her pedestal; chorus girls were replaced with women whose appearances were ordinary, but whose ability to express emotion through movement was extraordinary. In a little over a year, de Mille caused an ideological shift in the function of dance on Broadway and opened a portal on a fertile creative landscape.

The most significant arrival to Broadway, post-de Mille, was Jerome Robbins, who choreographed *On the Town* (1944), based on his ballet *Fancy Free* (1944). Robbins would become de Mille's staunchest competition and would with her define the production of musical theater dance in the "book musical." In his first two shows, *On the Town*, and *Billion Dollar Baby* (1945), de Mille's influence is apparent in the psychological ballets he created, but a greater influence on his work would be revealed in his strict adherence to accurate depictions of time, place, and character—lessons he learned as a member of Gluck Sandor's Dance Center.[15] Sandor, a choreographer for the Group Theater, an American acting company inspired by the work of the Russian director Constantin Stanislavsky, employed actors and directors from the Group to instruct his troupe of dancers on contemporary acting techniques. Robbins remembered his time in Sandor's company saying, "We never did anything on stage without knowing who we were, where we were, & why."[16]

Committed to the ideas of time and place in relation to character, Robbins, first relying on Stanislavsky and later employing Method Acting techniques learned at Lee Strasberg's Actors Studio, engaged in painstakingly extensive research whenever he embarked on a new musical theater project. Explaining his choreographic process for *Billion Dollar Baby*, set in 1920s New York, Robbins told *New York Post* reporter Harriet Johnson,

> I studied all the cartoons of the period I could lay my hands on. I went to the Museum of Modern Art and looked at all the possible movies of the 20s. I talked to everyone who remembered the period to find out what people were, thought, felt, said, and did. I wanted my dances to portray the kind of people who were typical of the time.[17]

By basing his choreographic inventions on authentic sources, Robbins supplied himself with made-to-order movement vocabularies to set within the dramatic structures of his dance numbers (⏺ Example 4.4).

For his ballet "Small House of Uncle Thomas" from Rodgers and Hammerstein's *The King and I* (1951), Robbins engaged Cambodian dance scholar Mara Von Sellheim to assist him in creating dances for the show (Jowitt, 181). Film recordings of Von Sellheim's company demonstrate how closely Robbins followed her instruction in terms of movement vocabulary and costuming, but it was Robbins's ability to infuse the movement with an American musical comedy sensibility that makes the dance a success in the framework of the show. By developing comic moments, for example, when the ballet's heroine, Eliza, reaches the icy river and is met by an angel who escorts her across the ice by way of a charming duet that fuses images from Frederick Ashton's *Les Patineurs* (1937) with Cambodian dance to create a delightfully humorous movement interlude, Robbins provided Broadway audiences with an entry point into his excursion into Cambodian dance and made the ballet accessible and entertaining in a musical theater context (⏺ Example 4.5).

As his musical theater career progressed, Robbins became increasingly invested in dances that made logical sense, supported dramatic intent, and provided a stylistic continuum from the libretto. With the exception of *West Side Story* (1957), which stands as an anomaly in Robbins's musical theater career (see below), Robbins had a chameleon-like ability to absorb dance styles so completely that his own particular movement style was obscured. As his success grew, so too did his frustrations with the lack of control afforded choreographers in the musical theater, which operates as a hierarchical system in which the director and writers occupy the upper rungs of the ladder and choreographers the lower. It was a condition he sought to alter with *Look Ma I'm Dancin'* (1948), a parody of his days touring with Ballet Theater, which he wrote and co-directed with George Abbott. Serving twice as co-director to Abbott before his solo directorial debut with *Peter Pan* (1954), Robbins became the first in the modern line of director-choreographers, a group that also would include Bob Fosse, Gower Champion, and Michael Bennett. As Robbins's power and control increased, so too did his method of weaving dance into the fabric of the librettos.

In Jule Styne and Stephen Sondheim's *Gypsy*, a musical based on the memoir of Gypsy Rose Lee, Robbins was faced with the task of creating dances for a vaudeville child act. Rather than simply creating dances that would be appropriate to the period and genre, Robbins gave himself the additional task of constructing the musical numbers as if they had been created by Gypsy's overbearing mother Rose (Jowitt, 319). The task provided Robbins with a choreographic method to support his central tenet, that "movement is always dictated by character, situation and material."[18] The result was two brilliantly witty vaudeville numbers, depicting a cloyingly cute child star, Baby June, backed by a ragtag group of boys that included her sister Louise (the future Gypsy Rose Lee) dressed as a boy. Although the numbers feature the pampered Baby June, they also tell the story of Louise, disguised and out of step, dismissed by her mother as no more than a tagalong burden. As examples of dance, the numbers are unremarkable, but within the context of the show they serve as searing illustrations of Rose's ambition and narcissism (▶ Example 4.6).

In 1964, with the exception of revivals and *Jerome Robbins' Broadway*, a retrospective of his choreography in musicals (1989), Robbins embarked on his last book musical for Broadway, *Fiddler on the Roof*. "The Bottle Dance," which occurs at a wedding celebration, imitates a traditional Jewish wedding custom in which guests are obligated to entertain the bride and spontaneously perform tricks, comedy routines, and acrobatics for her pleasure.[19] Robbins witnessed this custom at a Hasidic wedding ceremony in New York in which a Jewish comedian did a dance with a bottle on his head.[20] Expanding the moment to involve a group of men overtaking the celebration, Robbins created a brilliant dance that emerges seamlessly from the dramatic action and appears improvised by the characters. It represents the ideal manifestation of Robbins's legacy in the musical theater genre and serves as a model for his integrated brand of musical theater choreography (▶ Example 4.7).

West Side Story (1957), created with Leonard Bernstein, Arthur Laurents (book), Stephen Sondheim (lyrics), and co-choreographer Peter Gennaro, stands as an aberration in Robbins's musical theater career because the dances, while adhering to Robbins's requirements in terms of time, place, and period, were also examples of movement innovation in a modernistic sense. By his own admission, Robbins, who concurrent to his Broadway career maintained an active career in the field of classical ballet, worked differently in the musical theater than he did when creating a ballet, a fact that he hoped to amend with *West Side Story*. In a Dramatist Guild symposium almost thirty years after *West Side Story*'s creation, Robbins explained what he, Leonard Bernstein, and Arthur Laurents were trying to accomplish with the show:

> I wanted to find out at that time how far we three, as "long-haired artists,"…could go on bringing our crafts and talents to a musical. Why did we have to do it separately and elsewhere? Why did Lenny have to write an opera, Arthur a play, me a ballet? Why couldn't we, in aspiration, try to bring our deepest talents together to the commercial theater in this work? That was the true gesture of the show. (Jowitt, 266)

Robbins's fusion of ballet, jazz, and 1950s social dance idioms (see Figures 4.2 and 4.3) was so astonishing in terms of dance that after the opening of *West Side Story* he formed a new company, Ballets: U.S.A., and continued to develop *West Side Story*'s movement vocabulary for the concert stage (Jowitt, 293).[21] In terms of musical theater dance, *West Side Story* was the first and last of its kind to be created by Robbins (⊙ Example 4.8).

The generation of choreographers spawned by de Mille and Robbins, including Jack Cole, Michael Kidd, Bob Fosse, Peter Gennaro, and Gower Champion, used the methodologies established by the form's ostensible parents as a template on which to base their own unique choreographic systems. Cole defined a jazz dance vocabulary for musicals with his fusion of Bharata Natyam, African American vernacular dance, and Latin forms.[22] Writing for the *New York Times* in 1948, John Martin expounded on Cole's technique,

> Cole fits into no easy category. He is not of the ballet, yet the technique he has established is probably the strictest and most spectacular anywhere to be found. He is not an orthodox "modern" dancer, for though his movement is extremely individual, it employs a great deal of objective material—from the Orient, from the Caribbean, from Harlem. Certainly, however, he is not an eclectic, for the influences that he has invoked have been completely absorbed into his own motor idiom.[23]

Engaging in extensive movement research, Cole was known to travel to remote locations in order to develop authentic dances.[24] However, despite his best intentions, it is difficult to reconcile his pursuance of dance authenticity with the fact that for *Kismet* (1953), which is set in ancient Arabia, he employed his particular fusion of swing music and Bharata Natyam, ignoring both the period and setting of the musical play (⊙ Example 4.9).

The tension between a drive toward authenticity and a disregard for it at the same time is a central element in musical theater dance creation. Negotiating that tension is one area in which the musical theater choreographer demonstrates artistic vision and creative choice. Whereas Robbins grounded his dances within the boundaries established by the libretto, Cole, with his *Kismet* dances, disregarded the time and place of the libretto, drawing from a movement lexicon that did not, in terms of authenticity, relate to the musical play. His choreography is the embodiment of what music critic Irving Kolodin called "the fruitful anachronism and the relevant absurdity."[25] And it was in the anachronistic and absurd facts of Cole's work that his choreographic voice emerged.

Cole was not the first in this generation to choreograph anachronistically. De Mille, for E. Y. Harburg and Harold Arlen's *Bloomer Girl* (1944), created "The Civil War Ballet" using American country-dance vocabulary and formations as the basis for her movement invention. The choice is notable since by the 1860s country-dance in America had been replaced by the polka, the mazurka, and the waltz as popular social dances.[26] Why then did de Mille choose the historically inaccurate American country-dance? As described by Kate Van Winkle Keller and Genevieve Shimer, country-dance is

Figure 4.2 *N.Y. Export: Opus Jazz* (1958), created for Jerome Robbins's company Ballets: U.S.A., further developed the movement ideas he formulated in his choreography for the "Jets" in *West Side Story* (1957). (Photograph reproduced with permission of the Jerome Robbins Dance Division, The New York Public Library for the Performing Arts, Astor, Lenox and Tilden Foundations)

Figure 4.3 In contrast to the photograph of Jerome Robbin's *N.Y. Export: Opus Jazz*, this photograph from the film adaptation of *West Side Story* (1961) demonstrates a less formalized and more dramaturgically organic use of the movement idioms Robbins elaborated on and continued to explore in his Ballets: U.S.A. (Photograph reproduced with permission of the Billy Rose Theatre Division, The New York Public Library for the Performing Arts, Astor, Lenox and Tilden Foundations)

a group dance in which there is interaction between two or more couples and it is a democratic dance in that the couples often change positions in the set and take turns leading the figures. Only in a culture in which the absolute power of the king had been tempered by the demands of democracy could such a dance form flourish.[27]

De Mille was clearly less interested in historical authenticity than in creating a met-aphoric dance language evoking democratic ideals. Creating the ballet in the final days of World War II, de Mille was intent on making a dance that offered her audi-ence a cathartic expression of hope and renewal, rather than an accurate depiction of the social dance of the period (⏺ Example 4.10).

Another important choreographic voice in the Golden Age was Michael Kidd, who began his career as a dancer and choreographer in the early days of American ballet, working with Eugene Loring's Dance Players and Ballet Theatre. Transferring his talents to the commercial genre, Kidd created robust, vigorous dances that required highly trained ballet and modern dancers willing to perform choreogra-phy demanding strong resilient bodies. His men portrayed a sort of hyper-masculinity wielding axes in "I'm a Lonesome Polecat" from the film *Seven Brides for Seven Brothers* (1954), and whips in the "Whip Dance" from *Destry Rides Again* (1959). "Runyonland" and "Havana" in *Guys and Dolls* (1950) maintained narrative through lines while sending out strands of danced scenarios, adding idiosyncratic texture in movement and layering mood, tenor, and character. Like Robbins he was able to create dance in a wide range of movement styles, but unlike Robbins his dances always bore his particular movement style, characterized by high knees and chest, impish perkiness, spectacular lifts, and muscular athleticism (⏺ Example 4.11; ⏺ Example 4.12; ⏺ Example 4.13).

Bob Fosse, who bridged the Golden Age and the post-Golden Age periods, had the most powerful influence upon the dance zeitgeist of the late twentieth century. He was inspired by Fred Astaire's classic song-and-dance-man flair, Jack Cole's idio-syncratic use of jazz dance lexicons, de Mille's drive toward movement innovation, and Robbins's ability to engage song, dance, and text within a cohesive whole. In a career that began with "Steam Heat" from *Pajama Game* (1954; ⏺ Example 4.14)—an exciting reenvisioning of a movement lexicon popularized by, among others, vaudevillian Joe Frisco—Fosse developed one of the most imitated movement styles in musical theater dance, in particular with the erotic renderings of women, pre-sented in *Pippin* (1972) and *Chicago* (1975). Fosse's obsession with overt sexual images and the objectification of women found an audience in the musical theater as his career ascent coincided with the 1960s sexual revolution. The theater com-munity that in 1957 rejected his "Red Light Ballet" from the musical *New Girl in Town* (see Figure 4.4), an explicit romp through a nineteenth-century bordello fea-turing Gwen Verdon, applauded the slithering and writhing of his female chorus in *Chicago*.[28]

One of his most innovative choreographic moments occurred in *Sweet Charity* (1966) with the musical number "Big Spender" in which a group of worn-out dance hall girls tries to entice a patron to purchase a dance. Closely resembling the quality

Figure 4.4 This photograph of "The Red Light Ballet" from *New Girl in Town* (1957) features Gwen Verdon atop a chair and a chorus of women in poses demonstrating Fosse's early fascination with placing the female body in overtly sexual positions, a characteristic that became a signature feature of his work. (Photograph reproduced with permission of the Billy Rose Theatre Division, The New York Public Library for the Performing Arts, Astor, Lenox and Tilden Foundations)

and intent behind both de Mille's "Postcard Girls" and Antony Tudor's "has-been" goddesses in *Judgment of Paris* (1938), Fosse succeeded in creating a minimalistic, narrative dance with a literal chorus line of women who, posing side by side, move in a kind of trance punctuated with pointed isolation. Rife with innuendo, his dancers project insolent disdain and demonstrate a purely original choreographic voice. The musical theater has yet to recover from Fosse's persistent influence on choreographers and his seeming ownership of the musical theater jazz dance lexicon (⏺ Example 4.15).

Peter Gennaro also bridged the period during and after the Golden Age. As a performer he danced in the chorus of *Guys and Dolls*; shared the stage with Carol Haney and Buzz Miller in "Steam Heat"; and originated the role of Carl in *Bells Are Ringing* (1956; choreography Jerome Robbins and Bob Fosse), dancing "Mu Cha Cha" with Judy Holliday. Robbins was so impressed by Gennaro's mastery of Latin dance forms, techniques learned as a student at the Katherine Dunham School of Arts and Research, that he asked him to co-choreograph *West Side Story* and assigned him the task of creating the dances for "the Sharks." Gennaro's success was based on an exuberant dance style characterized by fast footwork, isolation, and complex rhythms. Like Robbins's dances in *Fiddler on the Roof*, Gennaro's work possessed the quality of improvisation, as if the characters were acting on a spontaneous urge to dance.

Gower Champion began his theatrical career as a tap and ballroom dancer and gained popular success in the 1940s and '50s in Hollywood and on television with his wife and ballroom dance partner Marge, nee Belcher.[29] Their danced narratives portrayed the postwar desire for a return to normalcy and the reestablishment of male dominance in the workforce and at home, promoting the heteronormative ideology of the 1950s (⊙ Example 4.16). As a Broadway director and choreographer, Champion introduced a cinematic sensibility to the musical theater stage by employing "continuous choreographed staging," a transitional device first used by Robbins in *West Side Story* (Gilvey). The device allowed for a seamless flow from scene to scene replacing blackouts and "in one" numbers (scenes or musical numbers performed downstage of the first wing in front of a painted drop or curtain) which enabled set changes to occur upstage. "In ones" were discontinued as soon as technology caught up with the imagination of theater artists who craved fluid transitions between scenes. Champion's further use of dance as a scenic element was evident in the opening of *Hello, Dolly!* (1962) for which he created an 1890s New York City street scene by developing a movement style based on period photographs. When interspersed with song and dialogue, this style served as a frame establishing a sense of place and style for the production. Champion used dance as a catalyst for ushering in a new era of musical theater production that sought to disguise old-fashioned stage mechanizations.

In the decades following 1964, the most common end point of the Golden Age, Broadway creators preferred reality-based dance and Robbins's late-career method of dance at the service of the libretto to de Mille's method of inserting multilayered, daedal dance structures. Consequently, dance in the "book musical" was increasingly employed in realistic terms, as in *A Chorus Line* (1975; director-choreographer Michael Bennett, co-choreographer Bob Avian), in which dancers and dance propel the story; backstage musicals such as *Dreamgirls* (1981; director-choreographer Michael Bennett, co-choreographer Michael Peters); and *42nd Street* (1980; director-choreographer Gower Champion); and theatrically stylized productions such as *Once on This Island* (1990; director-choreographer Graciela Daniele), in which dance plays a primary role in the overall gestalt of the presentation.

The 2006–07 Broadway season witnessed a change in this trend with the advent of Bill T. Jones's Tony Award–winning choreography for *Spring Awakening*, based on the play of the same title by Frank Wedekind (1891), which condemns the hypocrisy of oppressive nineteenth-century attitudes toward the body and sexuality. The writers of *Spring Awakening*, Steven Sater and Duncan Shiek, along with director Michael Mayer and Jones, freed themselves from the confining precepts of musical theater production by ignoring the historical setting of the play in terms of movement, music, and language. The production design is drawn from the period, but not authentic to it, and the music and performance style, complete with hand held microphones, borrows from a rock-concert aesthetic. Despite the absence of trained dancers, Jones used dance innovatively to express sexuality, repression, longing, and anger.

Creating a movement theme that underlines the sexual repression of the play's characters, Jones establishes a set of choreographed gestures to which he returns throughout the show. In a conversation with the author, he explained how studying Wedekind's original text and experiencing the "absurdity and symbolism" of the play gave him the courage to approach his work

> in the experience of the expressionists, [as] something that would be at once psychological and literal, that could be used like a decor that changes....I was trying to understand how to set up a field of gestural movement that could track through the bulk of the piece and could be in counterpoint to the heavy psychology of the writing and the rock-and-roll nature of the music...the gestures were a challenge between that which is literal and that which is abstract...that was the biggest contribution that I made.[30]

Jones's approach to dance and movement, with its tension between the literal and the abstract, echoes de Mille's complex structures and her core belief that dance as an essentially abstract form could interact with literal narrative, thereby providing a unique layering of kinetic expression in innovative dance movement (a belief that Robbins ultimately abandoned for a more realistically integrated use of dance in musicals).

The 2007–08 season saw yet another innovative use of dance in the Tony Award–winning choreography for *In the Heights* created by choreographer Andy Blankenbuehler. Blankenbuehler allows the setting of the show, Washington Heights in New York City, a predominantly Latino (both Dominican and Puerto Rican) neighborhood in which dance is an important aspect of the culture, to permit dance to flow into the streets as both a scenic element (pedestrians moving fluidly through their day) and as spontaneously erupting dance numbers. Blankenbuehler's hook is the prevalence of dance in Latino culture, and although people do not regularly dance their way through city streets, within the context of a musical, such activity seems plausible. His fusion of hip-hop and break dance movement lexicons, both improvisatory in nature, with a formalized Broadway aesthetic, result in a joyously innovative fusion.

These examples demonstrate how the "book musical" offers choreographers a creative dance venue separate from the concert arena and requires skills often outside the realm of dance makers, including storytelling ability; character-specific movement development; ability to communicate with actors and nondancers—all while maintaining an adaptable working style that places the overall success of the show above the individual success of the choreography. The Golden Age choreographers established paradigms for choreographing the "book musical," and each subsequent generation of musical theater choreographers, cognizant of his or her predecessors' contributions to the genre, has enlivened the form with contemporary dance lexicons and theatrical strategies. Like all art, the form is in a constant state of invention and evolution. What makes musical theater challenging as an art form is that box-office receipts measure success, which can inhibit artists' innovative impulses. It is to the credit of musical theater choreographers that they continue to reinvent and redefine the use of dance in the "book musical," persevering under the constant pressures of time and money as they embrace the unique qualities that a body moving in space, free from the concrete expressiveness of language, can offer an audience.

NOTES

1. Barbara Stratyner, *Ned Wayburn and the Dance Routine: From Vaudeville to the Ziegfeld Follies* (Studies in Dance History No. 13, Madison: University of Wisconsin Press for the Society of Dance Scholars, 1996).

2. Ned Wayburn, *The Art of Stage Dancing: The Story of a Beautiful and Profitable Profession* (New York: Belvedere, 1980), p. 6.

3. Frank W. D. Ries, "Albertina Rasch: The Broadway Career" (*Dance Chronicle* 6:2 [1983]: 95–137), pp. 95, 99, 101.

4. See Brenda Dixon Gottschild, *Digging the African American Presence in American Performance* (Westport, CT: Praeger, 1996).

5. Jacqui Malone, *Steppin' on the Blues: The Visual Rhythms of African American Dance* (Urbana: University of Illinois Press, 1996), p. 73.

6. Marshall Stearns and Jean Stearns, *Jazz Dance* (New York: Macmillan, 1968), p. 139.

7. John Murray Anderson, *Out without My Rubbers* (New York: Library Publishers, 1954), p. 77.

8. Agnes de Mille, *Martha* (New York: Random House, 1991), p. 68.

9. Richard Kislan, *Hoofing on Broadway: A History of Show Dancing* (New York: Prentice Hall, 1986), p. 57.

10. ªFrank W. D. Ries, "Sammy Lee: The Broadway Career" (*Dance Chronicle* 9:1 [1986]: 1–95), p. 66.

11. Camille Hardy, Popular Balanchine Dossiers 1927–2004. "*Boys from Syracuse*" (Box 15, New York Public Library for the Performing Arts, Dance Division, New York, NY), p. 13.

12. Constance Valis Hill, Popular Balanchine Dossiers 1927–2004. "*Babes in Arms*" (Box 14, New York Public Library for the Performing Arts, Dance Division, New York, NY), 2002.

13. Barbara Barker, unprocessed papers, box 18, box 5, box 6 (Research materials of Agnes de Mille, New York Public Library for the Performing Arts, Dance Division, New York, NY).

14. Louis Horst, *Modern Dance Forms and Its Relation to the Other Modern Arts* (New York: Dance Horizons, 1961), p. 98.

15. Deborah Jowitt, *Jerome Robbins: His Life, His Theater, His Dance* (New York: Simon & Schuster, 2004), p. 16.

16. Amanda Vaill, *Somewhere: The Life of Jerome Robbins* (New York: Broadway Books, 2006), p. 43.

17. Harriet Johnson, "The First Steps in a Robbins Dance: It's Planning Says *Billion Dollar Baby* Choreographer" (*New York Post*, January 4, 1946).

18. Arthur Gelb, "Robbins and His 'Courage'" (*New York Times* [April 28, 1963]: 127).

19. Judith Brin Ingber, "Dancing into Marriage," *Arabesque* 7.4 (1982): 8–9, 20–21.

20. Greg Lawrence, *Dance with Demons: The Life of Jerome Robbins* (New York: Berkley Books, 2001), p. 342.

21. Jerome Robbins used 1940s and '50s jazz dance from his earliest ballets *Fancy Free* (1944) and *Interplay* (1945 [New York City Ballet premiere 1952]). My focus is on how his interest in combining ballet and jazz found its way to the Broadway stage and to ponder why he did not continue to explore that idiom in the commercial theater after *West Side Story*.

22. Constance Valis Hill, "From Bharata Natyam to Bop: Jack Cole's 'Modern' Jazz Dance" (*Dance Research Journal* 33.2 [Winter 2001–2]: 29–39).

23. Glenn Loney, *Unsung Genius: The Passion of Dancer-Choreographer Jack Cole* (New York: Franklin Watts, 1984), p. 242.

24. Ethel Martin, interview by Liza Gennaro, February 26, 2003, transcript (Oral History Collection, Lincoln Center Library of the Performing Arts, New York, NY).

25. George Beiswanger, "New Images in Dance: Martha Graham and Agnes de Mille" (*Theatre Arts* 28.10 [October 1944]: 609–14), p. 614.

26. Kate Van Winkle Keller and Charles Cyril Hendrickson, *George Washington: A Biography in Social Dance* (Sandy Hook, CT: Hendrickson Group, 1998), p. 109.

27. Genevieve Shimer and Kate van Winkle, *The Playford Ball: 103 Early Country Dances* (Chicago: A Cappella Books and the Country Dance and Song Society, 1990), p. viii.

28. Harvey Evans, interview by Liza Gennaro, March 3, 2003, transcript (Oral History Collection, Lincoln Center Library of the Performing Arts, New York, NY; ◗ Example 4.17).

29. John Anthony Gilvey, *Before the Parade Passes By: Gower Champion and the Glorious American Musical* (New York: St. Martin's Press, 2005), p. 7.

30. Bill T. Jones, telephone interview with Liza Gennaro, May 18, 2007.

PART II

TRANSFORMATIONS

CHAPTER 5

....

MINSTRELSY AND THEATRICAL MISCEGENATION

....

THOMAS L. RIIS

THE word "minstrel" derives from the Latin term *ministerialis*, an official of the Roman imperial household. From about the twelfth century, the English word denoted a professional entertainer of any kind, but chiefly one who danced, juggled, and played instruments. Up to the late sixteenth century, minstrels were frequently attached to royal courts. Since that time the term has come to suggest a wandering singer or lyric poet equipped with lute, harp, or other portable stringed instrument, since romanticized as a light-hearted rover traversing a pseudo-Medieval landscape. Minstrelsy evokes for modern readers the allure of an idyllic past, often masking the hardscrabble existence of traveling performers.

American minstrelsy—synonymous with blackface minstrelsy because its participants used black face paint (typically a mixture of grease or water and burnt cork from bottle plugs)—arose in the early nineteenth century as a form of mass entertainment. Performers who adopted the name "minstrel" seem to have viewed it as the best moniker at hand to suggest talented artists who upheld professional standards or, ironically, used subversive, carnivalesque elements, or both. The idea to present a *group* of "Ethiopian delineators" (another euphemism for blackface acts) arose from the efforts of innovative circus entertainers to distinguish themselves from competitors.

In June 1842, three white men, Edwin P. Christy, George Harrington, and T. Vaughan, calling themselves the Virginia Minstrels, gave their premiere performance in Buffalo, New York (Harrington's hometown). Christy later attached his own name to the troupe, which enjoyed a long-running success in New York City.

The more famous ensemble to use the same name included banjoist Billy Whitlock, songwriter Dan Emmett, and dancers Dick Pelham and Frank Brower, staging a celebrated opening at the Bowery Amphitheater in February 1843. As Dan Emmett later reported the story, they had observed the success of a European singing troupe in America, the Rainers, billed as "the Tyrolese Minstrel Family," and so added the name to a famous Southern state to form the Virginia Minstrels. Both Christy's and Emmett's groups spawned a legion of imitators and within a remarkably short time minstrel fever seized the nation. Formal minstrel companies sprang up, worked steadily across the country, and traveled abroad. Crowds flocked to theaters to see minstrel shows throughout the rest of the nineteenth century.

American minstrelsy was the most influential and long-lived musical-theatrical development in the antebellum period with lingering effects that can be traced to the present. No form of popular entertainment created in the United States since the early nineteenth century has been untouched by it. Thousands of books, songsters, scripts, and music sheets catering to both professional and amateur minstrels were published well into the 1930s. Grounded in what W. T. Lhamon, Jr., has described as "the blackface lore cycle," minstrelsy's basic gestures, expressive patterns, musical incipits, dance steps, and labile attitudes coalesced during the 1820s and 1830s, were transformed and tamed in the 1840s and 1850s, and were further stretched and exploited through the remainder of the century. Although banned or suppressed for its virulent racial stereotyping during the second half of the twentieth century, elements of blackface minstrelsy have repeatedly resurfaced in environments where underclass theatrical expression could come out and be expressed safely—though often indirectly or covertly—in the same venues that fostered ragtime, jazz, rock-and-roll, and hip-hop. Minstrelsy has been and remains a slippery, paradoxical, and tenacious phenomenon.

MISCEGENATION

Because American minstrelsy arose when slavery and the future of social relations among blacks and whites in the United States was being strongly contested, this particular form of blackface theater, more so than any previous one, was preoccupied with the idea of "miscegenation," defined as interracial marriage with the intention of producing mixed-race children. The word was coined in 1863 by Democratic Party propagandist David Goodman Croly, whose anonymously published pamphlet, *Miscegenation: The Theory of the Blending of the Races, Applied to the American White Man and Negro*, alleged that widespread marriage between whites and blacks was the overriding goal of Abraham Lincoln and the Republican Party, as the ultimate solution to interracial conflicts. Although this screed, released during the 1864 presidential campaign to stoke panic among whites, was discredited by the end of the election season, the word nevertheless worked its way into common circulation.

Its Latinate flavor (*miscere*, to mix, plus *genus*, a biological type) lent an air of scientific credibility to the hoax, but "race" as a fixed category was widely accepted as a "natural" and unchangeable human state. To advocate interracial marriage seemed to its detractors to be tantamount to playing God. The scientific basis for racial types is groundless, rooted on surface appearances rather than fundamental genetic differences; all human beings are now classified as *Homo sapiens* and share over 99 percent of their DNA. But the idea was persuasive nonetheless. A rigid set of racial classifications confirmed master-subaltern power relations already established during the slavery period. The common perception of race as an empirical category has determined much American law and custom ever since. Between 1913 and 1948, a majority of American states forbade interracial marriage, although no federal statute was ever enacted to this effect. Only in 1967 did the United States Supreme Court rule all anti-miscegenation laws unconstitutional.

In such a fraught environment, theatrical representation of racial elements and mixing of races on stage (a kind of theatrical miscegenation, which was also illegal in many states), whatever the motive or audience, was bound to be provocative. Every generation of Americans has produced a slightly different reading. Constance Rourke in a famous analysis of American national character detected three archetypal American comic figures: the Yankee peddler, the braggart frontiersman, and the black minstrel.[1] The first two have long since faded from the cultural landscape (or merged with newer types), but the last—being such a mischievous, potent and multivalent figure—is still with us in unsuspected locations.

BLACKFACE BEFORE 1843

The minstrel show, which by 1844 began adhering to consistent formats and advertising itself as a full night's entertainment, comprised a variety of interwoven elements: jokes, dances, patter, topical skits, eccentric instruments, sentimental and comic songs, mimicry of familiar and prominent persons, and much more. With white actor-musicians allegedly imitating the habits and attitudes of African Americans, blackface minstrelsy has been viewed most often as a racist travesty pure and simple. But the roots and the history of minstrelsy are both problematic and complex, and remain the subject of heated debate.[2]

King Richard II reportedly hosted an English royal entertainment that featured characters made up to resemble African potentates in 1377, and Ben Jonson's *Masque of Blackness* (1605) offered a similar conceit, but the most famous of all African or Moorish characters played in blackface by English-speaking actors was Shakespeare's *Othello* (1603), "a general in the service of Venice." This heroic but flawed Moor, created roughly a century after the expulsion of the Moslems from Spain, spawned a variety of serious and comic successors, including musical versions of Aphra Behn's story, *Oroonoko* (1688); George Colman and Samuel Arnold's *Inkle and Yarico* (1787);

the comic servant, Mungo, in Bickerstaffe and Dibdin's ballad opera *The Padlock* (1768); and Monostatos in Mozart and Shickaneder's *The Magic Flute* (1791). None of the actors in these plays participated in minstrel troupes as they emerged later, but their conventional black makeup, a mask that enabled the representation of exotic customs or peculiar behavior, laid the foundation for public acceptance of minstrelsy later on. Narratives written by or about escaped slaves further sustained public fascination with African lore and eyewitness travel accounts. But minstrelsy did not take off as a distinctively American phenomenon until the charismatic day-to-day behavior of ordinary African American citizens added another—perhaps the most important—reminder of its immediacy and appeal to the working class.

Folk theatricals or seasonal holiday celebrations with ancient roots also employed blackface performance in unscripted but widely practiced rituals of chaos, such as *Mardi Gras* or Carnival, where all is topsy-turvy. In such celebrations of "misrule," rich and poor, white and black, weak and powerful change costumes and change places—at least for a day—in jovial but sometimes disruptive and even debauched circumstances. Like modern Hallowe'en trick-or-treaters or the saucy exaggerated characters of Italian commedia dell'arte, blackface players in rustic festivals were disguised for fun and profit, but also for protest against social norms. In such a context, blackness was primarily a disguise for safety's sake rather than a racial statement per se.

The creation of the United States in 1789 based on principles of equality for its citizens, New York's Gradual Manumission Law of 1799 (which freed all Negroes born in New York after July 4, 1799), the abolition of slave trade in the British Empire in 1807, and trade patterns established between the United States, England, and the Caribbean islands continued to place the social/political status of dark-skinned and marginalized immigrant peoples at the center of public consciousness. The construction of the Erie Canal (1817–25), which required mass employment of unskilled labor, brought darker working-class newcomers inland, affecting northern and western regions of the country as well as the South. Canals historian Peter Way reports that the work was "performed by the lowest of the low, Irish immigrants and slaves. [Done by] these two pariah groups,...canalling [became] one of the first truly lumpen proletarian professions in North America."[3] Yet these workers, along with other riverboat men, itinerant tradespeople, trappers, and explorers were heroic in their way and lived on as romantic figures in later nostalgic song. Songs and plays of the time manifested both sympathy for the enslaved or newly freed workers, and fearful suspicion about their place in the social order.

Andrew Jackson's election in 1828—closely following complete emancipation in the state of New York in 1827—marked another sea change, as America's elite old guard was visibly contesting with a restless underclass and working class hoping for advancement. The movement of the American national boundary to the west, and the accompanying influx of Easterners, new European immigrants, and former slaves—ever more deeply encroaching into Native American territory—and the disappearance of massive agriculturally based slavery above the Mason-Dixon line fed sectional debates about slavery, miscegenation, and the significance of racial difference across the country. Huge population increases during the first decades of the nineteenth century complicated life in the cities, forcing the issues of urban subsistence, family formation, patriotism, and personal identity. Minstrels of the 1830s sang about the yearnings of all racial groups. Some took up the cause of Andrew Jackson, especially his opposition to the rechartering of a national bank, and of struggling northern black workers, by means of the foppish figure known as Zip Coon. Apart from and yet related to English scripted stage traditions were folk-inspired improvisational ones. Minstrel shows drew from both streams, featuring soloists, duets, trios, and larger ensembles performing on noisy, eccentric instruments, dancing wildly in tattered costumes, and singing raucous comic songs such as "Buffalo Gals" (referring to the city, not bison), which probably dates to 1844:

> Buffalo gals, won't you come out tonight,
> Come out tonight, come out tonight.
> Buffalo gals, won't you come out tonight
> And dance by the light of the moon.

Well before the advent of the mass-marketed minstrel show, American improvisational actors were busy imitating African Americans—not only exotic Africans—in broad and memorable gestures. They claimed to have encountered their models for impersonation on southern plantations, western riverboats, and in northern urban neighborhoods. The roots of many minstrel controversies lie in the credibility of these claims. One of the earliest paradoxes of minstrel research is that minstrel shows, while claiming southern Negro roots—seem to have first appeared and had their greatest impact in northeastern cities performed by white men during the 1840s. Minstrel-like ensembles developed in many locations, but minstrelsy became a mass cultural phenomenon with the help of modern technology, transportation, and communication networks provided by cities, especially port cities such as Buffalo, Albany, Philadelphia, and New York.

The neighborhood of Five Points, near Catherine Market, a formerly bustling commercial crossroads on the East River between Brooklyn and south Manhattan, was an especially fecund spot for pre-minstrel doings. A place where racial groups intermingled in the late eighteenth and early nineteenth centuries, this area thrust together its inhabitants and facilitated cross-cultural contact and exchange. Participating in the bustling life on the wharves and markets of New York's Seventh Ward, black men contested with each other and were paid in money or in goods to entertain and drum up business for shopkeepers. Black step-dancers went about this activity and were sketched by a local witness as early as 1820. By 1848, their demonstrations—"dancing for eels" as it was termed at the time—were taken up as theatrical skits in plays by Frank Chanfrau in the nearby Chatham Theatre and were preserved in genre paintings by William Sidney Mount (1807–68).

Outside observers of Five Points during the 1850s raised objections to what was plainly normal everyday behavior for the residents—not only the mixing of people of different races in public markets and social spaces, but the free and easy attitudes of the local women in their exchanges with men, at a level of frivolity that disrupted the habits favored by merchants who depended on a large group of docile factory workers from this same laboring class. Class critics noticed and scoffed at the deliberate use of theatrical devices—peculiar dress, accents, perfume, and makeup in places of amusement or public gatherings—which further muddy the waters of identity and imitation. As is clear from many accounts, poor white residents of Catherine Market were not dressing down simply to mock their dark-skinned neighbors but rather to flatter them or pay compliments by trading songs, jibes, jokes, and stories in a free-flowing exchange that touched observers within and without, high, low or middle in status.

While outsiders may have viewed the whole spectacle of rough fun as devoid of middle-class decorum, evidence for minstrel vitality is everywhere apparent, in their lyrics, repetitive choruses that invite participation, the illustrations provided in songsters, and the newspapers and police records when ebullient spirits erupted violently or spilled over disruptively into more genteel venues.

> I come to town de udder night.
> I hear da noise, den saw de fight.
> De watchman was a runnin' roun'.
> Cryin' Old Dan Tucker's come to town.
> So get out de way! Get out de way!
> Get out de way! Old Dan Tucker
> You're too late to come to supper.

T.D. RICE

Thomas Dartmouth ("Daddy") Rice (1808–60), a resident of the Bowery and frequent denizen of Five Points and Catherine Market, was centrally important to the rise and spread of blackface entertainment. Born into a poor Anglo-American Protestant family, Rice trained as a ship carver's apprentice but also acted in modestly appointed local theaters—often these were little more than saloons with raised platforms for the performers—which offered farces, melodramas, and topical skits. He would soon be playing to vast crowds in New York and London, having perfected his unusual talent on the road.

Rice's lasting impact was made with the songs and acts he developed as a traveling showman beginning in 1828. The most sensational was "Jim Crow," a dancing song in which he mimicked country or street characters. The faithfulness of his imitations were attested by those professionals closest to him, but the power of his unique impersonations seems to have come from an intense combination of elements: motley clothes, a blackened face, a twisted and turning body (knees bent, left hand raised, and right arm akimbo); and transgressive ideas sung and spoken in the manner of an ancient court jester, albeit in rough quasi-black dialect. He often spoke for and not against the black race and found a sympathetic audience among the white working class as well. Jim Crow in Rice's depiction was a proud, free, defiant, and slippery trickster, impossible to account for and never accountable to authority figures or powerful institutions.

> Weel about and turn about and do jis so;
> Eb'ry time I weel about, I jump Jim Crow

Speaking on behalf of the marginalized and against the rich and prominent, Rice's fame spread dramatically throughout America and England during the 1830s. He almost always played to audiences mixed by race and class. As one of his managers, Frank Wemyss, reported in 1848, "Mr. Rice crossed the Atlantic [during 1837], and turned the heads of the chimney sweeps and apprentice boys of London, who wheeled about and turned about and jumped Jim Crow, from morning until night, to the annoyance of their masters, but the great delight of the cockneys." It was Rice's peculiar brand of acting that helped to reveal the vast potential for developing more extended full-evening shows, minstrelsy that encompassed plays with interpolated songs, vocal ensembles, group dances, and circus specialties.

As Dale Cockrell has extensively documented, blackface theater was not restricted to or developed solely on the minstrel stage.[4] Rice was only one of several white actors engaged in blackface antics. Others included theater manager/comedian Englishman Charles Mathews who in 1822 claimed to be satirizing a black American actor (probably James Hewitt) in his London acts, and white American George Washington Dixon (1801–61) whose vehicles included dialect songs such as "Coal Black Rose" and "Zip Coon" (also known as "Turkey in the Straw"). Gradually in the 1830s, other singing actors began to add dancers and instrumentalists to their acts with African instruments or instruments associated with southern slaves, such as bone castanets, fiddles, tambourines, banjos, and sometimes accordions or concertinas. Solo turns became ensemble acts with four or more members. For individual singers, the term "minstrel" could still be loosely applied until 1843, but the arrival of Dan Emmett's quartet in New York established a prototype for the term and its synonyms, "harmonist" and "serenader."

FROM 1843 TO THE CIVIL WAR AND BEYOND

In the antebellum era, blackface minstrelsy dominated the American popular theater to the exclusion of all other forms. A variety of formats were introduced, but all included a few essential ingredients. A small group of men in blackface played noisy instruments, sang lively dialect songs—often parodies—and performed satirical skits. Most shows concluded with a vigorous dance finale. Many troupes took to the road and many others established themselves full-time in locations and theater buildings reserved for minstrelsy exclusively. Within a year of the Virginia Minstrels' New York debut, another minstrel troupe, the Ethiopian Serenaders, was appearing in the White House (see Figure 5.1). By 1846 this ambitious ensemble set out to perform in England and was well received. Minstrel troupes blanketed towns along the Ohio and Mississippi rivers, set up shop in all large cities, and traveled to California with the Gold Rush of 1849. The most prominent companies before 1850 included the Virginia Minstrels, Christy Minstrels, Ethiopian Serenaders, Buckley's Congo Minstrels, and the New Orleans Serenaders. Ordway's Aeolians, Wood's Minstrels, White's Serenaders, and Sanford's Opera Troupe, among many others, flourished through the 1850s.[5]

By the late 1840s, as minstrel show production methods became more settled and established, managers sought to widen their audience and soften the edginess of their repertory. The irreverence of the early days was mitigated, though not replaced, by aspirations for respectability and a larger number of paying customers, including women and children. The descriptions of comfortable theater interiors of the time also imply that a more genteel audience was being sought. Emphasis continued to be placed on dialect songs and burlesques—the latter often focusing on English and Italian operas (for example, Balfe's *The Bohemian Girl* or Bellini's *Norma*)—but more instrumental solos and sentimental parlor songs were interpolated as well. Theater seating capacity was expanded and liquor was banned. The intensely parodic quality of minstrel humor was maintained. No prominent persons, political figures, foreign groups, or exotic ideas were exempt from ridicule. All current events and upper-class fashions became objects of fun. Stump speeches and tall tales were the order of the day, the wilder the better.

Roles were designated for the instrumentalists on the front line. The tambourine player (Mr. Tambo) and the bone castanet player (Mr. Bones) stood on either end of a semicircle of anywhere from four to eight men and joked with each other as a prelude to a series of musical or other specialties. To underline the increasing impulse to control eccentric minstrel movements and manners among polite audiences, a third character, Mr. Interlocuter, who always spoke with perfect diction and unctuous tone, arose in the 1850s to stand center stage and serve as master of ceremonies. His traditional opening line underscores his task to rein in potentially disruptive forces: "Gentlemen, be seated!" In the 1850s and 1860s, pro-black sentiments were less in evidence than they had been in T. D. Rice's shows, and blackface performers became blank slates inscribable with any sort of comic twist.

Minstrel humor, while certainly racist after 1843, was not invariably so, although stereotypical markers of blackness were consistently employed. Minstrelsy held up to ridicule foreign performers such as violinist Ole Bull or singer Jenny Lind, but it also exposed pompous preachers and greedy capitalists, and spoke to various issues with no direct tie to African American culture. If, for example, the idea of phrenology—reading bumps on the head to gauge character and personality—were a fashionable topic, then minstrels would deliver absurd dialect speeches on the subject. When the flashy French conductor Louis Jullien (1812–60) brought his eighty-seven-piece orchestra to New York in 1853, the same season as opera diva Anne Seguin appeared, with both charging the public large fees to attend their concerts, they were roundly put down by Buckley's Serenaders' skits about "the Black Jew-Lion" and "Mme. Anna See-Her." Since tickets to

Figure 5.1 Sheet music cover: "Music of the Ethiopian Serenaders." (Reproduction courtesy of the American Music Research Center, University of Colorado, Boulder)

the Serenaders show were only twelve-and-a-half cents, the class-based critique of elevated European tastes and exhibitions was especially pointed.

Because of its commanding place in mid-century American culture, minstrelsy—not unlike television in a later era—had occasion to weigh in on every conceivable subject from temperance to women's rights. Minstrel scripts and period playbills address an array of topics related to gender, class, politics, and musical taste, as well as race. Typical minstrel show "finales" found in advertisements in the 1840s and 1850s allude to other theater pieces as well as fads and current events, and include, for example, "Fireman's Chaunt," "Burlesque Tragedy of Damon and Pythias," and "Burlesque of the Bohemian Girl."

Blackface minstrelsy grew and changed with a protean character that defies full explanation. It did far more than borrow surface racial features or allow itself to be limited to a single signifier. Minstrelsy rarely if ever attempted to say much about Africa or "the old plantation" as a real place, but it often provided a disguise or mask behind which actors could comment on the American scene—urban, suburban, rural—in the form of a burlesque. Any claims that minstrelsy portrayed "authentic" African American culture must be weighed against its essentially satirical character. Minstrels were never trying to score serious aesthetic points or make idealistic declarations. Rather, they subjected all types of foreignness, pretension, or posturing to close scrutiny and broad lampoon. How to explain the strong presence of operatic parody embedded in 1840s and 1850s minstrelsy but from a need to critique the strong presence of European visitors on American stages?

Such was the power and flexibility of the minstrel format and its reputation for rambunctious irreverence that African Americans themselves began to form minstrel companies in the 1850s, although most of the early troupes were short-lived. Immediately following the Civil War, however, minstrelsy became one of the most important points of entry for young, ambitious Negro men seeking a nonfarm livelihood and a ticket to the big city. Brooker and Clayton's Georgia Minstrels emerged in 1865, closely followed by a series of companies created by Lew Johnson and Charles B. Hicks. These African American impresarios traveled the world—from South America and Australia to Asia and of course Europe—in treks that sustained the fame of "genuine" black minstrels for decades. Ike Simond in his autobiographical "reminiscence and pocket history of the colored profession," published in 1891, names hundreds of minstrels unrecorded in any other source.[6] The history of African American minstrelsy in the late nineteenth century is still largely untold.

GENDER AND MINSTRELSY

Misogyny was an especial preoccupation of mid-nineteenth-century minstrel shows. Offered primarily to male audiences by male actors, minstrel shows consistently instructed men on the wiles, charms, moods, ruses, and demands of women in and out of marriage and the home. Many men specialized in cross-dressing parts to establish the illusion of a feminine presence or to set up scenes of romance gone awry. George Harrington, one of E. P. Christy's first partners, was famed for his "wench" roles, as was Tony Hart (1855–91), partner of Ned Harrigan.

Few real women worked in minstrelsy, but opportunities for men to do cross-gender burlesque were plentiful. As early as 1847, an ensemble calling itself "Female American Serenaders," probably only female in costume, performed a noisy minstrel finale entitled "Railroad Overture." Minstrel men regularly imitated the attitudes and dances of famous women performers, such as Jenny Lind and Fanny Elssler. The minstrel show remained men's business, and cross-dressing actors were common in the 1840s and later. Francis Leon, the most prominent of female impersonators, who trained as a minstrel before the war, was billed as "the Only Leon," and had perfected the role of prima donna by 1870. By giving complete attention to every facet of his elaborate wardrobe (including dozens of custom-made dresses and expensive jewelry), makeup, and movement, he portrayed a subtle and serious image of ideal femininity, not a farcical take-off.

THE MUSIC OF THE MINSTREL SHOW

One of the bedeviling aspects of minstrel show history, partly accounting for its hold on successive generations despite repulsive racist and sexist elements, is its large and attractive musical repertory. By the mid-1840s, minstrelsy had come to be understood by many as a basic framework, hospitable to the latest musical novelty. Much of the music was composed by performers in shows who needed to dance, sing, and play at the same time, and the numbers were stitched together from a mixture of elements. Audience preference for a busy stage presence encouraged a less complex musical structure within individual numbers than would have been required for, say, a solo concert recitalist.

Such popular favorites as "Old Dan Tucker" had many verses with a relatively short and repetitive melody (⊙ Example 5.1). The song could accommodate a nearly endless series of tempos, poses, asides, and elaborations. Minstrel songs not only allowed but required a sustained intensity in performance in order to make the most of their basic material. Only the performers who could ratchet up a song's energy succeeded on a large scale. This combination of simple musical building blocks and broad physical gestures defined the quintessentially American quality of minstrelsy. More than mere musical medleys interspersed with comic dialogues, minstrel shows presented a crescendo of intensity realized through a concatenation of events. It riveted audiences with a rich interactive rhetoric of gesture and movement, lively tunes, and humorous speech.

Many minstrel songs from the early years have survived in memory into the twenty-first century, having become a permanent part of America's collective consciousness. Stephen Foster (1826–64) was arguably the finest native-born song-writer of the minstrel era. His melodies were reprinted in European sources as early as the 1850s. He wrote specifically for the Christy Minstrels, although many other groups adopted his most popular numbers, including "Gentle Annie," "Oh Susanna," "Camptown Races," "Old Folks at Home," and "Old Uncle Ned." Many of his lyrics capture the manic absurdity of the minstrel persona as well as its sentimental turns.

> It rained so hard the day I left,
> The weather it was dry.
> The sun so hot, I froze to death.
> Susannah, don't you cry.

Minstrel songs enabled expressions of pathos, satire, and energetic good fun, within singable melodies with regular rhythms, punctuating chords, and accompanying percussion. Much of the raw material was original, but much was also reshaped from preexisting sources: banjo and fiddle tunes from the oral/aural tradition, Irish melodies, current favorites from the opera stage, and parlor songs. As harmonized choral concerts of Negro spirituals became the rage in the 1870s and 1880s, inspired by the success of the Fisk Jubilee Singers, traveling minstrel companies wasted no time in incorporating them into their repertory and making fun of them as well (◖ Example 5.2).

Rag music was first published during the 1890s, when it became a national craze. The new *style*—first understood as a rhythmically inflected type suitable for exuberant and syncopated dancing (as opposed to a *genre* of music called ragtime)—had unquestioned roots in midwestern African American communities. It differed from minstrelsy, at least for black composers, in its refusal to be identified as imitation or parody of something else. Yet because it was understood as a black genre, whites wrote and sang ragtime songs in blackface, adding words that reinscribed hackneyed racial stereotypes. The specific subgenre of ragtime songs that uses insulting dialect verses is referred to as "coon song."

By the 1890s minstrelsy had ceased to command the attention of crowds in theaters devoted to that purpose. No new music was being composed for the genre. But the explosion in sheet music publication, including colorful cover illustrations—with both drawings and photographs—proved that the visual legacy of minstrel grotesques remained (see Figure 5.2). Distorted faces, wildly gesticulating characters, clothed apes, razor-wielding toughs, chicken-stealing hoodlums, and sultry females ushered in a new era of hard-edged and brutal images, bespeaking anxiety about overcrowded ethnic enclaves in American cities at the turn of the century. Many of the lyrics and covers amount to racial slander. By the 1920s, this type of song lyric had been supplanted by the blues and less virulent verses in Tin Pan Alley products, but the exaggerated images persisted on title pages, posters, songsters, and films.

The 1890s also saw the creation of the first all-black cast and black-created musical comedies, many of which made a point of not using burnt cork even while incorporating "coon" songs and every other kind of ethnic humor imaginable. Robert "Bob" Cole and his partner Billy Johnson in their landmark show, *A Trip to*

Figure 5.2 Sheet music cover: "Oh! Didn't It Rain," featuring Eddie Leonard. (Reproduction courtesy of the American Music Research Center, University of Colorado, Boulder)

Coontown (1898), featured a succession of ethnic imitations by popular comedian Tom Brown, including an Italian, a "Chinaman," and an Irish policemen. Cole himself took the role of a lovable hobo who appeared in *white* face makeup—possibly a model for both Charlie Chaplin and circus clown Emmett Kelly.[7] Offering both farce comedy and a parody of the popular contemporary musical *A Trip to Chinatown*, Cole and Johnson's effort lasted only a few seasons on the road but proved that black actors and creators could successfully challenge the long-lived stereotypes of minstrelsy, spawning at least two dozen similar shows over the next two decades.

The most successful African American actor at the turn of the century, famous for boldly crossing the color line at the highest level, retained blackface for his entire career. The Ziegfeld Follies star, Bert Williams (1874–1922) could have followed the lead of his friends Bob Cole and Ernest Hogan (the self-proclaimed "unbleached American"), but Williams confessed to never having felt comfortable onstage *without* burnt cork—such was the strength of the convention throughout his early career. Personal accounts of those who saw him, as well as surviving film clips of his most famous skits, give powerful evidence of a superbly skilled actor who managed to transcend the limited realm of contemporary white minstrels with his own personal gestures and style, underlain by a deep strain of melancholy. W. C. Fields famously called Williams, "the funniest man I ever saw, and the saddest man I ever knew."

MINSTRELSY IN FILM

The earliest films about African American life, from the late 1890s, were short newsreels or documentaries capturing brief moments of unscripted action (e.g., a watermelon-eating contest, West Indian boys at play, African American soldiers disembarking from ships returned from the Spanish American War). But "black" characters were acted by whites in blackface so frequently that the appearance of real African Americans onscreen assumed a parallel, but distinctly different, path for blacks than for whites playing black roles.

Because much of early moviemaking was about getting the product to market rapidly and cheaply, filmmakers tended to adopt the most vivid images already in circulation, including stereotyped figures from the minstrel stage: olive-complexioned women with "tragic" (i.e., mixed race) personal histories, predatory young men adrift in the city, and hordes of dancing, singing "darkies" at every street corner. For nostalgia fans—who were many—the movies provided familiar plantation characters and antebellum scenarios featuring full-figured mammies, docile Uncle Toms, and happy hyperactive children. Minstrel images were transferred directly from the stage to films, dominating the portrayals of most real African American characters in the first two decades of the twentieth century even as independent black filmmakers William Foster and Oscar Micheaux made their first movies.

The most important film in the pre–sound era to include black characters, both real and blackface, was D. W. Griffith's *The Birth of a Nation* (1915). It astonished its first viewers by telling a sweeping Reconstruction-era story of the founding of the Ku Klux Klan, heroically reclaiming the South from heartless Yankee carpetbaggers and freedmen run amok. Using virtuoso cinematic techniques studied by film students to this day, *The Birth of a Nation* flagrantly perpetuated degrading stereotypes of hulking, frenzied black males raping, pillaging, and generally wreaking havoc. Black women were either scheming seductresses or repulsive hags. Griffith's wish to convey the devastation of civil war and its aftermath was realized, ironically, to the detriment of some of its most oppressed victims.

The overwhelming success of *The Birth of a Nation* gave new life to the most loathsome minstrel images for at least a generation. White vaudeville headliner Al Jolson in blackface famously sang "Mammy" in *The Jazz Singer* (1927) as he inaugurated the new era of sound films. Director Erich von Stroheim courageously placed African Americans in complex roles within a biracial cast in such films as *Wedding March* (1928), and King Vidor would feature musical African Americans in *Hallelujah!* in 1929, but not until more subtle technical effects were possible on screen in the 1930s did a few independent Hollywood filmmakers expand their horizons and invite individual actors to discard minstrel-based stereotypes. The work of Nina Mae McKinney, Clarence Muse, Bill "Bojangles" Robinson, Willie Best, Mantan Moreland, Eddie "Rochester" Anderson, Paul Robeson, Louise Beavers, Fredi Washington, and Rex Ingraham was prominent in this period. Herb Jeffries, as "The Bronze Buckeroo," appeared in black-cast Westerns. Black gangster films were made by Apollo Theater entrepreneur Ralph Cooper. Hattie McDaniel, as a classic minstrel mammy—albeit more humanely realized than most—won the Academy Award for Best Supporting Actress for her performance in *Gone With the Wind* (1939). Films of the late 1940s and '50s were still dominated by African American characters whose chief job was to sing, grin, and dance.[8]

After the radical displacements of World War II, besides the enhanced visibility of the real black community in America and the internationally recognized heroism of black troops, more significant changes appeared to be possible. Hollywood gradually showed itself willing to treat racial issues seriously. The Academy Award nomination of Dorothy Dandridge in the title role of *Carmen Jones* (1954) and Sidney Poitier's appearance in the *Edge of the City* (1957) were positive signs of change. Black agency in the television and film industry was enhanced gradually with the increase in number of African American actors of the first rank and the emergence of young independent black filmmakers, most prominently Melvin Van Peebles (*Sweet Sweetback's Baaadasssss Song*, 1971) and Spike Lee (*Do the Right Thing*, 1989; *Jungle Fever*, 1991; and *Bamboozled*, 2000—the last film imagines a successful recreation of a blackface minstrel show on modern television).

CONCLUSION

Although the diversity of visual representations of race has increased in complexity across the United States and around the world during the last third of the twentieth century and into the twenty-first, and while many old-fashioned minstrel stereotypes have lost their ability to shock (or even surprise) us, the association of blackface makeup with motives of racial mockery and denigration is by no means dead. In 2004, gay white comedian Chuck Knipp created an outrageous black female stage character named Shirley Q. Liquor and drew howls of protest from feminists and antiracists who happened to notice the show in a downtown New York nightclub. (Incidentally, Knipp also found enthusiastic support from the black drag queen Ru Paul.) Clearly minstrelsy as a site for parody, comedy, and burlesque in the classic sense is still very much with us. Blackface remains a lightning rod for expressions of opinion about larger sociopolitical questions. The sprightly musical residue of early minstrelsy has largely been separated out from its racialized images and texts (now habitually bowdlerized), so as to facilitate the incorporation of the tunes into generic folk song histories appropriate for children.

NOTES

1. Constance Rourke, *American Humor: A Study of the National Character* (Garden City, NY: Doubleday, 1953; originally published 1931).

2. On this subject, see especially Eric Lott, *Love and Theft: Blackface Minstrelsy and the American Working Class* (New York: Oxford University Press, 1993).

3. W. T. Lhamon, Jr., *Raising Cain: Blackface Performance from Jim Crow to Hip Hop* (Cambridge, MA: Harvard University Press, 1998), p. 62.

4. Dale Cockrell, *Demons of Disorder: Early Blackface Minstrels and Their World* (Cambridge: Cambridge University Press, 1997).

5. William J. Mahar, *Behind the Burnt Cork Mask: Early Blackface Minstrelsy and Antebellum American Popular Culture* (Urbana: University of Illinois Press, 1999), pp. 355–63.

6. Ike Simond, *Old Slack's Reminiscence and Pocket History of the Colored Profession from 1865 to 1891* (Reprint edition, Popular Press: Bowling Green, OH, 1974; originally published 1891), pp. xvii–xxiii.

7. This suggestion comes to me from David Krasner, author of *Resistance, Parody and Double Consciousness in African American Theatre, 1895–1910* (New York: St. Martin's Press, 1997), and Marvin McAllister, author of *White People Do Not Know How to Behave at Entertainments Designed for Ladies and Gentlemen of Colour* (Chapel Hill: University of North Carolina Press, 2003).

8. See Donald Bogle, *Toms, Coons, Mulattoes, Mammies, and Bucks: An Interpretive History of Blacks in American Films*, 4th ed. (New York: Continuum, 2001).

CHAPTER 6

TIN PAN ALLEY SONGS ON STAGE AND SCREEN BEFORE WORLD WAR II

RAYMOND KNAPP

MITCHELL MORRIS

TIN PAN ALLEY has suffered from a bad reputation, and the company it has kept has not helped it any: Broadway, Hollywood, and the American musical on the one hand, and jazz (back when it was disreputable), radio crooning, and popular singers and groups on the other. Indeed, jazz's practitioners, fans, and historians, in elevating jazz to its latter-day position of "America's classical music," have tended to overlook or downplay its awkward dependence on Tin Pan Alley, which provided many of the tunes that brought jazz its mainstream popularity. But whereas jazz historians might easily claim, if disingenuously, that Tin Pan Alley's tunes provided only a starting point for a jazz number, and only in some cases, those tunes in their original versions were most often the core attraction in the Broadway and Hollywood musicals that figure most prominently in historical surveys. As a result, historians of the musical have had to perform their own quaint dance around Tin Pan Alley, focusing mostly on revivable shows and films with enduring repute, and placing their focus on what the songs in such shows accomplish, usually through being "integrated" (see chapters 3 and 7). Like jazz historians, they rarely bother to note how often those songs also serve—deliberately and even proudly—a broader marketplace.

In this chapter, we consider the extensive overlap, before World War II, of Tin Pan Alley with Broadway, vaudeville, and post-1927 Hollywood, a convergence that includes not only the well-known shows and films from this period, but also those shows and films that are most frequently overlooked by historians: revues, variety shows, and musical comedies whose musical numbers were only loosely held together by a plot or theme. On Broadway, such shows included not only Ziegfeld's Follies and similar "annual" fare[1] but also book shows that counted on hit tunes for their sustainability—in other words, almost everything except operetta, and even some of that repertory. In Hollywood, there were first of all the correlatives of staged revues, such as Busby Berkeley's "Gold Digger" films (1933–1937), the "Big Broadcast" and "Broadway Melody" films (1936–1940), and *The Goldwyn Follies* (1938). But there was also the rampant practice, within the Hollywood studio system, of song substitution in adaptations of stage shows, which, before cast albums stabilized the song lists of stage shows (beginning in the 1940s), most often resulted in fewer than half of a film's songs coming from the show it ostensibly adapted for the screen. These films all fall irretrievably on the disdained side of the dichotomy evoked by John L. Sullivan, the would-be idealistic film director of Preston Sturges's *Sullivan's Travels* (1941) who is eager to move on from *Ants in Your Plants of 1939* to the social realism of *O Brother, Where Art Thou*. For better or worse, Sullivan's dichotomy is one we seem to be stuck with, despite the realization that comes to Sullivan himself in his "travels": "There's a lot to be said for making people laugh. Did you know that that's all some people have? It isn't much, but it's better than nothing in this cockeyed caravan."

These shows and films don't (for the most part) have a privileged place in histories of the American musical, nor can their neglected history be captured in an essay of this scope. Fortunately, the basic events of this era may be easily researched in Gerald Bordman's compendious *American Musical Theatre* and/or the Internet Broadway Database.[2] More consistent with the aims of this collection, and with our desire to throw emphasis toward the songs themselves, is for us to place this extensive oeuvre within those histories that are better known, by briefly describing the forces that shaped venues for popular song during the Tin Pan Alley era, establishing the cultural function of the songs thus produced, and explaining how the quintessential type of Tin Pan Alley song developed so as to serve not only shows and films but also other markets, including sheet music, recordings, radio, and jazz-based venues and markets. To this end, we will probe the cultural work done by some of the highly problematic songs of this era, sketch the historical basis for the intertwined histories of Broadway and Tin Pan Alley both before and after the "Great War," query the codification of the mature Tin Pan Alley type between the wars, and discuss—following Rose Rosengard Subotnik's brave lead—the ways in which the songs of this era, largely *because* of their quotidian nature, have continued to provide essential "Equipment for Living."[3]

EARLY TIN PAN ALLEY AND THE SOCIAL FABRIC

A quick survey of any large list of songs performed in musical plays and revues on the New York stage at the turn of the century reveals a bemusing concentration of numbers that project clusters of racial and ethnic stereotypes. "Coon songs," in particular, owe the majority of their musical and lyrical styles as well as their customary performance practices to minstrelsy, but over and above their ways of imagining the appearance and habits of African Americans, they also decisively shape the ways that other minorities appear in the popular music of the time. The lavish array of social (stereo)types was perhaps especially important because of the mileu in which they were generated. New York City's overwhelming importance as a destination for immigrants, along with the population density created especially by the city's tenement system,[4] guaranteed that citizens would frequently cross paths with a wide assortment of people who could be sorted into racial or ethnic "groups."[5] (The modes of social identification/recognition cut across class and economic lines as well, but by and large immigrants tended to start out very poor.) In an oft-cited remark, progressive journalist Jacob Riis in his 1890 book *How the Other Half Lives* asserted that a map of New York coded by ethnicity "would show more stripes than on the skin of the zebra and more colors than the rainbow."[6] And, regrettably but not surprisingly, interactions among the ethnic groups settled in the city could become vicious. The most famous instance of this was the New York City Draft Riot of 1863, in which immigrant resentment against the draft—especially sharp because well-off draftees could pay their way out of enlistment and impoverished newcomers had no such option—led to numerous atrocities against the scapegoated African American population of the city. But this was only one of a series of episodes of mass violence that sporadically broke out during the nineteenth century (and well into the twentieth century); in between such times of uncontrollable hostility, there was a steady underscore of bad feeling, from distrust to dislike to outright hostility, always present.

In an environment of such persistent tension between groups, the ethnic caricatures that litter the New York stage may well seem to have been an improvement over homicidal rage and malice. That is, even ambivalent laughter (both with the figures and at them) could seem to have the potential to reduce ethnic tensions by substituting travesty for assault and battery. From another point of view, since such stock figures quite often carry attributes that could be treated as backhand compliments, attention to the positive aspects of these cartoons, though still stereotypical, might lead audiences to at least limited forms of tolerance as well. Moreover, it can be argued that one of the greatest challenges of an urban environment of such extreme variety as New York is acquiring the forms of social tact that will allow different groups to manage, if not avoid entirely, potential offenses against one another. To some extent this challenge is a question of "knowing one's place" literally as well as figuratively, but it also entails developing a template of routines—a system of manners—that enable further interactions with familiar groups as well as methods of coping with groups previously unencountered. The problem with such strategies is that their possible effectiveness in the theater may stop at the exit; there are no good reasons to have confidence that what works to defuse animosity onstage will also work offstage. But whether or not these ethnic songs had any beneficial effects in everyday life at the turn of the century, they carry historical importance for scholars of the musical not least because their

practical realizations can end up undermining the manifest content of the stereotypes that the songs project.

"How Can They Tell That Oi'm Irish?" was a successful song in the Broadway
show *The Jolly Bachelors* from 1910. The show was built on a wafer-thin plot in
which three men compete for the affections of an heiress, one Astarita Vandergould
(played by the popular vaudeville star Nora Bayes), who has taken a job as a drugstore clerk in order to find a boyfriend. But Bayes was well known (and well liked)
for her propensity to step out of character and simply sing popular songs to the
audience. It is clear that this is the case here.[7] The song's persona is that of a newly
arrived immigrant who is determined to pass as "American," and cannot understand why her masquerade does not work. The first verse sets the scene:

> I landed here from Ireland just a week ago today,
> And as soon as I had settled in the town
> I resolved to act entirely in a Yankee Doodle way,
> So I changed me name but not me emerald gown.

Unfortunately for the song's protagonist, her accent is quite broad—but she seems
not to hear that. Bayes puts on a brogue (a brogue that the song's persona denies
having) and decorates her performance with the occasional hoydenish yip and
yodel. The musical setting is not marked with any Irishisms: no bagpipe figures or
jiggish rhythms, nothing to connect it to overgeneralizations of Irish folk music.
Rather, the stereotype is situated firmly in the realm of accent and diction—details
of speech that it is implied the character is too naive or unintelligent to notice.
Instead, she wanders around her new town constantly puzzled that everyone she
encounters instantly knows her origins (🔊 Example 6.1).

To be sure, the humor here is not particularly pointed; its derogatory content
is more potential than actual. In this, it fits well with the trend of Irish stereotyping
at the turn of the century; nastier ethnic caricatures were much more common
earlier in the nineteenth century, and by the 1890s Irishness was increasingly an
excuse for effusive sentiment rather than ethnic denigration. The song's typing is
made considerably less stable, moreover, by the layering of Nora Bayes's own persona. A Jewish girl from Illinois (her birth name was Eleanor Goldberg), Bayes
anglicized herself by stage name and by several of her marriages.[8] As mentioned
earlier, her character in *The Jolly Bachelors* is named Astarita Vandergould—its
very implausibility does not detract from its function as a parody of "Old New
York" high society.[9] So what might it have meant for a Jewish comedienne passing
as Anglo, playing an "old money" New Yorker disguised as a shop girl, to step out
of character and take on an Irish persona? In any case, the possibilities of a kind of
ethnic delirium were quite high, and arguably such play with identity added significantly to the song's appeal.

Prejudices against other ethnic groups can be more tenaciously ugly in the comic
songs of the period. "Chin Chin Chinaman" was one of the most popular hits from
The Geisha, a British musical comedy that was first performed in London in 1896 and
was hugely successful in New York that same year.[10] A bargain-counter variation of

Gilbert and Sullivan's 1885 hit *The Mikado*, *The Geisha* tells a romantic story of court-ship between the handsome British naval officer Reggie Fairfax (already engaged to Molly, a girl back home) and the beautiful young geisha O Mimosa San. Shades of Cio Cio San! But no, the plot of this work does not take the tragic turn found in David Belasco's play *Madame Butterfly* (1900) and Puccini's operatic adaption (1904); instead, in *The Geisha* the kind of switched-identity shenanigans common in farce ensure that the romantic leads end up with partners of the appropriate social and racial position. The character Captain Wun-Hi, the Chinese proprietor of the Japanese Tea House employing Mimosa (against all historical likelihood), is clearly comic relief, and "Chin Chin Chinaman" is his one song.

One of the earliest recorded versions of the song is a rendition by James T. Powers, a New York comedian who found one of his major roles in revival productions of the show.[11] The recording begins with a histrionic fanfare of fake Chinese, after which the song settles into an absolutely regular 4×4 verse-chorus structure. The musical setting is quite minimal, probably to provide room for the performer's comic effects—not only the stream of faux-discourse that starts the number, but also especially the strange parodic cadenza that ends the recording. This is not "real" (i.e., Western) virtuosity, but a clumsy musical imitation. As for the lyrics, they are put into the style by which Chinese-accented English is usually derided (◗ Example 6.2):

> Chin chin Chinaman / Muchee Muchee sad!
> Me afraid allo trade / Wellee welle bad!
> Noee joke—/ Brokee broke—/ Makee shuttee shop!
> Chin chin Chinaman / Chop, chop, chop!

The strategy of mockery is obvious in the lyrics' jeering focus on the character's inability to distinguish between "l" and "r" and his addition of extra vowels on many of the words that end in consonants.[12] The inability to pronounce English correctly is the verbal equivalent of his unsuccessful musical aspirations. But it is worth not-ing as well that in the midst of all of this performed incompetence, the song draws our attention to the question of commerce. Wun-Hi's occupation as a "small busi-nessman" is as important to his stock character as his linguistic (and musical) infe-licities. One negative interpretation that could be drawn from the situation is that while Wun-Hi may be assimilated with respect to his work—a merchant like any other—his musical-verbal nature suggests that he will never truly be "Western/British/American." On the other hand, the play's structure depends on treating the Japanese characters as figures subordinate to but much more allied with the British characters; Wun-Hi then becomes the figure most likely to carry the negative ste-reotypes of Asian people; he is the scapegoat whose comic abjection allows the other interracial exchanges to be tolerated. Although the basic structure of prejudice is left intact, in other words, its lines of demarcation may be able in the right circum-stances to shift, however slightly, toward greater inclusiveness.

Inevitably, the ethnic songs that focused on more recent immigrant ethnic groups referred back to minstrelsy for their primary strategies of masquerade. And at the turn of the century, minstrelsy, though greatly transformed from its earlier historical incarnations, had in no way vanished. In the hands of especially gifted performers, "coon songs" of many types could carry substantial sub- and counter-texts in performance, ones that ironized the manifest stereotyping that was probably a requirement for any performance at all. The legendary team of Bert Williams and George Walker, who for a stretch of time billed their act as "Two Real Coons" (as opposed to the white folks who were obviously faking it), were famous for their subtle ways of transforming the conventions of minstrelsy in their routines. One of their great performances came in the 1901 show *Sons of Ham*, a comedy in which the two play hoboes who drift into Denver, Colorado, where they are mistaken for the long-lost children, home at last from boarding school, of a rich man named Ham. But then they learn that Ham's real sons, away trying to become acrobats, are about to return. More hilarity ensues. The songs contained in this musical range over topics familiar in minstrel shows, but many of the most standard racial clichés are either omitted from the action or noticeably undermined by aspects of the performance.

The love song "My Little Zulu Babe," for instance, was recorded by Williams and Walker in 1901, the year of the show's run.[13] There are a number of features worth noting, all having to do with the strikingly idiosyncratic way that the duo treat it. First, almost the only words that are completely clear in the recording are those of the (white) announcer giving the song's title and the performers' names. The sonic surface becomes a good deal murkier in what follows, and this is not entirely the result of the recording technology that was used. Williams, who is singing lead, employs a strong minstrel-show accent difficult for modern listeners to decipher, and his joyously messy singing, chock-full of vocal breaks, slides, and muffled syllables, masks the lyrics even further. Careful listening, however, reveals some details of what is present, as well as what is not: the song describes the charms of the eponymous "little Zulu babe," who lives "beside the Nile" (not geographically coherent, but good enough for a vaudeville audience c.1900), as well as the singer's determination to propose and celebrate the wedding in her town. What is *not* present are all the typical verbal markers of African primitiveness—aside from the surrounding "jungle," there is nothing particularly exotic in the lyrics of the song to place the Zulu maiden in a stereotyped position. Instead, Williams's performance can be taken as making him into something of a "fool for love." The comedy of his delivery is vastly amplified by Walker's background clowning: he interjects an assortment of wails, yodels, and other "jungle noises" into the background, sonically painting a cartoonish stylization of the Zulu babe's surroundings—but not of her (🔊 Example 6.3). And given that Williams is so audibly in on Walker's jokes, it may raise the question of just whom the joke is ultimately on. In fact, this kind of slippery humor was the norm for the routines that Williams and Walker had developed and in part accounts for the enormous influence that Williams, especially, had on comedians black and white alike.

These three songs, taken together, touch on some of the entanglements of racial and ethnic types as they appeared in New York performances. In a way, stock characterizations in these songs may be thought of as analogous to genres as defined by the formal properties of the music and lyrics: that is, these stereotypes set up a generalized set of characteristics that not only act as a container for the specifics of a given performer but also create a horizon of expectations in the audience. To the extent that we are conversant with a given set of conventions, we will be primed to look here, not over there; to hear this, not that. But at the very moment that conventions are stabilized, they become newly available for productive contradictions. This kind of stereotyping did not vanish with the spread of recording and the erosion of vaudeville, though it did begin to recede from the extremely blunt forms it took in the nineteenth century. One of the things its practical usage handed down to later Tin Pan Alley composers, however, was a sense that the artifice of a song was, after all, one of its major potential virtues.

TIN PAN ALLEY AND BROADWAY BEFORE WORLD WAR II

The first significant reference to a "Golden Age" of the American musical—a term that has now come to refer, most often, to the two decades or so before the mid-1960s—was by Gerald Bordman, who continues to locate this era between 1924 and 1937, coincident with the years George Gershwin was most active as a composer for Broadway and Tin Pan Alley. In being the first to apply this term to the musical, Bordman both claims a valuable history for Broadway and asserts a specific period of arrival, during which the tug of war between operetta and more distinctively American styles sorted itself out, generally in favor of the latter.[14] It was during this period that the "standard" 32-bar Tin Pan Alley type of song fully established itself, a type that accommodated all of the Tin Pan Alley venues and markets mentioned above, including not only Broadway, but also Hollywood, jazz, sheet music, recording, and radio. For Bordman, implicitly, the basis for this Golden Age was song, the element that placed all of these markets and venues (most importantly for Bordman, revues and book shows) in the same plane of existence, so that the relative value and impact of shows could be judged mainly by their songs and their effectiveness in putting those songs across.

The mature American musical emerged from the interweaving of, and competition between, two separate strands of theatrical music-making: adapted European operetta traditions (mainly English and Viennese) and a number of traditions that shared the practice of staging popular song, deriving in part from the English music hall and similar traditions. Tin Pan Alley—which, like the studio system in Hollywood with respect to film, grew to control the marketplace of song in America—grew up alongside the musical in New York, both literally and figuratively, and they long maintained a closely symbiotic relationship. Many date the beginnings of Tin Pan Alley to the spectacular success of Charles K. Harris's "After the Ball," a song interpolated into the touring version of *A Trip to Chinatown* in 1892. But Tin Pan Alley's connection to theatrical Broadway predated that success, as is clear from the way Tin Pan Alley followed the theatrical district as it migrated north from its earlier center near Union Square (East 14th Street), to 28th Street in the 1890s, and eventually to the Brill Building near Times Square, built in 1931. The term itself was coined by Monroe H. Rosenfeld in the 1890s in reference to its 28th Street iteration, but the classic "Tin Pan Alley" song emerged only in the 1920s and '30s with the generation of songwriters headed by Irving Berlin, George Gershwin (especially with his brother Ira as lyricist), Jerome Kern (with Oscar Hammerstein II and others), Cole Porter, and Richard Rodgers (with Lorenz Hart).

The musical styles and forms of Tin Pan Alley, while always responsive to the needs of the musical stage, also played to a popular marketplace, following a line of development from nineteenth-century waltz songs to ragtime and "Coon" songs in the early twentieth century, to later styles derived from jazz, at all times maintaining as well a spread from sentimental (maintaining a dual allegiance to the parlor-song tradition and operetta) to humorous and more rhythmically inflected songs. Both onstage and in the marketplace, songs also played to a wide variety of topical interests, including, as discussed, a now-discomfiting engagement with ethnic, racial, and gendered stereotypes. Their use of dance rhythms and styles, too, pointed toward a need for songs to succeed on many fronts, whether by making them easier to put over onstage, allowing them to serve as a vehicle for social dance, or helping them to catch on with the public as songs to be sung at home, where they might also be listened to (and possibly danced to) through radio or recordings.

The vast majority of Tin Pan Alley songs use a verse-chorus structure, in which the "verse" either narrates a story or establishes a dramatic situation, and the "chorus" either acts as a punctuating refrain or represents the song promised by the dramatic setup. While the narration-refrain type was more typical in Tin Pan Alley's first generation (e.g., in the classic waltz-song, such as "After the Ball," or in the ragtime-song, such as Bob Cole and J. Rosamund Johnson's "Under the Bamboo Tree" of 1902), the "dramatic situation" song type came to dominate in the 1920s, employing the "classic" Tin Pan Alley 32-bar form for the chorus. While in both types, broadly speaking, the refrain or chorus would have been understood as the "song itself," the dependency on the verse lessened considerably as the new type evolved, a development that served all relevant marketplaces and venues.

Charles K. Harris's "After the Ball" offers a good example of how the earlier type worked, employing a relatively lengthy narrative verse and relatively short refrain (as compared to the later type). The song's full narrative takes three verses to unfold, and it is only with the third iteration of the refrain-chorus that we fully understand that the singer-narrator's early jealousy and rebuke have in time turned to regret tinged with self-reproach. The success of the song depended both on the dramatic arch of its verse-based narrative and the memorable chorus, during which, in public performance, or while listening to radio or recordings, auditors might join in, enjoying the waltz-based lilt of the "After" that opens each of the first few lines, and savoring the wistful "feminine" endings on the key words "over," "leaving," "aching," and "vanished." The refrain thus presents a sonic image of the ball as a metaphor for the "vanished" promise of married bliss, a combination that became even more effective as the waltz-song, as a type, evolved into an emblem of nostalgia (⬥ Example 6.4).[15]

By 1927, indeed, this transition of the older type was officially complete. That year's *Show Boat*, in one of a handful of period musical references, brings in "After the Ball" as an emblem of the 1893 Chicago Fair, along with Sousa's "Washington Post March" and Broadway imitations of both spirituals and blues ("Ol' Man River" and "Can't Help Lovin' Dat Man"; ⬥ Example 6.5; ⬥ Example 6.6), the last two presented as a kind of African American "roots" music. In other ways, too, *Show Boat* positions itself as a kind of "threshold" show. Produced with extravagant staging by Florenz Ziegfeld, renowned impresario of the Ziegfeld Follies, *Show Boat* was originally to have included a mini-revue in the second act performed by Paul Robeson (who rejected the idea, and the role of Joe in the bargain, although he joined the show later and would become closely identified with "Ol' Man River").[16] In other ways, too, the show seems poised between operetta and revue, superimposing them in a way that was potentially (and in the long run, actually) transformative. In making life along the Mississippi the site of operetta-based nostalgia and intrigue, it also constructed a space to celebrate an African American musical heritage and gave that heritage an onstage, dramatic presence, where it is valued both through nostalgia and as a revitalizing presence, without (in the context of its era) over-sentimentalizing the role of blacks in the postwar South. Often thought of as the first classic "book" musical, *Show Boat* is equally important for completing the transition, on Broadway, from European operetta to American operetta, in the process effacing operetta as such by replacing its European musical core with an African American–styled musical panorama, encompassing spirituals, blues, characteristic dance, and ragtime (the latter oddly positioned as a white appropriation). It is this successful stylistic superimposition, along with *Show Boat*'s unprecedented success in revivals, that lends plausibility to the claim that it marks the beginning of the American musical's maturity as a genre.

But if *Show Boat* may be understood as a kind of new beginning, it remains unclear what exactly it might be seen to have either launched or displaced. In Bordman's configuration of the Golden Age (1924–37), *Show Boat* is but part of the broader emergence of a new kind of song that blended styles in a characteristic American way, and he is probably right to date this emergence back to 1924, when Gershwin began to enjoy real success on Broadway (although his ending with Gershwin's untimely death in 1937 seems a bit over-dramatic, especially since Cole Porter's star was then emphatically in the ascendant). But the continued success of the new style being developed by Gershwin, Berlin, Kern, and others during the mid-1920s and its easy transitions among venues and markets did not depend on what many historians have seen as the revolutionary aspect of *Show Boat*: its vaunted position in the evolution of the integrated book musical—which somehow had to wait until *Oklahoma!* sixteen years later to receive a sustainable echo. In light of this traditional if misguided focus, it is important to note both that *Show Boat*'s integrated book is scarcely unique for its time (although its durability in revivals is), and that it is the song type itself that truly mattered to audiences of the day. In this we may concur with Bordman, for it was indeed song that sustained *Show Boat* and countless other shows and films of the era, whatever their level of integration.

"Natural" Form versus "Formula"

In the second half of the Tin Pan Alley era, when the style developed an even closer connection to the Broadway stage while remaining the source of America's most popular music (roughly the 1920s through the mid-1950s), a number of factors combined to shift the form and expressive strategies of the basic song-type. Technology (especially radio and recording) imposed increasingly stringent demands on the length of a song. More subtly, the fecundity of the genre as a basis for jazz improvisations and arrangements, as well as for extended dance sequences, tended to dictate a standard, moderate-length formal structure, functioning much like binary forms in the eighteenth century. And while earlier Tin Pan Alley songs played into practices of song-interpolation, later types had to fit into particular dramatic moments, as what may be termed "fragments of expressivity" (Knapp, *National Identity*, 77–78). These forces conspired to shape the form and the potential of the song in fundamental ways and made its 32-bar form the standard for the type (although for many venues the 12-bar blues form, sometimes crossbred with the 32-bar form, worked at least equally well).

This standardization of 32-bar song form, however, has always had its detractors, who have used it and other recurring features of the Tin Pan Alley song to decry its "formulaic" aspect. Certainly there are songs from this era that seem formulaic, and to their detriment. But it is entirely possible to be thoroughly formulaic—that is, to employ formulas at nested lower levels within the basic 32-bar formula—and still engage listeners freshly, often through a deft deployment of lyrics. Cole Porter's "list" songs, such as "You're the Top" or "Anything Goes" (both from *Anything Goes*, 1934), provide ready examples. But the formulaic can serve aesthetic functions beyond humor; even in these "list" songs, the formula-driven humor deflects and disconcerts, cloaking the expression of genuine feeling with crucial deniability. More broadly, formulas may create a sense of containment for what might otherwise seem emotionally risky or impart a sense of naturalness or inevitability to what might otherwise seem strange or unlikely, in these and other ways lending ontological conviction to content that might not otherwise persuade. More subtly, and surprisingly often—surprising, that is, for those who have bought into the negative profiling of Tin Pan Alley as formulaic—creating a sense of a well-known formula can lull listeners into a sense of occupying a familiar, "natural" space, so that they might not notice how unformulaic things actually are within that space. Examples range from the structural freedom of the formula itself, to specific devices that deflect strict formula in one way or another, and to deft uses of formula to manage a potentially disruptive element, be it harmonic, melodic, or rhythmic.

To begin with, 32-bar form is not a single formula but an array of conventions, generally resulting in four balanced phrases of eight bars each, or an easily recognized variant of this arrangement (involving, for example, cadential extensions). The most common design includes two repetitions of the first phrase separated by a contrasting phrase (often referred to as the "bridge," "release," or "middle eight"), resulting in an AABA thematic structure—a design, often termed "song form," with a pedigree dating back to the eighteenth century. Somewhat less common is a two-part structure, ABAB, evoking "binary" or "period" structures, also standardized in the eighteenth century. In either type, the final phrase might be varied significantly (thus, AABC or ABAC); indeed, variations of material in repetition are quite common, so long as the gesture of repetition—and of returning, as if inevitably, to the familiar—is clear. Typically, an extension of the form in performance will include an instrumental interlude, sometimes danced, followed by a final repetition of the concluding phrase (thus, AABABA, where the second B is performed instrumentally and the final two "A" phrases are identical).

Within the conventions of 32-bar form, the apparently formulaic can disguise some surprising departures. The familiar song "Always" (Berlin, 1925) flirts with each of the formal types identified above but follows none of them, resulting in a form that might best be described as ABCD, while nevertheless providing a secure sense of balances maintained or restored, especially through its repetitions of the title word. Remarkably, "Always" thus imparts an extraordinary sense of comfort while surreptitiously violating most of the basic expectations of the form. And using a device shared with a few other songs, "Oklahoma!" (from *Oklahoma!*, 1943), doubles the basic dimensions of the form (16-bar phrases instead of 8-) while keeping to an 8-bar bridge ("We know we belong to the land..."), thus seeming to follow convention while heightening the song's sense of expansion through an internal contrast in phrase proportions.

As in "Always," the gesture of repetition in Tin Pan Alley songs is often deflected without disrupting the basic gesture, in some cases adding a patina of urgency or mystery and in others expressively shifting emphasis. "My Funny Valentine" (Rodgers and Hart, from *Babes in Arms*, 1937), for example, moves a third upward at the beginning of the second "A" phrase, angling toward the relative major (which arrives with the bridge). The final "A" phrase then moves through both keys at its outset, completing a process that adds crucial expressive energy and leads to an ending in a different key from the opening, all accomplished within phrases that will seem to be unproblematic repetitions to most listeners (◐ Example 6.7). Another device used in "Funny Valentine"—reaching a higher pitch with each repeated phrase—is used in many songs of this era (such as "Ol' Man River") and especially favored by Cole Porter, who used it, for example, in "All through the Night" and "I Get a Kick Out of You" from *Anything Goes* (1934; the latter song from 1931), and "So in Love" from *Kiss Me, Kate* (1948)—which, like "My Funny Valentine," ends in a different key from the opening. All of these songs employ the device with considerable subtlety, but "All through the Night" is particularly deft in its coordination of unpredictable upward leaps that spring free of the song's sagging chromatic lines to give additional emphasis to key words: "close *to me... You* and your love" (◉ Example 6.8).

While all of these devices preserve a *sense* of the formulaic while departing from actual formula, this kind of balance between order and disruption is probably never so crucial as with "rhythm" songs, a type of Tin Pan Alley song that employs a potentially disruptive (and often hard to sing) "hook" that is then contained within the strict phrasing dictated by the type. "Fascinating Rhythm" (George and Ira Gershwin, from *Lady Be Good*, 1924), "Puttin' on the Ritz" (Berlin, 1930, from the film of the same title), and "I Got Rhythm" (George and Ira Gershwin, from *Girl Crazy*, 1930) are three well-known "rhythm" songs that all lead with their distinctive and disruptive hooks and then depend on the 32-bar form to restore a controlling stability.

The hook for "Fascinating Rhythm" is an insistent melodic pattern of six eighth-notes followed by an eighth-note rest, yielding a three-and-a-half-beat pattern that pulls backward against the bar line, driven by the shifting accentual patterns of the lyric; briefly stabilized in the fourth iteration, the pattern is then repeated at a higher pitch level for the second half of the "A" phrase within an ABAC structure (◉ Example 6.9). The device in "Puttin' on the Ritz" is similar but paced more slowly; its seven-beat melodic structure (including an awkwardly placed syncopation) is sorted out, within each "A" phrase of an AABA structure, through a measured pause and a more straightforward presentation of the title phrase (◉ Example 6.10). "I Got Rhythm" places its title phrase within its rhythmic hook, a thrice-repeated, evenly spaced four-note phrase that cuts across the basic rhythm by virtue of its consisting entirely of dotted quarter-notes, starting off the beat and thus imposing a slower rhythm that coincides in alignment with its background only on the third syllable of each iteration ("I got *rhy*-thm"; ◉ Example 6.11). Interestingly, the rhythmic hook in each of these "formulaic" songs has a different significance; in "Fascinating Rhythm" it is imposed from without, as something (ostensibly) unwelcome that takes hold of the singer, whereas in "Puttin' on the Ritz" it reflects the inner awkwardness of described behavior (allied in its first version with an imputation of racialized difference)[17] and in "I Got Rhythm" it betokens a mastery of something difficult—even if more singers fail than succeed in rendering its rhythmic device accurately.

"Equipment for Living"

According to the scholar Philip Furia, the vast majority of Tin Pan Alley songs published during the 1920s and '30s were love songs.[18] In fact, during these decades questions of sexual desire and identity had become central to many understandings of modernity, especially among the bohemian crowd in New York City, whose elaborate participation in the artistic avant-garde (at this point, closely connected with many aspects of popular culture, particularly music) gave their widely publicized interpretations of modern love tremendous influence.

The advent of medical sexology in the late nineteenth century, for instance, had presented a painstakingly constructed taxonomy of sexual "dysfunctions"—which, ironically, offered the subjects under classification an opportunity to appropriate the medical labels, enabling a bewildering host of possible sexual identities.[19] The related discourse of psychoanalysis had placed questions of sexuality and its pervasive but hidden manifestations at the center of human subjectivity; not only was sexual content potentially everywhere, but there was also a much-expanded vocabulary with which to discuss it. Freud and his circle favored the rhetoric of science in presenting their account of sexuality as well, giving psychoanalysis the progressive luster of biology, chemistry ("yeah, chemistry"), and above all physics.

No less important were shifts in propriety and the laws that underwrote it. In the wake of nineteenth-century feminist actions such as the suffrage movement and the battles for access to birth control and family planning, and equal access to education, the protocols of feminine respectability began to shift and broaden considerably; in so doing, they revised the protocols of masculine respectability, as well. Modernist art movements, which placed challenges to bourgeois morals and tastes at the center of many projects, constantly challenged normative assumptions about what could and could not be explicitly represented—the best evidence of this in the United States was the obscenity proceedings brought against Gautier's *Mademoiselle de Maupin* (1922), Hall's *The Well of Loneliness* (1929), and, most famously, Joyce's *Ulysses* (1933). In each case, notions of artistic merit and "scientific" exploration contributed significantly to the arguments against censorship. And in the United States, these shifts in style took place within the milieu of Prohibition, which rather than elevating public morals by banning alcohol contributed to a widespread cynicism about all moral legislation.[20]

The effective collapse of the older models of gender, especially among the influential urban classes of America, meant that the protocols of love and courtship that helped realize those models quickly seemed out of date; but there were no alternative structures of affection and romance that would replace them. Instead, an array of possible models took the place of the old erotic regime; at the same time, the representation of modes of courtship became one of the major concerns of Tin Pan Alley songs. And so, by way of a conclusion to this chapter, we briefly consider a few points related to this development in two songs from Tim Pan Alley's Hollywood mode.

The 1932 musical *Gay Divorce* was Fred Astaire's last Broadway show before moving to Hollywood. Of the ten or twelve songs Cole Porter provided for the production, only one—"Night and Day"—survived the show's transformation into the 1934 film *The Gay Divorcee*.[21] Although the film alters elements of the scanty plot, it keeps the essential structure of a screwball comedy, in which a divorce sought out of boredom, faked adultery, a barely covertly gay gigolo, mistaken identity, and so on combine to comment lightheartedly on the travails of modern marriage. But "Night and Day" itself, though an elegant display of verbal and musical wit, takes courtship quite seriously. The terms in which it does so are apparent in the performance by Fred Astaire as he sings to Ginger Rogers. The song's verse sets up a series of similes that concatenate the primitive (jungles, tom-toms—a clear reference to jazz) with the technological (the clock) and nature (rain). The musical setting is melodically a chant-like reciting tone—Porter was well known for tailoring his songs to the capacities of specific performers, and in this case he had in mind Astaire's limited vocal range but also his sensitive phrasing and diction—not to mention his talent as a dancer. The repeated pitches, while they suit Astaire's skills well, also immediately start to establish an obsessive quality to the song's notions of courtship. It is also significant that, although the verse at first projects a steady rise in pitch level, suggesting urgency, just before the turn into the refrain the melody relaxes back to its initial pitch. Taken together with the refrain's propensity for gracefully drooping gestures, the melody establishes a fascinating tension between the suave wistfulness of possibly unrequited love and the thrum of underlying passion. As for the lyrics of the refrain, it is difficult to decide whether the omnipresence of the first person—the song is fundamentally not a set of compliments, as might be expected in romance, but instead a brilliant set of self-descriptions—is the result of tact or narcissism. If it is a plea for affection, then it is one that avoids ever making an outright proposition (⊙ Example 6.12).

Shall We Dance, released in 1937, was the seventh film featuring Fred Astaire and Ginger Rogers. Unlike The Gay Divorcee, it did not start as a stage musical: it arose from RKO's decision to create its own version of Rodgers and Hart's On Your Toes. The Gershwins were persuaded to sign on for what would be their first Hollywood musical. Again, courtship and marriage play a central role. In this case, the romantic leads, who are from different worlds (ballet and tap), are thrown together in a stunt marriage but gradually realize that what started out as a ploy has become "real." George Gershwin was reportedly excited about the opportunity to compose in a range of dance styles, and the score is stylistically quite rich. "They Can't Take That Away from Me," one of the film's most popular numbers, is a foxtrot, and its mode of courtship is complementary to that outlined in "Night and Day." That is, "They Can't Take That" is a not a self-description but a very detailed set of compliments. The beloved's style—clothes, hair, gestures—are listed as examples of the persistence of memory—and in this case, the repeated pitches in the melody (Gershwin's own acknowledgment of Astaire's particular skills?) becomes less a sign of romantic obsession and more a jaunty launching pad for the affectionate listing of details (⊙ Example 6.13).

Such short descriptions barely brush on the range of ways that Tin Pan Alley songs offered vehicles and models for constructing styles of courtship, but they nevertheless suggest how we might heighten our sensitivity to the kind of cultural work they participated in. In the authentistic moods of Cold War America, the stylish impersonality of such songs fell under suspicion: where was the truth of the performer's experience in a frothy commercial love song? But to a significant extent, many of the cultural battles fought in the United States over the last few decades have been less about "truth" and more about "impression management." They have in important ways been about negotiating a system of manners that we can collectively tolerate. Within this realm, it may be that Tin Pan Alley, with its elaborate romantic ad hocs, can offer us insights into our present as well as our past.

NOTES

1. The most important of these were Lederer's *The Passing Show*, Hippodrome "Extravaganzas," the Music Box "Revues," the "Grand Street Follies," the "Greenwich Village Follies," the "Garrick Gaieties," "Artists and Models," Earl Carroll's "Vanities," and George White's "Scandals."

2. See Gerald Bordman, *American Musical Theatre: A Chronicle*, 3rd ed. (New York: Oxford University Press, 2001) and http://www.ibdb.com

3. See Rose Rosengard Subotnik, "Shoddy Equipment for Living? Deconstructing the Tin Pan Alley Song," in *Musicological Identities: Essays in Honor of Susan McClary*, ed. Steven Baur, Raymond Knapp, and Jacqueline Warwick (Aldershot, UK: Ashgate, 2008), pp. 205–18.

4. "Tenement" in this sense refers to cheaply built structures, often without adequate plumbing or ventilation, into which vast numbers of impoverished immigrants were crowded. The disastrous condition of the buildings and consequences for their inhabitants were a central concern for journalistic and political reformers—the New York State Tenement House Act of 1901, which corrected problems in the predecessor laws of 1867, 1879, and 1887, was the result of vigorous campaigning by the Progressive Movement of the turn of the century.

5. For the rest of this discussion the term "ethnic" will also stand in for "racial." To be sure, the differences between these two sets of characteristics can be understood as quite different—"race" is commonly held to be fixed to a degree that "ethnicity" is not. But especially since we are dealing with a period in which scientistic theories of "race" typically blended into considerations of what we would call "ethnicity," and since "race" as a term carries a much heavier load of historical sedimentation, we opt for "ethnic" as the more easily generalized term.

6. Jacob A. Riis, *How the Other Half Lives: Studies among the Tenements of New York* (New York, 1890; reprinted New York: Kessinger Publishers, 2004); online at www.authentichistory. com/1865-1897/progressive/riis/index.html, accessed November 4, 2010.

7. Nora Bayes, "How Can They Tell That Oi'm Irish?" (Norworth/Bayes), recorded August 11, 1919 (78 Vic 700030 [mx C-9633-3]).

8. Husband #2 was the popular vaudevillian Jack Norworth (who co-authored the song under discussion); #3 was a dancer by the name of Harry Clarke; #4 was a New York businessman named Arthur Gordon.

9. "Astarita" is a thinly disguised jest at the Astors; "Vandergould" manages to send up the Vanderbilts.

10. *The Geisha*, music by Sidney Jones, lyrics by Harry Greenbank, book by Owen Hall; additional songs by Lionel Monckton and James Philip. In fact, the musical was even successful in continental Europe. The show was one of a sequence of so-called Gaiety musicals that made up a substantial share of the British shows successfully trans-Atlanticized at the turn of the century.

11. James T. Powers, "Chin Chin Chinaman" (Jones/Greenbank), recorded December 5, 1898 (78/Berliner 525-X).

12. These are actually genuine difficulties for some Chinese speakers who learn English as a second language. If learning went in the other direction, surely native Chinese speakers would be amused by English speakers' probable mismanagement of Sinic tonal systems. Once again, the problem is not the presence of such speech challenges between languages but their reductions to a symbol of maladroit Otherness. In "Yinglish" theater, such bumps in language shift are a major resource for witty wordplay.

13. Bert Williams and George Walker, "My Little Zulu Babe" (Potter), recorded August 11, 1901 (78 Vic 1086 [mx 1086]).

14. Bordman's *American Musical Theatre* has been expanded, corrected, and updated several times since its first edition in 1978, with an expanded edition in 1986, a second edition in 1992, and a third edition in 2001; all versions include, as "Act IV," a chapter headed "The Golden Age of the American Musical, 1924–1937."

15. For more detailed discussions of this song and several others discussed in this chapter, see Raymond Knapp's *The American Musical and the Formation of National Identity* and *The American Musical and the Performance of Personal Identity* (Princeton, NJ: Princeton University Press, 2005 and 2006).

16. See Todd Decker, "Black/White Encounters on the American Musical Stage and Screen (1924–2005)" (Ph.D. Dissertation, University of Michigan, 2007).

17. The original version's racialized text was rewritten for Fred Astaire in the film *Blue Skies* (1946), and the later "cleaned-up" version is now standard.

18. Philip Furia, *The Poets of Tin Pan Alley: A History of America's Great Lyricists* (New York: Oxford University Press, 1990), p. 15.

19. Possibly one of the most striking examples of this occurs in Radclyffe Hall's famous lesbian novel *The Well of Loneliness*, in which the protagonist discovers her sexual identity by reading: she pages through Richard von Krafft-Ebing's famous classificatory work *Psychopathia Sexualis*, learning to call herself a lesbian in the process.

20. The most lively generational social network in England during the 1920s was known as "the Bright Young People." Their attitudes and public styles closely resembled those of New York bohemia—not surprising considering how frequently the two worlds overlapped.

21. The Hayes Office was troubled by the musical's original title, since it suggested that divorce was a happy occasion. Since the parties getting divorced, however, could be happy without upsetting the censors' sense of propriety (and perhaps persuaded by the parallel with *The Merry Widow*), the slight shift in title was accepted.

CHAPTER 7

INTEGRATION

GEOFFREY BLOCK

In the decades after the Supreme Court infamously ruled that separate could be equal (*Plessy v. Ferguson*, 1896), debates over racial integration in America gradually spread to a broader American public, fueled by W. E. B. Du Bois's and Booker T. Washington's forceful arguments. In popular culture, where race lines were contested by generations of performers and athletes, "integration" acquired more layers of meaning. Nearly sixty years after *Plessy*, another historic Supreme Court decision, *Brown v. Board of Education* (1954), overturned its predecessor and endorsed the ideal of racial integration, establishing a new national formulation of racial *veritas*: that separate is *not* equal. Integration—at least of public schools—became the law of the land.[1]

During the years between *Plessy* and *Brown*, the Broadway musical made its own tentative moves toward racial integration. In the epoch-making musical *Show Boat* (Jerome Kern and Oscar Hammerstein, 1927), audiences saw and heard two choruses, one black and one white, separately but equally powerfully, supporting a story that depicted the unfairness of laws against miscegenation. Moss Hart's and Irving Berlin's revue, *As Thousands Cheer* (1933), achieved its most poignant moment when Ethel Waters sang "Supper Time," a lament for her husband who had been lynched that day. Despite such forays into racial politics, however, "integration" on Broadway was, at least until the 1960s, an aesthetic aspiration largely unconcerned with racial politics. From the decades before *Brown* and continuing through the decades of its implementation, creators of the musical—Kern, Hammerstein, Rodgers, Lorenz Hart, Jo Mielziner, Agnes de Mille, Jerome Robbins, Boris Aronson, Hal Prince, Stephen Sondheim, and Michael Bennett, to name only a few pivotal figures—deliberately strove for an integration of the spoken, musical, danced, and scenic dimensions of a musical.

INTEGRATING THE MUSICAL PLAY

Shortly after the premiere of *Oklahoma!* (1943), Hammerstein compared his treatment of songs from that of its source play, Lynn Riggs's *Green Grow the Lilacs*:

> The songs we were to write had a different function. They must help tell our story and delineate characters, supplementing the dialogue and seeming to be, as much as possible, a continuation of dialogue. This is, of course, true of the songs by any well-made musical play.[2]

Six years after *Oklahoma!,* in his most detailed treatment on the art of lyrics, Hammerstein revisited his first show with Rodgers and the marriage between words and music, a key component of what he now calls "well-integrated," rather than "well-made." After sharing his belief that the musical expression of a story is comparable and equal to its verbal component, Hammerstein uses the word "integrated" to explain the merging of words and music "into a single expression":

> This is the great secret of the well-integrated musical play. It is not so much a method as a state of mind, or rather a state for two minds, an attitude of unity. Musical plays, then, are not "books" written by an author with songs later inserted by a composer and a lyric writer.[3]

Near the end of his long career, Rodgers too shared his thoughts on the integrated musical in his autobiography:

> I have long held a theory about musicals. When a show works perfectly, it's because all the individual parts complement each other and fit together. No single element overshadows any other. In a great musical, the orchestrations sound the way the costumes look. That's what made *Oklahoma!* work. All the components dovetailed. There was nothing extraneous or foreign, nothing that pushed itself into the spotlight yelling "look at me!" It was a work created by many that gave the impression of having been created by one.[4]

By the time Rodgers and Hammerstein's *Oklahoma!* launched the so-called Golden Age in 1943, the principles of the "well-integrated" (or "well-made") musical play, although not invariably endorsed or practiced, had become a widely recognized and valued approach. The central characteristics of the "integrated" musical appear with ubiquity if not complete observance not only in *Oklahoma!* but also in many other critically acclaimed shows.[5] From the quoted Hammerstein and Rodgers passages, as well as from their musicals, we may glean the following Principles of Integration (following each Principle is an illustrative example or two from *Oklahoma!*):

   1. ***The songs advance the plot***. In "Surrey with the Fringe on Top," Curley improvises a seductive description of the surrey he plans to use to take Laurey to the box social. Laurey and Aunt Eller become caught up in this extravagant idea, and by the end of the song—before it is interrupted by dialogue—the young couple have moved on to a deeper place in their still-unacknowledged but inevitable pairing.

2. *The songs flow directly from the dialogue*. By the time Ado Annie's beau Will Parker tells Aunt Eller, Ike Skidmore, and the assembled cowboys that he arrived in Kansas City "on a Frid'y," the song "Kansas City" has already begun. A little later Ado Annie explains to Laurey the problem she has with saying no, and within a line, dialogue has merged almost imperceptibly with music in "I Cain't Say No."

3. *The songs express the characters who sing them*. Ado Annie's "I Cain't Say No" expresses her flirtatiousness in language and music utterly foreign to Laurey. It would be equally implausible for Ado to address Will in a song remotely like Curley and Laurey's "People Will Say We're in Love" or a song as lush and romantic as Laurey's waltz "Out of My Dreams."

4. *The dances advance the plot and enhance the dramatic meaning of the songs that precede them*. Dance in *Oklahoma!* is exemplified by the historic dream ballet "Laurey Makes Up Her Mind," but the dancing that follows other songs is similarly "integrated" with the meaning of its companion song and the fabric of the show as a whole. For example, the dance styles discussed in the lyrics are executed in the dancing to "Kansas City," and Laurey's friends dance out the independence they extol in the words and music to "Many a New Day."[6] Similarly, dance in "The Farmer and the Cowman" expresses civilized engagement of the two groups, whereas "Oklahoma!" expands choreographically (and musically) to suggest the settling of an empty space by a growing population.

5. *The orchestra, through accompaniment and underscoring, parallels, complements, or advances the action*. In the reprise to "People Will Say We're In Love," it is the orchestra, not the singers, that initiates the musical development of this important dramatic moment, by underscoring the kissing and affectionate banter between Laurey and Curley with nearly half of the song's chorus. After that, Curley, in contrast to his behavior during this song in act I, welcomes full disclosure of their love ("Let people say we're in love"). (Along with the enhanced role of dance, the orchestra as a dramatic player will be exploited further in works such as *West Side Story* and *Sweeney Todd*.)

None of these Principles of Integration made a sudden appearance with *Oklahoma!* The integration of book and score was readily evident in the operettas of Gilbert and Sullivan, Johann Strauss, Jr., and Franz Lehár, all of whom had a major impact on Broadway from the late 1870s until World War I. The American musicals of Victor Herbert, especially *Naughty Marietta* (1910), also demonstrated some of the Principles of Integration common to European opera, operetta, and symphonic music. The integrated *musical* ideal was already for several generations also a common aesthetic component of both European symphonic literature from Beethoven to Mahler (known to musicologists as organic unity) and much opera, especially Wagner. But while this technique can contribute to the musical and dramatic integration of a work, an integrated musical, in the sense of the well-made musical play, does not require an organic score. In fact, when an organic score fails to imbue its organicism with dramatic meaning the result might be a *poorly* made musical play.

In an interview published four years before *Oklahoma!*, Rodgers insisted that songs in a show "must bear a family resemblance to the other musical material in the piece."[7] This is another way of endorsing the principles of musical organicism. Kern's organic approach to *Show Boat* and his use of such Wagnerian techniques as the grouping of themes within a larger family of motives, was recognized by Robert Simon in a contemporary profile of the composer in *Modern Music,* when he wrote that "themes are quoted and even developed in almost Wagnerian fashion."[8] In numerous musicals that followed *Show Boat,* including works by Rodgers and Hammerstein, Bernstein, Sondheim, and Lloyd Webber, organic musical scores constitute a key component of integration.

Among American-born Broadway practitioners Kern was perhaps the first to articulate the view that the well-made musical play should exhibit the dramatic values expected of well-made nonmusical dramas and comedies. A decade before *Show Boat* he expressed this position, in a 1917 interview:

> Plausibility and reason apply to musical plays as to dramas and comedies, and the sooner librettists and composers appreciate this fact the sooner will come recognition and—royalties.[9]

Later in this interview Kern demonstrated that some of his goals as a musical theater composer were identical to those later allied with the "integrated musical" of the 1940s:

> It is my opinion that the musical numbers should carry on the action of the play, and should be representative of the personalities of the characters who sing them. In a scene of college life you would never today present students in songs which deal with piracy or cheese manufacture unless the action of the piece demanded such activities. In other words, songs must be suited to the action and mood of the play.

Three years before *Show Boat,* the hugely popular operetta *Rose-Marie* (Friml and Hammerstein) not only contained a murder but also provided a demonstration of the future ideal, the integrated score:

> The musical numbers of this play are such an *integral* part of the action that we do not think we should list them as separate episodes. The songs which stand out, independent of their dramatic associations, are "Rosemarie," "Indian Love Call," "Totem Tom-Tom" and "Why Shouldn't We" in the first act, and "The Door of My Dreams" in the second act.[10]

A program note in Rodgers and Hart's *Chee-Chee* (1928) informed audiences that the short musical numbers "are so interwoven with the story that it would be confusing for the audience to peruse a complete list" (Rodgers 1975, 118). From *Show Boat* to *South Pacific* to *West Side Story* to *Sweeney Todd,* some musicals before and many musicals after *Oklahoma!* possessed integrated scores rich in thematic or "organic" unity.

Some integrated musicals are more integrated than others. Moreover, makers of musicals and their critics do not generally put forward the integrated musical as a polemical ideal but as a potentially profitable as well as an artistic approach (as Kern emphasizes) to a varied popular entertainment genre competing alongside a newer popular entertainment, the motion picture. To the extent that elaborate, coherent narratives were becoming the critical norm in Oscar-winning pictures such as 1939's incredible crop (including *Gone With the Wind* and the film musical *The Wizard of Oz*), musicals that are presentational rather than cinematic became less appealing as potential Hollywood crossover fodder.

Increasingly, scholars express the view that integration is actually present in musicals formerly dismissed for alleged incongruities between dialogue and song (in short, a perceived lack of integration). Even Cole Porter's perennially revived— and perennially revised—*Anything Goes* (1934), described by Raymond Knapp as the show that "seems to exemplify the pre-*Oklahoma!*, pre-'integrated' era of the American musical," contains songs that "are carefully situated within the show, often carrying important dramatic and thematic weight, and consistently setting out the characters' sensibilities and relationships in vivid, yet subtle, fashion."[11] Probing and substantial dramatic themes prominent in the integrated musical plays of Rodgers and Hammerstein (e.g., spousal abuse in *Carousel*, racial prejudice in *South Pacific*) also occur regularly in the 1930s musical, for example, *Of Thee I Sing* (1931), *Face the Music* (1932), *Johnny Johnson* (1936), *I'd Rather Be Right* (1937), and *The Cradle Will Rock* (1938), all of which challenge audiences with political and social satire rather than (or in addition to) romance.[12]

Before *Oklahoma!*, dances, when they followed a song, were considered more an accessory than an essential to the development of the story. Critics of noninte-grated dance numbers are prone to accuse such numbers of stopping the show, when in fact these glorious extraneous moments *are* the show. Nevertheless, prior to *Oklahoma!* dance gradually came to exert a stronger dramatic and plot-related presence. As early as the late 1920s, *New York Times* dance critic John Martin paid serious attention to the "prodigious raising of the level of the dancing" in Busby Berkeley's innovative choreography in Rodgers and Hart's *A Connecticut Yankee* (1927) and *Present Arms* (1928), including Berkeley's artistic way "of utilizing to the fullest extent the actual material which author and composer have provided for him."[13] Although the claim that George Balanchine's "Slaughter on Tenth Avenue" advances the action in *On Your Toes* (1936) has been challenged, the hybrid ballet hardly seems extraneous to a musical whose subject matter to a large extent con-cerns the reconcilable differences between ballet and jazz dance.

Film historian John Mueller emphasizes the importance of the "Night and Day" dance sequence to the integration in the Broadway show *Gay Divorce* (1932), starring Fred Astaire, and soon thereafter in the Astaire and Ginger Rogers film adaptation with its less scandalous title, *The Gay Divorcee* (1934). For Mueller, "Night and Day" constitutes "the first of Astaire's major plot-advancing numbers in film, brought over from the stage play where it served a similar function," four years before "Slaughter on Tenth Avenue" and eleven before "Laurey Makes Up Her Mind."[14] In Mueller's view, Agnes de Mille's ballet "Laurey Makes Up Her Mind" from *Oklahoma!* enriches the plot but does not advance it. Such a position does not acknowledge that "Laurey Makes Up Her Mind" offered a dimension not present in *On Your Toes* or the integrated dancing of Fred and Ginger. More than

simply advancing the plot, "Laurey Makes Up Her Mind" employs dance to vividly explore the psychological dimension of a central character in ways that dialogue and songs could not. Through dreams and nightmares, dance conveys
Laurey's unspoken thoughts, unacknowledged sexuality, and fears that lie below
the surface in her waking (and nondancing) state. The self-aware Ado Annie
knows her mind; Laurey does not know hers until she has danced out her feelings
in her dreams. Not even the remarkable integrated dances of Fred and Ginger try
to accomplish so much.

While the demonstration of the Principles of Integration may be the exception rather than the norm before the 1940s, the principles appeared regularly and
increasingly in shows from the 1910s through the late 1930s before the integrated
ideal became the law for post-*Oklahoma!* aspirant musicals of the 1940s. In fact,
the Princess Shows of Kern, Guy Bolton, and P. G. Wodehouse, Kern and
Hammerstein's *Show Boat,* George and Ira Gershwin's *Of Thee I Sing* (book by
George S. Kaufman and Morrie Ryskind), and George Gershwin's anomalous
Porgy and Bess (book by DuBose Heyward, lyrics by Heyward and Ira Gershwin)
are familiar pre-*Oklahoma!* realizations of the integrated ideal. In the far lesser
known *Cat and the Fiddle* (1931) Kern, in tandem with librettist-lyricist Otto
Harbach, continued his efforts (according to the hype of its producer Max
Gordon) "to work artistically and with greater integrity in the medium than may
have been imagined" and "to make certain that there will be strong motivation for
the music throughout."[15] As Stephen Banfield argues, the successful solution to a
complex dramatic problem was to create "a plot and a treatment in which all the
musical performances would be diegetic" (i.e., "music from an identifiable source
within the fictional world of the film," a term increasingly applied successfully to
musical theater studies).[16]

Toward the end of their long association, Rodgers and Hart in *Pal Joey* (1940)
consistently used songs to explore character and enhance the story. *Lady in the Dark*
(1941; book by Moss Hart, lyrics by Ira Gershwin, and music by Kurt Weill) used
music dramatically to realize the dreams of its central character in a show that purposefully segregated nonmusical dialogue from continuous musical dreams.
Significantly, contemporary reviews used the term "integrated" to describe what
they saw and heard in these shows. It is not a term imposed by later historians and
critics. The word "integration" does not, however, appear regularly in print until the
arrival of *Oklahoma!*, after which it becomes ubiquitous.

First night *New York Times* reviewer Lewis Nichols, for example, wrote that
"Mr. Rodgers's scores never lack grace, but seldom have they been so well integrated
for *Oklahoma!*"[17] In a slightly later discussion of de Mille's choreography, John
Martin described why he regarded the act I dream ballet so highly:

> "Laurey Makes Up Her Mind" is a first-rate work of art on several counts. For one
> thing, it is so integrated with the production as a whole that it actually carries
> forward the plot and justifies the most tenuous psychological point in the play,
> namely, why Laurey, who is obviously in love with Curly, finds herself unable to
> resist going to the dance with the repugnant Jud.[18]

A couple of pages after Rodgers summarized "what made *Oklahoma!* work" (see above), he acknowledged that "*Oklahoma!* did, of course, have an effect on the musicals that came after it" and that "everyone suddenly became 'integration'-conscious, as if the idea of welding together song, story and dance had never been thought of before." In refreshing contrast to most musical theater historians (until relatively recently), Rodgers offered a less grandiose claim for the epoch-making nature of *Oklahoma!*, although he did see the work as innovative and helpful to writers and composers looking for "a new incentive to explore a multitude of themes and techniques within the framework of the commercial theater" (Rodgers 1975, 229).

As *Oklahoma!*'s innovations merged into the mainstream of Broadway history, it has become increasingly common either to place the word "integrated" in quotes or to preface integrated with the qualifier "so-called." In fact, straightforward use of the word "integrated" is probably the exception in recent scholarship. In *The Musical as Drama* (2006), Scott McMillin interprets the traditional book musical as inherently *non*-integrated because of the sharply defined and incompatible divisions between the normative book time (dialogue) and the interruptions from number time (song). McMillin sees the book and the score in *Oklahoma!* and musicals of the next twenty or thirty years as separate and oppositional. As a prime example he offers "People Will Say We're in Love" to illustrate a nonintegrated song interruption of book time. McMillin observes that some of the lyrics in this song do not truly fit the characters who sing them (e.g., Laurey's lyrical reference to her parents when in fact her parents are deceased), but he welcomes the opportunity to hear from Curly and Laurey at this late stage in act I even if the song does not advance the action.

The work of Stephen Sondheim demonstrates that it is possible to write "integrated" musical scores without paying allegiance to a Wagnerian ideal characterized by continuous orchestral underscoring beneath a through-sung melodic language that is neither recitative (sung speech) nor aria. For the most part, Sondheim maintains the formal distinctions common to the German singspiel, European and American operetta, and American musical comedies, with clear distinctions between dialogue and song. Unlike some works by Andrew Lloyd Webber, in Sondheim we usually have no trouble discerning the difference between musical speech and song. Even in a musical that exhibits the through-sung qualities of opera, such as *Sweeney Todd*, Sondheim offers considerable spoken dialogue, most noticeably at the climactic close of the work.[19] In Sondheim's *Sunday in the Park with George* (book and direction by James Lapine), the completion of Georges Seurat's painting at the end of act I also completes the musical ideas foreshadowed the moment he first faced his blank canvas. In *Into the Woods* (also with Lapine), the songs, like the intricate plot, derive from Jack's five-note "bean" theme, offer intricate motivic networks that are dramatically meaningful, and demonstrate the kind of organic unity that would be the envy of a Brahms symphony or Wagner opera.

Before the 1970s, the integrated musical maintained the separate but equal conventions of book and number time. Sondheim, arguably Broadway's leading lyricist-composer of his generation, favored this separation over the less differentiated merging of the two dimensions found in later Verdi and Wagner and in many post-1970 Broadway musicals. Although Sondheim embraced organicism in some of his shows, he also has demonstrated a consistent antipathy toward opera:

> I don't like opera, but I have a feeling that I wish I did. Because, I'll tell you something, it's much more satisfying and easier to write something like *Passion* than it is to write something like *Merrily We Roll Along*. To write a thirty-two-bar song that has freshness and style to it and tells the story is really hard. And nobody does it anymore. Everybody writes so-called "sung-through" pieces, and it's because anybody can write sung-through pieces. It's all recitative, and they don't develop anything, and it just repeats and repeats. And that's what most shows are. (Horowitz, 19–20)

CONCEPT

In the first "integrated" generation, despite the strong presence of choreographers (de Mille and Robbins) and directors (Rouben Mamoulian, Joshua Logan, George Abbott, George S. Kaufman, Moss Hart, and Robbins), composers and lyricists played a larger role than they would in a future era dominated by directors, choreographers, director-choreographers, and producers.[20] The controlling hand in the creation of *Oklahoma!* remained Rodgers and Hammerstein, not Mamoulian, despite the latter's distinctive and influential directorial stamp. In *Fiddler on the Roof* the primal roles of the librettist, lyricist, and composer were partly usurped by director-choreographer Robbins, to a far more visible extent than in *West Side Story,* where Robbins collaborated and grappled with two strong creative personalities, Arthur Laurents and Leonard Bernstein. In both *West Side Story* and *Fiddler,* Robbins's insistent question, "What is the show *about*?" led to major changes—for example, the replacement of a traditional opening number in *West Side Story* with an extended Prologue told entirely through dance. But *Fiddler* was more a Robbins show than its predecessor. After *Fiddler,* stagers had largely replaced librettists, lyricists, and composers as the dominant Broadway force.

West Side Story may have had dramatic meanings conveyed through song as well as dance, but *Fiddler on the Roof* also had a "concept," a central idea that governed the integration of the other dramatic elements (words, music, dance, and set design). To announce its presence, Robbins created an opening number in which the "concept," the breakdown of tradition, was made unequivocally clear and incarnate. Thereafter, the concept of tradition and its demise would occasionally reemerge during the course of the integrated book and number format, familiar from Rodgers and Hammerstein and Lerner and Loewe.

In the 1960s the idea of the "concept" musical thus began to replace "integration" as the critical encomium of choice, perhaps reflecting a broader social movement toward a modernist aesthetic that favored vision and subject matter to elaborate settings and narrative. As many musical theater historians have noted, the "concept" musical did not, however, first appear ex nihilo (or fully formed) in *Fiddler on the Roof* any more than the integrated musical made its debut with *Oklahoma!* Although with relatively short runs and seldom revived, Rodgers and Hammerstein's *Allegro* (1947) and Weill and Lerner's *Love Life* (1948) are well-known precedents, two earlier musicals organized around a central idea or concept. But the origins of the "concept" musical can also be traced back to loosely plotted revues organized around an idea such as newspaper headlines (*As Thousands Cheer*, 1933) or travel (*At Home Abroad*, 1935).

Two years after *Fiddler*, Hal Prince extended the "concept" musical to encompass elements of nonlinearity and extra-spatial dimensions in the "limbo" sections between reality and imagination in *Cabaret*. Since about half of *Cabaret* takes place outside of the Kit Kat Klub, however, the show as originally staged preserves the traditional book and number format. The metaphorical concept component—the cabaret as a metaphor for the moral decline of Germany that led to the rise of Hitler's Third Reich—shared its conceptual space with the book and number time of non-cabaret scenes.

The 1972 film version of *Cabaret*, which earned Bob Fosse an Academy Award for direction, marked the end of an era that generally featured more faithful adaptations, an era significantly framed, as with the staged Golden Age musical, by the films of *Oklahoma!* (1955) and *Fiddler on the Roof* (1971). For the most part, film adaptations before *Oklahoma!*—which despite its general fidelity and completeness omitted a powerful and dramatic song from the stage version, Jud Fry's "Lonely Room"—typically rewrote the original book and treated the score, however integrated, as a dispensable item subject to significant cutting. To take one example out of many, the 1939 film adaptation of Rodgers and Hart's *Babes in Arms,* a show packed with hit songs in its Broadway staging, retained a total of two.

In contrast to the stage original, which included both book numbers and diegetic numbers, Fosse's filmed *Cabaret* takes a more realistic approach and reserves nearly all the musical numbers for the Kit Kat Klub (the exception is a public group sing-along of "Tomorrow Belongs to Me" at an outdoor *Biergarten*). In general terms, film adaptations of Broadway musicals before 1955 for the most part increased realism without seeking to increase the integration of book and score. While film realism often produces imaginative, and sometimes surreal, results (e.g., the vaudeville routines growing out of Roxie's mind in the 2002 film adaptation of *Chicago*), the predilection for diegetic contexts generally leads to less rather than more integration of the musical's key component parts. On the other hand, the majority of film musical adaptations in recent years (*Dreamgirls, Hairspray, Mamma Mia!, The Phantom of the Opera, The Producers, Rent, Sweeney Todd*) have demonstrated a healthy tolerance for nonrealistic, even surrealistic, contexts for song and dance.

Four years after the staged *Cabaret*, Prince, along with Sondheim and choreographer Michael Bennett, recentered the role of the concept in the concept musical with *Company* (1970) by including a less straightforward narrative line. Based on a series of eleven one-act plays by George Furth, the musical's amorphous plot leaves audiences unable to detect whether the birthday gathering we see at the end of the show is the same as the one that opens the show. In his autobiography, Prince summarizes some of what made *Company* different from his earlier work:

> *Company* was the first musical I had done without conventional plot or subplot structure. The first without the hero and heroine, without the comic relief couple. There are, of course, plots, but they are sub textual and grow out of subconscious behavior, psychological stresses, inadvertent revelations: the nature of the lie people accept to preserve their relationship.[21]

The characters in *Company* invade the space and the number time of other characters and, in seeming contrast to the "integrated" covenant between words and music, many of the songs comment on the action or emotional developments rather than grow directly from the dialogue (some of the Kit Kat Klub songs in *Cabaret* had also served as commentary). Concept in this sense opposes integration; since the plot is fundamentally nonlinear, the songs cannot directly advance the plot. That said, in common with the integrated musical, all the elements (words, music, movement, and design) are interconnected and coalesce into a unified whole. Furthermore, by the end of the show Robert has grown as a character and has moved to a new *psychological* place in which he, like Laurey, makes up his mind and embraces the meaning and responsibility of marriage ("Being Alive").

INTEGRATION REVISITED

James T. Patterson concludes, in his survey of race in America from the years after World War II until the mid-1970s, that for those opposed to segregation, *Brown v. Board of Education* "conveyed profound moral legitimacy to the struggle for racial justice, not only in the schools but also in other walks of life" (Patterson, 390). But not everyone in America at the time thought that school integration was in the best interests of all concerned. The politically conservative black writer Zora Neale Hurston questioned the wisdom of black children being forced to attend schools where they would be unwelcome, even endangered. Other critics objected to the presumption that black children in segregated schools would receive social damage and feel inferior in a black school of exceptional quality. The main criticism of *Brown*, which continues to the present, however, was its slow and dilatory implementation.

Naturally, parallels between the story of racial integration and the development and reception of the integrated musical can go only so far, and they occupy vastly different realms of sensibility. The differences and stakes were and remain separate and not at all equal. Nevertheless, some of the parallels are instructive. For example, although the integrated musical became the unwritten law of Broadway starting in the 1940s, the years after *Oklahoma!* witnessed successful if less spectacular runs of more "segregated" shows, such as *Mexican Hayride* and *Follow the Girls* (both in

1944). Despite its great score and canonic status, the integration of the subplot in *Annie Get Your Gun* (1946) was so tenuous that its songs and the characters who sang them frequently vanished from revivals.

Furthermore, the integrated musical was not without its detractors—for example, the distinguished critics Eric Bentley and George Jean Nathan, neither of whom welcomed the integrated musical with its artistic complexities, seriousness of purpose, ambition, and dramatically meaningful themes. For Bentley, writing in 1954, "the best musicals at present are not those with the biggest intentions behind them but those with the simple virtues in them of singable tunes and sheer showmanship."[22] When comparing the current revival of *On Your Toes* with recent fare, Bentley preferred the old-fashioned show with its "breath of a less stuffy generation," and he agreed with James Thurber "that something was lost during the forties and early fifties" when the "cocky, satirical, devil-may-care philosophy" abundant in Rodgers and Hart's 1930s hit gave way to loftier approaches (Bentley, 192). Nathan, an early champion of the serious dramas of Eugene O'Neill and Sean O'Casey, felt that the Broadway musical merited its separate and unequal status. He defended Hammerstein's sentimentality (a critical judgment that became hard to shake after *The Sound of Music*) and Rodgers's relentless tunefulness, and appreciated their musicals not for their modernity or integration but because they knew their place in the theatrical hierarchy in which the "lighter stage occupies the same position in music that the cocktail does at the dinner table" (to whet "the appetite for the better things to come").[23]

Although it was possible after *Oklahoma!* for the integrated musical to merge with musical comedy (e.g., *Guys and Dolls* and *Gypsy*), the integrated musicals of Kern, Rodgers and Hammerstein, and Bernstein (*Candide* and *West Side Story*, if not *On the Town* or *Wonderful Town*), among others, favored more serious subjects and came to exhibit some of the musical complexities more frequently found in opera. Both Bentley and Nathan resented these attempts "to make the-musical-that-is-more-than-a-musical." Starting in the 1970s with the musicals of Prince and Sondheim and in the late 1970s and 1980s with the musicals of Lloyd Webber, Alain Boublil, and Claude-Michel Schönberg, many high-profile musicals continued to address serious dramatic subjects and to favor operetta or even opera over musical comedy. With the arrival of musicals such as *Les Misérables, The Phantom of the Opera, Miss Saigon,* and *Sunset Boulevard* in the 1980s and 1990s, musicals not only got more serious but also grew in size—hence the soubriquet, the "megamusical," or in Mark Grant's dismissive parallel with the McDonald's Big Mac hamburger, the "The Age of McMusicals" (Grant, 304–15).

Ironically, integration, when it came to musicals, could prove for some critics to be too much of a good thing. Scott McMillin has tried to replace the term "integration" with "coherence," believing it to be a more accurate term regarding musicals in the 1940s. As he, like Grant and other critics and historians, dismisses the so-called megamusical of the 1980s for its pretentions and over-reliance on technology "in order to preserve the illusion of a seamless whole," McMillin acknowledges that while Rodgers and Hammerstein fell short of integration, they had "mastered the principles of difference that formed the earlier musicals."[24] Although *Phantom* may have departed from these principles of difference to create a show he regarded as "pretentious and overblown," McMillin nonetheless is prepared to "see the logic of claiming that the drive for integration has finally been achieved in Lloyd Webber" (McMillin, 165). The problem remains, for many, that integration has evolved from an ideal to become a false god and a source of criticism and ridicule. Specifically, the increasingly through-sung integrated musical, with its abandonment of the separation between book and number, has in recent decades become thoroughly entwined with the mostly negative critical status of Lloyd Webber, an association that has diminished the positive view of critics, if not audiences, toward the integrated ideal. With the musical, the problem is not integration per se but that a musical too saturated with integration is more prone to a sameness that can result in dramatic meaninglessness (Block 2009, 394–95, 402–7). But this is not always the case. In the musicals of Sondheim the musically integrated score is invariably dramatically meaningful. And, as Wagner has demonstrated, it is possible for integration and the dramatically meaningful to coexist in through-sung opera, as well.

Phantom and *Les Misérables* constitute excellent examples of how the development of the integrated musical thwarted at least two of the five Principles of Integration presented near the outset of this chapter: "*The songs express the characters who sing them*" and "*The orchestra, through accompaniment and underscoring, parallels, complements, or advances the action.*" Both of these shows, extensively through-sung, use a relatively small repertoire of musical themes and motives and recycle these melodies continuously throughout the work, usually with new lyrics. The technique ensures unity and musical integration and provides opportunities to create new dramatic meanings for musical ideas. However—and this happens often, especially in the latter show—when characters (and their underscoring) in these musicals use each other's music without regard to the appropriateness of the appropriation, the increased integration is matched by decreased dramatic meaning.

Classic American musicals of the Golden Age between *Oklahoma!* and *Fiddler on the Roof* are not immune from the "devil-may-care philosophy" of a 1930s show such as *Anything Goes* or *On Your Toes*, the latter explicitly and the former implicitly favored by Bentley. A good example is the canonic classic *Kiss Me, Kate* (1948), lyrics and music by Porter and book by Sam and Bella Spewack. Despite its greater integration compared with *Anything Goes*, *Kate* ignores dramatic logic (in Fred's act II reprise of "So in Love," sung alone by Lilli in act I),[25] loses an opportunity for nuance when Porter presents his characteristic alternation between major and minor in both the *Shrew* numbers and the Baltimore numbers rather than confining this identifier to one group or another to distinguish the two (Block 1997, 184–85; 2nd ed. 221), and offers the show-stopping "Too Darn Hot" without even a fig leaf of an "integrated" rationale.

In his chapter on *Les Misérables*, Joseph P. Swain offers numerous telling examples of infelicities that plague the over-integrated musical, which collectively exceed the relatively unnoticeable violations of the Principles of Integration found in *Kiss Me, Kate*:

While it may be reasonable for Jean Valjean to recall Fantine's death song ("Come to Me") at his own demise, there is no reason for Eponine to convert it to a torch song ("On My Own"). Similarly, to sing again the evocative, half-mournful, half-hopeful melody by which Bishop Myriel charges Jean Valjean to change his life as a sentimental reminiscence of the dead students in "Empty Chairs" is a waste of a precious resource, musical semantics.[26]

The ideal of integration in the Broadway musical, which includes the European imports of the 1980s and 1990s, led to the super-integrated musical that has generated a split between critical and popular acclaim. In both the social and artistic versions of integration, ideals have led to disillusionment and cast doubt on the viability of the concept. Yet, despite disappointment in how the histories of racial integration and Broadway integration played out, both areas of American life can still point to demonstrable gains. At long last, America has elected a black president. And, whatever combination of good or ill may be ascribed to the integrated ideal on Broadway, the American musical, with some notable contributions from across the pond, has maintained its status into the present as one of the most vigorous, entertaining, popular, and challenging art forms.

NOTES

1. James T. Patterson, *Grand Expectations: The United States, 1945–1974* (New York: Oxford University Press, 1996), pp. 375–406.

2. Oscar Hammerstein II, "In Re 'Oklahoma!': The Adaptor-Lyricist Describes How the Musical Hit Came Into Being" (*New York Times* [May 23, 1943]: 11).

3. Oscar Hammerstein II, "Notes on Lyrics," in *Lyrics* (Milwaukee: Hal Leonard Books, 1985, 3–48), p. 15.

4. Richard Rodgers, *Musical Stages: An Autobiography* (New York: Random House, 1975; repr. New York: Da Capo, 1995, 2000), p. 227.

5. Geoffrey Block, "The Broadway Canon from *Show Boat* to *West Side Story* and the European Operatic Ideal" (*Journal of Musicology* 11.4 [Fall 1993]: 525–44), pp. 525–26.

6. Ethan Mordden, *Beautiful Mornin': The Broadway Musical in the 1940s* (New York: Oxford University Press, 1999), p. 75.

7. Richard Rodgers, "How to Write Music in No Easy Lessons: A Self Interview" (*Theatre Arts* [October 1939]: 741–46, p. 743; reprinted in *The Richard Rodgers Reader*, ed. Geoffrey Block [New York: Oxford University Press, 2002], 261–65).

8. Robert Simon, "Jerome Kern" (*Modern Music* 6.2 [January–February 1929]: 20–25), p. 24.

9. Louis R. Reid, "Composing While You Wait" (*The Dramatic Mirror* [June 2, 1917]: 5).

10. Hugh Fordin, *Getting to Know Him* (New York: Ungar Publishing, 1977), pp. 55–56 [italics mine].

11. Raymond Knapp, *The American Musical and the Formation of National Identity* (Princeton. NJ: Princeton University Press, 2005), p. 89.

12. Alisa Roost, "Before *Oklahoma!*: A Reappraisal of Musical Theatre during the 1930s" (*Journal of American Drama and Theatre* 16.1 [Winter 2004]: 1–35), p. 15.

13. John Martin, "The Dance: New Musical Comedy Talent" (*New York Times* [July 22, 1928]: Section 7, 6).

14. John Mueller, "Fred Astaire and the Integrated Musical" (*Cinema Journal* 24.1 [Fall 1984]: 28–40), p. 31.

15. Max Gordon, with Lewis Funke, *Max Gordon Presents* (New York: Random House, 1963), p. 147; quoted in Stephen Banfield, *Jerome Kern*. New Haven. CT: Yale University Press, 2006), p. 179.

16. Banfield, 179. The definition of "diegetic" is quoted from Steve Blandford, Barry Keith Grant, and Jim Hillier, *The Film Studies Dictionary* (London: Arnold, 2001), p. 67.

17. Lewis Nichols, "'Oklahoma!' a Musical Hailed as Delightful, Based on 'Green Grow the Lilacs,' Opens Here at the St. James Theatre" (*New York Times* [April 1, 1943]: 27). See also Tim Carter, *Oklahoma!: The Making of an American Musical* (New Haven, CT: Yale University Press, 2007), pp. 173–74.

18. John Martin, "The Dance: De Mille's Oklahoma" (*New York Times* [May 9, 1943]: Section 10, p. 6).

19. Banfield, 291–92; Mark Eden Horowitz, *Sondheim on Music: Minor Details and Major Decisions* (Lanham, MD: Scarecrow Press, 2003), pp. 125–26.

20. Mark N. Grant, *The Rise and Fall of the Broadway Musical* (Boston: Northeastern University Press, 2004), pp. 277–303.

21. Hal Prince, *Contradictions: Notes on Twenty-Six Years in the Theatre* (New York: Dodd, Mead, 1974), p. 149.

22. Eric Bentley, "The American Musical," in *What Is Theatre?* (New York: Athenaeum, 1968, 190–93), p. 191.

23. George Jean Nathan, *The Theatre in the Fifties* (New York: Alfred A. Knopf, 1953), p. 234.

24. Scott McMillin, *The Musical as Drama: A Study of the Principles and Conventions behind Musical Shows from Kern to Sondheim* (Princeton, NJ: Princeton University Press, 2006), pp. 170 and 165.

25. Geoffrey Block, *Enchanted Evenings: The Broadway Musical from "Show Boat" to Sondheim and Lloyd Webber* (New York: Oxford University Press, 1997; 2nd ed., 2009), pp. 227–29.

26. Joseph P. Swain, *The Broadway Musical: A Critical and Musical Survey* (Oxford: Oxford University Press, 1990; 2nd ed., Lanham, MD: Scarecrow Press, 2002), p. 404.

CHAPTER 8

AFTER THE "GOLDEN AGE"

JESSICA STERNFELD
ELIZABETH L. WOLLMAN

THE term "Golden Age" is riddled with unfair assumptions. It implies a consensus about when the American musical theater reached its aesthetic and cultural pinnacle, as well as when it began its alleged decline. In fact, the term is used loosely: depending on which history one reads, the Golden Age began anywhere between (or even before) Kern and Hammerstein's *Show Boat* (1927) and Rodgers and Hammerstein's *Oklahoma!* (1943). Similarly, the end of the Golden Age is placed anywhere between the mid-1950s and late 1970s.[1] There are, further, historians for whom the term has an entirely different emphasis: Allen Woll, for example, describes the 1920s as the "Golden Age" of black musicals.[2] The term is thus subjective and potentially applicable to a vast array of musical subgenres.

The phrase "After the Golden Age" is inherently negative: it implies that any musical to have opened in recent decades is by nature of its chronology somehow less artistically important or culturally resonant than those that opened in the past. Such judgments often extend to audiences, whose collective taste is seen to have declined precipitously since 1960.[3] Despite a growing number of writings that demonstrate the cultural importance of various contemporary musicals, examine how musicals have developed in style and sophistication, and explore ways that musicals have been adapted to reach larger, newly international audiences, even some recent histories exhibit hostility toward any post-1960 musical not written by Stephen Sondheim.[4] His work—often described as dissonant, intellectual, challenging—is frequently contrasted with the blockbuster hits that came to be known as megamusicals. Epic in scope and staging, often featuring sung-through scores that draw on operatic and pop influences, and enormously popular with audiences, megamusicals such as *Les Misérables* (1987) and *The Phantom of the Opera* (1988) have had an enormous influence on the economy, audience, and reception of recent musicals in general.

While the term "Golden Age," for all its implications, is not ideal, its continued application is understandable. The American musical has undergone a number of monumental changes in recent decades, as a result of economic, technological, social, and aesthetic developments, all of which have affected the demands of a changing audience. Despite frequent insistence to the contrary, the American musical is not dead. But it is certainly different from what it was a half-century ago. Scholars who consider the contemporary musical must consider as well the many ways it has evolved. In the following pages, we discuss some of the more important developments that have affected the stage musical in the past half-century.

THE ECONOMICS OF PRODUCTION

Broadway has always been about making money: since musicals existed, there have been producers hoping to profit from them. In the early twentieth century, Broadway musicals were relatively inexpensive to mount, and most did not need to run for long to recoup investments. During the 1920s—Broadway's busiest decade—it was common for fifty or more musicals to open each season; even mildly successful ones spawned national tours.

The Great Depression and the advent of film both changed Broadway's economic landscape dramatically. Musical output after 1929 fell precipitously. The 1929–30 Broadway season offered only thirty-two new musicals; there would be only thirteen in the 1933–34 season (Bordman, 502, 534). In terms of quantity, Broadway would never bounce back: offerings would rise just slightly through the twentieth century, with only two seasons capping at twenty musicals.[5]

The amount of money needed to produce a musical has risen since the onset of the Depression, but especially since the 1960s. The cost of production, coupled with the introduction of several cheaper, more widely accessible entertainment forms, has forced the musical to struggle financially and aesthetically at various periods during the postwar era. Historians who argue that the so-called Golden Age ended in the late 1960s or early 1970s are likely associating the alleged stylistic decline of the musical with its economic struggles during this era.

The 1970s were problematic not only for the theater industry but also for New York City in general. Excessive spending by the city government through the 1950s and 1960s, combined with a declining stock market and period of stagflation in the early 1970s, caused New York to teeter toward bankruptcy by mid-decade. The economic slump exacerbated a slew of social ills that had plagued New York since the

1960s. Homelessness, drug abuse, and a sharp increase in crime had a profoundly negative impact on the city's image, and thus on tourism.

Socioeconomic woes were especially palpable in Times Square, which became a symbol of urban decay. The neighborhood's many "grinder" houses, porn shops, peepshows, and massage parlors—and the related rise of petty crime—alienated theatergoers, especially after the city fired 20,000 civil servants in 1975. Weak theater attendance, combined with skyrocketing inflation, forced producers to slash budgets while simultaneously boosting ticket prices. Through the early twentieth century, tickets for most Broadway shows were relatively inexpensive: orchestra tickets cost $1.50 to $2.00 until World War I. But between 1965 and 1969 alone, tickets rose from $6.00 to over $10.00; in 1990, they were $55.00 (Bordman, 723). By the end of the twentieth century, top seats for most productions cost over $100.00, with seats at some of the hottest shows above $500.00.

Inflation has affected the criteria for hit status: shows must now run for longer stretches to be profitable. Thus, while Broadway musicals that ran for more than a few years were comparatively rare in the 1940s, it is now common for musicals to run several years before recouping; conversely, shows running a year or more are often "flops" financially.

As the first resident of the Ford Center for the Performing Arts, for example, the 1998 musical *Ragtime* (music by Stephen Flaherty; book by Terrence McNally; lyrics by Lynn Ahrens) was expected not only to fill the huge stage but also to fill the 1,830-seat auditorium. Marketing for the show was particularly intense, and the spectacle aspect was strongly promoted by producer Garth Drabinsky, under the auspices of his Canadian production company, Livent. Despite relentless publicity and generally positive reviews, the enormously expensive show ran only two years. Although it now boasts a successful life as a regional and international property, *Ragtime* failed to recoup its investment on Broadway, thereby closing as a "flop" in 2000.

The longer average run of Broadway musicals depends in part on an increasingly international audience, which is seen as transitory and ever-renewing. In the prewar era, Broadway served a comparatively local audience; once locals stopped coming, a musical would embark on tour. Yet modern musicals court larger, international audiences by relying on new approaches to spectacle, sophisticated marketing, and more dependence on mass media.

This is especially true since Times Square was renovated in the 1990s. The overhaul of the famously seedy neighborhood began when the city struck a deal with Disney to restore the dilapidated New Amsterdam Theater in exchange for an exclusive lease on the building. This deal attracted other entertainment conglomerates, which have since joined Disney as theater producers.

The presence of such conglomerates has, on one hand, helped work the American musical back into the web of popular culture from which it was arguably severed in the mid-1950s and, on the other, affected the content of many musicals, a greater number of which rely on familiarity to attract audiences. Thus, there are more revivals on Broadway in recent years, as well as an increase in musicals based on movies; examples include *Footloose* (1998), *Saturday Night Fever* (1999), *The Full Monty* (2000), *Hairspray* (2002), *Legally Blonde* (2007), *Xanadu* (2007), *Billy Elliot* (2008), and *Shrek* (2008).Critics argue that the "corporatization" of musical theater has led to a decline in nuance and a shift toward crass commercialism—as if making money was not an objective on Broadway before 1990. Yet the American musical continues to enjoy enormous populist appeal in its increasingly varied forms. Despite charges that the American musical would fall prey to "corporatization," musicals huge and intimate, innovative and pedestrian, spectacular and simple, on Broadway and on film, in New York and across the country, continue to be developed, performed, and patronized.

SPECTACLE

Aural Spectacle

The term "spectacle" tends to connote the visual, and traditionally relates in some way to human bodies: enormous casts; throngs of leggy chorines in revealing costumes; arrangements of dancers into geometric shapes. Depending on the era and prevailing styles, the visual can range from subtle to spectacular, integrated to irrelevant.

For all its innovation, the 1968 Broadway production of *Hair* (music by Galt MacDermot; book and lyrics by Gerome Ragni and James Rado) was something of a throwback in its approach to visual spectacle. During the act I finale, cast members reenacted a human be-in by dancing naked beneath a huge, flowered sheet. Because the use of full-frontal nudity was a first for Broadway musicals, the scene generated enormous publicity and has since been cited as novel by many critics and historians. But nudity notwithstanding, there was nothing especially groundbreaking about the use of human bodies as a source for visual spectacle.

One innovation with which *Hair* was strongly associated, however—and not always positively—was in its contribution to *aural* spectacle, both in MacDermot's use of rock in the score and in the use of amplification. As purveyors and perpetuators of popular culture, theater composers have always incorporated contemporary sounds into their scores. While *Hair*'s catchy rock score helped earn the production particular acclaim, the musical's reliance on microphones was hardly as celebrated (◉ Example 8.1).

Amplification has become increasingly common since the advent of rock for several reasons. First, many actors need microphones to protect their voices and to be heard above the electric instruments that accompany them. Second, film and sound recording technologies have exerted significant influence on the stage musical.[6] Third, advances in sound design have allowed theatrical productions to offer cleaner, more balanced sound from the orchestra pit and stage.

Jesus Christ Superstar inadvertently marked an important juncture in this development. When Lloyd Webber and Rice could not get backing for a stage production, they instead recorded an album version, which went gold upon release in 1970. When Tom O'Horgan's stage version opened on Broadway in 1971, *Superstar* was forced to compete with its own aural predecessor. Despite several frustrating attempts to design a cutting-edge sound system in the Mark Hellinger Theater, O'Horgan and his team could not match the highly polished sound of the extraordinarily successful studio recording. This hurt the production, which—for all its amplification and lavish visual spectacle—struck many spectators as underwhelming when compared with the album (⬥ Example 8.2; ⬥ Example 8.3).

Though a relatively young field, sound design has become increasingly important since the advent of wireless microphones, computerized mixing boards, and digital sound. Whereas "sound design" was once roughly equivalent to placing microphones around the stage and orchestra pit, sound designers now oversee all sounds—both musical and otherwise—used in a specific production; some even compose and perform the sounds they design. Contemporary stage musicals thus can and often do emulate sound that was once possible only on film.

One recent trend in aural spectacle, however, suggests a retreat from "cinematized" sound. Director John Doyle's revivals of Sondheim's *Sweeney Todd* (2005) and *Company* (2006) departed radically from the original productions. In both revivals, actors all played instruments, and thus the cast provided its own accompaniment. Such productions not only create visual spectacle from what is traditionally perceived aurally but also help remind audiences of the propulsive centrality of a musical's score (⬥ Example 8.4).

Visual Spectacle

During the 1970s, visual spectacle took a turn toward the mechanical and electronic, and sets became increasingly elaborate as technology improved. Concerned that elaborate sets were drawing attention from the performers, many critics argued that theater was becoming too cinematic. Yet in spite of jokes about leaving the theater humming the scenery, some of the new sets served their shows beautifully: *Les Misérables*, with its furniture-turned-barricade, rests its complicated story on a set that, while large, is simple and fundamental to the telling of the saga (⊙ Example 8.5). *The Lion King* also effectively uses sets and costumes to convey its moods; one might even argue that spectacle lends gravity to this musical's thin plot (⊙ Example 8.6).

There are certainly productions that have gone awry despite—or because of—their cinema-sized sets. For example, Lloyd Webber's import *Starlight Express* (1987)—in which trains were embodied by roller-skating actors who zipped around a multitiered hydraulic set that extended above the stage and into the auditorium—failed to charm American audiences (🔘 Example 8.7). Similarly, a painstaking rendition of Bay Ridge—complete with miniature subways traversing a network of bridges—could not save the otherwise uninspired 1999 musical version of *Saturday Night Fever*. The set of the Benny Andersson-Björn Ulvaeus-Tim Rice flop *Chess* (1988) is often said to have been so unsightly that it actually deterred audiences.

With *Ragtime*, designer Eugene Lee needed to satisfy a number of challenges: his set had to support the sweeping narrative and simultaneously evoke the simple domesticity of the central characters. The plot of *Ragtime*—based on E. L. Doctorow's 1975 novel—revolves around three families: an upper-middle-class white family in New Rochelle (Mother, Father, and Mother's Little Boy); the Jewish immigrants Tateh and Tateh's Little Girl, who end up on New York's Lower East Side; and the African American family Coalhouse Walker Jr. (a ragtime pianist), Sarah, and their baby. The families and cultures in *Ragtime* clash, often violently, but eventually blend to a degree.

Ragtime has epic breadth, in megamusical fashion, but it also closes in on characters during quiet, reflective moments. The Broadway production balanced large and small, detailed and simple. When Mother gardened, the stage was bare but for a dollhouse-like cut-out of a Victorian home upstage and a row of flowers downstage. Because silhouettes were a recurring theme in the novel, they were integrated into the show's lyrics and staging: Coalhouse's beloved Model-T Ford is destroyed by racist firemen in silhouette against an orange background (🔘 Example 8.8). Other sets were more literal: the nightclub of vaudevillian Evelyn Nesbit (one of several historic figures woven into the story); the Atlantic City boardwalk. Yet during Mother's eleven o'clock number, "Back to Before," the boardwalk melted away, leaving her alone on the stage, thereby allowing the audience to focus entirely on her.

The most effective application of hugeness in *Ragtime* happens when Tateh and his daughter arrive at Ellis Island ("A Shtetl Iz Amereke"; 🔘 Example 8.9). Ellis Island is depicted as an enormous gate holding back groups of immigrants, who wave their papers and attempt to surge forward. The gate lifts as they sing, but they move only a few feet before another gate bars their way. This happens several times as they press forward, until the last gate lifts and the immigrants spill across the apron, which has become the Lower East Side. Here, spectacle adds tension and symbolism. *Ragtime's* design was never invasive or distracting. It was, instead, fluid. The set never inspired its own applause but rather helped convey the mood of each scene.

No amount of sparkle or flash has ever been able to sustain a show that fails to engage an audience emotionally, just as ugly productions tend not to command attention as effectively as those with attractive, appropriate sets. This remains the case regardless of what kind of spectacle is in fashion at any given time. As musicals like *Starlight Express* and *Saturday Night Fever* demonstrate, overreliance on spectacle is foolish. Nevertheless, the tendency to disparage musicals that incorporate technological innovations simply because they can is unfair. Musical theater has always aimed to entertain audiences aurally *and* visually. As technology continues to change, so will the approach to spectacle.

CHANGING RELATIONSHIPS IN NEW YORK CITY
AND BEYOND

The Times Square neighborhood has been home to the greatest concentration of commercial theaters in the country since the turn of the twentieth century. Because the American musical was developed and nurtured on Times Square's many stages, the terms "American musical" and "Broadway musical" are often used interchangeably, even though the musical has become increasingly uprooted from its Broadway pedigree.

Steven Adler writes that Broadway is no longer "an isolated enclave of theatrical activity whose only connection to the rest of the nation [was] as a purveyor of goods. It is now inextricably linked to the network of American theatrical production that barely resembles its earlier incarnation of a few decades past."[7] Indeed, any study that focuses on the American musical as it has developed in the later twentieth century must consider the contributions not only of Off and Off-Off Broadway and the country's many regional theaters, but also a growing number of international concerns.

During the 1960s and 1970s, Off and Off-Off Broadway exerted profound influence on Broadway as an institution. This period was economically and aesthetically difficult for Broadway, but it galvanized the Off Broadway theater scene, which had grown from the Little Theater Movement during the 1950s, and especially the experimental Off-Off Broadway scene, which developed through the 1960s. The Off and Off-Off Broadway realms are responsible for a number of musicals to land on Broadway in recent decades and for several innovative rehearsal and performance techniques.

Hair, for example, had a life in all three theatrical realms, but even in its most famous incarnation on Broadway, it remained very much an Off-Off Broadway baby. *Hair* was written by Gerome Ragni and James Rado, two actors who were affiliated with Joseph Chaikin's experimental Open Theater. While they were performing in Megan Terry's collaborative anti-war piece *Viet Rock* (1966), Ragni and Rado began to document hippies in Greenwich Village. Their notes became a script about the counterculture, which they shopped around town. Producer Joseph Papp chose *Hair* to be the inaugural production of Off Broadway's Public Theater on the condition that Ragni and Rado find a composer to tame their lyrics. Galt MacDermot was hired for the job, and *Hair* opened at the Public for a limited run in 1967. Producer Michael Butler secured rights after the Off Broadway run and set about moving *Hair* to Broadway.

Under the direction of Off-Off Broadway director Tom O'Horgan, the enormously successful Broadway incarnation opened at the Biltmore Theater in 1968. *Hair* was lauded for its contemporary score and gentle depiction of a much-maligned subculture, as well as for its many innovations. In both rehearsal and performance, O'Horgan applied a number of techniques that were common Off-Off

Broadway but still novel on Broadway in the late 1960s. These included nontradi-
tional casting; the use of trust and consciousness-raising exercises and collective
collaboration in rehearsals; and improvisation, breaks to the fourth wall, performer-
audience interaction, and stage nudity in performance.

As a musical that was not cultivated on Broadway, *Hair* is hardly unique.
Countless others—including blockbusters like *A Chorus Line, Rent,* and *Spring
Awakening*—originated Off Broadway. In recent years, regional theaters as well have
nurtured early versions of productions that eventually reach Broadway.

In the 1980s, during the so-called British Invasion, Broadway became an international business concern as a result of a growing number of "highly capitalised,
globally competent and now often transnational players," including British pioneers
like composer Andrew Lloyd Webber and producer Cameron Mackintosh (Burston,
206). In 1982, Lloyd Webber imported his musical *Cats*—already a hit in London's
West End—to Broadway; the American production also proved enormously successful. Lloyd Webber's earlier Broadway productions—*Jesus Christ Superstar* (1971)
and *Evita* (1979), both with lyricist Tim Rice—had garnered plenty of attention, but
Cats was a cultural phenomenon that made Lloyd Webber a household name.

Thanks in part to intense publicity, *Cats* became an entity known even to those
who hadn't seen it. The first of many imported megamusicals, *Cats* ran for twenty-
one years in the West End and eighteen on Broadway, where it closed in 2002 and
2000, respectively. It has been seen in over twenty countries, and continues to enjoy
international success via productions that look remarkably like the original ones.

The idea of musical franchising—in which producers demand that any production hew as closely to the original as possible—is relatively new and strongly associated with the British Invasion. Lloyd Webber, especially when partnered with
hands-on producer Cameron Mackintosh, favors the practice. Disappointed by
O'Horgan's staging of *Jesus Christ Superstar* in 1971, he sought more control over
how his subsequent properties appeared, regardless of where they were staged or
who staged them.

Traditionally, when a property is licensed, directors are free to stage the production however they wish. For example, all subsequent productions of *Hair* in the late
1960s and '70s were custom-designed for each city. But with *Cats,* and even more
rigidly with Lloyd Webber's *The Phantom of the Opera* and Claude-Michel Schönberg
and Alain Boublil's *Les Misérables* (both Mackintosh productions), what one saw in
Berlin, Australia, or Japan was identical to what one saw on Broadway.

Theatrical franchising makes sense as a marketing strategy and proves an effective way of generating international exposure: interested audiences do not have to
travel to New York or London to see extravagant musicals, and people across the
world can experience something they never could before. But the practice has been
roundly condemned as "McTheater": a soulless chain of identical productions that
destroy local creativity and deprive individual companies of artistic freedom. In
response to this criticism, many international properties have held less strictly to
foreign staging rules since the 1980s and continue to thrive.

Broadway still serves as the musical theater's symbolic heart, but its grip on the genre has loosened, due to Off and Off-Off Broadway innovations and more recently by the "internationalization" of the musical. The result has allowed for different kinds of musical theater, broader audiences, and the chance for the musical to attain "mass media" status.

ADVERTISING AND MARKETING

Because of the international appeal of the American musical and because of the rising costs of putting on a show, the ways producers have attempted to attract audiences—thus, to sell theater to increasingly broad segments of the world's population—have intensified greatly in recent decades. Since the late 1990s, many new techniques have been applied to the practice of researching and targeting audiences, on both the grassroots and international level. In 1997, *The Audience for New York Theatre,* a landmark study by the company Audience Research and Analysis, was published, sponsored by the League of American Theatres and Producers. Since its appearance, an interest in profiling actual and potential audiences has grown substantially on Broadway and beyond.

Also newly popular is the practice of synergy, whereupon a company can simultaneously sell a particular product and any number of related products. Synergy allows companies like Disney to rely on familiarity to sell a musical version of, for example, the film *The Little Mermaid,* but also to use the stage version to generate continued interest in the film on DVD and all *Mermaid*-related merchandise. While familiarity has long been used to sell musicals—hence revivals, musicals based on films, and the Tin Pan Alley practice of dropping popular songs into numerous productions—the modern concept of synergy is particularly potent now that entertainment conglomerates are functioning as theater producers.

While the marketing of musicals has become more sophisticated, advertisements have been streamlined and, in some respects, simplified for international audiences. Once franchised musicals began opening in foreign cities, producers began to reinforce the idea that all productions, regardless of setting or language spoken, would be Broadway reproductions. Shows began to be sold like brands: musicals were reduced to simple, striking logos that could appear in the media and on billboards; repetitive musical themes that could saturate radio and television ads; and catchy slogans that would stick in the mind. Mackintosh's early ads for *Cats* teased, "Isn't the curiosity killing you?" The famous logo for the production featured two yellow cat's eyes—the pupils of which are dancing figures—against a black background (🅾 Example 8.10). For *Les Misérables,* the equally famous lithograph of young Cosette was adapted for every country (🅾 Example 8.11; 🅾 Example 8.12). *Rent*'s catchy slogan, "No Day But Today," exemplifies the power of simplicity in advertising. Of course, images and slogans alone do not sell Broadway shows. Producers have also become more reliant on mass media to sell musicals.

Since it was first televised in 1956, the annual Tony Awards ceremony has featured scenes from nominated productions, which help draw audiences to Broadway. Similarly, the occasional talk- or variety-show appearance has boosted sales for many productions; the numbers performed by the cast of *Camelot* on Ed Sullivan's "Toast of the Town" in 1961 resulted in an unprecedented $3.5 million surge in ticket sales. In 1972, the Broadway musical *Pippin* broke new ground by becoming the first Broadway musical featured in a television advertisement.

At present, musicals are advertised on television and radio, before films in movie theaters, and especially via the Internet. Web sites like Broadway.com feature extensive theater coverage and allow theatergoers to secure tickets to Broadway shows from anywhere in the world. It is also customary for each Broadway production to have its own Web site through which tickets can be purchased and production information gleaned. Internet fan sites, on which loyal audience members swap gossip and discuss their favorite shows, also abound; occasionally, as was the case with *The Scarlet Pimpernel*, such sites can support grassroots efforts to keep struggling shows alive.

Most recently, mass media have been employed to sell musicals via the reality show. In both the United States and the UK, "American Idol"-style programs have tracked audition processes over the course of a television season. Viewers vote on contestants; the winners earn roles in productions like the West End revival of *The Sound of Music* ("How Do You Solve a Problem like Maria?" 2006, UK) and the Broadway revival of *Grease* ("*Grease*: You're the One That I Want!" 2006, United States).

Because producers have always been invested in appealing to as many potential spectators as possible, marketing techniques may be more sophisticated, but the philosophy behind them is not new. As with the approach to spectacle, approaches to advertising and marketing have intensified, but only as the technology has allowed and the business of production has demanded.

Nostalgia and Revisionism
in the Postmodern Age

John Bush Jones notes that the precondition for widespread nostalgia—a collective desire to return to a "younger, more innocent, less jaded" time—is "severe discontent with the present" (Jones, 305–6). Musicals have long relied on emotional pull to connect with audiences, but nostalgia has an especially strong impact during or immediately after periods of national hardship. Certainly Rodgers and Hammerstein understood nostalgia's pull: *South Pacific* (1949) allowed American audiences to relive "the Good War"—and perhaps to reinvent it as less personally disruptive, frightening, or tragic—shortly after its resolution.

One of the most successful examples of nostalgia in the musical theater is *Grease* (1972), which capitalized on the '50s craze that developed in America in the early 1970s and lasted through much of that turbulent decade. A light romp through an era that was collectively idealized as relatively safe and innocent (if also socially conformist and politically conservative), *Grease* became the longest-running musical in Broadway history for its time. Audiences continue to embrace this idealized take on '50s teen culture, which was made into a successful film in 1978 and has been revived on Broadway twice: in 1994 and after the 2006 reality series discussed above.

Other postwar musicals that evoke nostalgic affection for their times include *Annie* (1977), *42nd Street* (1980), *Dreamgirls* (1981), *Little Shop of Horrors* (1982), *Miss Saigon* (1991), *Crazy For You* (1992), *The Who's Tommy* (1993), *Mamma Mia!* (2001), *Hairspray* (2002), and *The Drowsy Chaperone* (2006). These shows—and countless others—vary in the degree to which they draw on period-appropriate musical styles. But the sounds of the past trigger nostalgia, and thus an emotional connection. This is the driving logic behind the "jukebox musical," a subgenre that has become ubiquitous since the turn of the twenty-first century.

Instead of offering new songs evocative of past styles, jukebox musicals string together preexisting songs by a popular artist or group with the aid of a unifying (often frivolous) plot. Audiences of jukebox musicals tend to enter the theater familiar not only with the era but also with the songs themselves. As a result, the lure of familiarity is strong, gasps of recognition are frequent, and singing along during performances is common.

Jukebox musicals have clear precedents in film but are also influenced by shows like Tom O'Horgan's *Sgt. Pepper's Lonely Hearts Club Band on the Road* (1974) and the faux-concert *Beatlemania* (1977). The jukebox musical's own golden age began, perhaps unsurprisingly, after 2001, during a period of monumental uncertainty that caused a surge of collective nostalgia. Jukebox musicals that have opened since 2001 to varying degrees of success include *Mamma Mia!* (2001), *Movin' Out* (2002), *Jersey Boys* (2005), *All Shook Up* (2005), *Ring of Fire* (2006), *The Times They Are A-Changin'* (2006), *Rock of Ages* (2009), *Million Dollar Quartet* (2010) and *Baby, It's You!* (2011).

Some productions present a much subtler brand of nostalgia. *Ragtime*, for example, does not play on the audience's experience with an era but instead with the characters' experiences of their own past. While the Doctorow book is told by an omniscient narrator, the characters narrate their own lives in the stage version, in past tense and the third person, as if they are experiencing events and reflecting on them simultaneously: "The house on the hill in New Rochelle was Mother's domain," Mother announces in the prologue. "She took pleasure in making it comfortable for the men of her family."[8] The many historical figures (Evelyn Nesbit, Booker T. Washington, Harry Houdini, Emma Goldman, Henry Ford, J. P. Morgan) whose stories are woven into the musical introduce themselves similarly: "Evelyn Nesbit was the most beautiful woman in America." This narrative affectation frames the show: the audience watches the characters watch their own pasts, some from beyond the grave.

Flaherty's score refers to a variety of genres, most of which are rooted in turn-of-the-century styles: ragtime, the blues, the parlor waltz. Although there is a fair amount of belting, the general color of the score is bittersweet, gentle. *Grease*, like many jukebox musicals, features a score that is almost consistently upbeat; the audience generates its own nostalgia for the sound (◐ Example 8.13). Yet in *Ragtime*, fondness and a sweet sense of loss are built into the score. Consider, for example, Mother and Tateh's tentative meeting in "Nothing Like the City," or the preordained doom of Mother's Younger Brother in "He Wanted to Say" (◐ Example 8.14; ◐ Example 8.15). The music, like the action, is simultaneously nostalgic and present.

As with other musicals that play on a less immediate sense of nostalgia—*Fiddler on the Roof* (1964), for example—the events depicted in *Ragtime* are often violent and upsetting, but distance keeps us safe. Ultimately, musicals like *Grease* and *Ragtime* function similarly, despite different approaches: both allow audiences to long for an idealized past, but perhaps to be simultaneously thankful that the past is gone.

Nostalgia applies not only to musicals themselves but also to the legacy of many composers who have created them. The musical theater has its own canon, which is reflected in the constant flow of revivals that appear on Broadway stages. And nostalgia has colored the individual careers of, for example, Stephen Sondheim, who has earned the reputation among many critics and historians as the sole remaining representative of the mythic, storied past.

Sondheim has not enjoyed the international success experienced by some of his contemporaries. Most of his musicals are intimate in comparison with, for example, megamusicals or Disney spectacles. Both musically and dramaturgically, Sondheim's works tend to be denser and darker and are thus often perceived as less accessible. Because his musicals don't tend to translate to international audiences, they are not marketed aggressively to them.

What is misleading about Sondheim's placement in the musical theater canon is that while he was strongly influenced by the songwriting teams of the so-called Golden Age—in particular, Richard Rodgers and Oscar Hammerstein II—his sound is hardly rooted in the past; nor is he the last living practitioner of the sort of "authentic" musical that purportedly died when the Golden Age passed. Sondheim has always embraced bold, experimental, and contemporary sounds (◐ Example 8.16). The many young composers Sondheim has influenced—Jason Robert Brown, Adam Guettel, Jonathan Larson, and Jeanine Tesori, for example—have all clearly absorbed myriad musical influences that are reflected in their scores.

The fact that nostalgia involves collective revisionism is enormously important when it comes to the examination of contemporary musicals. The American musical is often seen to reflect American culture, but to some degree, the form simultaneously reinvents culture as well. Musicals depend on a collective—but also a *selective*—interest in the past. Thus, more work needs to be done on how musicals of the past fifty years have negotiated contemporary cultural demons: AIDS (*Falsettos, Rent*); race and class (*In the Heights, Passing Strange, Caroline, or Change*); sexuality and gender (*Hedwig and the Angry Inch, Wicked, Spring Awakening*; ◐ Example 8.17). Also relevant here are the ways older musicals are revisited. For example, the 1999 revival of Irving Berlin's *Annie Get Your Gun* (1946) altered several scenes seen as offensive to Native Americans, sparking debate about whether classic shows should be changed to fit contemporary sensibilities.

Scholars must keep in mind that not only nostalgia but also cultural memory can be selectively fabricated. Composers of musicals comment selectively on racial, sexual, economic, political, and sociocultural ups and downs. They have also begun to comment, often with great insight, on the musical's own history: a slew of self-referential, postmodern musicals, including *Bat Boy: The Musical* (2001), *The Producers* (2001), *Avenue Q* (2003), *[title of show]* (2004), *Monty Python's Spamalot* (2005), and *Musical of Musicals: The Musical* (2005) look back on their own legacy with affection and witty insight (◐ Example 8.18). In exploring the sociocultural relevance of contemporary musicals, the scholar must tease out what is cultural reflection and what is cultural revision.

Conclusions

Although set in the past and infused with nostalgia, *Ragtime* is a modern musical: it had huge (although not always complicated) sets, employed unusual narrative techniques, featured a pastiche of musical styles, relied on massive publicity, and while financially unsuccessful on Broadway, still achieved international success. The musical does not necessarily align itself with any previous or current tradition, except in the broadest of strokes: it was influenced by a century of tradition but also contains innovations and surprises. Yet in commenting on contemporary productions, many critics and scholars resort to comparisons with the past. In his review of *Ragtime* for the *Village Voice* (February 3, 1998), Michael Feingold evokes the Golden Age (he locates it between "the century's teens" and the early 1960s) in arguing that the musical—that "very unhappy art form"—is stuck in a "silver age." Feingold liked *Ragtime* but felt it lacked "the extra light-hearted spark that made the old musicals great." He mournfully concludes that "here and now, this is the best we can do."

It is our hope that the tendency toward simplistic comparisons of the "golden" past with the tarnished present will fall away as musical scholarship becomes more varied and sophisticated. Musicals are not what they were: time has elapsed; technology, economics, politics, and culture have shifted. Yet while perhaps not as central to popular culture as before, musicals have not stopped being relevant or influential, just as their audiences have not gotten stupider, lazier, or less emotionally connected. Contemporary musical theater draws from the past while simultaneously offering modern innovations. We scholars must continue to do the same.

NOTES

1. See, for example, Geoffrey Block, *Enchanted Evenings: The Broadway Musical from* Show Boat *to Sondheim* (New York: Oxford University Press, 1997), Gerald Bordman, *American Musical Theatre: A Chronicle*, 3rd ed. (New York: Oxford University Press, 2001), *The Cambridge Companion to the Musical*, 2nd ed., ed. William A. Everett, and Paul R. Laird (Cambridge: Cambridge University Press, 2008), Denny Martin Flinn, *Musical! A Grand Tour: The Rise, Glory, and Fall of an American Institution* (New York: Schirmer, 1997), Mark. N. Grant, *The Rise and Fall of the Broadway Musical* (Hanover, NH: University Press of New England, 2004), Gerald Mast, *Can't Help Singin': The American Musical on Stage and Screen* (New York: Overlook Press, 1987), and Ethan Mordden, *The Happiest Corpse I've Ever Seen: The Last 25 Years of the Broadway Musical* (New York: Palgrave Macmillan, 2004).

2. Allen Woll, *Black Musical Theatre from* Coontown *to* Dreamgirls (New York: Da Capo, 1989), p. 248.

3. Mordden, for example, regularly makes assumptions about contemporary audiences and their inability to appreciate musicals that he has deemed "sophisticated."

4. Bordman also includes Cy Coleman, Charles Strouse, and "possibly Jerry Herman" in his list of post-1960s composers "willing or able" to supply the theater with memorable scores (721).

5. John Bush Jones, *Our Musicals, Ourselves: A Social History of the American Musical Theatre* (Hanover, NH: University Press of New England, 2003), p. 83.

6. See Jonathan Burston, "Theatre Space as Virtual Place: Audio Technology, the Reconfigured Singing Body, and the Megamusical" (*Popular Music* 17.2 [May 1998]: 205–18).

7. Steven Adler, *On Broadway: Art and Commerce on the Great White Way* (Carbondale: Southern Illinois University Press, 2004, p. 4.

8. This and all other quotations from *Ragtime*: Lynn Ahrens, Stephen Flaherty, and Terrence McNally, libretto (Original Broadway Cast Recording, BMG Entertainment, 1998).

PART III

MEDIA

CHAPTER 9

THEATER

TAMSEN WOLFF

THE Polish director Tadeusz Kantor reportedly said that one of the main reasons people go to the theater is to sit down and stand up at the same time as other people. Certainly a defining aspect of theater is that it requires a group of spectators to come together in a room to watch performers. Live theater involves performer(s), spectator(s), and performance material; it is an immediate, transient, embodied, and unpredictable medium. The exchange between audience and performers has different dimensions for musical theater from those of straight theater. The relationship between an audience and musical theater is distinctive in at least two ways: in the communication, circulation, and shelf life of musical numbers; and in a pronounced focus in musicals on communal action, thematically, musically, and choreographically. Looking at these two features of musical theater and where they overlap helps illustrate what is unique about musicals in the theater.

If Kantor is right that people gravitate toward live theater because of a desire for a shared activity or to feel part of a group with a clearly defined role, then musical theater's regular use of ensembles reflects and magnifies that desire on the stage. A central question of musical theater is how do people come together? The question was integral first to the influential musicals of Rodgers and Hammerstein, in which the importance of community solidarity routinely outweighs individual concerns. Although romantic couples are at the heart of the narrative in most Rodgers and Hammerstein musicals, the couple's union is also a measure of the community's cohesiveness and usually, sooner or later, the chorus envelops individuals. In *Oklahoma!* (1943), the main couple, Curly, a cowboy, and Laurey, who belongs to a farming family, represent the two quarreling factions of citizens in the Oklahoma territory. When Curly and Laurey eventually marry, their union anticipates and parallels the alliance of the ensemble and formation of the state.[1]

Musical theater's thematic emphasis on community is inseparable from the most powerful expression of that community onstage: everyone's singing and dancing together. Ensemble singing and matching choreography are entrenched musical theater conventions. As Scott McMillin puts it in *The Musical as Drama*, "There is a drive toward ensemble effect in the musical dramatic form. . . . Legitimate drama has its large scenes, too, but the ensemble numbers of a musical do something that does not happen in legitimate drama. The characters express themselves simultaneously, and the build-up of a number to a simultaneous performance is often a dramatic event itself."[2] A crowded, synchronized musical number on stage is also different from the same big number performed on screen. In the theater, the physical proximity of the performers' bodies and their exertion is unmediated and unpredictable. Watching a large group of individuals performing in uncanny unison is often particularly thrilling for audiences, although it can just as easily be disturbing. Historically, large-scale simultaneous performance has been used to intimidate as well as impress spectators, especially in displays of military power—think of Stalin's processions of soldiers, or Nazi storm troopers' marches. Audience fascination with this kind of unified spectacle has deep roots, in everything from political rallies, to the chorus in Greek drama, to the apparently endless appeal of the Radio City Music Hall Rockettes.

Performers' singing and dancing skills are also exposed in the present tense, embodied theater. People may very well go to musicals for the same reason that they watch the Olympics: the stakes are high and live bodies can't fake the necessary effort. There's no logical explanation for what athletes and performers do, but both fulfill a human desire to test the limits and talents of the body, to see what it can do and what it can express. A performer can do the feat (the high dive, the javelin throw, the solo) only with a greater or lesser degree of proficiency. Singing ability is the first and most demanding requirement for musical theater performers. When a performer opens her mouth to sing, she can bomb. Singing and dancing are both measurable skills that always contain the riveting possibility of audible and visible public failure. Whereas on film and in recordings, singing and dancing can be edited and augmented in a variety of ways, this kind of intervention is harder, if not impossible, in live theater. Certainly performers can be miked and usually are, especially in bigger houses. This practice has generated plenty of controversy and has shifted the requirements for both the acting and singing skills of musical theater performers. Nonetheless, it hasn't changed the fact that performers reveal themselves when singing. It tends to be easier for audiences to agree on the quality of singing, even without a trained ear, than to do the same for acting, but audiences can see slips as well as hear them on stage—the wrong note, the dropped partner, the fudged line. The possibility of accidents or even fiascos in live performance, and the accompanying excitement for an audience, is raised exponentially in a musical, where such a wide range of skills—singing, dancing, and acting—are required.

The frequent movement among the basic dramatic elements of speech, song, and dance in musical theater not only underscores the many abilities of the performers on stage but also repeatedly reminds the audience that they are watching a performance. As McMillin argues, the unavoidable push-and-pull between elements on the musical theater stage creates a unique dramatic form and experience for the audience. The competition and contrast between the different elements means that songs and dance stand out in high relief from spoken dialogue on stage. This differentiation is further highlighted for the audience by the way in which speech, song, and dance often function in a hierarchy of authentic affect. A character becomes most articulate and emotionally truthful in song and dance (and characters are not necessarily in charge of their revealing, intuitive singing and dancing selves). This truth-telling convention dovetails with the exposure of a performer's ability, which is also revealed primarily in song. Songs that are characters' truthful asides or confessionals to the audience can allow audiences to feel closer to the characters and their dilemmas during musical numbers. The disjunction between song and speech doesn't exist on recordings (if there are snippets of dialogue, they usually occur during the lead-in to a song or as brief interjections) and it works very differently in film where there are multiple ways to suggest characters' emotional states and to gloss over or highlight shifts from speech to song to dance. In live theater, to watch performers jump between modes of performance is an exuberant, liberating exercise, one that audiences frequently celebrate by applauding at the end of numbers, which in turn reinforces the distinction between song and dialogue.

The relationships among song, dance, and book—the ways in which the elements collide and coexist in performance—mirror musical theater's common narrative focus on how characters come together to form a community and what kinds of communities they form. In many mid-twentieth-century musicals, the struggle to create a seamless community within the story corresponds to a structural effort to integrate song, dance, and book. Rodgers and Hammerstein's *Oklahoma!* is one of the most frequently cited examples of this development, in part because Rodgers directly and repeatedly addressed the aesthetic choices that the creators made. As he described *Oklahoma!* in his autobiography, *Musical Stages*, "No single element overshadows any other.... It was a work created by many that gave the impression of having been created by one."[3] Not only do song, dance, and book complement one another, but this harmony merges with the narrative focus on the joyful integration of the farmers and the cowmen (and, eventually, the merchants).

At the same time, musicals that devote themselves to the question of a community's coming together by way of singing and dancing include a wide range of works that offer diverse representations of communities. *West Side Story* (1957) marked a shift in musicals' portrayals of communities by focusing on society's outsiders who want in as opposed to social insiders solidifying their base. If in *Oklahoma!* territory folks stick together because they know they belong to the land and the land they belong to is grand, in *West Side Story*, the socially marginalized warring groups of the Jets and Sharks are deeply ambivalent about whether this land is grand, and they know for sure that they don't belong to it. This doesn't stop their fighting over it, but their failure to come together in *West Side Story* is depicted as society's failure and raises the question of how, whether, and what groups are brought together by singing and dancing.

This darker take on social harmony appears in musicals as dissimilar as *Assassins* (1991), and *A Chorus Line* (1975). *A Chorus Line* is a self-referential ode to performers auditioning to join a musical kick line while *Assassins* is an episodic, vaudeville-inspired, trans-historical story of assassins and would-be assassins of United States presidents. Both depict makeshift communities of outsiders looking for social inclusion. In *Assassins* and *A Chorus Line*, the route to social inclusion is through performance, celebrity, or public recognition. The stakes are higher than getting the girl or the boy. The minor love plot in *A Chorus Line* between the director, Zach, and his ex-leading lady, Cassie, is displaced by her focus on joining the chorus. The only semblance of a love plot in *Assassins* lies in John Wilkes Booth's wooing Lee Harvey Oswald to join the group of assassins. *Assassins* in particular offers what Raymond Knapp refers to as a "counter-mythology" to the romantic unification myths about America that are generally promoted in Golden Age musicals.[4] Community formation is still central, but now it is identified as deeply troubling, if not downright dangerous. Indeed, both "Another National Anthem" from *Assassins* and the musical number "One," in *A Chorus Line* offer cautionary comments on what is compromised when individuals join forces.

A number of contemporary musicals explicitly challenge the value of community. In *Parade* (1998) a community in Georgia in 1913 functions as the terrifying antagonist—eventually transforming into a lynch mob—that threatens the central romantic couple, Leo and Lucille Frank. Here the ensemble's collective force is meant to disturb the audience. The story is a direct inversion of the traditional communal embrace of the main couple. But it's not an exclusively new idea. Arguably, the classic *Music Man* (1957) also presents the couple of Harold Hill and Marian Paroo as unassimilated outsiders. Hill is a peripatetic con artist and Marian is a freethinking librarian at odds with her hometown in River City, Iowa. The romantic connection between Hill and Marian emerges in the linked melodies of "Seventy-Six Trombones" and "Goodnight My Someone," Hill's need to complete the duet of "Til There Was You" and the shared music of the "Trombones/Goodnight" reprise, but their union is not about their integration into the larger community. They remain individuals uniquely matched to each other and set apart from the general population of River City. The community itself is revealed to be a sham, a group formed only as a result of Hill's con game and united in fantasy rather than in reality.[5]

Already in the sentimental celebration of like-minded community that characterizes many of the musicals from the mid-twentieth century, happy unity frequently occurs at the violent expense of characters who threaten it for any reason. In the case of *Oklahoma!*, Jud Fry, the farmhand who repeatedly comes between the main couple of Curly and Laurey, is finally killed, conveniently falling on his own knife. But his death is only the most obvious instance of the violence necessary to create a unified community. Much of *Oklahoma!* is informed by fear of violence connected to romantic coupling, either comically (when Ali Hakim is threatened at gunpoint to marry) or potentially less so (when Aunt Eller points a gun at both the cowboys and the farmers, who will need to make a symbolic shotgun marriage of their own in order to form the titular state). Indeed, this element was even more pronounced in the original play (*Green Grow the Lilacs*, by Lynn Riggs), where Laurey's fear of the shivaree is given more play (Riggs at one time planned to title the play "Shivaree"). Thus, even within an early classic, jubilant promotion of community, cohesiveness is more complicated than it might appear.

The problem of representing the simultaneous pleasure and difficulty of community formation is well suited to live musical theater. Theater allows for unfixed, here-and-then-gone interpretations, which have the potential to challenge and reinvigorate individual shows and the whole form.[6] This can happen in a single actor's performance, in a musical number, or in a whole production. For example, the grand finale of *A Chorus Line*, "One," in which the individual dancers join the kick line and become indistinguishable, can be dehumanizing, but it can also be passionate and emotional, revealing the human beauty and power of both dance itself and the chorus line as a miraculous, organic, living being. While this contradiction is built into every performance of *A Chorus Line*, revisionist revivals tend to expose the underbellies of traditional musicals. An extreme example of this is Anne Bogart's unauthorized, revisionist 1984 production of Rodgers and Hammerstein's *South Pacific* (1949). Bogart set the show, one of the most popular romantic musicals of all time, in a disturbing, clinical rehabilitation facility for shell-shocked war veterans who were acting out the show as a kind of behavioral modification therapy. The production was almost entirely faithful to the score, but the setting and approach upended the original sentiments. In one instance, during the famous—and famously lighthearted—number "I'm Gonna Wash that Man Right Outa My Hair," the inmates got stuck on the line, "I'm in love I'm in love I'm in love I'm in love I'm in love" like a broken record, until romance looked and sounded like mental illness. Even highly restrained individual performances can illuminate productions. In the 2001 London revival of *My Fair Lady*, Nicholas Le Prevost's affectionate and understated portrayal of Colonel Pickering left no doubt that Pickering was gay. This choice—never clearer than when Pickering took charge of dressing Eliza for the ball—subtly reconfigured the relationships among the three central characters.

Because theater comes and goes so quickly and allows for play in interpretation even within every performance, more varied—if not always more daring—versions of musicals have the potential to show up on stage. While creative and revisionist interpretations are certainly possible on film, the movie market won't bear multiple versions of the same show, whereas revivals are the mainstay of the musical theater business. This gives directors and performers the opportunity to try new approaches to the same shows. It means, too, that audiences are often repeat customers who can anticipate the score with a thorough knowledge of the songs and of the songs' histories in multiple productions. What's more, these audiences can develop their own layered relationship to the songs and the characters.

Musicals often have built-in singing lessons, inducements to sing, and examples of how singing can open up unlikely lines of connection, all of which work together to strengthen an audience's understanding of and pleasure in what they are watching. Songs that explain within musicals either explicitly how music works or how it could work, simultaneously suggest to an audience what and how to think about music and how to respond to what they are hearing. These strategies can be straightforward and practical, as is true of the unambiguously named *The Sound of Music* (1959). Maria, as a new governess to the seven Von Trapp children, wins them over with song but also breaks down the basics of music for them and teaches them to

sing with the number "Do-Re-Mi." *Floyd Collins* (1996) offers another way of thinking about the singing voice and its powers. Floyd uses the echoes of his voice to
sound out caves in Kentucky. In the dark he tests his voice and its ability to reach
across undefined distances. Later when he is trapped in a cave, he makes the imaginative leap to connect to the outside world through singing. Many of the songs in
Floyd Collins emphasize vocalizing and mouth noises, as well as call-and-response.
For an audience, these musicals extend an invitation to make any kind of noise, test
the vocal waters, chant a musical scale, harmonize, and sing in order to open up
space and reach out to people and places that are unseen, or even unknown.

One of the most important measures of the success of a musical—if not the
only truly vital measure—is the power of the music onstage to inspire imitation.
The longevity of a musical has a lot to do with how singers put over songs—how
they communicate them—and whether those songs are then sung again offstage.
This may mean that an audience member sings along with performers in a production, but certainly that the audience *wants* to sing along then, and will sing the songs
at some point. At the 2001 London revival of *My Fair Lady*, a woman sitting behind
me sang every number, mostly quietly. (She hit top volume on "I Could Have Danced
All Night," which was a high point of the show.) Twice she apologized and whis-
pered, "I can't help it." But her response was a testament to the show's achievement,
and the relative equanimity of her neighbors suggested that they sympathized with
the urge. The pervasiveness of this impulse is recognized in a number of different
forums, including "musicals" karaoke and piano bars, and screening sing-alongs
like *The Sing-Along Sound of Music*. Since film doesn't allow for literal audience-
performer interaction, *The Sing-Along* goes a little way toward reinserting a live
exchange into or alongside viewing the film of *The Sound of Music*. Audience members wear costumes from the movie, are provided with props, are coached in ensemble responses (booing the Nazis, cheering Maria), and sing along with the subtitles
on the screen. *The Sing-Along Sound of Music* shares ground with a number of
hybrid, interactive events, most obviously *The Rocky Horror Picture Show*, as well as
TV shows like *Sing Along with Mitch*, *Mystery Science Theater 3000*, and, most
recently, the online event of Joss Whedon's *Dr. Horrible's Sing-Along Blog* (2008).

Musical theater frequently holds out an appeal, not only among characters
within the musical but also to the audience to participate. When the chorus sings,
"Join us!" in *Pippin* (1972), this is not only a direct invitation to the audience to witness Pippin's journey but also an indirect invitation to keep that story alive by singing the songs again. Consider the difference with straight plays: we generally do not
expect a play to inspire the desire to act or to prompt an imitative response (a more
common expectation might be that a good play will inspire an empathetic or critical response). Not everyone can be Hamlet—or would want to be—but anyone can
sing in the shower or to a child. While all theater is transient, musical theater is different because the music is the most memorable part of the show and the transmission of that music keeps the show alive. Participating is possible even for people
who don't own or play cast recordings and for people without anything reasonably
considered a passable singing voice. Since a show's survival depends on the audience's

desire to sing its songs, quantity and not quality of participation is what matters most offstage.

Musical theater's democratic, open-ended invitation to audiences is not simply to sing along, but even more to imagine themselves in any of the roles of the often dramatic, expressive characters who populate musicals. This extends the continued life of musical numbers because many people respond to the idea of imagining themselves in the role of the singer, publicly or privately. Musical theater circulates through offstage communities in ways that are at once unpredictable and surprisingly constant. This movement and maintenance relies on recordings, TV and film versions, reality TV shows about stage productions, and Internet versions of musicals. Nonetheless, the experience of singing musical numbers and thus spreading the music around is an embodied experience that originates in and is sustained by live performance. Musical theater has particular weight and currency in certain communities, notably among gay men, as has been insightfully detailed by D. A. Miller in *Place for Us*, and John Clum in *Something for the Boys*, among others.[7] But its circulation is not limited to any one demographic.

The movement of songs from musicals across generations, for instance, is also unexpectedly consistent. Students routinely mention being exposed to musicals by their parents' singing the songs to them at an early age. (This transmission can happen unwittingly. Once, when my eighteen-month-old daughter was attempting to hurl herself out of her high chair, I said, "Sit down," and she immediately chanted, "*Sit down, sit down, sit down, sit down, sit down, you're rocking the boat!*" I must have sung her the line from *Guys and Dolls*, but I had no memory of doing so. She latched onto the call-and-response gospel-inspired rhythm and repetition, as well as onto my pleasure in it, and sang it right back at me.) The practice of musicals being passed down through generations seems to be reflected in the omnipresence of nostalgia in musicals themselves. Musicals are notoriously backward looking in settings and stories, from *Oklahoma!* (1943), which is nostalgic for 1906 Oklahoma Territory, to *Grease!* (1972), which embraces the fifties, to *Hairspray* (2002), which grooves to the rebellious sounds of 1962 from a safe distance. Very few musicals are set in their present moment. The cross-generational pull is also present in the eruption of jukebox musicals, which cater to an audience's familiarity with previously recorded soundtracks and established recording artists, from Frankie Valli and the Four Seasons (*Jersey Boys*, 2005) to ABBA (*Mamma Mia!* 2001). Even satirical contemporary musicals with fantastical or futuristic story lines—*Bat Boy* (1997) or *Urinetown* (2001) for instance—hearken back to and play with musical theater's own history.

One musical that exemplifies the intersection of the issue of community, onstage and off, and the communication and circulation of musical numbers, is the rock musical *Rent* (1994). *Rent* is, in part, a retelling of Puccini's *La Bohème* set in the early 1990s in the East Village in New York, which follows a group of socially marginal, idealistic young people, who come together to deal with poverty, AIDS, heroin addiction, romantic difficulties, and homelessness. The cast of the initial workshop at New York Theater Workshop, who went on to Broadway, was made up of almost entirely unknown young actors. The musical and the production embraced cheap bohemianism, and a clever, similarly minded marketing campaign sold cheap tickets to anyone who wanted to camp out on the street outside the run-down Nederlander Theater, which is right up the street from the gritty Port Authority Bus Terminal and was frequently populated by homeless people at the time. An astonishing number of young audience members enthusiastically took up the challenge, often sleeping on the street all night, and often for a remarkable number of repeat visits. According to Elizabeth Wollman, the marketing campaigns for rock musicals often have to be particularly innovative because of the difficulties of selling this kind of musical, and *Rent* was no exception.[8] But the invitation to join the onstage community of *Rent*—the invitation for the audience to imagine themselves as the offstage counterparts to the characters—was an easy leap. That invitation is built into the story, the lyrics, and the performance style of the songs in the show, which were sung either directly to the audience, at standing microphones set downstage left and right, or into the obvious radio microphones the actors wore on their heads, with the accompaniment of an onstage rock band.

Before embarking on multiple national and international tours, *Rent* ran for twelve years on Broadway, the eighth longest run in Broadway's history. The die-hard fans of the show who helped sustain its run, self-named Rentheads, formed Internet groups based on, among other things, the camaraderie that resulted from the ticket buying on the street; the number of times people had seen the show, in how many cities and countries; and quizzes devoted to all the lyrics and music of the show.[9] This community's delight in the show was bound up in their lived experience of going to the theater and in their understanding of themselves as an extension of the show's characters.

Rent answers the question of how people come together this way: through shared hardship, a message of the story that was readily adopted by the show's most dedicated audiences. All theater brings people together in a room, but musical theater regularly brings people together to contemplate the spectacle of people coming together, in book, song, and dance. Musical theater also encourages and relies on the audience's desire to perform the songs that they have heard performed, and to form communities based on that desire. In its examination and staging of the problems and pleasures of community on stage to a group of people offstage, live musical theater offers an experience unlike anything else.

NOTES

1. This device, termed the "marriage trope" by Raymond Knapp, has been described by Rick Altman as a fundamental structure of musicals: "The marriage which resolves the primary (sexual) dichotomy also mediates between two terms of the secondary (thematic) opposition"; see Rick Altman, *The American Film Musical* (Bloomington: Indiana University Press, 1987), p. 50, and Raymond Knapp, *The American Musical and the Formation of National Identity* (Princeton, NJ: Princeton University Press, 2005), p. 9 and elsewhere.

2. Scott McMillin, *The Musical as Drama* (Princeton, NJ: Princeton University Press, 2006), pp. 78–79.

3. Richard Rodgers, *Musical Stages: An Autobiography* (New York: Random House, 1975; reprinted New York: Da Capo, 1995, 2000), p. 227.

4. Knapp 2005, 162–76; see also his "*Assassins, Oklahoma!*, and the 'Shifting Fringe of Dark around the Campfire'" (*Cambridge Opera Journal* 16 [2004]: 77–101).

5. For a related discussion, see Scott Miller, *Deconstructing Harold Hill: An Insider's Guide to Musical Theatre* (Portsmouth, NH: Heinemann, 2000), ch. 5.

6. For an extended discussion of this dynamic, see Bruce Kirle, *Unfinished Show Business: Broadway Musicals as Works-in-Process* (Carbondale: Southern Illinois University Press, 2005).

7. D. A. Miller, *Place for Us (Essay on the Broadway Musical)* (Cambridge: Harvard University Press, 1998), and John Clum, *Something for the Boys: Musical Theater and Gay Culture* (New York: Palgrave, 1999).

8. Elizabeth L. Wollman, *The Theater Will Rock: A History of the Rock Musical, from Hair to Hedwig* (Ann Arbor: University of Michigan Press, 2006), p. 174.

9. Regarding the growing importance of Internet groups to sustaining a fan base for individual shows, see Stacy Wolf, "*Wicked* Divas, Musical Theater, and Internet Girl Fans" (*Camera Obscura* 65 22.2 [2007]: 39–71.

CHAPTER 10

THE FILMED MUSICAL

RAYMOND KNAPP

MITCHELL MORRIS

INTERACTIONS between staged and filmed musicals have, since the beginning of commercially viable synchronized sound, been thoroughgoing and powerful, shaping the development of both. Given the longer existence of stage musicals, filmed musicals would naturally seem to be the derivative genre. Yet for the *American* musical, this "natural" understanding is dubious, since almost all staged musicals that still hold significance for American audiences were created within film's "sound" era. Whether it was due to coincidence, kismet, or some complex causal web, 1927 saw the births of both the "sound era" in film (with *The Jazz Singer*) and, by some reckonings, the "Golden Age" of American musicals on stage (with *Show Boat*). Later developments of either type require some consideration of the other.

Despite this intertwining of intimately shared histories, most studies consider staged and filmed musicals as separate genres, an academic habit bred more by the drawing of disciplinal boundaries than anything else. Thus, scholarly engagements with the former mostly ignore the latter (or consign it to secondary status through token consideration), whereas Rick Altman's *The Film Musical*—the landmark monograph on its topic—although full of insight and valuable readings of particular films, virtually ignores all relevant staged versions and models.[1]

In this chapter, rather than focus narrowly on the filmed musical's specific historical contributions, which would reinforce the filmed musical's "token" status, we examine selected areas of intersection between stage and screen, as sites where fusions and fissures between them have enlivened or beset one or the other (or both). We begin, after a brief exposition of some vocabulary essential to the study of film musicals, by addressing a set of practical issues related to race, stars, and adaptation, as grounded in the commercial realities of the film industry. We then proceed to a consideration of the separate and sometimes interactive worlds created by film musicals, choosing to focus on three specific aspects of those worlds: (1) modes of evoking the "real" (and the "artificial"), (2) the presentation of song, especially when tending toward the intimate, and (3) the specific role of camp, both in presentation and reception.

THE MUSICAL AS FILM

Because of the ubiquity of blends, hybrids, and fusions that compose the filmed musical, an acquaintance with basic stylistic concepts used in cinema studies is crucial to their formal analysis and interpretation.[2] Four domains seem most immediately relevant:

Mise-en-scène. This term, derived from theater criticism, encompasses all aspects of the "look" within the film's frame: setting, whether specially constructed or found in the everyday world; lighting, both artificial and "natural"; costumes and makeup; special effects (if any); and all modes of actorly performance such as gesture and stance, speaking, and singing. All of these aspects tend to combine, with greater or lesser success, with the others, and to acquire additional significance through the way their changes are articulated through performance time. In sum, mise-en-scène refers to how the scene is "staged." And in the case of musicals, the mise-en-scènes appropriate to theatrical productions are often apt to play an important role in the structuring of their films.

Cinematography. A film is always shot in a particular way that shapes the affective charge of particular moments and their combination into the whole. Analysis of cinematography typically attends to three things: (1) photographic qualities of the "shot" such as color, hue, speed, perspective, focus, and field depth; (2) framing, or the way that the borders of the particular image focus viewer attention, particularizing the image; and (3) duration, or "take," the length of the camera's view of a specific scene before cutting to another. Each of these factors can be broken down into many subcomponents in the course of an analysis, and more detailed study of the particulars of filmic language is invaluable in consolidating interpretations.

Editing. A film comprises a series of shots, and the way that these are combined (montage) decisively shapes viewers' interpretations.[3] Shots may be joined by devices such as fade-outs and fade-ins, dissolves and wipes, and most commonly by cuts—the direct juxtaposition of two shots. Qualities of the mise-en-scène and cinematography, the rhythmic play that comes from lengths of shots, and the spatio-temporal relations that they may imply are all relevant to a consideration of the editorial process, not least because they help determine a viewer's sense of the degree of continuity and discontinuity present in the narrative.

Sound. A film musical's numbers are generally recorded separately before they are shot and are thus subject to alterations that are difficult or impossible to make in live performances. Before the advent of amplification and the widespread use of prerecorded music in live theater, this was one of the most distinctive features of film musicals. The production of *My Fair Lady* (1964), where almost all of Audrey Hepburn's songs were "dubbed" by Marni Nixon, and Jeremy Brett's by Bill Shirley,[4] illustrates this difference well. But more subtly, the necessity of recording sound for film musicals meant that performers who did not sound well in live theaters could more easily participate in film musicals, whereas performers who flourished before the coming of the microphone (Ethel Merman comes to mind) arguably found themselves disadvantaged in film by the very skills that served them well in the theater. The expansion of studio techniques of sound manipulation in the 1960s as well as the rise of cinematic sound design at the end of the 1970s, coupled with the introduction of amplification in live musical theater from the 1970s on have further complicated analysis of both live and film musicals, as people bring expectations fostered by one venue to the other. In any case, the particulars of a film musical's sound design—the timbres of voices, their relationship to the arrangements they inhabit, and their place in the overall sound design—are perhaps best analyzed as working synergistically with the more visually oriented aspects of the overall work.

Managing Race and Stars

As discussed elsewhere in this volume (see especially chapters 5 and 14), race has played a huge role in the history of the American musical, especially regarding the black/white "color line" and the practices of blackface. The latter helped launch the sound era, figuring prominently in *The Jazz Singer*, and continued to play a part in filmed musicals until well into the 1940s—long after its use in Broadway musicals had waned—with a few stars specializing in blackface and many others taking at least an occasional turn in blackface.

Perhaps the most startling example is Fred Astaire's "Bojangles of Harlem" in *Swing Time* (George Stevens, 1936; ⊙ Example 10.1). Because it pays specific homage to a then still-active screen star, Bill "Bojangles" Robinson, the usual signifying elements of blackface have a specific point of reference rather than functioning as a generic mask. Yet several things complicate this number and contemporary reactions to it. As Todd Decker has shown, in other films Astaire took box-office risks in his forthright integration of black musicians into his musical numbers, making it difficult to cut them out of the picture for distribution in the American South (a standard practice for musical numbers performed by blacks).[5] Astaire's decision to "honor" Robinson with a number that not only uses blackface but also partakes of other stereotypical race-based images and emphases, then, seems odd. Especially problematic is the doubly offensive opening visual joke, when a large caricature of the blackface persona, with cheap bowler hat and exaggerated painted lips, turns into a pair of exaggeratedly large feet—a visual reference, perhaps, to the "educated feets" of minstrel performers. The centrality of race to the number is reinforced by stark oppositions of black and white throughout the scene (and elsewhere in the film), as in the contrasting outfits of the dancers, who alternately evoke segregation and miscegenation in their deployments, and in the giant black shadows of Astaire dancing, eventually recreating a kind of "challenge" dance evocative of early minstrelsy. Further, his dance, while overtly an homage, comes across quite differently, especially in his free use of hands, arms, and upper body, contrasting vividly with Robinson, who was criticized (reportedly by Astaire himself) for dancing only from the waist down. Intriguingly, Astaire's blackface resonates with Ginger Rogers's entrance in "The Way You Look Tonight," when she appears, distracted by Astaire's song, in a whitening shampoo lather (⏵ Example 10.2). While it is possible to trace a liberating narrative in the mixing of races and Astaire's dismissal of the shadows in "Bojangles," and to understand the parallel scene with Rogers as part of a coordinated claim that color is only skin deep, it is just as easy, and probably more common, to take the references at their offensive (black)face value, especially as they are reinforced by the sprinkling throughout the film of such elements as "jungle" drumming and a brief "indefinite talk" routine (with sidekick Victor Moore).

Astaire's struggles to make good on a debt he and many other white dancers felt toward a systematically excluded population of black performers—given that tap dancing was grounded in black and blackface traditions—found institutional echo in the war years, when *Stormy Weather* (Andrew Stone) appeared as one of two all-black musicals produced by major Hollywood studios in 1943. While its central story line falls flat, based on the unconvincing romantic pairing of an aging Bill Robinson with an oddly restrained Lena Horne, the trajectory of its musical numbers, as with Astaire's blackface number, points both to a tainted legacy in minstrelsy (thus the cakewalk, indefinite talk, and jungle numbers) and the evolving makeover of these elements, especially in Cab Callaway's "Jumpin' Jive" and its climactic dance turn by the Nicholas Brothers (⏵ Example 10.3).[6] If such gestures were inadequately reparative and largely ineffective in changing Hollywood race-based practices, in *Singin' in the Rain* (Stanley Donen and Gene Kelly, 1952) those practices could nevertheless be brushed aside as period curiosities, with Donald O'Connor's brief reference to Jolson's "Mammy" number in *The Jazz Singer* and Kelly's throwaway greeting to a white actor whose elaborate jungle makeup makes him unrecognizable.

Singin' in the Rain and *Stormy Weather* are each concerned with enacting a specific historical moment within the context of a "backstage" musical, and so, naturally enough, strikes a particular attitude toward "stars" and the "star system." While stars and teams (usually comic or romantic) were common enough on Broadway, and perhaps even more common in vaudeville and related venues, they were still more important in Hollywood, where they were aggressively marketed as such by the studios. Like most backstage musicals, the narratives of both of these films center on the prospects of an unknown "making it" and becoming a star. And because they are adult-oriented musicals, that quest combines easily with a romantic quest, in which the other half of the romantic pair is already a star and serves emblematically as stardom itself, with success in both realms achieved at one stroke.

While star teams were often the preferred marketing tool of the studios because of their multiple points of appeal—offering two or more stars individually and a familiar interactive dynamic—many stars tried to break away from this sometimes limiting pattern, with differing degrees of success. Judy Garland, for example, was effectively paired, as a "juvenile," with Mickey Rooney and struggled for years to emerge as an adult star in her own right. Ironically, *The Wizard of Oz* (Victor Fleming, 1939), in which she played a girl younger than her actual age, probably held up this process somewhat; five years later, in *Meet Me in St. Louis* (Vicente Minnelli), she was still playing "young," although in many respects more mature than her romantic partner, "The Boy Next Door" (played by Tom Drake).

Among the most successful star teams of the 1930s was that of Fred Astaire and Ginger Rogers, who enjoyed considerably more success together than either seemed destined to achieve individually in Hollywood (although each achieved individual success as their pairing played itself out). *Swing Time*, filmed at the height of their partnership, with songs by Jerome Kern and Dorothy Fields, and often cited as the most satisfying overall, exemplifies how their films tended to work. Astaire was easily the better dancer and, although rather thin of voice, more capable of "delivering" a song. Yet in both song and dance they proved both compatible and effectively complementary. It was thus in their musical numbers that their romance evolved, overcoming the frictions established by plot situations and their wise-cracking personae. Ironically, while *Stormy Weather* attempts something like this strategy, the crackling energy of its "real-life" partners and ensembles—especially in the case of the Nicholas Brothers—easily overwhelms the film's "official" center of interest.

ADAPTATIONS

Adaptations represent the most direct point of contact between Broadway and Hollywood and have been a mainstay of the latter ever since *The Jazz Singer* first showed the potential for sound film to bring a Broadway star in a Broadway show to a wider public. Critical views of adaptations depend on the perspective taken, on whether the resulting artifact is regarded as a filmed *version* of a stage show, or as a *film musical* that happens to derive from a stage show. We will consider these somewhat opposed perspectives in order.

While audiences have tended more often to see film adaptations as *versions* of the stage show, there are often large differences between them. Until the 1940s, for example, song substitutions and omissions were not only common but rampant, before the growing popularity of show-based albums after *Oklahoma!* (1943) made audiences invest more heavily in a stage show's specific song list and come to expect a more faithful version of the show on screen. Apart from this basic difference in song content, Hollywood was always eager to emphasize differences, often specifically cinematic; thus, they relied on naturalistic settings, added songs, larger-scale dance numbers, more fluid scene and act structures, and established film stars, among other strategies, to provide "more" than the stage version could and to compensate for the absent vitality of live performance.

The Music Man (Morton DaCosta, 1962) is a classic example of a film that remains fairly faithful to its stage predecessor, although it interweaves a new song and strives to create a fuller sense of the town of River City. But its train sequence illustrates the limitations of taking staged material to a "naturalized" screen. Here, the signal triumph of the stage's patter number, "Rock Island," depends on the actors bouncing in rhythm to create the illusion of a train's motion. This technique, though blatantly artificial, is brought intact to the screen, despite the "naturalized" setting of a "real train" emphasized by occasional cuts to train wheels (⏺ Example 10.4). Just as this scene is thus so clearly about reproducing a *stage* effect, filmed musicals in general, and especially adaptations, must often deliberately forgo the cinematic in order to provide adequate space for the artificialities of stage musicals. *Guys and Dolls* (Joseph Mankiewicz, 1955), another fairly faithful adaptation, is perhaps more forthright in mixing the artificial and the real, adding actual cars and pavement to what is clearly a stage set, and recreating much of the stage choreography for the screen. The latter film also exhibits other—to some, more transgressive—differences: using film star Marlon Brando despite his limitations as a singer, redistributing songs to accommodate the demands of Frank Sinatra, and dropping "Marry the Man Today" and "Bushel and a Peck" to make room for new songs.

Considered more distinctively as films, adaptations lie on a continuum between poles: filmed versions of theatrically staged productions, and versions that translate stage works into more distinctively cinematic styles. The first of these poles is not as straightforward as it has often seemed, which is an important consideration since for a significant number of musicals, it creates a primary object of study. One of the challenges that a filmed staging presents arises from its apparent documentary function: the film can seem implicitly to claim the status of an "innocent eye," offering simple secondary reportage of the genuine primary staged event. As such, the filmed staging is a surrogate for the theatrical performance, and the film itself might be taken to be interpretively transparent, with the particularities of its realization irrelevant to any close study of the show. But this is not true. A quick canvass of several filmed stagings will show that film as a medium exerts significant influence over the shaping of our experience of a staged work through the placement of shots, the choice and pacing of cuts, and other technical devices. Even the most minimal apparatus (such as a single camera aimed at center stage and including the entire stage picture in the frame) by its fixed point of view and exclusion of subsidiary senses such as touch and smell, frames the work in a way that does not occur in staged performances. Thus, Stephen Sondheim's *Passion* (1994), which was filmed and first broadcast on the PBS series "American Playhouse" in 1996, assumes a largely documentary point of view with respect to the way that it is filmed. But again, any form of cinéma vérité is always a necessarily stylized sampling of live performance, evident especially in the film's use of dissolves that superimpose images of the show's writers and recipients of letters as they share the dramatic act of singing them. However valuable the filmed staging may be in providing details of the theatrical performance, it is not identical to the theatrical work and must be treated as a work in its own right.

At the other pole lie films that create versions of musicals in which the theatrical apparatus is wholly absent. In a case such as *The Sound of Music* (1965), for instance, the picturesque environs of Salzburg are instrumental in creating a mise-en-scène of realism within which the song-and-dance of von Trappish courtship-and-politics takes place. That is, when songs are not in play, the film operates as a standard sound film shot on location, with interactions between characters managed largely as they would be in any nonmusical film of its period. The musical's status as a theatrical object is largely irrelevant to the shape of its filmic realization. In other films, such as *Cabaret* (1973) and *Chicago* (2002), nearly the reverse happens, as montage during songs allows realms of cinematic reality and fantasy to permeate more explicitly what was originally a theatrical space.

Especially in the case of musicals, a large number of intermediate forms between these poles loom large in the film tradition. They do not seek the modified cinematic realism of a film such as the *Sound of Music* nor the strictly theatrical milieu of *Passion*, but rather blend cinematic realism with various forms of stylization. The subgenre of the "backstage musical," for instance, establishes a stage world and a "real world" so that it can play on the difference between "life" and "performance" (but in backstage musicals such as *Broadway Melody of 1936*, or a more recent example such as *Fame* [1980, remade in 2009], performances end up occurring offstage as well as on). A particularly interesting case of a middle ground can be found in the film version of *South Pacific* (1958), which was shot in Technicolor, an intense process that amplifies color past the standards of realism in the late 1950s. In order to vary the intensity of the color, director Joshua Logan sought to use color filters during the performance of songs (this was a technique directly borrowed from the lighting effect used in the stage production). The process was enormously time-consuming, however, and Columbia Pictures refused to allow time to adjust the color from its lurid original. The result is spectacularly unrealistic, all the more so because of the role given the on-location sites of Kauai and Fiji. Thus, the visual aspect of *South Pacific* has been a source of critical dispute ever since the film's release and unquestionably exerts pressure on the ways that viewers understand the relationship between the musical numbers and the rest of the narrative (⊙ Example 10.5).

The increasing tendency to adapt films to the musical stage intertwines with the parallel rise in revivals and "revisals," and speaks also to the importance of film adaptations in building audiences for the latter. This co-dependency is especially evident when "revisals" are remade to resemble more closely the film versions, as in the 1998 Broadway staging of *Cabaret*, which incorporated many elements of Bob Fosse's 1973 film, or in revivals and repertory performances of *The Rocky Horror Show* that accommodate audience predilections to "call back" and otherwise participate in the show, continuing practices that bloomed during the film version's run at New York's Waverly Theater and other venues (*The Rocky Horror Picture Show*, Jim Sharman, 1975). In such cases, the filmed version effectively becomes the definitive version, a claim that may also be made for other filmed adaptations, even when, as in *Gentlemen Prefer Blondes* (Howard Hawks, 1953), song omissions and substitutions are more the rule than the exception.

THE WORLDS OF FILMED MUSICALS

Cinematic Realism and MERM

Narrative sound film typically maintains what André Bazin terms "the illusion of reality" through deploying its combination of images and sounds so as to seem natural to audiences, whether by directly simulating experienced reality or by following familiar conventions of cinematic storytelling. In classic Hollywood film and its derivatives, this mode of cinematic realism depends on such things as continuity (a consistent look and feel to the filmic world), maintaining a consistency of acting styles across the field (tending mainly toward restraint, so as not to seem to be playing to an audience), an aspect of cinematography that Bazin calls "cinematic tact" (maintaining a close relation to the human perspective), a seeming naturalness in the structure of narrative events, and the general subjugation of montage (especially associative montage) to a unity of space created through mise-en-scène.[7]

Musicals adjust the default aesthetic of cinematic realism at nearly every turn, because—on the most obvious level—in musical numbers characters appear to sing and dance their feelings in open violation of the restrained acting fostered by cinematic realism. Although these behaviors are often naturalized in various ways (particularly in backstage musicals), they nevertheless routinely depart from "the natural" in key respects. Thus, even if a character has a legitimizing reason to sing or dance, doing so brings into play a number of familiar tropes from musicals, such as the conceit that while singing in a musical number, a character is more honest than normal, more intensely present, more capable of interpersonal connection, more empowered, more empower*ing*, and generally better able to effect transformative change. Musical numbers, however they might be justified in terms of cinematic realism, thereby invoke what has been termed MERM (Musically Enhanced Reality Mode; see Knapp, 67–70 and *passim*), which is both a matter of the associated psychological dimensions of musical numbers and actual enhancements to the visual and aural experience of musical performance that have become typical of musical numbers in film.

MERM derives from stage musicals, where it has a similar profile in reception, but it has become even more vital to film musicals, because of both its challenges to cinematic realism and the capacity of film to intensify the presentation of musical numbers. Thus, regarding the latter, filmic MERM almost always includes lip-synching to prerecorded, studio-based singing, with non-diegetic instrumental and/or vocal support (that is, music that has no apparent source in the film's world). Through the device of performing to "playback" (the prerecorded track), not only might characters seem capable of singing effortlessly, regardless of how strenuous their physical activity might be, but the sound we hear will also remain uniformly good however the setting and positioning of the actor might change during a number: even a number filmed outdoors will, by default, have the focused, well-rounded sound of the studio. MERM might also include post-production manipulation of the performance's audio field—for example, through overdubbing taps to a dance routine, or by adding Foleys (sound effects) to enhance the cinematic reality of the scene, but which also (if they are done well) make the performance itself seem more immediate, if not fully believable as a filmed live performance. Other cinematic techniques may also be deployed more extravagantly to align with MERM (especially but not only in the work of Busby Berkeley). These might involve more elaborate camera positioning (crane shots and the like); montage; overt violations of the film's mise-en-scène (as when an actual stage mutates invisibly into an enormous sound stage in *42nd Street*, 1933); broader acting styles; otherwise unexplained adjustments to costume, sets, and lighting; an increased use of closeups; or other enhancements to the presentation whether or not an audience might be expected to notice them. Paradoxically, despite the blatant artificiality of the world created by and in coordination with MERM, the result is usually designed to create a heightened sense of reality, giving an extra charge to the performance of a musical number. This paradox provides the means by which MERM, especially through its capacity to highlight performance as such, might serve as a gateway to camp, allowing it to acquire a secure foothold in film musicals.

The differential between cinematic realism and MERM heightens the potentially difficult "reality" threshold that must be crossed to enter or leave the musical number. This threshold exists also in stage musicals, between the spoken play's dialogue and the sung (and/or danced) number, and it has been much discussed in that context.[8] But its disruptive capacity is even greater in its filmic form, with many possible consequences. Most common, perhaps, is the intensification of the pleasures afforded by the musical number's excursions from cinematic realism, perhaps releasing overtly into camp but in any case often veering toward the immoderate in both gesture and duration. More unusually, the threshold between cinematic realism and MERM may involve a collision of sensibilities or worldviews sufficiently extreme that it can overturn the genre itself. In some cases, "reality" becomes, in a sense, too "real" to support escape into a musical number, so that a film musical stops being a musical; examples include *The Wizard of Oz* (1939), where the last song, "If I Were King of the Forest," occurs just before Dorothy and her cohort have their audience with the Wizard, and *Meet Me in St. Louis* (1944), which stumbles forward with only an occasional song after Alonso Smith's announcement that the family will soon be moving to New York. (Notably, parallel examples for this phenomenon in stage musicals are extremely rare.) On the flip side of this phenomenon are traditionally narrative films that suddenly become musicals (generally, at or near the end). In one familiar example, *The Life of Brian* (1979), "Always Look on the

Bright Side of Life" is sung by a hillside of crucifixion victims, culminating the film's long series of outrages against cinematic realism. But there are more subtle examples, as well, such as *Bagdad Cafe* (1987) and *Bread and Tulips* (*Pane e Tulipani*, 2000), in which the final song-and-dance number both surprises and confirms the element of fantasy that has underwritten each film from the outset, however it may otherwise have behaved according to the conventions of cinematic realism.[9]

Sung Intimacy

Musicals on both stage and screen try to do two sometimes contradictory things through their musical numbers: to be intimately revealing of a character's inner life, and to indulge an audience's taste for opulent spectacle on a large scale. Although musicals on film lose the edge of immediacy and risk-taking that can add excitement to both intimacy and spectacle on the stage, film offers compensating opportunities to both realms. MERM, for example, can be used to augment both extravagant and intimate dimensions in a film's musical numbers. This is perhaps more obvious with the former; spectacle has from the beginning been a Hollywood specialty, and its capacity to indulge that predilection has been steadily enhanced by technology. In filmed musicals, there are few restraints on what might be used to pump up the (mostly non-diegetic) aural dimension of a large production number or to make a more modest number come across as "big"—although in their eagerness to outdo stage musicals, some films too readily abandon the framing that can make a full-scale ensemble number seem overwhelming on stage. Because MERM's capacity to enhance intimacy may on the other hand often pass unnoticed, we will focus here on the "small" rather than the "big."

In *Singin' in the Rain*, Don Lockwood overtly highlights the capacity of MERM to manage and enhance the expression of inner feelings by adding lighting effects, mist, and wind to the set as he prepares to sing "You Were Meant for Me" to Kathy Selden. But what may well pass unnoticed in this sequence is the way musical underscore and orchestration support these and other intimately drawn visual moments as the song and dance number gets under way, since orchestral underscore has long been a central device of Hollywood films, as dependable as lighting as a means to enhance intimacy (or withdraw from it, as when we pan out during the dance number for a breakout passage; ◉ Example 10.6). That we are more likely to notice this manner of scoring when it is absent than when it is present is deftly exploited to comic effect in *Moulin Rouge* (2001); thus, we may not even notice the faint musical background that continues to support Christian and Satine's moment of intimacy just after "Your Song"—until it is audibly "turned off" (that is, imitating the effect of stopping a record turntable) with the revelation that he is not a duke.

Even more subtle, and probably more common than not, is the effect of sudden intimacy that will accompany the movement into song on film (unless it is deliberately counteracted), as we leave the world of set- or location-generated sound (even if Foleyed in after the fact) for the world of prerecorded studio sound. In "Somewhere

Over the Rainbow" in *The Wizard of Oz*, for example, the studio recording gradually eclipses the background sounds of the farmyard as Dorothy begins the number, helping to effect the transition into Dorothy's inner world from the annoying, oblivious bustle of everyday reality (only to be displaced immediately after the song by a return to the mix of leitmotivic and familiar/generic "background" music provided by journeyman operetta composer Herbert Stothart, as the film cuts to Miss Gulch on her bicycle; ⊙ Example 10.7).

Musically framed intimacy has become the special province of film, always ready to be exploited by filmed musicals, especially in duet numbers. A particularly good example of the latter—even if, in sung terms, it is not exactly a duet—is "Over the Bannister" in *Meet Me in St. Louis*, which moves an increasingly intimate post-party progression from bustle to quietude as the guests leave, from light into shadows as Esther dims the lights, and from separation to proximity as, during the song, Esther descends the stairway to face John Truitt within a single frame. John has been our proxy until this moment, stammeringly in awe of Esther's beauty—her face lit by each dimming lamp in turn, the reduced lighting then circling around her auburn hair, creating a double halo for her softly bedimmed features—and cajoling her into prolonging the moment through song. Although one is likely to remember "Over the Bannister" less as a song and more for its surrounding qualities and John's comic inability to follow through, its somewhat stilted lyric and sweetly arched melodic lines fully support those qualities, especially by providing Judy Garland's voice and exquisitely nuanced visual delivery the opportunity to provide the aural equivalent for the caresses John is too timid to offer (⊙ Example 10.8).

Camp

The term "camp" has been used since the early twentieth century to refer to a style of performance and reception that favors the ostentatiously theatrical, the gaudily stylized.[10] As an attitude toward art, it may be understood as a democratization or carnivalization of the stance of the late nineteenth-century "dandy." In England, particularly, the Aesthetic movement, with its public relations slogan of "Art for Art's sake," was commonly equated with the complex associations of artists and attitudes that often carried labels such as "Symbolist" or "Decadent" in their French incarnations. In any case, in these cultural styles we typically find a rarefied attention to aesthetic nuance and detail coupled with a canny sense of public effect; consider the arch pronouncements of such fin-de-siècle figures as James Abbott MacNeill Whistler, Aubrey Beardsley, and especially Oscar Wilde. A sampling of Wilde's aphorisms points our attention toward the characteristic flavor of camp: "Music makes one feel so romantic—at least it always gets on one's nerves—which is the same thing; Illusion is the first of all pleasures; If you want to tell people the truth, make them laugh, otherwise they'll kill you." The role of paradox in these pithy one-liners translates into camp taste's preference for highly artificial "performances" that fail in one respect or another. For instance, if a style of theatrical acting prizes "realism," a camp point of view might tend willfully to elevate an instance of realism that has somehow gotten away from itself. Virtuosic skill in musical performance, for instance, is best for camp listeners if it is joined with completely implausible acting, or ludicrously inappropriate body type, or an unexpected and hilarious failure of costuming, scenery, or stage business.

The point of camp is not mockery by itself, but mockery that actually disguises an enormous tenderness toward the object or event under consideration. A camp appreciation of a great performer such as Ethel Merman, for instance, will probably pay special attention to Merman's well-known habit of moving to center stage and facing the audience directly whenever she was singing: dramatic plausibility, interactions with other performers, all such details of "realism" tended to be jettisoned in the interest of hurling that formidable sound toward the audience as overwhelmingly as possible. It seems likely, from Merman's own comments, that she saw this performance choice as a question of "giving the audience their money's worth." But for many listeners, the full-frontal sonic assault seems a capitulation to a spectacular narcissistic complex—and it's that very narcissism that wins the affection and sympathy of an audience predisposed to camp.

The example of Ethel Merman also raises the question of performers' intentions. In critical writings on camp, a distinction frequently appears between nonintentional and intentional camp. The nonintentional camp object is camp because a particular audience says it is, not because the creator strives to make it so. Intentional camp arises when the performer, clued into the interpretive practices of the specific marginal audience, deliberately plays to them. In-jokes and sly subcultural references are thickly constellated around an ostensibly "straight" performance.

Whether intentional or not, such modes of performance and appreciation operate by projecting a dualistic structure that distinguishes between essences and accidents, that is, between "real interiors" and "artificial exteriors." In musicals, for instance, there is "the character" being performed, but there is also a "real person" playing that character, and a camp moment represents the place where the concerns of the "real person" suddenly override, and hilariously sabotage, the decorum of performance that allowed "the character" to be formulated in the first place. Thus, the "failure" of performance represents on another level the triumph of the "true self" that crafted that performance. This also helps explain the preference of camp attitudes for styles of presentation and performance that are just slightly outmoded: when a hairstyle, for instance, is just beginning to be out of date, it looks silly, but when it has been out of date for a significant period, it tends to look merely "historical." What is happening in this case has to do with conventions and stylizations— they begin to seem passé because the fashion shifts, but they cannot go along for the ride. Thus, the very details that once passed unnoticed, because they merely seemed to be "natural," begin to become uncomfortably apparent and anything *but* "natural." The revelation of forgeries by the passing of time has become something of a cliché in art connoisseurship, primarily because it depends upon this consensus understanding of conventions' historical nature. But unlike the dubious objet d'art, which becomes less valuable because its failed conventions expose its meretricious "inner nature," the camp artifact becomes all the more funny and yet touching because its inadequacies seem like deeply human failings. Nearly everyone has at one time or another experienced an embarrassing failure of what the sociologist Erving Goffman called "impression management"; camp tastes tend to take such failures as the very incarnation of the values they hold most dear. As the façade cracks open, we may have a chance to glimpse the truth of interiority.

Not surprisingly, these modes of representation and interpretation have been especially appealing to stigmatized social groups who were able to "pass." Since the very notion of passing posits a "real self" that is prior to, more important than, and more vulnerable than the social self, the dualistic structure outlined above models the tensions and embodies the risks inherent in such social strategies. Jews and especially homosexuals, as the exemplary passing minorities of twentieth-century America, tended to adopt camp positions as a form of "in-house" culture-making. But with all due respect to Susan Sontag, whose famous essay "Notes on Camp," asserted a contrast between "Jewish moral seriousness" and "homosexual aestheticism and irony," these two "forms of modern sensibility" turn out to overlap in remarkable, intricate ways that would require a separate study to discuss.[11] For our purposes here, what matters is the imbrication of aesthetico-political concerns especially poignant for Jews and for queer folks in the texts and performances that constituted the musical as a genre. "Realism," to the extent that it underwrites a tendency to regard cultural norms as "natural," is the enemy of all marginal(ized) social groups and identities; and because the musical gave only lip service (at best) to the practices and moral commitments of "realism," it was one of the most hospitable of genres to camp styles and receptions. And to the degree that audience members who occupied less socially marginal positions accommodated themselves to the characteristic practices of the in-house audiences, they became proficient at camp reception as well. And the camp reading practices thus absorbed were relevant to film and stage musicals alike.

A striking example of intentional camp in film musicals is MGM's 1948 vehicle *The Pirate* (produced by Arthur Freed, songs by Cole Porter, directed by Vincente Minnelli, starring Judy Garland and Gene Kelly). From the film's first frames, the musical sets up a spectacle of marvelous visual and sonic gaudiness. Technicolor was always the most strenuously vivid of the color film processes, but everything in the mise-en-scène—especially the crazy costumes—amps up the chromatism. The arrangements of the songs, too, are timbrally polychromatic, especially to the degree that Latin influences enfold themselves into the score. Both Garland and Kelly are terrifically sly about the details of performance: pacing and intonation of lines, gestural complexes and postures (especially facial ones—viewers may often note a tendency for different parts of the actors' faces to express opposed emotions, a sure tip-off to their performance of serious frivolity). That is, at nearly every level of the film's construction, there is a bias toward anti-realism—a kind of anti-realism, moreover, that was by 1948 distinctly on the wane.[12] To add to the contexts of reception, the audiences who were "in the know" at the time of the film's premiere would have been aware of some off-camera details about the lives of the film's creators—

Freed's taste for hiring gay men to work in his MGM production unit (Freed's Fairies), the complicated sexual orientations of Porter and Minnelli, Garland's evolving status as a gay icon—that would likely have facilitated camp readings of the film (⊙ Example 10.9; ⊙ Example 10.10). The case was otherwise with audiences not-so-marginal; *The Pirate* met with mixed critical reactions and tepid box office, and its reputation has improved only gradually.

But it would be a mistake to assume that camp practices of presentation and interpretation maintained themselves unchanged over the course of the twentieth century. Sontag's 1964 essay, along with the critical treatment of the work of avant-garde filmmakers such as Jack Smith or Kenneth Anger, and most important, nearly everything associated with Andy Warhol, reveal the translation of camp stances into a more mainstreamed cluster of interpretive attitudes. This could be considered typical of the ways mainstream commercial culture harvests motifs, styles, and attitudes from various American subcultures over the course of the twentieth century.[13] But in the wake of the Stonewall Rebellion in 1969, when a more active and confrontational phase of gay politics began to exert major pressure on the customary social arrangements of American society, the mainstreaming impulses that in Sontag or Warhol seemed avant-gardishly rarefied were brought to a much wider public.

One of the most influential post-Stonewall musicals to articulate a camp point of view is *The Rocky Horror Picture Show* (1975). Although space does not permit a detailed analysis, a number of its aspects that attract camp can be observed. The film begins with a nostalgic recollection of 1950s science fiction films—by the beginning of the 1970s, a kind of film that would be available only as a late-night film or a television rerun. In either case, such science fiction films were, even when first released, relatively low in status,[14] and, especially because the genre is so preoccupied with technology, the mise-en-scéne of science fiction films erodes more quickly than in almost any other genre. The rapid obsolescence of these films, together with the second-rate status of their later broadcastings, made science fiction an ultra-powerful camp-magnet (⊙ Example 10.11). Similarly, the musical style, which tends toward the démodé (most overtly in the song "Hot Patootie—Bless My Soul," but in numerous less foregrounded musical details as well), attracts campish attentions and affections. The generic and musical framework of recycling resonates strongly with the frequent reference in the plot and dialogue to precedents from 1950s films ("normal, healthy kids," "juvenile delinquents," and so on), but just as strongly with the peculiar erotic bricolage of the Transylvanians, eventually revealed to be space aliens passing as humans.

The most critical difference between the camp attitudes of *The Pirate* and those of *The Rocky Horror Picture Show* have everything to do with the vast amount of social change that separates their periods of genesis. Dr. Frank-N-Furter can flash his corset and fishnets, and serially seduce everyone who takes his fancy, because by 1975, a panoply of tastes and styles that were unrepresentable even a decade before had become public and voluble. By contrast, the exotic desires expressed in *The Pirate*—especially the marvelously steamy dance-dream sequence—had to be expressed mostly by connotation. For that matter, the number "Voodoo" was famously cut by Mayer because it was far too overtly sexual for his sense of what the censor would allow.

But in both cases, the central point remains: by their affection for conventions—those agreements of social style that seem so powerful until toppled, as they inevitably are by their inherent weaknesses—camp attitudes make up one of the most powerful modes of interpretation in the musical, especially the musical film. Though Hollywood may thunder, "Pay no attention to the man behind the curtain," the musical on film is prone to pull the curtain back. And to the extent that we experience camp as one of the central possibilities of the musical on film, we can respond to its pleasures in toto, too.

NOTES

1. Rick Altman, *The American Film Musical* (Bloomington: Indiana University Press, 1987); a similar narrowness of focus may be found in Jane Feuer, *The Hollywood Musical*, 2nd ed. (Bloomington: Indiana University Press, 1992), among other studies.

2. A useful guide to these and other elements central to the study of film is David Bordwell and Kristin Thompson's *Film Art: An Introduction*, 8th ed. (Boston: McGraw-Hill, 2008).

3. *Montage* can refer in general terms, as here, to the assembly of shots (or cuts) within a film, although it has a number of more specific applications as well. Soviet filmmakers in the 1920s (e.g., Lev Kuleshov, Vsevolod Pudovkin, and Sergei Eisenstein) practiced and theorized montage as a means for creating filmic meaning through the juxtaposition of images, often in violation of continuity. And montage, used as a singular noun, is frequently used to refer to a filmic sequence (a "montage sequence") in which a quick succession of images suggests the passage of time, or a series of simultaneous occurrences, often to the accompaniment of music. A "musical montage" uses a musical number (song and/or dance) to frame a montage sequence, whether temporally based (as in a classic montage sequence) or associative (as in Soviet montage). The final reprise of "Let Me Entertain You" in the stage show *Gypsy* (1959) offers an example of musical montage, as a device, being imported to the stage, reminiscent of "Fit as a Fiddle" in *Singin' in the Rain*, among others.

4. While this process of substitution is often called "dubbing"—which would mean recording elements of a soundtrack to add to (or replace) the soundtrack of an already edited film, as is common with sound effects, or as an alternative to subtitles in foreign-language films—it is almost always used inaccurately when applied to musical numbers (the central plotline of *Singin' in the Rain* notwithstanding).

5. See Todd Decker, *Music Makes Me: Fred Astaire and Jazz* (Berkeley: University of California Press, forthcoming); see also his "Black/White Encounters on the American Musical Stage and Screen (1924–2005)" (Ph.D. dissertation, University of Michigan, Ann Arbor, 2007). Decker also details Astaire's own role in shaping the number, citing Kern's lack of affinity for the type of rhythm number Astaire wanted in this spot ("Bojangles" was a late addition to the score), and Astaire's lack of real involvement with choreographing the song itself, focusing instead on his own dance, in which Kern's "Bojangles" song plays no part.

6. For more on this dimension of *Stormy Weather*, see Raymond Knapp, *The American Musical and the Performance of Personal Identity* (Princeton, NJ: Princeton University Press, 2006), pp. 79–94.

7. Although the list of attributes here is of our own devising, they overlap with many described and discussed by Bazin in a series of seminal essays, including "The Evolution of the Language of Cinema" (1950, 1952, and 1955), "The Virtues and Limitations of Montage" (1953 and 1957), and "An Aesthetic of Reality" (1948). See André Bazin, "The Evolution of the Language of Cinema" and "The Virtues and Limitations of Montage" (*What Is Cinema? Essays Selected and Translated by Hugh Gray*, Vol. 1 [Berkeley: University of California Press, 2005, originally published 1967], pp. 23–52), and "An Aesthetic of Reality: Neorealism (Cinematic Realism and the Italian School of Liberation)" (*What Is Cinema?: Essays Selected and Translated by Hugh Gray*, Vol. 2 [Berkeley: University of California Press, 2005, originally published 1971], pp. 16–40).

8. See especially Scott McMillin, *The Musical as Drama: A Study of the Principles and Conventions behind Musical Shows from Kern to Sondheim* (Princeton, NJ: Princeton University Press, 2006).

9. For more on the phenomena described here, see Raymond Knapp, "Getting Off the Trolley: Musicals *contra* Cinematic Reality" (forthcoming in *From Stage to Screen*, ed. Massimiliano Sala, vol. 18 of *Speculum Musicae* [Turnhout, Belgium: Brepols Publishers]).

10. The term is popularly supposed to derive from slang usage of the French verb *se camper*, "to encamp, plant onself; *slang*—to pose in an exaggerated fashion," but this is not very well supported by research.

11. Sontag's often-reprinted essay probably owes much of its fame to the way that it turned one of the major cultural practices of a then-despised minority culture into a tool of high modernist critical scrutiny. This is not to say that the essay was generally welcomed by the gay people whose sensibility was being characterized.

12. The way that Kelly manages a waggish version of Errol Flynn's swashbuckling, even more than the vaudevillian orientation of the film's musical numbers, aims to establish the prevailing mood of hilarious anachronism. The creak of the conventions is not only deliberate but it is also central to the film's overall aesthetic.

13. Queer styles, black styles, and Jewish styles have historically been the most frequently exploited resources for mainstream renovation, though other liminal types (Latinos, poor Southern whites) have also come in for a degree of appropriation as well.

14. The genre's prestige rose dramatically after the 1977 release of *Star Wars*.

CHAPTER 11

....

THE TELEVISION MUSICAL

....

ROBYNN J. STILWELL

THE musical is a genre split between two dominant media, theater and cinema. While the dialogue and lead sheets may be nearly identical between the two, the differences are stark and can significantly effect the *affect* for the audience. Those medium-specific differences are highlighted by the fact that theatrical musicals tend to be studied by theater and performance scholars, cinematic musicals by film scholars; the creative heart of the genre, the music, is studied by musicologists, if at all—that in itself is a recent development, and all these groups are only just beginning to talk to each other.

One of the manifestations of the musical that has been left out of the discussion almost entirely is the television musical. The reasons for the relative neglect are manifold, interlocking, and conditioned by disciplinary boundaries. In addition to the strong divide that has existed between the studies of film and theater (and music), television has been largely the province of communications, in which interest was significantly slanted away from textual analysis toward institutional structures and ethnography.

Television musicals have also been a relative historical blip, at their most pertinent in the 1950s and into the 1960s. Many of the original broadcasts during the 1950s were either not recorded or are too inaccessible for most scholars, let alone for a casual audience; moreover, they increasingly became targeted toward children, based on fairy tales, often starring performers familiar from Hollywood musicals like the *Pied Piper of Hamelin* (1957) starring Van Johnson, or *Jack and the Beanstalk* (1967) starring and directed by Gene Kelly. The musical, across all media, receded in importance to the mainstream of entertainment—although that impression has been amplified because of the amount of attention given to the rise of rock music and youth culture in the media of the time and certainly in the scholarship since, a tendency only now beginning to be redressed.

Television was also a new medium in the 1950s, and in terms of its own specific qualities, it was still finding its way. Like many new technologies, particularly those that were in some way in a circular/spiraling relationship between perception and representation, television began by mimicking older technologies;[1] though photography emulated painting and cinema emulated theater and photography, television had at least three primary antecedents: live theater; film, which had developed its own language in the half-century before the widespread embrace of television; and, as is often lost in the discussion, radio. Television is as at least as much an audio medium as it a visual one.

The presentation of musicals on television began by most closely mimicking live theater. Within a decade, the development of videotape and more fluid camera technique led to a distinctive television language. Over time, television became more and more like film in many respects, while still retaining some native elements, and by the 1980s, the techniques of music video were the cutting edge of cinematic language, infiltrating film from television. Arguably, such television shows as *Miami Vice* and *Moonlighting* are more uniquely television musicals than the more obvious *Cop Rock*, *Ally McBeal*, *Scrubs*, and *Eli Stone*, or special "musical episodes", particularly those in such late 1990s fantasy fare as *Xena: Warrior Princess* and *Buffy the Vampire Slayer*. However, no single television musical better allows us the opportunity to explore a developing medium than Rodgers and Hammerstein's *Cinderella*, first produced as a major event in 1957 starring a rising young singer-actress, Julie Andrews. It was revived twice, once with Rodgers's participation, in a 1965 televised performance that was repeated annually for a decade; and in a 1997 version for Disney television, as part of a cycle of revivals that also included *Annie*.[2]

The three different versions of *Cinderella* offer a chance to look not only at the specificity of a musical made for television but also at the medium as it changes over the forty years between the first and third—and indeed, perhaps even more significantly in the seven years between the first and second. A case study such as this demonstrates some of the key questions that may arise when dealing with a television musical.

THE THREE PRODUCTIONS: AN OVERVIEW[3]

Cinderella was part of a cycle of televised musicals in the 1950s, whether versions of Broadway musicals (*Annie Get Your Gun, Kiss Me Kate, Peter Pan*) or newly composed (1956's *High Tor* starred Bing Crosby and a pre-*My Fair Lady* Julie Andrews). Richard Rodgers and Oscar Hammerstein II were the reigning kings of Broadway, and the initial production was a significant prestige event, broadcast on CBS in 1957.

This first version was performed live in a complex soundstage set. The liveness and the integral set meant that the performance was closest to a theatrical production (although the use of cameras also meant that the audience was moved around several "fronts" on the stage). The actors were primarily from Broadway, though some supporting actors (notably stepsisters Kaye Ballard and Alice Ghostley) also became important players in the new medium. The acting style is theatrical, slightly restrained to the small scale of the television screen, particularly the small screen of the 1950s. The story is the spun-sugar fantasy of a classic fairy tale. The King and Queen, played by Broadway veteran couple Howard Lindsay and Dorothy Stickney, are benevolent monarchs, but also recognizably a middle-class, middle-American, middle-aged couple. Edie Adams is a young fairy Godmother who straddles the theater, television, and popular recordings/nightclub singing. All of the supporting characters have more delineation than the central couple; Julie Andrews's Cinderella is clearly the antecedent of Disney's searching Belle from *Beauty and the Beast*, but she is also much more demure and composed. Jon Cypher's Prince is commonly tagged with the obvious "cipher," but, well . . . it's true. He is so generic as to be almost invisible; the couple does not meet until the ball, and the love-at-first-sight plot is acceptable as a fairy tale.

The 1965 version was shot on soundstages, with much simpler and more spacious sets. While the 1957 version has a rococo design aesthetic, the 1965 is a combination of the modern and the medieval. The minimalist sets are clearly artificial and in some cases simply flat cut-outs. The designs recall less Charles Perrault than the Brothers Grimm. The older cast members are movie stars—Walter Pidgeon and Ginger Rogers play the King and Queen, Celeste Holm is the Fairy Godmother, Jo Van Vleet (also, of course, a theatrical actress) is the Stepmother, and television actresses Barbara Ruick and Pat Carroll play the sisters. Newcomers Lesley Ann Warren and Stuart Damon are at the beginnings of lifelong careers in (mostly) television. Unlike in the 1957 production, we get a sense of both Cinderella and the Prince; they meet and connect early in the plot, and therefore the falling in love seems much more plausible.

The Disney version is strongly centered on the voice. The property was purchased by Whitney Houston as a starring vehicle for herself; by the time it went into production, she was in her early thirties and looked to find another Cinderella while she herself took the role of the Fairy Godmother. As a consequence, the latter role is more prominent in this version than in the other two. The casting of Brandy (Norwood) further emphasizes the voice, as she was primarily identified as a singer (though also the star of the sitcom *Moesha*), and Paolo Montalban (the Prince) is a Broadway performer. The role of the Prince is considerably more "generic adolescent" than the Prince of the 1965 version, while not being quite as much of a cipher as the 1957 Prince. Compared to the 1965 version, the relationship between the Prince and Cinderella is both more and less developed: in terms of musical theater convention, their sense of being destined for each other is strengthened structurally by a parallel introduction; unlike the Prince and Cinderella in the 1965 version, however, they are introduced more as a couple and less as two individuals: instead of each getting a song, they perform a duet across a crowded market square, creating their bond through the voice.

Book

Hammerstein expressed respect for the classic fairy tale, but a number of 1950s stereotypes appear in his teleplay, most notably in the "comic" supporting characters: the King and Queen are a typical middle-aged, middle-class mid-century couple familiar from the family sitcom of the era—he is vaguely oblivious to the family dynamics and his expanding waistline, she is seen mending his trousers and tidying the ballroom with a feather duster and a kerchief tied around her hair beneath her crown while worrying about her dreamy son; the stepsisters are less mean than stupid and thoughtless.

The characterization of these two pairs of characters changes perhaps most in the three versions; the King and Queen move with the times, not least in the portrayal of their relationship to one another and the expectations of middle-aged love. If Lawson and Stickney are an old married couple, Rogers and Pidgeon (appropriately, given their status as beloved romantic movie leads of an earlier era) are nostalgic and romantic; and Whoopi Goldberg and Victor Garber have a bantering affection with glimpses of actual sexual attraction. Goldberg's Queen is the flightiest and most comic of the three, and yet she seems to want her son's happiness the most. The stepsisters have a simpler trajectory, becoming increasingly comical and ridiculous through the three productions. Veanne Cox's gawky Calliope and Natalie Desselle's enthusiastic Minerva are superficial and exaggerated, more broadly comedic. Pat Carroll's Prunella and Barbara Ruick's Esmeralda are almost as exaggerated as Cox and Desselle in their character traits, but both also betray a humanity that stands out in relief to their more cartoonish aspects. This is particularly notable in the post-ball kitchen table scene, in which Prunella admits that the Prince danced with her only for a moment, and Esmeralda admits the same: in both other versions, the stepsisters claim that they each danced with the Prince for an hour or more. While Ghostley's Joy and Ballard's Portia also have their moments of vulnerability, they somehow seem more beaten down and pathetic. Robert L. Freedman's 1997 script, particularly in dealing with the Stepmother and Stepsisters, combines a number of lines of dialogue from both earlier versions, leaning more heavily on Hammerstein's in terms of word count, but hewing closer to Joseph Schrank's 1965 version in emotional tone.

The 1965 version is, arguably, *more* fairy tale–like than Hammerstein's book. In design and mythology, it is medieval in setting. And in perhaps the most drastic difference between the original and the 1965 version—and indeed, the 1997 version—this Prince Charming is a genuine character with a sense of humor and more concrete desires. Stuart Damon's Prince (the only one never called Christopher or Chris in the dialogue) is not a courtier or a student, but a knight. He's been off slaying dragons and rescuing damsels and is bored.

Schrank's book makes the story less about Cinderella than about this couple, as is evident from the beginning. We actually meet the Prince first, returning from a year of travel. Tired and thirsty, he stops by a thatched cottage, and a shy girl peeks out the window, her face smudged with soot—our first glimpse of Cinderella. Despite her fear of her Stepmother's retribution, she offers the Prince a dipper of cool water, and their dialogue is echoed throughout at structural moments:

PRINCE: "Thank you most kindly."
CINDERELLA: "You are most kindly welcome."

The exchange is a moment of connection between them at the ball, when he thanks her for the dance, and at the end when he has come with the glass slipper and she again offers him water.

This structural rigor—conventional, yes, but narratively powerful in creating a relationship in only an hour and twenty minutes—is fleshed out with parallel scenes. After the Prince leaves Cinderella's cottage, he pauses to sing the interpolated "The Loneliness of Evening" against the stylized backdrop of a ruined church in the distance. The placement, and Damon's fervent performance, recall "Something's Coming" in *West Side Story* combined with the "I wish" song familiar from the later Disney musicals. Thus, this Prince has an identity, a personality, and, most important, a *song* the equal of Cinderella's. Because it comes first, its relative shortness (two choruses) is not immediately noticeable, even though Cinderella's "In My Own Little Corner" (the opposite of an "I wish" song, in a way) runs to several choruses and an in-scene reprise. At the end of the musical, each lead also has a solo that features a non-diegetic reminiscence of the other, as is discussed in more detail later in the chapter.

This structural bonding between Cinderella and the Prince is used efficiently (if perhaps not as substantially) in the 1997 version, where the leads meet through Richard Rodgers's "The Sweetest Sound," interpolated from *No Strings*. This choice may have been cued by a line in the original Hammerstein book, in which the Prince says that Cinderella's voice is the sweetest sound he's ever heard (Block 198). The relationship between the Prince and Cinderella is still the catalyst of the plot, but more attention is given to other characters, particularly the Fairy Godmother, the Stepmother, and the major-domo of the castle, Lionel—undoubtedly a function of casting Whitney Houston, Bernadette Peters, and Jason Alexander, respectively. Perhaps due to casting, perhaps due to changed sensibilities, the romance between the Cinderella and the Prince in this version seems more youthful; at the end, the procession to the castle seems less like going to a wedding and more like going to the prom. While less of a fairy tale, it is also a more realistic contemporary depiction of young love.

MUSIC

"Cinderella" is a late Rodgers and Hammerstein show, their last but for *The Sound of Music* (1959), and while distinct Rodgers fingerprints exist in the score ("In My Own Little Corner" is first cousin, if not sibling, to "Whistle a Happy Tune"; the big love song is a waltz), it is also a bit less lush and romantic harmonically than previous scores, leaning toward the more astringent and linear harmonies of Rodgers's later scores, notably 1962's *No Strings,* Rodgers's first post-Hammerstein musical and source of "The Sweetest Sound," with its minor key and downward chromatic motion, easily interpolated into the 1997 version.

The songs of *Cinderella* seem to have a delicacy quite different from the bumptious Americanness of "Kansas City" or "I'm Gonna Wash That Man Right Outa My Hair," or even "Shall We Dance." The Fairy Godmother's "Impossible" has a trotting rhythm like that of "The Surrey with the Fringe on Top," but with a large leap down on the downbeat ("Impossible!"), rather than the upward escape at the end of the phrase ("scurry"). That melodic profile gives a very different feel, as does the inflection of the rhythm: whereas "Surrey" has a relaxed sway, "Impossible" pushes forward, creating anticipation. The melodic curve of "Impossible" reflects the lyrics' emotional progression remarkably well: "Impossible!" is an emphatic denial; the diatonic downward march "for a plain country bumpkin and a prince to join in marriage" over steady V–I repetitions composes a statement of inexorable logic; then, as "folderol" and "fiddle-dee-dee" are called on repeated notes, the pitch creeps upward chromatically at the ends of phrases, suggesting doubt, before "impossible!" asserts the new tonic. The bridge likewise stresses repeated notes on the tonic (G) which is now the dominant of a plagal-side excursion that oscillates between C major and minor—those "who don't believe in sensible rules" keep building up hopes in driving phrases of repeated pitches that eventually rise up and break through the B♭ to B♮ in the tonic major (G) of the title phrase. All this resistance to the pull of the tonic seems like hesitation, doubt, even sarcasm in "Impossible," but inexorability and exhilaration in the reprise, "It's possible."

Cinderella's two primary solo songs are "In My Own Little Corner" and "Lovely Night," Both have a light but emphatic duple rhythm and balance strong diatonic grounding with playful chromatic lines that add both wistfulness and intensity to the songs (◗ Example 11.1; ◗ Example 11.2; (◖ Example 11.3). While it is entirely possible that this chromatic tendency, especially toward the flat side, was an emerging trait of Rodgers's late style, it makes the interpolation of "The Sweetest Sound" all the more appropriate. The striking A section of the song relies heavily on emphasized dissonances that fall on ♯4 and ♭2/♯1. The melody descends chromatically, decorated by escape tones, but is otherwise very similar to the whole-tone descent in the coda-like extension of "Lovely Night," giving coherence to the interpolated duet while emphasizing Cinderella as a character. The chromatic sliding is a long-standing sign of feminine sexuality, and these short strands emerging out of a largely diatonic context may be a symbol of Cinderella's awakening yearnings out of innocence.

The major song for the Prince generates excitement in another, more linear fashion, remaining a "masculine" diatonic even in the context of a waltz, normally heard as a feminine rhythm (the Prince is a bit of a "new man," particularly in the later two adaptations; Jon Cypher's Prince doesn't have enough of a personality to tell either way). While not as famous as the elegantly balanced, chromatically inflected *Carousel* Waltz, "Ten Minutes Ago" is arguably one of Rodgers's finest moments as a dramatic composer.

The A section starts with a quiet, narrow, rocking melody under "Ten minutes ago, I saw you," which repeats, then sequences up a third. It feels like a much larger leap, in part because the harmony shifts from a solid tonic-dominant to a descending sequence, initiated with a secondary dominant.[4] Additionally, the melody does not take the balanced pause of the first half of the period—the rocking motion swings through the expected break (rather like the extended sequence of the A" of "Lovely Night"), creating a greater forward impetus. In the second repetition of A, this sense of swinging motion is emphasized, rather than impeded, by a sudden rest after the word "bells," allowing the word to "peal" out through the sudden cessation of accompaniment and sharpening of the rhythm. It is also a foreshadowing of the dramatic B section which sweeps up to "I have found" with a similar emphatic rest afterward, emphasized by the fall down to "her," a sixth lower, a phrase then sequenced downward on "she's an angel." The repetition gives similar emphasis to "danc-" and "fly-" while the drops on the "ing" part of the gerundial verb form keep the movement sailing across the rest. As with "Impossible" and "Lovely Night," the large leaps over a driving rhythm have a sweep that not only mimics the Prince's elated feelings but can also invoke them in the listener.

The songs are undoubtedly the focus of musical energy of the three versions, but other musical aspects also shape the productions. As much as the sets, the musical direction reflects the medium-specific aspects: the 1957 version is very close to a stage production, with a small, wind-heavy pit orchestra and little underscoring. The 1997 version has a full orchestra, lush orchestration, and a heavily leitmotivic underscore; very little is *not* underscored. The 1965 version is somewhere in between, with a pit orchestra but also more bridging cues and underscore than 1957.

CASTING AND PERFORMANCE

Casting can be crucial in any production, and the approach to casting in each of the three versions of *Cinderella* changed with the times, influencing the effect of each adaptation. The cast of the 1957 version is primarily from the stage; the cast of the 1965 version blends a leading couple new to television with an older generation from the silver screen; the 1997 version features singers above all, some from the stage but more significantly from popular music.

Cinderella was part of the constellation of roles that would, within a decade, make Julie Andrews an icon. At only twenty-one, she came to *Cinderella* as an established Broadway leading lady. The *My Fair Lady* original cast album had been a huge hit in 1956, and the roles of Eliza, Cinderella, Mary Poppins, and Maria von Trapp together created a strong star text by mutually reinforcing several qualities: a good heart, an impish sense of humor, and slightly varying rebelliousness, all nonetheless correct, polite, always easily contained in the socially acceptable. Andrews's voice is extremely precise in pitch, timbral clarity, and diction, strongly reinforcing the impression/illusion that she is a "good girl," not least because it betrays a training that is tinged with class privilege.[5]

Is it coincidence or a direct influence that the unknown chosen to play Cinderella in 1965 looks so much like Audrey Hepburn, the actress who controversially was cast instead of Andrews in the film version of *My Fair Lady*? Although slightly more robust than Hepburn in frame, Lesley Ann Warren is also a dancer and has the same triangular face, pointed nose, and large dark eyes. The resemblance is certainly emphasized by the parallel scenes in which Hepburn as Eliza and Warren as Cinderella appear at the ball—both are wearing empire-waisted gowns of ivory with touches of gold that emphasize their long necks, and their hair is wound on top of their heads inside a tiara (see Figure 11.1). Warren's imperfect voice (and teeth) and her obvious youth give us a heroine whom audiences might more readily recognize as a teenager, where Andrews seems already a grown woman (see Figure 11.2).

Warren and Norwood were both eighteen, though the difference in experience is significant. Compared to newcomer Warren, Brandy was already a pop star and had starred in two sitcoms, including her title role in *Moesha* (1996–2001).[6] The sitcom quality of Brandy's acting is obvious in her version, in overreactions and arch line readings, as if they were punch lines rather than emotionally generated phrases. The 1997 version is of a piece with the Disney animated musicals of the era, and Brandy's Cinderella is very much more like Belle than either of her predecessors, thoughtful and self-determined. Her most effective moments as an actress are when she asserts herself and the power of individuality.

The Princes were all unknowns when cast, but Stuart Damon has subsequently had the most successful career, in British and American television. His prince is practical and obedient, though still a bit of a dreamer, with a deadpan

Figure 11.1 Audrey Hepburn as Eliza Doolittle; Lesley Ann Warren as Cinderella

Figure 11.2 Julie Andrews and Lesley Ann Warren as Cinderella

humor that carried over into his later roles. He has a stronger, better-trained voice than Warren's, but as with her, his acting penetrates his voice, something that happens with neither other central couple. This is notable, for instance, in the first bridge of "Ten Minutes Ago," when his joy at finding his love stretches his vowels and adds a slightly tremulous undercurrent to his baritone, broadening and flattening the vowels. You can hear the exhilarated laughter trapped just beneath his larynx, pushing to escape, and it adds impetus to the releases on those high points in the B section in a melding of performance and song. The song hints at that performance, even encourages it, but neither of the other princes pull it off in the same way (▶ Example 11.4).

The performances of Norwood and Montalban are slightly more stilted, and they have less obvious chemistry—those nuances of body language and timing that are perceptible but hard to quantify or describe. They are primarily singers, performing for an audience most familiar with animated Disney musicals and music videos. A duet is a stronger choice than the paired solos in this version, lessening the burden on their simple screen presence and adding to the attraction of their voices. Unlike the live 1957 version or the half-playback (recorded backing track, live-recorded voices) of the 1965 one, the highly produced recordings of the 1997 version were made first and played back for filming. Brandy's relatively fragile voice can thus be boosted, particularly in duets, although it is also evident that Montalban is restraining his stage belt on occasion (▶ Example 11.5).

As mentioned earlier, the supporting casting causes shifts in the various productions: as King and Queen, Stickney and Lawson bring solidity and gravitas as old Broadway pros, whereas Rogers and Pidgeon recall the romantic films of the classical Hollywood period. Comedienne Whoopi Goldberg and versatile singer-actor Victor Garber create a more modern couple of two individuals, with both shifting power relationships and a spark of sexuality. The Stepsisters are always comic relief and become more exaggerated with each iteration, but certainly Alice Ghostley's dithering, glum Joy and Kaye Ballard's distinctly New York-Jewish Portia are recognizable manifestations of their individual personae.

Of the Stepmothers, Bernadette Peters has by far the biggest role, not surprisingly, given that she is the dominant Broadway musical star of her generation and well known to television audiences. She is given her own comical romantic partnering with Lionel—a part that *becomes* a part for sitcom and Broadway star Jason Alexander—and her own song. Another interpolation, Rodgers and Hart's "Falling in Love with Love" might seem an odd choice historically, given that it comes from an earlier stage of Rodgers's career, but it makes some musical sense in the fast waltz tempo that has the same anticipatory urgency as "My Own Little Corner" and "Lovely Night," but with more drive, as is appropriate for a conniving Stepmother who knows what she wants. Likewise, the Fairy Godmother role, for producer Whitney Houston, is strengthened, giving her a status recalling such interactive narrators as the Stage Manager in Thornton Wilder's *Our Town* or Che in *Evita*.[7]

The performances reflect their times and the media that shape the performers. While Cypher and Andrews perform like operetta stars—their body language at times strongly recalls Jeanette MacDonald and Nelson Eddy, stylized, conventional, polite (● Example 11.6)—and Norwood and Montalban perform like pop stars in a rock video that looks like a musical, with a mobile camera and multiple quick cuts, Warren and Damon perform like *actors*. Damon in particular looks at Warren with such intense adoration, more Gene Kelly and Judy Garland than MacDonald and Eddy. They remind us of the shifting terrain of musical production between the first two productions—without doubt, both are possessed of the talent and star quality to succeed in film musicals, but the genre is dying. And the subtlety of their performances, the flickers of emotion across their faces and the engagement of their eyes, together with the slight imperfections of their vocal performances, made them weaker candidates for the stage. They are meant to be seen on camera.

TECHNOLOGICAL FRAMES AND LENSES

The first, live broadcast version was preserved on a kinescope, though widely unavailable until the 2004 DVD release. Because it was a live broadcast, it has many of the same constraints as a live performance—quick changes, entrances and exits that have to be blocked and timed, a set that is constricted in space, for instance. The difference is that while the camera is not particularly mobile in 1957—dollies in and out are the major form of "camera movement" that are used, and those sparingly—the production employed multiple cameras, which allow different angles, and "editing" occurs live in a control room, as the director switches from one camera/set-up to another.

The camera does allow for a more three-dimensional set than would be possible on a stage. Some of the larger sets—the ballroom, the village square, the royal chambers, the palace gardens, and the downstairs area of Cinderella's home—allow a fairly fluent application of the multiple camera technique, deploying large master shots of the entire area with cuts in to individual close-ups and two-shots. Other areas (the gallery/balcony area of the ballroom, the tops of staircases) are cramped and often demand odd, high-angle shots that do not accord to the conventions of "film" cinematography of the era. To a modern eye, given the placement of most security cameras and the prevalence of their use by such filmmakers as Alfred Hitchcock and Michael Mann, they elicit an odd feeling of disruption or even sur-veillance. Another common feature of the camera technique demanded by the set and the live broadcast is efficient but can come off as blocky and clumsy to a mod-ern viewer: in some of the larger ensemble numbers, notably the first iteration of "The Prince Is Giving a Ball," the wide shots are mingled with cameo-esque shots of soloists (for instance, the girl who sings "And me, I'm in the second grade"—another example of Hammerstein's book being not only modern but also American in slant). The direct address of the "Stepsisters' Lament" is mediated by an ornate frame which suggests that they are looking in a powder-room mirror. Special effects are limited primarily to the superimposition of a sparkler over "magical" elements, such as the fairy godmother's transformation of Cinderella's dress (in one of the better examples of a quick change, the camera starts on her feet and pans up over a large wrap coat that could have been easily flung over Andrews, finally arriving at the tiara that could have been put on as the camera moves up her body). Andrews's dress looks very much like a contemporary 1950s "deb" dress—of course, the ball is essentially a debutante ball sans escorts.

The 1965 version has one great technical advantage—videotape. Gone are the spatial and temporal demands of live broadcast; this opens up the sets, and the cam-eras themselves are more mobile. Post-production editing allows for more fluency. Most important, the odd camera angles are smoothed out, and the somewhat jar-ring "cameo" close-ups in the ensemble numbers are handled by panning the cam-era across the characters in rhythm to the music. (It could be argued that the earlier cameo close-ups are more strongly rhythmic and create a stronger impression, but the converse is that they are choppy and impede the forward momentum that the pans actually amplify.) While the non-diegetic voices could have been managed technically in a live broadcast by an offstage microphone, they are undoubtedly easier to deal with on videotape.

The special effects in 1965 aren't much more sophisticated in concept, mostly the superimposition of a spinning sparkly effect (not unlike the "ruby slippers" effect for *The Wizard of Oz* from 1939) for magic and a cut-out animation of the horse and carriage carrying Cinderella to the ball during the reprise of "It's Possible." A simple cross-fade takes care of the transformations of pumpkin to carriage and bumpkin to princess.

By 1997, the technical differences between television and cinematic filming are minimal. The production is shot on film with more subtle special effects, and it certainly has the best choreography of the three, provided by Rob Marshall (later to direct and choreograph *Chicago* [2002]). The only element that really betrays the

Figure 11.3 The camera frames Cinderella and the Prince in "Ten Minutes Ago"

confines of television is the slightly cramped feeling of the sets, crammed onto a soundstage—although clever camera angles often minimize this, it's more obvious in the wide shots. The camera movement shows the influence of Gene Kelly's mobile, "dancing" camera as well as the faster cutting rhythms from music video, which also eases the possible "cinematic" anxiety of direct address. The Fairy Godmother opens the film with a sparkly wave of her wand, singing "Impossible" to the camera, which multiplies her functions: she's theatrical onstage narrator, television host, and music video performer, the role with which Houston is most strongly associated.

A quick look at the same moment in the three different productions—the beginning of "Ten Minutes Ago"—can illustrate how performance and technology meld with conventions of the distinct media over time (see Figure 11.3; see also 🎵 Examples 11.4, 11.5, and 11.6).

In 1957, technological limitations are exacerbated by the logistics of the cramped set. Although clearly blocked for the camera, the performers are in theatrical mode, projecting to the audience more than to each other or even to the camera. Cypher is singing for the back of the hall, and even though Andrews's bashful flirtatiousness is more natural in front of the camera, she is angled more toward the camera than him, and their interaction is almost contrapuntal, with moments of eye contact functioning like a higher-level harmonic rhythm that keeps them engaged with each other and carries across the more outward-projecting moments.

By 1997, the prerecorded music allows more freedom of movement and exertion without loss of vocal quality, so that Norwood and Montalban can converse and sing while in a conventional dance hold. Their focus is entirely and naturalistically on each other, while the camera whirls vertiginously around them.

Although traces of both theatrical and cinematic modes are evident in the 1965 version, I would argue that it is "televisual" as well as "teleauditory." Some of that is technological—the "look" of videotape, the resultant openness of the sets and camera movement, and the half-playback, which allows the security of the prerecorded orchestra as well as the immediacy of the live vocal performance, a kind of vocal "close-up" that captures Damon's above-mentioned acting-through-singing. Warren's performance is captured by the visual close-ups; where Andrews's nervousness is projected primarily by "business"—looking away, touching her hair—Warren's is in her body language and facial expressions. The counterpoint of touching and parting that we saw with Andrews and Cypher is still there, but the blocking is simpler, more open, and seemingly more naturalistic because their relationship to one another is always direct, even if not direct to the camera. They are moved onto the oblique of the shot-reverse-shot cinematic convention so that when she turns away in shyness, both of them are clearly and closely framed.

The 1965 version also has a structural feature that is highlighted by its cinematically influenced televisual production. A pair of scenes bonds Cinderella and her Prince even at a distance. As Cinderella and her Stepmother and Stepsisters talk about the ball, an instrumental reminiscence of "Ten Minutes Ago" is interpolated, and unique among the versions, Cinderella moves out into the garden to sing "Lovely Night" alone, highlighting Warren's dancing. Then the scene shifts to the Palace, where the Prince is wondering "Do I Love You," while his parents express concern about his sincerity. But as he moves outside (in parallel to Cinderella), he hears Cinderella respond to him in a non-diegetic reminiscence of the previous night, balancing her recall of "Ten Minutes Ago." A hint of echo on her voice invokes disembodied presence, and Damon's angle toward the left of the screen recalls their previous position. On a large-scale model of parallel editing, where two scenes in succession are read as simultaneity, these two scenes suggest that they are dueting across their physical (and temporal?) divide.

"DO I LOVE YOU BECAUSE YOU'RE BEAUTIFUL? OR ARE YOU BEAUTIFUL BECAUSE I LOVE YOU?"

I have wondered, as I return over and over again to the 1965 version—for which I'm sure you've noticed a decided bias—do I love it most because it was the one I saw every year as I grew up? Or is it really the best one? Of course, that depends upon your criteria for "best." I don't think there's a right or wrong answer; however, it does make us think more specifically about what elements influence our reactions.

There's no doubt that the 1957 version is closest to the "authorial intention" of Rodgers and Hammerstein; on a sheer technical level (most especially the quality of the choreography and camera work), there's no doubt that the 1997 version is superior. These are certainly valid criteria on which to judge. So why do I overlook the dated color schemes and cut-out sets of the 1960s design? The flip answer would be that I *like* those cut-out sets. Which I do. I've always been fond of the mid-century tendency toward schematic sets, like Isamu Noguchi's sparse sets for Martha Graham—but then perhaps that's because some of my earliest "design" memories are this production of *Cinderella* and the odd, spare (and false) false-front designs for the OK Corral dreamscape in the *Star Trek* episode "The Spectre of the Gun" (1967). It's distinctly possible those shaped my taste. But a more affective answer is that Lesley Ann Warren and Stuart Damon have a chemistry that neither of the other couples do—when it comes down to it, if there's a love story, I think it helps if the lovers convince me that they *are*. There's an energy and excitement in the performances that bubbles over into natural smiles and laughter in the singing, a balance of nostalgia and possibility in the casting, and a technology likewise poised between the past and the future.

The musical is a fascinating genre across which to consider those elements that are specific to the distinct media of theatrical performance, television, and cinema; television also offers us the opportunity to compare iterations. In the theater, challenges include not only the multiplicity of stagings and revivals but also the finer distinctions of re-castings and each individual performance—eight performances a week, even for a modest run, is an amazing amount of material, and there is still work that could and should be done about the mounting of a musical, including out-of-town try-outs and revisions. In cinema, musicals are a genre in which re-makes are relatively rare; Rodgers and Hammerstein's own *State Fair* is a significant exception, as is Hammerstein's earlier, seminal *Show Boat*, which has been filmed three times in substantially different forms. And cinema is a medium in which the "text" becomes frozen on film but not necessarily in performance: Gene Kelly's version of "Singin' in the Rain" may differ from Cliff Edwards's, Judy Garland's, and Jimmy Durante's, but it is always and forever the same Gene Kelly performance—although one could argue that the self-same recording playing over the end of *A Clockwork Orange* (Kubrick, 1968) is a different "performance" of the song because of its context.

These television performances give us a middle ground. The iterations are closest in tone to a revival, taking into consideration changes of technology as well as in musical style and cultural sensibilities.

NOTES

1. Rick Altman counters the conflation of technology and technique: "In order to represent properly, each new technology must therefore succeed in representing not reality itself, but the version of reality established by a previously dominant representational technology. In other words, there is no such thing as a representation of the real; there is only representation of representation." See "Toward a Theory of the History of Representational Technologies" (*Iris* 2.2 [1984]: 111–25), p. 121.

2. The all-black television musical *Cindy* (1978), although fascinating in itself, is an original production set in Harlem in 1943, not an adaptation of Rodgers and Hammerstein.

3. Geoffrey Block compares the three versions extensively in *Richard Rodgers* (Yale Broadway Masters Series, New Haven, CT: Yale University Press, 2003); my analysis does not disagree with his so much as stress other aspects.

4. I-III7-vi-iv-ii7—while this progression is not technically to the flat side, the prevalence of minor subdominant-function chords gives a similar impression.

5. For more extended discussions of this constellation of roles, see Stacy Wolf, *A Problem Like Maria: Gender and Sexuality in the American Musical* (Ann Arbor: University of Michigan Press,

2002) and Peter Kemp, "How Do You Solve a 'Problem' like Maria von Poppins," in *Musicals: Hollywood and Beyond,* ed. Bill Marshall and Robynn Stilwell (Portland: Intellect, 2000), pp. 55–61.

6. Norwood became a pop star under her single first name, "Brandy."

7. Block questions the multicultural casting of the 1997 version in terms of genetics—was Cinderella's father black? Were the two stepsisters fathered by different men because one is white and one is black? How do a black Queen and white King produce a Filipino son? While these questions are logical in reality, they are out of step with modern practices of race-blind casting. (Block himself asks "Should we not ask questions like this?" [199].) In an era when the American president is himself biracial and Disney has been seen as perpetuating racial and ethnic stereotypes in its animated films, it seems a positive step to present a multiracial cast as "natural."

CHAPTER 12

....

THE ANIMATED FILM MUSICAL

....

SUSAN SMITH

CONSIDER this sequence, arguably one of the most moving in the history of animation...

Dumbo has just been taken by his friend Timothy Q. Mouse to visit Dumbo's mother in the cage where she is being held in solitary confinement, branded mad for protecting her son from a boy's taunts about his outsized ears. On glimpsing Dumbo's little trunk through the bars of her window, Mrs. Jumbo moves toward him only to be held back by the shackles around her legs. As Dumbo looks up at her window, her trunk appears through its bars and, feeling around for him, touches the top of his head. The emotional force of this moment—as their trunks then meet and intertwine—is accentuated by the emergence on the soundtrack of the initial strains of "Baby Mine," sung by a female chorus in hushed tones. Following a shift to a closer view of Mrs. Jumbo's trunk lovingly caressing Dumbo's head while tears well out of his eyes, Betty Noyes begins her heartrending rendition of the lyrics of the song ("Baby mine, don't you cry/Baby mine, dry your eyes"). To Dumbo's delight, Mrs. Jumbo curls her trunk into a loop for him to sit in, and then rocks him gently from side to side while the lyrics offer reassuring testimony to her ability to soothe her child ("Rest your head close to my heart/Never to part, baby of mine";
⏵ Example 12.1).

Consider also the "Little April Shower" sequence from *Bambi* (Hand, 1942)...

Brilliantly encapsulating the film's "circle of life" theme in microcosm, this begins with the young deer being surprised by the sound of raindrops (rendered on the soundtrack by a series of single clarinet notes) tapping out a tune as they splash onto the leaves around him while a chorus of female (and, later, male) voices sings the lyric ("Drip, drip, drop/Little April shower/Beating a tune/As you fall all around"). The shower accelerates its pace, prompting the forest animals to scuttle for cover, eventually turning into a full-blown thunderstorm (accompanied by cymbal crashes)—only to return to a gentler mood as the storm dies out and nature emerges glisteningly refreshed by the rain, its drops gradually coming to a stop as the last three fall with a tinkling musical flourish onto a pool of water (▶ Example 12.2).

It's worth beginning with a discussion of these two sequences, since in different ways they raise important questions concerning what constitutes an animated film musical and how it may be considered distinct from its live action counterpart. Moreover, they also illustrate how Disney animated films in particular often contain songs that, while absolutely essential to the emotional fabric of their narrative worlds, wouldn't necessarily be considered musical numbers in the conventional sense. All of these factors suggest the value of making this studio's work a focal point for this chapter.

In the case of the "Baby Mine" sequence in *Dumbo* (Sharpsteen, 1942), much of its emotional richness stems precisely from the fact that Mrs. Jumbo doesn't perform the song as she would in a traditional number in a musical; indeed, her lack of access to the music and the latter's status outside of the diegesis reinforce her helplessness within the narrative and her physical separation from her son. Yet in resisting the temptation to have Mrs. Jumbo sing, the film exhibits a delicacy of restraint that enables her to express her feelings for her son on her own terms, as she uses the tactile properties of her trunk to overcome the physical confinement of her cage and reach out to her son. At the same time, there is also a sense in which the song *is* giving voice to Mrs. Jumbo's otherwise silent, soothing invocation to her son, and this intimacy of connection between song and character is suggested not only by the directness of address inherent in the lyrics themselves (which means that Mrs. Jumbo *could* have sung this song if the filmmakers had so chosen), but also by the manner in which the female chorus starts up just as mother and son's trunks intertwine for the first time.

In creating this harmonious fusion of tactile and vocal forms of expression, the sequence thus brings diegetic and non-diegetic layers together in a way that suggests some form of utopian bonding not just between mother and son but between human and animal sensibilities, and thereby provides a strong counterpoint to the more dominant view (expressed by one of the clowns moments later) that "elephants ain't got no feelings." Indeed, what we have here, arguably, are two parts of one overall musical performance, with the song bringing out the natural lyricism of the mother elephant's wordless lullaby and the gentle swaying of her trunk offering something analogous to the graceful movements of a dancer's body.

With *Bambi*'s "Little April Shower" sequence, the song is also non-diegetic but again there is a strong sense of its being intimately involved with the narrative world. Here, though, the song is not expressive of the animal characters' feelings in the way that it was for Mrs. Jumbo, but, rather, it acts as a kind of lyrical evocation of the music made by the sound of the raindrops falling. The non-diegetic song that we hear on the soundtrack is thus not construed as the *source* of the music as such but instead as a reflection of a natural musicality that, as the words themselves make clear, is already inherent within the narrative and superior to its own ("Drip, drip drop/Little April shower/What can compare to your beautiful sound?"). What we have here, in effect, then, is "Singin' in the Rain" but without Gene Kelly. In that live action number, Kelly both sings and dances while the rain functions more subserviently as the trigger and background for his character's expressions of joy, but here it is the raindrops themselves that dance across the screen, tapping out their own musical rhythms as they fall to the ground. The song, lacking a human figure to perform it, is projected instead onto the non-diegetic layer of the soundtrack, yielding to the rain itself as the main site of performance and focus of celebration.

What these two sequences suggest, then, is that the specific conditions of the animated film may require us to be more flexible in the way we think about the relationship between song and dance, performer and song. Indeed, the frequency with which these films have animals or some other nonhuman character at their center indicates that the animated film employs a much broader notion of performance and a greater range of performer types, some of whom (as in the case of the "Little April Shower" sequence) may not even have the kind of bodily presence that one takes for granted in the delivery of a live action musical number. When considered in relation to animation's ability to bring the inanimate to life, then, this makes it possible for anything to become endowed with a musicality of movement and expression all its own (something that Disney's first sound cartoon, *Steamboat Willie* [Disney and Iwerks, 1928], delights in right from the start; ◉ Example 12.3; ◉ Example 12.4). The presence of the human voice on the soundtrack pulls against any more radical decentering of the human figure from the field of performance, although the pairing of this with the animated body engenders further complexities specific to the animated musical genre. Thus, while some might argue that the "Baby Mine" sequence is not a musical number by virtue of the voice's non-diegetic status on the soundtrack, in animated films no voice ever really belongs to the performer we see on the screen, since the figure we see has no living entity outside of the text and its movements have no direct ontological equivalent in real life. The actions that constitute the performance (with the notable exception of the voice) are instead created through the manipulation of a set of drawings or other inanimate shapes and forms outside of the filming process, rather than from any physical action performed within the frame. As Hamilton Luske observes with regard to the cel-based form of animation that Disney developed and which became the dominant model against which other forms of animation were defined:

> Our actors are drawings. We cannot work on the inspiration of the moment as an actor does, but must present our characterizations through a combination of art, technique, and mechanics that takes months from the conception to the finished product.[1]

Animation's roots in the inanimate in turn raise the question of whether onscreen performance is actually a viable concept with this form, leading some to locate the identity of the performer outside of the film itself. Thomas and Johnston argue:

> Basically, the animator is the actor in animated films. He is many other things as
> well; however, in his efforts to communicate his ideas, acting becomes his most
> important device. (18)

They go on to highlight some of the special difficulties involved in trying to create a
performance under such conditions:

> But the animator has a special problem. On the stage, all of the foregoing symbols
> are accompanied by some kind of personal magnetism that can communicate the
> feelings and attitudes equally as well as the action itself. There is a spirit in this
> kind of communication that is extremely alive and vital. However, wonderful as
> the world of animation is, it is too crude to capture completely that kind of
> subtlety....
>   The live actor has another advantage in that he can interrelate with
> others in the cast. In fact, the producer relies heavily on this. When he begins
> a live action picture, he starts with two actors of proven ability who will
> generate something special just by being together. There will be a chemistry
> at work that will create charisma, a special excitement that will elicit an
> immediate response from the audience. The actors will each project a unique
> energy simply because they are real people.
>   By contrast, in animation we start with a blank piece of paper! Out of
> nowhere we have to come up with characters that are real, that live, that
> interrelate. We have to work up the chemistry between them (if any is to exist),
> find ways to create the counterpart of charisma, have the characters move in a
> believable manner, and do it all with mere pencil drawings. (18)

While these challenges are common to animation as a whole, they are particularly
an issue when it comes to thinking about this form in relation to the musical, given
the musical's heavy reliance on the abilities and charisma of its star performers,
together with its investment in notions of spontaneity and improvisation. In this
context, one could argue that what the voice brings to the animated performance is
a complexity and subtlety of expression that may be difficult to achieve through the
visual dimension of animation alone, while at the same time having the potential
(not always realized) to free the human actor from the constraints of her or his body
and even prompt a reconfiguring of the relationship between voice and star image.
But this reliance on the human voice has at times been considered a threat to the
creative potential of animation's visual dimension, owing mainly to the influence
that a well-known star may be deemed to have in over-determining the look and
personality of the character he or she is voicing. Even here, though, the voice's associations with a star personality can endow a character's otherwise entirely fictional
status with a quality of emotional reality that may be crucial in overcoming the
sense of implausibility arising from the sight of an imaginary figure bursting into
song and dance; in doing so it highlights the special capacity of the singing voice to
breathe life into the inanimate.

This power to bring the inanimate to life[2] is something that Sergei Eisenstein,
the Soviet filmmaker and writer, found fascinating about animation as an art form,
particularly the early short cartoons of Disney. What intrigued him most was their

capacity to enact a modern-day version of animism, namely, "'The belief [which goes back to early forms of human thought] that all objects possess a natural life or vital force, that they are endowed with an indwelling spirit.'"[3] Indeed, for Eisenstein, "The very idea...of the animated cartoon is like a direct embodiment of the method of animism" in the sense that inherent in its process is the "supplying of an inanimate object with life and a soul" (44). Eisenstein sees both forms of animism (the physical and the spiritual) operating in Disney's animated shorts, observing that not only are they "animated drawings" (41) brought to life but they also have a tendency to invest ordinary objects within the films with human traits and emotions (43). The latter is something that, according to Eisenstein, extends beyond animism to Disney's depiction of animals, this humanizing of them being evidence of a totemistic belief in "the unity of man and animal" (49) and something that Disney shares with other forms of art through the ages. As in other cases, this "'flight' into an animal skin and the humanization of animals" functions in Disney's work as "a displacement, an upheaval, a unique protest against the metaphorical immobility of the once-and-forever given" (33).

According to Eisenstein, this revolt against the fixity of one's human status also manifests itself in what he refers to as the "plasmaticness" of Disney's animated cartoons, which he defines as follows:

> We have a being represented in drawing, a being of a definite form, a being which has attained a definite appearance, and which behaves like the primal protoplasm, not yet possessing a "stable" form, but capable of assuming any form and which, skipping along the rungs of the evolutionary ladder, attaches itself to any and all forms of animal existence. (21)

This elasticity of form is something that Eisenstein considers capable of evoking an almost primordial state akin to what existed prior to the stabilization of human form and the fixing of boundaries between different species, containing within it a sense of endless possibility. The affective outcome of all this is one of "pure ecstasy" (42), which he defines as "a sensing and experiencing of the primal 'omnipotence'— the element of 'coming into being'—the 'plasmaticness' of existence, from which *everything* can arise" (46).

For Eisenstein, these traits of animism, totemism, and plasmaticness all contribute to what he calls the "pre-logical attractiveness" of Disney's work (41), a quality that he explains in terms of an investment in an "infantile, pre-human realm" (64) that allows Disney to create on a "conceptual level...not yet shackled by logic, reason, or experience" (2). He contrasts this with Chaplin's approach, which, while also infantile in nature, results in "a constant, agonized and somewhere at its core, an always tragic lament over the lost golden age of childhood" (2). For Eisenstein, Disney's infantilism is infinitely more hopeful and liberating, one that—in offering "a revolt against partitioning and legislating, against spiritual stagnation and greyness" (4)—allows the films to create a sense of "Paradise Regained," something that is otherwise "Unreachable on earth" and "Created only by a drawing" (2).

Eisenstein is extremely useful in helping us understand the potential of the animated film musical to offer something distinct from its live action counterpart. His use of the term "ecstasy" certainly suggests an affective dimension to the animated film that is compatible with the utopian sensibility of the musical. And his claims that Disney's cartoons convey a sense of "Paradise Regained" gestures toward the animated film's capacity to offer a more satisfying sense of what that utopia would look like, not just feel like (as Dyer famously contended).[4] The idea that an animistic impulse underpins the creative process of animation also seems absolutely crucial in understanding the special kind of utopian sensibility associated with this branch of the genre and helps explain why so many animated film musicals often find themselves devoted to expressions of joy at the bestowal or rediscovery of life, for in doing so they are celebrating something fundamental to the form itself.[5] Indeed, it is possible to see the relationship between animation and the musical as mutually enhancing, with the former's capacity to invest the inanimate with life finding its ultimate means of realization in the heightened physical vitality and emotional intensity of the production number, and the joyful spirit of the genre's utopian sensibility reaching its satisfying extension in the life-giving, not just life-affirming, nature of animation as an art form. It is important to acknowledge this compatibility, since in other respects animation's reliance on the painstaking manipulation of drawings, models, and other inanimate objects for its effects pulls against those notions of spontaneity of movement and expression on which the live-action musical depends.

Jane Feuer argues that the Hollywood musical is a capitalist, mass, prerecorded form of entertainment seeking to pass itself off as folk art through attempting (among other things) to create the illusion of spontaneity and improvisation in the performance of song and dance routines.[6] But this is difficult to sustain against the specific conditions of the animated film musical. This is especially the case in the field of stop-motion animation, where (as in the case of *The Nightmare before Christmas* [Selick, 1993]) it is possible to see the blatantly stitched-together nature of the characters' bodies, and where (depending on the sophistication of the technology) these figures' movements often have a jerky, unreal quality. It is precisely our awareness of such conditions that makes Jack Skellington's ability to achieve an Astaire-like grace of movement during his solo numbers seem all the more remarkable (▶ Example 12.5). Rather than relying on an effacement of its constructedness for its effects, then, or on an audience's forgetting the time and effort that goes into the production of its song and dance routines, the utopian pleasures of this branch of the musical seem more plausibly rooted in a self-conscious delight in animation's capacity for bringing things to life.

The other elements Eisenstein identifies can also enhance and extend the animated film musical's utopian sensibility. Plasticity offers unique opportunities in performance terms, with the animated human body (or human skeleton, as in the case of Disney's first "Silly Symphony," *Skeleton Dance* [Disney, 1929]), being capable of stretching, compressing, and changing shape in response to the rhythms and patterns of music to a degree that is impossible in the live-action musical (▶ Example 12.6). Totemism invests the utopianism of the animated film musical with another distinctive dimension, the potential freedom it offers being one of escape not just from the restrictions of ordinary society (as in the live-action musical), but also from the constraints of human identity itself, through a merging with animals and reconnecting with nature.

The "Pink Elephants on Parade" sequence in *Dumbo* demonstrates how all three of these elements may combine in an animated musical number. A tour de force of animation that has no equivalent in live-action musicals, it seems unhampered by the kind of conservative ethos and realist codes of representation that Disney has been criticized for. The fact that Dumbo is mute throughout the film (so that the singing must again be displaced onto the non-diegetic area of the soundtrack) makes him an unlikely figure to have at the center of a musical, yet it is precisely this that gives "Pink Elephants" its special rationale as a production number. Following soon after the "Baby Mine" sequence, its impact is heightened by that juxtaposition. Thus, whereas the soothing rhythms of the lullaby and Mrs. Jumbo's rocking of her son had earlier reinforced his child-like state of dependency on her, this gives way here to a much more unsettling realm of surrealist-inspired, free-form animation. It is this shift that allows Dumbo (now inebriated as a result of having unwittingly drunk from a bucket of water into which a clown has just accidentally knocked a bottle of champagne) to discover a newfound creativity and independent sense of self. Such a change is evident in the contrasting use made of the elephant's trunk: from Mrs. Jumbo's cradling of Dumbo in hers to his playful blowing of an assortment of bubbles of various shapes and sizes through his, at one point (egged on by Timothy) even molding it into a square concertina-like instrument in order to produce the desired effect, before finally blowing a giant bubble that suddenly morphs into a "live" pink elephant (⊙ Example 12.7). This form of creative expression links Dumbo with the life-giving powers of animation itself, as his trunk, functioning in analogous terms like an animator's pencil, projects onto the blankness of the night sky a circular shape that, in morphing into a moving elephant image, seems to enact the coming to life of the animator's drawing.

The malleable nature of the outline shape that Dumbo creates also exemplifies the "plasmatic" quality that Eisenstein valued in Disney's work. In exploiting this to the full through the morphing, dancing elephants that follow, the sequence can be understood to offer, from this infant protagonist's point of view, an imaginative release of all those feelings that he otherwise can't express. Branded a freak because of his oversized ears, Dumbo is able to explore here a much more liberating version of his own sense of difference, with the imaginary elephants' constant morphing—expanding, shrinking, and changing into different shapes and forms—constituting an extreme display of bodily deviance that is now defined in terms of creativity and freedom of expression rather than ugly abnormality or social failure. Early on, the free-form animation also gives vent to his feelings of oppression, as the bizarre image of a large elephant stamping on the head of a much smaller one renders literal Dumbo's own downtrodden state. Subsequent images enact a rebellion against such power structures, however, as the smaller elephant is shown kicking the large one from behind before responding to the four elephants that materialize in front of him by expanding into a giant version of his former self and crushing them between a large pair of cymbals.

Above all, the "Pink Elephants" sequence offers Dumbo an empowering release from the containing environment of the circus, as the entrapping, degrading forms of performance that both he and the other animals are forced to undergo there are replaced by more liberating ones. The fluidity of the elephants' movements and the plasticity of their bodies thus enable them to morph into a whole range of different animal and object forms while also appropriating, in the process, various human forms of dance, including Indian belly dance, classical ballet, ice skating, and Latin American rhumba. In also showing the elephants adapting their bodies to suit (dancing on two legs while retaining their trunks and other familiar features), this number pushes the "Baby Mine" sequence's idealized fusion of human and elephant forms of expression in other, more daring directions. Exploiting the plasticity and anti-realist properties of the form, "Pink Elephants" manages to generate a highly fluid, less representationally hidebound vision of totemistic union, one that involves the elephants "skipping along the rungs of the evolutionary ladder" (Eisenstein, 21) and exhibiting the skillful grace of a human dancer's body. It isn't just that elephants appropriate human forms of dance, moreover, as the hybrid nature of their physical features also gestures toward a more disruptive crossing of bodily boundaries. This finds its most disconcerting vision in the menacing image of a figure advancing toward the audience whose outline conforms to the human form but whose torso, head, and limbs are entirely made up of differently colored elephants' heads (⊙ Example 12.8). It is an image of totemistic union that inverts the power struc-ture of the narrative's circus world, departing markedly from the cozy, sentimental forms of anthropomorphism for which Disney has so often been criticized. The unsettling nature of this effect is accentuated all the more by our awareness that such a vision has purportedly emerged out of the mind of one of the studio's most genuinely cute animal characters.

Given how this surrealist sequence suddenly erupts out of an otherwise fairly conventional child's narrative, it is possible to regard this number as offering release not just for Dumbo but also for the animators themselves who, freed from the con-straints of the narrative feature film, are able to give vent to a more anarchic style of animation, closer in spirit to the innovative earlier phase of Disney's work. Indeed, the sequence almost feels like an animated short interpolated into a feature, although both the film and this surrealist-inspired piece gain much from their interaction. Dumbo's gradual recedence from view as the sequence progresses is suggestive of this fantasy sequence's increasing capacity to take on a life of its own. Yet what the closing segment goes on to imply is that what we have been witnessing all along is some form of hallucinatory buildup to—or even enactment of—Dumbo's first, undisclosed act of flight, the creative freedom of its images thus constituting a sur-realist flight of fancy that on some level seems to enable the discovery of his own ability to fly. The final sequence, showing the elephants morphing into cars, trains, dinghies, and rollercoaster cars, rushing chaotically across the screen, appears especially evocative of the chaos and excitement of those first few moments of flight. This is followed by the dream-like image of the imaginary pink elephants floating down and morphing into clouds that hang in the sky next to the tree where Dumbo and his friend are found sleeping, the effect of which is to negotiate the transition from number to narrative with an effortlessness that encapsulates the naturalness of their connection (⊙ Example 12.9).

The pastoral nature of this new setting highlights the impact of the "Pink Elephants" sequence in opening up a more utopian sphere, and this finds its culminating expression in the film's final number, "When I See an Elephant Fly." Initially performed by the crows as a jovial putdown of Timothy's claims regarding Dumbo's ability to fly, it first functions as an expression of the birds' resistance to the kind of deviant animal behavior that "Pink Elephants" wholeheartedly embraced. But this is completely reversed in the two reprises that follow, when the crows sing it in outright celebration of Dumbo's newfound abilities.

"Pink Elephants" thus seems to epitomize the qualities that Eisenstein extols in Disney animation, with its plasmatic, animistic and totemistic tendencies helping to pave the way for the film's utopian resolution. But Eisenstein's appreciation of Disney's films along such lines has not been echoed by many subsequent critics. In construing those aspects that Eisenstein so admired in entirely negative terms, their accounts are symptomatic instead of a growing application of media and cultural studies approaches to Disney's work, approaches that tend to seize upon what some regard as an increasing conservatism in the Disney studio's postwar era (which Eisenstein hints at himself). Thus, whereas Eisenstein celebrates Disney's innovative early animated films, seeing a direct causal connection between their formal creativity and their ability to offer a release from the standardization and mechanization of American capitalist society, more recent critics such as Jack Zipes have condemned the studio, as a corporate organization intent on maximizing profits, for its own standardization of the animated film and the fairy tale form on which it frequently draws. Any technical innovations are seen by Zipes as operating rather emptily, either as a means of promoting the Disney label or in the service of a deeply conservative ideological vision.[7] Eisenstein's extolling of the "plasmatic" quality of Disney animation for its ability to offer freedom from conventional modes of representation also finds its inverse reflection in the more common tendency nowadays for Disney to be criticized for not deviating enough from traditional live action codes of realism, and for thus stunting the development of animation as an art form (Wells, 21–28). Eisenstein's delight in Disney's totemistic outlook has similarly been supplanted in recent years by the view that Disney imposes its values on animals by anthropomorphizing them. And—most notably of all—whereas Eisenstein revels in what he sees as the socially liberating effects of Disney's investment in a child-like, pre-logical form of thought, Zipes and others accuse Disney of trading in a sentimental, regressive form of infantile escapism, diverting audiences from more radical utopian longings by encouraging them "to long nostalgically for neatly ordered patriarchal realms" (Zipes 1995, 40).

One of the challenges we face when studying the Disney animated film musical, then, is the need to be alert to these ideological issues while at the same time remaining open to the possibility of the films offering pleasures rooted in their animation and musical aspects, which may not be accessible through approaches based in a political or "representations" style of analysis. The crows' sequence in *Dumbo* offers a case in point. Labeled racist by some for its coding of these characters as African Americans, much of the controversy has centered upon the actors' use of an inaccurate black dialect, the naming of the lead bird "Jim Crow," the sequence's deployment of familiar racialized stereotypes such as preacher and jazz musician, and its borrowing of conventions associated with the popular 1940s' TV show *Amos and Andy*.[8] Considering *Dumbo* in terms of its musical and animation pleasures may produce a useful counterbalance to this kind of reading, prompting consideration of how the crows in fact occupy a privileged generic position as the only animals to perform a full-blown production number, the two reprises of which function as the defining expression of the film's utopian sensibility. The crows' privileged status in musical terms seems linked to their place outside of the circus environment, the freedom this grants them from the exploitative strategies and demeaning rituals of performance demanded from the other animals that work there enabling them (in a surprising inversion of the more typical containment of blacks and exclusion of them from the utopian spaces of the Hollywood musical) to engage in a number full of wonderful fluidity and jazz style inflections. The syncopated movements of two of the crows as they shimmy toward each other from opposite ends of the frame, together with the rousing harmonies achieved by the Hall Johnson choir and accompanying singers on the final two lines of the song, combine to convey a wonderful sense of brotherhood and communal spirit quite different from the (white?) middle-class snobbery and prejudice previously displayed by the adult elephants. The dynamic poses displayed by the lead crow, as he scats and struts his way across the screen, also exude an exuberant self-confidence and vitality of spirit refreshingly at odds with the film's earlier images of animal enslavement (▶ Example 12.10). The lyrics, too, are infused with an intelligent, inventive form of wit that pulls against the more stereotypical, folksy dialects used by the crows. In destabilizing the fixed meanings of certain words they even manage to display a plasticity of form and animism of spirit that are capable of transforming nouns into verbs and objects into active, sentient, musical beings ("I've seen a peanut stand/And heard a rubber band/I've seen a needle that winked its eye/But I be done seen about everything/When I see a elephant fly..."; ▶ Example 12.11).

Compared to the crows' sequence in *Dumbo*, the "I Wanna Be Like You" number from Disney's *The Jungle Book* (Reitherman, 1967) has been viewed by some as more irredeemably racist. As Susan Miller and Greg Rhode argue:

> Once we make the obvious connection between King Louie and African Americans—at least the African Americanism dear to white bourgeois liberal culture—the lyrics of his song become a humiliating revelation, for King Louie sings of his desire to be a man "and stroll right into town...ooo I want to be like you."[9]

The question arises again, though, as to whether such a reading is able to capture the full scope of the animated characters' performances (which arguably have a much greater degree of fluidity than Miller and Rhode seem prepared to allow) and the range of pleasures that these might in turn offer the film's audiences. A more rounded approach might begin, for example, by noting Louis Prima's initial scatting play with the opening line of the song ("I wanna be a man-man, mon-mon, lorang orang-utango jango"), which immediately destabilizes these categories of racial difference by running the words together and bringing out their rhyming properties (⊙ Example 12.12). This fluidity of performance continues in the next phase of the dance as King Louie's expressed desire to attain human status finds its inverse reflection in Mowgli's emulation of the orangutan's style of movement, as he slaps his hands down on the ground in delight and then uses his left hand to lift himself off the ground (⊙ Example 12.13). Mowgli's performance both here and during the main body of the number, where he is shown joining in with the other monkeys' dance around the ancient ruins, consequently becomes expressive of *his* resistance to his *human* destiny, forming part of a series of numbers in the film where he is shown trying on different animal identities (emulating elephants during "Colonel Hathi's March" and a bear while performing "Bare Necessities" with Baloo; ⊙ Example 12.14; ⊙ Example 12.15). Baloo's own entry into the dance poses another disruption to the jungle's carefully demarcated boundaries, his appearance dressed in a grass skirt and wearing a coconut over his mouth signaling a mode of performance that is capable of crossing both gender and species lines. The full impact of this is realized later on in the delightful scatting exchange that takes place between Baloo and King Louie and, as they begin to dance in lindy hop style, it is the orangutan who then takes on the female role by allowing Baloo to swing him between his legs (⊙ Example 12.16).

When considered in relation to the full range of the number's performance elements, the song's title thus becomes expressive not just of King Louie's aspiration to achieve human status but of a collective desire of all characters to break free from the restrictions of their fixed identities. What we are being invited to share in here is some kind of ultimate musical celebration of those totemistic and plasmatic impulses that Eisenstein deemed essential to the utopian spirit of Disney animation. The fact that Bagheera the panther is the only one of the main characters not to give in to the flow of the music during this number thus acquires a deeper logic, for although he may well be given a voice of authority within the narrative, and while he may exemplify how "the film invariably endows regal mannerisms and posh British accents to characters with power" (Miller and Rhode, 92–93), his well-spoken authoritarianism, like that of Colonel Hathi, is associated with a rigidity and inflexibility of approach that is presented as quite at odds with the "plasmatic" freedoms and animistic impulses of the animated film musical. This is depicted nowhere more clearly than when, just before a disguised Baloo bursts onto the scene, Bagheera attempts to hide from King Louie and his entourage by freezing suddenly, emulating the stone statue of a cat standing on the other side of the doorway. In adopting this static pose, he resists the music in a way that also constitutes a rejection of the life-giving powers it offers to him as an animated character—the "beat" of the music that Baloo so readily succumbs to being the very pulse of life that Disney animators used to time the movements of their characters' actions. His transformation of himself into a stone statue amounts to a symbolic death, in animation terms, as he allows himself to revert to the very condition of inanimate object from whence he came (Example 12.17).

I have tried—unlike Bagheera—in this essay to respond to the special properties of the animated film musical, so as to help open up for further study an area of the genre that has rarely been given the attention it deserves. There are, in particular, many subdivisions of this field still to explore, such as the short cartoon's role in the development of the animated film musical; the different effects that can be achieved through pairing the musical with non-cel-based forms of animation; and the significance of the practice, in recent years, of adapting Disney animated musicals for the stage. The complex question of how one thinks about performance or the relationship between body and voice within the animated film musical also warrants much further consideration. In pointing toward some of the issues raised by this and other areas, this chapter has sought to establish a creative platform on which to build.

NOTES

1. Quoted in Frank Thomas and Ollie Johnston, *Disney Animation: The Illusion of Life* (New York: Abbeville Press, 1981), p. 113.

2. As Paul Wells observes, "To animate, and the related words, animation, animated and animator all derive from the Latin verb, *animare*, which means to give life to, and within the context of the animated film, this largely means the artificial creation of the illusion of movement in inanimate lines and forms" (Paul Wells, *Understanding Animation* [London: Routledge, 1998], p. 10). Wells also cites Norman McClaren's definition of animation, namely, that it "is not the art of drawings that move, but rather the art of movements that are drawn. What happens *between* each frame is more important than what happens *on* each frame" (quoted in Wells, 10).

3. Quotation attributed to Webster's *Dictionary*, in Sergei Eisenstein, *Eisenstein on Disney* (London: Methuen, 1988), p. 95.

4. See Richard Dyer, "Entertainment and Utopia," in *Genre: The Musical*, ed. Rick Altman (London: Routledge & Kegan Paul, 1981), p. 177. Originally published in *Movie* 2 (Spring 1977): 2–13.

5. For a more melancholy meditation on the paradoxes involved in being an animated character, consider Emily/Helena Bonham Carter's moving rendition of the song "Tears to Shed" in Tim Burton's *The Corpse Bride* (2005).

6. Jane Feuer, *The Hollywood Musical*, 2nd ed. (Bloomington: Indiana University Press, 1992).

7. See Jack Zipes, "Breaking the Disney Spell," in *From Mouse to Mermaid: The Politics of Film, Gender and Culture*, ed. Elizabeth Bell, Lynda Haas, and Laura Sells (Bloomington: Indiana University Press, 1995), pp. 21–40; and Jack Zipes, *Happily Ever After: Fairy Tales, Children and the Culture Industry* (New York: Routledge, 1997), pp. 89–95.

8. See, for example, Mark I. Pinsky, *The Gospel According to Disney: Faith, Trust and Pixie Dust* (Louisville, KY: Westminster John Knox Press, 2004), pp. 43–45.

9. Susan Miller and Greg Rhode, "The Movie You See, the Movie You Don't: How Disney Do's That Old Time Derision," in *From Mouse to Mermaid: The Politics of Film, Gender and Culture*, p. 92.

CHAPTER 13

THE EVOLUTION OF THE ORIGINAL CAST ALBUM

GEORGE REDDICK

"When you listen to Pinza, you can only describe his voice—now silken is too weak. Velvet. Plush....When there is that rare combination of all the essentials of person and character and beauty and voice and image that you accept entirely as being true and real—those moments, whether in opera or in theatre, are treasured. And if one is fortunate enough to have experienced them, to have been there when it happened, I guess that's what life is made up of. Of moments."

As Saul waxed philosophical, I asked if his stereo system had been mainly a time machine designed to recapture those moments. "Oh no," he said. "It was not intended to recapture any of these, because it couldn't. It was parallel but separate. In other words, the pleasure I derived from recordings was independent of any pleasures I may have derived from the real thing. But I'm fortunate in having experienced so many real, that I can sort of trade off against what I enjoy from recordings. Because it's the real that stay. They are indelible. I don't know if I ever had any indelible recordings, do you follow me?...The beauty of listening to a recording is you *doooon't* see....You only hear and feel."[1]

—Evan Eisenberg, *The Recording Angel*

Otto Baensch wrote: "A work of art that gives eternal form
to a feeling thereby accomplishes its task, and thus fulfills its
function, no matter what kind of feeling it is that figures in
this fulfillment."

Eternal is surely a big word, and phonograph records
make no pretense to that. But they are, at least, a step in the
right direction; and one hopes that these records will serve
as a means by which the future listener will be able to sense
not only the accomplishment of the author and performers,
but the mood of the time in which they wrote, and acted,
and lived.[2]

—Goddard Lieberson

In the middle of the twentieth century, the cast recording enjoyed popularity so
widespread that of all the long-playing records released in the 1950s, the second
highest-selling album of the decade was of a Broadway musical. Though thousands
made the trip to New York to see *My Fair Lady* in person during its six years on
Broadway, millions who experienced it as a cast recording would never see it on
stage. But while its sophisticated music and witty lyrics appealed to a large market
in the 1950s, within a decade cultural tastes had so radically changed that the cast
album went from one of the most popular forms of entertainment in the world to
a small niche market that was often considered "out of touch." In this chapter,
I explore the development of the cast album, its rise to popularity, and its sudden
and seemingly permanent loss of cultural currency.

DEVELOPING TECHNOLOGY AND THE FIRST ORIGINAL CAST ALBUMS

At the beginning of the twentieth century, the burgeoning American music industry
was heavily influenced by musicals appearing on stages in New York. Many of the
hit songs of the day, sold as sheet music throughout the country, came from songwriters in New York, and many directly from shows being performed on Broadway.
The development of new technologies that made it possible to record and distribute
those hit songs on records began to revolutionize the way the country received its
music. By 1920, when broadcast radio began another revolution of the music industry, songs from Broadway hits were regularly being recorded and broadcast for an
even larger audience. Suddenly music and performances that had once been accessible by only relatively small numbers of people could be experienced by almost
anyone.[3] Moreover, performances that only a few years earlier would have survived

only in the memories of audience members at a particular performance could now be relived over and over again.

These technological advances did not make everyone happy. The American Federation of Musicians (AFM) was growing increasingly anxious during the 1920s and '30s that the work of the musician would become obsolete. Once a musician had recorded a single live performance of a work, that recording could go on to be used hundreds of times, across the country and even across the world, calling the value of live performance into question. Yet many consumers and critics felt that the recording age could provide a wide national audience with unprecedented access to good music. As early as 1924, Pauline Partridge wrote in the housekeeping journal *Sunset*, "The gracious response of the phonograph is untiring. No cajolery is necessary to persuade it to give of its richest treasure, it is never temperamental, needs no thanks, wishes no praise." Perhaps most important, the phonograph could bring "music, real music, good music, into the American home for the first time in history."[4] In a study of the integration of the phonograph into American culture in the first thirty years of the twentieth century, Mark Katz finds that Americans at the time did indeed seek to gain access to music of a higher cultural value, finding themselves lacking knowledge of "good" music and seeing the phonograph as the means through which they could acquire the "good" and "important" music their European counterparts took for granted. R. D. Darrell, critic for the *Phonograph Monthly Review*, wrote in 1926 that "the phonograph will in time do more for the cause of music than concert hall performances can ever do," concluding that "the phonograph is in the home," and "the home in which there is a phonograph is potentially a musical one."[5]

Meanwhile, James Caesar Petrillo, who had led the Chicago Federation of Musicians (CFM) in successful strikes for better terms regarding the broadcast and recording of musicians in Chicago in the 1930s, was strongly opposed to the idea that any phonograph could replace a live musician. "Since when is there any difference between Heifetz and the fiddler in the tavern? They're both musicians," he said.[6] Petrillo's past was a checkered one; he was connected with organized crime in Chicago and had once been kidnapped by the mob. Nevertheless, largely on the strength of his successes for the CFM, Petrillo was chosen as the new president of the AFM in 1940 (Anderson, 237–40).

As the possibilities offered by recorded music continued to appear, Petrillo led the AFM in a crescendo of protests that eventually resulted in the first of two major recording bans, beginning in August 1942. Musicians were on strike from that point, effectively banning any new music from being recorded. The record labels had stockpiled as much music as possible in the weeks before the ban took effect and as a result were able to hold out for a remarkably long time as musicians continued to perform only live or in live radio broadcasts. However, while records of classical music could be doled out over time, popular music had to be recorded and released in a relatively short period to capitalize on current trends and standards for popular music. Eventually, a series of pioneering records reintroducing popular music to the recording industry would contribute to the end of the strike.

Decca's 1943 cast recording of the original Broadway production of *Oklahoma!* is often cited as the first original Broadway cast album (◉ Example 13.1). This claim is also often disputed, since recordings of music from musicals performed by members of the stage cast had been heard on records since at least the turn of the twentieth century when Emile Berliner, inventor of the gramophone, recorded songs from *Florodora*, featuring members of the London cast.[7] *Oklahoma!*, however, in addition to its being a milestone in the development of the musical as an art form, was also a major landmark in recording history, since the success of its album release established the original cast recording as a staple element of the Broadway musical.[8]

Although many recordings of Broadway material appeared before *Oklahoma!*, they largely consisted of songs recorded by studio singers rather than by cast members of stage productions, and usually with different arrangements and different orchestras. Stars such as Ethel Merman and Gertrude Lawrence recorded songs from hit shows in which they had appeared, including *Panama Hattie* and *Lady in the Dark*, respectively.[9] Some scores were represented in studio-assembled recordings such as those of the Victor Light Opera Company, which released choral renditions of songs from a given score, including most of Jerome Kern's Princess Theatre musicals (Grant, 203–4). Several early British productions of musicals had been recorded in the early part of the century, and by the 1930s a few Broadway musicals received significant recordings, including a 1932 *Show Boat* recording featuring two members of the Broadway revival cast, and Victor's 1935 recording of *Porgy and Bess* featuring the Broadway chorus and orchestra and soloists Lawrence Tibbett and Helen Jepson from the Met.[10]

There were also a few musicals that actually received recordings of the original cast singing most of the songs of the show. Marc Blitzstein's *The Cradle Will Rock* (1937) was preserved on record with its original cast members accompanied by piano (as they had been in the first public performances).[11] However, Blitzstein's work did not appeal to a mainstream audience. The 1943 Decca *Oklahoma!* was a milestone in the history of the genre not only because it was essentially the first cast album to feature cast, chorus, and orchestra as heard in the theater, but also because it preserved what was, at that time, one of the biggest hit musicals in Broadway history.

Prior to the release of the cast album, several of *Oklahoma!*'s songs had already gained popularity, though its book writer and lyricist Oscar Hammerstein II apparently had attempted to promote the show and score as a whole and was not interested in pushing hit singles. The 1942 recording ban meant that while pop singers and other artists could perform songs from the show on the radio, they were prevented from recording pop "covers" with instrumental backing. Nevertheless, both Frank Sinatra and Bing Crosby got around the ban by recording two of the most popular songs, "People Will Say We're In Love" and "Oh, What a Beautiful Mornin'" in the summer of 1943 by using vocal, rather than orchestral, accompaniment.[12]

During the negotiation period prior to the end of the ban, Jack Kapp at Decca had taken advantage of a notable exemption. Petrillo effectively lifted his ban on any recordings made for servicemen,[13] so Kapp had recorded Irving Berlin's *This Is the*

Army, serving as another early example of a cast album. With that success behind him, *Oklahoma!*, the biggest hit show of the year, must have seemed like an irresistible follow-up, and Kapp struck a deal with Petrillo in late summer of 1943 to allow the original cast album of *Oklahoma!* to be made that fall.[14]

In 1943, when *Oklahoma!* premiered, the recording industry was facing difficult challenges in addition to the recording ban. Wartime shortages were cutting into the availability of materials to produce records, and experimentation with new formats and technology was intensifying competition among record labels. At the time, records were generally ten- or twelve-inch discs that rotated at 78 rpm. Each side could yield between two-and-a-half and four minutes of music. A group of related records could be sold together in an album—literally a bound book in which paper sleeves held separate records, much like a photograph album. The principal raw material used to make 78s was shellac, a resin secreted by an Asian tree insect. The war cut off supplies from the East, so records had to be rationed. In order to buy a new record, in some cases music lovers were required to turn in an old record to be reused (🔊 Example 13.2).[15]

As a label primarily known for popular recordings, Decca had weathered the recording ban less well than its competitors, who had been able to fall back on stockpiled recordings of classical titles. With the stunning success of *Oklahoma!* on record, Decca quickly capitalized on its exclusive deal with Petrillo and began to record and release other cast recordings, including *One Touch of Venus*, *Bloomer Girl*, *Song of Norway*, and *On the Town*. The other labels did not cave to the pressures of the ban until 1944, a full year after Decca's initial agreement,[16] and did not fully engage in the field of cast recordings until 1946 when Capitol released *St. Louis Woman* and Columbia entered the arena with its recording of Hammerstein's revival of *Show Boat* from that year, followed by *Street Scene* in 1947, the same year as Victor's first entry, Lerner and Loewe's *Brigadoon*. But Columbia would soon surpass Decca as the premier label for cast recordings.

GODDARD LIEBERSON AND THE LONG-PLAYING RECORD

During this time, cast albums consisted of cumbersome, weighty books binding several records together, and listening to the entirety of a show necessitated the constant changing of records after every couple of songs. In 1948, however, Columbia introduced a technological innovation that had been in development in different forms for years. The long-playing (LP) record could hold over twenty minutes on each side, allowing an entire cast album to fit on one record, about the same size as one 78.[17] The vinyl material used for the LP was also more durable and provided better sound than 78s (Elborough, 19–40). It was a watershed change for the recording industry.

The LP introduced a new era in music listening for 1950s America. Jazz artists were able to capture the elusive and ephemeral nature of a long improvised set in a format that anyone could revisit after that one single performance. Lengthy classical works that had previously existed in complete form only in a concert hall could now be heard in their entirety in one manageable set of LPs. John Culshaw's Decca recording of Wagner's *Der Ring des Nibelungen*, the first recording of the score in its entirety (released in installments between 1958 and 1966), eventually took up nineteen records.[18] Culshaw estimated that the same recording would have required 112 records on 78s (Elborough, 47).

Cast recordings were perhaps the ideal product for the LP. While a symphony or improvisational jazz performance could be almost any length, the approximate forty-five minute playing time of an LP, separated like acts into two sides, perfectly reflected the average amount of music in a two-act musical. At Columbia Records, where the LP was born, Goddard Lieberson eventually became recognized as a leader in the field of cast recordings, particularly with the release and wide success of *South Pacific* on LP in 1949. *South Pacific* was one of the earliest and most successful LPs of any kind and while *Oklahoma!* and *South Pacific* would have to wait almost a decade to be released for mass consumption as Hollywood films, these hugely popular musicals were by then already well known through their original cast recordings.

Goddard Lieberson became president of Columbia Records in June of 1956, just two months after producing the most successful cast album of all time, the original Broadway cast recording of *My Fair Lady* (⊙ Example 13.3). Lieberson is frequently credited, if not with the creation of the cast album, then with the promotion and solidification of the art form. In a 1973 tribute to Stephen Sondheim, when introducing Lieberson as a speaker, Leonard Bernstein described him as "the man who has done most to preserve and perpetuate the music of shows. Of course, that's only fractional. He is also the man who invented perpetuating the music of shows."[19]

Lieberson came to Columbia in 1939 as the assistant to the director of the Masterworks Division, eventually becoming the head of the division and vice president in charge of Masterworks artists and repertoire. He had attended the Eastman School of Music and had composed many of his own works; he even found time to write a novel, *3 for Bedroom C*, which was adapted into a Hollywood film starring Gloria Swanson.[20] Lieberson saw much of the popular music of the late '40s and '50s as a fad, and was at first reluctant to record rock-and-roll music during his tenure at Columbia. Lieberson saw the LP as a tool to bring "the university lecture hall, the theatre and the concert hall into the intimate possession of many who had never known them," establishing "a new consciousness in the art of listening" (Elborough, 68). Some of Lieberson's decidedly highbrow recordings included the works of Schoenberg, an extensive series of recordings featuring Igor Stravinsky conducting his own works, and the first recording of a stage play on LP, Shaw's *Don Juan in Hell*, directed by Charles Laughton. Other plays would follow, including the Broadway production of *Waiting for Godot* in 1956, which he not only produced for records but also provided what he called in the album notes "invented sounds of a more or less abstract nature."[21]

Lieberson's greatest legacy, however, lies with the musical cast recording. Lieberson saw the genre as an opportunity to bring the theater into the home, but he often required changes and alterations to scores of musicals in order to make the album work for the listener who would not have access to the show as it appeared on stage. By the time of his retirement, Lieberson claimed to have changed the "quality and style" of cast recordings:

> I'd usually be with a show since its inception, I'd go out of town two or three times, and by the time it came for the recording session, I'd know it pretty well. I sometimes changed the arrangements and tempos for the record—not always pleasing the arranger—but the sound you write for in the theater is quite different from the sound you need on an album....Another thing I did away with was dialogue lead-ins for songs unless they were absolutely necessary. I would have to explain patiently to the librettist and the composer and lyricist that you could listen to a song on a record forty times, but to hear some banal, spoken introduction to the song drives you nuts after the third time.[22]

Every album required some adjustment to make the album work for the home listener. Lieberson was interested in preserving Broadway scores which would otherwise disappear after their Broadway productions ended, but from the changes he made, we can infer that he did not see his role as a documentarian or historian, attempting to recreate shows exactly as they appeared on stage. Instead, he attempted to give the wider American public the best possible experience of a Broadway score through only its LP.

Lieberson dominated the era when original cast albums were popular. In the years he was regularly recording Broadway musicals, the practice became so common that fewer and fewer musicals went unrecorded. Some seasons, such as the 1957–58 and 1958–59 seasons, saw virtually no new book musicals that went without a recording (Mordden 1983, 199). Additionally, from the earliest days of the LP era, Lieberson, in collaboration with conductor Lehman Engel, began to record the scores of classic shows that were not tied to any production. Studio recordings of songs from shows were not a new idea. Popular artists had often recorded several tunes by a specific composer or from a specific show. But the Lieberson/Engel studio recordings were a new idea in that they began to take the scores of shows seriously as musical compositions. Some were recordings of shows that had pre-dated *Oklahoma!* and had not received original cast recordings, such as *Pal Joey*. Others were recordings of scores that had been previously taken down, but incompletely, such as *Porgy and Bess*.

The LP was a perfect new cultural product for an era in which the suburban lifestyle became the preferred choice for many Americans—the first time in the country's history that as many people lived in suburbs as in cities.[23] New York musicals were for them sophisticated cultural products that were not easily available, except through cast recordings on LP, which allowed access to thousands of people who might never see a Broadway show in New York. Like the earlier part of the century's interest in "good music," Americans in the late 1940s and 1950s began to be interested in status items, and Broadway musicals eventually came to be regarded as must-have items for what Ethan Mordden calls "the Informed Middle Class" (Mordden 1999, 261). Musicals became so popular with the general public outside of New York that when, in 1954, General Foods celebrated Rodgers and Hammerstein with a television salute, all three networks broadcast the show to 70 million viewers (Grant, 1). Three years later, when Rodgers and Hammerstein's television musical version of *Cinderella* premiered starring Julie Andrews, already a household name in large part due to the ubiquitous *My Fair Lady* LP, the viewership was 107 million.[24]

These telecasts made it possible for millions of people to experience Broadway talent in their own homes, and the cast recording on LP allowed constant in-home access. By the 1960s, however, a major sea change was afoot in the recording industry. Up to this time, the LP had represented largely contemporary "adult" tastes. Broadway cast recordings (most notably the original LP of *My Fair Lady*) were among the most popular LPs of the decade. Rock-and-roll was of course present and gaining popularity by then, but it was still dismissed by many critics and recording industry moguls as a passing fad, and relatively few recordings of the genre were widely popular on LP during the first years the format was in existence. But this was to change in the 1960s.

THE CONCEPT ALBUM AND POPULAR MUSIC ON LP

By the mid-1960s, the Beatles and other groups were beginning to have an impact not only with hit singles but also with LPs. By the end of the decade, the format that only ten years earlier had been almost totally dominated by show music and soft "adult" fare was now taken over by the country's "new" music. Between 1959 and 1970, the percentage of "rock" or "rock and roll" music sold on LP increased from below 10 percent of all LPs sold to over 50 percent.[25] Much of this radical change in music listening happened in the latter half of the decade. In 1968, the Beatles released *Sgt. Pepper's Lonely Hearts Club Band*, now often cited as the first "concept album." As *Reading the Beatles* authors Kenneth Womack and Todd F. Davis see it, the album suggested the idea that "the songs of an album [could] add up to a unified and coherent whole."[26] Paul McCartney would later suggest that he had no memory of an overt decision to write songs with a particularly "Northern" sound,[27] although the idea that the album consisted of songs by another group—alter egos for the Fab Four—gave the album a conceit, and the inclusion of a reprise of the title song gave it a cohesiveness that suggested a connection between all of the songs. Other popular artists would soon create even more elaborate "concept" albums, including The Who's 1969 double album, *Tommy*.

Of course, the idea of a group of interrelated songs, including reprises, was hardly something new for the LP. Besides Broadway show recordings, many artists had released albums of songs on a single theme or all by one composer. Sinatra is often given credit as the first artist to use the LP format to create an overall experience; as early as 1938, Sinatra's *The Voice*, released in an album of 78s, reflected an overall mood, and by the LP era, Sinatra began to make more complex choices, using his albums to portray himself as a character, described by biographer Chris Rojek as "the Zen master" of the game of love, with Sinatra "the very generalissimo of rejection."[28]

Other artists and genres also suggested the idea of a concept album long before the release of *Sgt. Pepper*, including jazz and comedy LPs all on one theme, but cast recordings and movie musical soundtrack albums were the most natural contributor to the form. There had also been Broadway-related concept albums since at least the 1940s—albums that would appear to represent a cast recording of a show but that had not yet appeared on stage; in some cases such albums actually did result in Broadway productions. The 1959 album *Clara*, for instance, starring Betty Garrett and James Komack, was produced on Broadway the next year as *Beg, Borrow or Steal*, a flop that lasted five performances.[29] But with the radical changes in popular culture during the 1960s, the idea of a concept album by a group like the Beatles was new. While most popular artists up to that time had found their widest audience through hit singles, the Beatles led the way for popular artists on LP. Though they continued to release singles after *Sgt. Pepper*, we as a culture, as Womack and Davis suggest, "came to recognize their albums as their principal form, as the ultimate goal for their artistic output" (16).

Changing ideas of what an album could be during the late 1960s had a profound effect on the role of Broadway cast recordings. At that time, a very young Andrew Lloyd Webber was attempting to break into the commercial theater as a composer. His collaborator and lyricist, Tim Rice, had begun his career working for EMI, which gave them an "in" with one of Great Britain's leading record companies.[30] At EMI, they released several songs together and in 1969 released a recording of their first larger work, a short musical originally written as a children's entertainment, *Joseph and the Amazing Technicolor Dreamcoat*. Their next collaboration would also materialize first on LP, though this time it would not be the small curiosity that the original *Joseph* recording had been.

Though Lloyd Webber later stated that it was always his intention for *Jesus Christ Superstar* to be a live theater piece,[31] the material was decidedly controversial. To test the waters, Lloyd Webber and Rice produced a single, "Superstar" (with "John 19:41" as the "B" side). The success of the single led to the recording and release of a double-LP concept album that became a phenomenon, particularly in the United States (⊙ Example 13.4). The success of the album launched an unprecedented theatrical history for the show. Rather than an original production being captured first on record and later remounted in duplicate stagings in various cities, following its initial popularity as a record, *Jesus Christ Superstar* was seen in various concert and live stagings across the United States prior to its first fully staged, fully sanctioned production. Lloyd Webber actually became involved in legal battles attempting to shut down various stagings prior to its first official production. The original Broadway production, staged by Tom O'Horgan (who had directed *Hair* on Broadway) lasted two years but was disliked by Lloyd Webber and many of the New York critics. A much less elaborate production directed by Jim Sharman opened in London in 1972 and became the West End's then longest-running hit, lasting eight years.

Lloyd Webber and Rice's second major collaboration also premiered as an album. This practice allowed the material to become first and foremost the property of its writers before it became associated with any particular director or production (Walsh, 100). But unlike *Jesus Christ Superstar*, *Evita* would eventually become highly associated with a single staging, that of famed producer-director Hal Prince. Though the concept album had presented the raw material, it was the stage production that remained the property's most successful incarnation.

As Lloyd Webber's musicals were making influential changes in the development of and expectations for musicals and cast recordings in the '70s, Broadway musicals and the world they reflected were also changing. Nineteen years after becoming president of Columbia Records, Goddard Lieberson announced, one day after his official retirement, that he would produce *A Chorus Line* for Columbia, one of his two final cast recordings (Marmorstein, 289).[32] Musical Director Donald Pippin later stated that he felt the show was "a little too contemporary" for Lieberson, which he felt marred the recording.[33] Lieberson, who had been a pioneer in the 1950s of promoting the music that Cold War era Americans could relate to, was perhaps too bound to that earlier era to be entirely successful with a youthful, contemporary work that not only was innovative in its creation and structure but also reflected the immense cultural shift that had occurred since Lieberson's heyday in the 1950s and '60s.

In *A Chorus Line*, a previously successful featured dancer comes to an audition in hopes of returning to the chorus. She does not want to be a star, she merely wishes to work. Cassie is perhaps the polar opposite of *Gypsy*'s Rose, who epitomizes the post–World War II obsession with capitalistic success through the most glamorous of all forms, Show Business. *Gypsy* remains one of Lieberson's most acclaimed cast albums, capturing Ethel Merman's equally electrifying and terrifying performance of songs that portray a woman so desperate for a piece of American stardom that she pushes away everyone who loves her. In contrast, John Lahr sees Cassie's desire to return to the line in *A Chorus Line* as a "new sound—the post-Vietnam sound of retreat." In Cassie, Lahr sees a reflection of "the culture's nostalgia for a simpler, happier life, one undamaged by the nation's imperialism, one that would replace the destiny of me with the destiny of we."[34] Between Lieberson's recording of *Gypsy* in 1959 and his recording of *A Chorus Line* in 1975, the country had become a radically different place, and Lieberson's consumer-based middle-class culture had disappeared.

The recording of *A Chorus Line*, the biggest hit show of the decade, never rose above ninety-eighth best-selling album of the week on the charts, reflecting the era's

diminishing interest in musicals on record. Music consumption in the years following would continue to develop further away from the standards set in the Lieberson
era (Marmorstein, 291). The LP itself eventually gave way to the compact disc (CD)
which remained standard format for music from the 1980s through the turn of the
millennium. But in the 2000s, the iPod and the downloadable MP3 have once again
changed the way consumers acquire music. In a sense, we have come full circle. In
the '50s, with the advent of the LP, cast recordings, soundtrack albums, and musicians like Frank Sinatra and Elvis so popularized the idea of the "album" as a concept that it was perhaps inevitable that the Beatles and other popular recording
artists would eventually adapt and take over the form. Today, however, we are back
to a jukebox style of music consumption, where listeners can choose to download
only the specific songs they want from any given album.

The Legacy and Future of the Cast Recording

In a recent discussion for the American Theatre Wing's "Working in the Theatre"
series, Decca Label Group executive Brian Drutman stated that the majority of sales
for cast recordings produced on the Decca label are sold "at the venue." Theatergoers
who visit the show in person want to take the recording home as a souvenir, as part
of the overall package they have purchased in going to see the show. Kurt Deutsch,
a former actor who represents the small label Sh-K-Boom/Ghostlight Records, got
started in the industry in part because the major record labels had become less
interested in producing cast recordings, a largely money-losing venture. Deutsch
states that many musicals on his label have done most of their business as digital
downloads, including youth-oriented musicals such as *Legally Blonde*.[35]

   With the current cost of creating a cast recording spiraling above $400,000 on
average, the likelihood of making a profit becomes less and less. Few records sell the
approximately 120,000 units necessary to recoup their costs. A new model for producing cast albums may be needed to make their future feasible. Mark N. Grant
notes that musicals have rarely been recorded live in the theater, while there have
long been live recordings of opera (204–5); however, this route might involve significant negotiations with the various unions involved.

   Whether the cost of making cast recordings will ultimately result in fewer
albums being recorded, their utility goes beyond their immediate uses in marketing
a show and selling albums. Cast recordings of musicals are, among other uses,
important tools for the thousands of productions of musicals that continue to
appear throughout the United States and abroad. Ted Chapin, president and executive director of the Rodgers & Hammerstein Organization, notes that he has learned
to be cautious when giving permission for new recordings of scores in the R&H

licensing catalog, since new arrangements will lead producing groups to request to alter their own productions to reflect these later recordings ("For the Record").

John Yap at TER/Jay Records started his "Complete Original Masterworks Editions" (full-score recordings of Broadway shows) largely, he says, because he was "somewhat disappointed by the fact that a lot of the music and songs were cut and abridged for…original cast albums as opposed to opera recordings, where the works were not only recorded complete, they were always of the original orchestrations and there were multiple versions of each opera." But while Yap hopes these recordings will be embraced by the musical theater-loving public in much the way that opera devotees value complete recordings, he also admits to "an inkling that the series would be very useful and helpful to the likes of musical directors, choreographers, conductors, directors and perhaps some actors who wanted to get the measures of the characters" (private correspondence).

Since the decline of Broadway musicals within popular culture, the significance of the cast recording has changed. Once, the cast album was a product for home consumption largely for a public who would never witness the musicals from which the albums were derived. Today, new recordings of musicals are primarily souvenirs of a particular show for audience members who have seen it, or tools for young practitioners to use in the mounting of a show. But the Golden Age of cast albums— roughly the years Goddard Lieberson was recording musicals at Columbia, from the late 1940s to the early 1970s—yielded what amounts to a living history of the Broadway musical. Cast albums were not recorded as legacy items, but that is what they have become. They are important in preserving not only the music but also the actual performances of musicals. As the life of a show goes on, its score may be recorded many times. What the original cast recording can reveal is a sense of the production itself—what made the show what it was, live on stage in front of an audience. Particularly as we listen today to cast recordings from the 1940s and '50s, when Broadway musicals were at the zenith of their popularity, it is possible to detect living moments that would otherwise be completely lost to time.

Anyone who has attended a show on Broadway will know that many of the most thrilling moments come from the experience of witnessing the performance live in the theater. The experience of hearing live music accompanied by the performance of actors and dancers in front of you is vastly different from the experience of listening to a cast album of the same show at home. But while the thrill of live performance can never be duplicated on record or CD, the cast recording, across several decades, remains our most lasting documentation of performances on Broadway.

NOTES

1. Evan Eisenberg, *The Recording Angel: Music, Records and Culture from Aristotle to Zappa*, 2nd ed. (New Haven, CT: Yale University Press, 2005), pp. 180–81.

2. Goddard Lieberson, liner notes from *Who's Afraid of Virginia Woolf?, an Original Broadway Cast Recording* (Columbia Records Masterwork Series, Monaural DOL 287, 1963).

3. For more on the birth of commercial radio, see Kathleen Drowne and Patrick Huber, *American Popular Culture through History: The 1920s* (Westport, CT: Greenwood Press, 2004), pp. 238–42.

4. Quoted in Mark Katz, "Making America More Musical through the Phonograph, 1900–1930" (*American Music* 16.4 [Winter 1998]: 448–75), p. 453.

5. Katz, 453; see also Mark Tucker, ed., "RD Darell Criticism in the *Phonograph Monthly Review* (1927–1931)" (*The Duke Ellington Reader* [New York: Oxford University Press, 1995]).

6. Quoted in Tim Anderson, " 'Buried under the Fecundity of His Own Creations': Reconsidering the Recording Bans of the American Federation of Musicians, 1942–1944 and 1948" (*American Music* 22.2 [Summer 2004]: 231–69), p. 237.

7. The first recordings were made of the London cast, followed by recordings of the American cast the following year; see Tim Brooks, "Early Recordings of Songs from *Florodora*: Tell Me, Pretty Maiden…Who Are You?—A Discographical Mystery" (*Association for Recorded Sound Collections Journal* 31 [2000]: 51–64), and Ethan Mordden, *Broadway Babies: The People Who Made the American Musical* (New York: Oxford University Press, 1983), p. 204. For blanket histories of the cast album, see Ethan Mordden, *Beautiful Mornin': The Broadway Musical in the 1940s* (New York: Oxford University Press, 1999), pp. 236–70, and Mark N. Grant, *The Rise and Fall of the Broadway Musical* (Boston: Northeastern University Press, 2004), pp. 203–7.

8. See, for instance, Leo N. Miletich, *Broadway's Prize-Winning Musicals: An Annotated Guide for Libraries and Audio Collectors* (New York: Haworth Press, 1993), p. 13, and Max Wilk, *Oh! The Story of Oklahoma! A Celebration of America's Most Loved Musical* (New York: Applause, 2002, 1993), pp. 240–41.

9. Mordden 1983, 217–19. Lawrence's recording is one of three early recordings of *Lady in the Dark*. RCA Victor released three ten-inch discs of Lawrence's six cuts, which featured a male quartet from the Broadway cast and mostly followed the score as it was performed on stage. Decca's preceding album of cuts featured Hildegarde, a popular radio singer, and Danny Kaye recorded six numbers for Columbia, including some of Lawrence's numbers, in pop arrangements. The show's composer, Kurt Weill, confided to Ira Gershwin (the show's lyricist) that he preferred Hildegarde's recordings to Lawrence's. See Bruce D. McClung. *Lady in the Dark: Biography of a Musical* (New York: Oxford University Press, 2007), p. 106.

10. Edward Jablonski, *Gershwin: With a New Critical Discography* (New York: Da Capo Press, 1998), p. 291.

11. Geoffrey Block, *Enchanted Evenings: The Broadway Musical from Show Boat to Sondheim* (New York: Oxford University Press, 2004), pp. 117 and 365. Block argues that the 1938 recording of *Cradle* was "the first Broadway cast album, a historical distinction almost always invariably and incorrectly attributed to *Oklahaoma!*" (117). For a fuller history of *The Cradle Will Rock*'s first public performances and the use of piano accompaniment instead of Blitzstein's original full orchestration, see, for instance, John Houseman, *Run-Through: A Memoir* (New York: Touchstone, 1980), pp. 242–81.

12. Tim Carter, *Oklahoma! The Making of an American Musical* (New Haven, CT: Yale University Press, 2007), p. 226.

13. Wanda Martin, "V-Disks Help Hasten V-Day" (*The Billboard 1944 Music Year Book* [Sixth Annual Edition]), p. 148.

14. Mordden 1999, 239. The album was recorded in October and released in December. It was so popular that three additional songs from the show were recorded the following May, released in January 1945, effectively creating an album with every major number from the show, excluding only dances and reprises (Carter, 227).

15. Travis Elborough, *The Vinyl Countdown* (Berkeley: Soft Skull Press, 2009), p. 25.

16. Gary Marmorstein, *The Label: The Story of Columbia Records* (New York: Thunder's Mouth Press, 2007), p. 120.

17. With the LP, most record "albums" were in fact no longer albums in the literal sense, since most releases consisted of single discs, which eliminated the need to set multiple discs into individual sleeves. But the term stuck to LPs that were collections of shorter numbers (such as original cast albums) by analogy and by habit, whereas the term was only rarely applied to recordings of longer works (opera, symphonies) even though these, too, were released in album form before the advent of the LP.

18. J. K. Holman, *Wagner's Ring: A Listener's Companion and Concordance* (Pompton Plains, NJ: Amadeus Press, 1996), p. 428.

19. Leonard Bernstein, unreleased segment of *Sondheim: A Musical Tribute* (Warner Brothers, LP No. 2WS 2705, 1973).

20. "Lieberson Sees A&R Exec as 'Heart' of Record Business" (uncredited, *Billboard* [August 4, 1956]: B-21).

21. Quoted in William Hutchings, *Samuel Beckett's Waiting for Godot: A Reference Guide* (Westport, CT: Praeger, 2005), p. 18. Lieberson had previously produced an eighteen-record set of 78s of the 1943 Broadway production of *Othello* starring Paul Robeson, José Ferrer, and Uta Hagen. Widely regarded as a landmark production for its casting of an African American in the title role, it was also one of the first full-length recordings of a Shakespeare play. It was also a result of the then-current recording ban; as a spoken word album, it required no musicians; see Barbara Hodgdon and William B. Worthen, eds., *A Companion to Shakespeare and Performance* (Oxford: Blackwell, 2005), p. 424, and Marmorstein, 117.

22. Quoted in Craig Zadan, *Sondheim & Co.*, 2nd ed. (New York: Perennial Library, 1989), p. 173.

23. "By 1960 as many people lived in the suburbs as in cities." Nigel Whiteley, "Toward a Throw-Away Culture. Consumerism, 'Style Obsolesence' and Cultural Theory in the 1950s and 1960s" (*Oxford Art Journal* 10.2 "The 60s" [1987]: 3–27), p. 7.

24. Richard Rodgers, *Musical Stages: An Autobiography*, updated ed. (New York: Da Capo Press, 2002), p. 293.

25. Philip H. Ennis, *The Seventh Stream: The Emergence of Rocknroll in American Popular Music* (Hanover, NH: Wesleyan University Press, 1992), p. 345.

26. Kenneth Womack and Todd F. Davis, *Reading the Beatles: Cultural Studies, Literary Criticism, and the Fab Four* (Albany: State University of New York Press, 2006), p. 16.

27. Barry Miles, *Paul McCartney: Many Years from Now,* 1st American ed. (New York: Henry Holt, 1997), p. 307.

28. Chris Rojek, *Frank Sinatra* (Cambridge, MA: Polity, 2004), p. 44. For more on Sinatra as one of the innovators of the "concept album," see Elborough, 147.

29. Steven Suskin, ed., *Opening Night on Broadway: A Critical Quotebook of the Golden Era of the Musical Theatre, Oklahoma! (1943) to Fiddler on the Roof (1964)* (New York: Schirmer Books, 1990), pp. 73–74.

30. Michael Walsh, *Andrew Lloyd Webber: His Life and Works*, updated and enlarged ed. (New York: HarperCollins: 1989), p. 31.

31. Episode Five of *Broadway! A Musical History with Ron Husmann* (Videotape). (Irvine, CA: Chesney Communications, 1988).

32. Lieberson's final cast recording was, serendipitously, the 1976 "Twentieth Anniversary" revival recording of *My Fair Lady*, starring Christine Andreas and Ian Richardson.

33. Quoted in Gary Stevens and Alan George, *The Longest Line: Broadway's Most Singular Sensation,* A Chorus Line (New York: Applause Books, 1995), p. 97.

34. John Lahr, "Toeing the Line: 'A Chorus Line' is back on Broadway" (*New Yorker* [October 16, 2006], http://www.newyorker.com/archive/2006/10/16/061016crth_theatre, accessed August 19, 2009).

35. Theodore S. Chapin, Kurt Deutsch, Brian Drutman, Thomas Z. Shepard, and Melissa Rose Bernardo, "For The Record: Inside Cast Albums" (American Theatre Wing's *Working In the Theatre* [April, 2009]), http://americantheatrewing.org/wit/detail/cast_albums_04_09, accessed August 19, 2009.

PART IV

IDENTITIES

CHAPTER 14

RACE, ETHNICITY, PERFORMANCE

TODD DECKER

> We deplore the evil of stereotypes in fiction, on the stage
> and on the screen—the crap-shooting, razor wielding
> Negro, the crafty and penurious Jew, the pugnacious,
> whiskey drinking Irishman. All these are on their way out as
> stock characters. When races are invariably symbolized by
> these types, the result is not only harmful but it is likely to
> make dull entertainment.[1]

Oscar Hammerstein II wrote this assessment in 1948, and in one sense he was right: negative theatrical stereotypes were on the way out in the immediate postwar years. Whether these stereotypes made for "dull entertainment" is debatable. Aimed at specific audiences, the stereotypes Hammerstein listed had been highly successful, and in their day they were the very antithesis of "dull entertainment." Throughout its history, the musical has relied on the dramaturgical shorthand stereotypes provide, chiefly as a means to enhance the entertainment value of a product being sold to particular audiences.

Hammerstein's short list of hateful stereotypes—the kind any enlightened person would see as wrong—fails to include others carrying more ambiguous meanings: the exaggerated smiles and good spirits of black mammy figures, "hot-blooded" Latin types, "wise" Asians, laconic Native Americans, "lazy" black males who avoid work by moving and talking slowly (exemplified by the African American actor Stepin Fetchit, a major Hollywood star in the 1930s), stuffy Germans, and accent-based characters from anywhere whose humorously incorrect use of a second language provokes laughter in an audience of native speakers.

Hammerstein's negative types and the more ambiguous "comic" types listed above together form an array of racial and ethnic masks familiar throughout popular culture history, including the musical. These combinations of costume, makeup, posture, accent, character traits, and narrative possibilities have gone in and out of fashion and acceptability. Some provided an excuse for exotic or spectacular display. Others offered cover for social or political satire. All are the products of particular social and historical circumstances. When circumstances change, typically, stereotypes do as well. Deeply embedded in the ever-changing social fabric of the nation, ethnic and racial stereotypes are frequently the most dated aspects of musical shows and films for later audiences, and while they can be softened or excised completely in later productions on stage, they live forever in films.

In musical terms, racial and ethnic masks might take the form of a melody that sounds foreign, such as the pentatonic "Oriental" sound of Richard Rodgers's "March of the Siamese Children" from *The King and I*, or complex rhythms suggesting a particular geographic origin, such as the "Latin" cross rhythms in Leonard Bernstein's "America" from *West Side Story*. These harmonic or rhythmic tropes assume a racially unmarked musical style to which the exotic effects are added. In similar fashion, racial and ethnic stereotypes are most often added to a show or film otherwise populated by ethnically and racially unmarked "white" characters with whom the broadest audience in a majority white nation can identify. Audiences for the Broadway and Hollywood musical have been consistently urban, middle and upper class, and white. It's no surprise that ethnic and racial others usually turn up as comic sidekicks rather than romantic leads or figures of authority.

The racial and ethnic masks prominent in the history of the musical are double-edged. Some have distorted particular groups in pernicious ways, causing lingering cultural effects as undeniable as they are immeasurable. Others did significant work helping select groups assimilate, facilitating passage into the unmarked collective called white. Andrea Most, among others, has argued that in the case of Jewish Americans, the opportunity to put on and take off a comic Jewish mask, among others in their repertoire, served performers such as Eddie Cantor well, allowing them to argue for the full inclusion of Jews as assimilated, racially unmarked Americans.[2]

Because the musical thrives on exaggeration, the ethnic and racial masks deployed throughout its history have represented racial and ethnic others in an altogether unsubtle fashion. This license to exaggerate is inevitably expanded if the audience has no real knowledge of the group being represented. Such is the case with blackface, easily the most influential mask in the history of the musical. For example, Sophie Tucker broke through on the vaudeville circuit in the 1900s by appearing as a blackface coon shouter. At the turn of the twentieth century, coon songs and shouters presented some of the harshest, most baldly racist stereotypes ever to appear in popular music. They were tremendously popular with audiences in northern cities that were experiencing an explosion in their African American populations as rural southern blacks migrated north, seeking greater opportunities and less racism. At the end of her coon-shouting act, Tucker would remove a single glove, revealing to the audience that she was, in fact, white. In her autobiography, Tucker reports that cries of amazement from her audiences followed the revelation of her actual racial identity.[3] That northern audiences could have mistaken Tucker for a black performer indicates that the derogatory stereotypes of blackface coon shouters were doing powerful cultural work. As Tucker's example shows, control over racial or ethnic masks is central to a performer's power over her career.

Pulling off a glove and provoking the audience's wonder at an act of racial mimicry—however false the stereotype—has not been an option for African American performers, who labor under a different set of assumptions in a nation historically obsessed with segregating black from white in all areas, including the musical. African Americans on the musical stage and screen have more often than not found their careers fundamentally shaped by their skin color. Their perceived black identity prevents African American performers from freely taking up or setting down ethnic and racial masks. This is not to say that performers with visibly Latin or Asian identities have not been similarly limited. In terms of musical style, however, Latin-inspired music has not affected the sound of the musical beyond its use as an exotic "tinge," and Asian-derived sounds have had little to no presence outside of "oriental" tropes drawn from European classical music and American popular song. Yet, as with virtually every kind of twentieth-century American popular music, the musical stage and screen has been intimately linked to African American musical styles; moreover, African Americans as a group have played defining roles as performers on the musical stage (as the long history of black-cast shows attests).

The distinction between black and white—a matter of perceived racial identity, of literally judging performers by their skin color—has had a structuring role across the history of the musical. This color line inevitably defines the history of the musical even as it defines the history of the nation. Often, but not always, the color line comes into focus when we attend closely to when and how black musical style and African American performers have been brought into the musical, a genre that has remained chiefly concerned with celebrating a functioning national community understood almost always to be, like the musical's primary audience, white.[4] To illustrate the central importance of race in American musicals, and especially the black/white color line, I focus for the remainder of this chapter on a series of case studies—selected stage and screen musicals and performers from the 1920s, 1940s, and 1950s—before concluding with a consideration of 1990s revivals.

NARRATIVE AND MUSICAL STYLE IN THE 1920S

The Broadway stage was at its peak in production activity and cultural power during the 1920s, a period when African American performers and musical style had a tremendous impact on the musical. The 1920s were ushered in by the first black-cast hit of the Jazz Age: *Shuffle Along* opened in 1921 and played 484 performances (placing it among the longest-running shows of the decade). Unlike most black-cast shows then and after, *Shuffle Along* not only starred African Americans but was written and produced by African Americans as well. In a score dominated by high-energy rhythm numbers, composer Eubie Blake and lyricist Noble Sissle took a risk with the song "Love Will Find a Way." This love duet for the romantic leads is unmarked by tropes of blackness and would easily fit into any operetta of the time. With a broad melody and sentimental lyrics in standard, rather flowery English, "Love Will Find a Way" characterized *Shuffle Along*'s black lovers as just like any other lovers—meaning white lovers—on the musical stage (🌑 Example 14.1). Sissle and Blake feared there might be a negative response from a Broadway audience unused to black characters presented in non-stereotypical ways. Contrary to these fears, the song was greeted respectfully, although it didn't become a hit. There have been few follow-ups to "Love Will Find a Way." For black performers, doing "white" musical numbers has never been as profitable as emphasizing the link between black performers and black musical styles.

The success of *Shuffle Along* led to a string of jazzy black-cast shows across the 1920s, which in turn created a sizable pool of experienced African American talent in New York. By the 1927–28 season, white producers were calling on black performers in unprecedented numbers. The only show still revived from this period is *Show Boat*, which opened in December 1927. Defying the pattern of segregating black and white performers from each other in different shows, *Show Boat* calls for an interracial cast of black and white performers (one of just a handful of such shows in Broadway history). With book and lyrics by Hammerstein and music by Jerome Kern, *Show Boat* was structured around the visible and audible differences between its black and white cast members. Racial identity defines everyone in *Show Boat*, an exceptional work that interrogates the absurdities and tragedies of racism even as it inevitably reinforces the racial stereotypes of the period.

Based on Edna Ferber's best-selling novel of 1926, the story of *Show Boat* centers on a white couple—Gaylord Ravenal and Magnolia Hawkes—who meet and marry in the romantic context of a floating theater on the Mississippi River in the late nineteenth century. Ravenal, a gambler whose luck finally runs out, abandons Magnolia in Chicago, leaving her to support and raise their young daughter. In the novel, the couple never reconciles. But the musical demands happy endings, and in the stage version *Show Boat* ends with the lovers reunited on the boat where they first fell in love. A secondary plot involving Julie, a light-skinned black woman trying (unsuccessfully) to pass as white, is skillfully worked into Magnolia and Ravenal's story. When Ravenal abandons Magnolia, she is able to earn a living singing on the stage, drawing on her experience as a performer on the floating theater, where she had learned how to sing from Joe, a black worker on the showboat and a decidedly minor character in the novel. Kern and Hammerstein saw the potential to expand the part of Joe on the musical stage and cast Paul Robeson in the part. Robeson, one of the most famous black performers of the time, had undeniable star quality with New York's white audience, having appeared in successful plays and sung sold-out recitals of Negro spirituals.[5]

While building *Show Boat* around the opportunity to feature Robeson in an operetta centered on a white romance, Kern, Hammerstein, and producer Florenz Ziegfeld expanded the black presence in the show, hiring an entire chorus of African American singers and dancers. There was no precedent in the novel for this decision. Numbering over forty, the black chorus performed a full range of '20s black musical theater types: serious spiritual-type numbers, high-spirited levee dances in modest southern costumes, jazzy dances in glitzy contemporary clothes, even an ironic "jungle" number as black New Yorkers hired to play African villagers for an anthropological exhibit at the 1893 Chicago World's Fair. The men of the black chorus opened the show singing "Niggers all work on de Mississippi/Niggers all work whil' de white folks play." This delineation of the color line was strong stuff then and proved unrevivable in later decades, when the opening words of both lines were replaced by "colored folks work," "darkies all work," and the racially neutral "here we all work."

Despite their being featured throughout the show, none of the black chorus's numbers connected directly to the story of the white lovers Magnolia and Gaylord: the black chorus added to the entertainment value of *Show Boat* but did not participate in the plot (except through Julie). In the subsequent revivals and film versions of *Show Boat*, of which there have been many, the story of the white lovers remained intact while many of the black chorus numbers so important to the 1927 original were cut, often because later audiences found these 1920s stereotypes to be unacceptably, irredeemably racist.

The first commercially successful sound film with synchronized lip movements opened in 1927 just a few weeks before *Show Boat*. *The Jazz Singer* remains one of the most intensely Jewish films ever released for a general audience: it is also a story that celebrates Broadway as the pinnacle of American success. The central character, Jakie Rabinowitz, grows up in an orthodox Jewish home on Manhattan's Lower East Side. His rabbi father forbids him to sing jazz, which in this context means American popular music. But Jakie wants to go on the stage, and he runs away to be a performer, eventually earning the chance to appear in a big-time Broadway show. Returning to his parents' home for the first time as an adult, Jakie finds his father gravely ill and unable to sing for services on the most sacred night of the Jewish year—the very night Jakie's Broadway show is to open.

Al Jolson, a seasoned Broadway star who built his success performing both in and out of blackface, played the part of Jakie. In *The Jazz Singer,* nothing in Jolson's performance style is typed as black (in other contexts, he did play a stereotypical "darky," although always with his signature style). Indeed Jakie's Jewish heritage— his "tear in the voice"—is understood to be the source of his extraordinary ability to sell a song: the blackface mask is simply part of the Jolson persona. The conflict at the heart of *The Jazz Singer* is lodged within Jakie's character: will he be true to his faith and family and sing on the holiest day of the Jewish year or will he honor the American show business creed that dictates the show must go on? In the end, Jakie—and the film audience—has it both ways: the opening is postponed while Jakie sings the Kol Nidre in his dying father's place; in the next scene, Jakie's knockin' 'em dead on Broadway, singing a mammy song to his teary-eyed mother in the front row. In this one instance in *The Jazz Singer*, it may appear that Jolson matches the blackface mask with a racial stereotype: the mammy singer. But he sings completely without an accent and, as noted, addresses the song directly to his Jewish mother (🔊 Example 14.2). For a late 1920s audience, the mammy singer was less a black stereotype that represented some essential quality of African Americans than a Jolson routine, a show-biz pose associated with a specific star performer. Of course, Jolson's power over the blackface mask—his ability, like Tucker's, to put it on and take it off at will—should not be overlooked.

The pain and pleasure of assimilation explored in *The Jazz Singer* became an enduring part of the affirming American story told again and again by the musical. It could be translated into almost any ethnic other (see the discussion of *Flower Drum Song* later in the chapter.). But it would be impossible to make a version of *The Jazz Singer* where Jolson's character was black. The African American experience is fundamentally unlike that of immigrant groups who came on their own terms rather than through force. And while the assimilation story at the heart of *The Jazz Singer* seems made for the celebratory mode of the musical, the very different historical experience of African Americans is not so easy to render in the simplified narrative patterns of the musical.[6]

Exotic "Other" Women in 1940s Hollywood

The contrasting careers of Carmen Miranda, the embodiment of a particular Latin stereotype, and Lena Horne, the only African American woman to sign a star contract with a major Hollywood studio, highlight how ethnicity and race played out during the glory years of the musical screen. Miranda and Horne attained Hollywood stardom at almost exactly the same time—Miranda in 1940, Horne in 1942—and their relatively brief careers ended around the same time as well. Both appeared in only one studio-era film after 1950. But the way Hollywood integrated Miranda and Horne into the world of the film musical was fundamentally different. While Miranda was able to bring an exaggerated ethnic color to both the music and the plot of the films she starred in—endearing her to the audience as an animated individual who spoke as well as sang—Horne's refined persona was confined to musical numbers only.

Carmen Miranda came to Hollywood from Brazil by way of Broadway. She appeared in fourteen films between 1940 and 1953, almost all in Technicolor, an expensive process suited to her signature lavish costumes and bright red lipstick. Miranda usually played a nightclub performer, which allowed her to offer several musical numbers and also take a supporting comic role in the plot. Most of her films provide ample space for Miranda's over-the-top persona as "the lady in the tutti-frutti hat." Miranda's musical numbers invariably involved the sights and sounds of an all-male Latin band: either the Bando da Lua, a group of light-skinned, middle-class Brazilians who traveled to New York with Miranda for her first Broadway appearances, or later, at MGM, Xavier Cugat's extremely popular band. Miranda was Brazilian (although born in Portugal) and Cugat, a classically trained violinist, was Spanish by way of Cuba: in the boiled-down logic of American popular music, they both made "Latin" music (🔊 Example 14.3). Hollywood made little attempt to distinguish between different national styles: South America was conceptualized as an undifferentiated cultural area, exuberantly colorful and filled with rhythms defined collectively as "Latin."

In her songs *con movimientos*, Miranda usually appeared surrounded by a group of men playing various Latin hand percussion instruments and guitars, dancing simple but (for that time) sexy steps, with lots of hip-swinging and leg-showing. Generic "Latin" rhythms packaged for a mass audience have periodically hit it big, and Miranda led the explosion of Latin-tinged music that coincided with the wartime Good Neighbor Policy, an effort to solidify U.S. ties with South America by cultural as well as political means. Miranda was often allowed a sexual role in her films as well, typically as an exotic figure of desire for older white male comic characters. In *The Gang's All Here* (1943), she manipulates Edward Everett Horton by covering his face with red kisses, marks indicative more of his desire than of any real danger posed by Miranda. Her playful, slightly naughty, in the end innocent and joyous sexuality was a key part of Miranda's attraction. However excessive and campy her persona might appear in retrospect, the films viewed whole tell a different story. Behind her malapropisms and frequent lapses into lightning-fast Portuguese lay a conniving mind that was frequently running the show. She provided a capable ally to the white ingénue at the center of virtually all her films—a bit of wishful political allegory, perhaps—and even if she wasn't at the center of the plot, a Carmen Miranda film is typically filled with the Brazilian bombshell's defining presence from start to finish.

Lena Horne made her first big splash in the early 1940s at Café Society, a New York nightclub that allowed black and white patrons to sit together at a time when nightlife, like most of American society, was segregated. Wartime pressure on the film industry encouraged the studios to expand the possibilities for black performers, and Horne was the primary beneficiary of this push to change Hollywood's presentation of African Americans. In 1942, Horne signed a star contract with MGM, but once they had her, the studio didn't know what to do with her. The Production Code, an informal agreement among the studios defining acceptable film content, forbade any suggestion of romance between black and white characters or actors. Horne could not flirt with her white co-stars like Miranda could, and without African American peers to play opposite her, there was little means to insert Horne into the plot. She did star in two black-cast films—*Cabin in the Sky* and *Stormy Weather*, both 1943—but these proved to be historical anomalies. And so, Horne appeared as herself in a series of minimally produced musical segments, inserted as specialty numbers unconnected to the plots of their films. An intensely photogenic subject, Horne typically sang one, sometimes two songs dressed in an elegant gown, usually standing almost entirely still. She always received a glamorizing close-up, treatment that created the aura of the star around her. But the limits on Horne's participation in these films were severe. Musically, Horne's subtle, rather personal style—shaped in the 1930s when she toured as a singer with both black and white bands—was ideal for the screen, and her solos, such as "Honeysuckle Rose" from *Thousands Cheer* (1943), remain highlights of the era (● Example 14.4). But since there was no possibility of tying Horne into the plots of her films, she languished as a specialty performer, boxed in by the realities of the movie business. Horne was deeply dissatisfied with the limitations Hollywood put on her talent, and after negotiating a contract that gave her most of the year free to perform elsewhere—highly exceptional for MGM—she asked to be released in 1950.

Living Rooms and Nightclubs in Flower Drum Song (1958 and 2002)

In the postwar decades, Hammerstein collaborated with composer Richard Rodgers on a series of musicals that brought Asians and Asian Americans into the Broadway musical in a substantial way for the first time. *South Pacific* (1949), *The King and I* (1951), and *Flower Drum Song* (1958) form a triptych of Asian-themed musicals, with Stephen Sondheim's *Pacific Overtures* (1976) serving as a lone response.[7] Asian stereotypes—comic, serious, or otherwise—have never been staples of the American musical and there has never been a sizable group of Asian American musical theater professionals. Given the outsized influence of Hammerstein, the musical with Asian characters is a writer's rather than a performer's tradition. In this light, the original and revised versions of *Flower Drum Song* offer an illuminating comparison, especially as this is the only one of the four "Asian" musicals set in the contemporary United States and directly concerned with questions of assimilation. And just as *The Jazz Singer* centered on the irreconcilable distance between the synagogue and the Broadway stage, *Flower Drum Song* turns on the contrast between a traditional Chinese home and an American-style nightclub.

Adapted from a 1957 novel by Chinese immigrant C. Y. Yee, *Flower Drum Song* opened in 1958, and a widescreen color film version followed soon after in 1961. Set in contemporary San Francisco, *Flower Drum Song* tells a multigenerational tale of tradition and assimilation by the gentlest of means. Largely lacking in spectacle and set almost entirely in domestic spaces, *Flower Drum Song* is the most play-like of Rodgers and Hammerstein's musical plays. While the revisal trend of the 1990s and 2000s saw the return to Broadway of many classic Rodgers and Hammerstein shows in slightly altered form, none were subjected to the comprehensive overhaul *Flower Drum Song* received. David Henry Hwang, the most successful Asian American playwright of his generation, worked with director/choreographer

Robert Longbottom to create an entirely new plot, retaining only the songs from the original. As Hwang noted in his introduction to the printed libretto, "I don't think a single line remains from the original book." The original production was modestly successful (seventeen months on Broadway followed by seventeen months on national tour); the revisal, which opened on Broadway in 2002, was a commercial failure.

The original *Flower Drum Song* tells the story of Mei Li, a Chinese girl who comes to San Francisco for an arranged marriage with Sammy Fong, owner of a Chinatown nightclub. Sammy doesn't want to follow thorough on the marriage contract—his mother arranged the match—and he convinces the father of Wang Ta to accept Mei Li as an ideal traditional Chinese bride for his son. Ta describes himself early on as "both" Chinese and American, saying "sometimes the American half shocks the Oriental half." He wants to choose his own bride and already has someone in mind, a Chinese American girl named Linda Low who, unbeknownst to Ta, works as a dancer at Sammy's nightclub and is, in fact, Sammy's lover. After Ta sees the assimilated Linda doing a Chinese-themed striptease at Sammy's club, his interest turns definitively toward Mei Li, who maintains a slight accent and modest demeanor throughout. Mei Li's appearance at a party scene in a glamorous yet tasteful American dress visually argues for her potential to assimilate just the right amount for Ta's sense of himself as "both" Chinese and American. Ta's father and aunt, gently comic elders, are major characters and Ta's family home— "architecturally Victorian with Chinese decoration superimposed"—is the primary setting. Traditional ways preserved by Chinatown's elders and the modern American ways of the children are juxtaposed throughout. In the end, the couples are sorted out in satisfactory fashion—Ta with Mei Li, Sammy with Linda—by way of the word "wetback," a contemporary racial epithet for an illegal Mexican immigrant. Spoken by Mei Li at the crucial moment—she learns the word watching late night TV—"wetback" assumes comic proportions as the children manage to get their way with their parent's blessings to boot, a thoroughly American result.

Two-thirds of the way into act one, we find ourselves at the graduation celebration of the Marina American Citizenship School. The scene typifies the gentle approach Hammerstein's version takes to questions of ethnicity and assimilation. Madame Liang, played by Juanita Hall, says, "I am proud to be both Chinese and American" and compares living in America to "that Chinese dish that the Americans invented." (Hall, a light-skinned African American, had played the much less subtly drawn Bloody Mary in *South Pacific.*) Liang then leads the group in "Chop Suey," a catalog song about late 1950s American life that is largely unmarked by Chinese examples. One can imagine almost any group of older ethnic "others" singing the song, which expresses excitement about citizenship in a modern country (⬤ Example 14.5). The only Chinese thing about the number is the title, which "Americans invented" after all. "Chop Suey" can be read as a reply to the more aggressive young Puerto Rican women of *West Side Story* (which opened in 1957 and ran concurrently with *Flower Drum Song* in 1960), a group of recent immigrants who sang a similar list of good American things in the song "America." The difference is the way Anita in *West Side Story* frames Puerto Rico as a place she never wants to return to. This never happens in *Flower Drum Song*, where respect for the homeland is taken for granted and a multigenerational new-world community modeled on the homeland is in place. "Chop Suey," like the original *Flower Drum Song* as a whole, is about America now, a place where immigrants are fitting in, where their children are marrying for love, and where even the older generation can sing show tunes the larger white audience can enjoy.[8]

The 2002 revisal retained the 1960 setting of the original, and so *Flower Drum Song*, originally a contemporary story, became a period piece. Hwang's version cuts the entire citizenship scene, along with the original's evocation of a solid middle-class Chinese American world with stable ties to the homeland. Instead, Hwang denies his characters any anchor in the new world. "Chop Suey" becomes the act two opener at the "Club Chop Suey." All Hammerstein's references to 1950s America were removed and the number redesigned along the lines of "Wilkommen," the decadent opening of *Cabaret* (1966). Uncle Sammy—an elder Chinese transformed from traditional opera singer to nightclub emcee—brings on the boy waiters and girl dancers, the latter dressed as dancing "to go" containers and introduced with the cry "And don't forget MSG for More Stunning Girls." All the sensitivity of the original is lost in this generic Broadway spectacle, where funny costumes stand in for Hammerstein's lyrics (which were perhaps too specific in their references to strike a chord with twenty-first-century audiences).

While domestic spaces dominate in the original, Hwang turned *Flower Drum Song* into a backstage musical where cultural tensions between Chinese and American values were dramatized as a contrast between traditional Chinese opera and the brash sounds of a Chinese-themed nightclub in 1950s San Francisco Chinatown.[9] While this conceit may work on a dramatic level, musically it proves problematic. Hwang had no access to music of a remotely authentic Chinese kind: he was limited to Rodgers's score. Rodgers's tunes for *Flower Drum Song* are largely unmarked by exotic "Oriental" tropes: only Mei Li's songs contain such touches. *Flower Drum Song* sounds, especially in its melodies, for the most part like a typical Rodgers and Hammerstein score. Preserving the potential for most of the songs to be sung out of context, Hammerstein seldom referred to the Chinese identity of the characters in his lyrics. The discrete addition of "Oriental" colors by orchestrator Robert Russell Bennett renders the score just slightly foreign. For the revisal, orchestrator Don Sebesky imported a small battery of instruments, mostly percussion, from the Peking opera tradition into the pit orchestra. These striking timbres are carefully introduced at the start of the revisal, giving the opening moments an exciting otherness (◉ Example 14.6). Still, these often delicate sounds do little to alter the forceful showbiz quality of the whole. When traditional Chinese opera is demonstrated with the tune "You Are Beautiful," Chinese flute and gongs are given prominence, but the tune is firmly in the Broadway tradition and the vocal style of the performers draws on the emotive power ballads of Broadway megamusicals and animated Disney films (◉ Example 14.7). Under these terms, the music cannot contribute to the storytelling or delineation of character. This didn't matter much in Hammerstein's version, which presents a world where assimilation is the goal and continuity with Broadway tradition is emphasized. But in the revisal, where stylistic contrast between traditional Chinese and American show biz is key, there simply isn't enough musical difference available in the Broadway idiom to make the point.[10]

ADDING THE BLACK GOSPEL VOICE IN 1990S REVISALS

Asians and Latinos have been less important in the history of the musical primarily because their occasional inclusion has not had a lasting impact on the music or dance content of the genre. In sharp contrast, identifiably African American musical styles have had, and continue to have, a formative impact on the sound of the musical. This is apparent in a minor trend of 1990s and 2000s revivals: the introduction of featured black characters into shows that were originally all white. In the film version of *Chicago* (2002), for example, rapper turned mainstream star Queen Latifah transformed warden Mama Morton into a blues queen. This felicitous casting decision allowed the 1920s figure of the blues queen—such as Bessie Smith—to find a place in a book musical. A white actress could not have used the song "When You're Good to Mama" to invoke the classic blues the way Latifah does. She draws effectively on both the cultural memory of the blues queens and her own past as a truth-telling female rapper. The highly theatrical nature of *Chicago*'s narrative and the anti-realistic nature of the musical as a genre permit Latifah to use her bona fide star power to play an authority figure with little period dissonance—although, clearly, a black woman working in a Chicago prison in the 1920s would not have been the warden.

Latifah's performance doesn't substantially alter the musical style of *Chicago*, which sounds like any number of Broadway scores evoking the 1920s. In a more transformative strategy, Broadway revisals of *Grease* (1994) and *How to Succeed in Business Without Really Trying* (1995) introduced black performers and gospel vocal style into shows that originally lacked both. In "Beauty School Dropout" from *Grease*, the falsetto stylings of the original Teen Angel were transformed into a ten-minute production number led by Billy Porter, who would go on to record the role of the soul-singing James Thunder Early in a live concert version of *Dreamgirls*. The original "Beauty School Dropout" was a Ziegfeldian costume parade, with girls parading around to the accompaniment of a singer channeling white 1950s teen idols such as Paul Anka. Casting a black gospel voice as the Teen Angel for the revival, "Beauty School Dropout" was turned into an ecstatic black revival production number fully twice the length of the original. In the revival of *How to Succeed in Business Without Really Trying*, African American actress Lillias White played the role of executive secretary Miss Jones. In the original, Miss Jones was a prim older white woman who let loose her operatic top notes while dancing on the boardroom table in the eleven o'clock number "Brotherhood of Man"—the joke of Miss Jones's presence as the only woman in the number turned on the sudden evaporation of her staid, self-possessed character (◑ Example 14.8). In the revisal, White as a black Miss Jones quickly takes control of the number by musical means. As the only black person in the room—by Broadway logic, she's the only one who's "got rhythm"— White alters the meaning of "brotherhood" and recasts the scene as a gospel number. She teaches the rhythmically challenged white executives how to clap off the beat and leads them in some cries of "sistah" in addition to all the "brothers" being passed around. The musical highlight—of the scene and arguably the show—comes when White takes the lead vocal, riffing on the song in a Broadway-gospel idiom (◑ Example 14.9) introduced most successfully in the black-cast musical *Dreamgirls* (1981). Broadway audiences for the *How to Succeed* revival would have known White's past roles—she played Effie in the 1987 revival of *Dreamgirls*—and they certainly would have anticipated her singing in her characteristic "black" style: why else would White be cast at all? Having to wait until almost the end of the show, and then hearing White let loose in only one number, proves to be the price exacted by a stage musical tradition that has so thoroughly and for so long invested in maintaining the color line.

NOTES

1. "Rodgers, Hammerstein Reply to Lee Newton on 'Show Boat'" (*Daily Worker* [October 25, 1948]: 13).

2. See chapter 2 in Andrea Most, *Making Americans: Jews and the Broadway Musical* (Cambridge, MA: Harvard University Press, 2004).

3. See chapter 5 of Sophie Tucker, *Some of These Days: The Autobiography of Sophie Tucker* (Garden City, NY: Doubleday, Doran and Company, 1945).

4. Part two of Raymond Knapp, *The American Musical and the Formation of National Identity* (Princeton, NJ: Princeton University Press, 2005) considers the nation-making functions of the genre in detail.

5. Although Robeson was not in the original production of *Show Boat*, which featured Jules Bledsoe as Joe, he played the part in London the following year and took over the role for the 1932 Broadway revival and the 1936 film. For broader discussions of Robeson's role in the development and reception of *Show Boat*, see Todd Decker, "'Do You Want to Hear a Mammy Song?': A Historiography of *Show Boat*" (*Contemporary Theatre Review* 19.1 [2009]: 8–21); and Todd Decker, *Show Boat: Race and the Making and Remaking of an American Musical* (New York: Oxford University Press, forthcoming).

6. The 1973 Broadway musical *Raisin* offers a rare example of a musical play examining African American contemporary life in a serious yet commercially viable manner.

7. The megamusical hit *Miss Saigon* was imported from London.

8. This is not to imply that Asian Americans have not had a conflicted relationship with *Flower Drum Song*'s representation of Chinese characters and culture. As the only prominent stage or film musical about the Asian American experience, the show has been widely discussed and often excoriated.

9. These two entertainment traditions were indeed opposing each other in Chinatown at the time.

10. For an opinionated history of both versions, see David H. Lewis, *Flower Drum Songs: The Story of Two Musicals* (Jefferson, NC: McFarland, 2006).

CHAPTER 15

GENDER AND SEXUALITY

STACY WOLF

THE representation and performance of gender and sexuality in musicals function as building blocks as basic to the form as song, dance, script, or design. Whether or not a musical seems to be "about" gender or "about" sexuality, these axes of identity invariably organize a musical's message, its ideological work, and its emotional effects, since all of the characters in a musical can be identified and analyzed in terms of their gender and sexuality.[1] We can ask, What do the characters, as male and female, do in the story? What do they sing? How do they move? How do they relate to one another as men and as women? How are characters' sexualities embodied and envoiced in a musical? What is the effect of characters' sexualities on the musical? Like any identity written on the body, gender and sexuality operate semiotically; actors and audiences rely on culturally and historically specific images of gender and sexuality to interpret characters, their actions, behaviors, and desires. Moreover, a character, as written on a page in words and musical notes and as inhabited by a performer who sings, dances, and acts, comprises innumerable additional identity categories, such as race, ethnicity, age, and even the body's shape and size. What emerges in the musical as a character's "personality" is inseparable from these identity categories.

This chapter offers several frameworks for analyzing gender and sexuality in musicals. With expanding spheres of focus, I first consider characters in themselves, or character types. I then look at characters in relation to one another, both within and across genders, and especially, the heterosexual couple, the figure that fundamentally organizes most musicals. I then move from text to performance, to examine the contradictions that bubble up when a role is embodied; the varying interpretations that actors bring to a given role; and the different readings that materialize at specific historical moments. At the end of the chapter, I briefly connect gender and sexuality to the musical as a genre.[2]

CHARACTERS AND CHARACTER TYPES

Characters in musicals are drawn in broad strokes. As Lehman Engel puts it, "Characters are always (to the audience) precisely who and what they seem to be."[3] Thus, characters as gendered fall into types, and often according to vocal range. For women, these include the ingénue, typically a soprano, such as Christine in *The Phantom of the Opera* or Marian in *The Music Man*; the comic sidekick, or bitch, or witch, typically a mezzo, such as Aldonza in *Man of La Mancha* or Sally in *Urinetown*. Altos are sometimes middle-aged principals, such as Rose in *Gypsy* or Mrs. Lovett in *Sweeney Todd*, or older character roles, such as Mme. Armfeldt in *A Little Night Music*.[4] Although many male romantic leads are tenors, such as Tony in *West Side Story* and the title character in *Pippin*, male roles are less typecast by vocal range than women's.

While every character is gendered, some musicals actually present the process of becoming gendered as the central narrative. *Gypsy*, for example, follows Louise from a disregarded tomboy who plays the back end of a cow to a rich and successful stripper. The story of the character's development—how she comes of age and finds her identity—is her gendering, or the process by which she becomes a woman. In addition, many mid- and late-twentieth-century musicals elide the process of becoming gendered with that of becoming heterosexual. Both *Funny Girl* and *The Sound of Music*, for example, feature central female characters, Fanny Brice and Maria, who begin as independent and somewhat childlike, and move toward romance and heterosexual coupling over the course of the musical. *The Sound of Music*'s story is Maria's Bildungsroman. As she comes to understand her life's true calling, she moves from one idealized image of "Woman" to another, occupying over the course of the musical the two stereotypical edges of the good feminine: nun/virgin and wife/mother. The musical wants the audience to see this process as Maria's natural, inevitable maturation from tomboy to woman. She was never meant to be a nun anyway, the musical argues, and her protestations to falling in love, which she enacts by leaving the von Trapp household and returning to the abbey at the end of act 1, emphasize both her guilelessness and the naturalness of her attraction to Captain von Trapp. The musical equates Maria's being a nun with entrapment (even though the nuns are portrayed as warm, good-humored, and intelligent) and being a mother and wife (especially of children who are nearly grown, and of a very wealthy man) with freedom and worldliness, albeit an unpretentious and tempered sociability compared to that of the Baroness. From a feminist perspective, Maria's trajectory is ultimately narrowing and conservative; she sacrifices her independence to be a mother. On the other hand, a feminist reading also observes that Maria makes her own choices and transforms the entire von Trapp household: she redirects the children's bad behavior by channeling their energy into play and music and reopens Georg to music and feeling. Maria, the star, dominates the family and the musical alike.[5] In contrast to Fanny Brice, whose marriage fails because she insists on staying in show business even when Nick is arrested (implying that Fanny wasn't an appropriately dutiful wife in the first place since she failed to protect her man), Maria's marriage succeeds because she gladly becomes a (step)mother and leads her family to freedom. The tone of each musical's ending, one tragic and one triumphant, corresponds to Fanny or Maria's matrimonial, or heterosexual, success. Like *Sweet Charity* and *Cabaret* on the tragic side, and *Guys and Dolls* and *The Music Man* on the triumphant side, *Funny Girl* and *The Sound of Music* naturalize the affiliation between maturity and heterosexual romance.[6]

Similarly, men in some musicals embark on a performative journey that intertwines gender and sexuality and moves from homosocial to heterosexual, from their buddies to a wife. Examples include Tony in *West Side Story*, Marius in *Les Misérables*, and Sky and Nathan in *Guys and Dolls*. Through the force of the narrative, told insistently in song and dance and script, many musicals convey the ideological message that proper maturity is becoming feminized/masculinized. Moreover, proper feminization/masculinization is inseparable from heterosexual awakening. In this way, musicals tie together psychological development, gender, and (hetero)sexuality.

Still, characters in many musicals are coded as gay, such as Moonface Martin in *Anything Goes*, Randy Curtis (first played by Danny Kaye) in *Lady in the Dark*, Henry Higgins and Pickering in *My Fair Lady*, the tomboy Anybodys in *West Side Story*, and to some commentators, Robert in *Company*.[7] Gay-signifying men in musical films include, for example, Adam (played by Oscar Levant) in *An American in Paris*, Cosmo Brown (played by Donald O'Connor) in *Singing in the Rain*, and Max (played by Richard Haydn) in *The Sound of Music*. Explicitly gay characters appear in the films *Cabaret*, *The Rocky Horror Picture Show*, and *Victor/Victoria*, and on stage in Jerry Herman and Harvey Fierstein's *La Cage Aux Folles* and William Finn's *Falsettos*, to name a few. A bevy of short-lived adult musicals sprang up in the 1970s, such as *Let My People Come*, which included gay characters for social activist as much as art-making purposes.[8] More typically, though, until the mid-1990s, when an explicitly gay character appeared in a musical, he (and it was almost always a man) had to bear the burden of representation, signifying more than simply an individual character, standing in for the very idea or whole category of gay people.

A Chorus Line, for example, introduced several characters (all men) who admitted they were gay, but only one whose story was told in detail. Paul's confessional monologue forms the emotional climax of *A Chorus Line*. What does Paul's gay identity mean in the musical? In an extended spoken "scene" near the end of the musical, Paul tells the heartbreaking story of his parents' discovery that he was performing in a drag show. He explains that, during the final show before the company went on tour, his parents came to the theater to say good-bye. They arrived too early and recognized him dressed as a woman. As Paul relates the story, "So I took a deep breath and started down the stairs and just as I passed my mother I heard her say: 'Oh my god.'" Stunned and horrified, his parents still stand by him, as Paul tells it, and his father commands the producer, "Take care of my son"; it's the first time he has referred to Paul as his son. By the end of the monologue, Zach, the director of the unnamed musical for which the characters in *A Chorus Line* are auditioning, and the lone witness to the story, comes onto the stage for the first time since the opening scene and puts his arm around Paul. This kind and sympathetic gesture is Zach's only one in the show, and compared to his shrugging cruelty toward Cassie, his ex-lover, it at once suggests his humanity as well as his homosocial (if not homosexual) affiliation. For the theater audience, Zach's attention and onstage appearance underline the importance of this moment and invite sympathy toward a gay character, too. During the next section of the audition, however, Paul's knee gives out, eliminating him from contention. The musical at once values, rouses sympathy for, and punishes the gay character.

Paul's ethnic identity as Puerto Rican is equally significant and inseparable from his homosexuality in *A Chorus Line*.[9] He is stunned that his traditional parents embrace him, and their steadfastness makes his story even more potent, since it suggests that he is such a sweet and loving son that his parents can't desert him in spite of his being gay. All of the characters in *A Chorus Line* identify themselves by their hometown per Zach's opening gambit, often referring to race and ethnicity. The significance of race and ethnicity in this 1975 musical reflects the era of its birth, when the push for racial and ethnic equality was very much a part of U.S. culture. Diana's charming and devastating solo, "Nothing," recounts her failure to do "improvisation" in an acting class, which she blames as much on her being Puerto Rican ("they don't have bobsleds in San Juan!") as on her skepticism of the whole enterprise. When Richie announces, "I'm black," it plays as a joke in the musical because he is visibly African American.

Although *A Chorus Line* writes characters' races and ethnicities into their lines and songs, every character in every musical is racialized, whether or not race is marked, and a character's race/ethnicity inflects what gender and sexuality mean at every turn. In some musicals, racial or ethnic identity is part of the very fabric of the story. For example, in *West Side Story*, Anita seems sexually available to the white boys in Doc's drugstore because they see her as a "spicy Latina"; in *The King and I*, Anna can challenge the King of Siam because she is an educated white woman and he is a "primitive" Asian man; in *Fiddler on the Roof*, Tevye is confronted with diminishing patriarchal power as a Jewish man; in *The Color Purple*, Celie's financial and emotional independence are extraordinary because she is an African American woman; in *In the Heights*, Nina struggles to adjust to Stanford because she is Latina. Moreover, in each example, the significance of a character's race/ethnicity is historically specific, both in relation to the musical's setting and to its time of production.

CHARACTERS IN RELATION: THE HETEROSEXUAL COUPLE AND HOMOSOCIAL COMMUNITIES

Heterosexual relationships, romance, and marriage provide the narrative spine of most musicals, typically the story of a couple's initial antipathy followed by a series of complications that eventually lead to their admission of love. Differences of origin, background, and temperament align with gender differences, and the musical's first duet, the subjunctive love song, foreshadows the couple's unification two or so hours later. In addition to presenting the meeting and mating of two characters of the opposite sex, the heterosexual imperative, or what Raymond Knapp calls the "marriage trope," performs Broadway musical theater's grander ideological project: to symbolically unite opposing forces in U.S. culture. When the couple admits their deep and abiding love for one another, their joining together represents a social, even political union. The ensemble's rousing finale in many musicals from *Oklahoma!* to *In the Heights* affirms how the couple is a synecdoche for the community.

Many musicals also introduce a secondary couple, sometimes comedic, forming a quartet of contrasting representations of masculinity and femininity. In *Guys and Dolls*, for example, the differences between men and women, signaled in the musical's title, is central to the plot. The musical concerns how "guys" and "dolls" occupy their own worlds and live by their own rules, but it also reveals how different guys and dolls can be from others of the same gender. Both leading men are inveterate gamblers, but that's all they have in common. The suave, elegant, but gentle Sky Masterson, introduced as the perpetual bachelor, sings two richly melodic duets with Sarah, the first the subjunctive love song, "I'll Know (When My Love Comes Along)" and later the openly romantic, "My Time of Day/I've Never Been in Love Before." Sky contrasts with the brash, bumbling, affectionate, and barely musical Nathan Detroit, Adelaide's longtime boyfriend, who sings only the opening of "The Oldest Established" and responds, half-speaking, to "Adelaide's Lament," "Sue me, Sue me, What can you do me? I love you." In a parallel construction, Sky unwittingly falls for and then seduces through a tricky bet and considerable alcohol the strait-laced, judgmental, sermonizing, Save-a-Soul mission doll Sergeant Sarah Brown, the musical's soprano ingénue. In contrast to Sarah, Nathan's match is the cold-afflicted, gum-cracking, husband-hungry, nightclub dancer/pseudo-diva, Adelaide. By the end, the women decide to accept the men's flaws, and the wayward men agree to marry, and with double weddings, the ensemble reprises the bouncy title song. The conventional architecture of two couples is also employed by, for example, *Oklahoma!*, *Wonderful Town*, *South Pacific*, *West Side Story*, *Bye Bye Birdie*, and *In the Heights*.

Another typical arrangement of story and romance occurs in triangulated relationships. Both Arthur and Lancelot compete for Guenevere's love in *Camelot*; both Curly and Jud Fry are in love with Laurey, and Ado Annie wants both Will and Ali Hakim in *Oklahoma!* Other characterological triangles that also include queer affections include Henry Higgins, Pickering, and Eliza in *My Fair Lady*; Oliver, Bill Sykes, and Nancy in *Oliver!*; Cosette, Marius, and Eponine in *Les Misérables*; and Don Quixote, Sancho, and Aldonza in *Man of La Mancha*. While homosocial relationships abound, more explicit homoerotic (or actually gay) connections occur in contemporary musicals, such as *Rent*, in which both Mark and Joanne bemoan their mutual attraction to Maureen (and they sing "The Tango Maureen"); or *Wicked*, in which Glinda and Elphaba each have a crush on Fiyero (and by the end of *Wicked*, both Glinda and Fiyero are in love with Elphaba); or *Spring Awakening*, where Wendla and Moritz are both in love with Melchior. In every case, duets chart the weightiness of the relationships, and the musical's concluding tone conveys its ideological project.[10]

Homosocial groupings in duets, trios, and chorus numbers at once foreground differences within one gender and blur individual characters' differences under the rubric of the feminine or masculine. In "Matchmaker, Matchmaker" in *Fiddler on the Roof*, for example, Tzeitl, Hodel, and Chava sing a lilting waltz about their hopes for a husband whom the matchmaker will bring. In the song's half-spoken middle section, Tzeitl imitates Yentl the matchmaker and teases her sisters about the old and ugly men whom they'll be forced to marry. The song allows each girl to express her own unique fantasy and also underlines how they're all the same in their desire to marry. Just as the romance narrative of many musicals reinforces heterosexuality as the norm, single gender musical numbers reaffirm social norms, which for women in most musicals means desiring marriage. Still, in *Fiddler*, the turn-of-the-twentieth-century Russian-Jewish young women choose mates that buck tradition. In *Sweet Charity*, which opened just two years after *Fiddler*, taxi dancers Helene, Nicky, and Charity sing and dance an exuberant, Latin-inflected number, "Something Better Than This," in which each outlines her escape from life as a taxi-dancer, whether to marry rich or become a respectable secretary. Charity's friends ably articulate their dreams; Charity can't quite envision hers. Yet all three women sing the chorus and each takes up a verse to announce her fantasies, however formed or not. Bob Fosse's choreography is expansive, alternating airborne leaps and kicks with angry and determined cha-cha stomps. In *A Chorus Line*'s "At the Ballet," Sheila, Bebe, and Maggie, isolated from the others, each sing about how ballet became her refuge from a troubled childhood. The three women stand on a diagonal, their stillness contradicting the joyful motion about which they sing in soaring harmonies. In the background in shadows, the rest of the cast enacts their memories, practicing simple exercises and stretching at the barre. Like the trio in *Fiddler* and *Sweet Charity*, this number connects femininity with desire and longing, but here to escape to the world of ballet.[11] Other numbers that perform femininity include "America" in *West Side Story*, "Lovely Ladies" in *Les Misérables*, and "Junk" in *Spring Awakening*.

To date, no musical has simply replaced straight characters with gay or lesbian ones in a conventional structure. Stephen Schwartz and Winnie Holtzman's *Wicked* comes closest, using the conventions established by Rodgers and Hammerstein and their contemporaries to create a feminist and queer musical. *Wicked* musically tracks Elphaba and Glinda's relationship from antipathy/attraction ("What Is This Feeling?") to common ground ("Popular") to relationship ("One Fine Day") to division ("Defying Gravity") to expression of devotion ("For Good"). While *Wicked* includes a heterosexual romance, a triangulated crush that both women have on Fiyero, and while Elphaba stages her own death and leaves Oz with him to pursue a heterosexual life, the end-run machinations of the plot hold less emotional sway than the sweetly wrenching final duet between the two women. In the final verse of "For Good," the women's voices wrap around each other, constantly switching voice parts and concluding the song in unison. The final dissonant chord of the musical, sung by the chorus, signals the community's dystopian state, since the proper romance has been denied. *Wicked* testifies to the flexibility of the formal conventions of the "Golden Age musical"—in other words, form doesn't determine content although it does determine narrative structure—and *Wicked*'s commercial success rejects the presumptive centrality of "boy meets girl."[12]

CONTEMPORARY MUSICALS AND GAY AND LESBIAN CHARACTERS

Rent creates new possibilities for characters' sexualities in musicals by representing multiple gay and lesbian characters with frank and casual openness. *Rent* is peopled with a gay male couple (Angel and Collins) and a lesbian couple (Maureen and Joanne) and it takes those sexualities for granted in the musical's world of NYC's East Village circa 1990. *Rent*'s structure—a single protagonist, Mark, surrounded by a close-knit community—borrows formal conventions of ensemble musicals of the late 1960s and 1970s, including *Hair*, *Company*, *Godspell*, and *A Chorus Line*. This structure enables the musical to nod to nonheterosexual identities and relationships, an ideological gesture that speaks to its (successful) intention to address musical theater's wide range of spectators and even make them feel politically progressive. This device of including a few gay characters in a community-based story is repeated with the gay male couples in *Avenue Q* and *Spring Awakening*, and perhaps foretells a musical theater future with a more consistent nod to gay people (or gay men, at least).[13]

Still, both *Rent* and *Spring Awakening* ultimately use gay characters to bolster heteronormativity. Angel serves as the emotional touchstone of *Rent*, endlessly generous and hopeful, caring and sensitive. All mourn his death, which compels the other characters to look at their lives and choices. That Angel's death enables the other characters to learn about themselves replicates a typical (tired) trope in which an Other (usually a person of color or with a disability) aids in the self-actualization of the principal character. Also, Collins and Angel have the most loving and healthy relationship, which the musical needs to eliminate so as not to valorize the gay male couple above all else. In addition, Joanne and Maureen sing a lively number, "Take Me or Leave Me," but the musical doesn't take their relationship seriously. Maureen is presented as a fickle, emotionally abusive, yet irresistible lover (Joanne and Mark's duet, "The Tango Maureen") and a less-than-accomplished artist (her "The Cow Jumped over the Moon" is a parody of performance art).[14] In contrast, Mimi and Roger's relationship lasts through the end of the musical, since Mimi comes back to life. This choice, one of the few that differs from Puccini's *La Bohème* (which provides the primary situational basis for *Rent*), shows how beholden twentieth-century musicals—even tragedies—are to the convention of a heterosexually happy ending.

Similarly, *Spring Awakening* offers a tacked-on celebrate-the-day ending that differs from its source material, even more jarring since it follows the suicide of one character and the death from a botched abortion of another. Like *Rent*, *Spring Awakening* affirms youth's hopefulness and the unstoppable passage of time, packaged with a seemingly progressive representation of homosexuality. Like *Rent* and *Hair*, *Spring Awakening* puts a male friendship in the center with a homosocial hue, heightened by Moritz's anxious and passionate admiration for and attachment to the confident, accomplished, renegade Melchior. The desire of the gay (male) characters, Hanschen and Ernst, is no more *verboten* than heterosexual attraction in the musical, as they repeat Melchior and Wendla's love duet, "Word of My Body." And yet, the gay scenes are played for laughs, with Hanschen a stereotype of a fey, arrogant cruiser. The presence of the gay couple effectively re-centers the straight couple as the norm.[15] A similar dynamic exists in *Avenue Q*, where the gay characters are sweet and silly but the center of the musical is Princeton and his love interest Kate. Even as these musicals show gay and lesbian characters, their ideological work is complicated and even contradictory.

In this way, these musicals' politics of sexuality echo earlier, pre-Stonewall musicals in which the gay-seeming characters, always part of the theatrical world, force sympathy and identification onto the heterosexual couple.[16] Typically, these queer characters sing little or not at all. In *The Sound of Music*, for example, Max is a gay stereotype (and perhaps Jewish, even though he is for a time accommodating to the Nazis), singularly obsessed with the niceties of life and a successful public image and not the least bit romantically interested in women. He is the friend/sidekick who is never a threat to the leading man. Nor is he a match for Else, the Baroness, who calls up her own vampirish lesbian stereotype. The presence of Max and Else sharpen the inevitability of Maria and Georg's union.[17] For a given musical, then, it's not enough to merely identify gay or gay-seeming characters; one should also consider what those characters do and how their existence and their actions contribute to the overall meaning and effect of a musical.

EMBODIED CONTRADICTIONS

While considerable information about gender in a musical can be gleaned from a script and a score, for audiences, musicals consist of embodied performances in real time. Performance analysis acknowledges this reality by examining what the men and women actors actually do over the course of the show. How often is the performer on stage? How many songs does she sing or dance and what kinds of songs and with whom? How, when, and with whom does he occupy space on the stage in song, dance, or spoken scene? While the script specifies such details, only in performance can an audience feel the dynamic effects of space, kinesthetics, and time, as well as the actor's performance choices and presence.

Dance's aestheticized, formalized movement, typically more symbolic than mimetic, defines gender as well. Diegetic waltzes in *Cinderella*, *The Sound of Music*, and *My Fair Lady*, mambo, jitterbug, and cha-cha in *West Side Story* ("The Dance at the Gym"), and athletic modern dance in *Wicked* ("Dancing through Life") also provide scenes of many bodies moving, enabling the couple to form through choreography. Other dances within single gender groups expand and define the meaning of masculinity or femininity, such as the Puerto Rican women in "America" in *West Side Story* as well as the male gangs, both the Jets and the Sharks, the nineteenth-century German schoolboys in "Bitch of Living" in *Spring Awakening*, or the jaded taxi-dancers in *Sweet Charity*'s "Hey, Big Spender," with each woman draped over a ballet bar in a unique pose of bored seduction, and then exploding in a rage-filled, gyrating frenzy of movement. Ensemble dance numbers such as "La Vie Boheme" in *Rent*, the extended "Hello, Twelve" sequence in *A Chorus Line*, or the opening number of *In the Heights* individualize the choreography for each dancer with movement vocabularies that express each character's identity.[18]

In some musicals, the onstage activities, or stage power, of the performer contradicts the written character's. The end of *Cabaret*, for example, finds Sally Bowles alone, having decided to abort her baby. Cliff leaves her to return to America, disgusted and fearful of the political situation and disappointed that she refuses to leave Berlin with him to marry him and raise a family. A "preferred" (that is, dominant or with-the-grain) reading of the musical sympathizes with Cliff, as the story is told from his perspective, framed (in the 1972 film version and the 1998 Sam Mendes-directed revival) by scenes of his arrival and departure from Berlin by train.[19] Over the course of the musical, Cliff grows from a naïve aspiring writer to a sharp observer of the Nazi's encroaching power. In the meantime, Sally's denial of the reality of the political scene is conflated with her refusal to marry Cliff: the musical frames both choices as her avoidance of reality, her immature, unreasonable resistance to conventional options. *Cabaret* presents Sally's insistence on remaining single and a performer as childish, especially since she is not especially talented or successful. But the musical works against itself, because Sally sings numerous charming songs, dances in the Kit Kat Klub in alternating scenes, and is a vibrant, active character compared to Cliff's quieter, less musical presence. The audience, then, understands Cliff's choices but is more drawn to Sally. By the end, Sally's heartrending rendition of the musical's title song cements her stardom. Although *Cabaret* wants the audience to judge her, Sally's belting voice and charismatic presence demand that the audience adore her.[20]

Like *Cabaret*'s treatment of the woman Sally Bowles, *A Chorus Line*'s treatment of the gay character Paul is contradictory. On the one hand, he is a main character and among the most memorable in the ensemble-based musical. When he admits his homosexuality, neither Paul's Puerto Rican father, nor Zach, the father figure, deserts him, which suggests his absolute goodness. Paul's beautifully wrought story takes up considerable stage time—a "number" made all the more effective for not being sung—and is central to the emotional movement of the musical. His subsequent injury is a key dramatic moment: it stops the action cold, compels Zach to ask the other dancers why they keep dancing, and leads into the penultimate number,

"What I Did for Love." On the other hand, Paul is a victim in the diegesis, his emotion-laden story "kills" him and renders him unable to dance, to perform, to finish the audition. He cannot finish what he started. Moreover, Paul's account is the only one with heft in *A Chorus Line* that is spoken rather than sung or danced, in contrast to the powerful memories of the women in "At the Ballet," "Nothing," and Cassie's "Music and the Mirror," another emotional high point in the show. The musical implies that Paul's story is so raw and honest that it exceeds music and dance, but in the conventions of musical theater's languages, this choice of communicative mode shows how Paul can't fit in; he can't express himself in the languages that are valued here. That he is gay and Puerto Rican—two non-normative identities—the musical (perhaps unconsciously) suggests, excludes him from the white and heterosexual musical theater of *A Chorus Line*.

Rent also compromises its progressive intentions when the characters are actually inhabited by actors. Because Angel cross-dresses and the role tends to be cast with an actor who is slim and effeminate, he and Collins look remarkably like a heterosexual couple on stage. This performance choice normalizes homosexuality but denies its visibility.

The performative energy of musical numbers, especially duets or trios, creates intimacy between and among actors and deepens relationships from how they read on the page. *The Sound of Music*, for example, complicates its heterosexual romance story with the infusion of homosocial connections. The songs between Maria and the Mother Abbess, "My Favorite Things" (a duet in the stage version) and "Climb Ev'ry Mountain" (the latter's solo act 1 finale that includes Maria in its purposeful address), along with the thunderstorm bedroom scene between Maria and Liesl and their reprise of "Sixteen Going on Seventeen," all portray close connections between women.[21]

Contradictions that emerge in performance are also built into the conventional scaffold of musical theater's heterosexual romances. That is, a musical is indeed "about" heterosexual romance in terms of its meaning and ideological work, but that doesn't describe what is actually performed on stage. Because a musical represents the developing romance of its heterosexual couple through a series of obstacles and conflicts, it may, ironically, spend more stage time revealing how thoroughly incompatible the couple is. Heteronormativity and narrative conventions may naturalize the romance and its matrimonial conclusion, but often in contrast to what is represented on stage.

Actors and Gendered Performances Historicized

Musical theater's history as a popular, commercial art form has meant that many characters were created for specific actors. Moreover, as Bruce Kirle has shown, exigencies of production, more than composers', lyricists', and librettists' idealized creative impulses, typically drive the creation of character and determine the details of a character's gender and sexuality. An actor in a role simultaneously creates the character and re-creates her, giving the character body and voice, so that a character is ultimately inseparable from the actor who plays her. For example, Nellie in *South Pacific* and Maria in *The Sound of Music* were written for Mary Martin, accommodating her vocal range and offering particular musical flourishes to flatter her voice. Similarly, *Gypsy* composer Jule Styne wrote songs to play to Ethel Merman's strengths as a singer, so that later actors must re-perform songs composed for Merman.

When we talk about "Rose" in *Gypsy*, then, which Rose do we mean? Merman, who originated the "mastodon of all stage mothers," as the *New York Times* review described her, and whose voice is captured (albeit in a recording studio and not on stage) in an original cast album and whose form is frozen in photographs (again, not from the performance itself but from a rehearsal specifically for photography)? Rosalind Russell, who made Rose permanent on film? Angela Lansbury, who performed the role in 1974 as librettist Arthur Laurents reimagined it (and directed it), bravely bowing beyond the audience's applause of the climactic "Rose's Turn" to reveal the character's slender tie to sanity? Tyne Daly, who revived the role to great acclaim in 1989 and gave Rose a new monstrous fierceness? Bette Midler, who brought a new Rose to audiences via film, ghosted by her campy star persona? Bernadette Peters, who found a vulnerable sexiness in the character that told audiences that Rose actually might have made a fantastic stripper herself? Or Patti LuPone, in a 2008 revival again directed by Laurents himself, who, as *New York Times* critic Ben Brantley put it, is "a laser, she incinerates."[22] To parse out who "Rose" is, then, a scholar gathers information by listening to cast albums, seeing photographs, viewing tapes of performances, or experiencing productions live. These materials, whether heard or seen, or both, whether taped or live, compose the archive that laminates the performer onto the character. Gender and sexuality are envoiced and embodied in the person of the actor playing the character.[23]

Each actor remakes a character anew, and both actor and character are tied to historical contexts and the historically available performance of gender. For example, Nellie Forbush in *South Pacific*, as rendered on the page, in the score, and in Mary Martin's 1949 performance, seems more than a little tomboyish. Martin's angular, guileless affect, the lack of a duet between Nellie and Emile (due to Martin's refusal to pair her musical theater voice with the opera singer Ezio Pinza's), and the quiet concluding tableau of the new interracial nuclear family, subsumed the romance within the larger story of race relations. Nellie, then, could seem to be an innocent southern girl whose racism merely stemmed from her lack of experience in the world.[24] In the twenty-first century, though, even as audiences acknowledged the musical's World War II setting, when Nellie sings, "I'm only a cock-eyed optimist/ Immature and incurably green," she seemed dangerously like a scatterbrain unworthy of Emile's love. In the 2008 Lincoln Center revival, Kelli O'Hara's exuberant yet grounded portrayal of Nellie never compromised the character Rodgers and Hammerstein created, yet she emphasized Nellie's openness and her sincere curiosity, rather than stupidity. When O'Hara sang Hammerstein's lyrics, her Nellie was wisely self-reflexive. Without apology or embarrassment, she nonetheless conveyed the recognition that the character was aware that her sheltered life was a deficit that needed to be made up.

Other productions of *South Pacific* offer a range of historically based portrayals of the famous role, albeit on film and television. The 1958 film version, for example, features Mitzi Gaynor as an excessively perky, not-very-bright Nellie, and the strangely hued scenes (director Josh Logan used tinted lenses to express the emotion of each scene) and awkward camera angles constantly remind spectators that the film is a relic, static and stagey.[25] Glenn Close played Nellie in a made-for-TV version in 2001. Not only is she older (a fact that rendered the character's naiveté unrealistic to some critics), but she is also serious and seriously convinced that each time she accepts or rejects Emile, it's for real. The different performances of femininity become especially clear in the famous "Gonna Wash That Man Right Outa My Hair" number. The Gaynor rendition, modeled on Martin's (both staged by Logan), consists of Nellie strutting around the stage, framed by the other women who mostly stand, sit, or kneel. Her minimal gestures include arm flapping and waving, and the song is capped off by the famous hair-washing scene, which Martin performed on stage eight times a week.[26] Martin's performance, captured on tape for a 1954 television tribute to Rodgers and Hammerstein,[27] and Gaynor's both portray Nellie as trying to convince herself that Emile is wrong for her; both are light on their feet and tentative in their gestures. In contrast, with Glenn Close, as choreographed by Vincent Paterson, all of the women participate, sing, and dance. Using everyday props of buckets of water, hoses, and a clothesline, the women express group solidarity through joyful exuberance, singing defiantly that they will "wash that man right outa (their) hair." While the choreography still relies on mundane movements such as walking, strutting, and swaying, the women are physically grounded and interdependent, as sections of the song move across trios or quartets. In this version, Nellie is fully integrated into the community of women, who support her, sympathize with her position, and join her. The force of the ensemble, with Nellie in the center, renders the number a vibrant expression of female community, and Nellie's rejection of Emile, while temporary, seems committed and sincere. This Nellie is fully capable of taking care of herself and making decisions for herself. Without changing a word or a note or the era in which the musical is set, Close's version updated Nellie for 2001, just as O'Hara did in 2008.[28]

The Musical as Feminine and Gay

While the musical continually presents performances of gender and sexuality as crucial aspects of character and so reinforces those social scripts, the form itself, as a genre, connotes femininity and gayness. Aside from the stereotypical and accurate observation that the musical is the cultural terrain of gay men, some of the most important, early analyses of the musical were written by gay men who argued that the very form of the musical is feminine and gay. D. A. Miller, in his evocative auto-biographical tribute to the musical, *Place for Us*, writes that the dominance of women in the musical encourages a feminine, empowering identification for gay men. He describes the musical as "a form whose unpublicizable work is to indulge men in the thrills of a femininity *become their own*."[29] In *Something for the Boys*, John Clum observes that many diva or strong female characters in musicals appeal to gay men, providing a feminine escape fantasy for those gay men who may not comfortably inhabit traditional masculinity. Clum finds musicals with explicitly gay characters ironically less compelling for gay men's identifications. Alexander Doty, whose *Making Things Perfectly Queer* takes on a number of cultural forms, of which the musical is one, writes that the exuberant performance style of the musical calls out to many gay men's sense of their own performances of gender. My study, *A Problem like Maria: Gender and Sexuality in the American Musical*, analyzes Martin, Merman, Julie Andrews, and Barbra Streisand and the musicals in which they starred from a feminist and lesbian perspective. From a materialist and historical perspective David Savran links gender and sexuality to musicals' cultural stratification.[30]

Even as the terms, definitions, and performances of masculinity and femininity in culture shift and morph into bi, trans, queer, and so on, the musical remains reliant on bodies and voices, movements and sounds, characters, and performers alone and in relation. These categories of identity and presence will always constitute a rich and important area of analysis and interpretation for the musical.

NOTES

Thanks to Ray Knapp and Jill Dolan for reading and responding to earlier drafts of this chapter.

1. Although for the purposes of this essay, I understand gender and sexuality to be stable and recognizable characteristics, certain performance traditions play with such presumed legibility. Breeches roles, for example, cast women as men, and their appeal in part relied on male spectators' desire to see women's legs. Drag roles, such as the title role in *Hedwig and the Angry Inch*, stress the way that gender is performative and also critique gender's normalizing force. See, for example, Judith Butler, *Gender Trouble* (New York: Routledge, 1990).

2. The keywords "gender and sexuality" might lead one, for example, to consider women and gay and lesbian artists of the musical. Other studies that take this approach include selected essays in *Passing Performances: Queer Readings of Leading Players in American Theater History*, ed. Kim Marra and Robert Schanke (Ann Arbor: University of Michigan Press, 1998), and *Women in the American Musical Theatre*, ed. Bud Coleman and Judith A. Sebesta (Jefferson, NC: MacFarland, 2008).

3. Lehman Engel and Howard Kissel, *Words with Music: Creating the Broadway Musical Libretto* (New York: Applause, 2006), p. 229.

4. http://tvtropes.org/pmwiki/pmwiki.php/Main/VoiceTypes?from=Main.TenorBoy, accessed May 8, 2010.

5. For a longer discussion of *The Sound of Music*, especially in relation to Mary Martin, who originated the role of Maria on Broadway, and Julie Andrews, the film's Maria, see Stacy Wolf, *A Problem Like Maria: Gender and Sexuality in the American Musical* (Ann Arbor: University of Michigan Press, 2002).

6. *Gypsy* posits another, more ambivalent position. Louise grows up, but she is narcissistic, still trying to separate from her mother, and so not yet (properly) heterosexualized. In addition, Rose, the actual star of the musical, is singular and post-heterosexual. See Wolf, *A Problem Like Maria*.

7. For readings of these characters as gay-signifying, see Raymond Knapp, *The American Musical and the Formation of National Identity* (Princeton, NJ: Princeton University Press, 2005) and Knapp, *The American Musical and the Performance of Personal Identity* (Princeton, NJ: Princeton University Press, 2006).

8. See Elizabeth Wollman, *Hard Times: The Adult Musical in New York City* (New York: Oxford University Press, forthcoming).

9. Most of the commentary on Paul has focused on the conjunction of his being gay and Puerto Rican. See, for example, Alberto Sandoval-Sanchez, *José, Can You See? Latinos On and Off Broadway* (Madison: University of Wisconsin Press, 1999); Frances Negrón-Muntaner, "Feeling Pretty: *West Side Story* and Puerto Rican Identity Discourses" (*Social Text* 63 18.2 [2000]: 83–106.

10. One might parse out the specific dynamics of two different kinds of romantic triangles: one in which two characters of the same sex vie for the love of a third person of the opposite sex, and one in which the pivotal character is currently homosocial but sees a heterosexual future.

11. Perhaps the feminine trio in musicals can be seen as a trope. As a trio, the women are less likely legible as "lesbian," and so are heteronormatively safer. These trios also depend on each individual's unique perspective, unlike the ensemble number that stresses community. Interestingly, many of these numbers express a desire to escape, while most ensemble numbers emphasize the characters' desire to belong.

12. For an extended version of this argument, see Stacy Wolf, *Changed for Good: A Feminist History of the Broadway Musical* (New York: Oxford University Press, 2011).

13. Gay-seeming characters also people the background of *Wonderful Town*.

14. The musical, perhaps unintentionally, expresses ambivalence about artists, since all of the art-making in the musical is bad, including Mark's film, Roger's song, and Maureen's performance art.

15. I saw the original Broadway cast with Jonathan Bradford Wright as Hanschen.

16. "Stonewall" refers to the Stonewall Inn, a gay bar in Greenwich Village and the location of the apocryphal birth of the gay rights movement. A riot ensued when police raided the bar and the gay and lesbian patrons fought back. On the history and significance of Stonewall, see, for example, Martin Duberman, *Stonewall* (New York: Penguin, 1993), and David Carter, *Stonewall: The Riots that Sparked the Gay Revolution* (New York: St. Martin's Press, 2004).

17. Knapp makes a similar argument in *The American Musical and the Formation of National Identity* (230–38). Also, the film centralizes the Maria/Georg romance event more by eliminating Elsa and Max's one song, "There's No Way to Stop It," a trio with Georg, from the Broadway version.

18. See Liza Gennaro, "Evolution of Dance," chapter 4 in this volume.

19. Among the numerous changes in the film version, Cliff is renamed Brian and becomes British and Sally (Liza Minnelli) is American.

20. For related discussions of *Cabaret*, see Knapp, *The American Musical and the Formation of National Identity*, and Mitchell Morris, "*Cabaret*, America's *Weimar*, and Mythologies of the Gay Subject" (*American Music* 22.1 [Spring, 2004]: 145–57).

A similar dynamic occurs in *Sweet Charity* and in *Funny Girl*. These characterizations are not unrelated to the period when these musicals opened—the mid-1960s—and they exhibit extreme cultural anxiety about gender at the time, simultaneously demeaning and empowering their female principal characters. Significantly, although Fanny in *Funny Girl* does become a star, her Jewishness complicates her success; she is not "white" enough to be a real star. For an extended discussion of single women in 1960s musicals, see Wolf, *Changed for Good*.

21. In the film version, the Mother Abbess delivers the news of Maria's new assignment without song, and Maria gains the solo, "I Have Confidence," which she sings during her journey. "My Favorite Things" is moved to the thunderstorm scene and "The Lonely Goatherd" is added as a puppet show to emphasize how Maria fosters the children's playfulness and imaginations. See Wolf, *A Problem like Maria*.

22. Ben Brantley, "Curtain Up: It's Patti's Turn as Gypsy" (*New York Times* [March 28, 2008]), http://theater.nytimes.com/2008/03/28/theater/reviews/28gyps.html?8dpc, Accessed March 14, 2010.

23. Envoicing is, of course, a form of embodiment, and the body could be inferred from the disembodied voice. One might argue that Merman always and forever ghosts the role of Rose. On actors and ghosting, see Marvin Carlson, *The Haunted Stage: The Theater as Memory Machine* (Ann Arbor: University of Michigan Press, 2003).

24. This characterization would in no way excuse the character's racism, but it would place her attitude within a cultural and historical context.

25. See also "The Filmed Musical," chapter 10 in this volume.

26. Martin became a representative for Breck shampoo, which suggests the visibility and importance of Broadway performers at the time.

27. The show was a "General Foods 25th Anniversary Show: A Salute to Rodgers and Hammerstein."

28. In addition, the earlier versions of the number, in which the women are weaker and less determined, read as more sexual and voyeuristic. In all versions of the song, the actor playing Nellie is subjected to the physical, real-life consequences of stripping, getting wet, and washing her hair in public eight times a week. While I put an optimistic, female-empowerment spin on the homosocial aspect of this number, such female bonding is also a well-worn trope of male heterosexual fantasy (cf. "June Bride" in *Seven Brides for Seven Brothers*), here underscored by Emile's catching enough of the final part of the number to parody it later.

29. D. A. Miller, *Place for Us [Essay on the Broadway Musical]* (Cambridge, MA: Harvard University Press, 1998), 90.

30. David Savran echoes many other scholars when he notes that "musical theatre… has in popular mythology been adjudged a sacred preserve of gay men" (59). See David Savran, *A Queer Sort of Materialism: Recontextualizing American Theatre* (Ann Arbor: University of Michigan Press, 2003). See also John Clum, *Something for the Boys: Musical Theater and Gay Culture* (New York: St. Martin's Press, 1999); Alexander Doty, *Making Things Perfectly Queer: Interpreting Mass Culture* (Minneapolis: University of Minnesota Press, 1993); Tim Miller, "Oklahomo! A Gay Performance Artist Vows that Musicals Shaped His Political Consciousness" (*American Theatre* 20.9 [2003]: 91–93); Wolf, *A Problem like Maria*. See also Matthew Bell's entry, "Musical Theater," in *Gay Histories and Cultures: An Encyclopedia*, ed. George E. Haggerty (New York: Garland, 2000), pp. 621–24, where he observes of the musical, "Perhaps no other modern art form succeeds so thoroughly in appealing, at the level of reception, to a gay (and implicitly male) 'sensibility,' and in refusing, at the level of denotation, gay content" (621).

CHAPTER 16

THE POLITICS OF REGION AND NATION IN AMERICAN MUSICALS

CHASE A. BRINGARDNER

ON February 28, 1999, after eighty-five performances and thirty-six previews, *Parade* closed its run at Broadway's Vivian Beaumont Theatre. Retelling the story of wrongly accused Leo Frank, a southern Jew killed by vigilantes in 1915 in Marietta, Georgia, *Parade* struggled throughout its run to fill seats. Some reviews hinted at the difficulties audiences might have in embracing its dark material and dramatic innovations. Still, the short run was a shock, given that *Parade* was conceived and directed by Hal Prince, received generally positive reviews from critics, featured the work of Tony Award winning playwright Alfred Uhry (book) and promising newcomer Jason Robert Brown (music and lyrics), and went on to receive nine Tony nominations. But its failure on Broadway was overshadowed when *Parade* opened its national tour the following year at the Fox Theatre in Atlanta, Georgia, where it drew large audiences. Despite (or perhaps because of) its being based on a racially charged incident and its aftermath, recounting events that took place a mere twenty minutes from the theater itself, *Parade* exceeded expectations, becoming, according to local producer Christopher Manos, "a success in every way."[1] The positive reception of *Parade* in Atlanta not only gave the show newfound popularity but also drew wider attention to musical theater productions outside the traditional New York market, highlighting the urgency for scholars to think anew about how musical theater relates to ideas of nation and region, and the role of politics in reception.

NATION AND REGION IN RELATION TO POLITICS

The terms "nation," "politics," and "region" intertwine deeply. The very process of defining a nation or region is political by nature, since it entails drawing physical or figurative boundaries. For the United States, as historians Edward L. Ayers and Peter S. Onuf remind us, American geography "recapitulates American history," affecting and reflecting how individuals and groups have "thought themselves across space."[2] In defining a nation or region, one reorders and recontextualizes space, memory, and history through a recurring process of forgetting and discovery, resulting in a politically charged construct specific to one's contemporary historical moment.

Nation and region have often been used as contrasting terms. Nation, as defined by the *Oxford English Dictionary*, describes "a people or group of peoples; a political state," and comprises a "large aggregate of communities and individuals united by factors such as common descent, language, culture, history, or occupation of the same territory, so as to form a distinct people."[3] In the United States, ideas of nation developed during the time of the Revolutionary War and solidified during the writing of the Constitution. Good citizens of the nation, besides owing allegiance, believed in a shared national experience as documented in the Preamble to the Constitution, the basis for a communal understanding of "We the people." Yet political strife and unrest have continually challenged notions of a cohesive union. As a result, regionalism—that is, emotional or political affiliation based on smaller geographical areas—rose out of distrust or disbelief in the nation as a transcendent, unifying concept. Proponents of regionalism, then and later, located and defined identities within specific understandings of more local regions, in opposition to the national. Political conflicts such as the American Civil War resulted in part from these clashing projects of identity formation, with conflicts between nationalism and regionalism couched in terms of states' rights, sovereignty, and slavery. Such conflicts played out on both national and international stages and supported developing regional movements that continue to thrive.

Across the twentieth century, scholars increasingly used region as a historiographic vantage point, giving scholarly credence to political passions that had festered since the formation of the United States. Persuasive regional narratives established particular regions as distinctive and identifiable, beginning, as argued by regional historian Henry D. Shapiro, with Appalachia.[4] The "discovery" and popularization of Appalachia by scholars and the popular press at the turn of the twentieth century brought the region national and international attention. Appalachian studies identified specific traditions, practices, and rituals (moonshine production, musical heritage, etc.), celebrating the unique and untamed nature of the region in relation to the rest of the United States, while simultaneously grappling with the question of how Appalachian culture fits within American culture more generally. This successful model led scholars to develop studies of other regions, such as the South, New England, the Sunbelt, the Pacific Northwest, and the Midwest, which supplemented and sometimes contradicted national histories, presented alternative identity constructions to challenge traditional understandings of nation, and remapped discussions of space and place within an American context.

NATION AND REGION WITHIN MUSICAL THEATER SCHOLARSHIP

Within musical theater scholarship, few scholars have traversed the complex terrain where national and regional identities converge and diverge in the American musical. Many texts celebrate the musical as the first truly American form, citing its continued fascination with projecting, championing, and challenging the American Dream. Both John Bush Jones's *Our Musicals, Ourselves* (2003) and David Walsh and Len Platt's *Musical Theater and American Culture* (2003) position the musical as distinctly American and argue that it offers an appropriate lens through which to view American history. Both texts helpfully link the musical to America's own processes of self-identification and its struggles to understand its global position, establish itself as a land of opportunity, and sell itself as a paragon of modern culture.[5] Raymond Knapp's *The American Musical and the Formation of National Identity* (2005) argues that the musical has "helped us envision ourselves as a nation of disparate people, functioning within a world of even more extreme differences," and reminds us that while this project often appears to celebrate cohesion and sameness, musicals tend to construct and (most often) reconcile difference within an American "melting pot," as a hallmark of American identity. More broadly, Knapp argues that musicals "frame and embody larger political issues" and thus provide rich texts to be considered, dissected, and studied.[6]

Stacy Wolf's *A Problem Like Maria* (2002) and Andrea Most's *Making Americans* (2004) similarly see the musical as a key element of America's cultural history, but emphasize its pivotal role as mediator of American identity, cultural history, and politics. For Wolf, the musical is a place where alternative understandings of gender and sexual identity exist within and alongside more traditional understandings, whereas for Most, it has provided cultural space for Jewish artists to negotiate their roles and positions within American society and promote a more ideal America. For both, the musical creates, exhibits, and maintains alternative identities in the service of re-inscribing, refining, and restructuring American cultural identity.[7]

David Savran and Bruce Kirle further interrogate the American identity of musicals. In *A Queer Sort of Materialism* (2003), "Towards a Historiography of the Popular" (2004), and elsewhere, Savran argues for the importance of the musical as a site of cultural production, its position within cultural hierarchies and at the intersection of several disciplines, and—most germane here—its role in identity politics.[8] While arguing for a similar centrality of the American musical to national identity, Bruce Kirle's *Unfinished Show Business* (2005) envisions new historiographies of the musical that focus on regional identities in addition to national.[9]

As Kirle's work indicates, a focus on region provides an important counternarrative to the project of nation building and nationalism that frequently informs discussions of American identity. The openness of the text in musicals, coupled with their ability to offer multiple meanings at once, makes them useful sites for tracing conflicting cultural forces and for witnessing changing understandings of American ideas and ideologies. But while nation has received due attention in musical theater scholarship, region has not.

One exception to this neglect has been the frequent tendency to see New York City as the center of musical theater in the United States. Supporting this tendency is a narrative of exceptionalism that marks New York as particularly appropriate for the creation and development of musical theater, drawing energy from Manhattan's bustling streets, towering skyscrapers, bright lights, ethnic neighborhoods, cultural variety, and concentration of talent. John Kenrick's *Musical Theatre: A History* (2008), for example, cites New York's long history with theatrical production, its abundant spaces, its access to technological innovations, and its proximity to popular music centers such as Tin Pan Alley as some of the many reasons that New York proved ideally suited for musical theater.[10] Despite such attention to place and space, however, New York too often becomes a placeholder for the entire country, with its narrative of exceptionalism becoming one of substitution and even erasure: as New York City goes, so goes the country. Musical theater histories tend toward an unreflecting and often unconscious focus on Broadway, neglecting national tours and alternative centers of musical theater production.[11] Such histories, as well as those that ignore region altogether, underestimate the potential benefits of analyzing a musical and its production history from the perspective of region.

What Region Offers the Musical Theater Scholar

A regional approach to musical theater encourages readings that center on space and place and puts specific performances or musical texts in conversation with national and global productions. Regional issues are often present within the text or lyrics of a musical, as with *Lil' Abner*, *Blood Brothers*, or *Flower Drum Song*, in which case the narrative already identifies or implies a specific region for analysis, be it Appalachia, Liverpool, or San Francisco. Just as musicals provide audiences opportunities to reflect on debates over American identity during various historical moments, they also offer them chances to reflect on regional concerns and identities as they relate to ideas of nation. From the Midwest identities in *Oklahoma!* and

The Music Man to the various New York identities in *Guys and Dolls* or the immigrant communities in *West Side Story*, the American musical has frequently used regional or otherwise local identities to address larger political issues such as racism, exoticism, or tolerance. Examining the ways region functions within texts can lead to a more nuanced understanding of identity politics and relationships in musicals and thereby enhance interpretations and meanings for performers and audience alike.

A regional focus can also address the effects of space and place on a musical once it goes on tour or gets produced in local venues such as colleges, high schools, and community centers. After a Broadway musical departs New York City and begins an often multiyear journey across the country, the show's meanings may shift with each performance location. For example, the musical *Wicked* takes on a different meaning in Dallas in a venue located on the Texas State Fairgrounds from the one it has in a Phoenix theater in the middle of summer or in a Chicago theater in the winter mere minutes from the home where Frank Baum wrote *The Wizard of Oz*. Examining both national and regional reviews in addition to any available production notes, blogs, interviews, or other accounts can reveal the different ways a particular city responds to a touring show, which may allow us to see the show or the city itself in a new light. Regionalism provides a vocabulary and context for addressing the experiences of touring productions and for tracing how a show might continue to develop and shift in response to local circumstances. For example, references and intonations that resonate in one region may not translate effectively to another, as was the case with *Parade*.

Regionalism also provides additional rationale for the openness of musicals' texts. A musical does not merely replicate itself exactly from town to town but becomes like a living entity, adapting to the character and culture of the regions it tours. Considering the ramifications of, responses to, and rationales for a performance of *Oklahoma!* in Oklahoma City or of *The Music Man* in Iowa places each show in relation to other performances of the same musical in other cities. More important, such an approach finds as much value in interrogating regional productions as in studying Broadway premieres or revivals, in part because a regional focus disrupts the typically New York–centered biases of musical theater scholarship. Further, it offers a more nuanced context for examining the relationship between the text of a show and the particular audience in attendance, allowing for discussions of how meanings are formed and of how interpretations and understandings shift according to circumstance. How might a musical create meanings in a high school gymnasium in rural Kansas different from those of a production in the university theater in Lawrence or the large civic center in Topeka, and how do those meanings relate to the original Broadway production?

Furthermore, this approach will encourage us to consider the implications of shows created outside the Broadway system altogether, which work their way to New York City via out-of-town tryouts in distinctive other regions, such as the Pacific Northwest or the Deep South. We must think about how a musical originating in a repertory theater elsewhere in the United States—such as *The Color Purple*

(Atlanta), *Shrek* (Seattle), *The Little Mermaid* (Denver), or *Passing Strange* (Berkeley)—might retain the flavor of that region. Through examining regional and national reviews, and production notes and narratives, among others sources, we can start to identify the traces of region that flavor Broadway productions.[12]

CASE STUDY: THE BEST LITTLE WHOREHOUSE IN TEXAS

To provide an example of what a regional approach might entail, I discuss *The Best Little Whorehouse in Texas* (1978) within a specific southern context. In approaching this musical from a regional perspective, I draw upon related work in American studies, cultural geography, and southern studies. Within American studies, for example, historian Pete Daniel (*Lost Revolutions*, 2000), reads the development of NASCAR and the Elvis craze, among other cultural events, as evidence of profound social, political, and economic changes in the South following World War II. Daniel explores NASCAR in the 1950s (including its moonshine-soaked roots), seeing it as a pastime that allowed traditional, God-fearing, lower-class Southerners to form communities of spectators that celebrated stock car racing in part as a refusal "to bow to the elite culture." Their support of the wild and often dangerous NASCAR, as opposed to the more refined racing traditions of Europe, indicated a "bending of culture to suit their purposes," thumbing their noses at larger national culture.[13] Thus, a specific regional cultural practice may be read as political resistance to the national. Likewise, southern scholars Gavin James Campbell (*Music and the Making of a New South*, 2004) and Tara McPherson (*Reconstructing Dixie*, 2003) emphasize performances in popular music, film, and television as sites where regional identities may be tested and contested. Campbell, for example, describes how productions by the New York Metropolitan Opera in Atlanta at the beginning of the 1900s "supplied a tune for a complex and sometimes macabre minuet between gender and race that only intensified after the Metropolitan Opera returned to New York."[14] Campbell emphasizes the way the Opera provided women and people of color a temporary opportunity to exceed their prescribed societal boundaries. McPherson argues that the television show *Designing Women*, while often perceived as progressive in its racial and gender politics, and while frequently addressing the "ways being Southern (of a place) intersects with being white, being a woman," remains trapped within a more problematic cultural hierarchy "where all the women are white, and all the blacks are men."[15] All of these examples provide models that easily translate to a musical theater context.

Traditional methods of musical theater analysis relegate *The Best Little Whorehouse in Texas* to a mere footnote in musical theater history, deeming it an unremarkable throwback to an older style of musical comedy. Conventional musical analysis would find that the show breaks little new ground aside from using a country-western sound, while a national analysis would erase the specificities of Texas and the South and let the whorehouse stand in for small-town America. Dance-based analysis, notwithstanding the lauded choreography by Tommy Tune, would tend to neglect the pointed political content of the book, whereas literary analysis might neglect to consider the preponderance of actual bodies on stage in a musical that revolves around the selling of bodily services. A regional analysis, on the other hand, addresses and incorporates many of these concerns while placing debates over regional identity at the center of discourse, thereby revealing the multiple layers of ideological construction within and around the show, and the multiple ways the show has conveyed meaning. Moreover, *Whorehouse* offers multiple layers for regional analysis: the text, the press surrounding the New York and several simultaneous touring productions, various audience responses to the touring show, and the subsequent Hollywood film.

Region dominates the musical's text (music and lyrics by Carol Hall, book by Larry L. King and Peter Masterson): "Texas has a whorehouse in it! Lord have mercy on our souls!"[16] In the small town of La Grange, Texas, "in the shadows of the state capitol," Miss Mona Stangley—madam extraordinaire—operates a whorehouse known as the Chicken Ranch, so named because during hard times desperate gentlemen lacking the standard three dollar fee could exchange a live chicken for the ladies' services (*Whorehouse*, 34). The local sheriff, Ed Earl Dodd, allows the whorehouse to operate both because of his love for Miss Mona and his perceived "small town" values of live-and-let-live. Melvin P. Thorpe, religious zealot and voice of the Watchdog radio program, however, makes it his personal mission to close the whorehouse and return morality to Texas. He enlists the help of the governor, a slick "sidestepping" politician more concerned with maintaining his power than serving his public (*Whorehouse*, 66). Meanwhile, the Aggies of Texas A&M have won a hard victory over the University of Texas and are treated—by a senator, no less—to an evening at the whorehouse as a reward for their efforts. The Aggies' visit marks the Chicken Ranch's last hurrah, as reporters and politicians then descend on it to close it down, forcing the women to leave, and Miss Mona to find a new home.

In telling the plight of Miss Mona, her employees, and her customers, *Whorehouse* places images of a southern traditional way of life against those of an encroaching modernity hell-bent on reform and change. These two opposing forces might be read as Old and New South or simply a simpler way of life in conflict with the speed and complexities of the contemporary. Historically, the concept of the Old South emerges in the mid-twentieth century in juxtaposition to the New South, an attempt to rebrand and reconfigure the region as a modern, civilized, and economically viable player in the national scene. The New South, according to historian Paul M. Gaston, relied on an image of the Old South as "poor, frustrated, and despised, because it had, by decree of history, become entangled in wrong policies."[17] To rescue the South from the depths of despair and ruin, New South proponents championed two main areas for reform: politics and religion. Yet in the musical, these two conflicting concepts of region take on different connotations. The Old South exists as the more desirable place, where people both mind their own business and maintain a sense of community through shared knowledge; thus, by tacit mutual agreement, the community remains silent about the whorehouse, allowing it to continue to operate despite the law. Conversely, the New South is configured as contemporary and over-mediated, reduced to two key terms or strategies: regulation and moralizing. These competing regional identities in the musical, reflecting actual political tensions, encourage audiences to reconsider traditional understandings of the conflict, so that *Whorehouse* can be read as a sharp, critical political commentary on southern regional history, with strong potential for progressive, transgressive performance.

Additionally complicating these contrasting regional identities is the setting of *Whorehouse* in Texas, which presents particular challenges to seeing the South as a coherent region. Some historians highlight "the ambivalence of Texans [to define] themselves as part of the South" and their preference instead to emphasize their independence; hence the nickname, the Lone Star State.[18] Yet others, such as Henry Grady, include Texas as a vibrant, prosperous part of the South in their work, praising the region for its contributions to a burgeoning southern economy through its profitable cotton and coal industries and linking its future to that of the entire southern region.[19] *Whorehouse* dramatizes this debate over Texas's inclusion in the South and links it directly to larger debates about the Old and New South.

These two ideas of the South are articulated early in the musical. When Miss Mona outlines the tenets of her business in her opening song, "A Lil' Ole Bitty Pissant Country Place," she details many rules and regulations for her girls, pointing to an idealized Old Southern regional identity in the construction of her ladies. Mona's rules on telephone usage, proper language, cleanliness, and general decorum assure a certain image for their customers, derived from a traditional antebellum picture of genteel, servile women, willing to please—the image of an alternative, reimagined older system. But Mona leaves space for maneuvering and some independence; in agreeing to "pay the food and the rent and the utilities" in exchange for their keeping "their mind on [their] work responsibilities," Mona allows the girls to maintain financial independence and a reprieve from the constraints of marriage and family (*Whorehouse*, 25). Through Miss Mona's business and its enactment of traditional southern ideals, these women embody the image of ideal southern womanhood while simultaneously defying social conventions and staking their own claims in a male-dominated society.

Positioned in direct opposition to Miss Mona and the ladies of the Chicken Ranch are Melvin P. Thorpe and the governor, the former a rabid religious reformer who wants to establish a new moral order at their expense, the latter a slick politician skilled in the rhetorical arts. *Whorehouse* uses Thorpe and the governor to emphasize the New South's desire to make the private public, as opposed to the Old South with its live-and-let-live attitude. Thorpe and the governor exist only within the public realm of the musical, always surrounded by large crowds of people, emblematic of their broad appeal and devoted followings. Their public personas highlight style over substance, typifying the overly mediated New South as presented in the show. These two public figures stand opposed to the private space and demeanor of Miss Mona's replication of the Old South.

Eventually, the New South regional identity represses and displaces the traditional Old South, as Thorpe's crusade compels the sheriff to close the whorehouse down. The New South imposes regulations and moral codes that replace the easygoing private roles suggested in Mona's house rules with a rigid hierarchical system with men on top, women beneath, and alternative identities eliminated altogether. With this bleak conclusion, the New South victory does not usher in a golden age; rather, its religious watchdog organization and corrupt political system simply destroys the Old South. True, men are re-inscribed as dominant, free to move about society; thus, the Texas A & M football team remain heroes despite their dalliances at the whorehouse. But the women must leave their home, abandoning their safe haven to face uncertain futures without the guidance of Miss Mona or Jewel, her assistant. In "Hard Candy Christmas," which they sing as they pack and prepare to leave, they do not sing about getting jobs or an education, but rather imagine, "Maybe I'll dye my hair," "Maybe I'll sleep real late," "Maybe I'll lose some weight," and "Maybe I'll just get drunk on apple wine" (*Whorehouse*, 81). They no longer have either the confidence expressed in earlier numbers or the independence to control their own futures.

For a musical that markets itself as a feel-good "musical comedy," *Whorehouse* leaves audiences with a rather forlorn vision: a nostalgic vestige of the Old South destroyed through corrupt political and religious figures embodying the influx of New Southern mentalities, who in effect "Northernize" the South through reform and governmental interference in a scenario redolent of post–Civil War "carpetbaggers." In the end, instead of simply celebrating a retrograde image of an antebellum South, *Whorehouse* offers a smart critique of the New South and its unquestioning enthusiasts.

WHOREHOUSE IN THE PRESS AND ON FILM

Newspapers and periodicals provide useful documentation of regional responses to particular musicals, offering box-office and production specifics as well as registering interactions with a given performance. For example, Clive Barnes of the *New York Post* recognizes the multiple forces at work within *Whorehouse*, calling it "a strange, old-fashioned, new-fashioned musical, full of simple sentiments, dirty words, political chicanery and social hypocrisy, decent jokes, indecent jokes, bubbling performances and music with a bustle."[20] Similarly, in the *Daily News*, Douglas Watt calls the musical "100% American," declaring it "both sunny enough and funny enough" to "change things with its cheerful disregard for reality" (Suskin, 93). Critics and audiences in New York responded to *Whorehouse* in a generally positive manner, refraining from painting Texas or the South as unsophisticated or banal. Reviews like these point to a feeling that the New York production presented a view of the region as down-home country. As Watt stated at the end of his review, "I'm only surprised they don't sell Girl Scout cookies in the lobby" (Suskin, 93).

Outside of New York City, reviews of the show begin to document the ways meaning shifted regionally. Ironically, one of the few negative reviews appeared in the June 1978 *Texas Monthly*, where W. L. Taitte criticizes the show for trying "to be too many things" and trying "to reach too many truths at once."[21] Taitte also reveals another level of regional critique, speculating, "When someone gets the gumption to mount a Texas production, I fear it is unlikely to be able to match the New York one, which is a model example of how to do a musical the right way." His frank assessment of the Texas theatrical community and its "more conservative institutional theaters" reminds readers that this musical, although created by Southerners, was workshopped and developed in New York, and thus has become a distinctly New York creation stripped of much of its potential to depict southern regional or Texan identities. In fact, he seems to argue that "real" facets of southern life, such as modesty and conservatism, will impede a straightforward presentation of the original material. Reviews such as Taitte's illustrate the possibilities of a regional analysis to deal with conflicting identificatory practices once musicals take to the road.

The press reaction to the Atlanta stop on the first *Whorehouse* national tour demonstrates how notices and reviews can help launch a regional analysis. Five days before its official opening, the *Atlanta Constitution* ran a series of articles about the production in the January 4, 1980, issue in an attempt to build audience investment in the production, thereby providing a performed interaction between the audience and the show even before it opened. One article, "Alexis Smith: Call Her Madam," profiles the actor portraying Miss Mona on the national tour and highlights her previous reputation as Broadway and Hollywood's "sophisticated lady"—almost as though juxtaposing this image to her role as Miss Mona will reassure readers that she is not actually a madam.[22] Smith is quoted as saying that the musical "has the greatest title in the world" (Litsch, 10-B). A companion article, "Atlanta Adds Spice to Salty Texas Comedy," profiles Amy Miller (portraying Ruby Rae) and Bob Moyer (newspaper man Edsel Mackey), emphasizing their ties to the city.

The final article of the series, "I Want Tickets to…Er…'The…Ah…Best,'" recounts the hilarious experiences of the Fox Theatre box office in dealing with patrons embarrassed to say the title of the show out loud. Box-office manager David Stewart recalls people referring to the show only as "The Best," "that play," or "that show about Texas."[23] "I Want Tickets" also recounts the troubles the advertising campaign ran into during the show's New York run. Bus placards in New York had proclaimed "come on down to the whorehouse" but were removed by order of the City Council. Other venues required a new title altogether, "The Best Little Chicken Ranch in Texas." And public relations coordinator Warren Knowles is quoted as saying that "some radio and TV stations don't want the ads to run during prime time" (Litsch, "I Want Tickets," 1-B). But Atlanta had no such objections. Large print ads ran in the *Constitution* and television spots hailed its arrival. Atlanta's treatment of the show, especially its decision not to censor the marketing campaign, indicates a desire to be seen as more sophisticated than other cities on the tour, perhaps even than New York City itself. After providing a summary of the production history of the musical, the article concludes by heralding the ability of the show to "destroy the colorful language barrier," noting that "far into the hinterlands, well removed from the supposed evils of New York and Los Angeles, people are lining up to get into *The Best Little Whorehouse in Texas*" (Litsch, "I Want Tickets," 1-B). This final statement again makes a claim for Atlanta's sophistication and positions the citizens of Atlanta as active participants in projecting this image to the rest of the nation through their attendance at the show.

With the release of the feature film in 1982, only two years after the Atlanta premiere, *Whorehouse* entered a new phase in its representations of conflicting southern identities. Just as the Atlanta production had allowed the story of the whorehouse to reveal larger hopes and concerns for the city and region, the film broadens the story to encompass the entire South, primarily through casting. Rather than casting native Texans to play the roles, the film's producers decided upon Dolly Parton, a native of Tennessee, for the role of Miss Mona, and Burt Reynolds, a native Georgian, for the role of the sheriff (a part Larry L. King originally wanted Willie Nelson to play). Their participation in the film necessitated a wider understanding of southern identity since Parton and Reynolds were both already closely associated with southern identity, Parton through her music and Reynolds through his films, including *Cannonball Run* and *Deliverance*. Though the film was a box-office flop, its interpretation of the story, with additional songs by Parton (including "I Will Always Love You"), contributed to its ability to be read as a commentary on the conflicting forces of an Old and New South. Parton's and Reynold's southern identities make the film a fascinating study in how an actor's identity interacts, in a complex negotiation, both with regional identities and issues of identity already present in a script or screenplay. For example, the interplay among Parton the serious movie actor, Parton the country music star, and Parton as Miss Mona illustrate the difficulties of reconciling an actor's regional identity with those of her character and of the musical itself.

While the theatrical production established more specific and nuanced embodiments of southern identity as it played before southern audiences on the stage, the film functioned differently in relation to region. The film, with its larger-than-life leads, saturated the southern identities in the piece and frequently treaded into an area of destructive caricature and exaggeration not present in the musical's original staging, while simultaneously sanitizing and cleaning up the material to suit a larger audience. Parton's larger-than-life personality coupled with Reynold's bad boy reputation exceeded the confines of their characters of Miss Mona and the sherriff, respectively, overshadowing any attempt at the subtlety and complexity of the stage musical. As Roger Ebert of the *Chicago Sun Times* observed, "The story has been cleaned up so carefully to showcase Parton and Reynolds that the scandal has been lost," replaced by "a hymn to romance"—a particular detriment to the film since critics almost universally cited the lack of chemistry between the leads as the film's chief failing.[24] For film audiences, the careful work of the musical to parse out a complicated ideological debate between Old and New South gave way to a star-studded, sterile romantic comedy between two extremely popular personalities—which is not to say that southern audiences may not have found pleasure or moments of identification in the film, simply that the level of discourse shifted. Moreover, the return to a more romanticized and caricatured version of the South only served to perpetuate negative stereotypes that the original musical had complicated and disrupted.

* * *

Seen through the lens of region, *The Best Little Whorehouse in Texas* becomes more than the sum of its bare mentions in musical theater history texts. *Whorehouse* stands at the crossroads of a debate between differing views of the South, grappling with the real political implications of national, regional, and state politics of the late 1970s. The Atlanta production of *Whorehouse* provides a particularly fascinating example of regional reception, reflecting residual tensions within that city concerning the New South project of reform and uplift. As the musical traveled state to state, region to region, from Broadway to Hollywood, it amassed an ever-growing collection of meanings that placed it at the center of a discussion about region and identity for those audiences in theaters across the country. In its travels from New York to Atlanta to Hollywood, in particular, *Whorehouse* gathered a variety of regional meanings and interpretations, beginning as an energetic, entertaining musical romp with southern flair, progressing to a lively debate between Old and New South mentalities, and coming to rest as a romantic star vehicle for two iconic southern personalities.

The wider implications of regional analysis for musical theater are rich and varied. Such an approach would unlock further avenues for the exploration of musical theater texts and of how they have different meanings for divergent audiences across states, regions, nations, and the globe. One might draw fascinating conclusions from comparing a production of *Oklahoma!* performed in Oklahoma City versus one in New York City, or a production of *Avenue Q* in New York City versus Las Vegas or Atlanta. A regional analysis of Baltimore productions of *Hairspray* might cast the piece in a different light and might reveal something about the city itself. A regional approach allows for an understanding of how a musical and its specific audience participate in the interpretive process for a show. By accounting for travel, venue, and identity (both regional and national), such an approach engages with the musical on an inherently political level as it positions the musical front and center in the processes of constructing, maintaining, and reconstituting cultural meaning.

NOTES

1. Dan Hulbert, "Theatrical Bright Side to Atlanta's Dark Story" (*Atlanta Journal-Constitution* [June 20, 2000]).

2. "Introduction," in Edward L. Ayers, Patricia Nelson Limerick, Stephen Nissenbaum, and Peter S. Onuf, *All Over the Map: Rethinking American Regions* (Baltimore: Johns Hopkins University Press, 1996), p. 1.

3. *Oxford English Dictionary Online* (http://www.oed.com/, accessed August 10, 2009).

4. Henry D. Shapiro, "How Region Changed Its Meaning and Appalachia Changed Its Standing in the Twentieth Century," in *Bridging Southern Cultures: An Interdisciplinary Approach*, ed. John Lowe (Baton Rouge: Louisiana State University Press, 2005).

5. John Bush Jones, *Our Musicals, Ourselves: A Social History of the American Musical Theatre* (Hanover, NH: Brandeis University Press, 2003), and David Walsh and Len Platt, *Musical Theater and American Culture* (Westport, CT: Greenwood, 2003).

6. Raymond Knapp, *The American Musical and the Formation of National Identity* (Princeton: Princeton University Press, 2005), pp. 7 and 283.

7. Stacy Wolf, *A Problem Like Maria: Gender and Sexuality in the American Musical* (Ann Arbor: University of Michigan Press, 2002), and Andrea Most, *Making Americans: Jews and the Broadway Musical* (Cambridge, MA: Harvard University Press, 2004).

8. David Savran, *A Queer Sort of Materialism: Recontextualizing American Theater* (Ann Arbor: University of Michigan Press, 2003), and "Towards a Historiography of the Popular" (*Theatre Survey* 45:2 [2004]: 211–17).

9. Bruce Kirle, *Unfinished Show Business: Broadway Musicals as Works-in-Process* (Carbondale: Southern Illinois University Press, 2005).

10. John Kenrick, *Musical Theatre: A History* (New York: Continuum, 2008).

11. Scott Miller's three "survey" books are an interesting partial exception, although his approach—offering focused discussions of shows that originated in New York, addressing themes and problems relevant to their being mounted elsewhere in repertory—rarely aligns with regional advocacy; see his *From Assassins to West Side Story: The Director's Guide to Musical Theatre* (Portsmouth, NH: Heinemann, 1996), *Deconstructing Harold Hill: An Insider's Guide to Musical Theatre* (Portsmouth, NH: Heinemann, 2000), and *Rebels with Applause: Broadway's Groundbreaking Musicals* (Portsmouth, NH: Heinemann, 2001).

12. A related issue concerns the "traces" that stem from authorship, which helps explain problems in reception, among represented constituents, of shows lacking such traces. Thus, we may note the troubled reception of *West Side Story* among Puerto Ricans, of *The King and I* in Thailand, or of *The Sound of Music* in Austria, which contrast sharply with how *The Music Man* plays in Iowa (book, lyrics, and music by Meredith Willson, a native of Mason City), *Oklahoma!* in Oklahoma (book derived, often verbatim, from *Green Grow the Lilacs*, by Lynn Riggs, a native of Claremore), or even *Guys and Dolls* to native New Yorkers (based on the work and language of Damon Runyan, Broadway's one-time authenticating voice).

13. Pete Daniel, *Lost Revolutions: The South in the 1950s* (Chapel Hill: University of North Carolina Press, 2000), p. 119.

14. Gavin James Campbell, *Music and the Making of a New South* (Chapel Hill: University of North Carolina Press, 2004), p. 65.

15. Tara McPherson, *Reconstructing Dixie: Race, Gender, and Nostalgia in the Imagined South* (Durham, NC: Duke University Press, 2003), pp. 35 and 187.

16. Carol Hall, Larry L. King, and Peter Masterson, *The Best Little Whorehouse in Texas* (New York: Samuel French, 1978), p. 34 (henceforward *Whorehouse*).

17. Dewey W. Grantham, *The South in Modern America: A Region at Odds* (New York: HarperCollins, 1994), p. 25.

18. Celeste Ray, "Introduction," *Southern Heritage on Display: Public Ritual and Ethnic Diversity within Southern Regionalism*, ed. Celeste Ray (Tuscaloosa: University of Alabama Press, 2002, pp. 1–37), p. 5.

19. Henry Woodfin Grady, *The New South, and Other Addresses, with Biography, Critical Opinions, and Explanatory Notes*, by Edna Henry Lee Turpin (New York: Maynard, Merrill, 1904).

20. Quoted in Steven Suskin, *More Opening Nights on Broadway: A Critical Quotebook of the Musical Theatre 1965 through 1981* (New York: Schirmer, 1997), p. 91.

21. W. L. Taitte, "Tarts of Gold" (*Texas Monthly* [June 1978]: 132).

22. Joseph Litsch, "Alexis Smith: Call Her Madam: Hollywood's Typecast 'Sophisticated Lady'" (*Atlanta Constitution* [January 4, 1980]: 1-B+.

23. Joseph Litsch, "I Want Tickets to…Er…'The…Ah…Best'" (*Atlanta Constitution* [January 4, 1980], 1-B+).

24. Roger Ebert, "*The Best Little Whorehouse in Texas*" (review in *Chicago Sun Times* [January 1, 1982]).

CHAPTER 17

CLASS AND CULTURE

DAVID SAVRAN

SINCE the decline of vaudeville and minstrelsy in the 1920s, the Broadway musical has been the only form of American theater that could reliably be considered a part of popular culture. It is also the one form that has been exported all over the world and continues to be performed in Berlin, Buenos Aires, Seoul, and myriad other urban centers. It is the only form of theater to make a significant mark on mass culture in the United States and abroad and whose anthems, from "Ol' Man River" to "Aquarius," "Climb Ev'ry Mountain" to "Seasons of Love," are sung and listened to worldwide. In 1964, at the height of the rock–and-roll craze, Louis Armstrong's recording of "Hello, Dolly!" even managed to dislodge the Beatles from the number 1 spot on the pop chart. *The Phantom of the Opera*, meanwhile, with a worldwide gross of more than $3.3 billion, represents a landmark in popular culture.[1] And lest we forget, the dearly beloved Rodgers and Hammerstein musicals are performed countless times every day in countless languages all over the world. Yet to say that the musical is a popular genre engenders the question, "What *is* popular culture?" For the "popular" is always changing. As Bertolt Brecht remarked, "What was popular yesterday is not today, for the people today are not what they were yesterday."[2] And the notoriously slippery category "the people" can be, and has been, mobilized for myriad purposes. Usually when we invoke the people, we mean the middle and working classes, or at least certain fractions of these classes. But because the middle class that listens to Beyoncé is not the same middle class that attends the 2008 Lincoln Center revival of *South Pacific*, claims to the Broadway musical's status as part of popular culture have to be qualified, for both its production and consumption distinguish it sharply from cinema, television, and other kinds of what is usually called popular culture.

Surveys demonstrate that middle-class Broadway audiences have considerably more economic and educational capital than most Americans. During the 2007–08 season, the average annual income of Broadway musical theatergoers ($141,600) was roughly three times the national average. Spectators were, moreover, one and one-half times more likely to have completed college (26.3% versus 17.2%) and four times as likely to have had some postgraduate education (41.1% versus 10%).[3] But studies of audience demographics date back no earlier than 1981, leaving us only anecdotal information about the public that attended Broadway musicals for most of their history. This information, however, does correlate with recent statistics. We know that since the end of the nineteenth century—when musical comedy separated itself from burlesque, minstrelsy, and vaudeville, on the one hand, and the serious, legitimate stage, on the other—the producers and consumers of the Broadway musical have been mostly middle class. Although some of its makers, such as Irving Berlin and George Gershwin, grew up in working-class immigrant neighborhoods, the vast majority has come from middle-class families, and many, such as Richard Rodgers, Agnes de Mille, or Stephen Sondheim, from the upper reaches of that class. Audiences, too, must have had a good deal of disposable income, because in the early twentieth century, as now, the cost of admission to a Broadway musical was many times that of a movie ticket. In 1928, prices for musicals ranged from 50 cents to $6.60 and for nonmusical plays from 50 cents to $4.40.[4] (In contrast, 99% of the motion picture audience paid between 10 cents and 49 cents.)[5] Even today, a musical on average costs a theatergoer between five and ten times as much as a movie.

CULTURAL HIERARCHIES

To point out the Broadway musical's status as a middle-class phenomenon, however, only begins to analyze its relationship to popular culture. More important is to study how it has been positioned among forms of entertainment by its makers, audiences, and critics. Historians have pointed out that a clear-cut hierarchy of cultural forms did not become established in the United States until the end of the nineteenth century, just as musical comedy was developing its own distinctive character. It was during this period, Lawrence Levine reports, that the words "highbrow" and "lowbrow" were coined, the former "first used in the 1880s to describe intellectual or aesthetic superiority" and the latter, "first used shortly after 1900 to mean someone or something neither 'highly intellectual' nor 'aesthetically refined.'"[6] These terms, borrowed from a racially inflected phrenology, were used to accentuate the differences between a European-inspired, morally and spiritually uplifting art and an allegedly primitive, vulgar, commercialized art; the culture of the intellectual and economic elites (most of them of northern European descent) versus that of the working classes (many of them African Americans and recent immigrants from southern and eastern Europe). Opera houses, concert halls, theaters, and museums were constructed to look like classical temples to make certain kinds of art appear dignified—and completely dissociated from both the marketplace and the culture of the working classes. The older elite used the division between high-brow and lowbrow as a tool to organize and rationalize the social and economic realms and to buttress their own power. For in certain respects, the ability to fashion a hierarchy (cultural or otherwise) and police its boundaries is far more important than the specific content of categories like highbrow and lowbrow.

European concert music, opera, literary classics, and paintings by the old masters defined a highbrow culture at odds with an indigenous, turn-of-the-century popular culture. Then (as now) highbrow work tends to be wrapped in mystique, trading on its purported exclusivity, its authenticity, and its refusal to succumb to the commodity form. At the opposite end of the spectrum, captivating the largely foreign-born masses, were genres such as comic strips, jazz, nickelodeons, and, among theater forms, min-strel shows, burlesque, cheap vaudeville, and the like. Although these forms were not mass produced in the way that cinema was, they were usually deemed lowbrow inso-far as they were imagined to be fit for consumption only en masse by the working classes. This period also saw the emergence of the so-called little theater movement in the United States, which tried to create a highbrow theater by producing the work of European playwrights such as Ibsen, Shaw, and Galsworthy. For the reformers of United States culture, this art theater was vitally important for elevating the taste of the theatergoing minority. Accordingly, it dedicated itself, as one critic then wrote, to "the encouragement and support of an American drama, the giving voice and tongue to a neighborhood, the production of the great masterpieces of the world, [and] the elevation of taste of the community."[7]

In 1909, the *New York Tribune* began to discriminate among theatrical offerings by ranking them in a clear-cut hierarchy, with "Comedy and Drama" at the top, fol-lowed by "Musical Plays," "Variety Houses," and "Beach and Park." The most refined form, "Comedy and Drama," sold its orchestra seats mostly to "affluent audiences." The galleries, meanwhile, at least after 1910, were peopled by increasingly serious spectators, "earnest devotees of drama unable to afford orchestra seats," mostly "middle-class and mostly women."[8] Although no cheaper than "Comedy and Drama," "Musical Plays" thrived, attracting (then as now) larger and more diverse audiences. As developed by writers such as Irving Berlin, Will Marion Cook, and Jerome Kern, they adopted popular music styles—first ragtime, then jazz—and elaborated their own distinctive brand of romantic comedy punctuated by song, dance, and shtick. Yet musical comedy and musical revue—part play, part variety; part narrative, part spectacle; part drama, part song and dance; part opera, part "leg" show; part art, part glamour—have always been hybrid genres that resist easy categorization. The *Tribune*, for example, classified a high-toned revue like the Ziegfeld Follies not as variety but as a musical play.

The *New York Tribune*, however, was not alone in finding it difficult to catego-rize musical theater. Theater critics also were made uneasy by the lack of a clear boundary between variety entertainments and the legitimate stage, between "whipped cream" and the "roast."[9] Burns Mantle, the longtime editor of the Best Plays series, excluded musicals on principle from the "best plays" while another critic grouped musical comedy together with motion pictures and bedroom farces as genres that "dilut[e] the general average of intelligence and lower...the standard of demand" because they "are not yet really provocative enough...to tempt the taster farther into the theatre" (Sayler, 187 and 246). The dean of the critics, George Jean Nathan, was especially anxious that musical comedy know—and respect—its allotted position in the cultural hierarchy. An "outlet for our trivial moods," "the music show occupies to the theatre and drama the same relationship...that alcohol occupies to art: a convivial moment of forgetfulness." Problems arise when this amnesia-inducing tipple forgets its place and "takes itself with deadly seriousness."[10]

The musical theater—positioned between highbrow and lowbrow, between art theater and variety entertainments—has for almost a century epitomized the culture called middlebrow, an elastic category into which a great many artifacts can fall. The word was coined during the 1920s as a way of describing a rapidly growing species of art that emulated highbrow forms while attempting to make them more accessible. The middlebrow consumer was considered to be traditional at heart yet striving to be au courant, a middle-class man or woman with education and social aspirations who, Janice Radway notes, would "read the new book-review sections" in newspapers and subscribe to "innovative magazines like *Time* and the *New Yorker*."[11] Radway identifies the culture that attracted these people not as a "harbinger of new mass cultural forms" but as a distinctive by-product of American modernism, "a separate aesthetic and ideological production constructed by a particular fraction of the middle class offended equally by the 'crassness' of mass culture and by the literary avant-garde."[12] The middlebrow consumer was routinely described as—and condemned for—being a social-climbing parvenu trying to "pre-empt...the highbrow's function" and "blur the lines between the serious and the frivolous."[13]

The term "middlebrow" has generally been a mark of opprobrium, especially during the height of the Cold War (from the late 1940s through the 1960s) when the arbiters of taste were anxious about the position of United States culture vis à vis European highbrow art and eager that United States art should be as formidable as its military might. In April 1949, *Life* magazine published an article entitled "Highbrow, Low-brow, Middle-brow" that included a two-page chart that classified the public's taste in everything from clothes, drinks, and salads to entertainment, phonograph records, and reading. *Life's* article became so popular that pigeonholing one's brow level became "for many months" a "favorite parlor game."[14] This chart (which divides middlebrow into upper and lower) makes it clear that for postwar tastemakers, theater was *the* emblematic middlebrow art. *Life* puts it in the upper-middlebrow category (where it is designated by actors decked out in Shakespearean garb) along with *Harper's*, *Vogue*, and a dry martini. The pile of records in the upper-middlebrow's record collection includes Cole Porter's *Kiss Me, Kate* sandwiched between Chopin and Sibelius while the lower-middlebrow's includes Victor Herbert, Nelson Eddy, and Perry Como.[15]

The postwar critics were by no means the only ones to pigeonhole musical theater as a middlebrow form. Indeed, since the 1920s, musical theater has occupied what I would describe as an intermediate position in United States culture, recycling and recombining elements of, on the one hand, public amusements like jazz, vaudeville, and rock, and, on the other, more elite forms like opera and the serious play. Neither high nor low—or rather, *both high and low at the same time*—musical theater has consistently evinced those characteristics that have historically been branded as middlebrow: the willful mixture of entertainment and art, the profane and the sacred, frivolous and profound, erotic and intellectual. Even with the consecration of what used to be called the avant-garde and the invasion of former bastions of high culture by a proliferation of new media, the Broadway musical continues to epitomize a middle-class, middlebrow form beloved of suburbanites and tourists.

The categorization of musical theater as a middlebrow art is unquestionably related to the fact that it was long ignored or derided by university theater and music departments. To all but legions of enthusiastic theatergoers, musicals were considered, in Gerald Mast's pithy account, "essentially frivolous and silly diversions: lousy drama and lousy music."[16] By way of example, in a comprehensive, 780-page book on modernist theater, *Century of Innovation* (1973), historians Oscar Brockett and Robert Findlay devote a mere two paragraphs to the musical, despite their concession that it represents "the most popular form" of theater.[17] For many theater scholars and musicologists, the musical is embarrassingly commercial and too closely linked to high school drama clubs—as well as gay and lesbian subcultures. Indeed, the intense pleasure it arouses in its aficionados militates against it, in effect decreeing that it is too much fun to be worthy of academic study. I would argue, to the contrary, that its dubious legitimacy, its intermediary position between highbrow and lowbrow, is in fact symptomatic of its privileged status as a barometer of cultural and social politics.

MIDDLEBROW DISTINCTION

As an illustration of the musical theater's uncomfortable position in U.S. culture, let me consider the correlation between the Broadway musical and the Pulitzer Prize, an award that has functioned historically to define upper-middlebrow excellence. When the prize for drama was first given in 1918, it was explicitly charged with uplifting a stage that was then dominated by musical comedy, melodrama, and farce. Indeed, the drama award was the only one in the arts to mandate that the winning text should instill "educational value and power" and so improve the genre in question, "raising the standard of good morals, good taste, and good manners."[18] The clause about "raising the standard" was dropped from the description in 1929 thanks to the work of Eugene O'Neill and his contemporaries in institutionalizing a serious American theater. But the " 'uplift' clause" remained on the books until 1964 (Hohenberg, 102 and 266–69).

Given the Pulitzer Prize guidelines, musicals have comprised a contentious category, in part because the mixture of highbrow and lowbrow is more visible and, for some, unsettling, in them than in other dramatic genres. Only eight pieces of musical theater have won the award, roughly one per decade beginning in the 1930s: *Of Thee I Sing* (1931), *South Pacific* (1949), *Fiorello!* (1959), *How to Succeed in Business Without Really Trying* (1961), *A Chorus Line* (1975), *Sunday in the Park with George* (1984), *Rent* (1996), and *Next to Normal* (2010). Given the history of critical discomfort, it is little wonder that musicals have accounted for less than 10 percent of the awards. When the jury honored the Gershwins' *Of Thee I Sing*, it felt obliged to adopt a defensive posture: "This award may seem unusual, but the play is unusual. Not only is it coherent and well-knit enough to class as a play, aside from the music, but it is a biting and true satire on American politics." It is telling that although the librettists and lyricist were singled out, George Gershwin was ignored in the citation despite the fact that his score borrows liberally, if satirically, from the conventions of operetta and opera. But the music was deemed an "aside" that made the work distinctive but did not contribute substantially to its "admirable" qualities.[19] While most critics applauded the selection, Brooks Atkinson, the long-reigning drama critic of the *New York Times* (historically the most powerful proponent of upper-middlebrow taste) excoriated the committee for "turn[ing] its back on the drama" and for having stripped the prize of "a great deal of its value" (quoted in Toohey, 102).

Among the eight musicals, I want to look briefly at the cultural positioning of two, *South Pacific* and *Rent*.[20] The former is emblematic of the formally and politically ambitious musicals of the postwar years, the latter of a theater forced by changes in popular music, social mores, and conceptions of personal identity to loosen the postwar formulas. The former is the only Rodgers and Hammerstein musical to be awarded the Pulitzer Prize and remains, in Stanley Green's estimation, their "most universally admired achievement."[21] The latter, meanwhile, succeeded in reviving both the American musical and the rock opera at a time when both had been left for dead. Its critical acclaim and great popularity (especially with younger audiences) mark it as a telling index of a society in which cultural hierarchies have been all but overturned and abjection has been increasingly commercialized. Both plays are war stories that feature the death of a protagonist, one pitting its heroes against the Japanese, the other against poverty, exploitation, heroin, and AIDS. Both feature cross-race romances in which persons of color are exoticized and sexualized. Both oppose what is supposed to be an indigenous, authentic folk culture to American commercialism. Both were sensationally successful in appealing to politically liberal, middle-class audiences, chalking up long Broadway runs and spinning off popular recordings and movies. And both plays recycle musical and dramatic tropes associated with opera, combine them with the pop vernaculars of their day, and in part are precisely about that mixing. *Rent* suggests that despite the breakdown of the mid-century cultural hierarchy and an unprecedented diversification of media, the Broadway musical remains stuck in a middlebrow groove.

Rodgers and Hammerstein's fourth stage musical, *South Pacific* had the largest advance sale of any Broadway musical up to its time. Not only were Rodgers and

Hammerstein the leading brand name in the Broadway musical by 1949, but the musical's source, James Michener's *Tales of the South Pacific*, had also the year before won the Pulitzer Prize for fiction. So no one was surprised when the musical garnered almost unanimous rave reviews, became "the 'hottest' ticket that Broadway had ever known," and went on to become the then-second longest running musical, surpassed only by *Oklahoma!* (Toohey, 237). Although only implied in most reviews, critics seemed especially impressed by the writers' "courage" in making "the secondary love plot...a plea for racial tolerance," complete with a song ("You've Got to Be Carefully Taught") that, according to one commentator, "attacks the issue with a vehemence never before...seen on the stage."[22] And while the contradiction between an explicitly antiracist politics (one year after Truman desegregated the military) with the racist exoticization of the South Seas natives has made many people uncomfortable, *South Pacific* is celebrated in most critical accounts of musical theater as a "cherished legend" that, in Philip Beidler's words, makes "a courageous statement against racial bigotry in general and institutional racism in the postwar United States in particular."[23] Although this mythology vastly oversimplifies and whitewashes the musical's racial politics, it is also responsible for reconstructing *South Pacific* as a middlebrow masterpiece: a politicized, hence morally uplifting, example of a frivolous theatrical form designed to appeal to liberal fractions of the middle and upper-middle classes.

Although hailed as Rodgers and Hammerstein's most accomplished *Gesamtkunstwerk*, *South Pacific* is in fact a perfect illustration of the sleight of hand responsible for producing the illusion of the so-called integrated musical—for none of their other works is as much the jerrybuilt collage that *South Pacific* is. Beidler's list of its components ranges neatly from highbrow to lowbrow: the "grandeur of opera; the seriousness of 'legitimate' theatre; the comedic possibilities of the variety show and vaudeville; the emotionality of melodrama"(Beidler, 214–15). And it is hardly coincidental that the hero, Emile de Becque, happens to be French (although played originally by Ezio Pinza, a leading Italian basso), since the score is suffused by a French-inspired orientalism that gives it much of its highbrow appeal, including its echoes of the orientalist operas of Delibes and Saint-Saëns, the modernist exoticism of Debussy and Ravel, and the sexualized yet innocent South Seas women popularized by Gauguin. Uncharacteristically for Rodgers and Hammerstein, however, the main plot is somewhat less highbrow in tone and structure than the subplot, despite its more Europeanized music. (In almost all their other musicals, a more vaudevillian subplot is subordinate in brow level.)[24] For while the main plot pits an American "hick," Nellie Forbush, against a cosmopolitan, rich European, the subplot could have come out of any number of nineteenth-century French operas that feature a white hero who ventures into a mysterious land filled with dark-skinned natives and succumbs to the seductions of a native temptress. And as in most every orientalist narrative, Western liberal, humanist values finally triumph over oriental despotism, despite—or perhaps because of—Lieutenant Cable's death. Sacrificed both to the American war effort and the then-unforgiving laws of cross-race desire, Cable can resolve an otherwise unresolvable plotline only by dying.

Like *South Pacific*, *Rent* aims to ennoble a popular form by making a political statement. Unlike the scrupulously plotted Rodgers and Hammerstein music drama, Jonathan Larson's multicultural rock opera is a deliberately disheveled affair. *Rent* takes pleasure in mixing musical, poetic, and dramatic styles and in bringing together all those persons that give social conservatives the heebee-jeebees: "faggots, lezzies, dykes, cross dressers," junkies, anarchists, the homeless, people with AIDS, and artists of all stripes.[25] Moreover, its translation of *La Bohème* into a "Lower East Side story" mixes high and low more aggressively than any other musical of the 1990s, turning the frail Mimi into an S/M-club stripper and junkie, the musician Schaunard into a transvestite who dies of AIDS, and "Musetta's Waltz" into a few feverish guitar licks. Unlike Puccini's opera, which does not take up explicitly political issues, Larson's first act ends with a celebration of "going against the grain," of "Revolution,.../Forcing changes, risk, and danger," of "Tear[ing] down the wall" (Larson, 1996, 1: 23).

Like *South Pacific* before it, *Rent* mixes elite and popular cultures, despite the fact that its appeal across generations and classes testifies to the deterioration of the cultural hierarchy that had been in place fifty years before. On the one hand, the piece appropriates the plot and characters of what continues to epitomize old-fashioned, high-culture: opera. On the other hand, it cops a hipper-than-thou attitude, recycling the forms, technologies, and conventions of new media and performance; taking up for its guiding philosophy a kind of pop existentialism ("There is no future/There is no past/I live this moment/As my last," 1: 15); and exploiting the chic of "anything taboo," particularly when it is embodied by a sexual avant-garde that comes in all colors and flavors (1:23). At the same time, *Rent* is unabashedly populist in its use of music best described as commercial, corporate rock with touches of rhythm and blues, house music, techno, and club. Unlike *South Pacific*, which borrows musical styles conscious of their histories and associations, *Rent* uses a more disorderly and at times arbitrary mélange of styles.

Rent's unique positioning in the cultural field and its proven appeal to white, middle-class adolescents and young adults lies in its claim to a kind of gritty authenticity. For the production team was especially anxious that *Rent* not be seen to exploit and commodify the experiences of persons who, by any measure, must be numbered among the abject. They were very nervous, for example, that the musical should present an "honest" picture of the homeless rather than an "insulting" "chorus of cute homeless people."[26] Michael Greif, the director, was particularly concerned that *Rent* maintain the balance that has long characterized middlebrow: "I think the issue has always been preserving authenticity…in the way we present these characters, and also presenting them in ways that make them very identifiable and sympathetic and human."[27] In order to make *Rent* a commercial property, Greif and the producers made several decisions. Although the cast of the first New York Theatre Workshop reading had been "nearly all-white," it became "increasingly racially diverse" as the play neared production (quoted in Larson, 1997, 35). Greif's singling out of Daphne Rubin-Vega for seeming "like she really lived in that world—not in the world of musical theater," betrays an assumption on the part of the production team that persons of color—who play five of the eight major roles—give the musical the aura of authenticity they so desperately wanted it to have. For like *South Pacific*, *Rent* uses persons of color to turn what would otherwise be just another Broadway commodity into "the real thing" (Michael Greif, quoted in Larson, 1997, 26). Unlike *South Pacific*, however, *Rent* completely sidesteps issues of racial discrimination, using its persons of color to provide an audience the *New York Times* describes as young, middle-class, and "not exactly rainbow-colored" with an exotic, multicultural experience guaranteed to make it feel liberal and hip.[28] Moreover, although it was written during a period when hip hop had become the most popular music form in the United States, *Rent* remains as white as *South Pacific* in its musical pedigree and, with the exception of Angel's house-music-inspired "Today 4 U," virtually ignores the unprecedented richness of both African American and Latino musical forms.

Although musicals continue to win Pulitzer Prizes in the twenty-first century, the Broadway demographic has altered considerably since the 1990s, due in part to very real changes in the production and consumption of live theatre in the new, cleaned-up, family-friendly Times Square. Surveys show that since the opening of *Rent* in 1996, the Broadway audience has become not only richer but also younger. The number of spectators under twenty-five has grown from 20.9 percent to 23.9 percent, while the number between the ages of thirty-five and forty-nine has declined from 31.8 percent to 25.1 percent. At the same time, Broadway has become a major tourist destination, as the number of tourists both from the United States and abroad has skyrocketed from 47.2 percent to 64.5 percent.[29] Much of this growth is a result of the invasion of Broadway by Disney Theatricals, beginning with *Beauty and the Beast* in 1994. Since then, Disney has opened five other musicals, none of which, except perhaps Julie Taymor's *The Lion King*, aspires to the kind of upper-middlebrow prestige that the Pulitzer Prize rewards. In an age of hyperconsumerism, these musicals have significantly changed the economics of Broadway. For the Disney musical—like the other new genre, the jukebox musical—does not require star performers or directors. Indeed, star performers would be liabilities because they would distract attention from the true stars of the show, which are the intellectual properties. In the case of most of the Disney musicals or Dreamworks' *Shrek*, the point is the near reproduction of the cinematic original. With the notable exception of Taymor, stage directors aim to recreate an animated film onstage while actors are fired if they deviate from their cartoon doppelgangers. And a musical that does not require a Patti LuPone or Nathan Lane is far more economical for producers because they can pay Equity scale rather than $4,000 a week. (It is important to note here that Disney has the economic clout to have been able to negotiate a 6 percent lower pay scale with Equity than the League of American Theaters and Producers [$1,465 minimum versus $1,558]).[30] Consumers are willing to pay $125 a head because they know they are getting a consumer-tested and familiar brand— satisfaction guaranteed by Disney or Dreamworks. The star power that used to be associated with writers, actors, and directors has been displaced onto corporations, which are the true Broadway stars in the twenty-first century. They are the bestowers of identity, community, and the magical power of the franchise.

In contrast to the Disney musical, the jukebox musical finds its star in an absent singer/songwriter. Affluent tourists go to *Mamma Mia!* or *Jersey Boys* not for the leading actor or plot or mise en scène, but to see performed the now classic pop songs featured in the show. (Both Disney and jukebox musicals are more appealing to non-anglophone spectators than traditional book musicals because audiences are likely to know the films on which the Disney musicals are based and the songs featured in jukebox musicals.) Since *Buddy—The Buddy Holly Story* in 1990, about twenty jukebox musicals have opened on Broadway, from the wildly successful *Mamma Mia!* based on the music of ABBA (which has grossed over $360 million) to expensive flops like *Good Vibrations* (the Beach Boys) and *Ring of Fire* (Johnny Cash). In comparison with the success of the Disney formula, the jukebox musical has proven a more hit-or-miss affair. And it, too, is difficult to place generically because it represents a hybrid of a rock concert (an already theatricalized event) and a play that might or might not be based on the life of its subject. But in all cases, the allure of the jukebox musical is largely nostalgic—one goes to *Mamma Mia!* in part to dance in the aisles and so relive one's youth or indulge in a fantasy reconstruction of the 1970s. The power of nostalgia suggests to me that the jukebox musical produces a different kind of star: *you*—for it provides a certain narcissistic gratification by evoking memories of "Dancing Queen" or "Money, Money, Money" and in the process making your own past a part of the performance. Unlike the old-fashioned back-stage musical, such as *Follies*, which is haunted by *its own* past, the jukebox musical is haunted by *yours*.

Despite the invasion of Broadway by multinational corporations and simulations of mass culture, musicals remain an archaic mode of production that seems almost embarrassingly quaint in a culture of hyper-marketing and instant celebrity. Moreover, because stage musicals are still handmade, even Disney and Dreamworks have been unable to replicate on Broadway the kind of mass distribution on which their Hollywood empires thrive. And until choruses, theater orchestras, and stage-hands are replaced by robots or machines, the musical will remain the most labor-intensive of Broadway theater forms. Despite its archaic, handmade quality, however, it seems incapable of amassing the cultural cachet that other long-established art forms enjoy. The bourgeois consumers who flock to *Jersey Boys* and *Shrek* continue to unnerve the guardians of what remains of high culture despite these audiences' economic and educational capital (Broadway League and Hauser, 31 and 29). Lincoln Center Theatre may have produced a widely acclaimed revival of *South Pacific*, but even this most prestigious among New York theaters is eclipsed by ballet and opera companies, symphony orchestras, and art museums, which retain a more verifiably highbrow patina and are more adept at enticing the social and economic elite to their boards of directors. The cultural stratification enshrined in the 1949 *Life* magazine chart may have become infinitely more complex in the intervening years, but the Broadway musical, I believe, remains a problematic affair—neither popular nor esoteric, hip nor sophisticated, trivial nor consequential *enough*—condemned to a middlebrow purgatory.

NOTES

1. See Gabriel J. Adams, "A Quick History of the Phantom of the Opera," *Ezine Articles*, http://ezinearticles.com/?A-Quick-History-Of-The-Phantom-Of-The-Opera&id=689698, accessed May 23, 2008.

2. Bertolt Brecht, "Against Georg Lukács," in *Aesthetics and Politics*, ed. Ronald Taylor (London: Verso, 1980), p. 83.

3. Broadway League and Karen Hauser, *The Demographics of the Broadway Audience, 2007–2008* (New York: Broadway League, 2008), pp. 31 and 29.

4. See Jack Poggi, *Theater in America: The Impact of Economic Forces, 1870–1967* (Ithaca, NY: Cornell University Press, 1968), p. 71.

5. See Richard Koszarski, *An Evening's Entertainment: The Age of the Silent Feature Picture 1915–1928* (Berkeley: University of California Press, 1990), p. 15.

6. Lawrence W. Levine, *Highbrow/Lowbrow: The Emergence of Cultural Hierarchy in America* (Cambridge, MA: Harvard University Press, 1988), pp. 221–22.

7. Thomas Herbert Dickinson, *The Insurgent Theatre* (New York: Benjamin Blom, 1972 [1917]), p. 83.

8. Richard Butsch, *The Making of American Audiences: From Stage to Television, 1750–1990* (Cambridge: Cambridge University Press, 2000), pp. 125 and 127.

9. Oliver Martin Sayler, *Our American Theatre* (New York: Brentano's, 1923), p. 247.

10. Walter Prichard Eaton, *The American Stage of To-Day* (Boston: Small, Maynard, 1908), p. 324; George Jean Nathan, *The Popular Theatre* (New York: Knopf, 1918, revised 1923), p. 81.

11. Janice Radway, "On the Gender of the Middlebrow Consumer and the Threat of the Culturally Fraudulent Female" (*South Atlantic Quarterly* 93:4 [Fall 1994]: 871–93), p. 872.

12. Janice Radway, "The Scandal of the Middlebrow: The Book-of-the-Month Club, Class Fracture, and Cultural Authority" (*South Atlantic Quarterly* 89:4 [Fall 1990]: 703–36), p. 733, n. 7.

13. Russell Lynes, "Highbrow, Lowbrow, Middlebrow," in *The Tastemakers* (New York: Harper & Brothers, 1954), p. 318.

14. Michael G. Kammen, *American Culture, American Tastes: Social Change and the 20th Century* (New York: Knopf, 1999), p. 96.

15. "High-brow, Low-brow, Middle-brow" (*Life* [April 11, 1949]: 100–101).

16. Gerald Mast, *Can't Help Singin': The American Musical on Stage and Screen* (Woodstock, NY: Overlook Press, 1987), p. 1.

17. Oscar G. Brockett and Robert R. Findlay, *Century of Innovation: A History of European and American Theatre and Drama since 1870* (Englewood Cliffs, NJ: Prentice-Hall, 1973), p. 567.

18. John Hohenberg, *The Pulitzer Prizes: A History of the Awards in Books, Drama, Music, and Journalism, Based on the Private Files over Six Decades* (New York: Columbia University Press, 1974), p. 19.

19. John L. Toohey, *A History of the Pulitzer Prize Plays* (New York: Citadel Press, 1967), p. 99.

20. For a more extensive analysis of these two musicals, see David Savran, "Middlebrow Anxiety," *A Queer Sort of Materialism: Recontextualizing American Theater* (Ann Arbor: University of Michigan Press, 2003), pp. 3–55.

21. Stanley Green, *The World of Musical Comedy* (New York: Da Capo, 1980), p. 216.

22. David Ewen, *Complete Book of the American Musical Theatre* (New York: Henry Holt, 1959), p. 265; Mark Kirkeby, liner notes to 1998 CD reissue of original cast recording of *South Pacfic* (Sony SK 60722), p. 9.

23. Philip D. Beidler, "*South Pacific* and American Remembering; or 'Gosh, We're Going to Buy This Son of a Bitch!'" (*Journal of American Studies* 27 [1993]: 207–22), p. 213.

24. Richard Rodgers writes: "If the main love story is serious, the secondary romance is usually employed to provide comic relief—such as Ado Annie and Will Parker in *Oklahoma!* or Carrie Pipperidge and Mr. Snow in *Carousel*. But in *South Pacific* we had two serious themes, with the second becoming a tragedy when young Cable is killed during the mission." Richard Rodgers, *Musical Stages: An Autobiography* (New York: Random House, 1975), p. 259.

25. Jonathan Larson, *Rent* libretto, Dreamworks compact discs DSMD2–50003, 1996, pp. 1: 23. Because there are no page numbers, I identify the source of lyrics by citing act and song number. All further references are noted in the text.

26. Michael Yearby and Jim Nicola, quoted in Larson, *Rent*, with interviews and text by McDonnell and Silberger (New York: William Morrow, 1997), pp. 40 and 23.

27. Quoted in Larson, *Rent*, with interviews and text by McDonnell and Silberger (New York: William Morrow, 1997), p. 25.

28. Weber, "Renewing the Lease on the Innocence of Youth" (*New York Times* [August 18, 2000]: E2).

29. Broadway League and Hauser, 20 and 10. These statistics cover the changes from the 1997–98 season to 2007–08.

30. See http://www.actorsequity.org/AboutEquity/contracts.asp, accessed March 15, 2009.

PART V

PERFORMANCE

CHAPTER 18

THE INSTITUTIONAL STRUCTURE OF THE AMERICAN MUSICAL THEATER

DAVID SANJEK

In 1866, New York producer William Wheatley found himself in a difficult position. He had contracted a melodrama—*The Black Crook*, by Charles M. Barras—which turned out to be a limp imitation of Weber's *Der Freischütz*. Simultaneously, however, another theater, set to present a ballet troupe newly arrived from Paris, burned down. Wheatley seized the opportunity to hire the stranded dancers, grafting their repertoire onto Barras's borrowed plot in an effort to salvage the situation. As the material evolved in rehearsal, the music director added music by Guiseppe Operti, an immigrant band leader, and interpolated songs by other composers, as well, many with little or no connection to the story. To top it off, Wheatley purchased elaborate—and expensive—stage machinery for the show in London.

The first performance of this goulash of ingredients occurred at Niblo's Garden in September 12, 1866, and lasted five and a half hours. One might imagine the public would have felt suffocated by this avalanche of tenuously interconnected elements, but they instead overlooked the emptiness of Barras's imaginings, applauded the opulent production, and ogled the corps de ballet, whose hundred members were—as the *Evening Post* grumbled—"perhaps less concealed than would be deemed proper by those of stout views as to where dresses should begin or end."[1] The three-thousand-seat theater was filled to capacity for the next sixteen months, with Wheatley alluring repeat customers by regularly inserting new production numbers (military drill, "Baby Ballet," ballroom masquerade), even further unhinging *The Black Crook* from its dramatic underpinnings. The show ran for 474 performances, and touring companies kept it playing across the continent for the next fifty years, with eight revivals in New York City alone. As late as 1929, *The Black Crook* played in Hoboken, with a young Agnes de Mille in the role of Queen Stalacta.

It seems appropriate to begin with the cockeyed creation of *The Black Crook*, not only because it has been traditionally dubbed the "first American musical" but also because its evolution from probable bomb to blockbuster incorporates a number of elements that constitute the supporting structure of individuals and agencies through which the American musical has thrived for nearly 150 years. The convulsive manner in which its disparate elements came together recalls the now-clichéd notion of stage production represented in the four Mickey Rooney–Judy Garland musicals released between 1939 (*Babes in Arms*) and 1943 (*Girl Crazy*). These films reinforce the popular belief that concocting a piece of musical theater is mostly a matter of adolescent pizzazz and egoless collegiality, a view promulgated as well by such endearing encomiums to the entertainment profession as Irving Berlin's "There's No Business Like Show Business" (1946). And it's easy to see why these views persist, given the spirit of conviviality instilled by a personal or professional investment in this repertoire. Even if one regards this conviviality as little more than the camaraderie of kitsch, the sense of social adhesion inspired by the American musical has proven hard to resist, especially for those many who are involved in a long-term love affair with the genre.

But such a wide-eyed perspective overlooks the more mundane and possibly mercenary agencies that support and maintain the musical theater as one of the nation's preeminent creative achievements. Even the short narrative of *The Black Crook* illustrates the activity of four of those agencies: producers, publishers, publicists, and property owners. For a piece of musical theater to come into existence, money must be raised; music must be written and protected; audiences must be enlisted to attend; and physical performing spaces must be built and maintained. While this list is not exhaustive, an examination of each of these functions in turn will give some sense of the elaborate superstructure dubbed the "art world" by sociologist Howard S. Becker, at least as it operates in this domain. Becker defines this superstructure as "the network of people whose cooperative activity, organized via their joint knowledge of conventional means of doing things, produce(s) the kind of art works that the art world is known for."[2] In order for someone to put on a show, these networks must marshal their forms of expertise, access to capital, understanding of public opinion, and possession of physical property. Before those individuals whose talents we revere can entertain us, these networks initiate the forces that permit their forms of expertise to have a public forum and enjoy an enduring audience.

THE PRODUCERS

Watergate's "Deep Throat" communicated an abiding truth to Woodward and Bernstein when he advised them to "follow the money." Similarly, it should not be construed as economic determinism to view the checkbook as the principal agent in the creation of a piece of musical theater. Simply put, the producer must collect any necessary number of those checks, by any available means, for a piece of musical theater to be developed, workshopped, previewed, and eventually premiered. Mel Brooks's outlandish exaggeration of the function of these individuals in *The Producers* (1968, 2001) cannot diminish the fact that mounting any piece of theater requires contributions from a pool of investors, even if that pool does not, as in Brooks's fevered imagination, comprise an endless parade of debauched female senior citizens. Professional theater is an innately speculative form of commerce, as much in the financial as the creative sense.

Figures are not available regarding the current average cost of an individual musical or the number of successes versus failures, but the percentages are surely not in the creators' or producers' favor. One might take as a potential benchmark the statistics William Goldman offers in his revelatory analysis, *The Season: A Candid Look at Broadway*, which chronicles the fates of the theatrical premieres mounted during the season 1967–68. Twenty-two percent of the offerings he discusses made money, a seemingly upbeat calculation until one looks more carefully. Of the twenty-five dramas that opened, only five were hits; of the nineteen comedies, five once again; but of the fourteen musicals, only two succeeded. Goldman concludes,

> Probably no season ever lost more, but I don't know that any of the above should be either surprising or disheartening. The theatre is a high-risk business, and it always has been. And more than that, unlike many businesses, the downside risk in the theatre is greater than almost anywhere else: in most industries you don't stand quite so great a chance of being wiped out completely. But in this decade, if a little over 21% of the productions show a profit, then a little under 78% [*sic*] show a loss. And most of the shows that do end up being profitable do so only in a small way.[3]

Could it be those seemingly insurmountable odds that have made so many impresarios of the musical theater so idiosyncratic? And "idiosyncratic" is putting it mildly. The most reasonable of them have been downright cockeyed, and some of the most celebrated have been close to pathological. The foremost exemplification of the latter was David Merrick (1911–2000). Acrimony seemed as routine to him as his dour-faced entrepreneur's trademark pinstripe suits. Collaboration in his mind took a back seat to confrontation; the production process was little more than a pretext for transforming allies into adversaries. Merrick seemed to assume that success came only when the participants were routinely made to squirm, fearful that they might be fired without warning; their contributions abandoned without pretext; and their paychecks delayed as long as the most elastic reading of the law would allow. Howard Kissel's 1993 unauthorized biography, *The Abominable Showman*, chronicles the uninterrupted antics of this serial abuser, climaxing with the notorious episode of Merrick's saving the news about the sudden death of director-choreographer Gower Champion until the initial curtain calls of the 1980 production of *42nd Street* in order to milk the maximum publicity out of the tragedy. Merrick reportedly stated, "Most people are weak. I respect no one but myself.... There is no such thing as unfair. It is simply a matter of inferiority and superiority. I know more than most people and I use it."[4] Unappetizing as such sentiments might be, the roll call of Merrick's successes indicates that fractiousness can sometimes fuel harmony: *Fanny* (1954), *Gypsy* (1959), *Carnival* (1961), *Hello, Dolly!* (1964), and *Promises, Promises* (1968). At the same time, the sequences of slip-ups that produced such notorious flops as *Breakfast at Tiffany's* (1966) and *Mata Hari* (1967) amply illustrate that aiding and abetting a creative meltdown provides an appetizing spectacle only to those predisposed to schadenfreude.

Florenz Ziegfeld (1869–1932) might have lacked Merrick's most unseemly mannerisms, but he nonetheless possessed his own idiosyncrasies. Impenetrable as an individual, he was selectively consumed by the various elements that made up his lavish productions. Costuming, décor, and casting took precedence over scores, and the verbal element sometimes seemed little more than an afterthought. Repeatedly, he turned to an unregenerate hack, William Anthony McGuire, rather than seek out more sophisticated writers to craft plot and dialogue. Ziegfeld furthermore thought of songwriters as more or less interchangeable employees; Ethan Mordden states, "Historians ask, 'Who wrote the songs!' Ziegfeld asked, 'Who will put them over, and let me see the dress against the backdrop.'"[5] As far back as the operettas featuring his paramour Anna Held through the various permutations of the *Follies* (1907–31), he sought to dazzle audiences with sexual spectacle and stupendous décor rather than leave them with tunes they might whistle as they headed home. One of his most essential employees was designer Joseph Urban, whose elegant and masterful craft can only be appreciated today through the remaining interiors of the producer's eponymous theater, now a single screen film house. Ironically, even his celebrated promotion of comedy had its limits. Though the *Follies* featured some of the major clowns of the age—Bert Williams, Fanny Brice, Eddie Cantor, and W. C. Fields among others—Ziegfeld is said never to have comprehended their appeal until it was recognized by audiences. His on-call talent scout, lyricist, and jack-of-all-trades Gene Buck often protected these talents when Ziegfeld seemed ready to abandon them in rehearsals.

The unique exception to his blinkered notion of production was the landmark 1927 show, Jerome Kern and Oscar Hammerstein's *Show Boat*, notable as the musical theater's most radical transformation of the genre to that date. But the odyssey of the work's emergence illustrates how both contention and collaboration spurred its completion, reflecting not only the array of these individuals' respective temperaments but also the complex function of the producer as but one of the many agencies engaged in the formation of the American musical theater. Kern was the first of the trio to see musical possibilities in Edna Ferber's novel, published in 1926. He communicated these sentiments to the critic and broadcaster Alexander Woollcott, knowing he was friends with the writer and fellow members of the Algonquin circle. Woollcott introduced novelist to composer at the opening of Kern's *Criss Cross* on October 12, 1926. Ferber expressed doubts about the proposed venture, but Kern felt he could crack the material along with Hammerstein, who had successfully collaborated as both lyricist and libretto writer (along with Otto Harbach) over the past three years with Vincent Youmans (*Wildflower*, 1923), Rudolf Friml (*Rose Marie*, 1925), and Sigmund Romberg (*The Desert Song*, 1926). The two had also worked together once before, on *Sunny* (1925), one of the period's typical grab-bag concoctions with only the most tenuous threads of dramatic logic connecting action and song. Ferber reports in her autobiography that her anxieties evaporated when she heard "Make Believe" and "Why Do I Love You?" and any residual doubts were extinguished altogether when Kern played "Ol' Man River": "The music mounted, mounted, mounted, and I give you my word my hair stood on end, the tears came to my eyes, I breathed like a heroine in a melodrama. This was great music. This was music that would outlast Jerome Kern's day and mine" (Mordden 1976, 103).

Kern and Hammerstein signed a contract with Ferber on November 17, 1926, and nine days later played a portion of the score for Ziegfeld. In a letter written the next day, the producer exclaimed, "This is the best musical comedy I have been fortunate to get hold of....This show is the opportunity of my life."[6] Kern and Hammerstein separately signed contracts with Ziegfeld on December 11, 1926, with the stipulation that the script would be delivered on January 1 of the following year and the work premiere on April 1. These daunting deadlines coincided with the producer's own shift to greater autonomy. For years, the *Follies* had occupied the New Amsterdam Theatre on 42nd Street, which the impresario owned along with theatrical magnates Marc Klaw and Abe Erlanger. With the support of newspaper tycoons William Randolph Hearst and Arthur Brisbane, Ziegfeld financed the building of his eponymous space on 54th Street and 6th Avenue. The cornerstone was laid in an elaborate ceremony, broadcast over the radio and attended by 800 people, on December 9, 1926. On February 2, 1927, the first production, *Rio Rita*, took the stage. Announcements of the immediately forthcoming "*Showboat*" appeared in the program but proved premature. A collision of sensibilities ensued. Ziegfeld was accustomed to libretti being concocted virtually overnight and with little regard to the dramatic or narrative logic of the material. Hammerstein recognized not only the inherent difficulties of accommodating the multigenerational dimension of Ferber's story but also the demands of making the songs and the saga intermingle. For Ziegfeld, the impasse could only be attributed to Hammerstein's refusal to accommodate audience expectations over his own aesthetic standards. He complained to Kern that the work "has not got a chance except with the critics" and worried in particular that the portion that followed Ravenal and Magnolia's wedding proved "too serious, not enough comedy" (Kreuger, 26).

Ziegfeld held off, however, giving Hammerstein enough time to develop the ambitious scenario we know today. *Show Boat* had its world premiere in Washington,

D.C., on November 17, 1927, and its New York debut on December 27. The producer, nonetheless, retained his time-honed concern with ostentatious production values virtually up to the last minute, complaining that the dances choreographed by Sammy Lee lacked oomph, whereas they had been intentionally designed to serve the movement of the plot rather than—as in the *Follies* or Ziegfeld's other musicals—stop the production dead in its tracks. Only when audiences and critics alike recognized the coherence and dramatic ambitions of *Show Boat* did Ziegfeld relax and revel in the box-office receipts. Interestingly, the initial reviews recognized those very qualities of the show that we today revere as a historical precedent. Brooks Atkinson characterized it in the *New York Times* as "one of those epochal works about which garrulous old men gabble for twenty-five years after the scenery has rattled off to the storehouse" and drew attention to the work of the principals: "They blend into the sort of joined, harmonized performance that we extravagantly commend in good dramatic productions" (Kreuger, 53). Even when critics later sometimes objected to what Kern and Hammerstein had accomplished, they underscored the transformation that had taken place, as in George Jean Nathan's lament: "The best musical comedies…are those in which sense is reduced to a minimum, the worst, those which aim at rationality….What we want…is a return to the old-time absurdity, the old-time refusal to reflect life and reality in any way, the old-time razzle and dazzle and the incredible" (Mordden 1976, 105–6). Ironically, what he describes are precisely those characteristics that typified Ziegfeld's career and that, not altogether with his approval, he helped to eradicate on the occasion of the premiere of *Show Boat*.

PUBLISHERS

If the producer provides the financial and logistic support for the creators of the musical theater, the publisher solicits and merchandises the songs featured in those productions. The relationship between the two groups has always been symbiotic, even if the balance of power may sway according to the relative commercial clout of the creators. For a considerable period of time after the premiere of *The Black Crook*, theatrical songwriters focused mainly on producing their material and left its promotion and legal protection to others. Working out a contractual obligation to a publishing firm allowed them to be single-minded about their craft. These obligations differed from individual to individual, although during the early years of the genre, most negotiations tended to be short and direct. Many would not even pursue a long-term association, selling their songs outright, while others recognized the benefits of a regular paycheck and worked out a system of advances. Whether contract employees or freelancers, most theatrical songwriters have been beholden to publishers in order to maintain their presence in the musical theater and were treated much like workers on an assembly line. Only a few, Irving Berlin most notably, were able to eradicate the middleman and inaugurate their own businesses.

To predict which of the pieces submitted to them might possess commercial viability, publishers needed to act something like social seismologists, attendant to modulations in the public mood and the vagaries of those performers to whom they hawked their wares. Publisher Edward B. Marks's memoir, *They All Sang*, opens with a depiction of the businessman, accompanied by his acolyte Louis the Whistler, ambling from theater to theater in lower Manhattan to convince prominent players to adopt items from his catalog. Hyperbole was the businessman's modus operandi: as Marks states, "We never had anything less than a sensation in those days. Some of them were tremendous, but sensational was moderate praise."[7] John Shepherd stipulates three criteria that needed to be in place for a song to have even a modicum of potential: "It had to be written in a musical style that was in fashion at the time. It had to be about something that was in the public's mind. Or it had to appeal to the public's emotions."[8] In his history of the institution most prominently associated with these practices, Tin Pan Alley, Isaac Goldberg draws attention to how personal emotion played little to no part in this process. Songs were rarely equated with self-expression but rather presumed to serve the requirements of the marketplace. He characterizes the system as "the paradise of Pseudo," for, "In the alley, song became synthetic; one wept, one laughs, at so many per cent."[9]

Publishers realized that they could increase their chances of success by placing their material in the hands of a popular figure on the stage, one who could add it to their act or even interpolate it into a theatrical piece, whether or not it had any bearing upon the plot or the overall tenor of the score. Al Jolson, for example, was famous for stopping a show, coming to the footlights, and letting loose with his best-known repertoire. Early publishers seemed to revel in the competition, thinking of each new composition as something to launch upon its commercial trajectory. Songs were merchandise, not potential masterpieces. Publishers agreed with Ziegfeld and Nathan that the musical theater strayed from its purpose when it failed to emphasize spectacle and sensation. The transition led by *Show Boat* toward the integrated score bemused and befuddled some of them. Some of their shared animosity comes across in Marks's sarcastic denigration of the new narrative format that began to emerge, however raggedly, at the start of the twentieth century: "The new musical comedies, however, marked a distinct retrogression in wit. They were romantic, pretentious; they bequeathed to us the terms 'musical comedy plot' to denote the artificial and saccharine, 'musical comedy heroine' for an insipid girl in tulle and organdie, and 'comic opera kingdom' for a nebulous and absurd locale" (Marks, 114). Over time, publishers accommodated the transformation in form, yet to this day the privileging of hits remains a reflex in the industry. Thus the repeated assertion that Stephen Sondheim does not write with the audience in mind, or the assumed efficacy of wrapping theatrical narratives around commercially proven material, as in jukebox musicals like *Mama Mia!* or *Jersey Boys*. Indeed, while creators of contemporary musical theater may not wish to reside in the "paradise of

Pseudo," many would be willing to drum up a set of emotions if it assured the audience's attention and added to ticket sales.

PUBLICITY

Public fascination with American musical theater arguably reached its peak between the 1920s and the 1960s. During this period, the emotional consensus of the nation was that Broadway represented the epitome of glamour and creative ferment. Many yearned to be First-Nighters and thereby to consort with all that was alluring, audacious, and original. Any number of factors fueled these shared feelings, but one of the most influential was the emerging array of journalists, publicists, and others who adopted the entertainment industry as their precinct. They concocted a novel brand of hyperbole, at times nearing hysteria, to embellish the aura that enveloped the stage and the surrounding geography and population of Broadway. The special lexicon of that discourse was a composite of street vernacular, theatrical lingo, and more than a smidgen of Yiddish, laced with striking neologisms that began as part of a minority vocabulary and eventually entered mass culture. For example, the "stix" were the boondocks, "shtick" encompassed an individual's unique behavior, and the "Death Trail" characterized the string of undesirable, cheap hotels that stretched from Chicago across to the West Coast.

No one person originated this phenomenon, but it took root in the pages of the industry publication *Variety* as much as anywhere. Founded by Sime Silverman (1873–1933) in 1905, *Variety* engaged in the dispersal of what he dubbed "slanguage." The boldness and irreverence he brought to the task quickly led to the identification of *Variety*'s pages with not only the activities of the entertainment industry but also a way of life and an emotional disposition. Its reporting remained rooted in the present tense and endeavored to immortalize the immediate, all the while recognizing (if only implicitly) that success was a momentary condition. It acknowledged as well that for most people show business, though nothing more than a circumscribed universe, represented within its narrow precincts limitless energies and ambitions. Both this vocabulary and its accompanying point of view reached an audience unacquainted with *Variety* through the wildly popular short fiction of Damon Runyon (1880–1946). Born in Lawrence, Kansas, Runyon lost his mother before he turned eight, was left on his own by his father, and ditched school before completing the fourth grade; no wonder he retained a lifelong fascination with outlaws and outsiders, while maintaining an aloof exterior and hiding his feelings. Runyon triumphed initially as a reporter, specializing in sports as well as flamboyant murder trials, and soon became one of the best-paid and most widely read contributors to Hearst's *New York American*. Runyon transferred his earlier attraction to cowboys and saloon habitués to the gangsters and chorus girls who flourished in the theatrical district of New York City: the *Guys and Dolls* of his most famous 1932 short story

collection and the source of Frank Loesser's 1950 hit musical.[10] Runyon rarely incorporated the physical attributes of that environment but instead rendered both the
mood and motivations of his characters through the voice of interchangeable and
typically unnamed narrators. His work became synonymous with both the territory
and a sophisticated way of life, but as much as anything, it was Runyon's point of
view, hardboiled but ultimately emotionally vulnerable, that others responded to. It
allowed them to remain both wide-eyed onlookers and smart-aleck insiders, simultaneously seduced by the Great White Way and cynical about its shabbiness.

The person who most successfully perpetuated this perspective, while epito-
mizing for many Americans the quintessence of American entertainment, was
Walter Winchell (1897–1972). Contemporary audiences may remember him as the
gruff-voiced, off-screen narrator of the television series *The Untouchables* (1959–63).
In his day, Winchell was ubiquitous, a presence in print and films, and on stage,
radio, and television. His sign-on catchphrase, "Good evening Mr. and Mrs. America
and all the ships at sea," reached as many as 50 million listeners, and his newspaper
column was syndicated in over 2,000 venues. Known as "The Bard of Broadway,"
Winchell rose from youthful poverty through a hardscrabble stage career to the pinnacle of an environment where his imprimatur made reputations and his dismissal
terminated them. Both egocentric and anxious about his professional eminence,
Winchell unreflectively kept the machinery of celebrity operating on all cylinders
for nearly forty years until age, alterations in social attitudes, and the wreckage
strewn by his vindictive temperament unplugged him from the battery of public
opinion. Winchell may not have invented gossip, but he crafted and commanded
many of its nuances. He introduced the now inescapable practice of piquing the
public's fascination with a particular individual or phenomenon, but then just as
readily pricking their credulity by revealing just how much of what had bewitched
them was as common as dirt. While this process might seem the very opposite of
celebratory, it had the undeniable consequence of making the environment Winchell
covered continually mesmerizing to his audiences. It is not so much that Winchell
enriched the career of any single performer, creator, or production as that he gave a
kick-start to the national consensus that entertainment and celebrity were the principal commodities of American society. In the words of his biographer Neal Gabler:
"Winchell had helped inaugurate a new mass culture of celebrity—centered in New
York and Hollywood and Washington, fixated on personalities, promulgated by the
media, predicated on publicity, dedicated to the ephemeral and grounded on the
principle that notoriety creates power."[11]

Since Broadway remained one of the touchstones of achievement that
Winchell considered fundamental to his beat, he helped thereby to keep the public focused on the achievements of the American musical theater. Who has succeeded him in this function? Parallel with a portion of his long career, Ed Sullivan
(1901–74), whom Winchell loathed immoderately, performed a comparable role,
particularly when he shifted from print journalism to television with a degree of
success that outdid his rival. During the time he ruled the 8 P.M. Sunday night
time slot (1948–71), Sullivan was one of the nation's sanctioning authorities; John

Leonard persuasively observes, "Never before and never again in the history of the republic would so many gather so loyally, for so long, in thrall to one man's taste."[12] Sullivan revered the theater, and where else did the American public have such easy access to full-dress, uninterrupted segments of hit Broadway shows? *Bye Bye Birdie* (Charles Strouse-Lee Adams, 1960) offers a clever tribute to his influence, when a suburban family sings his praises in mock-ecclesiastical tones. Following Sullivan's departure, there has been only the occasional repetition of this phenomenon, as for example on the Rosie O'Donnell daytime talk show (1996–2002), which served a similar function. The absence of a successor to either Winchell or Sullivan or even O'Donnell fuels the prevailing assumption of Broadway's imminent demise or at least its ongoing desiccation, reminding one as well of how influential such a national discourse can be in promoting forms of commercial entertainment as mass culture.

PROPERTY

In investigating any form of commercial entertainment, one may easily become so enthralled by the final product that one overlooks its mundane causes. For Broadway, one of the most easily bypassed of these is the very space in which it takes place. Obviously, you cannot launch a performance before securing a venue. Creative acts remain flights of the imagination without being anchored in a physical location, which, in the case of the musical theater, requires all the paraphernalia provided by a well-equipped stage. Throughout the history of the genre and its long-term attachment to the real estate of New York City, the principal location of those stages has shifted corresponding to the gravitation of both population centers and centers of public influence from the lower portion of Manhattan to midtown and thence the precinct surrounding Times Square. That migration did not occur without its advance scouts. Although his name and achievements have long since been eclipsed by those of his grandson, Oscar Hammerstein (1847–1919) may well lay claim to being the progenitor and imaginative architect of modern Broadway, as he built five theaters in and around Times Square (before it was so named), beginning with the Olympia in 1895, and thereby founded what Anthony Bianco has described as "the most entertainment-intensive block in the city that is America's once and future cultural capital."[13]

Debates over the commercial fate and physical decay of Broadway have simmered ever since the opening of Hammerstein's venture, accumulating even greater vehemence and ideological baggage when virtually all the live venues transformed into sites for motion picture exhibition after 1930. This led in turn to an influx of what some considered a less desirable clientele, and consternation increased when the sale of drugs and pornography as well as the staging of live sex shows permeated parts of the district. Over time, many in a position of power became convinced that the sophisticated veneer of Broadway had become tacky and tawdry. This interfered as well with marketing the city as a tourist Mecca, and some complained that the advertising motto "Fun City" had become offensively fraudulent. Fervent efforts to oust the interlopers led to the filing of legal briefs and back-room bargaining. Others argued, however, that the theater district provided many citizens with a welcome outlet for letting off steam, and that efforts at censorship and plans for wholesale redesign were informed more by class anxiety than business savvy. The question of who had a right to occupy public space was eventually answered when various parties to the debate conceded the clear-headedness of urban planner and development official Rebecca Robertson, who asserted, in 1990, "Do right by the old theatres and the rest will follow" (Bianco, 6). Those who followed her precept endowed the neighborhood with new or refurbished showcases, as did the management of Playwright Horizons, who engineered the erection of Theatre Row on the western extremity of 42nd Street. More recently, and more controversially, the Disney Corporation renovated the New Amsterdam (1997), the block's 1,800-seat site built by Klaw and Erlanger in 1905. While Theatre Row has been felt to redefine the scene's diversity, many worry that Disney's efforts, and the musical adaptations they have staged, add to both the dumbing-down of the profession and the tackiness of the district as a whole.

Ownership of physical space does not lead necessarily to the (sometimes controversial) imposition of (usually conservative) taste in theatrical exhibition. The activities of the Judson Memorial Church in Greenwich Village, and in particular their staging of Marie Irene Fornes's play with music *Promenade* (1965), represents one of several departures from this expectation. The performances at the church were part of the flourishing Off-Off Broadway scene that began in the 1950s following Actors Equity's 1949 ruling that actors could perform in small venues for lower rates. In that first decade, revivals dominated these venues, but the 1960s brought an explosion in experimental pieces staged in small spaces with even smaller casts and few elaborate accoutrements other than could be provided by the imagination. Venues such as Café Cino, La Mama ETC, and St. Mark's Church in the Bowery, in addition to Judson Memorial, opened their doors without charging admission, asking only for donations. Little thought was given to mainstream audiences, as the evolving community conceived itself as separate and self-supporting, even antithetical to the economic and institutional imperatives of mainstream culture. Those in charge of the physical spaces where this community met encouraged their integrity and provided it a refuge. Judson Memorial Church, founded in 1892, stood on the downtown side of Washington Square Park, adjacent to the sprawling campus of New York University and in the midst of a flourishing café, gallery, and club culture. Its director, Howard Moody (appointed in 1956), felt their mission was to serve the immediate neighborhood and initiated an outreach to artists and performers in 1961 by appointing minister-composer Al Carmines as intermediary. They agreed to open the space to any who applied without prior censorship with the only stipulation being that the annual budget for all appearances was $200. Over time, the institution made its setting even more performance-friendly, as the progressive congregation chose to remove all the pews as well as the altar.

The libertory energies unleashed by such decisions are paralleled by the gleefully off-kilter construction of *Promenade*. Fornes pioneered a form of composition that depended upon the operation of chance and randomness. She created *Promenade* by using three packs of cards: one with scene locations; the second listing character types; and the third containing possible opening lines. Whenever inspiration flagged, she drew from them and continued. Fornes also dispensed with customary forms of character motivation and instead stressed the transformations permitted by sudden revelations and turnabouts of action. Naturalism took a back seat to the free flow of invention. As Stephen J. Bottoms states, "the familiar dynamics of cause-and-effect narrative logic were far less important than the physically limited, but imaginatively limitless potential of the stage event itself."[14] Nothing therefore dictated how an audience ought to respond to her writing, and, ironically, this could be said to have reinaugurated some of the "old time razzle and dazzle and the incredible" that George Jean Nathan felt had fled the stage with the inauguration of the book musical. Furthermore, the songs that Fornes created along with Carmines were equally and eloquently unhinged in their ebullient wrenching from convention. Her lyrics frequently intercut radically disconnected statements— "Chicken is he would does not love me; for there's more to the cake than the icing"— to the tune of Carmines's sprightly melodies.[15] *Promenade* consequently comes across as a one-of-a-kind jeux d'esprit that left downtown denizens delighted. It became one of the exceptions to the rule of appealing only to an insular audience, for it transferred uptown in an elongated version and played for over a year. One cannot imagine such a piece emerging other than in an environment like Greenwich Village and a physical space such as the Judson Memorial Church, a combination that challenged predetermined notions of what a church or a theater or a musical ought to be. Sometimes, real estate can come without any impinging attachments and liberate rather than inhibit its inhabitants.

These four agencies—production, publishing, publicity, and property—have contributed to the repertoire and development of the American musical theater for more than 140 years. But even if one firmly believes they can encourage its continuation, they cannot either guarantee its evolution or outflank its possible extinction. Of course, rumors of the musical's demise are as rife as a cocked hat in a piece of Bob Fosse choreography. Still, there are distressing implications to the rationale behind the recent announcement that the long-standing parody series *Forbidden Broadway*, founded in 1982, shut its doors in March 2009: founder and principal writer Gerard Alessandrini believes that nothing remains to be ridiculed, as Broadway has come to resemble a theme park. An eventual return is not out of the question, but, until then, he waits until Broadway finds a means of renewing itself.[16] In the meantime, might these four agencies, among others, encourage and not disrupt that process.

NOTES

1. Quoted in Ethan Mordden, *Better Foot Forward: The History of American Musical Theatre* (New York: Grossman, 1976), p. 12.

2. Howard S. Becker, *Art Worlds* (Berkeley: University of California Press, 1982), p. x.

3. William Goldman, *The Season. A Candid Look at Broadway* (New York: Limelight Editions, 1984), p. 391.

4. Howard Kissel, *David Merrick: The Abominable Showman* (New York: Applause Books, 1993), p. 190.

5. Ethan Mordden, *Broadway Babies: The People Who Made the American Musical* (New York: Oxford University Press, 1983), p. 36.

6. Miles Kreuger, *Show Boat: The Story of a Classic American Musical* (New York: Oxford University Press, 1977), p. 20.

7. Edward B. Marks, *They All Sang: From Tony Pastor to Rudy Vallee*, as told to A. J. Liebling (New York: Viking, 1935), p. 6.

8. John Shepherd, *Tin Pan Alley* (London: Routledge & Kegan Paul, 1982), p. 2.

9. Isaac Goldberg, *Tin Pan Alley: A Chronicle of American Popular Music*, with a supplement: Edward Jablonski, *From Sweet and Swing to Rock 'n' Roll* (New York: Frederick Ungar, 1961), p. 140.

10. Damon Runyon, *Guys and Dolls and Other Stories* (London: Penguin, 1956).

11. Neal Gabler, *Winchell: Gossip, Power and the Culture of Celebrity* (New York: Alfred A. Knopf, 1994), p. xiii.

12. John Leonard, *Smoke and Mirrors: Violence, Television and Other American Culture* (New York: New Press, 1997), p. 17.

13. Anthony Bianco, *Ghosts of 42nd Street: A History of America's Most Infamous Block* (New York: William Morrow, 2004), p. 7. Modern Broadway is but one of Hammerstein's contributions to New York's cultural map; he also designed, built, and managed nine other venues during the course of his visionary if fiscally erratic career, during which he gained and lost three fortunes, dying penniless but rewarded by his permanent contributions to the metropolitan landscape.

14. Stephen J. Bottoms, *Playing Underground: A Critical History of the 1960s Off-Off-Broadway Movement* (Ann Arbor: University of Michigan Press, 2004), p. 141.

15. Maria Irene Fornes, *Promenade and Other Plays* (New York: PAJ Publications, 1987), p. 16.

16. Julie Bloom, " 'Forbidden Broadway' Curtain to Go Down" (*New York Times* [September 13, 2008]: B-9.

CHAPTER 19

ORCHESTRATION AND ARRANGEMENT: CREATING THE BROADWAY SOUND

DOMINIC SYMONDS

There are three basic types of orchestration in the Broadway musical. The first comes out of old vaudeville and from military bands; it's what orchestrators call the "Broadway sound" and may be best typified by *Hello, Dolly!* The second, the "academic school," is based mainly on classical operetta. *Candide* would be a case in point. Finally, there is the "interpretive style"…where the arranger draws from many sources to interpret the lyric in a dramatic sense. Russell Bennett's orchestration of "Lonely Room" in *Oklahoma!* is a great example of an orchestration that helps set the mood and character, much like a piece of theatre design, like sets and lighting.[1]

Orchestration in musicals is an area that has received little attention.[2] In this chapter I consider the orchestrator's role in crafting the distinctive Broadway "sound," from the work of composer Victor Herbert—one of the last to orchestrate his own material—to orchestrators such as Frank Saddler, Robert Russell Bennett, Hans Spialek, and Don Walker, who scored many classic musicals. Finally, I consider several related matters: copyright, union agreements, amplification, the virtual orchestra, and actor-musicianship, all of which have influenced the sound of the Broadway show.

ORCHESTRATION AND ARRANGEMENT

Despite its being a dominant part of musical theater, orchestration is seldom discussed or even defined. Orchestrator Robert Russell Bennett clarifies it as "the rounding out and filling out of the melodic line by means of instrumentation, harmonic color (and all that goes with it) and rhythmic emphases."[3] Don Walker notes that this involves three main stages: arranging—"fitting a song to a dance pattern, the composition of introductions, interludes, modulations, codas and other special material needed for the dance; the decision on the vocal keys and the type of accompaniment for a voice"; orchestration—"the translation of this 'arrangement' into sound…by writing notes on pages of score"; and extraction—"the copying of the individual parts for the various instruments of the orchestra from the score."[4] In classical music, orchestration is considered an integral part of composition; certain composers are renowned orchestrators, and Berlioz's *Treatise on Orchestration* has become a seminal text. Broadway composers, however, do not orchestrate their own material. Although some (Jerome Kern) had the ability, others (Irving Berlin) were remarkably illiterate in musical scoring; the composer typically hands over melodies, annotated to varying degrees, and thus much of the "Broadway sound"—and the decision making over how it is created—can be attributed to the orchestrators. Nonetheless, successful collaborations have existed between Jerome Kern with first Frank Saddler (including the Princess Shows) and later Robert Russell Bennett (including *Show Boat, Music in the Air, Roberta*), Rodgers and Hart with Hans Spialek (*On Your Toes, Babes in Arms, Pal Joey*), Rodgers and Hammerstein with Robert Russell Bennett (*Oklahoma!, South Pacific, The King and I, The Sound of Music*), and later Jerry Herman with Philip J. Lang (*Hello, Dolly!, Mack and Mabel, Mame*), Stephen Sondheim with Jonathan Tunick (*Company, Follies, A Little Night Music, Sweeney Todd, Into the Woods, Passion*), and William Finn with Michael Starobin (*Falsettos, Spelling Bee*).

THE OPERETTA SOUND

A useful starting point is Victor Herbert, the last of the "old-school": a composer who also orchestrated his music. Herbert's experience both as instrumentalist and orchestral conductor made him an "expert at instrumentation"[5] who "conceived everything orchestrally."[6] That Herbert was steeped in the classical tradition is evidenced by his demands for large ensembles: fifty instrumentalists for Broadway and thirty-four when on the road (Gould, 240)—significantly reduced from a symphonic ensemble but enormous by today's standards. These ensembles were modeled on a classical sound:

> the strings massed and predominant; the woodwinds marshalled to speak their
> humors in choir; the brass discreetly in hand, awaiting a grand tutti; and behind,

the simple percussion of tympani and drums, with glockenspiel and triangle for accent, the cymbal for exclamation point.[7]

In scoring for the stage, though, the orchestrator has to consider that a single principal instrument—the voice—demands dominance in the ensemble; Herbert's orchestration was carefully arranged to allow the voice to be heard, using sizable vocal choruses to aid the blend.

Herbert's vocal numbers show typical orchestration of the period: dominant strings supported by wind and brass for color (● Example 19.1). This provides both space and balance for the vocal line: balance from well-blended instruments close in tone and timbre to the voice; space in the layout over several octaves of a chordal structure replicating the harmonic series and using extreme registers (violins at the top of their pitch) to leave room in the vocal register for the voice to carry (●Example 19.2). Herbert's technique stems from traditional musical training— and he was certainly traditional, a musician from the nineteenth century who rebuffed the beginnings of jazz. Herbert's adherence to tradition underscores a persistent cultural tension—"a dual development to suit the tastes of a dual audience"— in the developing landscape of American popular music:

> Those who still dominated society by reason of wealth and prestige still demanded from their entertainment the eccentricities of the European model.... The new major players in American society, the new moneyed professionals, demanded a theater more to their own taste: the musical comedy. (Gould, 253)

Musical comedy of the period was typified by vaudevillian George M. Cohan, and the orchestration of his shows was strikingly different from Herbert's. Vaudeville instrumentation, known as "11 and piano," was more focused on brass, woodwind, and percussion, and very distant from the classical European sound (● Example 19.3).

> The basic Broadway pit orchestra of the time consisted of two violins (for the melody), viola, cello (for tender countermelodies), bass, flute (skipping decoratively around the fiddles), clarinet, two cornets (brightly underlining repeats of the violin melody), trombone (swooping up and down), percussion and piano.[8]

It was the classic ragtime band, sometimes decried as "the commonplace rooty-toot of most musical comedy orchestras" with its "blaring brasses, so common in theatrical pits of the time."[9] The next few decades would pit these extremes—and their very different orchestras—in a battle for musical theater dominance.

THE BROADWAY SOUND

Ultimately the Broadway style developed a compromise between the European and vaudeville sounds. "It was the achievement of the [orchestrators] to take the operetta ensemble as Victor Herbert left it and the vaudeville band as George M. Cohan knew it, to weld them together and to make them over in a new image" (Beiswanger, 42). This new "American" music swiftly became "a combination of what was happening in jazz at the time and the basic orchestrational principles anybody who worked in Vienna would know."[10]

For economic reasons, the size of Herbert's orchestra had to be reduced, and orchestrators had to find ways of maintaining both the balance of instruments and the diversity of sounds that gave the score "color." Frank Saddler, "champion of small orchestras" (Bennett, 1999, 279), was the first recognized orchestrator (rather than composer) for Broadway and was Jerome Kern's collaborator for most of his early shows. He "used comparatively few musicians, and his work was contrapuntal and delicate, so that the sound emanating from the orchestra pit was very much in the nature of chamber music."[11] Saddler found ways to reduce the orchestra while still maintaining color, balance, and movement, merging instruments from the vaudeville pit—such as the piano—with a significant but reduced string section.[12] The piano could be used for rhythm, to replace the second violin and viola, or to release them to a lyrical countermelody (🔊 Example 19.4).

Saddler created a number of characteristic techniques, such as his adapted-piano devices, including the "mandolin and banjo attachment" ("a metal tackboard that approximates the sound of a harpsichord")[13] and the "newspaper mute" (a "dull 'thwacking' sound...accomplished by laying a thick wad of newspaper over the strings"; McGlinn, 5). Saddler and Kern are also credited with the first appearance in the Broadway pit of saxophones—in *Oh, I Say!* (1913)—though Bordman concedes that "any pride Kern took in this progressive innovation was tempered by an eventual distaste for the abuses of jazz orchestras" (90). Saddler's setup became known as "Fifteen and Piano," though this arrangement did not represent just fifteen instruments, since strings usually had several on a part. Typically, he would use six violins (split conventionally in parts), two violas, two cellos, bass, flute, oboe, two clarinets, bassoon, two horns, two trumpets, trombone, and piano, harp, or drums, an orchestra of eighteen to twenty-four players,[14] with eighteen for the tiny 299-seat Princess Theatre (*Zip, Goes a Million!*; 1919), and twenty-six for *Have a Heart* (1917) at the larger Liberty Theatre (Bordman, 138). Bennett explains the arrangement:

> An arrangement of a song was: a loud introduction, a vamp-soft, with oom-pahs, a soft verse, a soft chorus (refrain) and a loud chorus made by repeating the same arrangement with the brass and drums added and the first violin up an octave. The first violin played the tune throughout, the second violin and the viola played after-beats (the pahs), the violoncello...had some kind of sustained counter-melody or doubled the bass, who played the ooms. The flute and the two clarinets did "noodles," the oboe played the melody and the bassoon either played in unison with the cello or played ooms and sometimes oom-pahs. The horns were mostly concerned with pahs, but also might reinforce a cello counter-melody; the first trumpet played the melody (on the repeat), the second trumpet found thirds and sixths under the first and the trombone doubled the bass, helped the trumpets to make a triad, or played the tune an octave under the top trumpet. The drums did oom-pahs and kept the whole thing from dying, just about as they do now.[15]

Saddler's effects "sparkled" (Bennett, 1999, 65), the main vocal melody and its accompaniment ornamented by instrumental "fills" ("noodles"). Take for example Kern's "Till the Clouds Roll By," from *Oh, Boy!* (1917; ◐ Example 19.5). The short phrases of the vocal line combine long sustained notes ("rain"; "like") with lightly tripping faster motifs ("comes a"; "to be"), a feature of the entire song:

> Oh the rain comes a-pitter patter.
> And I'd like to be safe in bed…(McGlinn, 17)

Saddler exploits this in the chorus, filling in the sustained notes with two closely harmonized flutes playing extensions of the faster motif. Not only does this provide interesting instrumental "noodles," but it also provides a complementary rhythm to the pulse of the double bass "ooms," reminiscent of the pitter-patter of rain. The lower strings and horn provide a more lyrical, sustained counterpoint.

THE CLASSIC ORCHESTRATOR

As operetta waned and the Tin Pan Alley style came to dominate on Broadway, a corps of orchestrators, including Robert Russell Bennett, Hans Spialek, Don Walker, and Ted Royal, introduced important developments. Bennett was the first of these and the most prolific, orchestrating over 300 Broadway shows as well as film scores and TV series. In Banfield's words, "If Saddler was the man who gave Broadway its musical color, it was Bennett who sealed its musical glamour" (2006, 44). Bennett was a traditionalist and a self-confessed snob, traits that colored both the instrumentation and technique of his scores. His sound—featuring classical instrumentation rich in strings and harp—evoked classical Europe even as Broadway was developing its own sound. To him, Broadway was second-rate, and his cherished ambitions to conduct symphony orchestras, his acquaintanceships with Stravinsky and Rachmaninov, and his creditable classical compositions all reveal a serious musician who simply found his metier on Broadway. Bennett's work, however, represents the epitome of one characteristic style of Broadway orchestration (◐ Example 19.6).

First, the vocal line is doubled by a melody instrument, reflecting a tendency toward softer vocals ("crooning"). Second, a countermelody (or "thumb-line," the middle line often played by composers on the piano with their thumbs) offers a chromatic counterpoint to the diatonic melody. Bennett is the master at this sort of counterpoint, and his work with Richard Rodgers benefits especially from chromatic resonances. Third, carefully spaced families of sounds (strings, winds, brass for effect) produce a rich harmonic balance. Finally, a combination of bass and off-beat "oom-pahs" provide the rhythm, typically from the harp or piano. But while these traits consolidated the conventions of the "classical" orchestration style, many of Bennett's colleagues were embracing the jazz sound, making Bennett's work begin to "sound surprisingly old-fashioned, and he admitted that he was slow in grasping the 'three trumpet sound' that began to revolutionise musicals with the advent of swing around 1930" (Banfield, 2006, 44).

This development reflected the "battle" (Beiswanger, 40) in the 1920s between two prominent aesthetics of the Broadway sound: the classical sound and the dance band sound. The battle was not just over aesthetics but also entailed an ideological contest between cultural discourses of value, race, and class. While the orchestra represented the accepted elegance of European culture, jazz band instrumentation represented a different and denigrated ethnicity, connotations of sexuality, questionable morals and—in an era of prohibition—the taboo of illicit entertainment. Where orchestras had been established as large ensembles with an acoustically balanced blending of instruments, the jazz band operated as a much smaller group of often competing individual sounds—cornet, trombone and clarinet, and a rhythm section of double bass, banjo and drums; sometimes a violin, later (around 1900) a piano, and later still (around 1920) saxophones (Beiswanger, 43).

Many of the songsmiths—often of immigrant stock and Jewish heritage—related to and embraced jazz (as they had ragtime twenty years earlier), not least George Gershwin, a pianist whose rhythms, cadences, and harmonies derived from composing on piano. The piano became even more prominent in the pit for shows such as *Lady Be Good* (1924), *Tip-Toes* (1925), *Oh, Kay!* (1926), and *Funny Face* (1927), which featured two pianos and two regular pianists, Victor Arden and Phil Ohman.

It was around this time—"beginning with such De Sylva, Brown and Henderson shows as *Good News* [1927] and *Hold Everything!* [1928]"—that the now enlarged jazz band "solidly entrenched itself in the pit" (Wind, 65; ◢ Example 19.7). It was well suited to the developing tendencies of songwriters, whose music was becoming increasingly syncopated and chromatically experimental. The principal difference between earlier pit instrumentation and this, "classed as either 'legitimate' or 'non-legitimate'" (Wind, 67), reflected the "choice of woodwind instruments. Operettas used the European light opera complement (flutes, oboe, clarinets, bassoon), whereas dance shows included saxophones, whose assertive tone had become an essential part of the jazz sound."[16] The dominance of three saxophones in the mid-low range and three trumpets on top provided a new punch. And even traditionalists adopted the sound: "It took Bennett a couple of shows to learn how to give the producers the crooning saxophone ensembles and three screaming trumpets, but after doing *Girl Crazy* [1930] he was on easy terms with the lick, rip and break" (Wind, 65; ◢ Example 19.8). By the mid-thirties (Gershwin's later shows, the classic Rodgers and Hart musicals), the sound of the dance band was established and expected, and prominent bands such as Paul Whiteman's were used as pit orchestras, with now-legendary names playing (Benny Goodman) and even co-orchestrating (Glenn Miller).[17]

The Golden Age

While—or perhaps because—developments in orchestration largely settled down following these rapid changes, the postwar period is characterized by two predominant orchestrational styles.

The first aligns with the classic integrated musicals of Rodgers and Hammerstein and Bennett's typical orchestrations, using "traditional" orchestral groupings relying heavily on strings. *Carousel* (principally orchestrated by Don Walker) used an enormous thirty-nine-strong orchestra with twenty-two strings, which competes with the orchestras of Victor Herbert or even Berlioz's outline of an opera ensemble (🔊 Example 19.9).[18] Given the option, many orchestrators preferred larger numbers, and recordings and concert performances have regularly inflated the number of strings: "When it comes to orchestration, there are never enough strings."[19] However, the predilection for a full orchestral sound is only in part aesthetic: it also assists the ideological claim to high-art status that the musical has always encouraged (alongside the terms "musical play" or "rock opera"). If musicals use classical or "legit" frameworks and terminology, they become increasingly valued artistically and culturally. Tellingly, a classical sound has also formed the basis for more recent megamusicals, from *Evita* (1978, Andrew Lloyd Webber and Hershy Kay) to *Miss Saigon* (1989, William D. Brohn).

The second style is best typified by Robert Ginzler and Sid Ramin's arrangement for *Gypsy* (1959), the "apotheosis of pit band instrumentation," voted by ASCAP the best ever orchestration for a Broadway musical (🔊 Example 19.10).[20] This stems directly from the dance band shows, and along with work by other orchestrators including Walker and Lang captures the quintessence of "Broadway's final era of razzmatazz, through an alchemy of songwriting, orchestration and voices, all of them long on brass."[21] This sound embraces the iconicity of Broadway, incorporating brash performances of stars like Ethel Merman: "that uniquely throat-catching, hair-raising Broadway sound" (Gottfried, 5).

The Microphone Era

The introduction of microphone technology (as early as 1937)[22] redefined the acoustic limitations of instruments and voices. Balance had always been a key element of orchestration, and the orchestra had been a brilliant tool for both fortissimo climaxes and sensitive underscoring beneath which dialogue could be heard—"perhaps the most difficult mechanical problem in the business" (Bennett, 1999, 281). But the jazz band's solo instruments threatened to compete with singers in timbre, tone, and volume, and partly in response to this, producers began amplifying both vocals and instruments.

While this offered many benefits, the reconfiguration of sound that the technology introduced disrupted the balance, "the natural color" that reflects "the art of orchestrating" (Pareles, 4): "a solo, muted violin can be made to drown out a full orchestra" (Bennett, 1999, 290). Techniques developed to accommodate this balance had in part defined the Broadway sound: "Stylish singers with small voices like Fred Astaire thrived on Broadway...because composers wrote songs suited to his style of delivery and kept orchestrations light."[23] The "noodles" interject *between* vocals specifically so that singers are not drowned out; likewise, orchestrators traditionally doubled the vocal line to support the melody.

Thus, amplification has been blamed for "unbalancing the score": "subtlety is impossible to achieve. The sound is smoothed out, bigger than life, with hardly any dynamics. Everything seems to be at that same mezzo-forte to fortissimo level" (Schonberg, 1); "the louder the orchestra gets, the louder we have to make the singers to ride over the orchestra."[24] Moreover, "inadequate sound design [sometimes] drowned out dialogue and lyrics, leaving audiences confused and frustrated."[25] Since Broadway embraced "rock" orchestration, however, rejecting amplification has not really been practical. Many instruments rely on it, and the mix of acoustic voice against amplified instruments becomes problematic.

ROCK AND THE MEGAMUSICAL

The "rock musical" initiated a trend toward a completely different pit setup, related to the rock band (guitar, bass, drums, keyboard). Surprisingly, shows relying purely on this orchestration or derivations of it have subsequently been relatively rare after the first few (*Hair*, 1967; *Godspell*, 1971; *Grease*, 1972; *The Rocky Horror Show*, 1973). Even classic "rock musicals" have more conventional instrumentation; *The Wiz* (1975) includes harp, woodwind, strings, and brass. On the other hand, the use of rock instruments within a more conventional pit orchestra, as in *Jesus Christ Superstar* (1971), has become common, creating the idiomatic sound of the "megamusical."

> The megamusical, then, offers not only more sophisticated sound than its predecessors, but also a more thorough blend of popular music and traditional theatre fare. Whereas rock musicals often feature raw, amplified voices backed by electric instrumentation throughout, rock's direct influence on megamusicals tends to be comparatively tame: an occasional guitar riff, the occasional use of twelve-bar blues form; an electric guitar, keyboard, or bass guitar intermingled with an otherwise standard pit orchestra; the occasional use of vocal techniques that might be heard on FM radio, amid songs otherwise performed by conservatory-trained vocalists. (Wollman, 128)

Synthesizing the Orchestra

Yet megamusicals have caused no little controversy, largely through scaling down the number of "live" instruments in favor of synthesized sounds. In fact, the use of synthesizers for some shows was part of the original conception: *Phantom of the Opera* (1987) used two synthesizers in David Cullen and Andrew Lloyd Webber's original orchestra of twenty-seven players, partly for the show's crucial pipe organ sound, partly for specialist sound effects such as "glassy lake," and partly to augment other instruments, particularly the strings.[26] In this decision, the economic restraints of even the most lavish shows are revealed, as in the standard Broadway practice of reducing the size of the orchestra after six weeks, once the "full" orchestration of a show is established. While some revivals enjoy the luxury of a return to original orchestrations, such as those of New York's City Center *Encores!* series, many establish new, often reduced orchestrations, using synthesizers. *Sweeney Todd*'s orchestra (1979, Jonathan Tunick) was reduced from twenty-six players to nine for the 1994 Royal National Theatre production (synthesizer, violin, cello, double bass, trumpet, horn, clarinet, bassoon, and percussion).

Although the synthesizer is often used simply to provide a thick string texture otherwise requiring several individual players, it is just one of the "new" instruments that has also developed its own aesthetic:

> The synthesizer is a wonderful tool. Because it can imitate other instruments, the biggest mistake that people make is to use it as an economic means to eliminate instruments. It's fine to use it sparingly to beef up a small orchestra. An ersatz trumpet can be fun. But you have to remember that it has its own personality, and if you write for it as if it's a real trumpet, you're going to get a very tinny, unsatisfying sound. (Winer, 5)

Assassins orchestrator Michael Starobin used the synthesizer as part of the orchestration process: "Starobin, playing the synthesizer, was able with his increasing familiarity with the score to add layers of color (now fixed as an orchestral score on the cast recording)."[27] Banfield suggests that this approach to orchestration may have led to some of *Assassins*' characteristic aesthetic. This is unusual, however, in an idiom that celebrates authenticity. As Maury Yeston puts it, "Musicians have been virtual Luddites at the inception of any electronic simulation of sounds, beginning with electronic pianos" (Yeston, 25).

The Unions

One influence on orchestration has been the Musicians' Union, whose agreements with the League of Broadway Producers stipulate that if live musicians were to be used at all for a theatrical performance, there would be a minimum number set for each theater, proportional to its seating capacity. The precise agreements have changed over the years, but as an example, "twenty-five was the legal minimum for the Shubert in 1973," when Sondheim's *A Little Night Music* was produced. Tunick's orchestrations for the show were therefore destined to be scored for twenty-five players, particularly since the "minimum...becomes effectively the maximum" (Banfield 1993, 82). As this highlights, the makeup of the sound is often a compromise between the producer's budget and Musicians' Union regulations, rather than compositional or orchestrational design. As Yeston asserts, "It is sometimes possible, and stylistically appropriate, to accompany Broadway shows with smaller ensembles." Bizarrely, on shows requiring fewer players than the stipulated number, sometimes "nonplaying 'walkers' [are] paid to meet the minimums" (Yeston, 25). More regularly, numbers are reduced when shows play at touring venues with lower minimums, compromising the orchestrator's original work and the "authentic" sound of the show.

One entrenched practice has been to "double" playing responsibilities, particularly among wind players, "a virtuoso speciality not just on the part of the players but for the orchestrator as well" (Banfield, 1993, 85). Doubling arrangements were often written with specific players in mind whose combination of instruments was known; while this expands the possible variety of sounds in the score, particular combinations will inevitably remain impossible if played by the same instrumentalist, since the orchestrator must leave breaks in the score for players to change instruments.

"Virtual Orchestra Machines"

More recently still, technology has developed the virtual orchestra, an artificial replacement for live musicians. "Played" from a computer, the machines replicate not just the notes and sound of the instrument(s), but also follow the phrasing, dynamic, and tempo indications of the live conductor. While the Musicians' Union has claimed that this will threaten jobs, manufacturers and producers insist on the reverse: "The show probably wouldn't have toured at all had it been required to maintain the full complement." Indeed, they point out that the software itself is operated "by a live musician."[28]

Perhaps the most compelling argument for the use of such technology is in amateur and school productions of the classic large-ensemble shows, many of which have neither the skill-base nor budget to provide full orchestration. As a supplement to existing musicians, "virtual orchestra machines" at least introduce regional audiences to the true orchestral sound of the Broadway shows. Musicians must trust that the wave of new technology will, in the hands of artists, enhance artistry. There can, and must be, a compromise—one that preserves the large live Broadway ensemble when appropriate (and, essentially, the minimums) but also gives smaller shows the flexibility to make the most of virtual enhancements (Yeston, 25).

New Aesthetics

The notion of the "authentic" in theater orchestration, though, is only a recent phenomenon; historically, the score was updated as shows were revived. Thus, Richard Rodgers assigned Don Walker to reorchestrate both *On Your Toes* and *Pal Joey* for revivals in the 1950s to give the shows a more contemporary feel; when Hans Spialek was called out of retirement to oversee *On Your Toes* in its 1983 revival, the original orchestrations began to be considered integral to the show (🔊 Example 19.11; 🔊 Example 19.12). Subsequently, particularly after the 1987 discovery of hundreds of authentic scores in a Secaucus warehouse,[29] the practice of reviving original, full orchestrations became common: the work of John McGlinn (particularly his 1988 *Show Boat* recording) is especially notable.

Yet the reorchestration of a show need not just be a response to production costs: director John Doyle and musical director Sarah Travis specialize in reconceiving classic shows as actor-musician shows, in which onstage performers provide not only the vocal but also the instrumental performances. Although originally an economic necessity, the reorchestrations required by this have created an aesthetic recognized for "knitting more closely together musical values and narrative shape."[30] Doyle's production of *Sweeney Todd* was particularly effective, and won a Tony award for its orchestration (🔊 Example 19.13; 🔊 Example 19.14).

Tunick's original orchestration of *Sweeney Todd* used twenty-six players in the classical style and has been recognized for its skill in creating "psychological and harmonic complexity." "String harmonics, woodwinds scored in the extreme upper and lower registers, and a whole spectrum of unusual brass sounds are an integral part of the score... the instrumentation is as much an identifying factor as the tunes themselves" (Parrent, 35). Yet Sarah Travis's adaptation of the orchestration for just ten versatile instrumentalists gives the show a Grand Guignol, chamber effect whose "sound tilts the production from blockbuster musical towards cabaret."[31] The shift in the audience's experience of this rescoring is palpable, as Sondheim observes:

> The variety of sounds [Travis] has gotten out of the instruments and also the practical way in which they allow [Doyle] to work with the performers onstage is extraordinary. But what got me most about the orchestrations is what they did for the play's atmosphere. These are wonderfully weird textures. The sound of an accordion playing with a violin—it's very creepy....What you gain is a swiftness and intensity that draws the audience into this macabre world, and that is created by a unified ensemble working in one tone. Here it's as if the audience is drawn into a tunnel. (Quoted in Isherwood, 1)

Actor-musicianship not only works in terms of aurality; it makes visible both the instruments and the physical bodies of the instrumentalists, elements conventionally marginalized from the dramatic space. "What is normally latent, unconsciously symbolic, [becomes] manifest, and a whole new dimension of interaction in music theatre [opens] up" (Banfield, 1993, 85). The music and its orchestration become voiced by characters, part of their expression and integral rather than just an accompaniment to the drama: "Because the performers are the musicians, they possess total control of those watching them in a way seldom afforded actors in musicals. They own the story they tell, and their instruments become narrative tools."[32] Elsewhere this has led to musical theater work wholly conceived for the aesthetic of actor-musicianship.[33]

Of course, there are practicalities involved in the negotiation between score and staging: "If, for instance, the score calls for a tuba (played by [Mrs. Lovett]), to complete a bass harmony, and Mrs. Lovett finds herself embroiled in a dramatic scene, an alternate [sic] musical solution must be found."[34] Similarly, a change of cast may involve changes in orchestration, even if the instrumentation remains consistent. Thus, the Watermill's original Mrs. Lovett, Karen Mann, played trumpet, while Patti LuPone in New York played tuba. As Doyle remarks,

> When the orchestration changes, the physical use of the stage changes as well, because if you're moving a violin around, it's different from moving a flute around, and you have to put it down in different places and use it in different ways, which inevitably means that the whole jigsaw puzzle changes.[35]

COPYRIGHT

Although *Sweeney Todd* is a Sondheim musical, the musical aesthetic of Doyle's production can be attributed to his work with Travis, just as the sound of the original Broadway show can be attributed to Tunick. As is clear, the sort of collaborative and interpretive arrangements that exist between composers and orchestrators complicate the notion of ownership; the orchestration often "creates a sound and feel with which the show will always be associated,"[36] and in this respect, issues of copyright arise.

While certain preemptive contractual arrangements have been made among producers, composers, and orchestrators, Joel Friedman notes a "measure of confusion" regarding this legal arrangement.[37] Some suggest that orchestrators are simply commissioned by composers or producers to fulfill a prescriptive task and that their orchestrations thus constitute "work made for hire," whereby "the employer or other person for whom the work was prepared is considered the author [and] owns all of the rights comprised in the copyright."[38] A second argument explicitly refers to "musical arrangements" in a category alongside translations, dramatizations, and so on, claiming that the work has a degree of originality and is therefore part-copyrightable to the orchestrator but is a "derivative work," one "based upon one or more pre-existing works."[39] The counterargument, claiming full recognition for the authorial rights of the orchestrator, labels the whole score a "joint work of authorship":

> Unlike a translation, a movie adaptation of a book, or a musical arrangement of an existing piece of music, an orchestration is not intended to take an already

complete underlying work and re-release it under a new form. Rather, the orchestration is meant to be a part of the entirety of the production as intended by the authors. A Broadway musical is not finished or ready for production until the orchestrations have been completed. (Perkins, 495)

The issue of copyright also affects subsequent arrangements of theater music, traditionally by dance bands—indeed, Jerome Kern prohibited any of the material from his 1924 show *Sitting Pretty* from being "distorted" in this way (Bordman, 249)—but nowadays by electronic sequencing and sampling. In some senses, the increasing use of existing musical material by other creative practitioners has highlighted the issue, and therefore copyright protection for composers is relatively secure. The rights of the orchestrator, however, remain an issue largely unaddressed:

> It is obvious that the official composer of a show produces only a small, though let us say, decisive part of the sounds an audience hears at a musical show. To this man alone go the sometimes fabulous rewards from a smash hit....His associate composers, often protected by unions, collect their adequate fees even if the show fails; but if it clicks, they get nothing more....The music staff's sole extra benefit accruing from helping to make a roaring theatrical success is the honor of being connected with it.[40]

Undoubtedly, the association of any collaborator with a major success will in part recompense the hard work and precise technique that has contributed to it. At last orchestrators are beginning to receive the recognition they deserve for their crucial role in creating the iconicity of the Broadway sound.

NOTES

1. Laurie Winer, "Theater; Orchestrators Are Tired of Playing Second Fiddle" (*New York Times* [July 29, 1990]: 2–5, citing Jonathan Tunick.

2. Recently, however, this topic has received increasing scholarly attention, most notably in "The Sound of Broadway Music: A Symposium on Orchestrators and Orchestrations" (Library of Congress, May 6–7, 2009) and the publication of a comprehensive new book by Steven Suskin, *The Sound of Broadway Music: A Book of Orchestrators and Orchestrations* (New York: Oxford University Press, 2009).

3. Robert Russell Bennett, *"The Broadway Sound": The Autobiography and Selected Essays of Robert Russell Bennett*, ed. George J. Ferencz (Rochester, NY: University of Rochester Press, 1999), p. 293.

4. Don Walker, "Music Goes 'Round: A Gentleman Who Arranges Theatre Tunes Tells How He Works," (*New York Times* [April 12, 1942]: X–1).

5. Joseph Kaye, *Victor Herbert: The Biography of America's Greatest Composer of Romantic Music* (New York: Crown, 2007), p. 7.

6. Neil Gould, *Victor Herbert: A Theatrical Life* (New York: Fordham University Press, 2008), p. 162.

7. George Beiswanger, "After Victor Herbert: The Battle of the Orchestras" (*Theatre Arts* 28.1 [January 1944]: 40–45), p. 40.

8. Barrymore Laurence Scherer, "Benjamin's Ragtime Band Captures the Real Cohan" (*Wall Street Journal* [July 2, 2008]: D-7).

9. Gerald Bordman, *Jerome Kern: His Life and Music* (New York: Oxford University Press, 1980), pp. 211 and 138.

10. John Pareles, "What Is the Sound of Broadway? Hans Spialek Knows" (*New York Times* [April 17, 1983]: 2–4).

11. Richard Rodgers, *Musical Stages: An Autobiography* (New York: Da Capo Press, 2002), p. 20.

12. Stephen Banfield, *Jerome Kern* (New Haven, CT: Yale University Press, 2006), p. 43.

13. See Bordman, 140, and John McGlinn, "Foreword" (Sleeve Notes), *Jerome Kern Treasury*, (Angel D 101,715, 1993), p. 5.

14. Herbert Warren Wind, "Profiles: Another Opening, Another Show" (*New Yorker* [November 17, 1951]: 46–71), p. 67.

15. Robert Russell Bennett, *Instrumentally Speaking* (Melville, NY: Belwin Mills, 1975), pp. 8–9.

16. Jon Alan Conrad, "Let the Drums Roll Out" (Sleeve Notes), *Strike Up the Band* (Elektra Nonesuch 7559–79, 273–2, 1991), p. 44.

17. See Joan Peyser, *The Memory of All That: The Life of George Gershwin* (New York: Billboard Books, 1998), pp. 170–73.

18. Hector Berlioz, *Berlioz's Orchestration Treatise: A Translation and Commentary*, trans. Hugh MacDonald (New York: Cambridge University Press, 2002), p. 321.

19. Maury Yeston, "The Lullaby of Broadway" (*New York Times* [February 28, 2003]: A-25). On recordings, see Amy Parrent, "From 'The Beggar's Opera' to 'Sweeney Todd': The Art of the Broadway Orchestrator" (*Music Educator's Journal* 66:9 [May 1980]: 32–35). On concert performances, see Stephen Holden, "Make It Proud and Loud, with Strings" (*New York Times* [May 22, 2008]: E-7).

20. Martin Gottfried, "Sleeve Notes," *Gypsy: A Musical Fable* (Original Broadway Cast Recording, Sony Classical/Columbia/Legacy SMK 60,848, 1999), p. 6.

21. Frank Rich, "Catching That Fading Sound of Razzmatazz" (*New York Times* [October 10, 1993]: 2–34).

22. According to Harold C. Schonberg, "Stage View: The Surrender of Broadway to Amplified Sound" (*New York Times* [March 15, 1981]: 2–1).

23. Anthony Tomassini, "Pipe Down! We Can Hardly Hear You" (*New York Times* [January 1, 2006]: 2–1).

24. Otts Munderloh, sound engineer for *A Chorus Line*, quoted in Schonberg, 1.

25. Elizabeth Wollman, *The Theater Will Rock* (Ann Arbor: University of Michigan Press, 2006), p. 203.

26. John Snelson, *Andrew Lloyd Webber* (New Haven, CT: Yale University Press, 2004), pp. 103 and 89.

27. Stephen Banfield, *Sondheim's Broadway Musicals* (Ann Arbor: University of Michigan Press, 1993), p. 84.

28. Jesse Green, "Theater's Alive with the Sound of Laptops" (*New York Times* [March 25, 2007]: 2–1).

29. Tim Page, "Broadway Song Trove Tops Original Hopes" (*New York Times* [March 10, 1987]: A-1).

30. Charles Isherwood, "Cutting 'Sweeney Todd' to the Bone" (*New York Times* [October 30, 2005]: 2–1).

31. Stephen Leigh Morris, "John Doyle's *Sweeney Todd*; Who's Your Barber?" (*LA Weekly*, March 17, 2008, http://www.laweekly.com/2008–03–20/stage/major-barber, accessed July 10, 2009).

32. Ben Brantley, "Grand Guignol, Spare and Stark" (*New York Times* [November 4, 2005]: E1–1).

33. See my discussion in "The Corporeality of Musical Expression: 'The Grain of the Voice' and the Actor-Musician" (*Studies in Musical Theatre* 1:2 [2007]: 167–81).

34. Anon, "John Doyle's Production of Sweeney Todd to Open A.C.T.'s 41st Season" (*American Conservatory Theater*, August 5, 2007, http://www.act-sf.org/site/News2?page= NewsArticle&id=5205&news_iv_ctrl=-1, accessed July 23, 2008).

35. In Robert Simonson, "John Doyle's Malicious Musicians: A Chat with the Director" (*New York Sun* [October 31, 2005]: Arts & Letters, 10).

36. Patrick T. Perkins, "'Hey! What's the Score?' Copyright in the Orchestrations of Broadway Musicals" (*Columbia-VLA Journal of Law and the Arts* 16 [1991]: 475–503), p. 494.

37. Joel L. Friedman, "Copyright and the Musical Arrangement: An Analysis of the Law and Problems Pertaining to This Specialized Form of Derivative Work" (*Pepperdine Law Review* 7 [1979]: 125–46), pp. 145–46.

38. 17 U.S.C. 101, 201(b) (1988), see Perkins, 481.

39. 17 U.S.C. 101 (1988), see Perkins, 493n.

40. Don Walker, "Who Says 'Arranger'?" (*Theatre Arts* 34:11 [November 1950]: 53–54), p. 54.

CHAPTER 20

MUSICAL THEATER DIRECTORS

BARBARA WALLACE GROSSMAN

In the end, practically and artistically, there can be only one voice to call the shots: the voice of the commander-in-chief. That is the voice of the director.[1]

It is not until almost halfway through Michael Kantor's six-part documentary, *Broadway: The American Musical* (2004) that the word "director" appears in the spoken narrative. The first two episodes of the series, covering 1893–1933, present a cavalcade of performers, composers, lyricists, librettists, and producers but do not mention any directors. Even that one-man theatrical conglomerate George M. Cohan is introduced as a playwright, songwriter, and star who "helped define the Great White Way in a series of shows over forty years," not as someone who also directed many of them. Near the end of Episode Three: "I Got Plenty of Nuttin'" (1929–1942), viewers hear a snippet from John Mason Brown's *New York Evening Post* review of the premiere of *Porgy and Bess* (1935):

It is a Russian who has directed it, two Southerners who have written its book, two Jewish boys who composed its lyrics and music, and a stage full of Negroes who sing and act it to perfection. The result is one of the far-famed wonders of the melting pot: the most American opera that has yet been seen or heard.

Excepting this oblique reference to director Rouben Mamoulian, however, directors remain tangential until the start of Episode Five: "Tradition" (1957–1979), which states emphatically, "A new generation of creative talent re-imagined what the musical could do. Songwriters like Stephen Sondheim, Bock and Harnick, Kander and Ebb, along with directors Hal Prince, Bob Fosse, and Michael Bennett created astonishing new work, new sounds, and a bold new tradition for Broadway."[2]

Though perhaps startling in an era when the primacy of directors is indisputable, their invisibility in the first part of Kantor's series accurately reflects their status—but not their actual importance—in the early twentieth century. According to Stephen Citron, directors were simply "hirelings, allowed very little creative input. Their productions were not much more than packages. Even the most successful directors' names are forgotten, and the shows they pied-pipered, if recalled at all, are only remembered for their composers and producers....Directors were not much more than glorified stage managers."[3] That unfairly dismissive comment fails to acknowledge the contributions of such prolific talents as Julian Mitchell (1854–1926) and Ned Wayburn (1874–1942), both director-choreographers in these formative decades, although that term was probably not applied to them during their lifetime. Mitchell directed more than eighty musicals including *A Trip to Chinatown* (with Charles H. Hoyt, 1891), *The Fortune Teller* (1898), *The Wizard of Oz* and *Babes in Toyland* (1903), and several editions of the *Ziegfeld Follies* beginning with the first, the *Follies of 1907*, which he choreographed. Wayburn, too, was part of Ziegfeld's stable for several years and directed seven *Follies*—among them the *Ziegfeld Follies of 1916*, which gave Fanny Brice two of her most memorable numbers, "Nijinsky" and "Becky's Back in the Ballet"—as well as other productions including *Star and Garter* (1900), *Mother Goose* (1903), *Tillie's Nightmare* (1910), *The Passing Show of 1912* and *1913*, *The Honeymoon Express* (1913), and *Hitchy-Koo* (1920).[4] Nevertheless, it is easy to lose sight of the accomplishments of these early directors because their work, if it received program credit at all, was usually not called directing but was described by a variety of other terms instead: "staged by," "conceived by," "devised by," "supervised by," "musical staging by," "dances and musical numbers staged by," "play staged by," "book staged by," and "dialogue staged by."

The rise of the director as a central artistic figure dates from the nineteenth century, but the emergence of the director as the most powerful member of a musical's creative team, whose vision shapes an entire production and whose authority delivers it, is more recent. This has to do, in large part, with significant changes in the form and content of musicals themselves. It would be a mistake, however, to underestimate the quality of early twentieth-century productions, or to privilege the integrated "book" musical over other forms such as the revue, since, as Bruce Kirle argues, the collaborative process through which musicals are created precludes the ultimate authority of the text.[5] Nevertheless, an accepted paradigm is that the book was the least important element in musicals before World War II. Whether revue, musical comedy, or operetta, the emphasis was on showcasing stars and offering audiences lively, upbeat, romantic and/or sexually titillating entertainment. With some noteworthy exceptions—*Show Boat* (1927), *Of Thee I Sing* (1931), *Porgy and Bess* (1935), *Pal Joey* (1940), and *Lady in the Dark* (1941)—books, in Harold Prince's words, "were there to string together really terrific scores."[6] Scripts were considered of far less value than the songs they supported or the talent they featured, so that authentic texts rarely survived from production to production.

The partnership of Richard Rodgers and Oscar Hammerstein II marked a critical moment in the musical's development. Determined to make musical theater a more serious art form, Rodgers and Hammerstein placed new emphasis on a well-crafted book as the basis for a unified, artistic whole. Beginning with *Oklahoma!* (1943) and continuing through *The Sound of Music* (1959), the story became preeminent in their productions. "From that point on," critic John Lahr asserts, writers provided a show's "creative drive."[7] Writers alone, however, cannot take a work from page to stage, ensuring that it will have maximal audience impact. Telling a story effectively, shaping it into a show with coherent structure, focus, and rhythm, is the director's responsibility. Not surprisingly, given the importance of the book—and hence the director—to Rodgers and Hammerstein, the first person to garner a Tony Award for directing a musical was Joshua Logan (1908–88) for their *South Pacific* (1949), which was named best musical in 1950 and swept most of the other relevant prizes as well. A "writer-director," Logan also shared the award for "Authors (Musical)" with Hammerstein, while Rodgers won as best composer.

The Tony Awards were presented for the first time in 1947 (which is one reason the names of earlier theater artists are so elusive), but a separate category for musical theater direction was not established until 1960. In that year, George Abbott (1887–1995) won it for *Fiorello!*, which he had both written and directed; he received the prize again for *A Funny Thing Happened on the Way to the Forum* in 1963. After "generations and generations of experience," lyricist Sheldon Harnick explained, this legendary director "was still in his prime" (Rosenberg and Harburg, 243). Known for his disciplined, forthright, pragmatic approach to directing as well as his versatility, "Mr. Abbott" was active as a director, producer, writer, "play doctor," and occasional choreographer for more than seven decades. He specialized in sprightly musical comedies including *The Boys from Syracuse* (1938, writer, director, producer), *Pal Joey* (1940, director and producer), *On the Town* (1944), *High Button Shoes* (1947), *Where's Charley* (1951, writer and director), *A Tree Grows in Brooklyn* (1951, writer, director, producer), *Wonderful Town* (1953), *The Pajama Game* (1954, writer and co-director with Jerome Robbins), *Damn Yankees* (1955, writer and director), *New Girl in Town* (1957, writer and director), and *How Now, Dow Jones* (1967). Yet his work defies easy categorization. According to director Arthur Masella, Abbott "was in his heyday as great as he was because he was a man who developed. If you look at what he did over his life as a director, you get the sense that he started in this genre, then he moved on to that. He was *constantly changing*" (Rosenberg and Harburg, 104).

Although the eclectic variety of his productions and the longevity of his career make it difficult to describe an Abbott "style," he was a formative influence on subsequent directors, including Harold Prince. In reflecting on his own distinguished career, Prince acknowledged his profound debt to the two men he considered his mentors: Abbott and director-choreographer Jerome Robbins (1918–98). As co-producer of *West Side Story* (1957) and producer of *Fiddler on the Roof* (1964), both of which Robbins directed and choreographed, Prince had ample opportunity to watch Robbins work. According to scholar Miranda Lundskaer-Nielsen, "Trained as a ballet dancer,…Robbins…introduced Prince to the idea of a unified production vocabulary and to a more fluid use of the stage,.…[as well as to] the effectiveness of improvisation and empathy techniques—elements of 'the method' that he had learned under Lee Strasberg at the Actors Studio."[8]

Dance had always been an essential part of musicals but emerged as a key element in dramatic storytelling with the work of Agnes de Mille, who brought ballet to Rodgers and Hammerstein's *Oklahoma!* and *Carousel* (1945). Notwithstanding the importance of her contributions as choreographer for these shows, however, Rouben Mamoulian was their director. It was not until Robbins that the director-choreographer became a powerful force in the creation of new work once again. As critic Frank Rich explained, "Jerome Robbins was the prime example of the idea that someone could direct and choreograph a Broadway musical, that they weren't two separate jobs, but the whole thing could move as one.... Other people like Agnes de Mille had done it before him, [but] he took the *Oklahoma!* dream ballet and applied it to the whole piece." According to Arthur Laurents, "When the director of a musical is also the choreographer, his power is absolute; the show is totally in his hands. Or so it would seem if the hands belonged to Jerome Robbins."[9]

In *Bells Are Ringing* (1956, co-choreographed with Bob Fosse), *West Side Story* (which he also is credited with conceiving), *Gypsy* (1959), and *Fiddler on the Roof,* Robbins was integral to shaping and staging all aspects of the production. In Lundskaer-Nielsen's view, he and other director-choreographers in the 1950s, '60s, and '70s—most notably Gower Champion, Bob Fosse, and Michael Bennett— "helped to raise the status of the director in the creative process" and secured the director's preeminent position in the creative team.[10] Each had begun his career as a dancer and had worked his way up through the production hierarchy, graduating from the chorus line to featured dancer, dance captain, assistant or associate choreographer, choreographer, and finally choreographer-director. As Citron notes, "some of them eventually even bypassed the official production system and went directly to record companies for financing of their projects [so that] it became Michael Bennett's *A Chorus* Line or Bob Fosse's *Dancin'* and, assuring his name as part of the logo and title, *Jerome Robbins's Broadway*" (Citron, 86). However idiosyncratic or autocratic their methods may have been, their ability to express a cohesive vision through dance and to make movement of paramount importance in conceptualizing and realizing a production had a transformational impact on musical theater.

The controversial Robbins, known as much for his reputedly tyrannical rehearsal techniques and his testimony as a "friendly" witness before the House Un-American Activities Committee (May 1953) as for his directorial brilliance, made his Broadway debut with *On the Town* (1944), a musical he conceived and choreographed.[11] Inspired in part by his ballet *Fancy Free* (1944), his collaborators were composer Leonard Bernstein, librettists/lyricists Betty Comden and Adolph Green, and set designer Oliver Smith. After choreographing *Billion Dollar Baby* (1945)—a show in which the company supposedly disliked him so much that no one stopped him during a rehearsal as he fell backward into the orchestra pit (Lawrence, 101)—Robbins won his first Tony Award three years later for choreographing *High Button Shoes* (1947).

Alternating between the dance and theater worlds for the next two decades, his accomplishments in the 1950s included choreographing dance sequences for *The King and I* (1951), collaborating with George Abbott on *The Pajama Game*, and creating *West Side Story* with Leonard Bernstein (music and uncredited lyrics), Stephen Sondheim (lyrics), and Arthur Laurents (book). Although *West Side Story* lost to Meredith Willson's *The Music Man* in almost every category at the 1959 Tony Awards, Robbins won his second for choreography. Along with Bernstein's brilliant score, Robbins's choreography remains the most memorable part of that production. According to Harold Prince, who co-produced *West Side Story* with Robert Griffith, "Robbins's choreography is authorship in that show. I don't think all choreography is, but certainly Robbins's was in [*West Side Story*]. The marriage of dance movement and storytelling was new to the theater."[12] Beyond that, the show was noteworthy for another reason. In Laurents's words: "Many said *West Side* forever changed the American musical…because of its use of dance and music. To me, it used those elements better than they had ever been used before; but what it really changed, what its real contribution to American musical theater was, was that it showed that any subject—murder, attempted rape, bigotry—could be the subject of a popular musical" (Laurents, 145).

Notorious for his dictatorial methods in directing *West Side Story*, which included keeping cast members playing Jets and Sharks apart and mutually distrustful during rehearsals, Robbins deserves recognition for his innovative approach to his dancer-actors. Chita Rivera (Anita in the original stage production) recalled his "genius" in an interview decades later:

> Jerry…really challenged you. If he told me to jump off a building and land on my left foot, I knew it was possible if I did what he told me to do. We used to sit on the steps of the 52nd Street Theatre and talk about my character in colors and textures. Dancers weren't used to this kind of delving. He made us go back into our own histories and make up stories that belonged to us and to the show. Yes, it was tense at times, but it was also amazingly exciting and you felt yourself grow. Suddenly dancers weren't just physical. They were thinking. They were using their own minds. A lot of us came out of that as better actors, better dancers, using ourselves so much more.[13]

Her comments convey a sense of Robbins in rehearsal, with the absolute authority he established and the total control he exerted seen as positive factors in the creative process rather than as inhibiting negatives. Like any director, he understood that he could realize his vision only if he succeeded in embedding his ideas in his actors' bodies. However autocratic he may have been, his reliance on fear as a motivational technique notwithstanding, he also was collaborative with and empowering of many of the performers with whom he worked.

Fiercely protective of his creations, Robbins ensured that his choreography was contractually regarded as part of *Fiddler on the Roof*, for which he won twin Tonys in 1965. (His fifth and last came in 1989 for directing *Jerome Robbins's Broadway*.) Years after his death, his choreographic stranglehold precludes directors from reinterpreting the dance sequences, as was the case with David Leveaux's 2004 Broadway revival. Denied permission to remove Robbins's choreography, he was forced to re-create it within an otherwise reimagined production. In Leveaux's words, "If he was here, he would be completely ruthlessly redoing and reediting his own work. That's hard for people whose job is to protect his legacy to understand" (Lundskaer-Nielsen, 168). It certainly raises concerns about the restrictions such provisions place on directors who hope to express their own vision in staging the work. In 2009, Arthur Laurents's reconceived Broadway production of *West Side Story* featured Robbins's choreography "reproduced" by Joey McKneely, but Laurents, the author of its original book, evidently did not seek to replace it. In McKneely's words, "If you remove Jerome Robbins's choreography, you lose significant plot, storytell-ing moments, and you lose characterization elements that are set in the dance....It's rare that shows have dance as that kind of signature. It's the emotional glue."[14]

As revolutionary a figure as Robbins was, he was not the first person to garner Tony Awards for directing and choreographing the same show. That honor belongs to Gower Champion (1919–80) who won for his work on *Bye Bye Birdie* in 1961. He received that twin recognition twice more, for *Hello, Dolly!* in 1964 and *The Happy Time* in 1968, and was honored posthumously with his eighth Tony as choreogra-pher for *42nd Street* in 1981. Of the major director-choreographers, his particular talent seems the most elusive, perhaps because he neither changed the form nor established a signature performance style. His energetic, ebullient choreography and skillful direction ably served the shows they enlivened, but did not aggressively scream "Champion."[15]

In that respect his polar opposite is Robert Louis "Bob" Fosse (1927–87) whose now much imitated style is immediately recognizable and remains more distinctive than some of the shows it animated. "When you see his work, you know immedi-ately it's Fosse, like when you see a Picasso," Graciela Daniele explained.[16] Heavily rhythmic music appealed to this award-winning director-choreographer and suited his jazzy idiom, characterized by its intense yet sophisticated sexuality and accentu-ated by the suggestive use of bowler hats, gloves, and canes. The slinky shuffling of leggy dancers with turned-in toes, thrusting pelvises, and curved, lowered shoul-ders, sitting seductively astride chairs or locked in erotic couplings is all "Fosse" and infused productions from *The Pajama Game* (1954) to *Chicago* (1975) to *Big Deal* (1986) with a pulsing energy. *The Pajama Game* brought him his first Tony for cho-reography, followed by five more: *Damn Yankees*, *Redhead*, *Sweet Charity*, *Dancin'*, and *Big Deal*. Rewarded with Tonys for both directing and choreographing *Pippin* (which he also essentially rewrote) in 1973, he became the first person to win Tony, Academy, and Emmy Awards in the same year when he earned an Oscar for direct-ing the film version of *Cabaret* and an Emmy for *Liza with a "Z."*

If Fosse may be credited with forging a style, Michael Bennett (Michael Bennett DiFiglia, 1943–87) was recognized by producer Gerald Schoenfeld for saving the Shubert Organization, revitalizing Broadway, and sparking the renewal of the then-squalid 42nd Street area with *A Chorus Line*, the 1975 Tony Award– and Pulitzer Prize–winning musical. The show he originally called "The Dancers' Project" and developed through a series of workshops over eighteen months allegedly "made dancing so popular that leg warmers became a fashion statement"[17] and was for much of the 1980s and '90s the longest-running show in Broadway history. Transforming the traditional chorus kick-line into a vehicle for self-revelation, Bennett evoked the pain and the exhilaration professional dancers experience in their challenging, unpredictable careers. Dancers, he seemed to say, have no control over their lives and that may well have been what propelled him from Broadway "gypsy" to choreographer and finally director. Although he often spoke of the joys of collaboration, as a director he sought control over all aspects of a production. He saw his role as that of "a leader who makes everything calm, gives everyone a sense of purpose," engages the audience "from the moment a show starts" and provides "the emotional experience that an audience expects and that is...attached to what they consider a great live theatrical experience" (Rosenberg and Harburg, 103).

Bennett's other distinguished work includes *Promises, Promises* (1966, choreography), *Coco* (1969, choreography), *Company* (1970, choreography), and *Follies* (1971, Tony Awards for co-direction with Harold Prince and choreography), *Seesaw* (1973, book, direction, and Tony Award–winning choreography). *Ballroom*, which he produced, directed, and choreographed in 1978, was a disappointment, although Bennett won his sixth Tony Award for choreography (sharing it with Bob Avian). His seventh (with Michael Peters) came three years later for *Dreamgirls* (1981), which he also produced and directed. A critical and popular success, the show ran on Broadway for almost five years. Based on the story of the Motown singing group the Supremes, it, like *A Chorus Line* and *Follies*, evoked the dark underside of American show business and the corrupting power of stardom. While not as groundbreaking as *A Chorus Line*, it was a production in which Bennett found innovative ways to explore stage space. According to critic John Heilpern, he "choreographed the set." Through his manipulation of four large, movable towers designed by Robin Wagner and lit by Tharon Musser, Bennett created "constantly changing perspectives and space, like an automated ballet....Dance and movement were organic to the entire action. But Bennett had made the mechanical set his dancers." As *Wicked* choreographer Wayne Cilento recalled two decades later, whereas Bob Fosse was "meticulous about being very precise about finger turns and hand turns and little wrist movements,...Michael Bennett was a genius with choreographing the whole stage, just moving it around and making the whole thing dance."[18]

Some viewed the ascendance of the director-choreographer negatively, claiming that this "hybrid type" exercised undue influence on both script and score and always privileged dance over text. As playwright Peter Stone declared in the early 1990s, "Here was the director or the director-choreographer as 'auteur,' organizing production values (sets, lighting, costume, technology, dance)." With the exception of Jerome Robbins, they were "deadly antagonists to bookwriters," uncomfortable with text. "They are like abstract painters," he explained, "except their forte is movement." They have no interest in words "that can be directed but can't be *staged.*" Unwilling to be part of a creative team, they wanted control of "the whole thing."[19]

Since directorial style is so individual, such generalizations seem unfair to the director-choreographers already discussed as well as to their successors, among them Thomas James "Tommy" Tune, Graciela Daniele, Kathleen Marshall, and Susan Stroman, the first woman to win twin Tony Awards as director-choreographer (*The Producers*, 2001).[20] Notwithstanding the prominence of director-choreographers in the historical narrative of musical theater, moreover, the two roles are not inseparably fused. There are other kinds of directors of comparable significance, who have exercised artistic control just as stringently. Whether director-producer, director-playwright, director-dramaturg, director-designer, or simply director, he or she is the artistic leader of a production, no matter how collaborative the art form is understood to be. According to Laurents, "In the end, the look of the musical is the director's look. He chooses the designers, he conveys his vision, he guides and edits. He can inspire the best to be even better or he can hamstring them into being less" (Laurents, 11).

The difference in perceived "creative muscle" may stem from the fact that the work of a director-choreographer is so palpable. Even without as distinctive a style as Fosse's, he or she shapes a large part of what the audience sees: the musical numbers as well as the dramatic scenes. When the duties are divided between a director and a choreographer, as Kathleen Marshall explains, "with a lot of directors, if there's music, the choreographer is in charge."[21] Because the musical numbers tend to be the most memorable parts of a production, the contribution of a director, as opposed to a director-choreographer, may be difficult for the average theatergoer to appreciate unless the director is also associated with some other tangible element such as the book (Laurents, *Gypsy* and *West Side Story*), the costumes (Julie Taymor, *The Lion King*), or the set (John Doyle, *Sweeney Todd*, 2005 revival). Doyle, in the last, placed his chilling modern-dress interpretation within what appeared to be a psychiatric ward and put his stylistic imprimatur on the production with his brilliant use of actor-musicians, who served as the show's orchestra, with every cast member responsible for at least one instrument. Whether cello (Joanna) or tuba (Mrs. Lovett), each instrument became an extension of the person playing it, creating great emotional resonance.[22]

As Lundskaer-Nielsen convincingly argues, "It is essential to recognize the vital contribution of a group of American and British theater directors who have infused the mainstream musical with new ideas, techniques and approaches," beginning with "the work of Broadway producer and director Harold Prince in the 1960s and 70s" and continuing with "Trevor Nunn, John Caird, Nicholas Hytner, James Lapine, George C. Wolfe, Tina Landau, Sam Mendes, Matthew Warchus, and David Leveaux" (Lundskaer-Nielsen, 7–8). That list should expand to include Michael Blakemore, Stephen Daldry, John Doyle, Richard Eyre, Thomas Kail, Arthur Laurents, Joe Mantello, Adrian Noble, Jack O'Brien, Diane Paulus, John Rando, Julie Taymor, Deborah Warner, and many other theater artists who have made the musical a viable forum for creative expression and imaginative exploration in the twenty-first century.

Lundskaer-Nielsen correctly sees Prince (b. 1928) as a seminal figure in the development of the postwar Broadway musical, owing to his "dual identity as the inheritor of Broadway showmanship and as a pioneer in bringing darker themes to the Broadway musical theatre." Beyond his important work as a producer (*West Side Story, Fiddler on the Roof*) and then as a producer-director (*Cabaret, Follies, A Little Night Music, Pacific Overtures, Sweeney Todd*), she credits him with broadening the boundaries of the musical in form and content "through his active participation in the development process, his need for social relevance, and his incorporation of structural formats and staging techniques beyond the traditions of the American musical theatre." Prince imbued musical drama with a new credibility and, in the words of *The Producers'* irresistible Roger De Bris, proved that musicals could be more than "silly entertainments. Dopey showgirls in gooey gowns. Two-three-kick-turn! Turn-turn-kick-turn!"[23] Determined to engage and challenge his audiences, Prince's work has embraced difficult topics and sobering themes—perhaps none more so than *Parade* (1998), which dealt with a shocking episode of anti-Semitism, the 1915 lynching of Atlanta pencil factory manager Leo Frank, as a cautionary tale for a nation still struggling with hatred, prejudice, and intolerance.

A collaborative director, Prince has explained, "You must listen to everything, which means to everyone.... There's no way of knowing where advice that hits a responsive chord will come from. You've got to be the censor, the editor." He is, however, collaborative only to a point. Although he has often been overshadowed by such creative partners as John Kander and Fred Ebb, Andrew Lloyd Webber and Tim Rice, and Stephen Sondheim, it is clear that he considers his directorial authority sacrosanct: "I must have the final word. People have walked away from that..., which is their prerogative. Choreographers can leave or accept the finality of my word. There's no halfway house" (Rosenburg and Harburg, 80, 103). Beginning with *Cabaret* (1966), for which he earned his first Tony Award for Best Direction of a Musical, his directorial concept has shaped all aspects of a production and determined its style. To date he has won twenty-one Tonys (eight for directing, two as Best Producer of a Musical, eight for producing the year's Best Musical, and three special awards). His career has not been without its critical or commercial failures—among them *Merrily We Roll Along* (1981), which ended his storied partnership with Sondheim, *A Doll's Life* (1982), *Roza* (1987), and *Parade*—but his many more successful productions have validated the musical as an art form worthy of serious consideration and intellectual engagement.[24]

Musical theater now attracts directors who consider it culturally and socially relevant, as credible a creative forum as the other dramatic works they explore. No longer dismissed as frothy, trivial entertainments, musicals have become respectable, while their directors—both British and American—have gained prominence, drawing on a variety of staging traditions to challenge their audiences. In addition to generating new work, moreover, Prince and his successors have sparked an upsurge of interest in musical revivals. Rather than simply recreating classic texts, they have reinterpreted them from a contemporary perspective and have demonstrated that canonical works must be explored as *living* texts. In Bruce Kirle's words, "Historical context not only influenced the texts of these musicals but also helped shape the way these productions were performed and received by their audiences.

New productions...will inevitably adapt to new cultural moments and to new audiences. As such, the musical is innately open, subject to a plurality of readings" (Kirle, xix).

British and American directors alike have embraced the challenge of reimagining them. In the 1990s especially, such Tony Award–winning productions as Hytner's *Carousel*, Jerry Zaks's *Guys and Dolls*, Prince's *Show Boat*, Walter Bobbie's *Chicago*, Sam Mendes's *Cabaret*, and Michael Blakemore's *Kiss Me, Kate* electrified audiences with their stunning theatricality and proved that mounting revivals is far more than an exercise in nostalgia. As Mendes explains, "*Cabaret* is up there with *The Crucible* or *The Homecoming* or any other great play of the twentieth century that deserves to be reinvented and rediscovered generation to generation. It's a great piece of theatre." For Laurents, "The goal of a revival is to add a fresh take on the material while not losing what made the original worth reviving. The key is to look at the material with fresh eyes rather than merely with the desire to do something different."[25]

Concomitant with these changes and undoubtedly contributing to them is the emergence of American nonprofit theaters as a venue for the development and production of new musicals. Although some shows, such as *Hair* and *A Chorus Line*, originated Off Broadway and Off-Off Broadway in the 1960s and '70s, the 1980s saw a significant increase in the number of theaters committed to nurturing artists, creating experimental new pieces, and cultivating audiences for them. They attracted intrepid directors seeking an alternative to Broadway, including Des McAnuff (*Big River*), Graciela Daniele (*Once on This Island, Marie Christine*), and Michael Greif (*Rent*). In Lundskaer-Nielsen's view, most influential among them was Tony Award–winning writer-director James Lapine (b. 1949) whose *March of the Falsettos* (1981) helped pioneer nonprofit chamber musicals and whose *Sunday in the Park with George* (1983), which won the 1985 Pulitzer Prize for Drama, introduced the seemingly oxymoronic concept of a noncommercial musical (Lundskaer-Nielsen, 77–78). Lapine has also used his considerable skills as playwright and director to structure, shape, and stage *Into the Woods* (1987), *Falsettos* (1992), and *Passion* (1994), each of which garnered a Tony Award for the Best Book of a Musical.

Whereas Lapine's emphasis has been on story, characters, and songs rather than opulent staging or inventive choreography, George C. Wolfe (b. 1954) is a renowned writer-director and producer who has embraced Broadway staging traditions and whose directorial role models include Jerome Robbins and Michael Bennett. Even more significant, as an African American in a field largely dominated by white men, he has brought the politics of race as well as the provocative portrayal of African American history and culture to mainstream audiences. From *Jelly's Last Jam* (1991) to *Bring in 'da Noise, Bring in 'da Funk* (1996), for which he earned his second Tony Award for directing, and *Caroline, or Change* (2004), he has succeeded in combining what Lundskaer–Nielsen calls "the traditions of black sociopolitical drama with the storytelling techniques of Broadway choreographer-directors," often in "a new and discomfiting context" (Lundskaer-Nielsen, 89–94, 99). In his words, "the kind of theater I want to craft [is] a theater that's full of delight but also has edge and a sense of responsibility to the world....My theory about musicals is that there is a dark world just waiting offstage and the people are singing and dancing to keep that dark world from coming onstage. The main thing you have to do as a writer or director with this kind of material is to keep things buoyant."[26]

If Wolfe has helped to shatter racial barriers, Julie Taymor (b. 1952), the first woman to earn a Tony Award for directing as well as for costume design, for *The Lion King* (1998), Susan Stroman (b. 1954), Tina Landau (b. 1962), Kathleen Marshall (b. 1962), and Diane Paulus (b. 1966), among others, have shown that gender equity may finally be within reach for women directors and director-choreographers. Both Stroman and Marshall began as choreographers and moved "up" to directing. As Stroman explains, "It was a natural stepping stone for me....Because I established myself as a credible choreographer, people then believed that I could direct" (Bryer and Davison, 211). Paulus, who became artistic director of the American Repertory Theatre in Cambridge, Massachusetts, in 2008, the year before her acclaimed production of *Hair* won the Tony for Best Revival of a Musical, has demonstrated that it is possible for women as well as men to move between the nonprofit and commercial theater worlds. Whatever the venue or the vehicle, she asserts that her focus as a director is on the audience. In her words: "It's just always been my passion. Whenever I've been asked to direct something, whether it's an opera or it's a musical or a play, I'm always interested in, who is the audience for this? Why are we doing this? Why are we creating this event? And why should I ask people to come and see this? What's the need to do this project now?"[27]

These are questions that any director of musicals should ask and answer. According to Tony Award–winning director Joe Mantello (b. 1962), whose musical theater projects include *Wicked* (2003), *Assassins* (2004), *Pal Joey* (2008), and *9 to 5* (2009):

> The director answers all of the questions, takes all the blame. The director's a combination probably of Dad or Mom, a therapist—hopefully someone who has a little vision and someone who can just lead the troops. You really have to find a way to marshal the troops at all times and say "We're going in this direction, let's go!" And you can't hesitate or they can smell it.[28]

Arthur Laurents (1917–2011), also in martial mode, considers the director the "commander-in-chief." Director, writer, composer, and producer Martin Charnin (b. 1934), best known for his award-winning production of *Annie* (1977), uses similar terms to explain what a director does. Calling him "a visionary who ideally knows everything there is to know...about how to make orchestrations match costumes, dialogue, scenery and performance," he waxes militaristic in likening a show to "an armada, a large fleet, with many ships." The director is the person whose responsibility is to "bring them into port at different times because they arrive at different times. Once that fleet is docked, it's the show." For Prince, taking an aerial view, "the director must see it from a distance, to see the whole arc of the show" (Rosenberg and Harburg, 75, 101, 138).

Given the artistic breadth that characterizes musical theater today, there is no template for directors. Effective directors will have their own individual styles of expression and ways of making a particular production work. In Laurents's view, whether "therapist," "seducer," "psychologist, or lucky," the director is responsible for everything seen, said, or done on the stage. "No musical, no matter how good, can survive a misdirected, misconceived production." A director's work "begins long before the first day of rehearsal—at the moment when he opens the script." At that point, "the first question" should be: "what is it about? The answer tells where to put the focus." Whatever the response, however different each director's approach and techniques may be, the "key always is emotional reality," the ultimate goal to move an audience. For Laurents, "The first five minutes of a musical are crucial; either the audience can be captured, in which case they are the director's, no matter what he or she does, until at least halfway through the first act; or they can be lost, in which case it will take some stage magic to get them back" (Laurents, 3, 7, 29, 31, 76, 132, 154–55).

According to Laurents, who directed into his nineties and who wrote with the authority that only age and experience could bring, "Why? is the most important of questions, certainly the most important a director could ask. Beginning with himself: why is he a director?" He continues thoughtfully, "Why do directors direct? To be in control? To achieve the success they couldn't as actors? To produce theater that gives the audience an experience only theater can—moves them, excites, and entertains, illuminates, and always makes them want to see more theater, that's the desired answer" (Laurents, 175). For every musical theater director, aspiring or seasoned, that edifying answer should be an inspirational first principle as well as a daily mantra.

NOTES

1. Arthur Laurents, *Mainly on Directing: Gypsy, West Side Story, and Other Musicals* (New York: Alfred A. Knopf, 2009), p. 14.

2. *Broadway: The American Musical*, a film by Michael Kantor (Educational Broadcasting Corporation and the Broadway Film Project, Inc., 2004), Episode Three, track 9, *Porgy and Bess*, and Episode Five, track 1, Introduction.

3. Stephen Citron, *The Musical from the Inside Out* (Chicago: Ivan R. Dee, 1991), p. 85.

4. Other directors and choreographers on whom Ziegfeld relied were George Marion, Joseph W. Herbert, Leon Errol, Edward Royce, William Anthony McGuire, Sammy Lee, and Zeke Colvan. See Ethan Mordden's *Ziegfeld: The Man Who Invented Show Business* (New York: St. Martin's Press, 2008).

5. Bruce Kirle, *Unfinished Show Business: Broadway Musicals as Works-in-Process* (Carbondale: Southern Illinois University Press, 2005), pp. 7 and 23.

6. Kirle, 23; Bernard Rosenberg and Ernest Harburg, *The Broadway Musical: Collaboration in Art and Commerce* (New York: New York University Press, 1993), p. 120.

7. *Broadway*, Episode Four ("Oh, What a Beautiful Mornin'," 1943–1960), track 2, *World War II/Oklahoma!*

8. Miranda Lundskaer-Nielsen, *Directors and the New Musical Drama: British and American Musical Theatre in the 1980s and 90s* (New York: Palgrave Macmillan, 2008), p. 23.

9. *Broadway*, Episode Five, track 2, *West Side Story*; Laurents, 93.

10. Lundskaer-Nielsen, 7. Others include Joe Layton and Michael Kidd.

11. Greg Lawrence, *Dance with Demons: The Life of Jerome Robbins* (New York: G. P. Putnam's Sons, 2001), 200. Chapter Five, "Betrayals, Triumphs, and Fairy Dust," is particularly informative.

12. *Broadway*, Episode Five, track 2, *West Side Story*.

13. *Broadway*, supplementary material.

14. Julie Bloom, "Rekindling Robbins, a Step at a Time" (*New York Times* [March 4, 2009]), http://www.nytimes.com/2009/03/08/arts/dance/08bloo.html, accessed July 22, 2009.

15. Ironically, producer David Merrick's dramatic announcement of Champion's death after curtain calls on opening night of *42nd Street*, shocking both audience and cast, is what many people now seem to remember Champion for.

16. *Broadway*, Episode Five, track 9, *Bob Fosse*.

17. *Broadway*, Episode Five, track 8, *A Chorus Line*.

18. John Heilpern, "Bennett's Breakthrough: *Dreamgirls* Remembered" (*New York Observer* [January 7, 2007]), http://www.observer.com/node/36503?observer_most_read_tabs_tab=2, accessed July 11, 2009; *Broadway*, supplementary material.

19. Rosenberg and Harburg, 133–34; for a similarly negative evaluation, see "Act Five. Wagging the Musical: How Director-Choreographers Co-opted a Writer's Medium," in Mark N. Grant's *The Rise and Fall of the Broadway Musical* (Boston: Northeastern University Press, 2004).

20. Stroman also won Tonys for choreography in 1992 (*Crazy for You*), 1995 (*Show Boat*), and 2000 (*Contact*). In addition to two Tony Awards for choreography, one for direction, and two for acting, Tune has won twice as a director-choreographer: in 1990 for *Grand Hotel* and 1991 for *The Will Rogers Follies*.

21. Quoted in *The Art of the American Musical: Conversations with the Creators*, ed. Jackson R. Bryer and Richard A. Davison (New Brunswick, NJ: Rutgers University Press, 2005), p. 160.

22. The same technique worked less effectively in Doyle's revival of *Company* (2006), in which some of the musical numbers left the unfortunate impression of a frenetic marching band, its members in dire need of a choreographer. Yet here, too, the device does important dramatic work, enhancing the teeming, oppressive dimension of Bobby's friends, as he experiences them; see Raymond Knapp, "Temporality and Control in Sondheim's Middle Period: From *Company* to *Sunday in the Park with George*" (*Speculum*, 2010 [forthcoming]).

23. Lundskaer-Nielsen, 15, 20, 23, 28; Mel Brooks and Tom Meehan, *The Producers: The Book, Lyrics, and Story behind the Biggest Hit in Broadway History! How We Did It* (New York: Hyperion, 2001), p. 130.

24. Lundskaer-Nielsen, 57. Sondheim and Prince did not work together again until *Bounce* (2003), which was not a critical success. When the revised version opened in New York in 2008 as *Road Show*, John Doyle, not Prince, directed it.

25. Quoted in Lundskaer-Nielsen, 117; Laurents, 15.

26. Quoted in Bryer and Davison, 286, 292. Wolfe won his first Tony for directing Tony Kushner's *Angels in America: Millennium Approaches* (a drama, not a musical) in 1993.

27. Interview with Matthew Small (*Talkin' Broadway Regional News* [April 13, 2009]), http://www.talkinbroadway.com/regional/boston/boston128.html, accessed July 9, 2009.

28. *Broadway*, supplementary material.

CHAPTER 21

SETS, COSTUMES, LIGHTS, AND SPECTACLE

VIRGINIA ANDERSON

Give 'em the old razzle dazzle
Razzle dazzle 'em
Give 'em an act with lots of flash in it
And the reaction will be passionate
Give 'em the old hocus pocus
Bead and feather 'em
How can they see with sequins in their eyes?
　　　　　　　　—Billy Flynn, *Chicago*[1]

Color and light.
There's only color and light.
—George, *Sunday in the Park with George*[2]

Over the history of musical theater, tendencies in design have swung, pendulum-like, between glittering spectacle and simplicity. This oscillation reflects a symbiotic relationship across the footlights; what the audience has seen on stage has contributed to the success—or failure—of many musicals. Design trends reflect changes in both popular taste and economic investment, even if, ultimately, each theatrical design has been developed to serve the story or mood at the heart of the production as determined through collaboration with writers, composers, and directors. As the economic, social, and political climate in which productions have taken place has in turn determined the definition and feasibility of "spectacle," design trends have moved from the extravagant to the comparatively simple and back again.

As an introduction to the subject of design, this chapter discusses only original productions, not revivals, and focuses on technological and artistic advancements within scenic and lighting design, sometimes incorporating discussion of costumes as they relate to the changing nature of spectacle. A genealogy with a wider scope would also address the work of such costume artists as William Ivey Long and Jane Greenwood, as well as the contributions of hair and makeup artists such as Michael Ward and Candace Carell, and wig makers such as Paul Huntley, each of whom has contributed significantly to characterization and the visual dimension of the stories being told in musicals.[3] In addition, the advancement of design and spectacle would not be possible without the often unsung engineering prowess of individuals such as Edward Kook and George Izenour, lighting technicians who installed the first electronic lighting control system in a professional theater and thereby reduced the amount of time it took to program a lighting cue from hours to seconds.[4]

Real experimentation in musical theater design began in Europe at the turn of the twentieth century with the dance-based work of Adolph Appia and the atmospheric designs of Edward Gordon Craig. Moving productions away from previously established expectations involving lavish sets and lights, these designs brought the notion of spectacle directly to the body. Since then, the presentation of the actor's body has been the central point from which the design pendulum swings. From the silky legs of chorus girls in *The Black Crook* (1866) to the complete baring of the tribe in *Hair* (1967), the revealed body of a performer has captivated musical theater audiences throughout the history of the American musical. The performer's body as it relates to other scenic elements often illuminates evolving tastes and technological innovation.

COLOR AND LIGHT: EARLY INFLUENCES AND INNOVATIONS

The stagecraft that proved most influential to the American musical developed in Germany in the late nineteenth century. Georg II, Duke of Saxe-Meiningen (1826–1914), was arguably the first modern stage director, with his touring theatrical company laying much of the foundation for modern musical theater. With careful attention to lighting and sound effects, the Duke strove for artistic unity through scenic design, costumes, and intricately choreographed crowd movement.[5] Also in Germany at this time, composer Richard Wagner (1813–83) developed an equally influential approach to design with his theory of the *Gesamtkunstwerk*, or total art work. Wagner called for the complete synthesis of artistic elements, pointing toward opera as the vehicle with the greatest potential for such a totalizing effect. To further his ideas, he opened the *Festpielhaus* (Festival Playhouse) theater in 1876 in Bayreuth, Germany, where he channeled the focus of his audience through several lasting innovations, including a darkened house and surround-sound reverberation. Music, movement, and design further contributed to the total art Wagner desired, and his work profoundly influenced designers who followed. This influential approach to design distinguished itself from the heavily detailed stages of nineteenth-century Realism and Naturalism.

Adolph Appia (1862–1928) drew inspiration from Wagner's *Gesamtkunstwerk*, devoting his designs to the essential mood of a piece as it complemented the embodied actions of performers.[6] He found a muse in Émile Jaques-Dalcroze, a dancer whose art derived from rhythm. Working with Dalcroze, Appia designed sets from pillars, shapes, and objects in a sculptural, nonrepresentational manner (⊙ Example 21.1). He eliminated walls and elaborately painted drop cloths, replacing them with abstract forms to emphasize the actors' movement in space. He simplified costumes to serve the total work and replaced scenic painting with moving projected colored light, always at the service of the actor. Indeed, Appia was one of the first to see the artistic potential of electric light, only recently introduced into theaters.[7] Instead of illustrating a story arc, Appia's approach to design, particularly lighting, intensified the mood and emotion of musical pieces and became the basis for lighting practices that followed.[8]

Like Appia, Edward Gordon Craig (1872–1966) moved theatrical design toward simplified abstraction, paring down his scenic designs to the most essential elements of the stories being told. Also like Appia, Craig found inspiration in dance, but he used light to emphasize scenic design rather than the movement of actors. He ultimately called for the director's complete control over the design of sets, lights, costumes, and choreography, and famously referred to his ideal actor as an "über-marionette," an ego-less performer capable of fulfilling the artistic demands of the director.[9] Over the course of his career, Craig's influential designs were recognized for their simplified scenes, creative use of curtains, emphasis on vertical architecture, and movable screens that allowed space to be redefined from scene to scene.[10]

While Craig and Appia communicated through abstraction in Europe, director/producer/playwright David Belasco signaled the imminent pendulum swing toward the extravagant. Like their European counterparts, Belasco's electrician, Louis Hartmann, with technicians John H. and Anton Kliegl, were devoted to the creation of mood through light, but they strove to create unparalleled realism through lighting. They famously enabled a sunrise to coincide with approximately twenty minutes of action within the saloon setting of Belasco's 1905 play *The Girl of the Golden West*, using tightly controlled lighting cues (⊙ Example 21.2).[11] Hartmann's innovations began in 1879 with the practical lensed spotlight, a device regularly used to separate the stars of musical theater from the chorus. Within an intricate lighting laboratory, Belasco, Hartmann, and the Kliegls developed multiple forms of electronic equipment to advance significantly the lighting technology of the early twentieth century. Belasco wrote, "Lights are to drama what music is to the lyrics of a song. No other factor that enters into the production of a play is so effective in conveying its moods and feeling."[12] Convinced of this principle, Belasco fit lights and their operators into every conceivable place around the stage in order to achieve the desired heavily atmospheric realism. His attention to detail suited well the elaborate artistry of the scenic designs for the musicals of the early twentieth century.

THE SPECTACLE OF THE BODY: THE EARLY CONTRIBUTIONS OF COSTUMING

Before innovations in scenic and lighting design drew their own attention, costumes dazzled audiences. The long-lasting popular success of *The Black Crook*, considered by some to be the first American musical, derived in no small part from the immodest attire of its dancing chorus girls. Advancements in stage machinery also enabled audiences to experience a remarkable and precedent-setting "transformation scene," in which a rocky cavern became a fairyland throne room before their eyes. But it was the daring provocation of nearly-nude dancing girls that brought audiences to this wildly successful show, whose extravagant and often revealing costuming for its leggy chorus members soon become characteristic of the American musical.[13] Direct testimony to the early influence of *The Black Crook* was the wild Broadway success of Lydia Thompson and her English Blondes, who caused a stir with their silky flesh-toned tights in the musical extravaganza, *Ixion* (1868).[14]

Florenz Ziegfeld (1867–1932) capitalized on such lucrative voyeurism in becoming one of the most influential producers of the Broadway musical, famous for sparing no expense while creating spectacular shows with unparalleled production values.[15] Although Ziegfeld's name is well known, those of his chief designers have been widely overlooked. Scenic designer Joseph Urban, along with costume designers Lady Lucile Duff Gordon and John Harkrider, provided significant contributions and innovations to the aesthetic hallmarks of musical theater.

Thirty years before Ziegfeld established the *Follies*, he built a career on the cult of the body, often enshrouded in meticulously designed costumes. With the examples of *The Black Crook* and Lydia Thompson's English Blondes pointing the way, Ziegfeld learned a valuable lesson early in his career: the nearly nude, physically attractive body could serve as a lucrative spectacle in and of itself. His first star, body-builder Eugen Sandow, was famously (barely) dressed in silk trunks or, as some photographs have documented, a strategically placed leaf (🔘 Example 21.3; 🔘 Example 21.4). This approach to costuming proved to be at least as true for feminine beauty, a fact exploited by decades of *Follies* productions, commencing in 1907.

Not all of Ziegfeld's "*Follies* girls" were presented in dishabille. From 1915 to 1921, Lady Lucile Duff Gordon, a high-society women's shop owner in both London and New York, designed elegant gowns for the *Follies*, after her ability to captivate buyers came to the notice of Ziegfeld through his young mistress and star, Anna Held. Lady Duff Gordon introduced the concept of the showgirl whose only responsibility was to look beautiful in spectacular clothing, a mode of presentation quite distinct from that of the singing and dancing chorus girl. As the arbiter of women's fashion in the early years of the twentieth century, she dressed both society ladies and *Follies* girls in extravagant and figure flattering—yet rarely revealing—gowns. Contributing to an enduring trend of emulation, variations of Lady Duff Gordon's stage creations were often on display at society events. Notably, Ziegfeld felt that each gown celebrated individuality, at a time when mass-produced clothing was taking over the fashion industry (◉ Example 21.5; ◉ Example 21.6).

John Harkrider served as Ziegfeld's costume designer throughout the showman's later years, but he owed a great deal to his predecessor. Lady Duff Gordon's gowns for the *Follies* were based on those worn by "living mannequins" who displayed them for the viewing pleasure of New York's elite. These stunning models were cool and detached, providing a prototype for the commanding poise of the *Follies* girls who later, under Harkrider's artistic command, donned the trademark feature of the *Follies*: architecturally extravagant, sculpturesque headdresses. Later parodied in such numbers as "The Money Song" of *Cabaret* and "Springtime for Hitler" in *The Producers*, these headdresses stretched the boundaries of how costumes and the body itself could contribute to spectacle.

Like Lady Duff Gordon, and most likely nurtured by the similarly minded Ziegfeld, Harkrider indulged a passionate affinity for the highest-quality materials, whatever the cost. Wresting control over all aspects of design, the notoriously difficult Harkrider sacrificed professional camaraderie for his own personal achievement in the creation of spectacle. At the age of only twenty-five, Harkrider designed the 1926 *Follies* revue, originally titled *Palm Beach Nights* for its Florida premiere. Feeding Ziegfeld's desire for lavish spectacle, the production's costume costs exceeded $90,000, and scenery expenses reached nearly $50,000 at a time when a loaf of bread cost approximately ten cents. Also in 1926, Harkrider introduced the egret-feather headdresses and costumes that established his place in Broadway history (◉ Example 21.7; ◉ Example 21.8; ◉ Example 21.9).

While Lady Duff Gordon and Harkrider created the look of the world-famous Ziegfeld girls, scenic artist Joseph Urban designed the equally extravagant sets. A noted Viennese architect of pavilions and palaces, Urban had designed operas throughout Europe and was designing for the Boston Opera in 1914 when his work came to Ziegfeld's attention. The designer's opulence and precision in artistry struck the producer immediately as the sort of sophistication he sought for his *Follies*. He immediately wooed Urban for the *Follies* and quickly commenced what proved to be an enduring collaboration, which culminated in Urban's contributions to the architectural and aesthetic design of the Ziegfeld Theatre in New York, an opulent performance space with every available technological extravagance (◉ Example 21.10).

Often relinquishing credit to his producer, Urban devised scenic innovations crucial to the development of musical theater stagecraft. Like other European designers of his time, Urban experimented with light and scenic painting. Although the lines of his sets were simple, they were frequently complicated by pointillist applications of vibrant color. This technique provided for the appearance and disappearance of shapes and images as well as radical changes of general hue according to the color of light used for illumination. He was among the first to employ platforms and portals in his designs, which allowed him to create an inner proscenium of whatever size best suited the action. Urban championed artistic unity and strove to focus his audience's attention upon a nearly seamless, total production, inspired by Appia and Craig abroad. A key link in an important chain of influence, Urban later inspired Robert Edmond Jones and Norman Bel Geddes, who were trained in scenic construction and painting at the Urban Studio, which he established in 1919 (🔘 Example 21.11; 🔘 Example 21.12).

As collaborators, Urban and Harkrider were often at odds, yet with Ziegfeld's nearly continuous ego-mending assistance, the pair contributed significantly to the watershed musical of their time: *Show Boat* (1927). As the first American musical to present serious themes and highly developed characters, *Show Boat* affected the perceptions and expectations of audiences that had been accustomed to the lighter or more romanticized themes of musical comedy and operetta. With Urban's massive moving set and atmospheric lights, and Harkrider's meticulously period-specific clothing, the designers contributed significantly to a unified generational story of those working on the *Cotton Blossom*, a Mississippi River showboat, between the 1880s and 1920s (🔘 Example 21.13).

BACK TO BASICS

With the economic collapse of 1929, the pendulum on Broadway was to swing again, this time away from spectacle and toward a renewed simplicity.[16] While Urban, Harkrider, and Belasco had emphasized beauty through extravagance to mirror popular tastes, visual trends in theater changed, as much of American society was forced to pare down to essentials during the Depression and war years. Seemingly simple and comparatively abstract designs represented a new wave in design, led by Robert Edmond Jones, Norman Bel Geddes, and Lee Simonson, who simultaneously captured the essence of the stories being told and reflected the changing mood of audiences (🔘 Example 21.14).

Even prior to this, while spectacle dominated the American musical stage, designers steeped in the work of Appia and Craig introduced the "New Stagecraft," an American design movement defined by the power of simplicity and suggestion, lasting from approximately 1915 through 1930.[17] Chief among these designers, Robert Edmond Jones (1887–1954) was considered "the father of American scenic design."

Although he designed relatively few musicals, his influence remains unsurpassed. Turning away from both the ornate designs of Urban and the hyperrealism promoted by Belasco, Jones strove to employ the imagination of his audiences by creating simplified, suggestive settings. He sought to communicate a *feeling* concerning the world of the play rather than construct a concrete reality.[18] Jones was heavily involved in the Little Theatre movement, especially the Provincetown Players and the Theatre Guild (which would produce *Oklahoma!* in 1943). He shared an interest in experimenting with naturalism and expressionism with Donald Oenslager, who contributed a lyrical elegance to even the harshest expressionistic lighting and scenic designs. Norman Bel Geddes (1893–1958) designed both sets and lights, and as with Jones his often "industrial" designs were emblematic rather than realistic. Bel Geddes influenced the focused appearance of later stage productions through his pioneering work with lenses in stage lighting.

Lee Simonson (1888–1967) called for a further simplified realism, eliminating any scenic elements that were not necessary for atmosphere or important information. Perhaps nowhere was Simonson's style felt more keenly than in the original production of the theatrical epitome of American Expressionism, Elmer Rice's 1923 play, *The Adding Machine*, which told the story of Mr. Zero, who murders his employer in a fit of fury when, after twenty-five years of service, he loses his job to new technology. Tried and executed, Mr. Zero awakes in Elysian Fields, where he is forced to work another adding machine before being sent back to Earth. Simonson's designs included a distorted courtroom, an adding machine big enough to walk on, and large numbers that spun across the stage with Mr. Zero's reeling thoughts. Simonson and other designers of the New Stagecraft imparted a less costly but conceptually rich aesthetic to the theater world, which proved invaluable during the troublesome economic period ahead.

Following the stock market crash of 1929 and the ensuing economic depression, most musicals and revues were forced to cut back, if not altogether eliminate expensive scenery and costumes. Instead, a renewed focus on music, choreography, and clever satire created a fertile atmosphere for the creation of a number of shows, including Cole Porter's *Anything Goes* (1934), the Gershwins' operatic *Porgy and Bess* (1935), and Rodgers and Hart's *On Your Toes* (1936). Spectacle was often created not through lights and sets but in other ways, such as with a live elephant in Rodgers and Hart's *Jumbo* (1935). When Marc Blitzstein's *The Cradle Will Rock* (1938), set to open at the Maxine Elliot Theatre with elaborate sets and costumes, was shut down due to budget cuts to the Federal Theater Project (reportedly in reaction to its core communist message), it was performed nearly extemporaneously in the New Century Theatre without the spectacular production values director/designer Orson Welles had created for it. Audiences cheered as Blitzstein told the story from the piano on stage as actors in street clothing sang to one another from across the theater, observing union rules that prohibited them from performing on stage.

While the move away from extravagance conditioned popular taste to a certain degree, musical theater was still associated with leggy showgirls, no matter the setting in which they appeared. Bearing in mind the continued influence exerted by the extravagant sets and costumes of successes stretching from *The Black Crook* to the *Follies*, which continued apace in Hollywood musicals, one may well understand the shock of the audience when the curtain first rose on *Oklahoma!* (1943) to reveal, not a rousing dance number performed by young chorus members, but an older woman in a conservative, floor-length skirt, churning butter in a generally open space. Lemuel Ayers's set and Miles White's costumes, like Urban and Harkrider's designs for *Show Boat*, contributed significantly to the story. Their roots in the Little Theatre movement were evident in sometimes abstract settings and costumes, which, while far from haute-couture, were highly expressive of individual character traits. With the design's emphasis on atmosphere as well as story, the influence of the New Stagecraft was readily apparent.[19]

Jo Mielziner brought the New Stagecraft further into the realm of musical theater, emphasizing a visual metaphor for the essence of each play and musical he designed, creating worlds on stage defined by a sense of poetic realism. He manipulated the styles of painted scenery from the past, adding his own fantastical images, decorations, and softly curved lines. Keeping tight artistic control over sets and lights, Mielziner worked carefully with color, gauze, and scrim to evoke mood, fantasy, dream, and memory. The flow of action from one scene to the next depended not upon the movement of scenery but on the raising and lowering of lights on his often fragmented sets, comprising multileveled playing spaces. This fluidity lent itself to the dream-like quality of the pieces for which he designed. In addition to plays such as *The Glass Menagerie* (1945), *A Streetcar Named Desire* (1947), and *Death of a Salesman* (1949), Mielziner designed such pivotal musicals as *Pal Joey* (1940), *Carousel* (1945), *South Pacific* (1949), and *The King and I* (1951).[20] Mielziner's significant artistic legacy is evident not only in the renderings and production photos he left behind but also through the influential work of his disciples, including Ming Cho Lee, who in turn trained contemporary designer John Lee Beatty and others who have contributed significantly to the way contemporary audiences experience the world of musical theater.

Mielziner's use of lighting to facilitate smooth, cinematic transitions inspired a wave of designers. William and Jean Eckart matched this fluidity with scenic innovations used to facilitate beautifully choreographed set changes. The designers of such musicals as *The Golden Apple* (1954; the first musical to move from Off Broadway to Broadway), *She Loves Me* (1963), *Anyone Can Whistle* (1964), *Flora the Red Menace* (1965), and *Mame* (1966), the Eckarts remain noteworthy for both their technological advancements and their minimalist aesthetic. Eckart designs were highly stylized, often deriving from symbol-laden modern art. The team introduced a winch-driven device that used hidden tracks to guide set pieces silently into place. They also developed a system for flying in set pieces, or mini-drops, which could drastically change the scenic picture while occupying little space when not in use. Laying the foundation for John Napier's design of *Les Misérables*, the Eckarts developed a system of often overlapping and concentrically revolving turntables. The lengthy breaks in performance required for Joseph Urban's spectacular sets for Ziegfeld were a thing of the past.[21]

The Eckarts and Mielziner contributed to the pendulum swing toward abstraction using color and light to replace the "razzle dazzle" of the earliest musicals, and their work prompted some designers to specialize in lighting for the first time. In the past, even the most intricate use of lights fell under the auspices of the designer of scenery or resident electricians. Lighting pioneers such as Abe Feder (1909–97) and Jean Rosenthal (1912–69) struck out on their own to establish lighting design as an independent craft. Rosenthal is most often credited with the earliest great achievements in lighting design for musical theater. Following an early start working under Orson Welles and John Houseman in the Federal Theatre Project, Rosenthal served as dancer/choreographer Martha Graham's lighting and production supervisor. This early experience illuminating dance prompted Rosenthal to experiment with the communication of mood through light, independent of the space in which it is perceived. Her experiments with light culminated in the 1950s and 1960s with the groundbreaking design collaborations for *West Side Story* (1957), *The Sound of Music* (1959), *Fiddler on the Roof* (1964), and *Cabaret* (1966), traversing the pendulum swing in design trends from spare to decorous once again.[22]

A RETURN TO OPULENCE

The New Stagecraft left a permanent mark on the design aesthetic of the American musical, but as technology advanced, the opportunities and demand for the grandiosity of yesteryear increased accordingly. Following World War II, a renewed artistic interest in spectacle through scenic and costume design emerged. The original production of *My Fair Lady* (1956) embodied this phenomenon, with lighting by Abe Feder, scenery design by Oliver Smith (1918–94), and costumes by Cecil Beaton (1904–80). As with lighting designer Jean Rosenthal, Smith found inspiration for his scenery designs in dance, working throughout his career with the American Ballet Theatre and frequently collaborating with Jerome Robbins. Smith, like the Eckarts, emphasized the graceful choreography of set changes, favoring quick and unobtrusive transitions. His aesthetic combined painting and sculpture, and Smith firmly believed that scenery for musical theater should be bright and entertaining in and of itself. Beaton's costumes for *My Fair Lady* contributed to a pivotal moment in musical theater history. In a brief return to spectacle for spectacle's sake, the scene at Ascot showcased Beaton's neo-romantic designs, placing ladies of the highest fashion on display in a manner unseen since the Ziegfeld *Follies* (◉ Example 21.15).

While the pendulum remained within the realm of extravagance, the influence of the New Stagecraft continued to be felt in terms of atmosphere, powerful simplicity, and metaphor, all of which were taken to new heights by scenic designer Boris Aronson (1898–1980). Aronson offered strong, clear, and ultimately simple design concepts while making full, expert use of available production values. Born in Kiev and with work experience in Russia and Germany, he designed a number of notable Broadway plays, from Clifford Odets's *Awake and Sing* to Arthur Miller's *The Crucible*. His greatest contributions, however, came in the conceptually driven designs for musical theater throughout the 1960s and 1970s including *Fiddler on the Roof* (1964), *Cabaret* (1966), and four of the Sondheim-Prince collaborations: *Company* (1970), *Follies* (1971), *A Little Night Music* (1975), and *Pacific Overtures* (1976). The early influence of the constructivist aesthetic popular in Eastern Europe during Aronson's youth is apparent throughout his work. Constructivist principles called for strictly functional scenery, often with exposed scaffolding, ladders, and multiple levels that contributed to a kind of celebration of machinery. Aronson employed such techniques to expose cold isolation within the mechanized frenzy of Manhattan society in his design for *Company*, which used steel and Plexiglas to create skeletal apartments complete with a functional elevator timed precisely to match the longest held chord in the musical's opening number.

Aronson's greatest achievements occurred through experimentation with form. One example is the primary drop he designed for the original production of *Pacific Overtures*, which portrays—from the Japanese perspective—the American Commodore Matthew Perry's opening of the island nation. Aronson ran a fine traditional Japanese print through a color-saturated Xerox copier (all the rage in the United States in the late 1970s). Combining the distorted delicacy of the print with tie-dyed fabric, which itself suggested a recent era of change in the United States, Aronson's set communicated, through what his audience saw, the show's central cultural clash. While Aronson also proved himself a master of lavish design, simulating the Ziegfeld era for his Loveland sets in *Follies*, this was not what separated him from other designers of musical theater. Rather, through his clear presentation of an essential concept, Aronson served as a powerful influence on the new generation of scenic artists.[23]

A Renewed Simplicity

Aronson's work prompted designers to reexamine the contribution of individual visual elements to the story. Designers of the 1970s taking this approach engendered a renewed simplicity that echoed the earliest years of the New Stagecraft. Over his extensive Broadway career, scenic designer Robin Wagner, like Aronson, proved himself capable of both minimalist and lavish designs, contributing the original designs to *Hair* (1977), *42nd Street* (1980), *Dreamgirls* (1987), *City of Angels* (1989), *Crazy for You* (1992), *Side Show* (1997), *The Producers* (2001), and many others. His design for *A Chorus Line* (1975) captures this shift in aesthetic toward powerful simplicity. Collaborating with Michael Bennett, Wagner distilled initial ideas for an expansive and detailed set to the famous black box with a mirror and a line. Aronson had effectively used a mirror in his set for *Cabaret* (1966), and Wagner similarly employed the device to implicate the audience, at the same time serving the practical purpose of evoking a dance studio setting. The famous line, the solitary stage ornament, became the visual focus of the production, with each character's motivation and fate balanced precariously upon it. Powerfully menacing through its simplicity, the line became the spectacle (⊙ Example 21.16).[24]

A Chorus Line also brought radical innovation in lighting from pioneer Tharon Musser (1925–2009), who introduced an entirely computerized lighting system to Broadway for the first time, marking an important shift away from slower, less consistent, manually operated "piano boards." From her Broadway debut with the mood and atmosphere-driven nonmusical play A Long Day's Journey into Night (1956), she meticulously researched the light quality of inspirational sources such as paintings and photographs; indeed, Musser insisted that she "painted with light." Musser collaborated with the Eckarts on Mame (1966) and with Boris Aronson on Follies (1971), A Little Night Music (1973), and Pacific Overtures (1976), in addition to her further work with Wagner on 42nd Street (1980).

CHANDELIERS AND HELICOPTERS: A SPECTACULAR BRITISH INVASION

While audiences grew accustomed to decoding deceivingly simple conceptual designs by the end of the 1970s, the following decade brought another drastic change in design. The "British invasion" of musical theater also brought an epic, and costly, scope in design to Broadway, reflecting the consumerism that dominated the 1980s. John Napier's set designs for Cats (1982), Starlight Express (1987), Les Misérables (1987), Miss Saigon (1991), and Sunset Boulevard (1994) each centered on a central scenic element and then expanded to fill the rest of the space with a feast for the audience's eyes. A combination of glitz and practicality, Napier's sets employed the latest scenic innovations to dazzle his audiences while suiting the needs of the musical. For Les Misérables, Napier began with what he deemed "the centre of the play's biggest moment": the barricade. Comprising objects that could be used as properties by the actors, the barricade was part of a revolving set (echoing the innovations of Eckarts) and was designed to detach into separate levels. Like early scenic designers who also coordinated lights to achieve their artistic visions, a number of set designers for the elaborate musicals of the 1980s and early 1990s also designed costumes. Napier designed sets and costumes for Starlight Express and Cats, while Maria Björnson designed both costumes and sets for The Phantom of the Opera (1988). Björnson, in particular, left a lasting imprint on spectacle through the famous rising—and of course, falling—chandelier, and the visually stunning costumes for the masquerade ball that opens the second act. Her design represented a hybrid less of practicality and innovation (like Napier's) than of spectacle and atmosphere, recalling the work of Jo Mielziner.[25]

During this period of dazzling spectacle, the scenic environment itself began to change. Often in the hands of Eugene Lee (1939–), who designed musicals well into the twenty-first century, the entire theater was adapted to provide audiences with a carefully conceived experience from the moment they walked through the door. This development also provided ample space and opportunities to sell memorabilia, both providing additional revenue and enhancing mass visibility of Broadway musicals. Even as perceptions of spectacle were to shift again, this total theater experience carried over into the musicals of the twenty-first century.

An Aesthetic Backlash and Hybrid Designs: Musical Theater Today

In 1996, Jonathan Larson's *Rent* represented an aesthetic backlash against the illusory extravagance of the Lloyd Webber and Boublil-Schönberg musicals that preceded it on Broadway. *Rent* was not unique in its rejection of massive spectacle—witness the simple, actor-driven unit set of Lynn Ahrens and Stephen Flaherty's Caribbean fable, *Once on This Island* (1989)—but it represented the greatest critical and commercial success of this new era of design. With echoes of Aronson's constructivist influence, Paul Clay's scenery consisted of multiple levels of pipes and city grates, establishing locales only through introducing props and set pieces. Through this means as well as exposed lighting instruments, Clay visually refused to let audience members retreat fully into the world presented to them—a design well suited to the presentational style of the show (⊙ Example 21.17; ⊙ Example 21.18). This kind of *verfremdungeffekt* (alienation effect), perhaps modeled on the designs of longtime-Brecht collaborator, Caspar Neher, altered the aesthetic of Broadway musicals after *Rent*. *Urinetown* (2001) and *Spring Awakening* (2006) similarly fight illusion through their alienating set designs and deliberately harsh lighting. Even the production design of the puppet-driven *Avenue Q* (2003) follows this trend of stylization and comparative simplicity.

While production design was pared down to place the emphasis of spectacle on the performers themselves, spectacle through lush design clung tenaciously to the Broadway musicals at the turn of the twenty-first century. As a corporation, Disney Theatricals, like Ziegfeld one hundred years earlier, has invested heavily in an assumption that audiences come to a Broadway musical to be dazzled. Beginning with *Beauty and the Beast* (1994), Disney Theatricals has brought several of its most successful animated film musicals to the stage, recreating effects of animation through stage spectacle. The corporation took a huge but ultimately highly lucrative risk when it hired avant-garde director-designer Julie Taymor for *The Lion King* (1997; ⊙ Example 21.19; ⊙ Example 21.20). Conveying influences of time she spent in Asia and parts of Africa, Taymor's designs were far from illusory, determinedly resisting "fuzzy animal costumes" and instead showcasing the (human) actor as much as the highly stylized costume and mask he or she wore. Richard Hudson's scenery and Donald Holder's lights complemented this aesthetic approach, creating painterly effects that further distanced the New York audiences from the African Serengeti. Despite the artistic and financial success of *The Lion King*, most of the previously animated Disney stage musicals that followed—*Aida* (2000), *Tarzan* (2006), and *The Little Mermaid* (2008)—returned to the kind of spectacular and semi-illusory effects popular during the 1980s. This trend culminated in the hiring of a "magic/illusion designer," Joe Eddie Fairchild, for *The Little Mermaid*.[26]

Perhaps because audiences today have been conditioned to expect both highly conceptual and elaborately designed productions, only a few individuals have proven themselves as cross-over artists à la Aronson. Eugene Lee mixes core conceptual elements with the grandiosity of design. With a career of theatrical design including the 1974 revival of *Candide*, *Sweeney Todd* (1979), *Merrily We Roll Along* (1981), *Ragtime* (1998), and *Wicked* (2003), Lee's sets are large, include moving parts, and tend to sweep into the area conventionally belonging to the audience. Nodding to the grandiose sets common when he launched his career, Lee's sets range from simple, bare, and abstract to elaborate, detailed, and realistic, sometimes within the same production (as for *Ragtime*).

Designers today often visually acknowledge their predecessors, to the delight of knowledgeable theater audiences. A quarter century after his minimalist design for *A Chorus Line*, Robin Wagner's lavish design for *The Producers* (2001) included notable tributes to both Ziegfeld's designers and Aronson. Thus, "Along Came Bialy" clearly echoes the doily-esque valentine of Aronson's set for Loveland in *Follies*, whereas the costume design for "Springtime for Hitler" offers scantily clad women costumed as if in the *Follies*, complete with massive head pieces in the shape of Bavarian pretzels and sausages that would have pleased (or perhaps insulted) not only John Harkrider, but also such inspired descendents as Busby Berkeley and Carmen Miranda. Whether such tributes are overt or subconscious, they display the chain of influence in design that forms the backbone of the history of musical theater, a history which, in turn, reflects the changing world in which performances take place. With the pendulum of design trends poised to swing again, one may look to the gravitational pull of popular tastes and the economic climate to predict the designs of the future, yet such predictions cannot encompass the spirit of theatrical innovation that has always propelled the pendulum itself.[27]

NOTES

1. Fred Ebb, Bob Fosse, and John Kander, *Chicago: A Musical Vaudeville* (New York: Samuel French, 1976), p. 75.

2. James Lapine and Stephen Sondheim, *Sunday in the Park with George* (New York: Applause Theatre Book Publishers, 1991), p. 38.

3. The American Theatre Wing offers readily accessible information on these and related topics through online seminars and interviews with contemporary designers, directors, actors, and producers. See http://americantheatrewing.org/wit ("Working in the Theatre") and http://americantheatrewing.org/downstagecenter ("Downstage Center"), accessed September 8, 2009.

4. George C. Izenour, *Theater Technology*, 2nd ed. (New Haven, CT: Yale University Press, 1997).

5. For more on Georg II's use of scenery, costumes, and lighting, see Ann Marie Koller, *The Theater Duke: Georg II of Saxe-Meiningen and the German Stage* (Stanford, CA: Stanford University Press, 1984), pp. 85–113.

6. See George R. Kernodle, "Wagner, Appia, and the Idea of Musical Design" (*Educational Theatre Journal* 6.3 [October, 1954]: 223–30).

7. Here, the innovator was impresario Richard D'Oyly Carte, whose Savoy Theatre in London opened in 1881 with Gilbert and Sullivan's *Patience*, becoming the first theater to be lit entirely by electricity. His focus, however, was more on safety and comfort than on enhancing potential for innovative stage design.

8. For an overview of Appia's career, see Richard C. Beacham, *Adolphe Appia: Artist and Visionary of the Modern Theatre* (Philadelphia: Routledge, 1994).

9. See Edward Gordon Craig, *On the Art of the Theatre* (New York: Theatre Arts Books, 1956).

10. For a close examination of Craig's aesthetic and career, see Christopher Innes, *Edward Gordon Craig: A Vision of Theatre* (Amsterdam: Routledge, 1998).

11. For more on this production, see Richard Leppert, "The Civilizing Process: Music and the Aesthetics of Time-Space Relations in *The Girl of the Golden West*," in *Musical Meaning and Human Values*, ed. Keith Chapin and Lawrence Kramer (New York: Fordham University Press, 2009, 116–49).

12. David Belasco, *The Theatre through Its Stage Door* (Whitefish, MT: Kessinger, 2006), p. 56.

13. For more on this production, see Leigh George Odom, "'The Black Crook' at Niblo's Garden" (*Drama Review: TDR* 26.1 [Spring 1982]: 21–40).

14. For more on Thompson and her English Blondes, see Kristen Pullen, *Actresses and Whores: On Stage and in Society* (Cambridge: Cambridge University Press, 2005), and Faye E. Dudden, *Women in the American Theatre: Actresses and Audiences 1790–1870* (New Haven, CT: Yale University Press, 1994).

15. The myriad resources concerning Ziegfeld and his Follies include Randolph Carter, *The World of Flo Ziegfeld* (New York: Praeger, 1974); Marjorie Farnsworth, *The Ziegfeld Follies* (New York: G. P. Putnam's Sons, 1956); Richard and Paulette Ziegfeld, *The Ziegfeld Touch: The Life and Times of Florenz Ziegfeld, Jr.* (New York: Harry N. Abrams, 1993); and Linda Mizejewski, *Ziegfeld Girl: Image and Icon in Culture and Cinema* (Durham, NC: Duke University Press, 1999).

16. This swing was in sharp contrast to the increasing grandiosity of Hollywood movie musicals during this period, particularly those of Busby Berkeley, which flourished throughout the 1930s. While Hollywood offered distraction and escape from the economic reality of the Depression era through spectacular sets and elaborately costumed production numbers, Broadway reflected the changing experience of its patrons through comparatively stark designs.

17. For an overview of the New Stagecraft movement, tracing its origins in Appia's work and its legacy, see Orville Kurth Larson, *Scene Design in the American Theatre From 1915 to 1960* (Fayetteville: University of Arkansas Press, 1989).

18. See Jones's manifesto on the theater: Robert Edmond Jones, *The Dramatic Imagination* (New York: Duell, Sloan, and Pearce, 1941).

19. Tim Carter, *Oklahoma! The Making of an American Musical* (New Haven, CT: Yale University Press, 2007).

20. The breadth of Mielziner's work is addressed in Mary Henderson, *Mielziner: Master of Modern Stage Design* (New York: Back Stage Books, 2001).

21. For more on the Eckarts, see Andrew B. Harris, *The Performing Set: The Broadway Designs of William and Jean Eckart* (Denton: University of North Texas Press, 2006).

22. For more on Rosenthal's career and aesthetic, see Jean Rosenthal and Lael Wertenbaker, *The Magic of Light: The Craft and Career of Jean Rosenthal, Pioneer in Lighting for the Modern Stage* (Boston: Little, Brown, 1972).

23. For a comprehensive and lushly illustrated treatment of Aronson's career, see Frank Rich and Lisa Aronson, *The Theatre Art of Boris Aronson* (New York: Alfred A. Knopf, 1987).

24. For more on Wagner's career, as well as other influential scenic designers, see Arnold Aronson, *American Set Design* (New York: Theatre Communications Group, 1985), pp. 153–67 for Wagner; and Ronn Smith, *American Set Design 2* (New York: Theatre Communications Group, 1991).

25. For an overview of design trends within the "British Invasion," see John Goodwin, ed., *British Theatre Design: The Modern Age* (New York: St. Martin's Press, 1989).

26. The use of such a designer is not entirely new, as Roy Benson had served as the "designer and supervisor of magic and illusion" for *Carnival!* (1961), which features a love triangle involving a magician.

27. For additional essays on scenography and developments in design, see Arnold Aronson, *Looking in the Abyss: Essays on Scenography* (Ann Arbor: University of Michigan Press, 2005), and Christopher Baugh, *Theatre, Performance, and Technology: The Development of Scenography in the Twentieth Century* (New York: Palgrave Macmillan, 2005).

CHAPTER 22

ACTING

JOHN M. CLUM

ANDREA Most has written that "the musical comedy is a celebration of acting, and particularly of American acting."[1] This statement raises a number of questions. How do you define and evaluate acting in musical theater? Lyricist Lynn Ahrens (*Ragtime*, *Seussical*) wrote of the casting process for *The Glorious Ones*, a musical she co-wrote: "What mattered most to us in casting each role was how well the actor could act, how well he or she embodied the role and whether or not the actor understood the specific world we were trying to create."[2] I am sure that Ahrens assumed that the candidates for her cast had the voices and training to sing the songs she and composer Stephen Flaherty wrote for the musical. Given that, she could be choosy about their acting abilities. Ahrens's criteria may hold for a number of contemporary musicals and major revivals of past classics, such as the 2008 revivals of *Gypsy* (1959: book, Arthur Laurents; music, Jule Styne; lyrics, Stephen Sondheim) and *South Pacific* (1949: book, Oscar Hammerstein II and Joshua Logan; music, Richard Rodgers; lyrics, Oscar Hammerstein II), but the same criteria do not apply to recent rock musicals such as *Spring Awakening* (2006: book and lyrics, Steven Sater; music Duncan Sheik) or *Passing Strange* (2008: book and lyrics, Stew; music, Stew and Heidi Rodewald) which rethink (in the case of the former) or defy (in the case of the latter) the usual conventions of musical theater regarding continuity of character between dialogue and song and the relevance of realistic acting to a rock musical. Nor were Ahrens's criteria for casting relevant to the producers, directors, and performers of Golden Age musical comedy who put "star turns" before characterization. Notions of acting, then, have to be considered in terms of the history of musical theater and the various subgenres that fall under the name "musical." Furthermore, discussions of theories of acting are inextricably linked with historically inflected concepts of character. In the musical, more than in "straight drama," these discussions also connect to the relationship between character and actor and the contrast between *acting* and *performing*.

Very little has been written directly on the subject of acting in musical theater. The only comprehensive textbook on the subject, Joe Dear and Rocco Dal Vera's *Acting in Musical Theatre: A Comprehensive Course*, underscores the subordinate position acting has had in the training of performers for the musical stage. *Acting in Musical Theatre* begins with basic Stanislavskian concepts of acting, though it is careful to delineate the differences between acting in musicals and "straight plays." The authors discuss key concepts, such as the importance of understanding a character's moment-by-moment objectives and her overall character objective and the obstacles that deter the character from reaching her objective. At the same time, the authors understand that the basic concepts of realistic acting will take the actor in musical theater only so far. They emphasize that "musicals operate on a heightened dramatic scale.... [T]he feelings will be large enough when it feels like life or death for your character" (Dear and Dal Vera, 44). This maxim suggests that acting in musicals needs to be set at a higher emotional pitch than in a play. Even so, there is always a difference in intensity between speech and song. The actor's task is to make both the dialogue and musical numbers real for the audience by finding a balance of scale between dialogue and song. This is a challenge in musical theater because singing requires a different level of physical energy than acting. For there to be a convincing transition between singing and acting of dialogue, the acting must have a different energy than that usually required for spoken theater.

The authors of the textbook also point out that unlike characters in realistic drama, "the characters in musicals...respond to adversity by becoming extraordinarily articulate" (Dear and Dal Vera, 76). Characters in musicals, in other words, tend to sing their subtext. Feelings or motivations may be hidden from other characters onstage but seldom from the audience. The imaginary fourth wall of realistic drama seldom exists in musicals. Characters take the audience into their confidence, which gives them a stronger rapport with those on the other side of the footlights. However, this articulateness is usually in the songs, not the book, for the dialogue of musicals is often far more condensed than that of a play. As actress Joan Copeland, a veteran of many musicals, notes: "In a way, you have to capsulize the characters more in a musical than in a straight play. You have to get to the character more quickly and precisely. You have far less dialogue to establish and develop the character."[3] Most of Dear and Dal Vera's textbook focuses, as it must, on how basic principles of acting are used to sing.

Acting in musical theater has a variety of meanings. It can mean, as we have seen, creating a believable character through speech and song, a criterion that is relevant only if character believability is a goal of the creators of the musical. It can mean the interpretation of the "book scenes" as opposed to "performing" the musical numbers. It can also mean interpreting a song so that it fits character and situation, which is sometimes difficult even in a character-driven musical by someone like Stephen Sondheim. For instance, do the same criteria of performance apply to *Sweeney Todd*'s (1978: book, Hugh Wheeler; music and lyrics, Stephen Sondheim) "Epiphany," a quasi-operatic mad scene that defines Sweeney Todd's state of mind as he madly resolves to expand his list of victims from Judge Turpin to anyone who sits in his barber chair, and "A Little Priest," the ensuing clever patter song that seems totally "out of character" for the demented man who just roared through "Epiphany"? The challenge for any singing actor who takes seriously playing the role of Sweeney is to find a way of playing his character so that it justifies both songs. But we're talking here about a musical created by artists for whom character was paramount and that demands excellent singing actors. The very term I use, "singing actor," is problematic, for it implies that acting in a musical is more important than singing. Perhaps the term should be "acting singer." In opera nowadays, we expect excellent singers who can also act. The criteria for musicals are actually the same. The singing style may be different, but we expect good singers who are also good actors. Unless one is totally inexperienced at acting, most of the challenge of acting in a musical comes through the singing, not through speaking the lines.

Like most acting texts, Dear and Dal Vera's is most interested in helping performers be *believable* as characters in a musical. However, the issue of believability in a musical raises even more questions. In his book, *The Musical as Drama*, Scott McMillin celebrates the unreality of musical theater performance and suggests that our conventional criteria of "acting" are inappropriate in discussing musicals:

> We do not think of real people while we watch the performance. We think of performance people, people who can sing and dance, numbers people. Chekhov and Shakespeare characters are performance people too, but the song-and-dance performance is not the same as the Chekhov or Shakespeare performance. If a suspension of disbelief occurs when we watch characters in a Chekhov play, it occurs twice when we watch characters from the book scenes of a musical open themselves into musical performance in the numbers. They are changed by the music.[4]

Are the characters in a musical really "changed by the music"? They are certainly most alive and often most convincing when they are singing. Yet the intensity of those musical moments is stronger when they are contrasted with spoken dialogue. Nonetheless, McMillin is correct in seeing that audiences enjoy the various disparities in a musical. Andrea Most has noted that the musical is more Brechtian (self-consciously performative) than realistic:

> Musical comedy is distinctly *not* realist, and the advent of a musical number—the switch in theatrical modes [from speaking to singing]—does, like Brecht's alienation effect, remind the audience that they are in a theater. But this reminder does not create the alienation effect Brecht describes. Quite the opposite. We might call the result of the separation of elements in a musical an *assimilation effect*. (Most, 9)

Both Andrea Most and Scott McMillin emphasize the paradox of disparity and unity in a musical that makes believability for an actor a challenge. Scott McMillin was also correct in seeing that a discussion of acting in musicals cannot be separated from questions about the very nature of this hybrid art form.

In the history of musical theater, acting was not always a primary concern. In the 1920s and 1930s *musical comedy* meant just that—a genre in which the book was not particularly important, and credible integration of musical number and dramatic situation was not a concern for creators or audience. Stars of musical comedy, as the generic term implies, were either singers (such as Ethel Merman), or comedians who could sing competently (such as Bob Hope, who quickly moved to Hollywood after appearing in a few musical hits in the 1930s) or who couldn't sing at all (such as Victor Moore, who moved back and forth between Broadway and Hollywood in the 1930s). Traditional musical comedy was a hybrid performed by specialists. The chorus was split into singers and dancers. Comics didn't have to be very good singers. Big-voiced singers weren't expected to be great actors. Dancers such as Fred and Adele Astaire did specialty numbers. The baritone who sang the big ballads wasn't expected to have comic timing. Serious actors usually avoided the musical entirely since there was enough serious drama on Broadway to keep them busy. Singers with legitimate voices weren't expected to belt. Operetta, extremely popular in the 1920s, was built on stock characters: the exotic romantic leading soprano and baritone, the comic mezzo and bass, the wistful tenor, and the perky soubrette. These same characters appeared again and again in different settings and costumes. Acting was definitely secondary to quasi-operatic singing. The work we consider the first great "serious" American musical, *Show Boat* (1927: book and lyrics, Oscar Hammerstein II; music, Jerome Kern), combined the conventions of 1920s musical comedy and operetta. The book was by Hammerstein, who had before then been associated with operettas. Magnolia and Gaylord were played by "legit" singers, for the most part performing scenes that could have been out of operetta until Magnolia starts jazzing it up a bit in the middle of the second act. Julie, originally played by Helen Morgan, got the torch numbers, though they are written to be sung with a real, quasi-operatic voice—the belt voice had not yet moved from vaudeville houses and nightclubs into the legitimate theater (which it would do with Ethel Merman in 1930). The older comic characters, Andy and Parthy, don't sing much. In revivals over the years, Captain Andy has become a plum role for an aging comic, the sort of performer who used to be the centerpiece of musical comedy. The song-and-dance team is given specialty numbers. The older black characters, Queenie and Joe, demand more musical versatility, though Queenie, Joe, and mixed-race Julie are doing sophisticated versions of the sort of blackface numbers ("coon songs" as they were called) that had been around since the minstrel show. There are no great acting challenges in *Show Boat*—no one in 1927 assumed that musical comedy performers would be particularly strong actors.

Show Boat is important because it combined musical comedy and operetta to create something more "serious," more character-driven, but for a dozen years after its premiere in 1927, the dominant form of musical would still be the traditional musical comedy driven by star comics (Eddie Cantor, Jimmie Durante, Ed Wynn), who usually had a fixed persona developed in vaudeville, burlesque, and revue. Audiences expected to see that persona, which meant that book writers had to create plots and "characters" built on the pre-packaged characteristics of their stars. Other roles were also types in which performers specialized: the ingénue, the romantic leading man, and so on. A singing star such as Ethel Merman was expected to sing and wisecrack with the comics, which she did in a succession of musicals in the 1930s and early 1940s. Often the book did not provide any consistency of character.

Take for instance, one of the most revived shows of the period (albeit with rewritten dialogue), *Anything Goes* (1934: book, Guy Bolton, P. G. Wodehouse, Howard Lindsay, Russel Crouse; music and lyrics, Cole Porter). The most richly "dramatic" song in the show is the one Reno Sweeney (originally played by Ethel Merman) sings at the opening, "I Get a Kick Out of You," a brilliantly written ballad about unrequited love. Here is a song that cries out for a performer who can act a song as well as sing it, the bored woman of the world who only comes alive at the sight of her beloved's "fabulous face." The lyric specifies the social milieu in which this woman lives and the argot of her world. The problem is that the character the song defines isn't the wisecracking nightclub chanteuse turned evangelist who sings the song. Exactly who owns the "fabulous face" she sings about? Certainly none of the leading men in the original cast had one. When Patti LuPone's leading man is the handsome Howard McGillin (in the 1988 revival) or Elaine Page and Sally Anne Triplett are paired with John Barrowman (in the 1989 and 2005 London revivals) one can think for a moment that Reno pines for her Billy Crocker. However, nothing in the dialogue suggests that is the case. Their duet, "You're the Top," is hardly "You Are Love." Reno ends up with the comic toff—clearly she isn't the romantic lead—and Billy gets the vapid ingénue he has chased throughout the show.

"I Get a Kick Out of You" is thus just a good song inserted into the musical with no character motivation. "Acting" the specifics of this song works against acting the character who sings it. Because *Anything Goes* is constructed as a farce rather than a romantic comedy, feelings and motivation don't matter much. Billy gets the love ballads and no one thought of Ethel Merman as the appropriate object of "Easy to Love." The general problem, then, for thinking about acting in traditional musical comedies of this period is that the songs are self-contained and often have little relationship to the characters who sing them or the overall action of the musical. Indeed, the same could be said of a musical hit like *Phantom of the Opera.* Do the songs of the Phantom, Raoul, or Christine really tell us anything about the specifics of their characters or situation?

No one thought of Ethel Merman, the original singer of "I Get a Kick Out of You," as a great actress. In fact, Merman personifies the problems of discussing acting in musicals. She was famous for facing the audience rather than her partner during dialogue scenes. Fernando Lamas, her leading man in *Happy Hunting* (1956: book, Howard Lindsay and Russel Crouse; music, Harold Karr; lyrics, Matt Dubey), famously asked, "Am I going to read my lines to Miss Merman and Miss Merman read hers to the audience?" The answer, of course, was "Yes." One can even see that trait in some of her film work, which may be one reason she did not become a big Hollywood star. Merman "performed" during both book and musical numbers. Playing a teenaged country girl like Annie Oakley in *Annie Get Your Gun* (1946: book, Herbert and Dorothy Fields; music and lyrics, Irving Berlin) was going to be a stretch for her in the best of circumstances, even more so in the 1966 revival when she was decidedly middle-aged, but Merman knew people went to see *her*, not Annie

Oakley, and certainly not anyone else on stage with her. She could belt wisecracks with the same energy and efficiency that she belted her big numbers, but since no one cared about writing a coherent character for her, at least until *Annie Get Your Gun*, there was no need for her to study acting. She was a singer who occasionally said lines. Merman was a great success in *Annie Get Your Gun*, which she played for over 1,000 performances, but part of the frisson of the show was the disjuncture between the performer and the teenage country girl she played.

When Merman triumphed as Madame Rose in *Gypsy* (1959: book, Arthur Laurents; music, Jule Styne; lyrics, Stephen Sondheim), some of her advocates thought she had suddenly become an actress. What really happened was that for the first time she was given a three-dimensional character to play that perfectly fit her personality and hard-driving musical style. Her Rose wasn't as madly driven and unhappy as Tyne Daly's (1989: who acted the role better than she sang it) or as multifaceted as the Roses of Angela Lansbury (London, 1973; Broadway, 1974) or Patti LuPone (2008), who were able to make Rose in turns sexy, funny, manic, and sad. Lansbury and LuPone—and Betty Buckley (Paper Mill Playhouse, 1998) and Bernadette Peters (2003)—under the leadership of directors who saw the musical as character-driven (the original director, Jerome Robbins, saw it as director- and star-driven) made acting both dialogue and songs the most important aspect of *Gypsy*, which has become the musical version of an operatic vehicle, like *Tosca*—a classic aficionados go to see again and again because they want to see what different great performers will do with its central role.

Hearing Ethel Merman sing "Everything's Coming Up Roses," a perfect belt number for the veteran diva, one was witnessing a singing style that already was passé. Pop music by the late 1950s had moved either to the mellower sound of male and female crooners or the sound of '50s rock. Within a few years, Broadway singers would be wearing wireless microphones. Belters were part of old Broadway, which was to go through a period of experimentation before resolving its split with pop and rock music. Merman could make the moment frightening because the sheer power of her voice, combined with the drive of the Styne-Sondheim song, made the song seem like the utterance of an indomitable will, but was that drive for self-assertion Rose's or Merman's? I don't remember specific details of the original production, but photographs show Rose singing the song as a solo while Herbie and Louise clutch each other in the background. Merman, as usual, did her thing on stage with everyone else in the background. Was this an acting choice or Merman's usual modus operandi? Singers who "act" the song as well as sing it often play more on its irony and its relationship to Louise. Tyne Daly stood apart, as Merman did, but hit herself on "Roses" as if it were "Rose's," thus making the song say something about the driving ego of the character who sang it: everything would come up Rose's way. Patti LuPone's Rose grabs onto Louise as if trying to imbue her with some of Rose's tawdry vision of show business success. The sad thing about Madame Rose is not that she is a stage mother driving her daughters to realize her own ambition but that her dreams are so limited. Vaudeville is dead and burlesque is dying; in response, Rose moves away from Los Angeles, not toward it! In a way, with all her limitations,

Merman was perfectly cast to play this character, not because of her acting ability, but because she fit the original conception of the character. She, too, was a representative of a different era of show business. It is no surprise that *Gypsy* was the last musical she originated and one of the last musicals we consider classics.

The star power of Ethel Merman raises other issues about character and actor in musical theater. Audiences went to see Ethel Merman. Did they ever forget that it was Merman, not the character she played, that they were watching and hearing? In her book *Making Americans: Jews and the Broadway Musical*, Andrea Most defines two styles of acting in musicals: what she calls "the performative" and "the psychological." In the former style, "The theatrical characters, comfortable with performance, have control over their self definition. Their singing and dancing styles, their costumes, and their modes of behavior both determine who they are and to which community they belong. They are self-conscious about performance, acknowledging that they are on stage and gleefully making full use of the conventions the stage allows them for self definition" (Most, 31). Ethel Merman would fit into this category, as would most stars of Broadway musicals from the 1920s to 1940 and, in some cases, beyond.

Even in the post–Rodgers and Hammerstein era, many hits were star vehicles that were performer- rather than character-driven. Sometimes these vehicles would show that a star had more versatility than audiences and critics expected. Dancer Gwen Verdon was a passable singer and comedienne who became a star by playing the comic sex-driven females in *Can Can* (1953) and *Damn Yankees* (1955). In her next outing, *New Girl in Town* (1957), a musical adaptation of Eugene O'Neill's *Anna Christie*, she demonstrated real talent as an actress. Nonetheless, the rest of her Broadway musical vehicles (*Redhead*, *Sweet Charity*, *Chicago*) took her back to her "type." Does one "act" Dolly Levi in *Hello, Dolly* (1963: Book by Michael Stewart, music and lyrics by Jerry Herman)? Does Carol Channing, the original Dolly, ever act? Like many musical stars before her, she adapts parts to fit her fixed persona. There is a long list of Dollys who followed Channing during the Broadway run, on tour and in London (Ginger Rogers, Mary Martin, Betty Grable, Phyllis Diller, Pearl Bailey, Yvonne DeCarlo, Ethel Merman, among others, plus a miscast Barbra Streisand in the elephantine film). Most of these replacements for Carol Channing were established stars with identifiable personae rather than actresses. Star turns were popular as long as there were stars.

Nonetheless, different demands were made on performers to act, as specialties and character types combined and broke down when, around 1940, book writers became interested in characters rather than types. Here, what Most calls the psychological mode of performance came into play: "The psychologically defined characters, while more detailed and realistically drawn, have much less control over their identity. These characters have a consistent costume, accent, and gestural style that are fundamentally based on *who they are*. . . . These characters do not redefine themselves every time they sing; rather, the songs form a natural extension of the dialogue" (Most, 31). One could define Most's distinctions as between *performing*, based on the individual style of the performer, and *acting* a coherent character. Joey Evans

(*Pal Joey*, 1940: book by John O'Hara, music, Richard Rodgers; lyrics, Lorenz Hart) was not the first lead character who was a dancer as well as a singer (Junior in *On Your Toes* [1936: book, Richard Rodgers, Lorenz Hart, George Abbott; music, Rodgers; lyrics, Hart] made a star out of song and dance man, Ray Bolger), but Joey combined a number of types. He was at once the sexy leading man, like Antipholus in *The Boys from Syracuse* (1938: book, George Abbott; music, Richard Rodgers; lyrics, Lorenz Hart), and the comic con man William Gaxton played so often in musicals of the 1930s. Joey had to sing ballads and comic numbers, and perform jazzy song and dance routines. But Joey also had to be a loser who overreaches. Joey had complexity. Above all, because *Pal Joey* is a musical about sexually driven characters, Joey has to be sexy. It is no wonder the role sent its first incarnation, Gene Kelly, straight to MGM. Joey is a three-dimensional character in an art form where such depth had not appeared before. The same can be said of the complex, psychologically troubled career woman, Liza Elliott, in *Lady in the Dark* (1941: book, Moss Hart; music, Kurt Weill; lyrics, Ira Gershwin). More than most musicals, the experimental *Lady in the Dark* is written for an actress who can sing. The first half of each of the three acts is totally spoken. Legend has it that the original Liza, Gertrude Lawrence, was said to be a variable singer with pitch problems, though her recordings suggest that she was better than that (alas, there is no complete recording of the original production of *Lady in the Dark*). She was considered sui generis, charismatic, and a superb comic actress who moved back and forth between musicals and sophisticated comedies. For its time, *Lady in the Dark* was a hit, and Lawrence stayed through the entire run of a year and a half; producers considered her, like Ethel Merman, irreplaceable, but in a role that really did require a singing actress.

From the beginning of their collaboration in 1943, Rodgers and Hammerstein proudly dubbed their creations "musical plays." This separated their work from the musical comedies they knew well and had mastered separately in the decades before *Oklahoma*. The term "musical play" suggested that the material was to be more character-driven, which meant that more acting would be required of the performers than had been the case before then. Hammerstein had already shown in *Show Boat* that he wanted to create a hybrid of operetta and musical comedy. Now that hybrid would be merged with drama as Rodgers and Hammerstein created adaptations of works that had already appeared as straight plays (*Oklahoma!* was based on Lynn Riggs's folk drama, *Green Grow the Lilacs*, and *Carousel* was based on the Hungarian play *Liliom* by Ferenc Molnar, which appeared successfully on Broadway in 1932 and 1940, and had been adapted for film multiple times), serious films (*The King and I*, based on the book and 1946 film *Anna and the King of Siam*), or fiction (*South Pacific*, based on James Michener's *Tales of the South Pacific*). This involved a modification of previous fixed character types rather than a rejection of them. Laurey in *Oklahoma!* and Julie Jordan in *Carousel* are in some ways typical ingénue roles, sisters of Magnolia in *Show Boat*, but they are also individualized characters whose socioeconomic status is a driving force in their motivation. Ado Annie isn't much different from the man-hungry comic women of previous musical comedies, though she fits more convincingly into the social milieu the musical depicts.

Celeste Holm, the first Ado Annie, was more an actress than a singer. Though *Oklahoma!* is mistakenly thought by many to be the first musical in which character complexity is important and songs and narrative are truly integrated, there is only one role in the musical that demands serious acting—that of Jud Fry, played originally by Howard da Silva, a veteran of the Group Theatre. Clearly, the creators felt that this brooding character needed to be played by someone from a different theatrical background than Curly, Laurey, Ado Annie, and Will Parker.

Musicals that require what we conventionally call "acting" are seldom star vehicles. The original casts of the first two Rodgers and Hammerstein musicals contained no established stars. The role was to be more important than the person who played it. It was only in *South Pacific* and *The King and I* that Rodgers and Hammerstein, who now were producing as well as writing, felt the need to find a balance between character and star, although *South Pacific* ran for years after Mary Martin and Ezio Pinza left the cast and *The King and I*, at first a vehicle for the versatile, charismatic Gertrude Lawrence, has gone through several revivals in which her role has become secondary to the King, which is more an acting role than most musical leads. Both the roles of Nellie Forbush and Anna Leonowens demand more versatility than the usual type, and characterization beyond star persona. Clearly, as musicals became more character-driven than performer-driven, lead performers became more replaceable. Rodgers and Hammerstein's hits of the 1940s and 1950s could survive major cast changes in ways star vehicles could not. Ethel Merman's vehicles closed when she was tired of doing them: *Oklahoma!* and its successors went on for years with a succession of leads. Today, when musicals must last for years just to break even, the star vehicle of old is not economically feasible. Performers are now replaceable parts, asked to give more or less a reproduction of the performances of the original cast. What is being "acted" by a replacement has thus become an imitation of the performance of the original cast member. Star performers in Golden Age musicals were celebrated for their eccentricities, their inimitability. Acting singers in character-driven musicals are not allowed to stand out in the same way. Character comes before performer.

For a brief period in the 1950s and early 1960s, a series of successful musicals were built around leading actors who were at best passable singers (Yul Brynner in *The King and I*, Rex Harrison in *My Fair Lady*, Richard Burton in *Camelot*, Robert Preston in *The Music Man*). In the case of the two Lerner and Loewe musicals (actually, the leading role in their unsuccessful 1951 musical, *Paint Your Wagon*, was also written for an actor who could barely carry a tune), the nonsinging male lead supported the notion that these shows were more "serious" than their competition. One could also speculate that the creators thought that the leading men of contemporary musicals weren't good enough actors for the roles they had written. They wanted actors, not singers. Given the attitudes about gender in the 1950s, these older nonsingers who became mentors and lovers for younger women may have been considered more manly than their singing counterparts. As I write elsewhere, "If you want to be a [male] star in a musical, don't sing the ballads. That's sissy stuff."[5] The long-running 2001 London revival of *My Fair Lady* featured a succession of distinguished actors who could actually sing playing Henry Higgins (Jonathan Pryce, Alex Jennings, Anthony Andrews). As singers are now expected to be good actors, so actors are no longer above singing in musicals.

However honestly and effectively a performer acts the dialogue—in the 2008 revival of *South Pacific*, for instance—we come to hear the songs, and it is in the songs that the characters most come to life for us. After all, both the original creators of *South Pacific* and the director of the 2008 revival cast as their leading man opera singers who had no experience of acting dialogue, particularly dialogue in English. Like all good opera singers, however, Ezio Pinza and Paolo Szot (in the 2008 revival) know how to act a musical number. Daringly, *South Pacific* ends in a silent tableau, as a new family is forged. There is a lot of dialogue in the work, but it is in song or silence that characters reveal who they are and what they feel most deeply. Do we even remember the names of the nonsinging military men who take over the stage for much of act II? Nellie speaks of her racial prejudice but sings of her optimism and her love, which ultimately prevail. The woman behind me at the 2008 revival of *Gypsy* told me that she had come to "hear Patti LuPone sing those songs." She didn't say anything about her expectations of LuPone's acting of the dialogue. As I noted earlier, most of the acting challenge in a musical comes through singing, not speaking the lines. What we expect in a "musical play," then, is someone who can act the songs as well as sing them, someone who can present the songs as utterances of a specific character with specific objectives. Only then are music and spoken dialogue tied together in a meaningful way.

Our criteria for acting in musicals have been changed by the microphone. In the days before body and head mikes, a strong singing voice that could reach the back row of the largest Broadway house was essential. Expertise in naturalistic acting was less important. Many critics have decried what the microphone has done to singing in the musical, but few discuss its effect on dialogue. With the microphone, acting can be less mannered, more naturalistic. This also means that singers are concerned less about volume and more with interpretation. The quasi-operatic legitimate voice and the Merman-like belt voice are no longer necessary to reach the back rows of large Broadway theaters. As a result, there can be more seamless integration of dialogue and song. The trade-off is that musicals and performers lose some of their spontaneity when the sound is coming from speakers over and around the proscenium rather than from the singing actor's mouth. How "live" is theater without live sound?

Some contemporary rock-inflected musicals emphasize the difference between acting and performing the musical numbers. Michael Greif's original 1996 production of Jonathan Larson's *Rent* had the band on stage, minimal scenery, and a presentational style more like a rock concert than a conventional Broadway musical. In *Spring Awakening* (2006: music, Duncan Sheik; book and lyrics, Steven Sater), directed by Michael Mayer, a character developed in the dialogue pulls a microphone out of his pocket, even though he is wearing a head mike, and performs the song as if he were on *American Idol*. Mayer obviously wants to emphasize the disconnect between the show's source, the period drama written by Frank Wedekind, and the contemporary pop songs the characters sing. (Can't the audience hear this contrast without the visible presence of microphones?) *Spring Awakening* in effect has two styles: the "acting" style required by the book scenes and the rock performance style required by the songs. Mayer and his writing team are fighting the notion of "integration" championed by the advocates of Oscar Hammerstein and Stephen Sondheim (though the latter and his collaborators fought integration in many of their musicals). The performers in *Spring Awakening* need to be both actors and singers, though not simultaneously. Perhaps the kind of performance required by rock music works against a traditional concept of acting. Directors of rock musicals like *Rent* and *Spring Awakening* assume that audiences who are used to rock concerts expect a particular kind of performance associated with rock music.

In her book on rock musicals, Elizabeth Wollman notes that because the rock musical was created out of the desire to capture the sense of immediacy and authenticity, however artificial, of a rock concert, "staged rock musicals have always reflected an interest in finding ways to connect with audiences that are not typical of mainstream theater productions."[6] This may include creating the sense of an improvised performance with the band visible, or a different rapport with the audience than a conventional musical offers. This rapport isn't that different from the relative freedom offered a performer in a musical in the 1920s or 1930s. Rock musicals such as *Spring Awakening* support Scott McMillin's thesis that for all the talk of integration, the inescapable fact of any musical is the "incongruity between book and number" (McMillin, x). Most teachers of acting in musicals will encourage their pupils to reduce that incongruity in their performance.

The relative importance of acting in musicals, then, depends on the style of the show being performed. To a great extent, it depends on the style of the music the actors are required to sing. It is, after all, the songs that define the character and situation more than the dialogue.

NOTES

1. Andrea Most, *Making Americans: Jews and the Broadway Musical* (Cambridge, MA: Harvard University Press, 2004), p. 10.

2. Quoted in Joe Deer and Rocco Dal Vera, *Acting in Musical Theatre: A Comprehensive Course* (London: Routledge, 2008), p. xxii.

3. Dennis McGovern and Deborah Grace Winer, *Sing Out, Louise: 150 Stars of the Musical Theatre Remember 50 Years on Broadway* (New York: Schirmer Books, 1993), p. 51.

4. Scott McMillin, *The Musical as Drama* (Princeton, NJ: Princeton University Press, 2006), p. 59.

5. John Clum, *Something for the Boys: Musical Theater and Gay Culture* (New York: Palgrave, 1999), p. 128.

6. Elizabeth L. Wollman, *The Theatre Will Rock: A History of the Rock Musical from* Hair *to* Hedwig (Ann Arbor: University of Michigan Press, 2006), p. 70.

CHAPTER 23

SINGING

MITCHELL MORRIS
RAYMOND KNAPP

THE American musical, as compared to other theatrical genres that involve singing, such as opera and operetta, is extremely eclectic in its deployment of vocal types and song styles. Musicals not only offer the full range of classic "Broadway" types but may also include "quality" voices and operatic styles, derivatives from popular song, and a variety of comedic, specialty, and character-based vocal types whose entertainment value comes in some measure from vocal inadequacies of one kind or another. While this eclecticism may be understood in part as a legacy of vaudeville and other variety-based genres, it also stems from the musical's responsiveness to emergent popular styles, its penchant for pastiche, and its middlebrow aspirational profile, all of which have conspired to develop a steadily enriching mix of vocal possibilities. To do some justice to this wide range, we will here consider the basis of vocal production in the human body, delineate generally accepted typologies regarding voices and styles, and survey representative examples drawn from two shows especially rich in their deployment of distinctive song and voice types, *Kiss Me, Kate* and *Sweeney Todd*.

BODY TALK

Vocal production has been described in a number of ways, not all of which are commensurate. In the interest of establishing some common points of reference, this section briefly sets out some of the terms that seem most useful in describing singers and singing. This discussion is neither comprehensive nor exhaustive; rather, it establishes a few conceptual markers for the sake of further discussion.

The human vocal apparatus is a complex system involving a number of muscles and organs. The lower part of the system is the less intricate. The (thoracic) diaphragm, for instance, is a large muscle that forms a sheet supporting the chest and abdominal cavities. Above the diaphragm are the lungs and heart, below it the viscera. The diaphragm contracts to expand the lungs, creating inhalation. It expands to push air out of the lungs in exhalation (also assisted by the muscles of the abdominal wall). When vocal instructors speak of "support," they are primarily focused on control of the abdominal wall to better manage the controlled release of air necessary to speaking and singing. Support has a significant effect on singing technique, not only because consistent support helps establish a relatively homogenous sound but also because divergences from this homogeneity then acquire expressive meaning. An "unsupported" sound might strike the ears of listeners as wavering, uncertain, dubious, fragile; and it might be employed by a careful singer for dramatic effects. The lungs, in addition to their necessary functions in ventilation, also act as the reservoir for air that will be used to vocalize. Lung capacity is to some extent a matter of biology: men typically have larger lung capacity than women, taller people tend to have more than short people, those born and living at high altitudes usually have greater capacity than those born and living at sea level, and so on.

Moving from the lungs through the bronchial tubes, air enters the more complex areas of the larynx and the oral cavity. The larynx, composed of cartilage, muscle, and tendon, is an organ that guards the entrance to the trachea and sits just below the hyoid bone, above which lies the pharynx—the place where esophagus and trachea divide. Inside the larynx are the the vocal cords, also called the vocal folds, which produce pitch and manage volume. The folds themselves are a pair of mucous membranes that stretch across the interior of the larynx; they produce pitch when air moves across them, causing them to vibrate. The length and thickness of the folds, which determines the pitch produced, is managed by the musculature of the larynx, which shifts the cartilages to control their shape. The size of the vocal folds is the central element in determining vocal range.

The components of the oral cavity take the sound generated in the larynx and shape it in an astonishing variety of ways. The most important features of the oral cavity are the palate or roof of the mouth, the tongue, the teeth, and the lips; the nasal cavity plays a substantial role in managing sound production as well. The soft palate, for instance, can be raised or lowered, not only to make the oral cavity larger or smaller but also to influence the particular overtones that help determine a sound's timbre. The tongue, in addition to its role in articulating consonants, also shapes the oral cavity to produce vowels. (Vowels can be distinguished from one another because each vowel reinforces specific parts of the overtone series.) It is in the oral cavity, in particular, that the concerns of singing merge with those of speaking.

DESCRIBING THE VOICE

The anatomical details just outlined constitute the material grounding of vocal production. Singing, as the term is usually understood, depends upon using the vocal apparatus to create sustained pitches, more or less stable frequencies. ("Middle C," as it is called with respect to the piano keyboard, can also be named as C4 in scientific notation, or c' in the system commonly used by music scholars; middle C is defined as approximately 261.626 cycles per second, or Herz.) In speaking, the voice typically ranges within a general area of frequencies rather than keeping one frequency more or less stable.[1] But musical systems around the world are very often constructed by selecting out a set of frequencies to form some kind of articulated system—often called a scale or a mode, depending on the strategies used in a particular kind of music. Musicals, since they are overwhelmingly based on the systems inherited from Western European music, work mostly within the 12-pitch chromatic scale.[2] Within the usual space occupied by human voices, a number of distinctions have been established that allow us to move beyond the specificity of unique voices and classify them and the ways they work. The terms of greatest use in describing singing are type, register, and production.

Vocal Type

This term refers to the combination of characteristic range and timbre (or vocal "color") of an individual voice. Male singers are named by the vocal types *bass*, *baritone*, and *tenor*, in order of ascending range; the female equivalents are *alto*, *mezzo-soprano*, and *soprano*. By convention each voice type centers on a particular segment of the musical system. The bass type spends most of its singing time in the octave-plus-fifth of F2/F-C4/c', though for the sake of special effects some bass parts extend down to C2/C; bass parts also can extend up as high as G4/g' but this is uncommon in the repertory of musicals. The baritone vocal type typically covers the area from F2/F to G4/g', although most singing will occur in the middle of this range. It is distinguished from the bass voice not as much by the range of possible pitches it can sing, but more by the quality of voice—for most listeners, a baritone voice will sound "lighter," and will tend to be written in the higher parts of its range more often than would be usual in a bass part. The baritone type is considered the most common type of male voice, and this is true for much of the repertory of musicals. Tenor voices are the highest standard male voice type, usually written within the range C3/c-A4/a'. Operatic writing in particular makes some use of the brilliant effects of extensions above A4/a', up to C5/c', the tenor's famous "high C."

The standard complement of female voices parallels that of the male voices. The alto type, occasionally called contralto, is the lowest female voice, with music usually falling between G3/g to F5/f'; in addition, alto voices are often described as "thicker" or "heavier" in timbre. The mezzo-soprano is roughly equivalent to the male baritone and is probably the most common female voice type. Its characteristic range is

A3/a-A5/a'. (Note that the range is quite large, and significantly overlaps that of the typical alto range. Once again, the distinction of vocal types is a matter not only of range but also of timbre.) The soprano voice lies within the compass of C4/c' and A5/a', with frequent extensions up to C6/c'; specialists in opera or recent popular music with the necessary skill set can sing even higher.

Especially in the world of opera, subdivisions can be established within each basic voice type. Thus, in the German *Fach* system, which depends on subclassification of voice types and their most suitable operatic roles, it is possible to describe high female voices as lyric coloraturas, dramatic coloraturas, soubrettes, lyrics, young dramatics, dramatics, and Wagnerian dramatics (in order from "highest" and "lightest" to "darkest" and "heaviest").[3] But even the German *Fach* system does not exhaust the roster of possible voice types. In particular, the male vocal type that relies to an especially great extent upon the falsetto register (see below), called *countertenor*, finds wide use in both "classical" and "popular" styles. The highest voice in male quartets is especially likely to be occupied by countertenors. Formerly something of a rare specialty in high- and middlebrow music, associated there primarily with antiquarian or ecclesiatical genres, the countertenor voice type has become much more common, expanding out of the gospel, soul, and rock contexts where it used to flourish most widely.

Register

This word may be used to refer to vocal range, the characteristic feeling of resonance in a specific section of the upper body, a timbre, or a given segment of a singer's range defined by the location of vocal "breaks."[4] Speech pathologists, since they base their classification on physiological distinctions, offer a convenient system through which to offer an overview. There are four registers that differ by the vibratory patterns used to produce them. These registers can be ordered from lowest to highest; if a singer moves from the lowest possible pitch in his or her voice to the highest, the vocal cords will exhibit these vibrational patterns in sequence—though with a degree of overlap between each register and those contiguous to it. The lowest register is called *vocal fry*, and is produced by loose glottal closure, that is, keeping the tension of the vocal folds loose enough to allow air to seep through the apparatus slowly, creating a distinctive buzzing or creaking sound of low frequency. Vocal fry is used in singing to reach low pitches more often than is recognized; it is more common as a technique for bass singers than for the other vocal types.[5] Above the register of vocal fry is the register of *modal* voice, the type of resonance that is used in the majority of singing and speaking. The modal voice typically occurs over the span of an octave and a half or two octaves, depending on the amount of vocal training a singer has had. The *falsetto* register overlaps the modal voice by as much as an octave. In contrast to the modal register, where the entirety of the vocal folds is energized, in falsetto only the edges of the folds vibrate. Falsetto tends to produce fewer overtones than the modal register, giving a "lighter" or more "transparent" result. The difference between modal and falsetto registers is much more audible in men, thanks to their longer and thicker vocal folds, but the difference in women is significant in the musical (discussed later in the chapter). At the top of the register system is the *whistle* register; at present its means of production is imperfectly understood, but it seems that only the front part of the vocal apparatus is employed. The whistle register is rarely used by men but is often used by women.

It is worth noting that the distinctions offered here do not reflect the most common usages in vocal pedagogy. There, the terms *head* and *chest* voice are more commonly used. Rather than focusing on the specific vibrational patterns occurring in the larynx, these terms draw attention to the subjective experience of the singer. Chest resonance is most commonly experienced when singers are moving through the lower parts of the modal register; head resonance, on the other hand, is typical of the upper part of the modal register. (Some teachers and vocal coaches additionally distinguish further between chest, head, and falsetto voices.)

Production

This is the term used in this chapter to cover the local details of a singer's sound. It is at this point in description that technical vocabulary referring to physiology and bodily sensation tends to recede in favor of a much more figurative language. A whole host of words that may join sound synesthetically to vision (such as "clear," "crystalline," "murky," "dark") or touch ("syrupy," "thin"), or smell and taste, are all just as common and evocative as descriptors that refer one sound to another sound. (It may be that such language tends to proliferate in descriptions of voice because our vocabularies for sound are much less extensive and specific than those for sight, in particular.)

This kind of figurative language is probably the most useful way of describing the singing voice from the point of view of listeners. In addition, however, any quick survey of a selection of musicals will reveal that, quite frequently, performers may employ moments of speech within songs, as well as a huge range of vocal productions that lie somewhere between speech and song as those terms are usually construed. In the history of "classical" music, such liminal styles of production are often collectively referred to as *Sprechgesang*, or "speech-song" (the German name accurately reflects the area of its greatest formal use). Musicals, since they offer a more spacious environment for skilled actors who may not be skilled singers (Rex Harrison comes to mind), tend to feature *Sprechgesang* more than operas do. But even with respect to performers who do have ability as singers, the selective use of speech and semi-speech remains an important dramatic resource.

Another distinctive kind of voice production, one that has been enormously important in musicals, is called "belting," especially important in the careers of performers like Ethel Merman or Judy Garland. Although there are complicated, finicky disagreements about what belting is and how its muscular sound is produced, the most plausible explanation is that belting comes from holding on to the characteristic vibrational pattern of the modal voice, but in a pitch range where the falsetto register would normally be heard. Belting offered one of the most certain ways, before the common use of amplification, of being heard even in the cheap seats of the theater; but more than that, the kind of physical effort that is audible in a belted voice intensifies the energy of the performance, making it viscerally exciting in all senses of the phrase. To the extent that belting is associated with extravagant, outsize female characters, it establishes a very close tie between the timbre of a voice and the kinds of character traits we are likely to read into that voice.

And this leads to the question of "bad" singing in the musical. One way of understanding the particular effects of operatic singing, most especially the powerful tradition known as *bel canto* singing, as well as its relatives, is to observe that the desired characteristics, such as even tone throughout the registers, great agility and flexibility in executing ornaments and passagework, careful control of breath and phrasing, and clear but standardized diction, all have to do with making the voice into something that blends effectively with the instruments of the orchestra (in an era without amplification) while still being able to project over them; furthermore, to the extent that virtuosity of execution is prized in opera, these characteristics make vocal athleticism much easier to manage. The goal of homogeneity within a particular voice is not a special value in most styles of popular music, however. Instead, vocal heterogeneity acquires expressive value: distinctive differences between vocal registers, variations of sound resulting from changes in vocal production, strongly marked accents as well as idiosyncrasies of diction—all kinds of "untrained" sound qualities tend to be heard as an index to the individuality of a singer or the character that the singer embodies. Because of this, singing in musicals is often subject to widely, even wildly varying criteria. Rather than attempting to maintain a single standard by which to judge a given performance or set of performances, it is usually more helpful to keep in mind the probability that in any show—sometimes even within a single song—multiple criteria may be operating simultaneously.

THE MATTER OF STYLE

Chapter 3 in this volume offers a historically based survey of song styles prevalent in the musical, although a truly comprehensive account could easily fill a separate volume. It seems useful, though, to augment that discussion here by discussing specifically *singing* styles, not only according to the characteristic ways of singing already discussed (belting, speech-song, falsetto, head voice, chest voice, and the like), but also as a representation of time and place. Broadway has always been about creating and enhancing illusions of often exotic temporal and geographic settings, whether through scenery, costume, gesture, and vocal accent, or, most tellingly, through evoking an appropriate "atmosphere" by adopting specific styles of song and of singing. Because of that traditional function of song on Broadway, it seems important to frame our discussion in those terms, even as we underscore that the resulting and potentially endless diversity engendered by the strategy of evoking time and place through song makes cataloging nigh impossible.

Historically, this evocative function of song is a carryover from operetta, where conjuring up a semblance of (often fictional) exotic locales through song, or engaging in nostalgic pastiche (thus with a heavy accent on the first syllable, on the *past*-ness of pastiche),[6] have aligned with common operetta themes. Many Broadway practices directly borrow from operetta, which provides access not only to "higher" styles familiar from opera (which on Broadway is also a matter of pastiche), but also provides the basis for easy extensions into other modes of evoking geography and pastness, through variations of what has loosely been termed *ethnic* song and dance, a broad category that may involve not only characteristic singing styles but also, as appropriate, jazz, blues, Latin rhythms, and scales borrowed from Jewish, Eastern European, or Asian traditions (among others), often allied with identifiable (and thus stereotypical) vocal accents and inflections.

Besides this quasi-geographic function of song, it may also evoke place in a more local context, by suggesting venue. A classic case is Kander and Ebb's *Cabaret*, which imitates the style of a Berlin cabaret circa 1930, but examples are legion and extend sometimes to suggest somewhat inappropriate conflations of place, as with the importation of revivalist and gospel styles into secular settings, such as the eleven o'clock numbers "Blow, Gabriel, Blow," "Sit Down, You're Rockin' the Boat," or "The Brotherhood of Man."[7] Venues such as the English music hall, vaudeville, nightclubs, café (or other folk-singing venues), the nineteenth-century parlor, and, more recently, street music (including rap and other contemporary types) are easily evoked through recreations of appropriate singing and musical styles.

The inverse of evoking distant times and places is, of course, creating a semblance of "now" through adopting contemporary styles—which is, again, a matter of pastiche, be it the imitation of rock-and-roll in *Bye Bye Birdie* or of rock in *Hair*, *Rocky Horror*, and later shows (and of more lately evolving styles). For many, the importation of rock to the Broadway stage in the 1960s and '70s was a watershed (see chapter 8), since it decisively institutionalized amplification as a permanent Broadway reality, complicating the purely biological account of vocal production given above with other modes of vocal "enhancement," ranging from simply allowing singers to be heard over the orchestra, to aiding them in evoking singing styles (such as belting), to helping a falsetto voice carry, to the correction of faulty pitch through auto-tune (which, using current technologies, effaces other aspects of timbre).

KISS ME, KATE AND SWEENEY TODD

This discussion of type, register, production, and style by no means exhausts the ways we may describe and discuss singing, but it offers some useful points of departure when examining specific performances. To open up this consideration to more practical use, the remainder of this chapter turns to two specific case studies. Both *Kiss Me, Kate* (1948) and *Sweeney Todd* (1979) combine a marked aspirational dimension with a deliberate indulgence in cultural "slumming," and their ambitious and deft deployment of a wide range of vocal types and singing styles may be seen to align with both sides of their divided personalities in turn. *Kiss Me, Kate*, being based on Shakespeare in the wake of the Rodgers and Hammerstein revolution, has always worn its gestures toward high(er) culture openly, but it is also based just as squarely on the often petty side of those who perform high culture and gives prominent play to loose living and gangsterism, long-standing affiliates of Broadway. *Sweeney Todd* likewise points in both directions. Its operatic tendencies have been often discussed, along with its political allegories and high tragic tone, whereas Sondheim himself has noted with admiration the blank verse with which Christopher Bond subtly elevated and dignified Sweeney's argot (a feature retained in the musical). But *Sweeney Todd* also panders dreadfully (perhaps campily), trading shamelessly in shocking violence, lurid situations, and crude humor, an outgrowth of Sondheim's originating desire to bring Grand Guignol to the Broadway stage, blood and all. The spread between aspiration and pandering provides each show with a wide field of potential musical styles, and both Porter and Sondheim met their respective challenges well—which is not surprising considering that they rank among the most sophisticated Broadway composers of their respective generations (although both tend to be more celebrated as lyricists than as composers). Thus, both *Kate* and *Sweeney* draw on the full richness of Broadway's voracious capacity to draw on any and all musical styles that suit its purpose, without needing to answer to the standards of aesthetic unity that opera and other "serious" musical genres seem to demand.

Kiss Me, Kate

Kiss Me, Kate employs a pervasive strategy of stylistic layering, first, to establish boundaries between both its strata of characters and its layers of performance, and, second, to overstep those borders repeatedly in order to collapse the difference between performer and character, and between performance on stage and performance in life. In this, it remains true to its origins in the observed intermingling of onstage and backstage drama during a Theatre Guild Production of Shakespeare's *Taming of the Shrew* by the Lunts some years earlier.[8] One of the distinct advantages augured by the decision early on to turn the show into a musical (as well as being able to recruit a reluctant Cole Porter for the project) was the possibilities that a musical could provide for making—and violating—these distinctions in vividly musical terms.

For example, the main couple, Fred Graham and Lilli Vanessi, are alike in aspiring to an artistic level higher than their sensibilities can sustain, and so their theatrical background and musical styles are operetta. Operetta, as a genre within American culture, is firmly ensconced in aspirational middlebrow culture, capable of coupling beautiful, quasi-operatic singing with grand gestures, and unconcerned about (or oblivious to) the yawning gap that separates operetta from actual opera. Thus, early on, Fred and Lilli reconnect through "Wunderbar," a number from an operetta they remember from their past—which is clearly not true operetta but rather an American facsimile of operetta, intermingling German words as an obviously phony marker of old-world authenticity (the song is rumored to have come readymade from Porter's trunk of unused songs). In singing this song together, the two reveal a level of comfort with each other and with themselves that they will not recapture, even in the happy ending that awaits them (◉ Example 23.2).

Within the musical production of *Taming of the Shrew* that Fred's company is mounting, he (as Petruchio) sings three songs, all deriving from lines in Shakespeare's play. The first, "I've Come to Wive It Wealthily in Padua," adopts an archaic style meant to evoke the Italy of Shakespeare's day, including the "canzona" rhythm that Porter was undoubtedly taught in his music classes at Yale as a hallmark of that style (◉ Example 23.3). His second song, "Were Thine that Special Face," borrows several operatic tropes, rendered more palatable to Broadway through the modified beguine rhythm that supports the return of the chorus. Porter here creates a kind of da capo structure (ABA) by delaying the recitative-like verse until after the first chorus and letting the verse's more direct text-setting function like a Baroque opera's "B" section, whereas he gives the vocal line an operatic quality through shaping, playing to the rich deeper notes and heroic higher notes of his singer, Alfred Drake, the quintessential "quality" baritone then singing on Broadway (◉ Example 23.4). Petruchio's third song, "Where Is the Life that Late I Led," is an operatic "list" song, a virtuosic blend of melodramatic and *buffa* elements that ends with an elaborate vocal cadenza across the final three words of the title phrase (◉ Example 23.5).

In contrast to Petruchio, Kate sings only two songs, near the end of each act, and in each oversteps the role she is supposed to be playing, bringing her (Lilli's) private quarrel with Fred on to the stage, and breaking down Fred's otherwise professional façade (thus, all three of Petruchio's songs remain earnestly in character). "I Hate Men," coming right after Lilli's discovery that the flowers she received from Fred were meant for someone else, gestures toward the "mad" scene by alternating gloomy minor-mode melodrama, set up by an "illogical" chord progression, with a flippant major mode in a more modern idiom (◉ Example 23.6). Porter withholds the rage aria that he might have opted for in this position, saving that style instead for Kate's interjections during the first act finale, which bring down the curtain in chaos. But her song that opens the second act finale, "I Am Ashamed that Women Are So Simple," derives more directly from the play's dialogue than any other song in the show, holding its simple and direct musical style until the end, where it briefly adopts a militaristic dotted-note (i.e., march-derived) motive ("So wife, hold your temper and meekly put/Your hand 'neath the sole of your husband's foot"), leading to a brief indulgence in the melodramatic scoops of romantic opera ("My hand is ready, ready,/May it do him ease"). It is only in the operatic excesses of the final lines that Kate's song reveals Lilli winking behind the vocal mask of what otherwise seems as earnest a song as any in the show (◉ Example 23.7).

"So in Love," which Lilli and Fred each sing in turn as a heartfelt soliloquy, she in the first act and he in the second (a reprise that comes across to some commentators as a lapse of dramatic logic),[9] directly links the two original singers, Alfred Drake and Patricia Morison, by playing directly to their mutual strengths: both singers had rich, covered voices, intimate in the lower register and carrying full-bodily into the higher register. Porter shapes the song accordingly, beginning three of the song's four 8-bar phrases at the lowest pitch and ascending an additional step with each phrase, while otherwise following the traditional AABA form common to Tin Pan Alley show tunes. Nevertheless, there is a subtle but telling dramatic difference between the two appearances of the song. Lilli, early on anticipating their reuniting as a couple, soars in her final phrase to the highest notes of the song ("I'm yours till I die"), and then falls away in waves from this vocal climax as if from sexual climax ("So in love, So in love, So in love with you, my love, am I"). Yet, when Fred begins this phrase of the song ("So taunt me and hurt me"), his rich lower register brings reality to the hurt, so that his own heroic ascent ("till I die") comes across as resolve in the face of a bleak future to be endured *without* the consummation Lilli seems to anticipate, brought about in performance by a sotto voce rendering of the final iterations of "so in love" (🔊 Example 23.8; 🔊 Example 23.9).

The vocal stratum occupied by the secondary couple, while clearly "Broadway," is not so elaborately developed. Harold Lang (the original Bill Calhoun) had to badger Porter to write him a song (owed to him by contractual obligation), and the result, "Bianca," despite its charm, gives credence to the anecdote that Porter deliberately wrote a song so hokey it would have to be cut. This and the second-act song of his counterpart, Lois Lane, "Always True to You in My Fashion," are novelty songs, setting up a dance number for Bill and providing a tour de force Broadway list song for Lois in the best Porter tradition. Lois's earlier song, "Why Can't You Behave?" briefly reprised as a lead-in to "Always True to You," is a conventionally bluesy number, replete with throaty scoops both up and down on the title phrase (🔊 Example 23.10). It is in the first-act quartet "Tom, Dick or Harry" that they define both their onstage and offstage relationships, through their mutual occupation of the same level of earthy sophistication, he through dance and she through flirtation and witty wordplay (thus, "Any Tom, Dick or Harry,/Any Harry, Dick or Tom"). As a singer, Bill's Lucentio is comfortably situated between the other two suitors, not only in register and temporally but because he pretends neither to money (as his lower predecessor Gremio) nor position (as his aristocratic successor Hortensio). As a dancer, he is able to offer the heightened physicality demanded by the (archaizing) rhythms and sexual innuendo of Lois's Bianca. Although occupying the middle (and with only a middling voice), he is thus on an even footing with the more stable bass of Gremio and the aristocratic high operatic tenor of Hortensio—the latter type in any case often marked as effeminate on Broadway (🔊 Example 23.11).

As markers for a Broadway (comic) sensibility, Lois and Bill also provide useful points of reference for the lead couple. "Bianca," for example, seems to parody "Were Thine That Special Face" in its overly simplistic recitative-style setting of self-deprecating words (respectively, "So I've written her a love song/Though I'm just an amateur," and "I wrote a poem/In classic style/I wrote it with my tongue in my cheek/And my lips in a smile"; ◉ Example 23.12; ◉ Example 23.13). And "Always True to You" tweaks "Where Is the Life" fairly directly, especially obvious for those who might recognize their mutual origin in Cynara (respectively borrowing the lines "I have been faithful to thee, Cynara! in my fashion," and "gone the wind"—the latter also the basis for the title of Margaret Mitchell's famous book; ◉ Example 23.14). Thus are the borders both patrolled and violated by musical style, in a trope of parallel construction that dates back at least to eighteenth-century opera.

The lowest musical tier belongs to the gangsters, who perform a vaudeville number, "Brush Up Your Shakespeare," in front of the curtain late in the second act. This is one of the most enduring—and endearing—of eleven o'clock numbers, reinforcing the already established basis for these characters in burlesque caricature, and (depending on casting) often revealing quite skilled performers lurking behind characters who have served mainly as comic relief and a convenient means to force the plot along. The singing style appropriate here has quite a wide range, since a comic effect can be achieved equally from actual singing or from a kind of speech-song (or something in between); as a waltz song, the number is ultimately as much about their surprising turn as comic dancers as about the broad humor of their pun-strewn lyrics (◉ Example 23.15).

Finally, the choral numbers of *Kiss Me, Kate* support and partake of nearly the full range of cross-cultural tweaking already observed between the secondary and lead couples. Fairly obviously, "We Open in Venice" tweaks "Another Op'nin', Another Show," by revealing, as the flip side of opening-night excitement, the dreary routine of a touring company. More subtle is the send-up of "I Sing of Love" by "Too Darn Hot," displacing the (really, too-) benign pastoral of the first act with the gritty, jazz-based opener to the second. But the chorus's most important function derives from opera, representing the public that underscores the embarrassment of the dysfunctional lead couple in the first-act finale, but also supporting the operatic excess of feeling that invigorates the second-act finale, for which Lilli's Kate substitutes Italian superlatives ("Carissimo!" "Bellissimo!") for the insults she interjected in the first-act finale (◉ Example 23.16).

Sweeney Todd

Sweeney Todd is a famously class-conscious musical, and differences in songs—both their styles and genres as well as the ways they are performed—are central to the musical's evocation of different social worlds. But the variation of social/musical levels takes place within an overall set of strategies that gives *Sweeney Todd* an operatic flavor: although there is some spoken dialogue, it is relatively sparse, and plot advancement as well as emotional amplification both take place through primarily musical means—a contrast to the Broadway tendency to place action in the book and feeling in the songs; the bitter humor underlying the words and music, however often it may pop up in Sondheim's earlier shows, pervades the entirety of *Sweeney*, darkening the show to a degree much more common in operas than in musicals;

although "popular," "lower," or "lighter" musical styles are mixed together with some more overtly modernist ones, they are all rather antiquated—nineteenth-century popular styles, not the jazz-tinted (more recently, rock-tinted) kind that usually mark Broadway works. Nevertheless, *Sweeney*'s operaticisms take place within a set of assumptions that govern musicals rather than operas. Most crucially, the roles of Sweeney and Mrs. Lovett (and to some extent the role of Judge Turpin) can be quite effectively executed by actors with only moderate musical skills—fabulous voices are not particularly necessary for them, but dramatic skill is paramount.

An overview of singing in *Sweeney Todd* can begin with the assignment of vocal types to characters. To some extent this follows the practices of much nineteenth-century opera: unquestioned romantic leads and younger characters get higher voice types, while more complex, ambivalent, or older characters are written for lower voices. Sweeney and Judge Turpin are cast as bass-baritones or baritones, suggesting that if baritones are cast, those whose voices are a bit heavier and/or darker will match the parts best. Mrs. Lovett is similarly designated as an alto or mezzo-soprano, the choice again signaling that a certain vocal heft is desirable. Joanna is a soprano, and by the evidence of her music, one who tends strongly toward the coloratura style or the soubrette type rather than the lyric or the dramatic sopranos—she is an ingénue first and foremost. The Beggarwoman is assigned to the mezzo-soprano type, which is probably meant to match her age and rough life. The tenor roles show the most interesting range of characterizations. Anthony Hope, as a stereotypical handsome young sailor—a Frederic from *Pirates*—is either a baritone or a tenor: a young Heldentenor (to simplify brutally, a baritone who has lots of good high notes) would be an effective compromise and would point up the youthful heroics that justify the character's presence in the show. Tobias Ragg is listed as a tenor, which taken together with his rather simple, folkish music, indicates his youth and naiveté. Most interesting of all with respect to vocal type are Adolfo Pirelli, the barber/con man who is cast as the most Italianate of tenors, and Beadle Bamford, whose allotted type of tenor/countertenor reinforces his unctuous foppery.

The most "musical" of *Sweeney*'s numbers is certainly Joanna's "Green Finch and Linnet Bird." To begin with, the song is unproblematically allegorical, commenting on the emotional situation rather than constituting itself as part of the direct action. Joanna is introduced standing on a balcony, in effect giving a little concert. The presence of high style is marked by the song's range of an octave plus fifth, its propensity for wide leaps and somewhat tricky turns of melodic phrase, and above all by the ostentatious trill that leads into the recapitulation of the song's opening material (🔊 Example 23.17). But just as important as all of these musical details is the simple choice of this voice type; for good or ill, the soprano voice type is the stereotypical operatic voice, and the decorum required to make "Green Finch" effective—careful pronunciation, a controlled sound that makes each pitch sound clearly, evenness of tone throughout the voice's range—marks the song as "cultivated." This is of course the character's natural state: as the genteel ward of Judge Turpin, Joanna is a well-brought-up young lady who has been kept "innocent," and the somewhat stock opera-operetta tone of her song signals this to the audience from the moment she opens her mouth.

By contrast, Mrs. Lovett's introductory number, "The Worst Pies in London," uses a bustling lower style with many modernist touches (unpredictable rhythms, some piquant dissonances) to sketch out her broadly comic character—the gruesome facets of her ferocious capitalism come later on. The song requires two kinds of singing. In the fast patter sections of the song, the music aims at rhythmic vivacity. Whether we take the unexpected pauses and sudden accents of the patter sections as syncopations or frequent shifts of meter, the song's bumpy progress comes across as an exemplification of Mrs. Lovett's tendency to chatter interrupted only by the occasional gasping breath or distracted exclamation. What is abundantly clear, as well, is that actual pitches matter less to the song's effectiveness than the accuracy of the rhythms. The more lyrical sections of the songs occur when Mrs. Lovett ruefully describes her wares. Because the deprecation is so broad, her melodic effusions will keep their humor whether the actress cast can sing well or not (◉ Example 23.18). Mrs. Lovett is an effective part for actresses who can act and count, whether or not they can produce beautiful tones. In fact, it is likely that this song, even more than the rest of Mrs. Lovett's numbers, will gain from being more spoken, less sung. The original cast album of *Sweeney* demonstrates Angela Lansbury managing exactly this kind of vigorous farce in an exemplary matter; specific sonic details might include her management of Cockney-ish vowels and glottal stops to increase the song's rhythmic vitality; her switch between the modal register for patter, and a carefully wobbly falsetto register for her lyrical effusions; and her ways of changing vocal production to increase the song's sense of nonstop breathlessness.

Sweeney's overwhelming mad scene, "Epiphany," is subject to many of the considerations that drive "The Worst Pies." A beautiful sound is not at all the point. "Epiphany" sets up a contrast between more spoken passages, where Sweeney rages at losing his chance with the Judge, and where he imagines slaughtering unwary customers for practice (◉ Example 23.19), and more lyrical stretches where he alternately pronounces sentence on the whole world and mourns his lost wife and child (◉ Example 23.20). It's worth noting that the lyrical moments in Sweeney's vocal part are always carefully supported by preparatory instrumental cues and/or helpful doublings. Len Cariou's performance on the original cast album, like Angela Lansbury's, reveals his great success at using vocal production to create many nuances of delivery in the vocal part.

The vocal worlds of Sweeney and Mrs. Lovett represent a demotic level of musical discourse in the musical: they are the equivalent of the show's urban common speech. Joanna and Anthony operate in a "higher" stylistic world, which is appropriate since of all the characters they are least implicated in the variously sordid and ghoulish happenings on stage. The vocal spaces occupied by both the Beadle and Pirelli, however, are set up to be audibly false instances of high styles. In Pirelli's case, the musical style evoked by his vocal type and his style of singing is distinctively foreign—Italian opera, and a very bad imitation at that. This is not only a matter of his caricatured Italian diction and his gracelessly set up high notes: the minor-mode parodic tone specifically conjures the operas of Rossini, creating an effect not unlike the famous Bugs Bunny/Elmer Fudd travesty "The Rabbit of Seville" (◉ Example 23.21). Although Sondheim has been criticized for this role, he deserves defending: after all, the whole point of Pirelli is that he is a *fake* Italian; his characterization is meant to be crude and embarrassing, and it makes him contemptible enough as a person that his murder and transformation into meat pies (the first one) does not alienate the audience. And, since this first one goes down so easily…The Beadle's musical world is different—he belongs to the sentimental, effusive, ultimately mendacious world of parlor song—but its effect is similar (◉ Example 23.22). Because he is presented vocally as precious, possibly even effeminate in vocal manner, and because of the way his self-importance merges so easily into his occupation as toady and panderer, the Beadle is, like Pirelli, a petty villain, one whose dispatch will not trouble the audience.

The point of all these stylistic juxtapositions, in the end, is their effectiveness at creating an elaborately layered world within which the penny-dreadful action takes place. Certainly, if one were to choose a generic designation for this musical, it would be melodrama. It is to melodrama that *Sweeney Todd* owes its most enduring and spectacular effects; and this is as true of its music as it is of its plot or staging.

NOTES

1. When linguists analyze the pitch systems of tonal language, for instance, they are concerned with relative pitch rather than absolute pitch; even a highly tonal language such as Hmong Der, for instance, defines its tonal levels in general terms such as "high, "middle," and "low" areas of pitch rather than by pitches as they are understood in music.

2. "Octaves" are defined as two notes whose frequencies display a 2:1 ratio. Thus, if A4/a' is the name for the frequency 440 Hz, then A3/a would oscillate at 220 Hz, and A5/a' at 880 Hz. The ear typically recognizes this ratio, hence these frequencies are designated by the letter a. For a more detailed discussion, see ◐ Example 23.1.

3. The *Fach* system is especially important for opera singers, but an acquaintance with it is helpful to those interested in musical theater as well. One account of this can be found in Pearl Yeadon McGinnis, *The Opera Singer's Career Guide: Understanding the European Fach System* (Lanham, MD: Scarecrow Press, 2010).

4. "Breaks" are those segments of a singer's range in which the vocal mechanism shifts between types of resonance. The most important of these breaks is the transition between modal and falsetto registers. The location of breaks is one of the traditional defining characteristics of voice types in vocal pedagogy.

5. Vocal fry is also characteristic of "creaky voice," a device encountered in some tonal languages of Southeast Asia and Mesoamerica.

6. "Pastiche" on Broadway refers to the practice of imitating specific, identifiable styles of song, whether of an era, a song type, or a specific composer, through allusion to or reproduction of key features of the evoked repertory. While the term "pastiche" is often used pejoratively, as part of a claim that a composer relies too much on imitation and not enough on imagination, it is in

fact basic equipment for composers on Broadway, who must communicate much in a few deft strokes.

7. The "eleven o'clock number"—so called because it is usually placed strategically late in the show—is designed to elicit extended applause and (usually) encores. For speculation regarding the dramatic import of this theatrical device, see Raymond Knapp, "Getting Off the Trolley: Musicals *contra* Cinematic Reality" (forthcoming in *From Stage to Screen*, ed. Massimiliano Sala, vol. 18 of *Speculum Musicae* [Turnhout, Belgium: Brepols Publishers]).

8. See Charles Schwartz, *Cole Porter: A Biography* (New York: Dial Press, 1977), pp. 230–31. For another discussion of the background, dramatic organization, and songs of the show, see Raymond Knapp, *The American Musical and the Performance of Personal Identity* (Princeton, NJ: Princeton University Press, 2006), pp. 273–84.

9. See, for example, Geoffrey Block, *Enchanted Evenings: The Broadway Musical from* Show Boat *to Sondheim* (New York: Oxford University Press, 1997), pp. 192–93.

CHAPTER 24

DANCE AND CHOREOGRAPHY

ZACHARY A. DORSEY

WARMING UP

My central task in this chapter is to articulate a methodology for analyzing dance in musical theater performance. I begin by discussing definitions of both dance and choreography in this context, assessing the existing body of writings on dance in musical theater, and offering a few observations as to why such scholarship has rarely been pursued. I conclude with an examination of Bob Fosse's 1979 film, *All That Jazz*, to demonstrate the challenges and the joys to be found in looking intensely at dance and choreography in musical theater.

Early in "The Line," Mark Steyn's chapter on dance in *Broadway Babies Say Goodnight!*, he quotes the lyrics to the Irving Berlin song, "Choreography":

> Chaps / Who did taps / Aren't tapping anymore
> They're doing / Choreography!
> Chicks / Who did kicks / Aren't kicking anymore
> They're doing / Choreography![1]

Steyn includes Berlin's song to underscore a major shift in the history of dance in musical theater, one that Liza Gennaro traces elsewhere in this book. Steyn relates that in 1936 for *On Your Toes*, George Balanchine became the first member of a production team for a Broadway musical to request that his work be described as "choreography by..." rather than "dances by..."; Balanchine saw himself as a "choreographer" rather than a "dance director," the title common to the industry at the time. In "The Line," Steyn traces the ascent of the choreographer on Broadway, as well as the relative importance of dance in the Broadway musical from that moment, noting how concert dance choreographers such as Balanchine and Agnes de Mille brought highbrow dance forms like ballet and modern dance to musical theater, paving the way for director/choreographers Jerome Robbins, Michael Bennett, and Bob Fosse, among others.

Berlin's song is just a divertissement for Steyn, but it is instructive, for those of us studying dance and choreography in musical theater, actually to look at the 1954 film *White Christmas*, in which "Choreography" is sung and danced (⊙ Example 24.1).[2] As the number begins, a small flock of ponytailed women clad in gray calf-length shifts form a tableau around a single male dancer (Danny Kaye) sporting tight-fitting black clothes and a black beret. Accompanied by music both dissonant and piercing, the women's dancing is asymmetrical, out of unison, and jerky. Their flat-footedness and frequent sinking or falling to the ground suggest a sort of earth-bound-ness, and their facial expressions make them seem alternately anguished and vacant. A few moments later, they stomp upstage to form and hold another tableau, even more angular and unnatural, reminiscent of two-dimensional figures frozen on an ancient vase. At the center of the tableau, Kaye wonders aloud, in a "posh" accent, "The theatuh [*sic*], the theatuh, what's happened to the theatuh, especially where dancing is concerned?" and then breaks into Berlin's song.

As he finishes the lyrics, a woman in a short hot pink skirt and tap shoes (Vera Ellen) descends into the frame from above (presumably lowered in on a trapeze). (⊙ Example 24.2) At first, only her legs are revealed, and the women in gray and Danny Kaye all surround her on the ground, eyes wide and faces nosed curiously toward these tapping pink feet, as if they were some alien object newly fallen to earth, filling them simultaneously with wonder and horror. Shortly, the camera pulls back to reveal this leggy pink and blond confection in her entirety (with hot pink muff on her hand and oversized pink feather in her hair), and she is joined by a male tap dancer in a white suit (John Brascia), who springs up through the stage floor. The two of them hoof it together, and intermittently, dance with Danny Kaye, while the chorus of women swarms around them.

The lyrics and the mise-en-scene make it clear that Kaye's character and his chorines represent the new wave, the "choreography" that is edging out the hoofing and other conventional dance steps of musical theater. Yet by watching the dance, one sees that it's all parody, all over-the-top send-up of both "dance" and "choreography," a fact that might be missed in reading Berlin's lyrics alone. These characters are all larger than life—not just Kaye and his chorus women, but also Ellen and Brascia, each of whom makes a spectacularly ridiculous entrance. And though the song itself might pit dance (or at least the old way of doing things) against choreography, this is not a cage match or a dance-off; Kaye's character reveals himself deft at partnering and well able to share the honor of lifting and twirling Ellen about with Brascia. And importantly, the two groups arrive in a tight tableau at the end of the song, the three leads framed by the chorus, all with arms thrust upward, neither group edging the other out of the spotlight despite their differences in movement styles and appearances.[3] One might imagine, upon listening to and watching this short song and dance, that musical theater would be ever informed by this convergence of dance forms, as well as reassured that the new dance is unlikely to ever replace the old.

I begin with this piece for a few reasons. First, to reiterate Steyn, it is an elaboration of a key moment in musical theater dance history. Even if an audience is lacking the full context—say, that the women in gray are only slightly exaggerated versions of dancers performing modern dance choreographer Martha Graham's technique—one can still see two vastly different dance styles in this number and understand from the spoken text and sung lyrics that change is under way in show dancing. Dance, certainly, can educate, parody, and crystallize a sociocultural moment, and it does all of these things in "Choreography," if only we're willing to look.

Also, I intend this assessment of "Choreography" to demonstrate that studying dance can be a joyful thing, and that this pleasure need not be absented from extensive analysis. "Choreography" might be dismissed as just an elaborate piss-take of pretentious choreographers, but as its staging places bodies on display, it can generate other narratives and hold other significances as well. Further attention to detail and interpretation, for example, might focus on the dancing bodies of the women in gray as juxtaposed to that of Vera Ellen, revealing two dynamically different versions of womanhood. When Ellen first descends, the other women seem mesmerized by her tapping feet, but the camera lens focuses on her bare legs all the way up to her waist. Who or what is being looked at here? And what contexts—gender roles in 1950s America, conceptions of beauty and sex appeal in show dancing, Vera Ellen's anorexia—might enrich our analysis? While dance in musical theater is fun just to watch, the intricacies of moving bodies demand a closer and more measured inspection of the dance itself, as well as considerable thinking about the contexts of the dance and the issues that rise out of it. This work, too, can be tremendous fun.

So what, then, is "choreography"? I examine this number from *White Christmas* not because I want to place choreography and dance as oppositional (as Berlin's song might comically imply), but rather, to show how interconnected they are. I have delayed the definitional aspect of this chapter purposefully, in part to gesture toward what I believe is the relative unimportance in most cases of parsing out the differences between dance and choreography. First, "choreography" literally means "dance writing" (from the ancient Greek), and as a term, it has become increasingly used since the eighteenth century when the practice of preserving dance steps by writing them down using assorted symbols and systems became popular. More generally, though, choreography refers to the composition of dance—not just putting the dance to the page but rather creating and assembling the dance structures and steps themselves. A choreographer, thus, is the person who creates choreography. I was drawn to using the number from *White Christmas* in part because there is a brief yet memorable moment right before Kaye's character starts singing when he reaches out and adjusts one of the dancer's hands, tugging it upward a few inches, presumably correcting her execution of his character's choreography. As a keyword, choreography is included in this chapter to spotlight the labor of the choreographer, to reiterate that dance steps for musical theater are purposeful creations.[4] Dance is almost never improvised or left to chance in musical theater performance on stage and screen; rather, it is methodically planned, rehearsed, and executed—and we should take for granted that these movements are there for a reason, even if we can't completely fathom what that reason might be.

So what, then, is "dance"? One of the first (and often, most frustrating) tasks in an introduction to dance studies class is the exploration of different definitions of dance. Roger Copeland and Marshall Cohen note that dance "is sometimes defined as any patterned, rhythmic movement in space and time."[5] Such a general definition allows for nonhuman dance, such as the migration of a flock of birds or the falling of leaves and snowflakes. Norman Bryson suggests the utility of looking at any "socially structured human movement," such as parades, weddings, and even bowing, as dance.[6] Joanne Kealiinohomoku, in an effort to define dance cross-culturally, specifies that "dance is a transient mode of expression, performed in a given form and style by the human body moving in space. Dance occurs through purposefully selected and controlled rhythmic movements; the resulting phenomenon is recognized as dance both by the performer and the observing members of a given group."[7] I cite these diverse definitions of dance not with any desire to be pulled into their debates but to suggest the wide range of activities that might be considered dance, depending on one's definition. I suggest not getting bogged down in attempting to define dance within musical theater; if the analysis and understanding of movement is the aim, all that is required from the viewer is the decision (before, during, or after the fact) of where to focus one's gaze.[8]

Thinking and writing about dance in musical theater is difficult, which is evident from the relatively few books and articles on the subject.[9] And yet, for the aspiring student, fan, or practitioner who wants an introduction to the subject of dance in musical theater, there are some fine places to begin. Most generalist books on the musical or its history do include some mention of dance and choreography, if not a complete chapter; beyond Steyn's book, Richard Kislan's *The Musical: A Look at the American Musical Theater* and Gerald Mast's *Can't Help Singin': The American Musical on Stage and Screen* provide balanced discussions of dance as one of the primary elements of the musical form.[10] Two books trace the history of dance in musical theater: Richard Kislan's *Hoofing on Broadway: A History of Show Dancing*, and Robert Emmet Long's *Broadway, the Golden Years: Jerome Robbins and the Great Choreographer-Directors*.[11] Biographies of choreographers are plentiful as well, and most provide not only rich context for the lives and careers of their subjects but also some description of these choreographers' aesthetics, their innovations, and their lasting influence on contemporary musical theater dance practice.[12] More scholarly studies on dance in musical theater are rare, though the last two decades have seen excellent work by scholars such as Andrea Most, Bruce A. McConachie, and Stacy Wolf, who analyze dance as evidence for their individual arguments about musical theater and its contribution to manifold dimensions of American culture, politics, and society writ large.[13]

Truly enterprising musical theater dance scholars will familiarize themselves with all that dance studies scholarship—dance history, world dance, dance

ethnography, and so on—has to offer. Though musical theater dance is often marginalized or ignored within these disciplines,[14] one can borrow and adapt methodologies from them for thinking and writing about various movement forms,
traditions, and histories. In particular, the work of dance scholars and critics can be
helpful in exploring how to write about and make sense of the complexities of dance
and choreography in performance. Writings about discourse on dance (whether
regarding scholarly research, dance criticism and reviews, or ethnography) by such
scholars as Joan Acocella, Janet Adshead, Sally Banes, Roger Copeland, Ann Daly,
Jane C. Desmond, Susan Leigh Foster, Deborah Jowitt, and Marcia B. Siegel have
been foundational to my own attempts to understand how movement works in
musical theater.[15] Beyond academic journals, anthologies about dance, and other
scholarly publications, there is great value in reading about dance and movement in
newspaper reviews, if only to see how others describe and make sense of live
performance.

Why aren't more people writing about dance in musical theater? I sense, first,
that nondance specialists may fear they lack either some sort of requisite technical
vocabulary or the experience of having danced much themselves. (This phenomenon is curious; fewer shy away from interpreting music, regardless of prior knowledge and familiarity.) All that is required for useful analysis of musical theater dance
is careful description of what one sees and a commitment to thinking logically and
creatively about it. Choreographers for musical theater, after all, aren't structuring
their dances so that only experts can understand them; dances are designed to serve
the story that is being told to a general theatergoing audience. In "Imagining Dance,"
Joan Acocella argues compellingly that the imaginative processes behind choreography have "a strong biological basis,"[16] and that dance is thus a language unto itself
that we can all understand without need of having the choreographer explain it to
us. She writes,

> So much of life is spent in the difficult task of trying to understand things, to see
> *through* them to what's on the other side. But the truths of dance are not on the
> other side. They are in the very bones of the dance, which our bones know how to
> read, if we let them. (Acocella, 16)

Certainly, the study of many different kinds of dance across cultures and performance styles may provide the viewer with an easier route into a piece of choreography. But movement vocabularies are something that we have all learned and been
immersed in since birth—both as spectators of the world around us and as participants moving through it—and this alone should give us much courage as we try to
interpret the way that movement, dance, and choreography bear meaning.

A second factor inhibiting musical theater dance scholarship is the ephemer-
ality of dance. Original cast albums make a show's music and lyrics convenient
to scholars, and the full scripts for some musicals are published even before the
show has closed. Except for a performance presented on the annual Tony awards
broadcast, a number excerpted for a variety show (such as the *Ed Sullivan Show*
or the *Ellen DeGeneres Show*), or the brief glimpse of a few dance steps recorded

illegally in the theater and uploaded to YouTube, dance is not as easily available for close study as the music and book to a show. True, one might write about the choreography in newer shows by attending a performance—or better still, multiple performances, if one can afford it—and scribbling frantic notes during and after. Yet it's frustrating to have the object of inquiry only briefly available, which may render the pursuit of dance scholarship altogether unattractive to even the most diligent of researchers.[17] Of course, in the absence of live or recorded dance performance, it's entirely possible to write about dance from deep archival work. Photographs, prompt books, others' descriptions and recollections of choreography, interviews, and dance notation in scripts, scores, and production notebooks all can reveal much about dance in a particular musical, although they are no substitutes for the movements themselves and require considerable time and energy to assemble, as well as great care and innovation to analyze in any coherent manner.

LEARNING THE STEPS

How then to overcome these challenges to musical theater dance scholarship? The simplest way to understand a live or recorded piece of musical theater choreography is to use what I describe in the next few paragraphs as "dance analysis," a process with which even a novice viewer of dance can address the work's rhetoric: what and how a given piece of choreography means. What follows is my own version of dance analysis, an adaptation of Janet Adshead's ideas laid out in her "An Introduction to Dance Analysis."[18] My methodology is influenced by the writing of dance critics and scholars like Roger Copeland, Ann Daly, and Deborah Jowitt, and is heavily informed by Stacy Wolf's "In Defense of Pleasure: Musical Theatre History in the Liberal Arts [A Manifesto]."[19]

Dance analysis intersects with the work of dance reviewers and critics, though it culminates in the formulation of one or more arguments or interpretations, and ultimately stops short of evaluating a dance. Some reviewers and critics similarly see it as their goal to help make sense of a piece of choreography for their readership, though many just settle for a sort of "thumbs-up/down" mode of criticism, judging a dance "good" or "bad" and making recommendations about whether or not one ought to attend it. Dance analysis is more in line with how Ann Daly delineates criticism: "Criticism...is about sorting out the morass of perception into something orderly and interesting. It's about discerning relationships and making meaning."[20] Dance analysis requires that the meaning we make out of musical theater choreography is not independent from the dance itself—that is, just our own subjective interpretive whims applied to a piece of movement—but rather, firmly grounded in the specifics of the dance and the context of the musical that it comes from. As a scholarly pursuit, dance analysis deepens our understanding of the role of the dancing body within musical theater and can help speak to social ideas and themes prompted by the musical but extending beyond the proscenium arch.

One misconception about musical theater dance is that it is all jazz hands, kick-lines, and corny smiles, and that it ultimately can bear little to no structural or thematic weight. Dance analysis forces us to work through this bias and overcome fears that we are reading too much into a dance by revealing its form and structure. Through dance analysis, we can engage with each of a dance's parts separately and then together so as to understand the dance in its entirety and to interpret it. As Janet Adshead states,

> To watch a dance and see and hear its complex interweaving of rhythms and patterns and to perceive the way in which these contribute to the imaginative significance of the whole construction is, similarly, both the excitement of, and justification for, engaging in analysis. (1998, 165)

Focusing on the minutiae of the dance's construction allows us to appreciate better the art form and to become more active viewers, collaborating with the musical's performers and creators to determine, critically and creatively, what a particular movement means within the musical and beyond.

The first step in dance analysis—and perilously, the most often ignored—is *description*, an extensive series of observations made by the viewer about the dance itself. What steps are taken? What gestures are made? Which parts of the dancing body move? In musical theater, dances are almost always performed by characters whom the audience has met (or will soon meet), and such details become vital to understanding the choreography's relationship to the musical as a whole. Which characters are dancing? Who are they dancing for? Where are they dancing? Because dance analysis doesn't happen in a vacuum, it's also appropriate at this stage to make observations about other elements of the musical during the choreography. What are the characters wearing as they dance? What lyrics are being sung? What does the music sound like? This stage of analysis alone is both exhausting and exhilarating; any eight counts of dance could conceivably result in eight pages of notes.

Description lays the groundwork for the analysis to come. Close observation of diverse elements of dance prevents the viewer from jumping to conclusions without evidence, and it allows for a vocabulary such that viewers can rely on more than just the type of knee-jerk responses consumer society has promoted—"It was good/bad, I loved/hated it." Description is also a way of preserving dance for the viewer, a way of holding on to bits of it despite its fleeting nature. Indeed, such observations, when carefully rendered and artfully assembled, can stand in (imperfectly) for the dance itself to those who haven't seen it. Dance writer Deborah Jowitt is correct in noting that "blow-by-blow accounts of physical actions are useful only in small, skilled doses,"[21] and as a work of criticism, literature, or history, can be deadly to read. But within the lengthy process of dance analysis, such attention to detail is crucial. Later, some notes will be used and interpreted and many others discarded, but as a first step, assembling a wealth of minute descriptions is the best strategy.

The next step in this method of dance analysis is to put these observations into conversation with one another—to begin a *synthesis* of these seemingly disparate descriptions. Here, one might juxtapose the shape of the dance with its speed, or consider together the movement vocabulary allocated to certain characters. One could also look at a repeated gesture or move as it surfaces throughout a musical number over time, with careful attention paid to the similarities and differences between each occurrence. Within this step, additional context can also be productively linked to observations about the dance, such as information about the plot and narrative of the song or the show, details about characters or themes, biographical or stylistic knowledge about the choreographer or performers, the history of a particular dance step, style, or genre, and so on. Though dance analysis doesn't require that one go out and research every aspect of a dance's context, it's clear that richer interpretations of the work might be prompted by the pairing of rigorous descriptions and insightful background material. However, it's important not to clutter an analysis with too much information on authorial intent or anecdotes about the musical's creation; context is meant to aid in the understanding of the dance rather than become the understanding itself. As with the previous step of dance analysis, not every partnering of observations and context will prove illuminating, and yet this methodical and inventive synthesis of observations and contexts is vital to arriving at a nuanced understanding of a dance.

Dance analysis achieves its purpose through *interpretation*, one or more arguments about what a given dance (or section of dance) says, means, or signifies. Interpretations may begin as hunches or suspicions, but when firmly rooted in the synthesis of numerous observations and bits of context, they blossom into compelling arguments that can contribute to better understanding and enjoyment of the work for others. Interpretations can be small or large, obvious or completely original. Again, the complexity of any given eight counts of dance begs for detailed study, and there is great value in being able to voice even the most pedestrian of arguments so long as its logic is made clear. Typically, many interpretations must be combined in analyzing a dance of any length or in understanding how dance functions throughout the entirety of a musical.

What then makes for a strong dance analysis? First, it's imperative to bear in mind that dance analysis is a process. It requires viewing and (if at all possible) reviewing a dance many times, composing and refining interpretations, and discovering which observations and contexts are most relevant and leaving the rest behind. Whether dance analysis is being used in a term paper, a class discussion, or a conversation in line at the bar during intermission, its aim should be a balance of description and ideas—a careful assemblage of observations that elucidate an argument about the dance. Though dance analysis has three distinct steps (description, synthesis, interpretation), these categories need not be relegated sequentially to separate paragraphs or even sentences. As in many forms of oral and written discourse, the argument or interpretation is often best presented up front so as to give those attempting to understand the dance some understanding of what is being discussed and why. And just as the best choreographers are precise and purposeful with every aspect of their dances, so must anyone analyzing dance be precise and purposeful with the language used to analyze these dances; particular attention should be paid to the exacting selection of verbs and adverbs, and to the mindful implementation of figurative language and rhetorical devices.

With a little effort, any "reader" of musical theater choreography can successfully carry out this sort of analysis, no matter how little dance vocabulary or context he or she has mastered. But the complexities of capturing movement in words that are capable of suggesting its significance require that we throw everything we have at the dance, including our own instincts, curiosities, pleasures, and emotional and kinesthetic responses. One might also briefly invoke literary and critical theories—large bodies of ideas, philosophies, and political thought, such as feminism and queer theory—to augment the study of a dance. If used well, these can inspire particular inquiries and might open up the musical's choreography to broader social significances. Not surprisingly, a number of dance scholars have expressed their distaste for analysis or criticism wherein the dancing body is completely eclipsed by the theoretical construct. For example, Susan Leigh Foster says, "These writings seldom address the body I know; instead, they move quickly past arms, legs, torso, and head on their way to a theoretical agenda that requires something unknowable or unknown as an initial premise. The body remains mysterious and ephemeral, a convenient receptacle for their new theoretical positions."[22] In dance analysis, theory should be used sparingly and imaginatively rather than as a replacement for a faithful description and consideration of the musical's choreography on its own terms.

Although there is value in conducting a comprehensive dance analysis for any given number or musical—that is, a description of the entirety of the movements throughout, along with extensive contextualization and the formation of multiple interrelated interpretations—this could easily stretch to hundreds of pages of written work, an undertaking unlikely to appeal to most readers. Whether carried out in a class discussion or put to the page as a term paper, newspaper review, or journal article, dance analysis is often most efficacious as a means of focusing an audience's attention on particular fragments or aspects of the dance through which some significance might be gleaned.

A Performance

To provide a brief case study, I conclude by exploring just a few key moments from "Bye-Bye Life,"[23] the nearly ten-minute finale from Bob Fosse's 1979 autobiographical movie musical, *All That Jazz*.[24] First I examine the dominant conventions of dance within the entirety of the film, and then I explore a pivotal piece of choreography from this number—a sequence that also echoes significantly throughout Fosse's career. I end by combining dance analysis with my own kinesthetic and identificatory response. This varied methodology allows me to model each step of dance analysis and to approach from different angles the challenge of figuring out the complicated ways that dance functions in Fosse's film. My choice of *All That Jazz* as a case study may seem obvious—it's all about dance and choreography in musical theater—and yet despite its winning numerous awards and being regarded as the last of Fosse's masterworks, it remains relatively unexamined in dance scholarship.

Joe Gideon, played by Roy Schneider, is Bob Fosse's onscreen stand-in in *All That Jazz*. He starts each day with a well-rehearsed routine of eye-drops, Alka-Seltzer, Dexedrine, and "It's show-time folks," a mantra that he intones to the mirror less and less enthusiastically as the film goes on. *All That Jazz* documents Gideon casting and choreographing a new Broadway musical, editing a film, and attempting to navigate relationships with his daughter, his ex-wife, his girlfriend, and his assorted one-night-stands. Even while in the hospital recovering from a heart attack, Gideon continues to smoke, to drink, to womanize, and to work himself quite literally to death. A sophisticated and self-involved foretelling of his own death, this biopic chronicles Fosse's own vexed relationship to show-biz, to women, and to his own mortality.

Much as he did in the film version of *Cabaret*, most every number within *All That Jazz* is diegetic, where the characters' singing and dancing fit naturally into the narrative as conscious performance for an audience, such as when Gideon's dancers perform his "Air-otica" number for the show's producers, or when his girlfriend and his daughter perform a practiced dance for him in his apartment. This is vastly different from typical musical theater fare, when characters break out into song and dance as a convention, sometimes with no apparent knowledge that they've done so. Near the end of the film and of his life, Gideon hallucinates bizarre and fantastical song-and-dance routines featuring his loved ones, which he himself watches and directs from behind a camera; his subconscious mind refuses to let someone else choreograph his own life or death. With Gideon at the helm, each of these hospital hallucinations suggests a well-rehearsed number, completely diegetic in its own illogical way—frantic last attempts to capture on film an idea, an aesthetic, an impulse before the ultimate deadline.

Yet "Bye-Bye Life," the final hallucination (if that's truly what it's meant to represent) is different. In it, Gideon emerges from behind the camera and, accompanied by frequent Fosse dancer and collaborator Ben Vereen as a kind of emcee named O'Connor Flood, sings and dances in a finale reminiscent of a surreal rock concert or a glitzy Las Vegas show. Lights of all colors flash and illuminate a multi-tiered metallic stage, including a pedestal that, with Gideon on it, slowly rises at multiple points in the song. Gideon sings into a microphone and performs in front of costumed band members and backup dancers. True, even in what Flood explains as a "final appearance on the great stage of life," Gideon is a performer who entertains 'til the last; his onscreen audience is made up of characters from throughout his life, all clapping, crying, and witnessing the last act in the spectacle that is Joe Gideon. But "Bye-Bye Life" is less clearly diegetic than every other song and dance in the film. Gideon's performance seems somehow unrehearsed and a bit of a personal journey; he occupies a relatively small kinesphere, and he sometimes dances facing away from the onscreen audience or with his eyes closed. The audience of *All That Jazz* has previously seen Gideon setting his movement vocabulary and style on others—which is easily recognizable as Fosse's own—and these are clearly on display here on the bodies of Gideon, Flood, and the other dancers. Importantly, however, and for the first time, Gideon is no longer shown choreographing anyone or consciously performing his own choreography, but just spontaneously dancing himself, and perhaps even for himself as well. "Bye-Bye Life" is evidence of Gideon finally relinquishing control, embracing the unknown, and just enjoying the ride.

Midway through the number—perhaps its first climax—the two cadaver-esque female backup dancers (who sport skin-tight white spandex with blue and white lines suggesting veins and arteries) wrap their arms around Gideon's torso, clinging to him, holding him down. As Flood repeatedly sings the lyric "bye-bye your life goodbye," a smiling Gideon thrusts both of his hands outward and upward, almost ecstatically shrugging them off. He then runs and slides feet first across the stage on his side and back, an astonishing way to move, almost transcendent as a departure from normal modes of human locomotion. This slide is expansive and powerful; it takes him far, and with great momentum (⏵ Example 24.3). This slide is also exuberant and uninhibited—as opposed to the calmer, more precise, and in-place movements we've seen from him throughout this song (and throughout the film)—and Gideon bursts into this motion with wild and joyful abandon. As he slides, one hand floats skyward triumphant, and the other retains an assured grip on his microphone; contrary to his earlier clumsy attempts to maintain control of his life, here he hurtles toward uncertainty with grace and great style. The onscreen audience goes berserk, of course, applauding Gideon and his apparent acceptance of his own imminent death. Gideon stands and as the rock star of his own hallucination, runs through the audience greeting and glad-handing his adoring fans and all those who have shared in his life.

Fosse's fans may recognize Gideon's athletic slide. Though less iconic than other mainstays of "the Fosse style," feet- and head-first slides turn up in many of his stage shows and films, such as *Damn Yankees* and *Dancin'.* Perhaps most memorable is the slide's appearance in the film version of *Kiss Me Kate* (1953; ⏵ Example 24.4).[25] Not content with just performing in a small role, the young Bob Fosse asked choreographer Hermes Pan if he could create a short section of dance for himself and fellow dancer Carol Haney for "From This Moment On." Pan agreed, and Fosse's minute-long choreography—which begins with his own spectacular slide onto stage—was one of the most visually stunning moments of the entire film. An early articulation of an aesthetic that he would return to throughout the rest of his career, this brief section of choreography helped him land his first job as choreographer on Broadway, for *The Pajama Game.* Considered in this context, Gideon's slide toward his exit in "Bye-Bye Life" resonates with Fosse's own entrance during "From This Moment On." As bookends to a career, these slides enunciate both a show-biz maxim and a life philosophy: that entrances and exits truly matter.

All That Jazz is the quintessential musical in which dance is posited as a metaphor for how one lives, and part of the reason that "Bye-Bye Life" is so striking is that it allows its off-screen audience so many ways to relate to it. If death is just a final performance, then those of us watching the film have likely been the audience for many such finales, including Fosse's own—like Gideon, he would later be struck down by a fatal heart attack. Watch *All That Jazz* after Fosse's death in 1987 and it's nigh impossible not to think of the generations of dancers and performers that he's influenced and who have borrowed heavily from his movement style.[26] And if we're willing and able to make these identifications and to reflect on what we've seen and gained from Fosse, then there is a place for us in Gideon's onscreen audience. For me, watching "Bye-Bye Life" also fosters a sort of sympathetic kinesthetic response. In at least three different moments after Gideon's slide, Flood and the two female dancers stand with their elbows near their torsos, their forearms outstretched to the side, and their wrists limp. Then, slowly, and somehow gloriously, their hands begin to rise, still in pronation, and their arms follow in accordance. This repeated ascending motion seems almost a benediction of sorts, and something about the elegance and ease of this particular movement makes me want to stand and join in the celebration, to help the dancers physically and lovingly usher Gideon into the beyond (⊙ Example 24.5). Finally, I would argue that in a surprisingly generous turn, "Bye-Bye Life" opens up a space for us to imagine ourselves in Gideon's position, particularly with the knowledge that we'll all die sometime. Even though Gideon has been a self-indulgent, womanizing, work-obsessed, selfish bastard throughout the film—all fairly well documented personality traits of Fosse himself—with "Bye-Bye Life" I suddenly identify with Gideon, and find that I want precisely what he wants: to choose how and when I'll leave this life, to be surrounded by those who love and know me best, and to go out singing and dancing to uproarious applause.

NOTES

1. Mark Steyn, *Broadway Babies Say Goodnight: Musicals Then and Now* (New York: Routledge, 2000), p. 179.

2. *White Christmas*, directed by Michael Curtiz and choreographed by Robert Alton (Los Angeles: Paramount Pictures, 1954; DVD release, 2007).

3. Ballet and modern dance have continued to inform musical theater choreography without subsuming it. For instance, although "dream ballets" briefly flourished in the wake of Agnes de Mille's success with "Laurey Makes Up Her Mind" in *Oklahoma!* (1943), they have proved faddish over the years and altogether inappropriate for some shows.

4. It's important to note, though, that particularly when "dance" is defined broadly, other members of the production team such as the director and the actors are also creating choreography, such as setting down entrances and exits (blocking), or even creating a gestural landscape for a character or a show. Choreography, like dramaturgy, is a collaborative act in performance and one that takes place even when there is not someone titled "choreographer" on the production team.

5. Roger Copeland and Marshall Cohen, *What Is Dance?* (Oxford: Oxford University Press, 1983), p. 1.

6. Norman Bryson, "Cultural Studies and Dance History," in *Meaning in Motion: New Cultural Studies of Dance*, ed. Jane C. Desmond (Durham, NC: Duke University Press, 1997, 55–77), p. 58.

7. Joanne Kealiinohomoku, "An Anthropologist Looks at Ballet as a Form of Ethnic Dance," in *Moving History/Dancing Cultures: A Dance History Reader*, ed. Ann Dils and Ann Cooper Albright (Middletown, CT: Wesleyan University Press, 2001), p. 38.

8. Much of this will be determined by a viewer's particular skill set and investments. Yet these definitions of dance indicate that there is much to be gained in looking beyond conventional dance steps during musical theater dance numbers. Actors' movements across the stage, their individual gestures, the motions of set pieces and lighting elements, and what might be referred to in dialogue and lyrics can all deepen one's understanding, interpretations, and appreciation for dance in musical theater.

9. For instance, Joseph Swain's *The Broadway Musical: A Critical and Musical Survey*, 2nd ed. (Lanham, MD: Scarecrow Press, 2002), is an important resource for learning how the composition of music shapes a musical, with over a dozen chapters, each looking in depth at the music and lyrics of a major musical. No correlate yet exists for musical theater dance studies.

10. Richard Kislan, *The Musical: A Look at the American Musical Theater*, revised, expanded ed. (New York: Applause Books, 1995); Gerald Mast's *Can't Help Singin': The American Musical on Stage and Screen* (Woodstock, NY: Overlook Press, 1987).

11. Richard Kislan, *Hoofing on Broadway: A History of Show Dancing* (New York: Prentice Hall, 1987); Robert Emmet Long, *Broadway, the Golden Years: Jerome Robbins and the Great Choreographer-Directors* (New York: Continuum, 2001).

12. For instance, there is a handful of books exclusively dedicated to the life and legacy of Bob Fosse: Margery Beddow's *Bob Fosse's Broadway* (Portsmouth, NH: Heinemann, 1996), Martin Gottfried's *All His Jazz: The Life and Death of Bob Fosse* (New York: Bantam Books, 1990), Kevin Boyd Grubb's *Razzle Dazzle: The Life and Work of Bob Fosse* (New York: St. Martin's Press, 1991), and Debra McWaters' *The Fosse Style* (Gainesville: University Press of Florida, 2008).

13. See, for example, Andrea Most's " 'We Know We Belong to the Land': The Theatricality of Assimilation in Rodgers and Hammerstein's *Oklahoma!*" and " 'You've Got to Be Carefully Taught': The Politics of Race in Rodgers and Hammerstein's *South Pacific*," chapters 4 and 6 in her *Making Americans: Jews and the Broadway Musical* (Cambridge, MA: Harvard University Press, 2004), Bruce A. McConachie's "The 'Oriental' Musicals of Rodgers and Hammerstein and the U.S. War in Southeast Asia" (*Theatre Journal* 46 [October 1994]: 385–98), and Stacy Wolf's " 'We'll Always be Bosom Buddies': Female Duets and the Queering of Broadway Musical Theatre" (*GLQ: A Journal of Lesbian and Gay Studies* 12.3 [2006]: 351–76) and " 'Something Better than This': *Sweet Charity* and the Feminist Utopia of Broadway Musicals" (*Modern Drama* 47.2 [Summer 2004]: 309–32).

14. For example, American musical theater dance is almost entirely exiled to the thirty-second and final chapter of *The Routledge Dance Studies Reader*, ed. Alexandra Carter and Janet O'shea (London: Routledge, 1998), and it is absent altogether from *Moving History/Dancing Cultures: A Dance History Reader*, ed. Ann Dils and Ann Cooper Albright (Middletown, CT: Wesleyan University Press, 2001).

15. In addition to the essays and books that I cite elsewhere in this essay, see Roger Copeland's "Between Description and Deconstruction" (*The Routledge Dance Studies Reader*, pp. 98–107), Jane C. Desmond's "Embodying Difference: Issues in Dance and Cultural Studies" (*The Routledge Dance Studies Reader*, pp. 154–62), Susan Leigh Foster's *Reading Dancing: Bodies and Subjects in Contemporary American Dance* (Berkeley: University of California Press, 1986), Sally Ann Ness's "Dancing in the Field: Notes from Memory" (*Corporealities: Dancing Knowledge, Culture and Power*, ed. Susan Leigh Foster [London: Routledge, 1995], pp. 129–54), and Marcia B. Siegel's "Bridging the Critical Distance" (*The Routledge Dance Studies Reader*, pp. 91–97).

16. Joan Acocella, "Imagining Dance," in *Moving History/Dancing Cultures: A Dance History Reader*, ed. Ann Dils and Ann Cooper Albright (Middletown, CT: Wesleyan University Press, 2001), p. 16.

17. And dance, I would argue, is seldom designed to be catchy, memorable, or easily repeatable for audience members after the performance. Music and lyrics, on the other hand, are often structured to stick in the audience's minds, to be hummed and sung on the way out of the theater, and to prompt the purchase of sheet music or a cast album for further repetition later.

18. Janet Adshead, "An Introduction to Dance Analysis" (*The Routledge Dance Studies Reader*, pp. 163–70). This essay was, in turn, adapted from her book, *Dance Analysis: Theory and Practice* (London: Dance Books, 1988).

19. Stacy Wolf, "In Defense of Pleasure: Musical Theatre History in the Liberal Arts [A Manifesto]" (*Theatre Topics* 17.1 [March 2007]: 51–60). In her appendix B, titled "Some Elements of Dance Analysis," Wolf presents a series of excellent questions that can further assist one's thinking about dance in musical theater. I see Wolf's questions as specific foci or particular avenues of inquiry that one might use to guide, frame, or organize, Adshead's dance analysis, which is more of a comprehensive methodology that emphasizes, first and foremost, the description of the dance itself.

20. Ann Daly, *Critical Gestures: Writings on Dance and Culture* (Middletown, CT: Wesleyan University Press, 2002), p. xiv.

21. Deborah Jowitt, "Beyond Description: Writing beneath the Surface," in *Moving History/ Dancing Cultures: A Dance History Reader*, ed. Ann Dils and Ann Cooper Albright (Middletown, CT: Wesleyan University Press, 2001), p. 9.

22. Susan Leigh Foster, "Dancing Bodies," in *Meaning in Motion: New Cultural Studies of Dance*, ed. Jane C. Desmond (Durham, NC: Duke University Press, 1997, 235–57), p. 235.

23. "Bye-Bye Life" is based on the 1957 song "Bye Bye Love," written by Felice and Boudleaux Bryant and made popular by performances and recordings by the Everly Brothers.

24. *All That Jazz*, directed and choreographed by Bob Fosse (Beverly Hills, CA: Twentieth Century Fox, 1979; DVD release, 2003).

25. *Kiss Me Kate*, directed by George Sidney, choreographed by Hermes Pan and Bob Fosse (Los Angeles: Metro-Goldwyn-Mayer, 1953, DVD release 2003).

26. For instance, Beyoncé recently admitted that the inspiration for her "Single Ladies (Put a Ring on it)" music video was seeing a YouTube video featuring Bob Fosse's choreography for "Mexican Breakfast," a number from a 1969 performance on the *Ed Sullivan Show*. In fact, many versions of this one performance now exist in cyberspace slightly altered; people have taken to trying to synch Fosse's choreography with contemporary music, from rap to pop to death metal.

PART VI

AUDIENCES

CHAPTER 25

BOX OFFICE

STEVEN ADLER

Money makes the world go around…
That clinking clanking sound
Can make the world go 'round!

Fred Ebb knew whereof he wrote when he penned these lyrics for the film version of *Cabaret*, capturing not only the crass cynicism of the cabaret but also the hothouse environment of producing musical theater on Broadway.[1] Much as Times Square sits at the confluence of Broadway and Seventh Avenue, the production of musical theater resides at the intersection of art and commerce and is exemplified by the term "box office." Whether one subscribes to the *Oxford English Dictionary*'s claim that the term refers, historically, to the office that books box seats or to the notion that the cash-box resides there,[2] "box office" is the literal and figurative locus of the essential transaction between seller/producer and buyer/audience. The cramped little booths are supplemented now by cyber-Doppelgängers, but the term is still fraught with meaning on Broadway. It reverberates with Ebb's "clinking, clanking sound"—raising, spending, and making money. Box office connotes ticket sales, also known as "the gate," quantified in dollar figures as "the take" or "the gross." *Variety*, the bible of the entertainment industry, employs a playful lexicon of Runyonesque terms—"crix" (critics), "auds" (audiences), "helmers" (directors), "tuners" (musicals), and "legit" (the theater, as opposed to vaudeville or burlesque)—to capture the idiosyncratic spirit of film, television, and theater. One salient page of each issue reveals "Legit Grosses." This compendium of audience attendance and ticket sales provides a graphic representation of the changing fortunes of producing on Broadway.

For much of the twentieth century, producing musical theater was a profit-making enterprise wrought by solo entrepreneurs with a penchant for showmanship.

The center of this activity was unequivocally Broadway. As the century waned, economic and artistic forces conspired to shift the nature of producing. Some institutional theaters in New York City and around the nation, once a bastion of the not-for-profit motive and offering an antidote to the perceived frivolity and pointlessness of Broadway, began to produce musicals with an eye toward burnishing their national reputations and sharing in the riches of the Great White Way.[3] On Broadway, raising money grew more challenging, and individual producers discovered that extensive partnerships, sometimes with the powerful real estate moguls who owned the theaters, provided the best means of mounting shows. Corporations, with extensive financial and marketing resources, recognized fertile territory in the hardscrabble terrain of midtown Manhattan and joined the fray. A Broadway presence might bolster the corporate brand, as with Disney, or enable exploitation of successful New York productions in corporate-controlled touring houses throughout the nation, as with Clear Channel.

Over the decades, the landscape changed dramatically, but through it all, "box office" has remained the sine qua non of producing. This chapter examines the critical link between money and art, and draws on new interviews with key players in the box-office arena—producers, attorneys, critics, general managers, and investors—providing valuable opportunities to look beyond the marquee and *Playbill* to evaluate how box office shapes the making of musicals.

ART AND COMMERCE

Jeffrey Seller (producer of the Tony Award–winning musicals *Rent, Avenue Q,* and *In the Heights*) offers his definition of box office with unhesitating precision:

> Box office is life and death. No matter how much we love the art form, we live and die according to how many people bought tickets yesterday at our box office. Life at a Broadway musical begins and ends at the box office. It begins the day you put it on sale and ends the day you close because you couldn't sell enough tickets. You have the sales, you're a winner; you don't have the sales, you're a loser, and that's all that matters.[4]

Paul Libin (producing director and vice president of Jujamcyn Theatres, which owns five Broadway theaters and frequently co-produces both musicals and straight plays) elaborates:

> In the last century, when a Broadway show opened and was praised with rave reviews from the critics, a long line of ticket-buyers at the theater quickly confirmed that the show was "box office." The meaning of "box office" is the unique collaboration of a playwright or composer, lyricist, book writer, director, cast of actors, designers, and many others. Theatergoers come to see the show, it triggers exuberant word of mouth, and suddenly it's difficult to buy

tickets—that's "box office." Nowadays, you have to have the same response, although theatergoers line up via their computers and telephones. The show still means "box office."[5]

He notes, in illustration, the particularly remarkable day after *The Producers* opened in 2001 at Jujamcyn's St. James Theatre:

> After the rave reviews came out, we had a line going all the way down 44th Street around Broadway, almost around the corner. I called the Shuberts.[6] I asked them if we could implement the computer system at their Majestic and Broadhurst theater box offices to take some ticket-buyers off our long line so we could relieve the pressure at the St. James box office. That, to me, is the essence of what box office is about. It's not that you go to a window to buy the ticket, but that there are long lines of theatergoers buying the ticket. That day we sold $3,029,179 worth of tickets to *The Producers,* a Broadway record to date.

The exuberant praise critics heaped upon *The Producers* helped propel the musical to a fiscally rewarding six-year run. But critics can also be parsimonious in their response, negatively affecting sales and precipitating a show's quick and humiliating demise. Box-office success is essential for the health and longevity of a Broadway musical.

To acknowledge that "box office" refers to the Rube Goldberg–like mechanism by which producers finance and market shows is to accept Libin's assertion that this complex commercial transaction links inextricably to the artistic development of a production. From *Show Boat* in 1927 (possible because of impresario Florenz Ziegfeld's belief that Kern and Hammerstein could deliver a blockbuster) to *The Little Mermaid* in 2008 (possible because Disney Theatrical exists primarily to reinforce the corporate brand), the production of professional musical theater presents a tantalizing opportunity to examine the cohabitation of art and commerce.

RISKS AND REWARDS

Until the 1940s, Broadway musicals were most often aimed at audiences seeking diversion in a bright score, romance, comedy, dancing, and perhaps a touch of scandal and sex. Producers, then as now, attempted to discover the alchemical formula that might ensure a hit and tried to repeat successes whenever possible; inevitably, there was much reinvention and rarely innovation. And today's theatergoers remain averse to paying hefty Broadway ticket prices for risky material; safe, tried, and true shows are more attractive to audiences and more lucrative for producers and investors. Much of what seems like the radically new on Broadway first saw life in a previous incarnation. Frank Rich, the *New York Times* lead drama critic from 1980 to 1994, explains:

The entire history of the Broadway musical is that people see a hit and try to imitate it. Then comes a period when those imitations are successful and attract more backers until the cycle passes, as it always does in show business. *My Fair Lady* brought in an epidemic of British or ersatz British musicals often set in period. *Cats* brought in the spectacle. *Rent* is a direct antecedent of several shows running now, like *Passing Strange* and *Spring Awakening*. It is what always happens in show business and not just in the Broadway musical. Someone sees something that works and money follows it because it is still a marketplace. After *Les Misérables,* we still have epic adaptations of classics, or pseudo-classics, with huge special effects. That has always been the way. The number of dollars may change. But *Hairspray* is a hit, so every John Waters movie or movie like a John Waters movie is turned upside down to be a musical. *Hairspray* has surely launched *The Wedding Singer, Legally Blonde,* and *Cry-Baby.*[7]

In Broadway's early years, new productions competed annually for available theater space, and very few shows ran for more than a year or two. According to *Variety,* in the decades prior to 1943, when *Oklahoma!* made its mark as the first truly integrated book musical, only two musicals ran more than 1,000 performances[8]—the Depression-era musical revues *Pins and Needles* and *Hellzapoppin.*[9] No book musical experienced such success, and few plays survived that long. However, musicals rarely needed to run very long to make a profit. Although ticket prices were much less expensive than today, when adjusted for inflation, production costs were proportionally lower than now, and a modest run could reap a tidy profit. Today, long runs are necessary if producers hope to recoup a production's investments and pay a profit.

Long runs, although usually profitable, present challenges. Seth Gelblum, a leading theater and entertainment attorney, observes that there were more theaters on Broadway in the first half of the twentieth century than at the start of the twenty-first:

> Today you can't mount that many shows a year; you can't easily raise that much money, and you can't find the space for the shows. Since shows started running for long periods of time—a phenomenon of the last twenty years—it has put a terrible pinch on theater availability. As a result, producers can't produce a new musical every year like some of the great producers did. They can't find a space and they're out raising money all the time. As a result, it's not a job anymore. It's an occasional killing, if it works.[10]

Producers evaluate a theater's location, stage size, sightlines, ambience, and seating capacity to determine where to house a production. When fewer theaters are available, musicals stack up like planes in a holding pattern, often circling for years to land at the right venue.

For much of the twentieth century, producing was a relatively lonely enterprise. Individual producers or small partnerships oversaw every aspect of the production process: identifying the property; luring backers, or "angels," who might share opinions with the producer but had no contractual artistic or managerial oversight; hiring the artistic team; and serving as arbiters of every element in the show. Today, the costs of producing a new musical render the solo producer an antiquated relic. Even

Cameron Mackintosh, producer of many spectacularly staged British imports that populated Broadway in the 1980s, collaborated when necessity demanded, most recently with Disney Theatrical on *Mary Poppins*.

From "Angels" to "Investors"

The names above the title in a contemporary Broadway musical's *Playbill* reveal the complex fiscal, personal, and artistic relationships that producers nurture in order to bring a musical to the stage. *Spring Awakening* received bountiful critical praise and eight Tony Awards in 2007. Modestly staged with a small orchestra and a cast of twenty young actors, it suffers nothing by the absence of impressive scenic effects or lavish costumes and was relatively inexpensive in comparison to larger-cast and more opulent musicals, costing, according to its general manager, Abbie Strassler, roughly $6 million.[11] (Lavish productions can cost $20 million or more.) Yet *Spring Awakening*'s producing credits speak eloquently to the necessity for producers to cultivate large investor networks to nurture a musical over several years through various incarnations. Its evolutionary path involved readings and workshops at La Jolla Playhouse, Sundance Institute's Summer Theatre Laboratory, Roundabout Theatre Company, and Lincoln Center, and a not-for-profit Off Broadway staging at the Atlantic Theatre Company, before it opened on Broadway. Each of those productions incurred expenses. Twenty-seven individual and partnership names appear above the title of *Spring Awakening*, most of them investors whose contributions earned them the cachet of a producing credit, although they enjoyed no artistic oversight. Attorney Seth Gelblum notes,

> *Spring Awakening* was a very risky thing to do, and as a result, it was hard to find people willing to write huge checks, so they had to go to more people. When it's a riskier show like that—a dark, "downtown" show—it takes more and more people, so the numerical threshold with respect to how much you have to invest to get your name above the title goes down. It's easier to get your name above the title on a show where they need the money.

The trend in billing inflation trumpets the ascendancy of the investor in a marketplace in which it grows increasingly difficult to capitalize productions. Jeffrey Seller and Kevin McCollum produced two of the more durable musicals around the turn of the twenty-first century, *Rent* and *Avenue Q*, as well as the 2008 Tony-winning *In the Heights*. Seller contrasts their approach with that of the producers of *Spring Awakening*:

> There is no such billing on *Rent* or *Avenue Q*, and although we have seven entities over the title of *In the Heights*, it is modest by today's standards. Kevin and I have been blessed with the ability to produce as we wish to produce and what we wish to produce, under terms that are very rewarding and satisfying to us. That is due

in large measure to our first success with *Rent* and the type of material we choose to produce. Kevin and I have made our living solely in the theater. We are certainly a rare beast on Broadway now; there are perhaps ten producers who also make their living solely from the theater. There have always been people endowed with money that they either had in their family or earned from other places, who like to play on Broadway. That has been enriching to Broadway. When a billionaire produces *Grey Gardens*, and takes it from [Off-Broadway theater] Playwrights Horizons to Broadway, that's good for Broadway. [But] it doesn't happen to be who I am.

In contrast to *Spring Awakening*, most musicals from the so-called Golden Age (roughly 1940s to 1960s) were the apparent creations of only one or two producers, but like their contemporaries, they were dependent upon investors. The wisdom that guides producing on Broadway is the more expensive the production, the longer it takes to pay back (recoup) the initial investment (capitalization). Investors do not earn a profit until the producer reimburses them for capitalization, which funds the development of the production through opening night. After opening, the production must survive on its weekly box-office gross, from which producers pay operating expenses such as salaries, royalties, theater rent, advertising, and equipment rental. If the gross receipts exceed the expenses—a large-scale, sold-out musical can earn more than $1 million a week but can cost more than $500,000 to run—producers distribute remaining funds to investors to pay back the capitalization. After a successful production recoups, producers and investors share any profits above weekly operating expenses. Producers forecast recoupment times based on projections of potential weekly box office. It can be difficult to attract investors if the recoupment time is long and the property risky.

Historically, about one of every five Broadway productions recoups its initial investment, a daunting statistic for a producer or investor. Broadway has never been a hospitable arena for speculators. The fanciful term "angel," once common parlance on Broadway, has yielded to the more prosaic but literal "investor." The evolution of terminology reflects a similar evolution in the landscape. Producing Broadway musicals is considerably more expensive in the twenty-first century than in the Golden Age. In 1943, *Oklahoma!*, which employed over fifty actors, cost roughly $100,000. Adjusted for inflation, this would equal about $1.25 million in 2008. If *Oklahoma!* were staged today, using contemporary stagecraft and a fifty-actor cast, it would cost close to $20 million—one reason that most revivals feature smaller casts than the original productions. Producers must consider theater rents, union-negotiated salaries, royalties, equipment, advertising, insurance, utilities, and development expenses for earlier versions of the show, as well as weekly operating expenses, when considering whether to proceed with a production.

Muscular box-office receipts and small capitalization result in rapid recoupment. *Rent*, according to producer Jeffrey Seller, recouped in about fifteen weeks because it was a hit of remarkable proportions. *Avenue Q*, another critical and box-office success, recouped in about forty weeks. However, as Seller notes, these were relatively inexpensive shows to produce. His more opulent production of Baz

Luhrmann's 2002 *La Bohème* was initially budgeted at $6.5 million and eventually cost about $9 million. Seller observes, "That was not responsible producing—but nevertheless we got back the whole $2.5 million overage, and we got back another half-million dollars. The rest of it [$6 million] we lost."

Roy Furman has had a hand in producing on Broadway since 1974, participating as investor and producer on *Parade, Sweet Smell of Success, Dirty Rotten Scoundrels, Spamalot, The Color Purple,* and the 2008 revival of *Gypsy*. Before he considers involvement with a production, he asks essential questions: "Who is going to see this? Does it have an audience? Will that audience pay one hundred [dollars] or more a ticket? Who is doing it—the creative side and the producing side? The right producers mean a great deal."[12] While a producer or investor might be inclined to assess a production's prospects only through the lens of sound financial strategy, Furman noted that there are moments "when there's a rationale that transcends economics. That is, this show is art and art deserves to be produced. I've done a few of those, where I'll make the judgment that this has to be seen, it must be done, and in that instance I'm willing to put my money on the line to make it happen." He cited the 2008 *Gypsy* as an example. Five years earlier, Bernadette Peters had appeared in a revival of the Styne-Sondheim-Laurents classic. It was too soon, said many, for another production. However, Furman thought highly of the 2007 staged-concert version of the show at City Center's *Encores!* series and concluded that a wider audience deserved to see it. "This made [the producers] think sometimes that willingness, that conviction, emboldens everyone to move forward. It was an instance where I thought the audience had to see this performance and production." Furman's passion, intuition, and willingness to fund a considerable portion of the capitalization helped mount a production that garnered critical accolades and a healthy box office. This *Gypsy* dazzled not only because of Patti LuPone's heralded star turn as Rose but also because the producers concluded that the score would suffer if not performed by a full-sized, albeit costly, Broadway orchestra. To reduce costs, producers of revivals of musicals orchestrated originally for acoustic instruments rely more frequently on smaller orchestras complemented by synthesizers. In this instance, the producers' willingness—unusual on Broadway now—to hire twenty-five musicians signaled their belief in the vitality of the score, which in turn contributed to the power of the production.

RISK MANAGEMENT, AND A NEW ROLE FOR NOT-FOR-PROFIT THEATERS

In 2008, San Diego-based investment banker Ralph Bryan chaired the board of trustees of La Jolla Playhouse, a not-for-profit institutional theater that, in partnership with commercial producers, launched several musicals that later enjoyed successful commercial Broadway runs. Bryan invested in a number of Broadway musicals, including *Jersey Boys,* a box-office success that premiered at La Jolla and recouped on Broadway after only eight months. According to Bryan,

> Anyone who invests in a commercial production with the idea that they're *going* to make a lot of money has the wrong focus. However, everyone does it because there is the *chance* to make a significant amount of money. It is binary; you either lose it all or do very well. There is rarely a solid return. If you're doing a straight play with a star in a limited run, you have a chance of getting your money back and maybe some return beyond that. In a musical, you take that all-or-none risk for the huge upside. [*laughing*] It would be fun to make money more often than you lose it.[13]

Max Bialystock, the down-on-his-luck producer *cum* con artist at the center of the Mel Brooks musical *The Producers,* cautions his protégé Leo Bloom that there are two ground rules for producing: "One: never put your own money in the show, [and, two]: NEVER PUT YOUR OWN MONEY IN THE SHOW!" For much of the twentieth century, many successful producers rarely invested their own money, offering instead their taste, skill, and experience as collateral against the angels' investment. Some of them, like George Abbott, Richard Rodgers and Oscar Hammerstein II, and Harold Prince were theatrical artists in their own right, with exceptional insight into the process of making theater. Now, it is rare for an artist to produce; the skill sets have grown more divergent and specialized. In today's fiscal climate, producers tend to invest in their own shows in order to demonstrate good faith to potential backers. Jeffrey Seller notes,

> I believe in putting my own money in shows; not so much that I'm going to have to sell my house if I fail, but I believe that a producer is showing confidence to the investors....Today, most big producers are putting their own money into shows. I can't say they're putting in a million dollars or 10 percent of the budget, but I do think they're putting in hundreds of thousands.

Ralph Bryan adds the investor's perspective. "It's probably easier to commit when you think the producer has skin in the game, but I don't know ultimately if it affects the success ratio. No matter how hard you try, only one in four or five shows recoups."

Although the great producers of the Golden Age relied on angels, they maintained a profile of individuality and idiosyncratic leadership that contemporary producers infrequently display. They were, to varying degrees, artistic and fiscal risk-takers. Today, the magnitude of production costs has shaped a landscape increasingly hospitable to wealthy corporations and consortiums, which, Frank Rich notes, are rarely inclined to take risks. "*The Lion King* may be daring by Disney standards, but it's hardly a bold risk. It was based on one of the best-selling movie musicals on the planet and it was a spectacle." Alan Levey, former senior vice president of Disney Theatrical, explains, "Corporations will always be more interested in producing franchise titles to take advantage of the built-in awareness."[14] Rich ventures that many of the innovative musicals on Broadway first saw light in not-for-profit productions:

No Broadway producer in the mid-1970s would have originated *A Chorus Line*, and I doubt any Broadway producer now would have originated *Spring Awakening* or *Passing Strange* [all three shows transferred from Off-Broadway, not-for-profit theaters]. It still takes certain guts to take risks, and producers often fail to put their money on something risky, even if it has gotten acclaim in a non-profit venue. The day of the producer with highfalutin' tastes seems to be over.

Production costs inhibit risk-taking because "things are decided by committee." As Paul Libin observes,

> One of the problems confronting the theater nowadays is that there are producers making decisions who may not have the experience or the expertise in the theater. These persons make choices that are costly, or are unable to negotiate reasonable contracts. The way shows are currently financed requires many people investing large sums of money. Hopefully, those producers are strong enough and smart enough to make the decisions both artfully and economically that are going to enhance the production.

Frank Rich contends that very few producers now conceive new musicals the way that David Merrick, the formidable and swaggering power behind many hits of the 1950s and '60s, did with the original 1959 production of *Gypsy*. Merrick was a larger-than-life mogul who famously browbeat and blustered his way to blockbuster productions like *Gypsy, Hello, Dolly,!* and *42nd Street*. Although a lawyer by training, he insinuated himself into every aspect of his productions, from writing and design to marketing and advertising.[15]

Jeffrey Seller draws some critical distinctions about producing styles:

> It is what I call the difference between top-down or bottom-up producing. Is this an idea generated by a producer who said, "I think this will sell tickets," or is this an idea generated by an author who comes to a producer and says, "I need help with this because I have a burning desire to do it"? There are top-down enterprises that have worked over the years. *Hello, Dolly!,* was David Merrick's idea. Cameron Mackintosh said to me that he had never done a show that was his idea. He does shows that artists bring to him. I took it to heart because none of the three shows that I produced that won Tonys for best musical was my idea in the least. They were shows that needed nurturing. Kevin [McCollum] and I got involved with them from the ground up and we helped them along, but their genius came from their authors. I believe history proves that this has been a better formula, but there are exceptions. Frequently, when a producer hires a writer to make a show, [the writer] doesn't bring to it that life because they did it for many reasons, some of which we know are financial. But it just doesn't burn with that kind of passion.

Seller and McCollum shepherded *Rent* from downtown workshop to resounding Broadway success. He and McCollum introduced the *Avenue Q* composer-lyricist team of Robert Lopez and Jeff Marx to librettist Jeff Whitty and director Jason Moore at a time when "the boys had only six songs and some sketch material." Harold Prince made a mark employing both methodologies. Director-choreographer

Jerome Robbins conceived *West Side Story* and developed it with Arthur Laurents, Leonard Bernstein, and Stephen Sondheim. Prince and partner Robert Griffith agreed to produce the show only when others dropped or passed on the property. However, Prince, as producer and director, generated the initial vision of *Cabaret* and engaged John Kander, Fred Ebb, and Joe Masteroff to write it.

In the Golden Age, producers rarely dared to open "cold" on Broadway with a new show; instead, they tried out musicals in cities close to New York, like New Haven, Boston, and Philadelphia, before plunging into the turbulent waters of Broadway. Now, musicals endure a longer process of development before they see the lights of Times Square. Few contemporary producers choose an out-of-town tryout due to the costs of mounting a show and then transporting it to another city. A typical approach now involves some combination of readings, workshops, and a less expensive, not-for-profit production before Broadway. This involves more time and planning than the older method and often extends the developmental period by several years. It also allows the creative team substantial time to refine the work, which was frequently impossible in rushed, out-of-town tryouts—*Spring Awakening*, for example, benefited greatly from multiple incarnations over a long gestation period. It is not without expense, however: a full-scale production at a not-for-profit regional theater, like La Jolla Playhouse or the Old Globe Theatre, can cost a commercial producer as much as $3 million in "enhancement money" in addition to several hundred thousand dollars from the institutional theater's budget.[16]

REDEFINING THE RELATIONSHIP BETWEEN ART AND COMMERCE

The relationship between commercial producers and not-for-profit theaters is a relatively new but vitally important factor. In strictly financial terms, commercial producers seek to earn profits for themselves and their investors; not-for-profit theaters return profits to the institutional coffers. The Public Theatre in New York City produced *A Chorus Line* and then transferred it to Broadway in 1975 without commercial involvement; the Public benefited from all profits. This musical, as groundbreaking for its developmental process as for its form and content, signaled to commercial producers that there was an attractive alternative to grooming a show for Broadway out of town. They sought less expensive, more hospitable venues in which to develop productions beyond the glare of the New York spotlight. Frank Rich highlights the difference between institutional theaters that serve as a testing ground for new musicals brought by commercial producers and institutional theaters that commission and create new work, citing artistic directors like Joseph Papp and George Wolfe of the Public Theatre and André Bishop of Lincoln Center as exemplars "who will take a chance using non-profit money and hope that someone will move it—or they'll move it themselves if it takes off." An institutional theater on Broadway, like Lincoln Center or the Roundabout, can run a successful musical indefinitely without transferring it to a commercial theater. This provides essential income, a necessity in the fiscally challenging world of producing not-for-profit theater. In most instances, commercial producers court institutional theaters, which recognize that there is much to gain from such a relationship. Steven A. Libman, former managing director of La Jolla Playhouse, acknowledges,

> We are devoted to the musical as a uniquely American art form and, therefore, we have a long history with musicals. We produce them primarily because they are artistically very important and, secondarily, because they generate a significant amount of revenue and allow us to grow our subscription base. We lose money on everything we do, but we lose less on a musical. We will lose less on a multi-million dollar, enhanced musical compared with a $500,000 straight show. Depending upon how long we run a musical, we can gross between $500,000 and $1 million in single-ticket sales alone, and I can convert a lot of those single-ticket buyers to subscribers.[17]

In the Golden Age, a commercial producer rolled the dice on an out-of-town tryout. Many productions closed in New Haven or Boston before ever playing Broadway, losing all of their capitalization. The commercial producer today will more willingly risk $2 million in enhancement money for an institutional production that may never transfer to Broadway, than $10 million to mount a commercial production that may flop out of town.

The potential risks for institutional theaters are more frequently organizational than fiscal. As Libman notes,

> You have to be very careful about how involved the outside producers get in the process of creating an enhanced musical or enhanced play. We are a non-profit and cannot be perceived as having the producers in the rehearsal studios telling the director what to do. We run the risk of adversely affecting our agreements with the unions. You have to be able to say to the producers, "You can attend some of the rehearsals but you can't attend all of them, and you really have to be invisible." The outside producers need to know that La Jolla Playhouse is in charge of *producing* the play, and has final say on all artistic matters.

Another threat is the strain that new musicals, because of their size and complexity, can impose. As Libman relates,

> They suck up more time. Our payroll can grow to an additional one hundred part-time employees. The new technology that we use is fascinating but expensive. Rehearsals take longer. You spend more money because you are doing a show where the potential single ticket income is at least $500,000, compared to up to $100,000 for a straight play. We have to constantly remind each other that we have other shows running at the same time so that the other show doesn't become the bastard stepchild of the large, enhanced musical.

The partnership of commercial and not-for-profit arenas was unthinkable a few decades earlier because of the perception of conflicting artistic and financial principles. Today, it offers a popular means of birthing new musicals. As Libman observes,

> In a sense, we have one foot in the non-profit world, but we're also part of the commercial theater world and the enhancement revenue that comes with it is significant. Sometimes, that makes it easier for us to say, "We can balance our budget if we do a big musical that's enhanced as opposed to a non-enhanced play." However, we always have to be careful and make sure the musical fulfills the mission of the organization. But it's like heroin, that enhancement money. It's wonderful for cash flow.

If successful on Broadway, the musical can return 1 to 2 percent of the gross to the institutional theater—perhaps $20,000 a week on a hit show

Regardless of the means of development, according to Alan Levey, "It all comes back to the story-telling. Without a good story, you have nothing." Good ideas may succeed in one venue but fail in another. Many new musicals that earn enthusiastic critical and audience reaction elsewhere fail on Broadway, where different expectations and audience demographics create a more challenging environment. In 2007, *A Catered Affair* was heralded at the Old Globe Theatre but lasted only three months on Broadway.

Producing wisdom, composed of equal parts experience and intuition, is essential in determining the future of new work. *Spring Awakening* played at the Off Broadway, not-for-profit Atlantic Theatre Company in spring 2006. Off Broadway, a designation that applies to a range of not-for-profit and commercial theaters throughout Manhattan, is a less expensive—and, with a maximum of 499 seats, less remunerative—venue than Broadway, where theaters can seat as many as 2,000. General manager Abbie Strassler explains the next steps in the producers' process:

> When the producers saw they had such good reviews, they started thinking, "Should we do it Off-Broadway [in a commercial venue] or on Broadway?" We started running numbers and it just didn't make sense to raise money for a production of that size Off-Broadway. It's very difficult to raise money for Off-Broadway, because [in the investors' view] there's nothing sexy about Off-Broadway. At the time, there were fifteen actors and four musicians, and that's a lot for Off-Broadway. When I started running numbers for Broadway, it did make a little more sense, but I thought, "Oh my God, there's teenage sex, nudity, the word "fucked"! Most "legit" money people said, "You're out of your mind." We were taking a crapshoot. But there was so much passion between [lead producers] Ira Pittelman and Tom Hulce for the piece itself. The feeling was that we might lose some money, but it was worth it. It's groundbreaking and we had to do it.

Musical theater is the mainstay of Broadway's box office. In 2007–08, Broadway grossed $938 million, a robust figure that would have been higher if not for a nineteen-day stagehands' strike. Musicals accounted for approximately $820 million of the box office.[18] Moreover, Broadway and New York City enjoy a symbiotic fiscal relationship. During the city's economic downturn of the 1970s and early 1980s, many theaters were dark because producers lacked capital, and audiences were

reluctant to venture into a blighted Times Square. Theater owners began to co-produce in order to populate their houses and generate income. The difficulty that producers encountered in raising money opened the doors to the so-called British
Invasion of lavishly staged productions such as *Evita, Cats, Les Misérables, Starlight
Express, The Phantom of the Opera*, and *Miss Saigon*. Many critics in the media and the
theatrically sophisticated segment of the theatergoing audience bemoaned the state of
the art and questioned whether the American musical would ever recover. The city's
subsequent economic rebound occasioned the reinvigoration of musicals created in
America. American-born hits like *Rent, Avenue Q, Hairspray, The Lion King, Jersey
Boys, Spamalot*, and *Wicked*, playing in tandem with highly praised revivals of *Gypsy*
and *South Pacific*, epitomize healthy Broadway box office at the beginning of this millennium. These productions reached Broadway by different paths and appeal to a
wide cross-section of theatergoers. However, history teaches that the fiscal and artistic
health of Broadway—once dubbed "the Fabulous Invalid"—is always unpredictable.
Will escalating costs and ticket prices drive producers and audiences to the apparent
safety of adaptations of mediocre movies and yet another iteration of *Grease*, or will
innovation flourish with shows cut from the cloth of *Spring Awakening* and *Passing
Strange*? Alan Levey, formerly of Disney, summed up the challenge. "Producers will
have to become more creative, controlling the economic challenges faced by Broadway
without stifling the creative process. Smart producing inspires creativity on both sides
of the equation—the economics and the creative."

NOTES

1. Fred Ebb, lyrics for "Money, Money," music by John Kander, in *Cabaret*, dir. Bob Fosse, 1972.
2. *Oxford English Dictionary*, 2nd ed. (Oxford: Oxford University Press, 1989), www.oed.
com/, accessed July 19, 2008.
3. Lincoln Center Theater, the Roundabout Theatre Company, and Manhattan Theatre Club
are, as of this writing, not-for-profit theaters with Broadway houses whose productions are
Tony-eligible. Second Stage may soon join their ranks.
4. Jeffrey Seller, telephone interview with the author, July 24, 2008.
5. Paul Libin, telephone interview with the author, July 23, 2008.
6. Author's note: the Shubert, Nederlander, and Jujamcyn organizations own or control
thirty-one Broadway theaters.
7. Frank Rich, telephone interview with the author, July 3, 2008.
8. At eight performances a week, 1,000 performances amount to a run of slightly under
two-and-a-half years, although some shows in the early twentieth century closed for the summer
because theaters lacked air conditioning.
9. "Broadway Long Runs" (Chart in *Variety* [June 9–15, 2008]: 50).
10. Seth Gelblum, telephone interview with the author, June 27, 2008. An old Broadway
maxim, attributed to playwright Robert Anderson, goes: "You can't make a living on Broadway, but
you can make a killing."
11. Abbie Strassler, telephone interview with the author, July 15, 2008.

12. Roy Furman, telephone interview with the author, July 17, 2008.

13. Ralph Bryan, telephone interview with the author, June 30, 2008.

14. Alan Levey, telephone interview with the author, June 11, 2008.

15. See Howard Kissel's excellent 1993 biography, tellingly titled *David Merrick: The Abominable Showman* (New York: Applause Books, 1993).

16. Since the mid-1980s, two institutional theaters in San Diego, for example, La Jolla Playhouse and the Old Globe Theatre, have launched several Broadway productions. La Jolla Playhouse: *Big River, Dangerous Games, The Who's Tommy ,,* the revival of *How to Succeed in Business Without Really Trying, Jane Eyre, Thoroughly Modern Millie, Dracula, the Musical, Jersey Boys, Cry-Baby, and Memphis.* Old Globe: *Into the Woods,* the revival of *Damn Yankees, Play On!, The Full Monty, Dirty Rotten Scoundrels , Dr. Seuss' How the Grinch Stole Christmas!, The Times They Are A-Changin', and A Catered Affair.*

17. Steven A. Libman., interview with the author, June 26, 2008.

18. The Broadway League, "Broadway Season Statistics at a Glance," www.broadwayleague.com/editor_files/Broadway%20Statistics%20at%20a%20Glance.pdf, accessed August 2, 2008.

CHAPTER 26

....

AUDIENCES AND CRITICS

....

MICHELLE DVOSKIN

THE terms "audience" and "critic" seem straightforward. The online *American Heritage Dictionary*'s first definition of audience is those "assembled at a performance ... or attracted by a radio or television program." Thus, an audience comprises people who engage with a particular performance text—for example, musicals. "Critic" is similarly uncomplicated: "one who forms and expresses judgments," in this case, about musicals.[1] By these definitions, every audience member is also, fundamentally, a critic. Everyone who attends a musical, has a response to it, and then shares that response has acted the part of a critic, even if the response was as basic as applause (or lack thereof).

Of course, typically when we talk about musicals and critics, we refer to published critics, individuals who make their living experiencing and responding to musicals, alongside other forms of performance. These are most often writers with some knowledge about and interest in the form, and throughout the musical's history they have been influential in regard to both audiences' attitudes and size. While this specialized role continues to exist, more and more audience members are beginning to share it, thanks to the Internet and the self-publishing possibilities it offers.

While defining both terms and recognizing their relationship is easy on this basic level, thinking about how to make use of them as a scholar of musicals is more complicated. How do musicals affect audiences, and how do audiences affect musicals? How do we make use of and understand the work of critics, both professional and recreational? These are the questions I begin to address in this chapter.

AUDIENCES

In considering musicals' relationships to their audiences, we may begin by acknowl-edging two key things. The first is that musicals are an inherently commercial form. Audiences are crucial to their existence because musicals depend on ticket sales to survive. In commercial venues, the typical goal is to run for as long as possible, or more aptly, as long as sufficient seats are filled with paying customers. Even when musicals play in nonprofit venues, with limited runs, they are typically seen as ways to raise money for less commercially viable material in the season. This need to appeal to audiences affects the choices made by producers and creative teams, par-ticularly as the cost of mounting a musical continues to grow rapidly. Historically, audiences directly influenced musicals' development via their responses during try-out performances. During musical theater's "Golden Age" (1943–approx. 1966), musi-cals were typically developed through out-of-town tryouts, when a new show played in other cities on its way to Broadway. Audience reaction served as feedback for the artistic team, who would then often make adjustments to the show to maximize its audience appeal. This dependence on popularity and responsiveness to audience appeal has tended to make people interested in "serious" theater view musicals with suspicion.[2]

The second key issue is the presence of musicals in a variety of media, since medium matters when thinking about reception practices. Musical *theater* is a live form, with performers sharing time and space with spectators. Like any live theater audience, musical theater audiences are part of a communal experience with other audience members as well as the performers and are "involved in a reciprocal rela-tionship which can change the quality and success of a performance."[3] Most audi-ences are aware of their influence and manage their responses accordingly.

Movie musical audiences are also part of a group but one traditionally under-stood as more privatized. While watching other audience members at a live perfor-mance has historically been an expected part of the event, watching other spectators at a movie is much less common. There are other important differences as well. At a movie musical, the performers are not physically present; the filmic text will be the same every time, regardless of audience composition or response. The medium of film also allows a heightened level of control over reception. Through close-ups and other cinematic choices, film directors can ensure that their audience notices what they want them to, when they want them to. Theater directors, though they can use design and blocking to emphasize key moments or images, have much less control over the audience's gaze.

Television, a medium in which musicals are becoming increasingly popular, shares these elements of fixity and control with film. Television audiences, however, are generally understood as even more privatized than movie audiences. Most tele-vision is viewed in the home, either alone or with small groups of family and friends. This paradigm also holds true for film musicals released on DVD or video. Musicals that occur as part of episodic series, however, have a slightly different relationship to their audiences as a result of the fandom and familiarity built up over time. Many shows also have established fan communities, often online, which offer a designated, preexisting place to share responses to the musical, if not the act of viewing itself.[4]

These differences affect how we think about audiences engaging with a given musical. Audiences watching *Chicago* on Broadway will have a different experience, and perform their responses differently, from audiences who saw the movie version in the theater, and their responses and performance will differ from those who watched it on DVD in their living rooms. For example, on Broadway one of the "merry murderesses" in "Cell Block Tango" might make eye contact with an audience member, who may then pay particular attention to her performances in group numbers. This kind of personalized connection isn't possible for a viewer of the filmed text. And while everyone who watches the movie version of *Chicago* will respond to the same text, audiences who see the live musical will see a different text each night, making generalizations about reception difficult even within a single production's run. One night, the actress playing Roxie Hart might be a little tired, lending a certain vulnerability to her characterization. Another night, a particularly exuberant audience might energize the whole company, creating entirely different nuances in the performances. And of course, in a long-running show like *Chicago*, cast members are frequently replaced. An audience member who saw Ann Reinking's Roxie responded to a different version of the character from one who saw Bianca Marroquin in the same role, in the same production, later in its run.

Despite these important differences, however, certain characteristics of musical reception tend to operate across media. One is the influence of cast albums, which extend aspects of the audience experience beyond the act of viewing the musical itself. Since *Oklahoma!* (1943), Broadway (and, increasingly, Off Broadway) musicals have typically recorded and marketed the original cast performing the songs, creating an often profitable artifact that can be purchased and enjoyed regardless of whether the listener has actually seen the production. Attachment to a cast album can follow from or precede attendance, and through this artifact, it becomes possible to understand oneself as a fan of a show without having seen it.[5] For those who do see a production, these albums grant some measure of permanence to the ephemeral medium of musical theater. While the actual experience of attending the show is impossible to replicate, cast albums allow audiences to relive their experience, offering not only the words and music but, in some measure, the performances of the singers.[6]

Although existing as artifacts themselves, movie musicals also typically release soundtracks that, like the album for a stage musical, allow audiences to engage in additional ways with the production in the space of their home. Even television musicals, which begin for audiences in the home, often take up this trend. For example, both *Xena: Warrior Princess* and *Buffy the Vampire Slayer* produced episodes framed as musicals, and each released a soundtrack. Joss Whedon, *Buffy's* executive producer and the writer/composer/lyricist of the musical episode, emphasized that the release of the album was as much about authenticating his episode as a "real musical" as it was about commerce. In his liner notes for the album, Whedon, a self-proclaimed musicals fan, made the association with authenticity clear: "Now I have a *real* soundtrack album of my musical.... This makes it *real.*"[7]

If audio recordings, and the extended connection they allow, are a common thread across media, so also is the way in which audiences tend to experience musicals. Whether watching live performance, film, or television, audiences engage with musicals in particular ways, ways that have everything to do with the body. Increasingly, musical theater scholars have begun to note the predisposition of musicals toward embodied reception, what Stacy Wolf terms a particularly "performative spectatorship" (Wolf, 2002, 33). Audiences for musicals do not simply watch and listen; they engage kinesthetically, from the most subtle head movement, to tapping fingers to the beat, to feet mimicking dance steps under a chair. And as D. A. Miller points out, this embodiment isn't limited to the actual moments of watching. Many audience members who might hum under their breath during the show offer their own performance of a number later on.[8] Of course, as musicals move into the home via television and DVD, official performances and audience performances can merge. If you are watching alone in your living room, singing full voice and dancing along with a number won't disturb anyone!

The 2008 Pixar film *Wall-E* offers an entertaining illustration of this concept. Wall-E, a trash-compacting robot left alone on earth after all humans have fled, has acquired and become attached to a recording of the musical film *Hello, Dolly*. As the film opens, we see that Wall-E sometimes collects and saves interesting objects during his compacting rounds, including, on this day, a round disc. When he returns home and plays the recording, we see why he chose this object: he wanted to be able to perform along with a sequence of the musical that involved hats. It's clear, watching this moment, that Wall-E has made a regular practice of performing along with the recording and that he has forged a deep connection to the movie that goes far beyond simple entertainment. Watching a musical isn't enough, even for a futuristic robot—the embodiment of reception is somehow essential.

Live, participatory screenings of film and television musicals, most notably *The Rocky Horror Picture Show* (1975), present a different type of embodied reception. This film adaptation of the stage musical *The Rocky Horror Show* was initially unsuccessful before it began to be presented at midnight showings in 1976. These screenings quickly became popular live performance events in their own right, with audience members participating by responding, vocally and physically, to the movie, as well as performing along with the film in floor shows, often in costume.[9] Like Wall-E, audiences for *Rocky Horror* seem compelled to perform along with the musical, but here those performances are social, interactive, and vocal, as well as physical. As both these examples indicate, musical theater scholars need to think more about what it means to take musicals into our bodies. How does this mode of reception affect the ways in which audiences make meaning from musicals? What are musical audiences embodying, as they tap their toes and sing along?

And who are the audiences for musicals? On one level, the answer is almost everyone in the United States—and beyond. Because musicals are a commercial, popular form, they are widely produced in community theaters, dinner theaters, and high schools, and are also a common mode of performance for churches and community festivals. When people ask about the audience for musical theater, however, they are most often referring to Broadway musicals. At the Museum of the City of New York, a placard in the ongoing exhibit *Perform: A History of Broadway and Theater in New York City* describes Broadway's audience as "relatively well-off, well-educated, and predominantly white and female. Visitors to New York fill the largest percentage of seats." Statistically, this assessment is probably true, at least in the early twenty-first century. According to a report by Broadway's national trade association, from June 2006 to June 2007 Broadway audiences were 64 percent female and 74 percent white; they had an annual household income averaging just under $100,000, and of those over twenty-five, 75 percent were college graduates. Tourists accounted for 65 percent of ticket sales.[10]

We should, however, think carefully about how this sort of quantitative data may (or may not) be useful. We might believe, for example, that we can draw significant conclusions about musicals and gender based on these demographics. We know from the statistics that more women than men attended Broadway musicals in 2006–07. We also know that in the popular imagination, the form is typically positioned as somehow associated more with femininity than masculinity, regardless of content, and it would be easy to assume that the audience numbers have created this perception of the form. It would be equally easy, however, to use these data to support an argument that musicals are *designed* to appeal to women and their assumed femininity, and are succeeding. The fact that both of these presumptions come easily to mind points out that the numbers themselves tell us only that a relationship exists; they can tell us almost nothing about how that relationship works, or where causation lies.

Also lacking from the picture created by the demographic study is any recognition of the relationship of gay men to musical theater, which also influences perceptions of effeminacy. The perceived feminization of musical theater accrues not only (or even, I would argue, primarily) from the majority-female audience but also from the affiliation of musical theater with gay men. David Savran echoes many other scholars when he notes that "musical theater…has in popular mythology been adjudged a sacred preserve of gay men."[11] More specifically, musicals are commonly affiliated with effeminate gay men, as in the stereotype of the "show queen." D. A. Miller, like John Clum and other scholars, emphasizes the interrelationship of musicals, gay men, and a queered experience of gender. Miller argues that musical theater functions as "a form whose unpublicizable work is to indulge men in the thrills of a femininity *become their own*" (Miller, 90). While Miller sees a femininity inherent in musicals that makes them appealing to gay male audience members, I would suggest that a more complicated, cyclical relationship is at play: musicals respond to audience interest *and* to perceptions of that interest, and audiences respond both to actual qualities of musicals *and* to perceptions about musicals. While statistics can tell us something about the sex (and sexuality, were that question added) of audience members, they can't unpack this cycle. Quantitative data, therefore, is of limited value in understanding the relationship of musical theater and gender to audiences.

The numbers we have regarding "the Broadway audience" also don't really address the distinct audience makeup for any particular show. The 2008 audience demographics for *Passing Strange* (2008), for example, a coming-of-age story about a young black musician featuring a rock score by its star, Stew, likely differed from those for *Phantom of the Opera* (1988), Andrew Lloyd Webber's operatic megamusical based on the novel by Gaston Leroux. When one is writing about a particular show, awareness of those demographics could potentially be useful. For example, research on *Passing Strange* might benefit from attention to the demographic makeup of the audience and how it differed—or not—from the larger Broadway audience, in order to investigate the show's particular appeal. However, the causation problem would remain. While we can make educated guesses, it's important to resist oversimplifying the relationship between show and demographic. For example, *Phantom of the Opera* has been running for decades, at this point offers very little in the way of theatrical innovation, and has had an enormously successful national and international marketing campaign, while *Passing Strange* had a short run that followed a successful Off Broadway engagement, considerably less aggressive marketing, and more experimental elements in its dramaturgy. All of these things play a role in who fills the theater seats, alongside any emphasis on identity markers like race or age within the show itself.

This points to what is perhaps the largest weakness of using statistics to study audiences. Statistics address questions relevant to marketing a musical, but they can tell us very little about how audiences find meaning in musicals. In the end, what does knowing that 68 percent of the audience for a given show is female tell us about how spectators engaged with the production? Identities are complex and intersectional; the category of "woman," for example, includes such an extraordinarily diverse range of identities and experiences that it becomes almost meaningless as a way of understanding viewing practices. Simply put, sharing a single identity category doesn't mean that spectators will have the same or even similar responses. As Stacy Wolf notes, engaging with a performance requires us to draw on our "cultural competencies," which "are developed in everyday life and can include identity positions...*as well as other kinds of knowledge*" (Wolf, 2002, 25, emphasis mine). While demographic identity markers influence some of our cultural competencies, others derive from experiences and knowledge bases outside traditional understandings of identity. For example, when I watch musicals, my knowledge of musical theater history and interest in directing typically influence my interpretation and response more than any of the traditional identity categories into which I fit.

It's also important to recognize that we can take up viewing positions that may not match our identity category. Perhaps the best example of this is the practice of "queering." In queering, spectators read, watch, or listen in queer ways to a text that officially contains no queer content. For example, an audience member watching *Chicago*'s Velma attempt to seduce Roxie into forming a double act might read her efforts as seduction of a more literal type. Alexander Doty asserts that queer readings are not limited to people who identify as gay, lesbian, bisexual, or queer, and he argues that queer readings and responses can occur "whenever *anyone* produces or responds to culture" (Doty, 3). In making her case for lesbian and feminist readings of mid-century musicals, Wolf makes a similar point, noting that these readings are not limited to lesbians and women (in fact, she acknowledges that some lesbians and women will have no interest in such readings at all) but are available to anyone with sufficient cultural competency and interest (Wolf, 2002, 5). In the end, queering offers an excellent example of the limits of identity's value in understanding reception practices.

None of this, of course, is meant to ignore the very real role identity politics can play in bringing audiences to the theater. We are often drawn to entertainment that features characters that we understand as somehow "like us," whether that means African American audiences attending *The Color Purple* (2005) or younger audiences flocking to *Rent* (1996). A production's marketing choices can also influence these trends. For example, *Rent* pioneered the practice of offering heavily discounted ($20) tickets for the first two rows of orchestra seats to whoever would wait in line for them.[12] This innovation encouraged younger audience members, who couldn't necessarily afford ordinarily high ticket prices but often had both the time and inclination to accept long, sometimes overnight, waits, to attend. It's also worth noting that a show's audience makeup may shift over time, as hits such as *Phantom of the Opera* or *Rent* accrue cultural capital and become "the thing to see," whether or not the show itself seems particularly interesting to a given spectator.

CRITICS

Critics, adversarial or supportive, have been essential collaborators throughout musical theater's history. Throughout the Golden Age of musical theater, New York had up to nine daily papers publishing theater reviews, including the *New York Times,* the *Herald Tribune,* the *Daily News,* the *Post,* and the *World-Telegram and Sun.* Critics' feedback could encourage changes in a show during its tryout period, influence a show's journey to Broadway, increase (or decrease) attendance, and help shape audience response. During out-of-town tryouts, reviews from local critics had two crucial effects. First, they offered the creative team outside perspectives on what was—or wasn't—working. Since revisions were an expected part of these tryouts, critics could have significant influence on how a show evolved. Second, they helped create expectations and word of mouth for the show as it moved toward Broadway.

For much of musical theater's history, critics' reviews were vital to a show's success once it arrived in New York. Unanimous bad reviews were typically enough to close a show, while strong reviews were seen as essential to creating a hit. Carol Channing, reminiscing about her first starring role, in *Gentlemen Prefer Blondes,* emphasizes the degree to which a show's success or failure was seen as dependent on the critics: "After the show, I could not leave my dressing room until…all the powers that be had advance notice from the newspapers that we were a hit."[13] The prestige of the reviewer, and particularly the paper he wrote for, mattered; if reviews were mixed, the *New York Times* often proved a decisive voice. The power of the *Times* has only increased in recent years, as the number of daily papers in New York has continued to drop. Still, as important as reviews have always been, they aren't perfect predictors of a show's box-office potential. Well-reviewed shows don't always have long runs—the original production of *Candide* (1956), for example, received mainly positive reviews but closed after a money-losing seventy-three performances.[14] While, as this suggests, reviews have never been 100 percent predictive of success or failure, the power of traditional print criticism has also waned over time. Some contemporary shows leave critics unimpressed but wow audiences and become smash hits. (I'll talk more about one example, *Wicked* [2003], at the end of the chapter.) Conversely, *Passing Strange* was a critical success, with strong reviews including a rave from Charles Isherwood in the *Times*, but it ran only 165 performances.[15] There is one area, however, in which critical power seems to have increased over time. While negative reviews no longer lead to automatic closure, today's critics can help a show open. Increasingly, musicals are developed off Broadway, often by nonprofit theaters. Strong reviews of these shows frequently encourage producers to invest in a Broadway production.[16]

While traditional criticism clearly retains some influence, in recent years the major print critics have ceased to be the only game in town. New media platforms have created increasing opportunities for criticism that can both add to the historical archive and influence an ever-wider body of potential audience members. In particular, the rise of the Internet has provided new forums for criticism. First, as most newspapers add online platforms to their print work, the "official" review becomes accessible to those who may not subscribe to the paper. Many papers' Web sites also allow readers to comment and post their own thoughts. The *New York Times*, for example, puts links to their critic's review and user reviews side-by-side on the page of show listings. Anyone who is interested can easily move from reading Isherwood's review of the hit musical *Spring Awakening* (2006) to perusing the ninety-two "user reviews" posted by interested audience members.[17] A more personalized criticism is available via e-mail. While people have always been able to obtain reviews from friends, the advent of e-mail makes the process quicker, simpler, and more easily archived. A request for reviews can be sent out once to a wide variety of friends and colleagues, who can respond immediately. Their responses, more easily than phone conversations, can then be saved for future use.

The advent of other online media have also increased opportunities for less official, but often no less astute, criticism. Blogs, for example, allow for more specialized criticism that explicitly takes up particular points of view. The immensely popular social networking site Facebook also offers opportunities for recreational criticism. While a Facebook account includes a profile with basic biographical information, users can also download applications to personalize their pages, including "Stage Door," which allows users to display their favorite shows and review them. Finally, a less textual but as easily archived online venue for criticism is the podcast. Podcasts are audio (and increasingly, video) recordings that interested listeners can download free of charge. Fairly easy to create, podcasts offer another avenue through which recreational critics can reach out to anyone with an interest in musical theater. Like blogs, podcasts tend to be ongoing affairs, allowing listeners to become familiar with the critic's point of view. It's important to remember, too, that these platforms can offer access to productions done in any venue a writer cares to address—from Broadway to small town high schools—thereby offering students of musical theater access to information on small, local productions that ordinarily might be difficult to study.

While the particulars of critics' power and the media through which they communicate have shifted over time, critics remain crucial to our understanding of musical theater history, as reviews provide what is often the only record of what a production might have looked and sounded like. However, we have to remember that those records are neither objective nor transparent windows onto the performance. In examining a given piece of criticism, it's crucial to consider the writer's goals. Different critics have different understandings of the critic's role. Some recognize that they are creating a historical record and emphasize details in order to archive what otherwise will exist only in memories. Many see themselves as a commercial service, helping audience members decide how to spend their money. Some consider themselves guardians of an art form and focus on enforcing what they see as its standards, "polic[ing] the boundaries of the cultural hierarchy" (Savran, 2003, 48). Still others are interested in using theater, and musical theater specifically, to hold conversations about larger world issues. Of course, these aren't mutually exclusive objectives, and most critics combine two or more of them. Given the limited word count available for their responses, critics' choices of goals have enormous influence on what they include in their writing.

Considering a critic's objectives is the first step in using his or her work productively. The second is paying attention to a particular critic's interests and strengths. For example, Walter Kerr, critic for the *Herald Tribune* from 1951 to 1966 and later for the *New York Times*, was a book writer for musicals before he was a critic, making his dramaturgical assessments particularly interesting. Awareness of a critic's tastes and biases is also helpful. Some critics mark these themselves. Clive Barnes's (*New York Times*) 1977 review of *Annie* offers an amusing example. He notes his surprise at finding the show "whimsically charming," since he typically has no patience for shows about "performing children and performing dogs." His positive review, he points out, should therefore be read differently from one by a writer who "customarily swoons at" such material.[18] In other cases, it may be necessary to do a little research. Does a critic typically adore a particular performer? Dislike deviation from the traditional book musical form? Find a given composer uninspiring? Reviewers' opinions on any specific show are best understood in the context of their larger bodies of work.

Finally, it's useful to look at as many reviews of a production as possible. Different reviewers may take entirely different views of a given show, or they may disagree on specific elements. Reviews of the 1980 revival of *Camelot*, for example, range from raves to absolute pans. Critics also split widely on Richard Burton's star performance. While Frank Rich, in the *Times*, rhapsodized about how Burton "seems to own [the stage] by divine right" and found his reprise of his 1960 performance magnificent, Clive Barnes in the *Post* was positively nasty: "he seems little more than a burnt-out dummy." Clearly we can't draw any conclusions about the overall quality of Burton's performance through these reviews. Several reviewers, however, mention the unique and powerful quality of Burton's "sonorous" (Barnes), "powerful yet vulnerable" (Rich), "distinctive, irresistible voice" (Watt, *Daily News*).[19] So while we can't judge his performance as a whole, we can safely assume that Burton's vocal performance was strong and distinctive, and we can begin to imagine what it might have sounded like. Through careful, thoughtful use of reviews, musical theater scholars can begin to recreate performances lost to time without inadvertently codifying a single individual's opinions or biases.

AUDIENCE–CRITIC INTERSECTIONS: *WICKED*

I conclude by looking briefly at a recent musical as an example of the complicated interactions among musicals, audiences, and critics. *Wicked*, the blockbuster success that opened in 2003, offers a useful perspective on these relationships, in part because of how the production constructs its audience. All theatrical performances, including musicals, address themselves to a particular type of spectator, with particular cultural competencies. This choice of address is not naïve or innocent; as I noted at the beginning of the chapter, as a commercial form, musicals are produced, particularly on Broadway, to bring in audiences large enough to fill houses and earn a profit. Still, shows are increasingly choosing to target spectators outside the traditional "white, middle-class, heterosexual, and male" (and, I would add, middle-aged) paradigm mainstream theater has typically emphasized.[20] Looking at *Wicked*'s engagement with its intended audience outside as well as inside the theater, alongside its relationship to critics, will clarify some of my earlier arguments and offer an example of how we might begin to think about musical theater audiences and critics in more nuanced ways.

An adaptation of Gregory Maguire's novel of the same name, *Wicked* reimagines the story of *The Wizard of Oz*'s Wicked Witch of the West. The musical focuses on Elphaba, the green-skinned girl who will become that feared figure—unjustly, in this version—and follows the development of her friendship with Galinda/Glinda, the Good Witch. While Glinda and Elphaba have heterosexual romances, it is their relationship that forms the spine of the show. *Wicked*, then, unapologetically focuses not just on women, but on young women. As Wolf notes, it taps into "a contemporary lexicon of 'girl power' images."[21] Additionally, by emphasizing Elphaba's role as an outsider, the show speaks to challenges most young people face as they move into adulthood. Attention to the show's merchandising strategies bears out an interest in attracting young, female fans: the "Ozdust Boutique" homepage, the hub for online sales of *Wicked* merchandise, primarily features young women in fitted T-shirts.[22] While T-shirts for male fans can be found deeper in the Web site, much of the merchandise is distinctly feminine—pink T-shirts, sparkly earrings and necklaces—and the models, particularly the women, generally seem much younger than the "average" Broadway audience member. *Wicked* aims squarely for a young, female audience.[23]

Indisputably a hit, *Wicked* continues playing as of this writing to nearly 100 percent capacity crowds in New York almost eight years after opening, with productions finding significant success in other cities and on tour.[24] Yet it opened to reviews that were mixed, at best. Brantley, in the *Times,* found things to admire—particularly Kristin Chenoweth's performance as Glinda—but in the end his review, tellingly titled "There's Trouble in Emerald City," described *Wicked* as a "bloated production" that "does not, alas, speak hopefully for the future of the Broadway musical."[25] Isherwood, writing for *Variety,* had similar feelings.[26] The *New Yorker's* John Lahr was also impressed by Chenoweth and a few other elements, but he found the score lacking and saw *Wicked* as "a morass of overproduction." He concluded his review by mocking audience members who "gave this fourteen-million-dollar piece of folderol a standing ovation."[27] In the *Village Voice*, Michael Feingold's scathing review labeled the show "a hideous mess of a musical."[28]

One critic, however, gave the show a glowing review. Elysa Gardner, theater and pop music critic for *USA Today,* declared *Wicked* a "triumph" and "the most complete, and completely satisfying, new musical I've come across in a long time."[29] There are likely many reasons for Gardner's divergence from her colleagues: her taste in music, her relative interest (or lack thereof) in upholding cultural hierarchies, or any number of other factors. Still, it's perhaps telling that she is the lone female critic represented here. Watching the 2007 documentary *Show Business: The Road to Broadway,* which follows four new musicals and a set of critics through the making of the 2003–04 Broadway season, it's impossible not to notice that almost all the critics chosen to represent their field are middle-aged (or older) white men.[30] It's equally impossible not to notice a certain tone of disdain (echoed in some of the reviews cited) for *Wicked* and its fans, a disdain that seemed absent when they questioned or doubted other shows. It seems plausible that at least some of this hostility may have come from being in the unusual position of finding themselves emphatically *not* the ideal, targeted spectator for this particular musical.

In considering why *Wicked* was able not only to survive these negative reviews but also to thrive like few other musicals in history, the difference in cultural competencies between the audience the show spoke to most directly and the official critics seems particularly relevant. Perhaps audiences were so willing to ignore the official reviews because they also recognized that *Wicked* wasn't aimed at those critics. Certainly, other factors helped make the show a success despite the sometimes nasty reviews. It's an adaptation of a very popular novel, itself an adaptation of a classic American film, based on a classic popular novel. It offers enormous spectacle, something that has often proven quite appealing to audiences. And the Internet allowed for the creation of an enormous fan community, building enthusiasm and extremely positive word of mouth from audience members who, knowingly or not, were taking on the role of critic themselves—and doing so from an ideal, rather than a marginalized, spectatorial position.[31] The convergence of all of these factors makes *Wicked* a useful example of the need for nuanced, multifaceted analysis in considering the inter-connected relationship between audiences, critics (professional and recreational), and musicals.

NOTES

1. http://education.yahoo.com/reference/dictionary/, accessed July 11, 2009.

2. See David Savran, "Toward a Historiography of the Popular" (*Theatre Survey* 45 [2004]: 211–17).

3. Susan Bennett, *Theatre Audiences: A Theory of Production and Reception,* 2nd ed. (London: Routledge, 1997), p. 21.

4. For more on the relationship of audiences to these popular culture media over time, see Richard Butsch, *The Making of American Audiences: From Stage to Television, 1750–1990* (Cambridge: Cambridge University Press, 2000).

5. In fact, beginning with *Jesus Christ Superstar* (1971), some musicals released cast albums prior to the production itself, creating fans before the show was ever performed.

6. Stacy Wolf, *A Problem Like Maria: Gender and Sexuality in the American Musical* (Ann Arbor: University of Michigan Press, 2002), p. 7. See also Michael R. Schiavi, "Opening Ancestral Windows: Post-Stonewall Men and Musical Theatre" (*New England Theatre Journal* 13 [2002]: 77–98).

7. Joss Whedon, "Liner Notes," *Buffy the Vampire Slayer: Once More, with Feeling, Original Cast Album* (Rounder Records, 2002), p. 3, emphasis mine.

8. D. A. Miller, *Place for Us: Essay on the Broadway Musical* (Cambridge, MA: Harvard University Press, 1998), p. 87.

9. See Raymond Knapp, *The American Musical and the Performance of Personal Identity* (Princeton, NJ: Princeton University Press, 2006), pp. 240–52. Among several book-length accounts of the *Rocky Horror* "phenomenon," see especially Jim Whittaker's *Cosmic Light: The Birth of a Cult Classic* (Altoona, PA: Acme Books, 1998).

10. "The Demographics of the Broadway Audience 2006–2007," Broadway League, http://www.broadwayleague.com/index.php?url_identifier=the-demographics-of-the-broadway-audience-2005–2006, accessed September 13, 2008.

11. David Savran, *A Queer Sort of Materialism: Recontextualizing American Theatre* (Ann Arbor: University of Michigan Press, 2003), p. 59. See also Miller; Wolf, 2002; John Clum, *Something for the Boys: Musical Theater and Gay Culture* (New York: St. Martin's Press, 1999); Alexander Doty, *Making Things Perfectly Queer: Interpreting Mass Culture* (Minneapolis: University of Minnesota Press, 1993); Frances Negrón-Muntaner, "Feeling Pretty: *West Side Story* and Puerto Rican Identity Discourses" (*Social Text* 63 18.2 [2000]: 83–106); and Schiavi.

12. Matthew Blank, "Broadway Rush and Standing Room Only Policies," *Playbill.com,* http://www.playbill.com/celebritybuzz/article/82428.html, accessed December 2, 2008.

13. Carol Channing, "Foreword," in *Opening Nights on Broadway: A Critical Quotebook of the Golden Age of the Musical Theatre,* Oklahoma! *to* Fiddler on the Roof, by Steven Suskin (New York: Schirmer Books, 1990), p. xv.

14. Steven Suskin, *Opening Nights on Broadway: A Critical Quotebook of the Golden Age of the Musical Theatre,* Oklahoma! *to* Fiddler on the Roof, (New York: Schirmer Books, 1990), p. 132.

15. Charles Isherwood, "It's a Hard Rock Life: Theatre Review of *Passing Strange*" (*New York Times* [February 29, 2008]). http://theater.nytimes.com/2008/02/29/theater/reviews/29stra. html?ref=theater. (accessed May 9, 2011).

16. I wish to thank Steven Adler for his assistance with this point.

17. "Broadway," http://theater2.nytimes.com/venues/broadway.html, accessed November 24, 2008.

18. Clive Barnes, "Stage: 'Annie' Finds a Home" (*The New York Times* [April 22, 1977]: 65).

19. As quoted in Steven Suskin, *More Opening Nights on Broadway: A Critical Quotebook of the Musical Theatre, 1965 through 1981* (New York: Schirmer Books, 1997), pp. 131–33. Both this volume and its precursor, *Opening Nights on Broadway*, offer useful overviews of the critical response to a vast array of Broadway musicals (although the reviews are heavily edited), as well as brief biographies of major critics.

20. Jill Dolan, *The Feminist Spectator as Critic* (Ann Arbor: University of Michigan Press, 1988), p. 1.

21. Stacy Wolf, "'Defying Gravity': Queer Conventions in the Musical *Wicked*" (*Theatre Journal* 60.1 [2007]: 1–21), pp. 4–5. Wolf also argues compellingly that the relationship the show builds between the two young women is a queer one.

22. "The Ozdust Boutique Online," Araca Merchandise, http://www.wickedmerch.com, accessed September 13, 2008.

23. *Wicked* was not the first show to address a young, female audience, but its success has inspired more shows with a similar approach. See Campbell Robertson, "Tweens Love Broadway, but Can't Save It Alone" (*New York Times*, October 2, 2007). http://www.nytimes.com/2007/10/02/theater/02twee.html?pagewanted=1&sq=tweens%20love%20broadway&st=nyt&adxnnl=1&scp=1&adxnnlx=1304978860-IUYelSXsiF3Nk8z0abvYWQ. (accessed May 9, 2011).

24. "Broadway Grosses: *Wicked,*" BroadwayWorld.com, http://www.broadwayworld.com/grossesshow.cfm?show=Wicked, accessed May 7, 2011.

25. Ben Brantley, "There's Trouble in Emerald City: WICKED" (*New York Times* [October 31, 2003]: E-1).

26. Charles Isherwood, "More Bothered than Bewitched by *Wicked*" (*Variety* [November 3, 2003]: 30).

27. John Lahr, "The Critics: The Theatre: Bitches and Witches: Ulterior Motives in *Cat on a Hot Tin Roof* and *Wicked*" (*New Yorker* 79.34 [November 10, 2003]: 126–27).

28. Michael Feingold, "Voice Choices: Theater: Green Witch, Mean Time: Both On and Off-Broadway, New Musicals Suffer from Severe Multiple Personality Disorder" (*Village Voice* 48.45 [November 5–11, 2003]: 77).

29. Elysa Gardner, "Something 'Wicked' Comes to Broadway" (*USA Today* [October 31, 2003]: 9E-6).

30. *Show Business: The Road to Broadway,* directed by Dori Berinstein, 2007 (Liberation Entertainment DVD release, 2007).

31. For an excellent discussion of *Wicked*'s relationship to its girl fans, see Stacy Wolf, "Wicked Divas, Musical Theatre, and Internet Girl Fans" (*Camera Obscura* 22.2 [2007]: 39–71).

CHAPTER 27

STARS AND FANS

HOLLEY REPLOGLE-WONG

Sawyer, you're going out a youngster, but you've got to come
back a star!

—42nd Street (1933)

American imaginations have invented numerous mythologies about the fledgling
Broadway star ascending to her or his rightful place in the show business firma-
ment. *42nd Street,* Busby Berkeley's Depression-era "backstage" film musical, tells
the quintessential "big break" tale. A young chorus girl, Peggy Sawyer (Ruby Keeler),
gets an opportunity of a lifetime when she is selected to replace the lead, who broke
her ankle the night before the premiere. With a singular stroke of luck, and a lot of
hard work to develop her raw ability, the chorus girl becomes a star on the Great
White Way overnight—and every member of the onscreen audience is thrilled that
they were the lucky ones who were able to witness, and participate in, the birth of
the star. The film ends with the audience leaving the theater abuzz with adulation
for the new leading lady.

Although Sawyer's exhilarating rise to fame is a fictional tale, it has several
points of articulation with a real and equally thrilling legend. Midway through the
evening of October 14, 1930, a young unknown singer and former secretary who had
purportedly "never had a singing lesson in her life" took center stage at the end of
the first act of George and Ira Gershwin's *Girl Crazy* and introduced her second
featured solo of the evening, "I Got Rhythm."[1] The fast-paced, rhythmically exhilarating tune played up Ethel Merman's best asset as a performer: her powerful belt
voice that she could project, loud and clear, straight into the back of the theater. On
the second time through the chorus, Merman omitted the first three lines of lyrics
and triumphantly belted a sustained C over the orchestra before demanding "Who

could ask for anything more?" Indeed, the audience decided that they couldn't, and Ethel Merman was an overnight sensation. Audiences responded to her ability and powerful presentation. Critics broadened audiences' acclaim with notices that drew in even more people wanting to be dazzled by the new talent. In short time, Merman's name would headline Broadway theater marquees.

Both of these star-making mythologies assimilate and reconcile seemingly paradoxical aspects of stardom. Sawyer and Merman are both "ordinary people"—an average city-dweller and a stenographer—with extraordinary raw talent. They work hard (in *42nd Street*, Sawyer works to near collapse; the consummate professional Merman sings her songs the same way every time and was famous for rarely requiring an understudy) but also win success because of a lucky "break"—one critical opportunity to show the world what they can do. Although stars have modest and relatable roots, they must also be exceptional enough to receive notice. Stars are accessible, but also extraordinary. Merman's "natural" vocal ability and alleged humble background (really a middle-class upbringing) provides hope to dreamers. And although they may have "what it takes" to be a star, they need the audience to accept them, identify with them, and idolize them in order to thrive.

Richard Dyer, who pioneered the field of star studies in his influential book *Stars*,[2] outlines some of the incongruities that form a star's persona. As Stacy Wolf points out, "The star persona is a public figure who is defined, often complexly and often with contradictions, in relation to the cultural politics and social practices of her time."[3] A star may reify the ideological status quo by reiterating or concealing dominant values, but he or she can also be a locus for resistance or subversion, a place of identification for the marginalized audience member (Dyer 1998, 26).[4] Star-making is a reciprocal project that is mediated between the star figure (including the entourage of agents, managers, and stylists), the media, the mass audience, and the individual fan. These elements work together to create the star's image, which is the persona that the public sees and consumes. Stories about stars enact a capitalistic American narrative of success. As Dyer writes, "The general image of stardom can be seen as a version of the American Dream, organized around the themes of consumption, success, and ordinariness" (Dyer 1998, 38). Star legends provide inspiration and optimism, but stardom does have its dark side as well. Dyer cites Judy Garland and Marilyn Monroe as two examples of the "soured" American dream, stars whose enduring mythologies are as much shaded by personal and professional tragedy as they are highlighted by success.

Success in the two star scenarios related here (one fictional, one not) relies as much on adoration from the audience as it does on the talent of the performer. A star's image is made up of media "texts," including not only roles and performances but also artifacts such as recordings, films, publicity pictures, and interviews. Fan practice and the relationship between fans and star texts are intricate and varied. In this essay, I outline an introduction to scholarship on stars and fan participation in stardom, and I address a variety of topics pertinent to the study of stars and fans of musical theater. What characteristics compose a star? How do stars operate socially and culturally? How does a star leave an imprint on a show text? How do audiences participate in fandom? I also consider the history of stardom in musical theater, detailing how facets of stardom and the relationships between stars and fans have been altered as recording technologies changed.

Star Qualities

So, what is a musical theater star? Perhaps it may seem silly to ask this question because much of what defines a star is obvious and easy to identify; audiences "know" who has achieved stardom. Although the "star," the "celebrity," and the "diva" often seem to be interchangeable terms, since they all suggest fame and power, these classifications have important differences. Celebrity suggests renown and notoriety but does not imply the talent, ability, and continued existence as a figure of importance that a star might have. A diva has an extraordinary aura of talent, endurance, and a strongly defined persona. More generically, a star is a public figure (often a performer) whose personal fame is foregrounded as much as or more than the roles he or she plays. Stars are multivalent personae; they are people who work as actors who portray characters. Stars combine distinctive talents with recognizable (and often imitable) looks and personalities that are spun and perpetuated as an image. A star's image is not limited to visual content; the voice, manner of speech, and patterns of behavior are all part of celebrity. It is not enough to be perfect for the role, or a gifted "triple-threat" (singer, dancer, and actor). Stars are unique. Their voices and personae are recognizable, and their abilities and charm are not only impressive but often somehow off-kilter: Ethel Merman's brashness and big belting voice, Julie Andrews's primness and carefully balanced vocals, Patti LuPone's quirky diction, George Hearn's hammy acting and booming lyric baritone.[5] Visibility is certainly a factor of celebrity; a star typically has a resumé filled with leading roles in successful and popular shows (although perhaps a few flops as well; one of the most important facets of a diva persona is her ability to triumph over failure with a spectacular comeback). Stars are marketable; their names come above the show title on the marquee, as an incentive for audiences to buy tickets. Successful stars like Bernadette Peters or Audra MacDonald sell tickets to solo concert performances with their names alone. Without star power, these performers might have successful careers, but they would not be the major draw; the show would take precedence.

Richard Dyer writes, regarding film stars, that image develops from media texts such as interviews, publicity photos, and recordings, which

> consist both of what we normally refer to as his or her "image," made up of screen roles and obviously stage-managed public appearances, and also of images of the manufacture of that "image" and of the real person who is the site or occasion of it.[6]

In Dyer's view, stars are always significations; the public never knows them as "real people," although the fact that stars are also people who have offstage lives raises questions of authenticity and authorship that the fan must process and reconcile. Celebrity media work hard to convince the public that what we are seeing is private and "real life." Behind-the-scene biographies and interviews practice acts of "authentic spontaneity." To what degree do stars author their images, and to what degree are the roles they play reflective of their selfhood? Audiences want to know who the person is, and they often believe that the star's image is representative of his or her actual self. Stars perform roles based on a "good fit" to their personae (playing types), and we map readings of the actor onto the character; but the oeuvre of accumulated roles also offers possible readings of the star.

Musical theater is full of female stars with strong, diva-like personae, and the repertory of shows favors strong women performers. But what is a "diva?" The term "diva," borrowed from both an Italian word ("goddess") and the Latin *divus* ("divine one"), was initially applied to late nineteenth- and early twentieth-century operatic sopranos. Historically, "divas" are women performers; the term is rarely applied to male performers except in reference to a gender-bending or queer performance (as with a drag queen, for instance). Not all female musical theater stars are divas, and it is possible for a diva's star to fizzle. In order to reach "divadom," a diva must have been a star at some point in her career, but she can still retain the diva label even if her star is no longer in ascendance.

The voices of past and current divas are inextricably bound up in notions of genius and embodiment. Divas are not only figures of fascination but potentially also figures of public identification through their public personal struggles and tragedies. In addition to diseases and addictions, career battles and personal strife, often publicized with reference to her appearance and weight, the diva must show resilience and the ability to make a comeback against steep odds. Judy Garland, with comebacks both tragic (her 1954 film *A Star is Born*) and triumphant (her 1961 Carnegie Hall concert) codified these tragic qualities of the diva for twentieth-century popular music audiences.[7] Beyond their highly iconic images and mannerisms, singer-divas have historically thrived on talent, extravagance, and unique, innovative vocal styles. The diva also displays an apparent indifference to reality, which may be a result of her total unawareness of how she is being received or a misunderstanding of what audiences find appealing about her.[8] However, this indifference often comes across to the public as courage and grit, and in the end the diva sometimes turns to a sort of rueful acknowledgment of her reception in her public persona.

A BRIEF HISTORY OF STARDOM

Historically, the emergence of stardom is often traced to eighteenth-century theatrical actors, particularly David Garrick, whose star mythology reads similarly to the ones above: his innovative naturalistic portrayal of Richard III in 1741 brought him fame nearly overnight. In the 1790s, actors following in the footsteps of Garrick toured popular roles (often Shakespeare) through Europe and the United States, promoting themselves just as much as, if not more than, the roles they played. They fused their names to the character so audiences could easily remember and spread the word about an individual actor's version of the character.[9]

Through the early nineteenth century in the United States, actors were typically employed as stock players attached to a particular theater. Actors specialized in certain types of role, and they would rotate between playing leads and character parts, depending on the cast list and genre of the play; an actor who played the romantic lead in one play with the company might have nothing to do with the next play, featuring a comic male lead. As more stars became known and toured more frequently (often European actors like Sarah Bernhardt), stock companies went into decline. Stars were a stronger audience draw, and they helped "legitimize" the theatrical profession to a public who had long been suspicious of actors' morality. Actors who were acclaimed for their interpretations of dramatic roles provided an image of greater stability than the nameless stock player, and through them the public slowly began to regard theater as a respectable profession and stable economic venture.[10]

In 1817, European vocal stars began to tour American theaters, singing selections from famous operas in variety shows and solo concerts. One of the most popular vocal stars was the "Swedish Nightingale," soprano Jenny Lind, who had a wildly successful American concert tour in 1850, engineered by circus impresario P. T. Barnum. She was famed as much for her charity, Victorian-era virtue, and "anti-diva" behavior as she was for her voice, which was celebrated for being pure and clear, possessed of very little vibrato or excessive emotion. Her voice was a reflection of her carefully constructed public persona; as Susan Leonardi and Rebecca Pope point out, Lind "provided middle-class ticket buyers with a model of their own ideals."[11] She performed only in venues appropriate to her image of respectability, such as concert halls and churches. Her image was part of the product audiences consumed, and it was both relatable and exceptional.

Through the nineteenth century, concert tours like Lind's and touring companies with hopeful performers crossed America. Variety and minstrel shows were itinerant, of irregular quality, and attracted varying audience demographics; some were held in community theaters, others in saloons. Minstrel shows in particular were geared toward a mostly white, male, working-class audience. In 1860, theaters across America started to organize a tour schedule for variety shows, and performers developed their acts to target family audiences, creating the genre of entertainment known as vaudeville. By the 1890s, vaudeville performers traveled to a set series of theaters—a "circuit"—and depending on their style and quality, they would be hired to perform in "small time" venues (low-paying contracts, frequent performances, rural theaters) "medium time" theaters, or the "big time" urban theaters that catered to the middle and upper classes. Theaters decided the lineup of the acts based on quality and popularity; the best acts went on second (when the audience was finally seated) and second to last, and the worst acts went on first (while people would be looking for their seats) and last (to clear out the theater). This system inherently leaned toward the development of a star system: acts that were familiar, well advertised, and reviewed were the ones that generated more revenue and word-of-mouth promotion.

Sheet music of popular songs, which were generally sold to middle-class amateur musicians, was marketed with a picture of the star who had made the tune famous on the cover. Performers rose and fell on the circuit—the more popular the act, the better lineups and bookings it received. The genre of American musical theater came into its own at the end of the nineteenth century, developing from both European operetta and forms of music theater such as minstrelsy, vaudeville, burlesque, and the spectacular extravaganza (the 1866 extravaganza *The Black Crook* in particular figures into the beginning of American musical theater).[12] Stars from vaudeville were often the first headliners in these productions. George M. Cohan, for instance, a "writer-director-star" who grew up touring vaudeville circuits with his family, was one of the early developers of Broadway shows in the 1900s.

Cinema took its first audiences and many of its first actors from vaudeville and the so-called "legitimate" stage ("artistic" theater, as opposed to "commercial" theater) where the star system was already in place. Janet Staiger points out that in early film studios, actors were not given name credit (they were labeled by a production company: for example, "The Vitagraph Girl"), but eventually studios were pressed by the public to adopt the cult of personality as the main source of publicity for their output. Audiences had a stronger curiosity about the stars—what their lives were like, where they shopped, whom they spent time with—than the production companies had anticipated. To audiences, stars had become a significant part of what defined entertainment.

With the advent of the "talkie" (films with synchronized sound), screen adaptations of musicals gave audiences across America the chance to enjoy professionally produced musicals with stars they might not otherwise have been able to see if their city was not big enough to warrant a national tour and if they lacked the funds and leisure time to visit Broadway. The first big success of sound film, *The Jazz Singer* (1927), starring Al Jolson (perhaps the biggest vaudeville star of all time), established this pattern. That film and many that followed gave even small-town audiences the opportunity to experience a star's "presence." Later breakthroughs in commercial recording technology each placed a different set of demands on the star and changes in the ways in which fans might engage with them. A significant swath of scholarship on stardom focuses on film, which has become the benchmark of stardom in American culture, the site where true stars test their box-office mettle. Musical theater has a number of important points of historical articulation with film studies— perhaps inevitably so, given the early run of successful filmed musicals.

Stars and Technology

The Jazz Singer established the musical as a commercially viable genre for the screen, and it also set a precedent for the musical to become a star-focused form of entertainment. Studios developed "stables" of musical stars, and studio musicals were crafted to showcase the talents of their most popular stars, who served as a kind of name-brand guarantee of a certain kind of product; audiences trusted stars to give them a quality product in their specialized genres. Fred Astaire had achieved stardom on Broadway when he signed with RKO, and the studio teamed him with Ginger Rogers as supporting players in *Flying Down to Rio* (1933). Their dance number in that film made them stars of the silver screen, and RKO went on to produce nine musicals for them within the span of six years (1933–1939). At MGM, Judy Garland, who started her career as part of a touring sister act in vaudeville, struggled against her studio-manufactured image of the unglamorous, extremely talented, eternal little girl. Gene Kelly, an established dancer and choreographer on Broadway, came to Hollywood in 1941 and became an innovator for cinematic dance in films such as *An American in Paris* (1951) and *Singin' in the Rain* (1952). Some musical theater stars did not transition well to the screen; Ethel Merman and Mary Martin each made a few films and left Hollywood, never achieving the kind of success they enjoyed on Broadway.[13] However, while Merman's and Martin's performance styles and personae did not translate well to the screen, they came across well as guest performers on live television.[14] Early television variety shows borrowed conventions of form and style from vaudeville and had live studio audiences; musical theater actors were accustomed to playing to an auditorium of spectators.

In the 1950s and '60s, starring roles in a handful of important film musicals went to Hollywood stars whose singing voices, inadequate by normal Broadway standards, were either overdubbed or left alone as an emblem of naturalness; the former included Natalie Wood in *West Side Story* (1961), Rosalind Russell in *Gypsy* (1962), and Audrey Hepburn in *My Fair Lady* (1964), and the latter Marlon Brando in *Guys and Dolls* (1955) and Lee Marvin and Clint Eastwood in *Paint Your Wagon* (1969). Ironically, Julie Andrews won an Academy Award for *Mary Poppins* (1964) in the same year she had been denied the lead role in the film adaptation of *My Fair Lady*, which she had originated on Broadway. Barbra Streisand became a film star with her 1968 screen debut as Fanny Brice in a film adaptation of *Funny Girl*, a role she created on Broadway, but she had already found popular success as a singer, stage actress, and recording artist. Liza Minnelli, another star who was involved in several kinds of media at once—live performance, recordings, film, and television—reached a pinnacle of fame in 1972 when she starred in a film adaptation of *Cabaret*.

More recent film musicals continue to cast current screen stars as their leads, some of whom lack the singing and dancing chops to do well on Broadway but still acquit themselves well on screen (e.g., Nicole Kidman in *Moulin Rouge!* [2001] and Johnny Depp in *Sweeney Todd: The Demon Barber of Fleet Street* [2007]; Catherine Zeta Jones in *Chicago* [2002], trained as a dancer but known primarily as a film star, was on the other hand a "surprise" talent). Other film musicals borrow celebrities from popular music, like Jennifer Hudson and Beyoncé Knowles for *Dreamgirls* (2006). This practice parallels a current trend on Broadway, where starring roles in running shows and revivals are occasionally filled by Hollywood stars (such as Brooke Shields in *Cabaret*), pop idols (Usher and Ashlee Simpson in

Chicago), and reality show favorites (Clay Aiken in *Spamalot*). Familiarity with Broadway stars no longer has the same level of mass culture currency as it did during the Golden Age of musicals; it has become a kind of specialized knowledge, and both film and musical theater producers look to mass media celebrities to energize their box office earnings.

Radio broadcasts reached mass audiences, and record sales brought stars' voices into people's homes, where the nuances of their voices could be consumed and enjoyed repeatedly. In 1943, Decca Records released a six-disc original-cast album of *Oklahoma!*, the first recording of a musical with the entire original cast and orchestra. The record was packaged with plenty of pictures of the stars and the stage production, and an insert describing the plot. The success of the *Oklahoma!* album spurred the production of cast albums for other shows, and cast albums have since become important artifacts to fans, who can imagine and recreate a star's performance in their homes, whether they were able to see the production or not. Recordings offer fans a sense of intimacy and familiarity with a star; listening at home can be both intimate (listening closely, perhaps with headphones) and interactive (singing and dancing along).[15]

Following the introduction of amplified sound in musical theater—first crudely with corded microphones in the first runs of *Hair* (1967) and *Jesus Christ Superstar* (1971), and more complexly with the headset microphones and mixing technology of the megamusical in the 1980s—stars no longer needed to have voices that projected into the back of a large auditorium, and audiences grew impatient with non-amplified sound. Although amplified performers' voices are disconnected from their bodies and physical locations—voice are picked up, mixed, and sent out into the theater through speakers—audiences have become more accustomed to amplified, mixed sound as emblematic of reality (as in film) and seem to prefer it to the realism of a voice directly produced from an actual body on the stage.[16]

STAR VEHICLES

The 1959 musical *Gypsy* was tailored from its inception as a vehicle for Ethel Merman, a show that would be written both to suit her talents and to stretch her dramatic chops (to convince critics to rethink their long-held complaints about her weak acting). The show was based on the memoirs of burlesque strip artist Gypsy Rose Lee, but the drama of the show focuses on Gypsy's mother, a stage mother to end all, Madame Rose. Ethel Merman had a significant role in the early planning stage of the show and used her power as a star to influence the selection of the creative team. Merman and producer David Merrick discussed the possibility of turning Lee's memoir into a show, and after Merrick obtained the rights to Lee's book, he approached Jerome Robbins to direct and Leland Hayward (at Merman's request) to co-produce. Arthur Laurents was eventually persuaded to write the book, and

Robbins asked Stephen Sondheim to write the score. Merman, however, did not want a then-unknown composer writing the music and brought in Jule Styne, confining Sondheim to the role of lyricist once again.[17]

As noted above, character narratives merge with star images, so that Rose was understood by audiences as an articulation of something essential about Merman's private self: "Merman's powerful sound is the perfect expression of Rose's character: loud, forceful, unyielding."[18] John Clum calls *Gypsy* a diva musical: a show that glorifies its female star, is authored in part by important gay artists (Stephen Sondheim and Arthur Laurents) and provides a locus of identification for the gay male spectator (especially the closeted audience of the 1960s). The narratives of this kind of show tend to eschew love stories in favor of tales about women's independence and survival—the specialties of the diva. Since its first run, *Gypsy* has had four Broadway revivals. Finding the right actress to play a role that was tailored to a star with very specific abilities is a complicated feat—how does a casting director find another Ethel Merman? The solution for all four revivals was to cast another diva possessing a similar larger-than-life persona, but with a different voice and acting style to bring to the role. *Gypsy* has since become a vehicle for other stars, an opportunity for them to reinvent Madame Rose. Only a woman of a certain age and status can do Rose, and it is a challenge to her divahood. To the fan, the character in the drama matters less than the opportunity to see how the star will take on the role.[19]

When *Gypsy* was adapted as a film musical in 1962, film actress Rosalind Russell was cast in the lead role, and her singing was dubbed. Merman was crushed when she did not get to play Rose on screen, but she took *Gypsy* on national tour while the film was in production. The first star to tackle the role on Broadway after Merman was Angela Lansbury in 1974. She was already an established actress in Hollywood, and a Broadway star since her career-defining turn in the title role of another diva-musical, *Mame* (1966). She had won a Tony Award for her star turn in the otherwise critically panned musical *Dear World* (1969). Her famed contribution to the performance practice of *Gypsy,* in collaboration with Jerome Robbins, was to "solve" the applause problem at the end of Madame Rose's climactic breakdown in "Rose's Turn." Although the music ends triumphantly, Rose is still desperately broken, and the writers felt that applause would be inappropriate for the drama. They had convinced Merman to continue with the scene and forfeit her applause, but Oscar Hammerstein II persuaded them to let the applause happen—at least to give the audience the chance to cathartically express their appreciation. When Robbins and Lansbury worked together on a London production, they allowed the applause to happen, but Lansbury's Rose remains lost in her fantasy and continues to bow after the applause has ceased, reminding the audience that they are watching a woman in the midst of an emotional crisis.[20] That Lansbury was the star who figured this out suggests that she is a different kind of star from Merman, resisting diva impulses for the sake of the drama. This anecdote reifies a broadly accepted "fact" about Merman's personality: that she is always concerned with being center stage, regardless of who or what she has to maneuver into the background.

In 1989, television actress Tyne Daly took on the role, and she self-consciously reimagined Madame Rose's stage mother as a woman who has spent half a lifetime convincing herself that she didn't make it as a stage performer because she was "born too soon and started too late"—although it becomes clear in her delivery of the monologue before "Rose's Turn" that she never made it because she simply wasn't good enough.[21] Bernadette Peters's 2003 Rose had the archetypical toughness but was also attractive and vulnerable.[22] Patti LuPone's performance, like Merman's, was tagged as monstrous (in Charles Isherwood's estimation, LuPone's interpretation was monstrously sexual).[23] In an important way, the performance is really no longer about the role itself, that is, the character in the drama, but rather about the audience's desire to watch a star taking on the role and making it her own, and seeing that reflexive give and take between the diva and the diva role.

FANDOM AND FAN PRACTICE

The two star stories at the beginning of this essay have an unsung key player: the audience. As I indicated above, audiences have a stake in a star's image, and the perspective of the fan is an important position to engage with when thinking about a star. Fans are much more than "spectators"—passive consumers of media texts.[24] Audiences and individual fans are interactive components in the creation and reading of stars; they are part of the image-making process, and although they may not have direct input in the signals stars send out, they can choose what they wish to engage with. A fan has a personal engagement with a star's image, and his or her perspective will be shaped by experience and personal demographics. Dyer argues that the allure of the star is in the ways that the star image is constantly in dialogue with the tensions between public and private spheres—the star embodies (or idealizes) certain social identities, and a star's performance of "social categories" helps individuals understand themselves within society.[25] Fans may also choose to share their experiences by participating in an interactive community developed from a shared attachment to a star. Fan community may be broadly defined; it may be a small group of friends with a shared passion, or an Internet message board with active members from around the world.[26]

Musical theater is a genre that is popular with both mainstream and marginalized audiences. It has historically had a significant gay male following; D. A Miller, in Place for Us, writes that nearly all the 1950s musicals—a genre that appears assuredly hetero-normative on the surface—have subtext that validates gay audiences.[27] Recently, teenage girl fans—an audience that has a history of being dismissed by mainstream critics—have emerged as a more visible audience for the musical with the blockbuster success of Stephen Schwartz's Wicked.[28] These diverse fan communities have varied and endless ways of interpreting musical theater star texts and engaging with their fandom. For instance, a fan may keep track of a star's career and personal life; he or she might study, imitate, and emulate a star's performance style or dissect the particulars of a performance (whether a recording, a stage production, an appearance in a film, or a live televised event) with fellow fans.

Scholarship on fans and fandom is a relatively recent development in academia, and one that produces considerable strain between the supposedly polarized "moral values" of the scholar and the fan. If a scholar is supposed to be "objective," how can she comprehend and fairly portray what it means to be a fan, and likewise, can a scholar trust fans to articulate what is important about their participation in fandom? It is important to note that the meaning of fandom changes among different social and cultural groups. As Matt Hills writes:

> I want to suggest that fandom is not simply a "thing" that can be picked over analytically. It is also always performative; by which I mean that it is an identity which is (dis-)claimed, and which performs cultural work. Claiming the status of a "fan" may, in certain contexts, provide a cultural space for types of knowledge and attachment.[29]

In academia, labeling oneself a fan carries the risk of having one's work disparaged for lack of critical engagement. However, as Alexander Doty argues, it may also be problematic for scholars to suppress their personal alignments for the sake of an imagined academic professionalism.[30] One solution taken by scholars has been to embrace their "scholar-fan" subjectivity and acknowledge their positioning as they theorize fandom, as in the work of John Clum, Henry Jenkins, or Matt Hills. Fan ethnographies are another method used by scholars such as Jackie Stacey and Janice Radway, who foreground the individuality of fans and allow their voices to shape their scholarship.[31]

Internet fan sites and discussion boards are important locations of community for fans, making ethnographic research over the Internet a useful way of engaging with fans from different geographic locations in dialogue within online communities. Community and school theater programs are also likely to have knowledgeable and passionate fans who aspire to emulate their favorite stars. Recordings of musical theater stars inspire ambitious young singers to imitate their sound and style—a complex consequence of technology. Original cast performers codify how the show is supposed to sound, and amateur performers typically choose to model their own styles on what they have experienced from the cast album. Imitating the voice allows the fan to own something essential of the performer that would otherwise be impossible to experience. Stars in turn summon aspiration and ambition from their followers. Would-be stars emulate the star's vocal style, delivery, and physical mannerisms while they imagine the glamour of the star's life and fantasize about their lives if they had the star's talent, beauty, wealth, and power. Fans desire to hear the voice, but in some way, they also want to *own* the voice.[32] Ownership may be earned in a number of different ways: repeated listening, publicly performing the diva's music in school or community shows, or in more private spaces, by lip-synching or dancing at home.[33]

Some shows develop fan cults that track favorite performers across national tours and replacement casts. In the cast of *Wicked*, young fans track their favorite actresses who have played Glinda and Elphaba and savor brief moments of difference from the "canonical" cast album, for these moments seem to unlock some small part of the performer's personality. Consider, for instance, the penultimate measure in the act I finale, "Defying Gravity." The commercially available sheet music and the original cast album have different versions of Elphaba's melisma, but it is Idina Menzel's melisma, which she likely devised to showcase her high belt to thrilling effect, that persists as "canon." However, different touring actresses devise their own melismas: a stamp of their individuality.

Part of the power of stars is the illusion that the fan can be intimately familiar with their lives; the fan with a certain level of vocal ability can own her voice, perform her music, relate to her, and share in her success. Following in the footsteps of Fox's "American Idol" and the recent placement of former Idol contestants in Broadway shows, the pop culture phenomenon of reality television has "gone Broadway" with shows like "Grease: You're the One That I Want" (2006) and "Legally Blonde the Musical: The Search for Elle Woods" (2008). Susan Smith, discussing the BBC contest show "How Do You Solve a Problem Like Maria?" (2006), posits the reality show as a possible solution to the problem of casting leads for a show such as *The Sound of Music,* which has an iconic star performance perhaps too difficult for the audience to overcome or "forget."[34] Although choosing the contestant most similar in image to Julie Andrews, the audience gets a seemingly real experience of "direct participation" in star-making; they get to know the contestant and watch the Sawyer- or Merman-like process from nobody to star, and in the case of the *Grease* and *The Sound of Music* shows, even vote for their favorite to win. The process of identification is thereby reified and intensified. After all, the reality show contestant could conceivably be any one of us; any one of us could become a star.

NOTES

1. A common feature of Merman's star mythology is that she had never received formal vocal training, and further, that George Gershwin advised her never to do so after her success in *Girl Crazy.* Caryl Flinn, *Brass Diva: The Life and Legends of Ethel Merman* (Berkeley: University of California Press, 2007), pp. 31–32.

2. Richard Dyer, *Stars* (London: British Film Institute, 1998).

3. Stacy Wolf, *A Problem Like Maria: Gender and Sexuality in the American Musical* (Ann Arbor: University of Michigan Press, 2002), p. 34.

4. Richard Dyer, *Stars* (London: British Film Institute, 1998), p. 26.

5. Within Andrews's persona, vocals always serve the role; see Peter Kemp, "How Do You Solve a 'Problem' Like Maria von Poppins," in *Musicals: Hollywood and Beyond,* ed. Bill Marshall and Robynn Stilwell (Portland: Intellect, 2000, pp. 55–61), and Stacy Wolf, *A Problem Like Maria: Gender and Sexuality in the American Musical* (Ann Arbor: University of Michigan Press, 2002).

6. Richard Dyer, *Heavenly Bodies* (London: Routledge, 2004), p. 7.

7. *A Star Is Born* (1954) was brutally edited for its theatrical release, in part because the studio worried about its running time and the attention span of the average audience member. The film did not make its expected profits. Garland was also denied the Oscar that year, even though the Academy went through the trouble of setting up a live feed into her hospital room so she could be "present" at the event. Her concert in Carnegie Hall on April 23, 1961, was one of the highlights of her career, and the recording won five Grammy awards.

8. Mae West, for example, is beloved for her audacity and her drag queen mannerisms, but nonetheless she insisted on her (decidedly nonmainstream) sexiness until the end of her career.

9. See Dyer, 1998, 91, and Jean Benedetti, *David Garrick and the Birth of Modern Theatre* (London: Methuen, 2001).

10. See also Janet Staiger, "Seeing Stars," in *Stardom: Industry of Desire,* ed. Christine Gledhill (London: Routledge, 1991), pp. 3–16, and Katherine K. Preston, "American Musical Theater before the Twentieth Century," in *Cambridge Companion to the Musical,* ed. William A. Everett and Paul R. Laird (Cambridge: Cambridge University Press, 2002), pp. 3–28.

11. Susan J. Leonardi and Rebecca A. Pope, *The Diva's Mouth: Body, Voice, Prima Donna Politics* (New Brunswick, NJ: Rutgers University Press, 1996), pp. 44–45.

12. Regarding *The Black Crook* and its historical importance to American musical theater, see Raymond Knapp, *The American Musical and the Formation of National Identity* (Princeton, NJ: Princeton University Press, 2005), pp. 20–29.

13. See Stacy Wolf, *A Problem Like Maria: Gender and Sexuality in the American Musical* (Ann Arbor: University of Michigan Press, 2002), for a consideration of why these women had trouble assimilating as Hollywood stars.

14. The two appeared on many television variety shows and in June 1953 sang a duet medley of their greatest hits for the Ford fiftieth anniversary special, remembered as a momentous event in musical theater star history.

15. The voice of the singer is a commodity indebted to the listener. Leonardi and Pope discuss the potential for a recording of a diva's voice to become a fetish object when separated from the body as a recording and "circulated in a masculine economy" (Leonardi and Pope, 195).

16. Regarding the "cinematizing" and changing aesthetics of sound in the megamusical, see Jonathan Burston, "Theatre Space as Virtual Place: Audio Technology, the Reconfigured Singing Body, and the Megamusical" (*Popular Music* 17.2 [1998]: 205–18).

17. See Meryle Secrest, *Stephen Sondheim: A Life* (New York: Alfred A Knopf, 1998).

18. John M. Clum, *Something for the Boys: Musical Theater and Gay Culture* (New York: Palgrave, 1999), p. 169.

19. See John Clum's analysis of the 1998 *Gypsy* revival at the suburban Paper Mill Playhouse in New York, with Betty Buckley playing Rose.

20. Arthur Laurents, *Original Story By: A Memoir of Broadway and Hollywood* (New York: Alfred A. Knopf, 2000), pp. 395–96.

21. Both Lansbury and Daly won Tony Awards for their turns as Madame Rose. Merman was nominated but lost to Mary Martin (Maria in *The Sound of Music*). There are two filmed versions of *Gypsy,* the 1962 adaptation starring Rosalind Russell and the 1993 version with Bette Midler.

22. Arthur Laurents, liner notes to *Gypsy* (original revival cast album CD, Angel Records 7243–5–83858–2–3, 2003).

23. Charles Isherwood, "Patti LuPone in *Gypsy:* Light the Lights, Boys! Mama Rose Hears a Symphony" (*New York Times* [August 15, 2006], http://theater.nytimes.com/2006/08/15/theater/reviews/15lupo.html, accessed April 9, 2011).

24. Jackie Stacey argues that film theories of spectatorship ignore the spectator's social context to study the ways that film texts produce "spectator positions," while cultural studies investigate "audiences' readings" of texts. Film theory regarding stars has historically given agency

to the "text" (i.e., the film) rather than the audience, privileging the term "spectator," which carries a connotation of audience passivity. Jackie Stacey, *Star Gazing: Hollywood Cinema and Female Spectatorship* (London: Routledge, 1994).

25. He also raises the possibility of reading stars as camp, since they exaggerate conventional "types," as in the hyper-sexuality of Marilyn Monroe.

26. For related arguments on fan culture, see Henry Jenkins, *Textual Poachers: Television Fans and Participatory Culture* (London: Routledge, 1992), p. 49.

27. D. A. Miller, *Place for Us* (Cambridge, MA: Harvard University Press, 2000). See also Clum.

28. See Barbara Ehrenreich, Elizabeth Hess, and Gloria Jacobs, "Beatlemania: Girls Just Want to Have Fun Beatles," in *The Adoring Audience: Fan Culture and Popular Media,* ed. Lisa A. Lewis (London: Routledge, 1992), pp. 84–106, and Stacy Wolf, "*Wicked* Divas, Musical Theater, and Internet Girl Fans" (*Camera Obscura 65* 22.2 [2007]: 39–71).

29. Matt Hills, *Fan Cultures* (London: Routledge, 2002), pp. xi–xii.

30. Alexander Doty, *Flaming Classics: Queering the Film Canon* (London: Routledge, 2000), p. 11.

31. Besides other work cited here, see Janice Radway, *Reading the Romance: Women, Patriarchy and Popular Culture* (Chapel Hill: University of North Carolina Press, 1984).

32. Wayne Koestenbaum argues that the diva's identity lies in her voice, a product of her effort that is also a component of her body. Wayne Koestenbaum, *The Queen's Throat: Opera, Homosexuality, and the Mystery of Desire* (New York: Poseidon Press, 1993).

33. See Miller. For closeted Golden Age Era boys, this practice is encoded as gay; see, for instance, Matt Damon's private lip-synching performance in *The Talented Mr. Ripley* (1999, dir. Anthony Minghella), and the reaction of Dickie Greenleaf (played by Jude Law).

34. Susan Smith, unpublished contribution to "You Gotta Have a Gimmick": Startexts and Voices" (panel presentation at "The American Musical on Stage and Screen: An Interdisciplinary Extravaganza," University of California, Los Angeles, October 2007).

CHAPTER 28

KNOWING YOUR AUDIENCE

JENNIFER CHAPMAN

THIS essay investigates the shared history and contemporary practices of community and high school musical theater in the United States, through which each has established a unique relationship to its audience—an audience that has in turn shaped its identity and informed its musical selections. Critical scholarship about amateur theater suggests its viability as a form of civic engagement,[1] as a subversive space where the "masses" own the means of production,[2] and as the primary disseminator of theater knowledge and experiences in the United States.[3] Documentation of practices in community and high school theater suggests that each offers an experience that is very different from, but equal in value to, professional theater.[4]

DOCUMENTING PRACTICE

Unfortunately, there are few case studies, personal narratives, or documentary studies of community and high school theater practices.[5] However, there is an abundant source that offers a kind of "back door" into the subject: "how-to" resource manuals written for teachers, directors, and producers of amateur theater.[6] Although they vary in quality and level of critical engagement, many of them are written by practitioners and so offer valuable anecdotal evidence about what "works" in amateur theater, how audience expectations shape ideological boundaries of community and high school musical theater production, and what practicalities amateur theater makers face in selecting, casting, and producing plays.

Between 2001 and 2004, the American Association of Community Theatres (AACT), with its umbrella organization, Theatre USA, collected documented histories of community theaters in the United States, including play and musical production since 1919. The resulting publication, *Millennium Theatres: Discovering Community Theatre's Future by Exploring Its Past*, includes theater members' personal memories, records of ticket sales, stories or descriptions of how theaters were restructured to meet economic or community needs throughout the years, and useful anecdotal evidence of the challenges and rewards of participating in community theater.[7]

Another resource for documenting practice is *Dramatics* magazine. Published by the International Thespian Society (ITS) and the Educational Theatre Association (EdTA), *Dramatics* targets high school students and their teachers, and compiles from member schools a "most produced play and musical" list annually. While *Dramatics* does not provide an exhaustive look at all high school theater work in the United States, it represents schools that have made a commitment to including theater in their curricula or after-school activities.

An inventory of the play lists in *Millennium Theatres* and *Dramatics* shows that the top shared musical titles for community and high school production are *Guys and Dolls* and *Oklahoma!* The remainder of this essay investigates why Broadway musicals are so popular in each venue and how these two shows offer possibilities and challenges when they function, in part, as a way of building community and facilitating civic engagement.

REACTING TO AND EMBRACING BROADWAY

The intersecting histories of community and high school theaters in the United States arguably bind them to similar ideological assumptions and expectations about their processes and products. Both forms developed alongside the "little theater" movement in the early twentieth century and were also influenced by the development and expansion of theater programs in universities. Both became popular, in part, because of a growing belief that theater's creative process has educational and social value.[8]

From about 1912–1920, theater companies known as "little theaters" were created throughout major cities in the United States, using professional directors and amateur actors and staff, who sought to provide an alternative to popular commercial (Broadway) productions and to experiment with European forms, especially the "free theater" movement. The little theater movement was an important nurturer of playwrights such as Eugene O'Neill and Susan Glaspell; it is regarded as a key contributor to the development of a uniquely American dramatic voice. It planted the seed from which other amateur theater forms grew, such as community, high school, and university theater.[9] These forms owed much of their public support to the little theater movement, which introduced the idea that amateur theater can have a powerful impact on its participants and broader grassroots community. Yet, although the little theater movement sought to offer an alternative to Broadway, community and high school theater has generally chosen to produce known Broadway titles.

Another reason for the growing popularity of theater at the local level, particularly in high schools, was the expansion of theater programs and classes at the university level. As more newly certified teachers graduated from universities after taking courses in theater, they disseminated that training into secondary classrooms and local communities.[10] According to Kenneth Macgowan, writing for *Harper's* in 1929, "drama is the new thing in the high schools," estimating that "probably a third of the twenty-two thousand high schools in America are studying and applying production methods to a rather decent grade of play." Macgowan commends the youth of 1928 for their work in theater, declaring that, based on his observations of high schools, "Broadway theatre may be dying, but never was the theatre so alive in the rest of the United States" (Macgowan, 1929, 774, 779). While it unclear how Macgowan arrived at his numerical estimate, his article highlights the role that theater and drama, particularly Broadway musicals, came to play in transforming the American high school and its local communities.

One History Becomes Two:
Organization and Expansion

Louise Burleigh introduced the term "community theater" in 1917, describing it in *The Community Theatre in Theory and Practice* as "a house of play in which events offer to every member of a body politic active participation in a common interest" (Burleigh, xxiii). By 1925, a community theater movement was thriving, with 2,000 companies registered with the Drama League of America, a professional organization formed in 1910 to support the development of community theater.

Theater work in American high schools appeared as early as the mid-1920s. The 1920s were a time of debate and change for secondary school curricula, primarily because of problems in recruiting and holding students. Early advocates of high school theater production and study argued that it benefited students' moral, social, and academic development (Hume and Foster, 1932; Law, 1936; Macgowan, 1921; W. Brown, 1947). The introduction of theater into the secondary curriculum was part of an effort to attract and retain a larger student body and to teach life skills that would make students "better" Americans in various ways (Chapman, 2005; Chapman, 2007; Hume and Foster, 1932).

By 1928, the national curriculum was revised to meet the needs of "all" students rather than just an elite, college-bound group. The new curriculum placed the social on a par with the scientific, and subjects were offered that taught "effective living." Twelve fields of instruction were available: English, foreign language, math, science, social studies, business, manual/industrial arts, agriculture, home economics, (visual) art, music, and physical education.[11] An emphasis on students' moral development as good Americans and their responsibilities to the welfare of society's future provided a rationale for theater to enter secondary school. Educators argued that by performing good citizenship and ethical decision-making in dramatic enactments, students could rehearse the roles of their future, adult selves.[12] Initially, theater was studied as part of "oral interpretation" in English classes, but in some schools this small subset of an academic course was expanded into play production, playwriting, and even schoolwide competitions (Macgowan, 1921, 174–75). The National Thespian Society, a nonprofit organization dedicated to the advancement of secondary school theater, was formed in 1928, gained a membership of seventy schools within its first year, and by 1939 tallied 33,000 student members.[13]

The period following World War II was one of the most economically expansive in American history, to the great financial benefit of community arts and arts education. The expansion of community and high school theater work during this period is evident in the establishment and growth of professional organizations to represent both forms and a growing critical interest in the role of amateur theater in local communities.

The American Community Theatre Association (ACTA) was created in 1956 to represent community theaters at the national level; at that time, there were an estimated 3,500 community theaters across the United States (Gard and Burley, 1959), a number that would grow to 15,000 by 1975.[14] Renamed the American Association of Community Theatres (AACT) in 1986, the group currently represents 7,000 member companies in the United States and in the armed forces overseas. It publishes resources, offers support to members in their organizational needs, sponsors an annual competitive festival of community theater performance, and sends select member companies to competitive theater festivals internationally (http://www .aact.org).

Since Burleigh's initial definition of "community theater," a number of amateur theater movements—such as "little," "tributary," "fringe," "community-based," and "alternative" theater—have blurred the boundaries of what constitutes "community" theater. The term today is used broadly to describe amateur theaters supported by local communities on stage, backstage, and in the audience. Currently, the AACT defines a community theater as a nonprofit, tax-exempt organization staffed (onstage, backstage, and in its administrative structure) primarily by volunteers (http://www.aact.org). However, this definition is merely a guidepost, since different communities provide different levels of financial support for local theater. Some community theaters have funds to pay one or more individuals, such as a full- or part-time managing director, or an occasional set designer, stage or musical director, or conductor. Rarely does payment represent a full-time livable salary, and it seems uncommon to pay performers. As nonprofit, tax-exempt organizations, community theaters may support themselves with local, state, or national grants; they may rely on community donations; and they likely depend heavily on ticket sales, particularly to subscribers.

During and shortly after World War II, the National Thespian Society saw a significant increase in school memberships and active participation. Between 1941 and 1950, schools reporting to the annual play survey increased from 729 to 1,548. With increased participation came more critical articles in *High School Thespian* (the official publication of the National Thespian Society, renamed *Dramatics* in 1944) about how and why theater should be practiced in school settings. Articles from the mid-1940s through early 1960s tend to focus on pedagogy and play selection, offering assistance to teachers looking to create or improve theater programs and giving students a sense of national solidarity. The latter concern is evident in the January 1951 "Dedication," which also documents an explosion in the number of schools participating in the play survey:

> This issue of *Dramatics*—our ninth Pictorial number—is dedicated to the *largest play cast in the world*—the *twenty thousand high school boys and girls*, who, as Thespians, practice our motto: "*Act well your part: there all the honor lies.*" By being loyal / To their fellow classmates / To their directors and teachers to their school / To their parents / To their community / To their country.[15]

Moreover, in 1945 and 1949, the "High School Committee" of the American Education Theatre Association (which would later become EdTA) published pedagogical guidelines for secondary theater study: "Teaching Dramatic Arts in the Secondary Schools" (1945) and "Course of Study Materials for a High School Dramatics Course" (1949). The latter was published in the *National Association of Secondary School Principals' Bulletin* and disseminated to its membership at their annual conference.[16]

Today, the National Thespian Society is called the International Thespian Society (to recognize a small Canadian membership), and its publication for members, *Dramatics* (titled *The High School Thespian* until 1944), is distributed to about 42,000 individuals, 80 percent of whom are high school students. The remaining 20 percent comprises theater teachers, librarians, and other interested individuals.[17] The International Thespian Society is currently under the umbrella of the Educational Theatre Association (EdTA), which publishes and distributes *Dramatics* and, along with the American Alliance for Theatre and Education (AATE), represents teachers of high school theater, guided by state and national theater arts standards that define "highly qualified" theater teaching under the No Child Left Behind Act.[18]

A COMMON CHALLENGE: NEGOTIATING EXPECTATIONS

As noted, community and high school theater differs from the little theater movement in tending to produce known Broadway titles, particularly musicals. Although community and high school theater programs face unique challenges in play selection, they share some important commonalities—particularly in their audience makeup—that lead to similar choices for production. In both, many audience members are likely to know (or have some personal connection to) a person who worked on the show and would not attend otherwise. Since many audience members are also likely to know one another, attendance may be thought of as a form of civic engagement. Audience makeup is likely broad; parents, grandparents, siblings, and children are all important supporters of friends and family members who worked on the show. Finally, since some audience members are potential future participants, productions serve partly as a kind of "audition" to the community they serve.

Guidelines in "how-to" texts for community and/or high school theater indicate that both spaces must consider similar audience expectations. Texts suggest that to be successful, programs should (1) offer shows that audiences of all ages can attend, (2) omit or criticize onstage behavior that may be viewed as inappropriate or immoral by the community at large (such as smoking, drinking, doing drugs, using vulgar language or violence, etc.), (3) sanitize images of sexuality and avoid references to homosexuality (except perhaps for the purpose of a joke, since making fun of homosexuals has often been sanctioned implicitly by schools that do not address homophobia and heterosexism with students), and (4) try to create entertaining and fun community-building events (Chapman, 2005, 2007). Community theater audiences seem to tolerate slightly racier material than high schools. (For example, *The Fantasticks*, a documented popular choice for community theater, includes a song about a rape, but several texts about how to produce high school theater suggest cutting this number.) Nevertheless, guidelines tend to reinforce heteronormative behavior in male and female characters and present courtships with predictably stereotyped gender behavior.

Historically, both community and high school theater have been identified as spaces of civic engagement and opportunities to teach or profess what it means to be a "good American."[19] Specifically, in 1921, observing the educational possibilities of high school theater, Kenneth Macgowan stated that "acting is being used deliberately by the teachers as a means to correct defects in the personalities of the students and to build a better citizenship" (774). And in 1932, Hume and Foster argued that the process of creating theater has educational value and the potential to uphold democratic principles when it is created for and by students (30–39).

Selecting material for community and high school theater has always been a careful negotiation between the needs of participants and audience members. Historically, community theater has had to compete with other forms of live entertainment, such as sporting events, fairs and carnivals, and traveling tent shows. High school theater has often been challenged by competing opinions about what is "appropriate" for that age group. In the past and present, familiar works from the commercial stage have helped guarantee an audience and excite potential participants.

Selecting material for community theater is often difficult. Sometimes it is done by a board of directors, sometimes by the directors and/or membership, and sometimes a combination of the two. The selection process can lead to conflicts over the mission and identity of the theater and the community it serves. Audiences have strong expectations that their community theater will produce Broadway musicals, at least occasionally, and reward them with high ticket sales when they do (Filichia, 2007).

Broadway musicals are also a staple of many high school theater programs in the United States. Parents, administrators, and student bodies expect a musical production to integrate music, dance, and drama departments (or clubs), with the drama teacher usually given the job of directing it. Ample evidence for this expectation may be found in the number of "how-to" teacher resource texts for directing high school musical theater and the recent inclusion of an "acting in musical theater" section in *Dramatics* magazine.

One of the unique problems of teaching and directing theater with high school students, both historically and in contemporary practice, lies in the question of what is "appropriate" material for the age group. This is a challenge faced by theater and drama teachers of all youth-age groups because often teachers, administrators, parents, and students hold different opinions. For example, in 1947, Wilhelmina P. Brown wrote in *Dramatics*:

> The fact remains that in a public school we of the teaching staff must cater, or at least defer, to the religious and moral sense of our parents and patrons. We must not permit any of the student actors to smoke on the school stage. We must not show the effects of, or indicate the drinking of alcohol. We must not use profanity. These are the unwritten requirements that a high school production must abide by.... Rarely will you find a parent who is proud to see his offspring caricature a drunk.[20]

Although audiences' tolerance of content may have shifted since 1947, the problem remains one of balance: is it possible to provide teens with quality artistic experiences while appeasing society's desire to preserve their childhood innocence? Broadway musicals, particularly those from the "Golden Age" of American musical theater, offer a safe choice, in addition tending toward large ensemble casts and offering opportunities for collaboration with dance and music departments.[21]

In contemporary practice, high school theater production tends to be guided by the following ideological assumptions: (1) theater has the potential to teach "life skills" and is thus important beyond its ability to teach within its discipline; (2) productions will be something that students, parents, and younger siblings can attend; (3) student actors should not engage in onstage behavior that is not allowed in the school at large (such as smoking, drinking, doing drugs, using vulgar language or violence, etc.); (4) plays should not be overtly sexual or have nonheterosexual characters (unless for the purpose of a joke); and (5) theater class or drama club is an alternative to playing sports and thus occupies an "unmasculine" space in high school society (Chapman, 2005, 2007).

Community theater is often affected, if not guided by, similar expectations. However, Leah Hager Cohen (2002) shows, in *The Stuff of Dreams*, how challenging these expectations can lead to productive dialogue. She tells the story of a conflict within the Arlington Friends of the Drama (AFD, a seventy-five-year-old community theater in Arlington, Massachusetts) over the desire of its younger members to produce David Henry Hwang's *M. Butterfly*. Older members object to the play's use of onstage nudity and its central characters' same-sex relationship. The younger contingency, led by a director with a vision to take the play to state and national competitions, wins the debate and the play is produced. Amazingly, members of the faction against producing the play do not abandon their volunteer work and continue to make coffee, clean the theater, and promote the show despite wholeheartedly being against it (189–217, 218–234). Cohen shows how a community theater's play selection process can be a site for public debate about the community's values and can serve as the vehicle through which a community can understand and articulate its changing identity (5–9). The same can be true for high school theater; when teachers negotiate with their principal, school board, and community to produce risky shows (such as *Rent*), they educate other adults about the issues that contemporary teenagers confront in real life.[22]

A SHARED CANON

The overwhelming popularity of certain shows, as documented by the AACT, Theatre USA, and the Educational Theatre Association, has created a de facto canon for musicals in community and high school theater; this canon in turn reveals some expectations that audiences have of each form. Broadway musicals from the Golden Age tend to dominate this canon, but note that focusing on the "most popular" musicals documented by these organizations does not consider either individual theaters' full seasons, which might also include riskier work, or nonmember school and community theaters. Looking at a documented canon provides merely one means for assessing popular trends in these venues.

In *Millennium Theatres*, AACT-member companies report the work of Gilbert and Sullivan (specifically, *H.M.S. Pinafore*, *The Pirates of Penzance*, *Princess Ida*, and *The Mikado*) as the most popular choices from 1919 to 1950 (*Millennium Theatres* does not distinguish between Gilbert and Sullivan societies and other community theaters). After 1950, the majority of reported musical productions are from Broadway. The ten most popular plays for community theater, as documented by Theatre USA and AACT, in order of popularity, are *The Fantasticks*; *Guys and Dolls*; *Oklahoma!*; *Fiddler on the Roof*; *The Sound of Music*; *The Wizard of Oz*; *South Pacific*; *The Music Man*; *A Funny Thing Happened on the Way to the Forum*; and *Godspell*. Many of these most popular titles are from the Golden Age and are categorized in Peter Filichia's *Let's Put on a Musical* as "good old reliable" shows:

> As Coca-Cola discovered some years ago, people like classics. So if you too are in
> a community that buys tickets only for the most famous titles in the Broadway
> canon, here are your bread-and-butter musicals. (Filichia, 2007, 7)

Clearly, most of the AACT-member theaters indeed have to make some bread and
butter with their musical productions. Catering to such needs, Filichia groups musicals according to considerations more practical than historical. For example, he discusses *The Sound of Music* and *The Wizard of Oz* in a chapter designated for shows
with large casts for children (173–190), *The Fantasticks* in a chapter about musicals
that do not require sophisticated production values (291–304), and *A Funny Thing
Happened on the Way to the Forum* in a chapter about musicals that do not require
sophisticated choreography (125–136). *Godspell* is in a chapter about post–Golden
Age musicals (primarily using rock or folk musical styles), titled "Can You Use Any
Money Today?" in which he discusses musicals that are reliable sources of income
(31–58). The organization of Filichia's text suggests that selecting musicals for school
and community theater is principally a negotiation between what is technically possible and what will attract audiences. That the latter issue is primary in most "how-
to" texts for school and community theater suggests that audiences of amateur
theater most want to see musicals that they are already familiar with.

The first two plays listed, *The Fantasticks* and *Guys and Dolls*, are reported by
AACT-member companies significantly more often than the remaining titles on the
list, and their popularity can be viewed as an indication of audience expectations
and community theaters' practical needs. Both are terrific shows with captivating
music—reasons enough for audiences to want to see them repeatedly (myself
included), particularly when they are performed well. Furthermore, *The Fantasticks*
uses minimal sets and costumes, making it suited to low-budget community theaters. Nevertheless, it is also worth considering that these top two productions offer
something in their stories that makes them consistent choices for community theaters across the United States. Both tell stories about heterosexual courtships, suggesting that gender relations are universal and that courtship rituals are something
that everyone can relate to; and both exploit gender stereotypes—specifically, both
present polarized images of female identity and suggest that women are either "low"
or "high" in character and stature, either sexually loose or virtuously virginal.

Dramatics magazine documents a somewhat different high school musical theater canon, as an extension of its annual most popular plays list (which includes
musicals, one-act, and full-length plays) from the reports of its member high
schools. In 2004, the magazine inventoried all of the lists and published the most
popular productions for high school theater in the United States and Canada from
1938 to 2004. From this list, the most popular musicals for high school theater production are (in order of popularity): *Bye Bye Birdie*; *Oklahoma!*; *Guys and Dolls*;
You're a Good Man, Charlie Brown; *The Music Man*; *Fiddler on the Roof*; *Once Upon
a Mattress*; *Grease*; *Godspell*; and *The Sound of Music*.[23]

All of these musicals have several qualities in common that make them suitable for high school production: they have large ensemble casts, strong vocal parts

for men and women, and in several cases smaller roles for nonsingers. Very few have vulgar language by contemporary standards, contain material that will likely be offensive to parents or younger siblings (with the exception of *Grease*, which is often cut to make it more palatable), or challenge heteronormative assumptions about gender and sexuality. Four titles have onstage drinking written into the script: *Bye Bye Birdie*, *Guys and Dolls*, *Fiddler on the Roof*, and *Grease*. A teacher would likely need to confirm that the context of the drinking was acceptable to the principal, school board, and local community, or apply for permission to cut it from the performance (Bennett, 2001; Gonzalez, 2006). Deciding whether the context is acceptable is often determined by the age of the character, the historical period of the play, and how essential the consumption of alcohol is to the storyline of the play. For example, *Fiddler on the Roof* features an essential song and dance number, "To Life!" in a tavern in 1901 Russia. Although many of the characters in the scene are "underage" by today's standards, it would have been acceptable for them to drink alcohol in the historical moment of the play. Furthermore, cutting "To Life!" would confuse the storyline, and it is a song that audiences popularly expect and recognize as part of this show. On the other hand, the teenage characters who drink alcohol in *Grease* do so illegally, and its use of drinking and smoking are often thought of as elements that can be cut without compromising the storyline.[24]

The top three titles, *Bye Bye Birdie*, *Oklahoma!*, and *Guys and Dolls* all celebrate heterosexual courtship and present fairly sanitized images of gender and sexuality. Although *Guys and Dolls* has characters who gamble illegally, their actions are treated as a character defect and in the end, the gamblers must redeem themselves. Also somewhat problematic is the scene in which the chorus of women performs a "strip" show down to leotards. However, the scene is meant to be funny, and a director would likely have to make a careful decision about how skimpy the costumes are. Like the popular titles from the community musical theater canon, all three shows have courtship rituals that reinforce gender stereotypes and all three have a wedding or offstage marriage as part of the plot.

The lists documenting community and high school theaters in the United States overlap in two of their three most produced titles: *Guys and Dolls* and *Oklahoma!* Both are Tony-award winning shows that have seen frequent revivals on Broadway, both have songs familiar to even the most infrequent theatergoer, and both have been acknowledged by critical scholars and popular audiences alike among the best that the American musical theater stage has to offer.[25] Both musicals tell stories about American identity and American values, and both present heteronormative images of gender roles and relationships.

Guys and Dolls was first produced on Broadway in 1950 and is set in a slightly earlier period. The plot concerns two heterosexual courtships, that of Nathan Detroit and his long-suffering fiancée of fourteen years, Adelaide; and that of Sky Masterson and Salvation Army Sergeant Sarah Brown. Nathan bets fellow-gambler Sky that he cannot get Sarah to fly to Havana with him; Sky succeeds, and he and Sarah fall in love. However, Sarah rejects Sky when she learns that Nathan has used her Save-a-Soul Mission for his floating crap game while they were away. To save Sarah's mission from being closed, Sky "wins" sinners in a crap game and requires that they attend a prayer meeting. When Sarah learns that Sky, in addition to saving her mission, has protected her reputation by claiming to lose his bet to Nathan, she reconciles with him. They marry, as do Adelaide and a somewhat unhappy Nathan.

Conflicts in *Guys and Dolls* depend on normalizing assumptions about gender roles, stereotypes of women as either "loose" or virginal, and of men as characters who are "tamed" by the women they love. Many of the songs reinforce these assumptions. In "Adelaide's Lament," Adelaide sings about how a girl can "develop a cold" from waiting for a man to marry her. A chorus of men sings about how "guys" get "licked" by "dolls": "When you see a Joe/Saving half of his dough/You can bet there'll be mink in it for some doll." Of course, getting "licked" is integral to the show's happy ending; in the final moments, the ensemble sings: "When you meet a gent/Paying all kinds of rent/For a flat that could flatten the Taj Mahal/Call it sad, call it funny/But it's better than even money/That the guy's only doing it for some doll!"[26]

Oklahoma! was first produced on Broadway in 1943 and is set in 1907 in the "Indian territory" above Texas, telling a story of American history, identity, and values that centers around two heterosexual courtships: Laurey and Curly as the primary couple, and Will and Ado Annie as the secondary couple. Although they are encouraged by Aunt Eller, Laurey and Curly are shy around each other. Ado Annie is on the other hand flirtatious, and sings "I'm just a girl who cain't say no" about the multiple men vying for her affection, though her father steps in and insists that she marry.[27] When hired hand Jud attempts to win Laurey's affection, Curly intervenes and marries her. Jud tries to kill Curly, but the fight ends with Jud's accidental death. In a short trial, Curly is found to have acted in self-defense, and the story ends with Curly and Laurey off to begin their honeymoon.

Oklahoma! celebrates characters who are surviving the challenges of America's expansion in the West through rugged individualism and a strong sense of how men and women should live their lives. Given the difficulty of life in the "new" West, it is not surprising that there is not room for a character like Jud, or for the child-like frolicking of Ado Annie. This is a story about people who have to work hard and depend on each other to survive; breaking social codes of behavior could be disastrous for the community and the chances of the territory becoming a state. *Oklahoma!* celebrates the foundations of the "American dream" and shows that part of that dream is heterosexual coupling, marriage, and family.

Both *Guys and Dolls* and *Oklahoma!* fulfill many of community and high school theater's technical needs: they have large, ensemble casts with multiple large roles; recognizable titles with familiar music to help sell tickets and recruit future participants; and integrated singing, dancing, and character work to allow performers with different talents and abilities to participate. The language used in both is generally inoffensive, with the possible exception of the historically and regionally specific dialect written into *Oklahoma!* Characters who engage in "objectionable" behavior, such as drinking, gambling, and violence, are either redeemed (Sky Masterson) or killed (Jud). Both shows celebrate American identity and values, supporting the idea that onstage and in the audience, community and high school theater are spaces of civic engagement, providing opportunities for people to feel a sense of belonging to something that is at once local, national, and universal. Finally, unsurprising given the time period in which they were written, both musicals contain normalized images of gender and sexuality, celebrate heterosexual rituals such as courtship and marriage, and reinforce some audiences' expectation that they should not be challenged to include nonheterosexual individuals in their community or worldview. However, even though both shows reinforce cultural assumptions about who is "normal" and what modes of gender performance are acceptable, when presented in a community or high school theater context, they are also opportunities for public debate about community membership and visibility, especially since their venues are historically understood as sites for civic engagement.

KNOWING YOUR AUDIENCE CAN BE PRODUCTIVE, BUT RISKY

The shared histories and contemporary practice of community and high school theater illuminate a unique relationship to audiences. Their history as sites of civic engagement complicates their frequent choices in musical theater production. When people in the audience and onstage know one another, the presentation of gender and sexuality—even as heteronormative stereotypes—poses questions to the community about who is valued, and who is visible. Furthermore, high school theater's historical role of teaching "life skills" and "effective citizenship" continues to challenge teachers in selecting material for production.

Guys and Dolls and *Oklahoma!* do not give nonnormative community members opportunities to see their own identities onstage, and in some contexts, it could seem as though the message of community and high school theater is that "good" and visible Americans fulfill heteronormative gender roles. However, Leah Cohen's documentation of the AFD's conflict over *M. Butterfly* demonstrates that although the "most popular" lists from AACT tend toward safe choices, selections across an entire season can be more diverse. The same is true for high school theater. Many "how-to" books for high school theater teachers encourage teacher-directors to take calculated risks with the support of their principal and school board, arguing that students' learning is at stake (Bennett, 2001; Gonzalez, 2006; Grote, 1997). To support teachers who might encounter resistance to risk-taking in their community, the American Alliance for Theatre and Education published "Freedom of Artistic Expression in Educational

Theatre" in 1993, and freedom of expression is an issue regularly addressed in publications by the EdTA.[28]

Regardless of whether a musical is "safe" or "risky" for a given community or high school, the intimacy between actors and audience in these theaters raises the stakes for everyone involved. Even if a show seems safe, playing a certain character, singing a solo, dancing, or wearing a particular costume might represent a risk for an individual actor. Cohen argues that this aspect of community theater creates a rich actor-audience relationship, one that makes the play event (regardless of the "riskiness" of the text) an opportunity for public discourse, with its issues refracted through the lens of storytelling. By considering the humanity of characters in a play, actors and audience come to know themselves and each other in new ways:

> Even in the safest, tamest production of the most banal old chestnut, relation-ships and conflicts unfold in public; people must make themselves more vulner-able than the daily code prescribes. The nature of theatre is to expose, and in partaking of theatre, whether as actors, crew, or audience members, we are ourselves made vulnerable, laid bare to feelings and reactions; to some degree we become participants in a story that asks something of us. (L. Cohen, 2002, xvii–xviii)

Other researchers and teachers of high school theater have made observations simi-lar to Cohen's (Bennett, 2001; Chapman, 2005, 2007; Gonzalez, 1999, 2006; Lazarus, 2004) and identified the development of empathy as one of the most important skills that theater can impart in the classroom, onstage, and in the audience (Gonzalez, 2006). Furthermore, the double meanings that can occur when actors and audience know each other allow for interesting moments of Brechtian distance, whether or not they were originally intended. Seeing a contemporary teenager play Adelaide in *Guys and Dolls* could illuminate the way that the performance of femi-ninity is historically specific. Casting the popular quarterback to play Curly in *Oklahoma!* could challenge the idea that theater is an "unmasculine" cultural space in high school. Seeing anyone from a local community sing and dance on stage, when he or she has never been known to sing and dance before, has an element of risk that distances the audience from the play text but may make them feel closer to their fellow community member.

Empathy toward others can be a starting point for building better school and local communities that not only tolerate differences but that also encourage mem-bers to treat one another with kindness and care, even when they cannot agree with or understand one another. Although popular texts for community and high school musical performance capitalize on heteronormative assumptions and gender ste-reotypes, the production itself may potentially serve as a medium for inclusion and as an opportunity for public dialogue (van de Water and Giannini, 2008). The moments of intimacy when actors and/or audience share a commitment to a the-ater, production, story, and/or performance can be delicate sparks of shared human-ity that set a foundation for expanding who is visible and knowable in communities and schools.

NOTES

1. See Louise Burleigh, *The Community Theatre in Theory and Practice* (Boston: Little, Brown, 1917); Leah Hager Cohen, *The Stuff of Dreams: Behind the Scenes of an American Community Theatre* (New York: Viking Penguin, 2001); Samuel J. Hume and Lois M. Foster, *Theatre and School* (New York: Samuel French, 1932); Lois Law, "Training in Citizenship through Play-Production" (*High School Thespian* 8.2 [October 1936]: 5, 16); and Joan Lazarus, *Signs of Change: New Directions in Secondary Theatre Education* (Portsmouth, NH: Heinemann, 2004).

2. See Sara Brady's review of Leah Hager Cohen's *The Stuff of Dreams: Behind the Scenes of an American Community Theatre* (*Drama Review* 46.1 [Spring 2002]: 170–74), and L. Cohen.

3. See L. Cohen; and Kenneth Macgowan, *The Theatre of Tomorrow* (New York: Boni and Liveright, 1921) and "Drama's New Domain—The High School" (*Harper's* [November 1929]: 774–79). For discussions of the dissemination of pre-professional knowledge and training in high school, see Tammy La Gorce, "High School Musical Actors Envision Being Rising Stars" (*New York Times*, March 15, 2009, http://www.nytimes.com/2009/03/15/nyregion/new-jersey/15papernj.html, accessed May 9, 2011), "At Home on the Stage" (*New York Times*, April 5, 2009, http://www.nytimes.com/2009/04/05/nyregion/new-jersey/05paper.html, accessed May 9, 2011), and "The Rising Star Awards: Singing! Dancing! Scholarships!" (*New York Times*, June 28, 2009, http://www.nytimes.com/2009/06/28/nyregion/28papernj.html, accessed May 9, 2011).

4. See L. Cohen; Robert E. Gard and Gertrude Burley, *Community Theatre: Idea and Achievement* (New York: Duell, Sloan, and Pearce, 1959); Jo Beth Gonzalez, *Temporary Stages: Departing from Tradition in High School Theatre Education* (Portsmouth, NH: Heinemann, 2006); Lazarus; Macgowan, 1921, 1929; and Manon van de Water and Annie Giannini, "Gay and Lesbian Theatre for Young People, or the Representation of 'Troubled Youth,'" in *We Will Be Citizens: New Essays on Gay and Lesbian Theatre*, ed. James Fisher (Jefferson, NC: McFarland, 2008), pp. 103–22.

Other amateur theater forms, such as college/university theaters and Gilbert and Sullivan societies, have also been instrumental in a grassroots dissemination of musical theater knowledge and experience. Although deserving of further attention, neither of these is considered at length in this chapter. For more information about Gilbert and Sullivan societies in and outside of the United States, see "The Gilbert and Sullivan Archive" at http://diamond.boisestate.edu/gas/, accessed September 8, 2009.

5. For exceptions see Cynthia Lynn Brown, "Longevity and the Secondary Theatre Arts Teacher: A Case Study" (Ph.D. dissertation, Arizona State University, 1997); Gonzalez, 1999, 2006; L. Cohen; Sonja Kuftinec, "A Cornerstone for Rethinking Community Theatre" (*Theatre Topics* 6.1 [March 1996]: 91–104), and "Staging the City with the Good People of New Haven" (*Theatre Journal* 53.2 [May 2001]: 197–222); Lazarus; Karlyn Love, "A Directorial Approach for a High School Production of *You Can't Take It with You* by Moss Hart and George S. Kaufman: Performed February 1, 2, 3, 2001 at Oregon City High School, Oregon City, Oregon" (M.F.A. thesis, University of Portland, 2001); Joe Norris, Laura A. McCammon, and Carole S. Miller, *Learning to Teach Drama: A Case Narrative Approach* (Portsmouth, NH: Heinemann, 2000); Carson Rothrock, "Our Own Junior High School Musical" (*English Journal* 61.8 [November 1972]: 1244–46); and Sharona Rozmaryn, "Producing a High School Production of Agatha Christie's *Ten Little Indians*: A Case Study" (Master's thesis, University of Maryland, 1994).

6. Select examples include Raina S. Ames, *A High School Theatre Teacher's Survival Guide* (New York: Routledge, 2005); Jeff Bennett, *Secondary Stages: Revitalizing High School Theatre* (Portsmouth, NH: Heinemann, 2001); Gary P. Cohen, *The Community Theater Handbook: A Complete Guide to Organizing and Running a Community Theater* (Portsmouth, NH:

Heinemann, 2003); Jean Dalrymple, *The Complete Handbook for Community Theatre: From Picking Plays to Taking the Bows* (New York: Drake, 1977); Peter Filichia, *Let's Put on a Musical! How to Choose the Right Show for Your Theater*, 2nd ed. (New York: Back Stage Books, 2007); Edwin Gross and Natalie Gross, *Teen Theatre* (New York: McGraw Hill, 1953); David Grote, *Play Directing in the School: A Drama Director's Survival Guide* (Colorado Springs, CO: Meriwether, 1997); Toby Heathcotte, *Program Building: A Practical Guide for High School Speech and Drama Teachers* (Glendale, AZ: Mardale Books, 2003); Hume and Foster; Margaret F. Johnson, *The Drama Teacher's Survival Guide: A Complete Tool Kit for Theatre Arts* (Colorado Springs, CO: Meriwether, 2007); Charlotte Kay Motter, *Theatre in High School: Planning, Teaching, Directing* (Lanham, MD: University Press of America, 1984); James Opelt, *Organizing and Managing the High School Theatre Program* (Boston: Allyn and Bacon, 1991); Jim Patterson, Donna McKenna-Crook, and Melissa Swick, *Theatre in the Secondary Classroom: Methods and Strategies for the Beginning Teacher* (Portsmouth, NH: Heinemann, 2006); William J. Rappel and John R. Winnie, *Community Theatre Handbook* (Iowa City, IA: Institute of Public Affairs, 1961); Lawrence Stern, *School and Community Theater Management: A Handbook for Survival* (Boston: Allyn and Bacon, 1979); Elizabeth Swados, *At Play: Teaching Teenagers Theater* (New York: Faber and Faber, 2006); Joy Verley, *An Essential Manual for High-School Theater Directors: How to Structure and Organize a Youth Theater Program* (Hanover, NH: Smith and Kraus, 2001); and John Wray Young, *Community Theatre: A Manual for Success* (New York: Samuel French, 1971).

7. *Millennium Theatres: Discovering Community Theatre's Future by Exploring Its Past*, ed. Shirley Harbin, Jennifer Roberts, Noelia Saenz, and Carl P. Grant (Detroit: Theatre USA, the American Association of Community Theatre, and the City of Detroit Department of Recreation, Empowerment Zone, 2004); also published online at http://www.aact.org/aact/Millennium_Theatres2b.pdf, accessed September 10, 2009.

8. Hume and Foster; Macgowan, 1921, 1929. For a contemporary look at this issue in schools, see Laurie Fox, "Staging *Phantom* an Epic Task for Southlake Carroll" (*Dallas Morning News*, December 8, 2007, http://www.dentonrc.com/sharedcontent/dws/dn/latestnews/stories/120907dn metphantom.4deb77.html, accessed May 9, 2011), and "Carroll Senior High Stages *Phantom of the Opera*" (*Dallas Morning News*, December 9, 2007, http://www.quickdfw.com/sharedcontent/dws/news/localnews/stories/DN-phantom_09met.ART.State.Edition2.3706394.html, accessed May 9, 2011.

9. For further information about the little theater movement, see Dorothy Chansky, *Composing Ourselves: The Little Theatre Movement and the American Audience* (Carbondale: Southern Illinois University Press, 2004); see also Burleigh; and Oscar G. Brockett and Franklin J. Hildy, *History of the Theatre*, 9th ed. (New York: Allyn and Bacon, 2003), pp. 457–58.

10. See Jennifer Chapman, "Heteronormativity and High School Theatre" (Ph.D. dissertation, University of Wisconsin-Madison, 2005) and "Heteronormativity and High School Theatre" (*Youth Theatre Journal* 21 [2007]: 31–40); see also Macgowan, 1921, 1929.

11. Edward A. Krug, *The Shaping of the American High School: 1920–1941* (Madison: University of Wisconsin Press, 1972), especially pp. 20–25.

12. See Earl W. Blank, "Why Boys Should Study Dramatics" (*High School Thespian* VIII [September/October 1936]: 6; 15–16); Lois Law, "Training in Citizenship Through Play Production" (*High School Thespian* VIII [November/December 1936]: 5, 16); Louise J. Lovett, "Dramatics in Negro High Schools" (*High School Thespian* VII [March/April 1936]: 9, 13).

13. "Membership Roll of the National Thespians" (*High School Thespian* 1 [October 1929]: 54); "National Thespian Roll" (*High School Thespian* 10.5 [May/June 1939]: 51).

14. American Association of Community Theatres (http://www.aact.org, accessed September 10, 2009).

15. "Dedication" (*Dramatics* 22 [January 1951]: 1); the uncited quotation is from Alexander Pope's "Essay on Man," Epistle IV.

16. American Educational Theatre Association, "Course of Study Materials for a High School Dramatics Course" (*Bulletin of the National Association of Secondary-School Principals* [December 1949]: 5–7, 23–25).

17. Educational Theatre Association, "Writer's Guidelines" (http://www.edta.org/pdf_archive/dramatics_writers_guide.pdf, accessed September 11, 2009).

18. See the U.S. Department of Education Web site (http://www.ed.gov/policy/elsec/leg/esea02/index.html, accessed September 11, 2009) for the full text of the No Child Left Behind Act, reauthorized in 2001.

19. See Burleigh; Heather Cousins, "Upholding Mainstream Culture: The Tradition of the American High School Play" (*Research in Drama Education* 5.1 [2000]: 85–94); Hume and Foster; Law; and Macgowan 1921.

20. Wilhelmina P. Brown, "Hints for the High School Director" (*Dramatics* 19.1 [September 1947]: 12–13).

21. These needs are also met by Gilbert and Sullivan operettas. However, a school with a sophisticated dance department (or with student dancers who train at a local studio) might find the choreography in these alternative "safe" choices somewhat bland because of their dependence on a double chorus.

22. For examples of how students, schools, and communities struggle over redefining what is "appropriate" for teenagers in high school theater, see Jeff Overly, "Instructor: Play Canceled Because of Gay Character" (*Orange County Register*, February 13, 2009, http://articles.ocregister.com/2009–02–13/cities/24657324_1_gay-characters-gay-and-lesbian-students-drama-teacher, accessed May 9, 2011); and Patrick Healy, "Tamer *Rent* Is Too Wild for Some Schools" (*New York Times*, February 20, 2009, http://www.nytimes.com/2009/02/20/arts/20iht-20rent.20328998.html?pagewanted=1&%2339&%2359;t%20Look%2040,%20Charlie%20Brown!&sq=You%20Don&st=Search&scp=4, accessed May 9, 2011).

23. Educational Theatre Association, "The Long Run" (*Dramatics* 76 [September 2004]: 19–20).

24. Bennett points out that there are other objectionable qualities about *Grease* that make it inappropriate for high school students, namely, its sexism and sentimentalizing of high school. For more discussion of this issue, see also Michael Criscuolo's online review of *Grease* from August 22, 2007 (http://www.nytheatre.com/nytheatre/showpage.php?t=grea5104, accessed September 12, 2009).

25. For example, see John Lahr, "Broadway Boogie-Woogie" (*New Yorker*, March 9, 2009: 78).

26. Quoted lyrics are from act I, scenes iv and v, and act II, scene vii; Frank Loesser, Jo Swerling, Abe Burrows, and Damon Runyon, *Guys and Dolls: A Musical Fable of Broadway* (London: Frank Music, 1951).

27. Quoted lyric is from act II, scene ii; Richard Rodgers and Oscar Hammerstein II, *Oklahoma!* (New York: Williamson Music, 1943).

28. American Alliance for Theatre and Education, "Freedom of Artistic Expression in Educational Theatre" (*Drama Theatre Teacher* 5.3 [1993]: A1–A3).

CHAPTER 29

PERFORMANCE, AUTHENTICITY, AND THE REFLEXIVE IDEALISM OF THE AMERICAN MUSICAL

RAYMOND KNAPP

The American musical, throughout its history, has proved capable of reinventing itself in countless, often unexpected ways.[1] In this capacity, it has mirrored one of its own dominant themes, allied closely to its most distinctive performance modes, singing and dancing. That theme is a kind of reflexive idealism, based on the implicit belief that renewal and redemption are always possible, that people can and should reinvent themselves as necessary, and in the process discover and unlock unexplored capabilities and capacities. In this final chapter of the volume, I first consider one of the negative dimensions of this thematic emphasis, which has placed the musical at odds with modes of musical authenticity long dominant in critical discourses. I then explore how reflexive idealism, as a transformative meta-theme, plays out both in performance generally and in the specific contexts of *Candide* and *Man of La Mancha*. Key to both prongs of my discussion is a transgressive dimension of performance especially evident in musicals, encapsulated in the carelessly affirmative response musicals give to the rather serious question, "Can either authenticity or idealism be advanced through the blatantly artificial modes of performance offered up in musicals?"

PERFORMING AUTHENTICITY

The musical has long provided fertile soil for American popular music, producing hit songs and jazz standards; fostering the song traditions of Tin Pan Alley; and accommodating elements of ragtime, jazz, blues, and other emergent popular styles. Yet the musical, while mostly ignored by those who work the "serious" side of the musicology and theater streets, is similarly marginalized within the burgeoning field of popular music studies. Within that realm, musicals belong to a large body of music—including Barry Manilow, disco, the Eagles, smooth jazz, Celine Dion, and so on—that, although manifestly popular, has been traditionally ignored or treated with disdain, amusement, or embarrassment.[2]

The reasons for this are many, but let's start with some history. The study of popular music arose in earnest during the long shadow of the 1960s and has ever since tended to reflect important issues and attitudes from that era, in many cases directly carried over from such periodicals as *Rolling Stone* or the *Village Voice*. To traverse some of that landscape: Youthful rebellion and the counterculture were establishing and reinforcing the boundaries of the generation gap. The civil rights movement and evolving notions of racial identity in America became politically energizing issues for the younger side of that gap. The sexual revolution was in full swing. The mainstream study of classical music was still ideologically opposed to serious engagement with the cultural and political foundations of music. The boundaries between American musicology and ethnomusicology were increasingly fluid regarding American music. And, enforcing and coloring the interactions of this potent mix of issues, attitudes, and circumstances, music's capacity to instill emotional fervor made questions of authenticity and relevance seem especially important.

Within this environment, two narratives of authenticity attached to popular music with particular force. Jazz and blues became seen as the foundational music of African Americans as a people, establishing along with spirituals a heritage that authenticated their claims to depth, emotional capacity, and cultural legitimacy during a time when that was at issue. And for many who were then coming of age, rock-and-roll emerged as an offshoot of blues and country, rapidly becoming the principal vehicle of youthful musical expression by offering sexualized, politicized, and directly *real* expressions of rock musicians' subjectivity, powerful enough to weld together a collection of causes, complaints, and compulsions into the semblance of a movement. Supporting these narratives was a centuries-old tendency to find musical authenticity among the working and peasant classes, which translated, in American terms, into whatever might be understood as "roots" music, especially when it expressed real or imagined experiences of victimhood.[3]

It is easy to see why Barry Manilow and the musical would seem just as irrelevant to all this as classical music. The area of popular music studies, especially as it tried to secure a foothold in the academy, engaged not so much with popularity, nor even with music per se, but rather with types of music within popular culture that seemed capable of engaging its broadly based, activist narratives.[4] Music that offered comfort, enforced the status quo, or gestured too strongly toward older mainstreams simply did not count, however popular or musically interesting. As for the *musical* study of musicals, it tended to retain the perspectives, methodologies, and borrowed prestige of traditional musicology, where it had long shared a ghetto with popular music more generally.

But why should a criterion such as "authenticity"—so obviously problematic and, well, *phony*—have the capacity to carry rock and jazz into academic legitimacy while so many other musical styles and practices languish in their various mixes of real-world popularity and academic obscurity? The answer has to do with a somewhat older academic history, that of musicology itself.

Musicology became established as a discipline during the nineteenth century in part as an outgrowth of German Idealism and German nationalism, which gave a direction and purpose to the young discipline: to foster a canon of serious, mainly German, musical works. The overriding standard of value was set by German Idealism, with its dual focus on subjectivity and the Infinite, and its ongoing difficulties regarding the real world, the "thing in itself." As German Idealism took hold, music became seen as the highest of the arts, capable of linking intense subjectivity directly to something much larger, be it nation, the world in some deep sense, or something beyond the world, such as God, universal consciousness, or the Will. These larger somethings were mostly interchangeable as far as music was concerned, allowing it to accommodate easily to the evolving constructs of German Idealism. But the focus on the musical *subject* as the generator of musical value—of music as such—and, from the other side, on music as the purest expression of subjectivity, became the foundation of a new understanding of music that has ever since dominated discourses on musical value.[5]

Within popular music studies, the cult of authenticity stems directly from this historically based valorization of subjective musical expression, and links up to both a related valorization of folk music as authentic within nationalist discourses and a strong latter-day emphasis on the recapturing of origins, whether in source studies, sketch studies, editions, or performance practice. All of these seek authenticity by reaching back to moments of inspiration or conception, of first thoughts and first performances or modes of performance, in order to bring us as close as possible to the unmediated expression of the originating subject or subjects.

In contrast with the hard-won authenticities of the classical canon and the projected authenticities of jazz and rock, musicals offer instead a multi-authored, highly collaborative, eclectic, star-driven commercial product in which roles are performed in the most artificial of modes: the glitzy glitter of song and dance, often with an admixture of camp. And these products are sustained not by artists steeped in a revered tradition but by a full gamut of performers, from Broadway casts performing the same routines every night, to musical neophytes lip-synching to playback that may or may not include their own voices, kids in high schools, college and community groups, and really, anyone who might want to sing or dance along to a cast album. How much further from the paradigms of authenticity could you get?

To illustrate how deep the divide between these worlds has been, historically, we might consider *Bye Bye Birdie* (1960), a show that addresses many of the issues I've identified, but especially the generation gap and the supposed authenticity of rock-and-roll. The show's parodic dismissal of the latter, welcomed by critics of the time, in retrospect seems a bit clueless, as if the show has not taken the full measure of what it parodies. This has partly to do with its timing; the show played between 1960 and 1961, when rock-and-roll seemed to have run its course, just before its dramatic resurgence and reification as rock. And this has partly to do with the unidimensionality of the show's faux-rock-and-roll songs, "Honestly Sincere" and "One Last Kiss," both of which devolve into excessive repetitions of simple-minded lyrics. Within songs that are fundamentally Golden Age Broadway layered with elements of rock-and-roll, this blatant repetition points in two directions at once: to the banality of directly expressed feeling as such, however authentic or "sincere," and to the vain pretensions of Conrad Birdie—the show's manipulated rock-and-roll icon, modeled on Elvis Presley—whose authenticity is clearly a pose (◉ Example 29.1; ◉ Example 29.2).[6]

These song parodies have not worn well on film or in revival, where they serve mainly as vehicles for slightly exaggerated rock-and-roll performances. In a sense, the rock-and-roll ethos itself rejects their parodic dimension, absorbing it into a mode of authenticating abjection, and so making their sharper barbs seem gratuitous. More basically, the parody of these songs fails because it takes rock-and-roll's claims to authenticity as the central issue, instead of querying how such claims *function* for those who invest in them. But to get at this dimension, we must indulge in some historical speculation.

Claims of authenticity regarding rock-and-roll began when teenagers who had become hooked on it in the '50s became adults and didn't want to let it go. To rationalize this desire, college students and other young adults developed what might be called a rhetoric of relevance, through which they attached this music directly to things that mattered, at least to them: to youthful idealism; or to forms of political and social protest, especially as they involved race, war, and sexual freedom. In the process, "rock-and-roll" became "rock," and there were four compelling reasons for the shift in terminology. Aesthetically, the shorter term seemed purer and more powerful, as if condensing rock-and-roll to its essence. Moreover, it freed this music from its function as dance music, foregrounding instead its capacity either to *em*power or to *over*power, and so to inspire a different kind of movement. And the new term made it seem as if the style itself were somehow elemental, obscuring its origins as a hybrid style. But more practically and decisively, rock became a term used in combination with other musical terms—as with folk-rock, an initially controversial fusion in which rock lent its power to a proven musical vehicle of political protest. Whether in combination or in one of its increasingly varied forms, rock thus became the basic music currency of the counterculture.

Which makes it particularly interesting to notice, regarding *Bye Bye Birdie*, not only its setting just *before* all this gets under way but also its near elimination of the college-age generation. It has teenagers and adults in large number, and a sprinkling of pre-teens who either feel left out or form alliances with the adults. But there are no college-age young adults to speak of—except for the show's leads. Albert and Rose are aging members of this cohort, fending off both generations at once, caught for eight years—that is, since around 1950—between the oppressive caricature of Albert's mother and, at least for part of that span, the callowness of Conrad Birdie. In the end, their dramatic project is to free themselves from both sides.

But anyone who's ever been involved with *Bye Bye Birdie* in repertory knows that for a significant swath of the cast and audience, the star of the show is neither Albert nor Rose, but Conrad. Conrad is, after all, more precisely part of the pivotal age group than either Albert or Rose, and he has the rapt attention of those who are at stake, especially Kim MacAfee, who—at least by aspiration—is coming of age when the show opens. But the issue is even more basic than that: how can Elvis—even a parody of Elvis—be *in* the show and not be its *star*?

And this gets directly to the heart of the problem: from the perspective of the preemptive authenticity of the rock aesthetic as it evolved in the years immediately following the show's run, Conrad—even as a parody—trumps the musical's core plot, no matter how extravagantly decked out with elements borrowed from *West Side Story*, *Gypsy*, and other shows from the recent past, and no matter that the show is basically right about role-playing in the rock-and-roll scene of the late '50s. Even if the bigger project in mounting *Bye Bye Birdie* is to put on a musical, you're also putting on a rock concert, and it's hard to keep the show's focus centered on Albert and Rose when most of the cast is modeling fandom directed elsewhere, whether to Conrad Birdie or to Ed Sullivan.

While this may seem to place musicals and "authenticity" at an impasse, there is, crucially, a dimension of German Idealism (and its American offshoots)[7] that I've sidestepped by focusing on the category of authenticity as it is generally understood (usually implicitly) in popular music studies. German Idealism is not about indulging the subjective position above all else but rather about the imperative to develop one's self so as to align with larger forces. It thus came to underwrite the German concept of *Bildung*, a term taken over in the late eighteenth century from Pietism, pointing to a deepened sense of education that encompasses character formation and the capacities for reflection and realizing individual potential. To the extent that ideals of authenticity seek to reify the presentation of self within some frozen, essentialized state, indulging one's feelings over one's potential, they are not based in German Idealism, but in a self-indulgent tributary. To borrow from the political scene of the recent past, the core of German Idealism is about *change*.

Now, this is not *inconsistent* with many elements of rock, which strikes a balance between the impulse to support either protest or progressive agendas, and the tendency to hold fast to particular modes of expression, which might be rendered impure if allowed to evolve and cross-breed with other modes of expression. But this transformative mode of authenticity is more fully and fundamentally consistent with the musical. As theater, the musical is about enacting change, and it is no coincidence that one of its most time-honored devices has been the transformation scene. In this, it plays not so much to German Idealism (with its aversion to transcendence) as to a characteristic American optimism, to beliefs about realizing potential and the capacity for redemption, or for responding to disaster by starting afresh. Corollary to this, musicals also do two other things: they involve music as a kind of fluid medium that facilitates change (and allows us to believe in it); and they also typically involve a dramatically delineated process of *earning* the desired change, through performance. These processes are part and parcel of how musicals work: characters have something to learn, and music teaches them what they need to know—including their capacity to learn it—while at the same time providing an environment that facilitates change. And except for the distraction of Conrad Birdie's insincere sincerities, *Bye Bye Birdie*, like most musicals, strives to work in precisely this way, especially with regard to Rose and Albert.

Further examples are legion: Magnolia in *Show Boat*, who early on is too enamored of appearances but learns to find and express shared truths through performance. Curly and Laurey in *Oklahoma!*, who early on *don't* learn enough from their shared songs, and emerge as a successful couple only by aligning—through song—with larger forces. Fred and Lilli in *Kiss Me, Kate*, who learn to perform themselves and their relationship through the characters they perform on stage, in song. Anna in *The King and I*, who teaches through both song and dance but also learns (most importantly, about herself) through performing the role of teacher. Most of the cast of *The Music Man*, who align with community through music. And Maria in *The Sound of Music*, who does it all: teaching through song, gaining courage through performance (at least in the film version), and, most extraordinary of all for a star on Broadway, attending quietly while someone else teaches her how one builds one's own character, in "Climb Ev'ry Mountain," the quintessential *Bildung* song.

In musicals, transformation, self-discovery, and self-expression all happen through performance. One may well argue that Broadway stars aren't really performing *themselves* but are instead performing *roles*.[8] But in truth, as I will explore more broadly in the following section, they *are* performing themselves, or at least that part of themselves that can be forged through performance. In merging their public personae with the roles they play on stage, stars demonstrate that one may perform selfhood much like any other role, internalizing it but directing it outward into specific action—a mode of performance perfectly in line with dramatic, vocal, and danced performance more generally. Musicals matter to people largely because they provide fluid musical texts that inscribe possibilities of social interaction and change, first observed in performance but then taken over through processes of internal modeling or external reenactment, which allows people to discover aspects of who they are, and (re)imagine who they might become.

PERFORMING IDEALISM

Because the musical is a highly collaborative, commercial art form involving both drama and music, its intertwining of creation and performance, on all levels, is distinctively rich. The so-called creative team—lyricist, librettist, composer, arranger, choreographer, director, set, lighting, and costume designers—all play to an audience as much, if less directly, as those on stage and in the pit. And the familiar claim that original cast members "create" their roles is not as grandiose as it sounds; indeed, in a literally vital sense all stage performers create their roles—bringing them to life through their own performing bodies and projected personae—even if they follow models, obey their directors, and adhere closely to their given texts. On a still broader level, *all* of the above are involved in a process of performance-based *re*-creation, contributing to a performed re-creation of the genre itself with every new mounting of a show, re-inscribing or overturning the practices and tropes of musicals on all levels.

Understood this way, interpretation and re-creation always already inform every facet of putting on a musical, combining to create a complex layering of performances at every stage. To perform a given role convincingly, an actor must make that role his or her own, merging identities as a performer and human being with those of an interpreted text. In situations that involve the mediating step of adaptation, this process of assimilation—sometimes devolving into a kind of performer-based imperialism of the present over the past—involves another layered stage. Authors who base a musical on a literary text are also in this sense performers, bringing to life the literary basis they are setting, adjusting it, whether consciously or unconsciously, to fit contemporary circumstances and their stars' capacities, and thereby creating a new text as a basis for performance in the more conventional sense. Nor does the layering stop there, since audience members (or auditors of recordings) quite often appropriate these performances, making them their own in various ways, by re-performing them or by performing their lives alongside, harnessing their rhythms, sentiments, and affects to their own purposes. Thus, they may sing the songs of a musical in the shower; sing along or lip-synch with the original cast recording on their phonograph, CD player, or iPod; or borrow energy by listening to show songs as they walk, drive, Web-surf, or perform other tasks. At each stage within this layered process of remaking and performance, identities are conceived and reconceived, formed and re-formed, and, above all, *per*formed, which is a matter of both assimilation and self-invention.[9]

Useful to consider alongside this performance-based dimension, and in extension, is the specific comic tone of the American musical, including camp, which persists even within musicals on serious subjects and both depends on and helps support the resolute belief, often presented as a specifically American attitude, that a "cockeyed optimism" is an appropriate response to adversity. We may think of this as the "happy-ending" expectation of musical comedy (and comedy more generally). Humor in American musicals tends to suggest that negative forces need not be taken seriously, or at least should not be allowed the final say, an attitude that emerges as a particularly American form of idealism. These two intertwined elements of the American musical—its performed re-creations on several layered levels and its comic tone—are largely responsible for what I term its reflexive idealism.

In the remainder of this chapter, I consider, in demonstration of this dual basis, the reflexive idealism that directs the hopeful narratives of the musicals based on

Cervantes's two-volume novel *Don Quixote* (1605 and 1615) and Voltaire's novella *Candide* (1759). Each of these source texts is vehemently anti-idealist, opposing a brand of idealism popular in its day—*Don Quixote* the persistence of a nostalgic longing for the age of chivalry, and *Candide* the optimism associated with the Enlightenment. Both texts' protagonists repeatedly survive extreme physical violence, humiliation, and deprivation, appearing more and more ridiculous as they persist in beliefs that run counter to the worlds they live in—worlds not so different from those of Voltaire's and Cervantes's first readers. And both were adapted for the musical stage during the final decade of Broadway's "Golden Age," *Candide* in 1956 and *Man of La Mancha* in 1965.

Despite the anti-idealism of their sources, both musicals are strongly idealist, and in three important ways. First, as with many Broadway shows during this period, *Candide* and *Man of La Mancha* reflect a desire to elevate the American musical by drawing upon venerated texts. This is, to be sure, the idealism of middle-brow culture, but it is firmly grounded in the optimism of eighteenth-century Enlightenment beliefs and aspirations—the very target of Voltaire's *Candide*, with its unbroken parade of human misery. This type of idealism, however, sometimes comes into direct conflict with a second type of idealism fundamental to musicals, as noted: their apparently reflexive impulse to instill hope and optimism, even when neither seems warranted. I explore this second idealist mode before introducing the third.

The reflexive idealism of the American musical has a specifically musical basis, relating to its comic tone and deriving from European musical comedy in the eighteenth century—borrowing in particular the sanguine assurances of tonality, the sustaining musical achievement of the eighteenth century. The familiar tautologies of tonality—embedded in its syntax and realized within a wide variety of new forms—carry with them the assurance that things will work out, that we will find our way home. Every single time, no matter what. True, those tautologies could be put to other expressive and narrative uses—for example, through irony, or through enforcing the sense that we cannot escape our given situations, however inhospitable, so that we *must* return home whether we want to or not. Thus, irony and fate-based tropes, among other archetypes, find ready expression in tonality. But the fundamental and most often exploited affect of tonality, at least on the popular musical stage, then as now, is a basic cheerfulness founded in optimism, even if that cheerfulness can, in its very ubiquity, seem insincere or jaded at times.[10]

In illustration, we may consider *West Side Story* and *The Music Man*, which opened in 1957, the year after the original short run of *Candide*. *West Side Story*—based like *Candide* on a venerated literary property—is a tragedy, yet it clings to the fundamental optimism that sustains the reflexive idealism of the American musical stage. It performs Shakespeare's *Romeo and Juliet* by grounding tragedy in contemporary gang violence, reinforced with a gritty urbanized musical syntax based in jazz, serialism, and other contemporary idioms. But it also performs its audience's need to experience hope, allowing its Juliet to live and ending with a reprise of the most hopeful music of the show, "Somewhere." Moreover, the extended audience for *West Side Story* has tended to perform an even more hopeful version of the show, displacing its tragedy with either its core of redeeming love—by singing "Maria"— or a more hopeful version of the future than the show itself allows, by singing "Tonight" without its counterpoint of incipient violence and sexual craving (sung in the show by the rival gangs and Anita, respectively). Even so, *West Side Story* initially proved less successful than *The Music Man*, a show that promotes its musical fantasies as a cure for all social problems and ultimately insists on the reality of its alternative world, asserting, essentially, that to lie to the accompaniment of music— even music as only *imagined*, through the "think system"—is to tell the truth.

This kind of ontological assertion is the mainstay of the American musical, which presents its fantasies as alternative realities, ultimately more important than whatever more conventional reality is being displaced. But the assertion is conditional; one must experience that music as true for its reality to emerge; which means, one must in some sense *perform* it, if only internally. In this way, the American musical is habitually both idealist and optimistically realist, creating an analogue of the idealist interior world through its capacity to project fantasy and providing the material for performing a version of those fantasies in the real world.

Candide initially fared poorly in this environment, its ironies buried beneath a heavy-handed book, its music pared back to bubbles and mirth, and its audience left wondering how to reconcile what the show's book was saying with what the music seemed to be saying. The subsequent history of the show has been about following the music, which is more immediate and richer than the original book, long since replaced. With the cult-based success of the original cast album as inspiration, the concert-repertory status of the overture as standard bearer, and a treasure trove of previously discarded music as fuel, the show was gradually developed from an uneasy operetta into the semblance of an opera, a culmination of sorts for the aspirational idealism that originally fueled the project.[11] The specific contribution of the music, both to the original failure and to the later success of the project, thus warrants some scrutiny.

To begin with, the overture flat-out lies to us about what to expect. Reasonably enough, it uses the two opening numbers as they were then—"The Best of All Possible Worlds" and "Oh, Happy We"—as the basis for a foreshortened "sonata form." Sonata form—the crowning achievement of eighteenth-century tonality— provides a structure for presenting and resolving conflicts that can be represented as contrasting themes, initially presenting those themes in contrasting keys, but eventually playing the second of them in the key of the first. From this structure, we know (or think we know) that everything will work out (🔊 Example 29.3). To be sure, the overture also tells us other important information: that it won't be easy; that it will involve carnivalesque exaggeration; and that the ending may not be quite as expected, since the resolution of the "love" theme does not bring the overture to a close but yields instead to a fast coda based on a later number from the show ("Glitter and Be Gay"). In its very mastery of tradition, form, and material, the overture reassures us, encouraging us to believe that the world we are about to enter, though a bit out of kilter, is "the best of all possible worlds"—a sentiment that the show in all its versions, like Voltaire's novella, turns squarely on its ear. And perhaps, so does the overture, by topping its innocent love theme with the cynical laughter of "Glitter and Be Gay"—in which case it is still lying, in pretending not to care about the innocence it mocks (◆ Example 29.4).

Candide's music also offers, as counterweight to this mix of idealism and mockery, a persuasive idealist trajectory set across the show, much of which has been restored only with the 1989 "opera" version. This trajectory records the protagonist's journey from idealism through disillusionment to wisdom, in a series of meditations framed by chorales in the style of Bach (◆ Example 29.5; ◆ Example 29.6; ◆ Example 29.7). The first chorale sets the text, "We have learned, and understood/ Everything that is, is good" (◆ Example 29.8; ◆ Example 29.9), and the final one concludes with "Life is neither good nor bad./Life is life, and all we know" (◆ Example 29.10), setting up the final number, "Make Our Garden Grow," with its sober commitment to life and work. That final number convinces in part because of its musical lineage from the meditations and chorales, but even more it depends on a single masterstroke within the closing section, when the orchestra falls away suddenly, leaving the choir to continue on its own. The gesture invokes traditions of a cappella singing as an emblem of community but also depends on the visceral effect of removing all external foundations from the singers, who must then do their best without help, a musical correlative for their dramatic situation. In this moment, the cast stands before us suddenly exposed, and the thorny counterpoint ensures that we hear them struggle a bit before they emerge together on the culminating phrase, "And make our garden grow" (◆ Example 29.11).

Yet, however well realized this core musical elaboration of *Candide*'s redemptive theme may be, it still matters that the overture has lied to us, because the overture and much of *Candide*'s music more generally (especially the cast album selections) indelibly imprint a world in which innocence somehow *can* be preserved through it all. Voltaire knew better. And so surely did Bernstein—why else would he have so carefully nurtured a musical narrative that entails the complete *disillusionment* of Candide's opening innocence? But despite this knowledge, the show's music, perhaps generically, tries to have it both ways.

Emblematic of the show's affective divergence from Voltaire's novella is the matter of Cunegonde's appearance at the end of the show. On Broadway and the opera stage she remains enduringly youthful and beautiful even then, but Voltaire renders her, more realistically, as having grown old and ugly before her time. Cunegonde's appearance as an operetta ingénue seems "naturally" to preempt the aging process, underscoring the music's assertion of unspoiled innocence, but there is another idealist mode at work—the third of my promised three— which offers a fuller explanation for this particular divergence.

Typically in musicals of this era, major themes are elaborated within coupled heterosexual relationships, as a way of making those themes directly performable.[12] In a musical that makes idealism its central theme, the central relationship will most often be a problematic or unsuccessful love story, serving as a "reality check" on the ability of the idealistic hero to realize his ideals; in one way or another, the idealized woman, who stands symbolically for the idealist dimension of the show, fails to live up to the demands of that symbolic function. A musical may thus bring dramatic emphasis to bear on idealist potentials, arguing through plotting and musical numbers that ideals are more valuable than their potential for realization and matter beyond the realities that prevent their fulfillment. According to this familiar trope of musicals, another lie that *Candide* indulges is that, despite the wisdom that Candide acquires, even about Cunegonde, the music itself does not admit—perhaps generically cannot admit—to Cunegonde's failures as the embodied ideal.

Man of La Mancha, on the other hand, by embracing more fully its responsibility to its time and place, emerges as more successful than *Candide*, despite the greater violence it does to its source material and despite the fact that *Candide*, for all its contradictions, is smarter, richer, and more ambitious. *Man of La Mancha* succeeds at all relevant levels of performance, in particular by speaking more directly to its contemporary audience through its hit tune, "The Impossible Dream," which became an international anthem of idealist striving.

Working backward through the three musicals-based idealist modes I've identified, we may note how much better the "ideal woman" trope works in *Man of La Mancha*, which awakens latent idealism in the brutalized Aldonza, as an emblem of the redemptive power of idealism; through her character, we see how identities might be reformed, *per*formed, and, finally, *trans*formed. Moreover, this mode extends and effectively overlaps the first idealist mode, giving dramatic presence to the "real-life" transformative potential of great literature, even if it must first be rendered accessible to the uneducated and illiterate. Through the example offered by Cervantes's fellow-prisoners, whose lives are changed by acting out his improvised account of his unfinished novel, the musical reinforces both the Aldonza-Dulcinea transformation and the larger aspirational project, of elevating the musical by drawing on great literature. Thus, in *Man of La Mancha*, these idealist modes are aligned, rather than opposed as in *Candide*.

The specifically musical idealist mode in *Man of La Mancha*, as is typical for this era, is built around the familiarity of the 32-bar Tin Pan Alley song type, which can most easily be seen in "The Impossible Dream." The song lays out the tenets of chivalry with a carefully balanced tension between internal ideals and outward action, couched in a characteristic Spanish idiom whose ostinato rhythms serve as an emblem of steadfast obsession. The song unfolds within a Tin Pan Alley form but with a "heroic" expansion of the bridge. Within this structure, the lyric at first maintains a careful alternation between inward-directed idealism and the heroic action it inspires ("To dream…To fight…"), throwing increasing emphasis to action ("To try…To reach…"; (◐ Example 29.12). Active verbs then carry us to a climax during the bridge, which dissipates in a series of idealist verbs; significantly, the verbs that mark the climax itself are idealist ("And I *know* if I'll only *be* true…"). Finally, the satisfying completion of the well-known form—the return to the melody of the first phrase, after the bridge—adds conviction to the lyric's concluding concern for legacy, for how the world itself might be transformed through the image of the inspired, idealist hero (◐ Example 29.13).

Part of what makes *Man of La Mancha* "work" better than *Candide* is the way it manages performance on every level. Whatever its strengths as a performable text, *Candide's* move to opera has confirmed that it is more about being a text than a show; not by coincidence, it has been published, at various stages in its development, more thoroughly than any other piece of American musical theater. As a text, it promises to outlive *Man of La Mancha*. But because the latter "performed" *Don Quixote* more appropriately for its intended venue and audience; because its onstage players so vividly enact its central metatheatrical theme and are redeemed, as characters, specifically through *performing* their redemption; and because it provided one of the central anthems through which its extended audience forged and performed the idealist component of their identities, its cultural impact has been much more powerful and lasting.

A central lesson to be learned from all reflexively idealist musicals is how lasting their moments of expressed idealism are, especially when sung, far outliving the cataclysms that often surround those moments. And in performing this reflexive idealism, both *Candide* and *Man of La Mancha* are, despite all odds, true to their originals, whose protagonists—at least in reception, and whatever Cervantes or Voltaire might have intended—have provided some of the key idealist images that have sustained Europe-based culture.

I have in this chapter addressed the need for a more congenial environment, especially within musicology, for the study of musicals, and argued for a perspective more centered on performance and less beholden to inherited notions of authenticity or text-bound standards of value. There has, indeed, been a broad surge of performance-based studies of the musical in the past few years, and a similar surge in studies that place performance at the center of musicological inquiry. One can only hope, with reflexive optimism, that these waves will be sustained, and that they will grow stronger in alignment.

NOTES

1. I have presented much of this essay's argument in a series of talks: "Cervantes, Voltaire, and the Reflexive Idealism of the American Musical" ("Musical Theater and Identity in Eighteenth-Century Spain and America," symposium held at the UCLA William Andrews Clark Memorial Library, Los Angeles, October 27–28, 2006), "Performing Authenticity; or, Why the Musical Doesn't Seem to Count as Popular Music" ("American Musical Theater," conference hosted by CUNY Graduate Center, April 2–5, 2008), and "The Musical, the *American* Musical, and 'Musical Comedy': Reflections on the Comic Inclinations of a Genre" ("Music and Humor," conference hosted by *Echo: A Music-Centered Journal*, UCLA, June 5–6, 2009). Additionally, my examples draw upon my discussions of *Candide* and *Man of La Mancha* in *The American Musical and the Performance of Personal Identity* (Princeton, NJ: Princeton University Press, 2006).

2. An important exception to this trend is Mitchell Morris's *The Persistence of Sentiment: Essays on Pop Music in the '70s* (forthcoming from the University of California Press), which considers several components of this list. Regarding the musical's lack of prestige, as theater, see David Savran's chapter in this volume, as well as his "Middlebrow Anxiety" (in his *A Queer Sort of Materialism: Recontextualizing American Theater* [Ann Arbor: University of Michigan Press, 2003]); and, regarding theater's intersection with jazz and the popular more generally, his *Highbrow/Lowdown: Theater, Jazz, and the Making of the New Middle Class* (Ann Arbor: University of Michigan Press, 2009); and "Toward a Historiography of the Popular" (*Theatre Survey* 45.2 [November 2004]: 211–17). See also Carl Wilson's extended discussion of Céline Dion in *Let's Talk about Love: A Journey to the End of Taste* (New York: Continuum International, 2007).

3. For a trenchant (and entertaining) account of this period, detailing its history while also querying its mythologies and what has motivated and sustained them, see Robynn Stilwell, "Music of the Youth Revolution: Rock through the 1960s," in *The Cambridge History of Twentieth-Century Music*, ed. Nicholas Cook and Anthony Pople (Cambridge: Cambridge University Press, 2004), pp. 418–52.

4. See, however, Elijah Wald's *How the Beatles Destroyed Rock 'n' Roll: An Alternative History of American Popular Music* (New York: Oxford University Press, 2009), which takes as its scholarly starting point an obligation to consider what music was actually *popular* at a given time, rather than what music best fits the conventional narratives of American popular music.

5. I consider some of this history, and its effect on the early development of American popular music, in my book *Surviving Absolute Music: Haydn, German Idealism, and the Persistent Dualities of American Music* (in progress).

6. For more on the background and rock dimension of *Bye Bye Birdie*, see Elizabeth Wollman, *The Theater Will Rock: A History of the Rock Musical from* Hair *to* Hedwig (Ann Arbor: University of Michigan Press, 2006), pp. 16–20. Elsewhere in the book, Wollman speaks directly to the question of authenticity as a contentious category within rock musicals; see especially pp. 24–41.

7. For an extended discussion of how German Idealism relates to the idealism prevalent in American musicals, see chapter 4 of my *The American Musical and the Performance of Personal Identity*.

8. Regarding the important connections between stars' personae and the roles they play (on stage and for their audiences), see Holley Replogle-Wong's contribution to this volume, and Stacy Wolf's *A Problem Like Maria: Gender and Sexuality in the American Musical* (Ann Arbor: University of Michigan Press, 2002) and "*Wicked* Divas, Musical Theater, and Internet Girl Fans" (*Camera Obscura 65*, 22.2 [2007]: 39–71).

9. In stressing the dynamic of performance and (re)creation in musicals, I am both indebted to Bruce Kirle's *Unfinished Show Business: Broadway Musicals as Works-in-Process* (Carbondale: Southern Illinois University Press, 2005) and insistent that the idea of performance be applied as broadly as possible. For related arguments, see Marvin Carlson, *The Haunted Stage: The Theatre as Memory Machine* (Ann Arbor: University of Michigan Press, 2003).

10. For an extended discussion of this aspect of tonality, see Susan McClary, *Conventional Wisdom: The Content of Musical Form* (Berkeley: University of California Press, 2000).

11. Among many accounts of the mismatch among *Candide*'s constituent parts, Stephen Sondheim's is especially memorable: "The book didn't belong with the score, the score didn't belong with the direction, and the direction didn't belong with the book. I thought Lillian [Hellman]'s book was wonderful, but it's very black. The score [by Leonard Bernstein] is pastiche, with bubble and sparkle and sweetness. The direction [by Tyrone Guthrie] was wedding cake, like an operetta" (quoted in Meryle Secrest's *Stephen Sondheim: A Life* [New York: Alfred A. Knopf, 1998], p. 120). For related accounts, see Humphrey Burton, *Leonard Bernstein* (New York:

Doubleday, 1994), p. 263 (quoting lyricist Richard Wilbur); Brooks Peters, "Making Your Garden Grow: Lillian Hellman and *Candide*" (*Opera News* 65.1 [July, 2000]: 38); and Ethan Mordden, *Coming Up Roses; The Broadway Musical in the 1950s* (New York: Oxford University Press, 1998). For accounts of how Harold Prince spearheaded the show's renovation, see chapter 26 of Prince's *Contradictions: Notes on Twenty-Six Years in the Theatre* (New York: Dodd, Mead, 1974); Carol Ilson, *Harold Prince: from* Pajama Game *to* Phantom of the Opera (Ann Arbor: UMI Research Press, 1989), pp. 212–25; and Foster Hirsch, *Harold Prince and the American Musical Theatre* (Cambridge: Cambridge University Press, 1989), pp. 149–56.

 12. For discussions and examples of what I term the "marriage trope," see my *The American Musical and the Formation of National Identity* (Princeton, NJ: Princeton University Press, 2005) and Knapp, 2006. Rick Altman succinctly describes this aspect of musicals: "The marriage which resolves the primary (sexual) dichotomy also mediates between two terms of the secondary (thematic) opposition" (*The American Film Musical*, Bloomington: Indiana University Press, 1987, p. 50). For revelatory discussions of how this entrenched trope has sometimes transferred to homosocial relationships, often similarly uniting opposites, see Stacy Wolf's "'We'll Always Be Bosom Buddies': Female Duets and the Queering of Broadway Musical Theater" (*GLQ: A Journal of Lesbian and Gay Studies* 12:3 [2006]: 351–76) and "'Defying Gravity': Queer Conventions in the Musical *Wicked*" (*Theatre Journal* 60 [2008]:1–21).

BIBLIOGRAPHY

Abbott, Lynn, and Doug Seroff. *Out of Sight: The Rise of African American Popular Music, 1889–1895*. Jackson: University Press of Mississippi, 2002.

Acocella, Joan. "Imagining Dance." In *Moving History/Dancing Cultures: A Dance History Reader*. Edited by Ann Dils and Ann Cooper Albright. Middletown, CT: Wesleyan University Press, 2001, pp. 12–16.

Actors Equity (Web site) http://www.actorsequity.org/AboutEquity/contracts.asp (accessed March 15, 2009).

Adams, Gabriel J. "A Quick History of the Phantom of the Opera." *Ezine Articles*, http://ezinearticles.com/?A-Quick-History-Of-The-Phantom-Of-The-Opera&id=689698 (accessed May 23, 2008).

Adler, Steven. *On Broadway: Art and Commerce on the Great White Way*. Carbondale: Southern Illinois University Press, 2004.

Adshead, Janet. "An Introduction to Dance Analysis." In *The Routledge Dance Studies Reader*. Edited by Alexandra Carter. London: Routledge, 1998, pp. 163–70.

Adshead, Janet, ed. *Dance Analysis: Theory and Practice*. London: Dance Books, 1988.

All That Jazz. Directed and choreographed by Bob Fosse. Beverly Hills, CA: Twentieth Century Fox, 1979. DVD release, 2003.

Altman, Rick. *The American Film Musical*. Bloomington: Indiana University Press, 1987.

———. "Toward a Theory of the History of Representational Technologies." *Iris* 2.2 (1984): 111–25.

American Alliance for Theatre and Education. "Freedom of Artistic Expression in Educational Theatre." *Drama Theatre Teacher* 5.3 (1993): A1–A3.

American Association of Community Theatres (Web site). http://www.aact.org (accessed September 10, 2009).

American Educational Theatre Association. "Course of Study Materials for a High School Dramatics Course." *Bulletin of the National Association of Secondary-School Principals* (December 1949): 5–7, 23–25.

Ames, Raina S. *A High School Theatre Teacher's Survival Guide*. New York: Routledge, 2005.

Anderson, John Murray. *Out without My Rubbers*. New York: Library Publishers, 1954.

Anderson, Tim. "'Buried under the Fecundity of His Own Creations': Reconsidering the Recording Bans of the American Federation of Musicians, 1942–1944 and 1948." *American Music* 22.2 (Summer 2004): 231–69.

Arlen, Harold, and E. Y. Harburg. *The Wizard of Oz: Original Motion Picture Soundtrack*. Turner Classic Movies Music R2 72755, 1995.

Aronson, Arnold. *American Set Design*. New York: Theatre Communications Group, 1985.

———. *Looking in the Abyss: Essays on Scenography*. Ann Arbor: University of Michigan Press, 2005.

Ayers, Edward L., Patricia Nelson Limerick, Stephen Nissenbaum, and Peter S. Onuf, *All Over the Map: Rethinking American Regions*. Baltimore: Johns Hopkins University Press, 1996.

Banfield, Stephen. *Jerome Kern*. New Haven, CT: Yale University Press, 2006.

————. "Popular Song and Popular Music on Stage and Film." In *The Cambridge History of American Music*. Edited by David Nicholls. Cambridge: Cambridge University Press, 1998, pp. 309–44.

————. *Sondheim's Broadway Musicals*. Ann Arbor: University of Michigan Press, 1993.

Barker, Barbara. Unprocessed papers, box 18, box 5, box 6. Research materials of Agnes de Mille. New York Public Library for the Performing Arts, Dance Division, New York, NY.

Barnes, Clive. "Stage: 'Annie' Finds a Home." *New York Times* (April 22, 1977): 65.

Bart, Lionel. *Oliver!* London, UK: Lakeview Music, 1960.

Barthes, Roland. "The Death of the Author." In *Image, Music, Text*. Edited and translated by Stephen Heath. New York: Hill and Wang, 1977, pp. 142–48.

————. "Introduction to the Structural Analysis of Narration." In *Image, Music, Text*. Edited and translated by Stephen Heath. New York: Hill and Wang, 1977, pp. 261–67.

Baugh, Christopher. *Theatre, Performance, and Technology: The Development of Scenography in the Twentieth Century*. New York: Palgrave Macmillan, 2005.

Bazin, André. *What Is Cinema? Essays Selected and Translated by Hugh Gray*. Volume 1. Berkeley: University of California Press, 2005 (originally published 1967).

————. *What Is Cinema? Essays Selected and Translated by Hugh Gray*. Volume 2. Berkeley: University of California Press, 2005 (originally published 1971).

Beacham, Richard C. *Adolphe Appia: Artist and Visionary of the Modern Theatre*. Philadelphia: Routledge, 1994.

Becker, Howard S. *Art Worlds*. Berkeley: University of California Press, 1982.

Beckerman, Bernard. *Theatrical Presentation: Performer, Audience, and Act*. London: Routledge, 1990.

Beddow, Margery. *Bob Fosse's Broadway*. Portsmouth, NH: Heinemann, 1996.

Beidler, Philip D. "*South Pacific* and American Remembering; or 'Gosh, We're Going to Buy This Son of a Bitch!'" *Journal of American Studies* 27 (1993): 207–22.

Beiswanger, George. "After Victor Herbert: The Battle of the Orchestras." *Theatre Arts* 28.1 (January 1944): 40–45.

————. "New Images in Dance: Martha Graham and Agnes de Mille." *Theatre Arts* 28.10 (October 1944): 609–14.

Belasco, David. *The Theatre through Its Stage Door*. Whitefish, MT: Kessinger, 2006.

Bell, Matthew. "Musical Theater." *Gay Histories and Cultures: An Encyclopedia*. Edited by George E. Haggerty. New York: Garland, 2000, pp. 621–24.

Benedetti, Jean. *David Garrick and the Birth of Modern Theatre*. London: Methuen, 2001.

Bennett, Jeff. *Secondary Stages: Revitalizing High School Theatre*. Portsmouth, NH: Heinemann, 2001.

Bennett, Robert Russell. *"The Broadway Sound": The Autobiography and Selected Essays of Robert Russell Bennett*. Edited by George J. Ferencz. Rochester, NY: University of Rochester Press, 1999.

————. *Instrumentally Speaking*. Melville, NY: Belwin Mills, 1975.

Bennett, Susan. *Theatre Audiences: A Theory of Production and Reception*. 2nd ed. London: Routledge, 1997.

Bentley, Eric. "The American Musical." In *What Is Theatre?* New York: Athenaeum, 1968, pp. 190–93.

Bergeen, Laurence. *As Thousands Cheer: The Life of Irving Berlin*. New York: Viking, 1990.

Berlioz, Hector. *Berlioz's Orchestration Treatise: A Translation and Commentary*. Translated by Hugh MacDonald. New York: Cambridge University Press, 2002.

Bernstein, Leonard. "American Musical Comedy." In his *The Joy of Music*. New York: Simon and Schuster, 1959, pp. 152–79.

———. *Candide*. New York: Boosey and Hawkes, 1994.

Bernstein, Leonard, and Stephen Sondheim. *West Side Story*. New York: Boosey and Hawkes, 2000.

Bianco, Anthony. *Ghosts of 42nd Street: A History of America's Most Infamous Block*. New York: William Morrow, 2004.

Blank, Matthew. "Broadway Rush and Standing Room Only Policies." *Playbill.com*, http://www.playbill.com/celebritybuzz/article/82428.html (accessed December 2, 2008).

Block, Geoffrey. "The Broadway Canon from *Show Boat* to *West Side Story* and the European Operatic Ideal." *The Journal of Musicology* 11.4 (Autumn, 1993): 525–44.

———. *Enchanted Evenings: The Broadway Musical from* Show Boat *to Sondheim and Lloyd Webber*. 2nd ed. New York: Oxford University Press, 2009.

———. *Richard Rodgers*. Yale Broadway Masters Series. New Haven, CT: Yale University Press, 2003.

Bloom, Julie. "'Forbidden Broadway' Curtain to Go Down." *New York Times* (September 13, 2009): B-9.

———. "Rekindling Robbins, a Step at a Time." *New York Times* (March 4, 2009), http://www.nytimes.com/2009/03/08/arts/dance/08bloo.html (accessed July 22, 2009).

Bock, Jerry, and Sheldon Harnick. *Fiddler on the Roof*. New York: Times Square Music, 1964.

Bogle, Donald. *Blacks in American Films and Television: An Encyclopedia*. New York: Garland, 1988.

———. *Toms, Coons, Mulattoes, Mammies, and Bucks: An Interpretive History of Blacks in American Films*. 4th ed. New York: Continuum, 2001 (originally published 1973).

Bordman, Gerald. *American Musical Theatre: A Chronicle*. 3rd ed. New York: Oxford University Press, 2001.

———. *American Operetta from H.M.S. Pinafore to Sweeney Todd*. New York: Oxford University Press, 1981.

———. *Jerome Kern: His Life and Music*. New York: Oxford University Press, 1980.

Bordwell, David, and Kristin Thompson. *Film Art: An Introduction*. 8th ed. Boston: McGraw-Hill, 2008.

Bottoms, Stephen J. *Playing Underground: A Critical History of the 1960s Off-Off-Broadway Movement*. Ann Arbor: University of Michigan Press, 2004.

Brady, Sara. Review of Leah Hager Cohen, *The Stuff of Dreams: Behind the Scenes of an American Community Theatre*. *The Drama Review* 46.1 (Spring 2002): 170–74.

Brantley, Ben. "Grand Guignol, Spare and Stark." *New York Times* (November 4, 2005): E1–1.

———. "There's Trouble in Emerald City: WICKED." *New York Times* (October 31, 2003): E-1.

Braudy, Leo. "Musicals and the Energy from Within." In his *The World in a Frame: What We See in Films*. Chicago: University of Chicago Press, 2002, pp. 139–63 (originally published 1976).

Brecht, Bertolt. "Against Georg Lukács." In *Aesthetics and Politics*. Edited by Ronald Taylor. London: Verso, 1980.

"Broadway." http://theater2.nytimes.com/venues/broadway.html (accessed November 24, 2008).

"Broadway Grosses: *Wicked*." BroadwayWorld.com, http://www.broadwayworld.com/grossesshow.cfm?show=Wicked (accessed September 13, 2008).

The Broadway League, and Karen Hauser. *The Demographics of the Broadway Audience, 2007–2008*. New York: Broadway League, 2008.

"Broadway Long Runs." Chart in *Variety* (June 9–15, 2008): 50.

"Broadway Season Statistics at a Glance." The Broadway League, http://www.broadway-league.com/editor_files/Broadway%20Statistics%20at%20a%20Glance.pdf (accessed August 2, 2008).

Broadway: The American Musical. A Film by Michael Kantor. Educational Broadcasting Corporation and the Broadway Film Project, 2004.

Brockett, Oscar G., and Robert R. Findlay, *Century of Innovation: A History of European and American Theatre and Drama since 1870*. Englewood Cliffs, NJ: Prentice-Hall, 1973.

Brockett, Oscar G., and Franklin J. Hildy. *History of the Theatre*. 9th ed. New York: Allyn and Bacon, 2003.

Brooks, Mel, and Tom Meehan. *The Producers: The Book, Lyrics, and Story behind the Biggest Hit in Broadway History! How We Did It*. New York: Hyperion, 2001.

Brooks, Tim. "Early Recordings of Songs from *Florodora*: Tell Me, Pretty Maiden...Who Are You?—A Discographical Mystery." *Association for Recorded Sound Collections Journal* 31 (2000): 51–64.

Brown, Cynthia Lynn. "Longevity and the Secondary Theatre Arts Teacher: A Case Study."Ph.D. dissertation, Arizona State University, 1997.

Brown, Wilhelmina P. "Hints for the High School Director." *Dramatics* 19.1 (September 1947): 12–13.

Bryer, Jackson R., and Richard A. Davison, eds. *The Art of the American Musical: Conversations with the Creators*. New Brunswick, NJ: Rutgers University Press, 2005.

Bryson, Norman. "Cultural Studies and Dance History." In *Meaning in Motion: New Cultural Studies of Dance*. Edited by Jane C. Desmond. Durham, NC: Duke University Press, 1997, pp. 55–77.

Burleigh, Louise. *The Community Theatre in Theory and Practice*. Boston: Little, Brown, 1917.

Burston, Jonathan. "Theatre Space as Virtual Place: Audio Technology, the Reconfigured Singing Body, and the Megamusical." *Popular Music* 17.2 (May 1998): 205–18.

Burton, Humphrey. *Leonard Bernstein*. New York: Doubleday, 1994.

Butler, Judith. *Gender Trouble*. New York: Routledge, 1990.

Butsch, Richard. *The Making of American Audiences: From Stage to Television, 1750–1990*. Cambridge: Cambridge University Press, 2000.

Butterfield, Herbert. *The Whig Interpretation of History*. London: G. Bell, 1931.

Cameron, Evan William, ed. *Sound and the Cinema: The Coming of Sound to American Film*. Pleasantville, NY: Redgrave, 1980.

Campbell, Gavin James. *Music and the Making of a New South*. Chapel Hill: University of North Carolina Press, 2004.

Carlson, Marvin. *The Haunted Stage: The Theatre as Memory Machine*. Ann Arbor: University of Michigan Press, 2003.

Carter, Alexandra, ed. *The Routledge Dance Studies Reader*. London: Routledge, 1998.

Carter, David. *Stonewall: The Riots that Sparked the Gay Revolution*. New York: St. Martin's Press, 2004.

Carter, Randolph. *The World of Flo Ziefeld*. New York: Praeger, 1974.

Carter, Tim. *Oklahoma! The Making of an American Musical*. New Haven, CT: Yale University Press, 2007.

Cartmell, Dan J. "Stephen Sondheim and the Concept Musical." Ph.D. dissertation, University of California, Santa Barbara, 1983.

Channing, Carol. "Foreword." In Steven Suskin. *Opening Nights on Broadway: A Critical Quotebook of the Golden Age of the Musical Theatre,* Oklahoma! *to* Fiddler on the Roof. New York: Schirmer Books, 1990.

Chansky, Dorothy. *Composing Ourselves: The Little Theatre Movement and the American Audience.* Carbondale: Southern Illinois University Press, 2004.

Chapin, Theodore S., Kurt Deutsch, Brian Drutman, Thomas Z. Shepard, and Melissa Rose Bernardo. "For the Record: Inside Cast Albums." American Theatre Wing's *Working in the Theatre* [April, 2009], http://americantheatrewing.org/wit/detail/cast_albums_04_09 (accessed August 19, 2009).

Chapman, Jennifer. "Heteronormativity and High School Theatre." Ph.D. dissertation, University of Wisconsin–Madison, 2005.

———. "Heteronormativity and High School Theatre." *Youth Theatre Journal* 21 (2007): 31–40.

Charyn, Jerome. *Gangsters and Gold Diggers: Old New York, the Jazz Age, and the Birth of Broadway.* New York: Thunder's Mouth Press, 2003.

Chauncey, George. *Gay New York: Gender, Urban Culture, and the Making of the Gay Male World, 1890–1940.* New York: Basic Books, 1994.

Citron, Stephen. *The Musical from the Inside Out.* Chicago: Ivan R. Dee, 1991.

Clover, Carol J. "Dancin' in the Rain." In *Hollywood Musicals: The Film Reader.* Edited by Steven Cohan. London: Routledge, 2002, pp. 155–73.

Clum, John. *Something for the Boys: Musical Theater and Gay Culture.* New York: Palgrave, 1999.

Cockrell, Dale. *Demons of Disorder: Early Blackface Minstrels and Their World.* Cambridge: Cambridge University Press, 1997.

Cohan, Steven. "'Feminizing' the Song-and-Dance Man: Fred Astaire and the Spectacle of Masculinity in the Hollywood Musical." In *Hollywood Musicals: The Film Reader.* Edited by Steven Cohan. London: Routledge, 2002, pp. 87–101.

———, ed. *Hollywood Musicals: The Film Reader.* London: Routledge, 2002.

Cohen, Gary P. *The Community Theater Handbook: A Complete Guide to Organizing and Running a Community Theater.* Portsmouth, NH: Heinemann, 2003.

Cohen, Leah Hager. *The Stuff of Dreams: Behind the Scenes of an American Community Theatre.* New York: Viking Penguin, 2001.

Cohen, Selma Jeanne. *International Encyclopedia of Dance.* New York: Oxford University Press, 1998.

Coleman, Bud, and Judith A. Sebesta. *Women in the American Musical Theatre.* Jefferson, NC: MacFarland, 2008.

Conrad, Jon Alan. "Let the Drums Roll Out." Sleeve Notes, *Strike Up the Band.* Elektra Nonesuch 7559–79273–2, 1991.

Copeland, Roger. "Between Description and Deconstruction." In *The Routledge Dance Studies Reader.* Edited by Alexandra Carter. London: Routledge, 1998, pp. 98–107.

Copeland, Roger, and Marshall Cohen, eds. *What Is Dance? Readings in Theory and Criticism.* Oxford: Oxford University Press, 1983.

Corbett, John. "Free, Single, and Disengaged: Listening Pleasure and the Popular Music Object." In his *Extended Play: Sounding Off from John Cage to Dr. Funkenstein.* Durham, NC: Duke University Press, 1994, pp. 32–55. Essay originally published in *October* 54 (Fall 1990): 79–101.

Cousins, Heather. "Upholding Mainstream Culture: The Tradition of the American High School Play." *Research in Drama Education* 5.1 (2000): 85–94.

Craig, Edward Gordon. *On the Art of the Theatre.* New York: Theatre Arts Books, 1956.

Craine, Debra, and Judith Mackrell. *The Oxford Dictionary of Dance*. Oxford: Oxford University Press, 2000.

Criscuolo, Michael. "Grease." Online review, http://www.nytheatre.com/nytheatre/showpage.php?t=grea5104, August 22, 2007 (accessed September 12, 2009).

Dalrymple, Jean. *The Complete Handbook for Community Theatre: From Picking Plays to Taking the Bows*. New York: Drake, 1977.

Daly, Ann. *Critical Gestures: Writings on Dance and Culture*. Middletown, CT: Wesleyan University Press, 2002.

Daniel, Pete. *Lost Revolutions: The South in the 1950s*. Chapel Hill: University of North Carolina Press, 2000.

Decker, Todd R. "Black/White Encounters on the American Stage and Screen (1924–2005)." Ph.D dissertation, University of Michigan, 2007.

———. " 'Do You Want to Hear a Mammy Song?' A Historiography of *Show Boat*." *Contemporary Theatre Review* 19.1 (2009): 8–21.

———. *Music Makes Me: Fred Astaire and Jazz*. Berkeley: University of California Press, forthcoming.

———. *Show Boat: Race and the Making and Re-making of an American Musical*. New York: Oxford University Press, forthcoming.

Deer, Joe, and Rocco Dal Vera. *Acting in Musical Theatre: A Comprehensive Course*. London: Routledge, 2008.

de Mille, Agnes. *Martha*. New York: Random House, 1991.

Delamater, Jerome. *Dance in the Hollywood Musical*. Ann Arbor: UMI Research Press, 1981.

"The Demographics of the Broadway Audience 2006–2007." Broadway League, http://www.broadwayleague.com/index.php?url_identifier=the-demographics-of-the-broadway-audience-2005–2006 (accessed September 13, 2008).

Desmond, Jane C. "Embodying Difference: Issues in Dance and Cultural Studies." In *The Routledge Dance Studies Reader*. Edited by Alexandra Carter. London: Routledge, 1998, pp. 154–62.

———. *Meaning in Motion: New Cultural Studies of Dance*. Durham, NC: Duke University Press, 1997.

Dickinson, Thomas Herbert. *The Insurgent Theatre*. New York: Benjamin Blom, 1972 (1917).

Dils, Ann, and Ann Cooper Albright, eds. *Moving History/Dancing Cultures: A Dance History Reader*. Middletown, CT: Wesleyan University Press, 2001.

DiMaggio, Paul. "Cultural Boundaries and Structural Change: The Extension of the High Culture Model to Theater, Opera, and the Dance, 1900–1940." In *Cultivating Differences: Symbolic Boundaries and the Making of Inequality*. Edited by Michèle Lamont and Marcel Fournier. Chicago: University of Chicago Press, 1992, pp. 21–57.

Dolan, Jill. *The Feminist Spectator as Critic*. Ann Arbor: University of Michigan Press, 1988.

Doty, Alexander. *Flaming Classics: Queering the Film Canon*. London: Routledge, 2000.

———. *Making Things Perfectly Queer: Interpreting Mass Culture*. Minneapolis: University of Minnesota Press, 1993.

"Downstage Center." Online interviews. The American Theatre Wing, http://americanthe-atrewing.org/downstagecenter (accessed September 8, 2009).

Drowne, Kathleen, and Patrick Huber. *American Popular Culture through History: The 1920s*. Westport, CT: Greenwood Press, 2004.

Duberman, Martin. *Stonewall*. New York: Penguin, 1993.

Dudden, Faye E. *Women in the American Theatre: Actresses and Audiences 1790–1870*. New Haven, CT: Yale University Press, 1994.

Dyer, Richard. "The Colour of Entertainment." In *Musicals: Hollywood and Beyond*. Edited by Bill Marshall and Robynn Stilwell. Exeter: Intellect Books, 2000, pp. 23–30 (originally published *Sight and Sound*, 1995).

———. "Entertainment and Utopia." In *Genre: The Musical*. Edited by Rick Altman. London: Routledge and Kegan Paul, 1981 (originally published in *Movie* 2 [Spring 1977]: 2–13).

———. *Heavenly Bodies*. London: Routledge, 2004.

———. " 'I Seem to Find the Happiness I Seek': Heterosexuality and Dance in the Musical." *Dance, Gender and Culture*. Edited by Helen Thomas. London: Macmillan, 1993, pp. 49–65.

———. *Only Entertainment*. Expanded from the 1992 edition. London: Routledge, 2002.

———. *Stars*. London: British Film Institute, 1998 (originally published 1979).

———. *White*. London: Routledge, 1997.

Eagleton, Terry. *Literary Theory: An Introduction*. 2nd ed. . Minneapolis: University of Minnesota Press, 1996.

Eaton, Walter Prichard. *The American Stage of To-Day*. Boston: Small, Maynard, 1908.

Ebb, Fred, Bob Fosse, and John Kander. *Chicago: A Musical Vaudeville*. New York: Samuel French, 1976.

Ebert, Roger. "*The Best Little Whorehouse in Texas*" (review). *Chicago Sun Times* (January 1, 1982). http://rogerebert.suntimes.com/apps/pbcs.dll/article?AID=/19820101/REVIEWS/201010305/1023, accessed May 10, 2010.

Educational Theatre Association. "Dedication." *Dramatics* 22 (January 1951): 1.

———. "The Long Run." *Dramatics* 76 (September 2004): 19–20.

———. "Writer's Guidelines." http://www.edta.org/pdf_archive/dramatics_writers_guide.pdf (accessed September 11, 2009).

Ehrenreich, Barbara, Elizabeth Hess, and Gloria Jacobs. "Beatlemania: Girls Just Want to Have Fun." In *The Adoring Audience: Fan Culture and Popular Media*. Edited by Lisa A. Lewis. London: Routledge, 1992, pp. 84–106.

Eisenberg, Evan. *The Recording Angel: Music, Records and Culture from Aristotle to Zappa*. 2nd ed. New Haven, CT: Yale University Press, 2005.

Eisenstein, Sergei. *Eisenstein on Disney*. London: Methuen, 1988.

Elam, Kier. *The Semiotics of Theatre and Drama*. 2nd ed. London: Routledge, 2002.

Elborough, Travis. *The Vinyl Countdown*. Berkeley: Soft Skull Press, 2009.

Engel, Lehman. *The American Musical Theater*. New York: Macmillan, 1975.

———. *The American Musical Theater: A Consideration*. New York: Macmillan, 1967.

Engel, Lehman, and Howard Kissel. *Words with Music: Creating the Broadway Musical Libretto*. New York: Applause, 2006.

Ennis, Philip H. *The Seventh Stream: The Emergence of Rocknroll in American Popular Music*. Hanover, NH: Wesleyan University Press, 1992.

Evans, Harvey. Interview by Liza Gennaro, March 3, 2003, transcript. Oral History Collection, Lincoln Center Library of the Performing Arts, New York, NY.

Everett, William A. "Romance, Nostalgia and Nevermore: American and British Operetta in the 1920s." In *The Cambridge Companion to the Musical*. Edited by William A. Everett and Paul R. Laird. Cambridge: Cambridge University Press, 2002, pp. 47–62.

———. *Sigmund Romberg*. New Haven: Yale University Press, 2007.

Everett, William A., and Paul R. Laird, eds. *The Cambridge Companion to the Musical*. 2nd ed. Cambridge: Cambridge University Press, 2008.

———. *Historical Dictionary of the Broadway Musical*. Lanham, MD: Scarecrow Press, 2007.

Ewen, David. *Complete Book of the American Musical Theater*. New York: Henry Holt, 1959.

Farnsworth, Marjorie. *The Ziegfeld Follies*. New York: G. P. Putnam's Sons, 1956.

Fehr, Richard, and Frederick G. Vogel. *Lullabies of Hollywood; Movie Music and the Movie Musical, 1915–1992*. Jefferson, NC: McFarland, 1993.

Feingold, Michael. "Voice Choices: Theater: Green Witch, Mean Time: Both On and Off-Broadway, New Musicals Suffer from Severe Multiple Personality Disorder." *Village Voice* 48.45 (November 5–11, 2003): 77.

Feuer, Jane. *The Hollywood Musical*. 2nd ed. Hampshire: Palgrave Macmillan, 1992.

Filichia, Peter. *Let's Put on a Musical! How to Choose the Right Show for Your Theater*. 2nd ed. New York: Back Stage Books, 2007.

Flinn, Caryl. *Brass Diva: The Life and Legends of Ethel Merman*. Berkeley: University of California Press, 2007.

Flinn, Denny Martin. *Musical! A Grand Tour: The Rise, Glory, and Fall of an American Institution*. New York: Schirmer, 1997.

Fordin, Hugh. *Getting to Know Him*. New York: Ungar, 1977.

———. *M-G-M's Greatest Musicals: The Arthur Freed Unit*. New York: Da Capo Press, 1996 (previously *The World of Entertainment! Hollywood's Greatest Musicals*. Garden City, NY: Doubleday, 1975; and *The Movies' Greatest Musicals, Produced in Hollywood USA by the Freed Unit*. New York: F. Ungar, 1984).

Fornes, Maria Irene. *Promenade and Other Plays*. New York: PAJ, 1987.

Forte, Allen. *The American Popular Ballad of the Golden Era; 1924–1950*. Princeton, NJ: Princeton University Press, 1995.

———. *Listening to Classic American Popular Songs*. New Haven, CT: Yale University Press, 2001.

Foster, Susan Leigh, ed. *Corporealities: Dancing Knowledge, Culture and Power*. London: Routledge, 1995.

———. "Dancing Bodies." In *Meaning in Motion: New Cultural Studies of Dance*. Edited by Jane C. Desmond. Durham, NC: Duke University Press, 1997, pp. 235–57.

———. *Reading Dancing: Bodies and Subjects in Contemporary American Dance*. Berkeley: University of California Press, 1986.

Foucault, Michel. "What Is an Author?" In *Textual Strategies: Perspectives in Post-Structuralist Criticism*. Edited and translated by Josué V. Harari (Ithaca, NY: Cornell University Press, 1979), 141–60.

Fox, Laurie. "Carroll Senior High Stages *Phantom of the Opera*." *Dallas Morning News* (December 9, 2007). http://www.quickdfw.com/sharedcontent/dws/news/localnews/stories/DN-phantom_09met.ART.State.Edition2.3706394.html, accessed May 9, 2011.

———. "Staging *Phantom* an Epic Task for Southlake Carroll." *Dallas Morning News* (December 8, 2007). http://www.dentonrc.com/sharedcontent/dws/dn/latestnews/stories/120907dnmetphantom.4deb77.html, accessed May 9, 2011

Frank, Rusty E. *Tap! The Greatest Tap Dance Stars and Their Stories, 1900–1955*. Rev. ed. New York: Da Capo Press, 1994 (originally published 1990).

Friedman, Joel L. "Copyright and the Musical Arrangement: An Analysis of the Law and Problems Pertaining to This Specialized Form of Derivative Work." *Pepperdine Law Review* 7 (1979): 125–46.

Friedwald, Will. *Stardust Melodies: A Biography of Twelve of America's Most Popular Songs*. New York: Pantheon Books, 2002.

Frye, Northrop. "Literary History." *New Literary History* 12.2 (Winter 1981): 219–25.

Furia, Philip. *The Poets of Tin Pan Alley: A History of America's Great Lyricists*. New York: Oxford University Press, 1990.

Gabbard, Krin. *Jammin' at the Margins: Jazz and the American Cinema*. Chicago: University of Chicago Press, 1996.

Gabbard, Krin, ed. *Representing Jazz*. Durham, NC: Duke University Press, 1995.

Gabler, Neal. *Winchell: Gossip, Power and the Culture of Celebrity*. New York: Alfred A. Knopf, 1994.

Gänzl, Kurt. *The Musical: A Concise History*. Boston: Northeastern University Press, 1997.

Gard, Robert E., and Gertrude Burley. *Community Theatre: Idea and Achievement*. New York: Duell, Sloan, and Pearce, 1959.

Gardner, Elysa. "Something 'Wicked' Comes to Broadway." *USA Today* (October 31, 2003): 9E-6.

Gelb, Arthur. "Robbins and His 'Courage.'" *New York Times* (28 April 1963): 127.

Gershwin, George. *An American in Paris*. New York: New World Music, 1930.

Gershwin, George, and Ira Gershwin. *Girl Crazy*. New York: New World Music, 1954. "The Gilbert and Sullivan Archive." http://diamond.boisestate.edu/gas/(accessed September 8, 2009).

Gilvey, John Anthony. *Before the Parade Passes By: Gower Champion and the Glorious American Musical*. New York: St. Martin's Press, 2005.

Gledhill, Christine, ed. *Stardom: Industry of Desire*. London: Routledge, 1991.

Goehr, Lydia. *The Imaginary Museum of Musical Works: An Essay in the Philosophy of Music*. Oxford: Oxford University Press, 1992.

Goldman, William. *The Season. A Candid Look at Broadway*. New York: Limelight, 1984.

Goldmark, Daniel. *Tunes for'Toons: Music and the Hollywood Cartoon*. Berkeley: University of California Press, 2005.

Gonzalez, Jo Beth. "Beyond the Boundaries of Tradition: Cultural Treasures in a High School." *Youth Theatre Journal* 10.3 (1999): 14–18.

———. *Temporary Stages: Departing from Tradition in High School Theatre Education*. Portsmouth, NH: Heinemann, 2006.

Goodwin, John, ed. *British Theatre Design: The Modern Age*. New York: St. Martin's Press, 1989.

Gordon, Joanne. *Art Isn't Easy: The Achievement of Stephen Sondheim*. Carbondale: Southern Illinois University Press, 1990.

Gordon, Joanne, ed. *Stephen Sondheim: A Casebook*. New York: Garland, 1997.

Gottfried, Martin. *All His Jazz: The Life and Death of Bob Fosse*. New York: Bantam Books, 1990.

———. *Broadway Musicals*. New York: Harry N. Abrams, 1979.

———. *More Broadway Musicals: Since 1980*. New York: Harry N. Abrams, 1991.

———. "Sleeve Notes." *Gypsy: A Musical Fable*. Original Broadway Cast Recording. Sony Classical/Columbia/Legacy SMK 60848, 1999.

Gottlieb, Jack. *Funny, It Doesn't Sound Jewish: How Yiddish songs and Synagogue Melodies Influenced Tin Pan Alley, Broadway, and Hollywood*. Albany: SUNY in association with the Library of Congress, 2004.

Gottlieb, Robert, and Robert Kimball. *Reading Lyrics*. New York: Pantheon Books, 2000.

Gottschild, Brenda Dixon. *Digging the African American Presence in American Performance*. Westport, CT: Praeger, 1996.

———. *Waltzing in the Dark: African American Vaudeville and Race Politics in the Swing Era*. New York: St. Martin's Press, 2000.

Gould, Neil. *Victor Herbert: A Theatrical Life*. New York: Fordham University Press, 2008.

Grady, Henry Woodfin. *The New South, and Other Addresses, with Biography, Critical Opinions, and Explanatory Notes*. Edited by Edna Henry Lee Turpin. New York: Maynard Merrill, 1904.

Grant, Mark N. *The Rise and Fall of the Broadway Musical.* Boston: Northeastern University Press, 2004.

Grantham, Dewey W. *The South in Modern America: A Region at Odds.* New York: HarperCollins, 1994.

Graziano, John. "Images of African Americans: African-American Musical Theatre, *Show Boat* and *Porgy and Bess.*" In *The Cambridge Companion to the Musical.* Edited by William A. Everett and Paul R. Laird. Cambridge: Cambridge University Press, 2002, pp. 63–76.

Green, Jesse. "Theater's Alive with the Sound of Laptops." *New York Times* (March 25, 2007): 2–1.

Green, Stanley. *Broadway Musicals Show by Show.* Milwaukee: Hal Leonard Books, 1985.

———. *The World of Musical Comedy; The Story of the American Musical Stage as Told through the Careers of Its Foremost Composers and Lyricists.* New York: Ziff-Davis, 1962 (reprint by Da Capo, 1980).

Greig, Charlotte. *100 Best Selling Albums of the 50s.* New York: Barnes and Noble Books, 2004.

Gross, Edwin, and Natalie Gross. *Teen Theatre.* New York: McGraw Hill, 1953.

Grote, David. *Play Directing in the School: A Drama Director's Survival Guide.* Colorado Springs, CO: Meriwether, 1997.

Grubb, Kevin Boyd. *Razzle Dazzle: The Life and Work of Bob Fosse.* New York: St. Martin's Press, 1991.

Hall, Carol, Larry L. King, and Peter Masterson. *The Best Little Whorehouse in Texas.* New York: Samuel French, 1978.

Hamm, Charles. *Yesterdays: Popular Song in America.* New York: W.W. Norton, 1983.

Hammerstein, Oscar II. "In Re 'Oklahoma!' The Adaptor-Lyricist Describes How the Musical Hit Came into Being." *New York Times* (May 23, 1943): 11.

———. "Notes on Lyrics," 3–48. In his *Lyrics.* Milwaukee, WI: Hal Leonard Books, 1985.

Harbin, Shirley, Jennifer Roberts, Noelia Saenz, and Carl P. Grant, eds.*Millennium Theatres: Discovering Community Theatre's Future by Exploring Its Past.* Detroit: Theatre USA, the American Association of Community Theatre, and the City of Detroit Department of Recreation, Empowerment Zone, 2004. http://www.aact.org/aact/Millennium_ Theatres2b.pdf (accessed September 10, 2009).

Hardy, Camille. Popular Balanchine Dossiers 1927–2004. "*Boys from Syracuse,*" Box 15. New York Public Library for the Performing Arts, Dance Division, New York, NY.

Harris, Andrew B. *The Performing Set: The Broadway Designs of William and Jean Eckart.* Denton: University of North Texas Press, 2006.

Harris, Cheryl, and Alison Alexander, eds. *Theorizing Fandom: Fans, Subculture and Identity.* New York: Hampton Press, 1998.

Healy, Patrick. "Tamer *Rent* is Too Wild for Some Schools." *New York Times* (February 20, 2009). http://www.nytimes.com/2009/02/20/arts/20iht-20rent.20328998. html?pagewanted=1&%2339&%2359;t%20Look%2040,%20Charlie%20 Brown!&sq=You%20Don&st=Search&scp=4, accessed May 9, 2011.

Heathcotte, Toby. *Program Building: A Practical Guide for High School Speech and Drama Teachers.* Glendale, AZ: Mardale Books, 2003.

Heilpern, John. "Bennett's Breakthrough: *Dreamgirls* Remembered." *New York Observer* (January 7, 2007), http://www.observer.com/node/36503?observer_most_read_tabs_ tab=2 (accessed July 11, 2009).

Henderson, Mary. *Mielziner: Master of Modern Stage Design.* New York: Back Stage Books, 2001.

Herman, Jerry. *Hello, Dolly!* New York: Edwin H. Morris, 1964.

Herman, Jerry. *Milk and Honey.* New York: Edwin H. Morris, 1963.

Hickey, Dave. "Buying the World." *Daedalus* 131.4 (Fall, 2002): 69–87.

"High-brow, Low-brow, Middle-brow." *Life* (11 April 1949): 100–101.

Hill, Constance Valis. "From Bharata Natyam to Bop: Jack Cole's 'Modern' Jazz Dance." *Dance Research Journal* 33.2 (Winter 2001–02): 29–39.

Hill, Constance Valis. Popular Balanchine Dossiers 1927–2004. "*Babes in Arms,*" Box 14. New York Public Library for the Performing Arts, Dance Division, New York, NY.

Hills, Matt. *Fan Cultures.* London: Routledge, 2002.

Hirsch, Foster. *Harold Prince and the American Musical Theatre.* Cambridge: Cambridge University Press, 1989.

Hodgdon, Barbara, and William B. Worthen, eds. *A Companion to Shakespeare and Performance.* Oxford: Blackwell, 2005.

Hohenberg, John. *The Pulitzer Prizes: A History of the Awards in Books, Drama, Music, and Journalism, Based on the Private Files over Six Decades.* New York: Columbia University Press, 1974.

Holden, Stephen. "Make It Proud and Loud, with Strings." *New York Times* (May 22, 2008): E-7.

Holman, J. K. *Wagner's Ring: A Listener's Companion and Concordance.* Pompton Plains, NJ: Amadeus Press, 1996.

Honzl, Jindřich. "Dynamics in the Sign in the Theater." In *Semiotics of Art: Prague School Contributions.* Edited by L. Matejka and K. Pomorsak. Cambridge, MA: MIT Press, 1976, pp. 74–93.

Horowitz, Mark Eden. *Sondheim on Music: Minor Details and Major Decisions.* Lanham, MD: Scarecrow Press, 2003.

Horst, Louis. *Modern Dance Forms and Its Relation to the Other Modern Arts.* New York: Dance Horizons, 1961.

Houseman, John. *Run-Through: A Memoir.* New York: Simon and Schuster, 1980.

Hulbert, Dan. "Theatrical Bright Side to Atlanta's Dark Story." *Atlanta Journal-Constitution*(June 20, 2000). http://www.jasonrobertbrown.com/press/shows/parade/theatrical_bright_si.php, accessed May 10, 2011.

Hume, Samuel J., and Lois M. Foster. *Theatre and School.* New York: Samuel French, 1932.

Hutchings, William. *Samuel Beckett's* Waiting for Godot: *A Reference Guide.* Westport, CT: Praeger, 2005.

Husmann, Ron. *Broadway! A Musical History with Ron Husmann.* Videotape. Irvine, CA: Chesney Communications, 1988.

Iggers, Georg G. *Historiography in the Twentieth Century: From Scientific Objectivity to the Postmodern Challenge. With a New Epilogue.* Middletown, CT: Wesleyan University Press, 2005.

Ilson, Carol. *Harold Prince: From* Pajama Game *to* Phantom of the Opera. Ann Arbor: UMI Research Press, 1989.

Ingber, Judith Brin. "Dancing into Marriage," *Arabesque* 7.4 (1982): 8–9, 20–21.

Innes, Christopher. *Edward Gordon Craig: A Vision of Theatre.* Amsterdam: Routledge, 1998.

Internet Broadway Database. www.ibdb.com.

Internet Movie Database. www.imdb.com.

Iser, Wolfgang. *The Act of Reading: A Theory of Aesthetic Response.* Baltimore: Johns Hopkins University Press, 1980.

Isherwood, Charles. "Cutting 'Sweeney Todd' to the Bone." *New York Times* (October 30, 2005): 2–1.

———. "It's a Hard Rock Life: Theatre Review of *Passing Strange*." *New York Times* (February 29, 2008). http://theater.nytimes.com/2008/02/29/theater/reviews/29stra .html, accessed May 10, 2011.

———. "More Bothered than Bewitched by *Wicked*." *Variety* (November 3, 2003): 30.

———. "Patti LuPone in *Gypsy*: Light the Lights, Boys! Mama Rose Hears a Symphony." *New York Times* (August 15, 2006). http://theater.nytimes.com/2006/08/15/theater/ reviews/15lupo.html?fta=y, accessed May 10, 2011.

Izenour, George C. *Theater Technology*. 2nd ed. New Haven, CT: Yale University Press, 1997.

Jablonski, Edward. *Gershwin: With a New Critical Discography*. New York: Da Capo Press, 1998.

Jasen, David A. *Tin Pan Alley; The Composers, the Songs, the Performers and Their Times*. New York: Donald I. Fine, 1988.

Jenkins, Henry. *Textual Poachers: Television Fans and Participatory Culture*. London: Routledge, 1992.

Jenkins, Jennifer R. "'Say It with Firecrackers': Defining the 'War Musical' of the 1940s." *American Music* 19 (2001): 315–39.

"John Doyle's Production of Sweeney Todd to Open A.C.T.'s 41st Season." Anon. *American Conservatory Theater* (August 5, 2007), http://www.act-sf.org/site/News2?page= NewsArticle&id=5205&news_iv_ctrl=-1 (accessed July 23, 2008).

John, Elton, Tim Rice, M. Lebo. Mark Mancina, Julie Traymor, and Hans Zimmer. *The Lion King: Original Broadway Cast Recording*. Walt Disney Records 60802–7, 1997.

Johnson, Harriet. "The First Steps in a Robbins Dance: It's Planning Says *Billion Dollar Baby* Choreographer," *New York Post* (4 January 1946). New York Public Library for the Performing Arts MWEZ/x/n.c./25,375.

Johnson, Margaret F. *The Drama Teacher's Survival Guide: A Complete Tool Kit for Theatre Arts*. Colorado Springs, CO: Meriwether, 2007.

Jones, Bill T. Telephone interview with Liza Gennaro, May 18, 2007.

Jones, John Bush. *Our Musicals, Ourselves: A Social History of the American Musical Theater*. Hanover, NH: Brandeis University Press, 2003.

Jones, Robert Edmond. *The Dramatic Imagination*. New York: Duell, Sloan, and Pearce, 1941.

Jowitt, Deborah. "Beyond Description: Writing beneath the Surface." In *Moving History/ Dancing Cultures: A Dance History Reader*. Edited by Ann Dils and Ann Cooper Albright. Middletown, CT: Wesleyan University Press, 2001, pp. 7–11.

———. *Jerome Robbins: His Life, His Theater, His Dance*. New York: Simon and Schuster, 2004.

Kammen, Michael G. *American Culture, American Tastes: Social Change and the 20th Century*. New York: Knopf, 1999.

Kander, John, and Fred Ebb. "Money, Money." *Cabaret*. Directed by Bob Fosse, 1972.

Kanter, Kenneth Aaron. *The Jews of Tin Pan Alley: The Jewish Contribution to American Popular Music, 1830–1940*. New York: Ktav Publishing, and Cincinnati: American Jewish Archives, 1982.

Kantor, Michael, dir. *Broadway: The American Musical*. Educational Broadcasting Corporation and the Broadway Film Project, Inc., 2004.

Katz, Mark. "Making America More Musical through the Phonograph, 1900–1930." *American Music* 16.4 (Winter 1998): 448–75.

Kaye, Joseph. *Victor Herbert: The Biography of America's Greatest Composer of Romantic Music*. New York: Crown, 2007.

Kealiinohomoku, Joanne. "An Anthropologist Looks at Ballet as a Form of Ethnic Dance." In *Moving History/Dancing Cultures: A Dance History Reader*. Edited by Ann

Dils and Ann Cooper Albright. Middletown, CT: Wesleyan University Press, 2001, pp. 33–43.

Keller, Kate Van Winkle, and Charles Cyril Hendrickson. *George Washington: A Biography in Social Dance*. Sandy Hook, CT: Hendrickson Group, 1998.

Kemp, Peter. "How Do You Solve a 'Problem' Like Maria von Poppins." In *Musicals: Hollywood and Beyond*. Edited by Bill Marshall and Robynn Stilwell. Portland: Intellect, 2000, pp. 55–61.

Kenrick, John. *Musical Theatre: A History*. New York: Continuum, 2008.

Kerman, Joseph. *Opera as Drama*. Rev. ed. Berkeley: University of California Press, 1988.

Kern, Jerome, and Oscar Hammerstein II. *Show Boat*. New York: T. B. Harms, 1927.

Kernodle, George R. "Wagner, Appia, and the Idea of Musical Design." *Educational Theatre Journal* 6.3 (October, 1954): 223–30.

Kirkeby, Mark. Liner notes to CD reissue of original cast recording of *South Pacific*. Sony SK 60722, 1998.

Kirle, Bruce. *Unfinished Show Business: Broadway Musicals as Works-in-Process*. Carbondale: Southern Illinois University Press, 2005.

Kislan, Richard. *Hoofing on Broadway: A History of Show Dancing*. New York: Prentice Hall, 1986.

———. *The Musical: A Look at the American Musical Theater*. Revised, expanded ed. New York: Applause Books, 1995.

Kiss Me Kate. Directed by George Sidney. Choreographed by Hermes Pan and Bob Fosse. Los Angeles: Metro-Goldwyn-Mayer, 1953. DVD release, 2003.

Kissel, Howard. *David Merrick. The Abominable Showman*. New York: Applause Books, 1993.

Kleinhans, Chuck. "Taking Out the Trash: Camp and the Politics of Parody." In *The Politics and Poetics of Camp*. Edited by Moe Meyer. London: Routledge, 1994, pp. 182–201.

Knapp, Raymond. *The American Musical and the Formation of National Identity*. Princeton, NJ: Princeton University Press, 2005.

———. *The American Musical and the Performance of Personal Identity*. Princeton: Princeton University Press, 2006.

———. "*Assassins, Oklahoma!*, and the 'Shifting Fringe of Dark around the Campfire.'" *Cambridge Opera Journal* 16 (2004): 77–101.

———. "Getting off the Trolley: Musicals *contra* Cinematic Reality" *From Stage to Screen*. Edited by Massimiliano Sala. Volume 18 of *Speculum Musicae*. Brepols Publishers (forthcoming).

———. "'How Great Thy Charm, Thy Sway How Excellent!' Tracing Gilbert and Sullivan's Legacy in the American Musical." In *The Cambridge Companion to Gilbert and Sullivan*. Edited by David Eden and Meinhard Saremba. Cambridge: Cambridge University Press, 2009.

———. "Temporality and Control in Sondheim's Middle Period: From *Company* to *Sunday in the Park with George*." *Time: Sense, Space and Structure*. Edited by Nancy van Deusen. Leiden, The Netherlands: Brill Publishers (forthcoming).

Knight, Arthur. *Disintegrating the Musical: Black Performance and American Musical Film*. Durham, NC: Duke University Press, 2002.

Knowles, Mark. *Tap Roots: The Early History of Tap Dancing*. Jefferson, NC: McFarland, 2002.

Koestenbaum, Wayne. *The Queen's Throat: Opera, Homosexuality, and the Mystery of Desire*. New York: Poseidon Press, 1993.

Koller, Ann Marie. *The Theater Duke: Georg II of Saxe-Meiningen and the German Stage*. Stanford, CA: Stanford University Press, 1984.

Koszarski, Richard. *An Evening's Entertainment: The Age of the Silent Feature Picture 1915–1928*. Berkeley: University of California Press, 1990.

Krasner, David. *Resistance, Parody and Double Consciousness in African American Theatre, 1895–1910*. New York: St. Martin's Press, 1997.

Krasner, Orly Leah. "Birth Pangs, Growing Pains and Sibling Rivalry: Musical Theatre in New York, 1900–1920." In *The Cambridge Companion to the Musical*. Edited by William A. Everett and Paul R. Laird. Cambridge: Cambridge University Press, 2002, pp. 29–46.

Kreuger. Miles. *Show Boat: The Story of a Classic American Musical*. New York: Oxford University Press, 1977.

Kreuger, Miles, ed. *The Movie Musical from Vitaphone to 42nd Street as Reported in a Great Fan Magazine*. New York: Dover, 1975.

Krug, Edward A. *The Shaping of the American High School: 1920–1941*. Madison: University of Wisconsin Press, 1972.

Kuftinec, Sonja. "A Cornerstone for Rethinking Community Theatre." *Theatre Topics* 6.1 (March 1996): 91–104.

———. "Staging the City with the Good People of New Haven." *Theatre Journal* 53.2 (May 2001): 197–222.

La Gorce, Tammy. "At Home on the Stage." *New York Times* (April 5, 2009). http://www .nytimes.com/2009/04/05/nyregion/new-jersey/05paper.html, accessed May 10, 2011.

———. "High School Musical Actors Envision Being Rising Stars." *New York Times* (March 15, 2009). http://www.nytimes.com/2009/03/15/nyregion/new-jersey/15papernj.html, accessed May 10, 2011.

———. "The Rising Star Awards: Singing! Dancing! Scholarships!" *New York Times* (June 28, 2009). http://www.nytimes.com/2009/06/28/nyregion/28papernj.html, accessed May 10, 2011.

Lahr, John. "Broadway Boogie-Woogie." *New Yorker* (March 9, 2009): 78.

———. "The Critics: The Theatre: Bitches and Witches: Ulterior Motives in *Cat on a Hot Tin Roof* and *Wicked*." *New Yorker* 79.34 (November 10, 2003): 126–27.

———. "Toeing the Line: 'A Chorus Line' is back on Broadway." *New Yorker* (October 16, 2006), http://www.newyorker.com/archive/2006/10/16/061016crth_theatre (accessed August 19, 2009).

Laing, Heather. "Emotion by Numbers: Music, Song and the Musical." In *Musicals: Hollywood and Beyond*. Edited by Bill Marshall and Robynn Stilwell. Exeter: Intellect Books, 2000, pp. 5–13.

Laird, Paul R. Personal interview with Stephen Schwartz, New York, NY, January 14, 2008.

Lamb, Andrew. *150 Years of Popular Musical Theatre*. New Haven, CT: Yale University Press, 2000.

Lapine, James, and Stephen Sondheim. *Sunday in the Park with George*. New York: Applause Theatre Books, 1991.

Larson, Jonathan. *Rent*. With interviews and text by McDonnell and Silberger. New York: William Morrow, 1997.

Larson, Jonathan. *Rent* libretto. Dreamworks compact discs DSMD2–50003, 1996, pp. 1: 23.

Larson, Orville K. *Scene Design in the American Theatre from 1915 to 1960*. Fayetteville: University of Arkansas Press, 1989.

Laufe, Abe. *Broadway's Greatest Musicals*. *1977*. Rev. ed. New York: Funk and Wagnalls, 1977.

Laurents, Arthur. *Mainly on Directing: Gypsy, West Side Story, and Other Musicals*. New York: Alfred A. Knopf, 2009.

———. *Original Story By: A Memoir of Broadway and Hollywood*. New York: Alfred A. Knopf, 2000.

————. Liner notes to *Gypsy*. Original revival cast album CD, Angel Records 7243–5-83858–2-3, 2003.

Law, Lois. "Training in Citizenship through Play-Production." *High School Thespian* 8.2 (October 1936): 5, 16.

Lawrence, Greg. *Dance with Demons: The Life of Jerome Robbins*. New York: G. P. Putnam's Sons, 2001.

Lawson-Peebles, Robert, ed. *Approaches to the American Musical*. Exeter: University of Exeter Press, 1996.

Lazarus, Joan. *Signs of Change: New Directions in Secondary Theatre Education*. Portsmouth, NH: Heinemann, 2004.

Lentricchia, Frank, and Thomas McLaughlin. *Critical Terms for Literary Study*. Chicago: University of Chicago Press, 1990.

Leonard, John. *Smoke and Mirrors: Violence, Television and Other American Culture*. New York: New Press, 1997.

Leonardi, Susan J., and Rebecca A. Pope. *The Diva's Mouth: Body, Voice, Prima Donna Politics*. New Brunswick, NJ: Rutgers University Press, 1996.

Leppert, Richard. "The Civilizing Process: Music and the Aesthetics of Time-Space Relations in *The Girl of the Golden West*." In *Musical Meaning and Human Values*. Edited by Keith Chapin and Lawrence Kramer. New York: Fordham University Press, 2009, pp. 116–49.

Lerner, Alan Jay. *The Musical Theatre; A Celebration*. New York: McGraw-Hill, 1986.

Levine, Lawrence W. *Highbrow/Lowbrow: The Emergence of Cultural Hierarchy in America*. Cambridge, MA: Harvard University Press, 1988.

Lewis, David H. *Broadway Musicals: A Hundred Year History*. Jefferson, NC: McFarland, 2002.

————. *Flower Drum Songs: The Story of Two Musicals*. Jefferson, NC: McFarland, 2006.

Lewis, David L. *When Harlem Was in Vogue*. New York: Vintage Books, 1982.

Lewis, Lisa A., ed. *The Adoring Audience: Fan Culture and Popular Media*. London: Routledge, 1992.

Lhamon, W. T., Jr. *Jump Jim Crow: Lost Plays, Lyrics, and Street Prose from the First Atlantic Popular Culture*. Cambridge, MA: Harvard University Press, 2003.

————. *Raising Cain: Blackface Performance from Jim Crow to Hip Hop*. Cambridge, MA: Harvard University Press, 1998.

Lieberson, Goddard. Liner notes. *Who's Afraid of Virginia Woolf?, an Original Broadway Cast Recording*. Columbia Records Masterwork Series, Monaural DOL 287, 1963.

"Lieberson Sees A&R Exec as 'Heart' of Record Business." Uncredited. *Billboard* (August 4, 1956): B-21.

Litsch, Joseph. "Alexis Smith: Call Her Madam: Hollywood's Typecast 'Sophisticated Lady.'" *Atlanta Constitution* (January 4, 1980): 1-B+.

Litsch, Joseph. "I Want Tickets to…Er…'The…Ah…Best.'" *Atlanta Constitution* (January 4, 1980): 1-B+.

Lloyd Webber, Andrew. *Joseph and the Amazing Technicolor Dreamcoat*. Borough Green, Sevenoaks, Kent: Novello, 1975.

Lloyd Webber, Andrew, and T. S. Eliot. *Cats: The Songs from the Musical*. London: Faber Music, 1981.

Lloyd Webber, Andrew, and Tim Rice. *Jesus Christ Superstar*. New York: Universal–MCA Music and Miami, FL: Warner Bros. Publications, 1970.

Loesser, Frank, Jo Swerling, Abe Burrows, and Damon Runyon. *Guys and Dolls: A Musical Fable of Broadway*. London: Frank Music, 1951.

Loewe, Frederick and Alan Jay Lerner. *My Fair Lady*. London: Chappell, 1956.

Loney, Glenn, *Unsung Genius: The Passion of Dancer-Choreographer Jack Cole*. New York: Franklin Watts, 1984.

Loney, Glenn, ed. *Musical Theatre in America; Papers and Proceedings of the Conference on the Musical Theatre in America*. Westport, CT: Greenwood Press, 1981.

Long, Robert Emmet. *Broadway, the Golden Years: Jerome Robbins and the Great Choreographer-Directors*. New York: Continuum, 2001.

Lott, Eric. *Love and Theft; Blackface Minstrelsy and the American Working Class*. New York: Oxford University Press, 1993.

Love, Karlyn. "A Directorial Approach for a High School Production of *You Can't Take It with You* by Moss Hart and George S. Kaufman: Performed February 1, 2, 3, 2001 at Oregon City High School, Oregon City, Oregon." M.F.A. Thesis, University of Portland, 2001.

Lovensheimer, Jim. *South Pacific: Paradise Rewritten*. New York: Oxford University Press, 2010.

Lundskaer-Nielsen, Miranda. *Directors and the New Musical Drama: British and American Musical Theatre in the 1980s and 90s*. New York: Palgrave Macmillan, 2008.

Lynes, Russell. "Highbrow, Lowbrow, Middlebrow." In his *The Tastemakers*. New York: Harper and Brothers, 1954.

MacDermot, Galt, Gerome Ragni, and James Rado. *Vocal Selections from Hair*. Los Angeles: United Artists Music, 1979.

Macgowan, Kenneth. *The Theatre of Tomorrow*. New York: Boni and Liveright, 1921.

———. "Drama's New Domain—The High School." *Harpers* (November 1929): 774–79.

Mahar, William J. *Behind the Burnt Cork Mask: Early Blackface Minstrelsy and Antebellum American Popular Culture*. Urbana: University of Illinois Press, 1999.

Malone, Jacqui. *Steppin' on the Blues: The Visual Rhythms of African American Dance*. Urbana: University of Illinois Press, 1996.

Marks, Edward B. *They All Sang: From Tony Pastor to Rudy Vallee*. As told to A. J. Liebling. New York: Viking, 1935.

Marmorstein, Gary. *Hollywood Rhapsody: Movie Music and Its Makers, 1900–1975*. New York: Schirmer Books, 1997.

———. *The Label: The Story of Columbia Records*. New York: Thunder's Mouth Press, 2007.

Marra, Kim, and Robert Schanke, eds. *Passing Performances: Queer Readings of Leading Players in American Theater History*. Ann Arbor: University of Michigan Press, 1998.

Marshall, Bill, and Robynn Stilwell, eds. *Musicals: Hollywood and Beyond*. Exeter: Intellect Books, 2000.

Marshall, P. David. *Celebrity and Power: Fame in Contemporary Culture*. Minneapolis: University of Minnesota Press, 1997.

Martin, Ethel. Interview by Liza Gennaro, February 26, 2003, transcript. Oral History Collection, Lincoln Center Library of the Performing Arts, New York, NY.

Martin, John. "The Dance: De Mille's Oklahoma." *New York Times* (May 9, 1943): Section 10, 6.

———. "The Dance: Jack Cole." *New York Times* (November 7, 1948): X-6.

———. "The Dance: New Musical Comedy Talent," *New York Times* (July 22, 1928): Section 7, 6.

Martin, Wanda. "V-Disks Help Hasten V-Day." *The Billboard 1944 Music Year Book*. 6th Annual Edition. New York: Billboard Publishing Company, 1944.

Mast, Gerald. *Can't Help Singin': The American Musical on Stage and Screen*. Woodstock, NY: Overlook Press, 1987.

Mates, Julian. *America's Musical Stage; Two Hundred years of Musical Theatre*. Westport, CT: Greenwood Press, 1985.

McAllister, Marvin. *White People Do Not Know How to Behave at Entertainments Designed for Ladies and Gentlemen of Colour*. Chapel Hill: University of North Carolina Press, 2003.

McClary, Susan. *Conventional Wisdom: The Content of Musical Form*. Berkeley: University of California Press, 2000.

McClung. Bruce D. *Lady in the Dark: Biography of a Musical*. New York: Oxford University Press, 2007.

McConachie, Bruce A. "The 'Oriental' Musicals of Rodgers and Hammerstein and the U.S. War in Southeast Asia." *Theatre Journal* 46 (October 1994): 385–98.

McGinnis, Pearl Yeadon. *The Opera Singer's Career Guide: Understanding the European Fach System*. Lanham, MD: Scarecrow Press, 2010.

McGlinn, John. "Foreword" (Sleeve Notes). *Jerome Kern Treasury*. Angel D 101715, 1993.

McGovern, Dennis, and Deborah Grace Winer. *Sing Out, Louise: 150 Stars of the Musical Theatre Remember 50 Years on Broadway*. New York: Schirmer Books, 1993.

McLamore, Alyson. *Musical Theater: An Appreciation*. Upper Saddle River, NJ: Pearson Prentice Hall, 2004.

McMillin, Scott. "Paul Robeson, Will Vodery's 'Jubilee Singers,' and the Earliest Script of the Kern-Hammerstein *Show Boat*. *Theatre Survey* 41 (2000): 51–70.

———. *The Musical as Drama: A Study of the Principles and Conventions behind Musical Shows from Kern to Sondheim*. Princeton, NJ: Princeton University Press, 2006.

McPherson, Tara. *Reconstructing Dixie: Race, Gender, and Nostalgia in the Imagined South*. Durham, NC: Duke University Press, 2003.

McWaters, Debra. *The Fosse Style*. Gainesville: University Press of Florida, 2008.

Melnick, Jeffrey. *A Right to Sing the Blues: African Americans, Jews, and American Popular Song*. Cambridge, MA: Harvard University, 1999.

Meyer, Moe. *The Politics of Camp*. London: Routledge, 1994.

Miles, Barry. *Paul McCartney: Many Years from Now*. 1st American ed. New York: Henry Holt, 1997.

Miletich, Leo N. *Broadway's Prize-Winning Musicals: An Annotated Guide for Libraries and Audio Collectors*. New York: Haworth Press, 1993.

Miller, D. A. *Place for Us [Essay on the Broadway Musical]*. Cambridge, MA: Harvard University Press, 1998.

Miller, Scott. *Deconstructing Harold Hill: An Insider's Guide to Musical Theatre*. Portsmouth, NH: Heinemann, 2000.

———. *From Assassins to West Side Story: The Director's Guide to Musical Theatre*. Portsmouth, NH: Heinemann, 1996.

———. *Rebels with Applause: Broadway's Groundbreaking Musicals*. Portsmouth, NH: Heinemann, 2001.

Miller, Susan, and Greg Rhode. "The Movie You See, the Movie You Don't: How Disney Do's That Old Time Derision." In *From Mouse to Mermaid: The Politics of Film, Gender and Culture*. Edited by Elizabeth Bell, Lynda Haas, and Laura Sells. Bloomington: Indiana University Press, 1995.

Miller, Tim. "Oklahomo!: A Gay Performance Artist Vows that Musicals Shaped His Political Consciousness." *American Theatre* 20.9 (2003): 91–93.

Mizejewski, Linda. *Ziegfeld Girl: Image and Icon in Culture and Cinema*. Durham, NC: Duke University Press, 1999.

Mordden, Ethan. *Beautiful Mornin': The Broadway Musical in the 1940s*. New York: Oxford University Press, 1999.

―――. *Better Foot Forward: The History of the American Musical Theatre*. New York: Grossman, 1976.

―――. *Broadway Babies: The People Who Made the American Musical*. New York: Oxford University Press, 1983.

―――. *Coming Up Roses: The Broadway Musical in the 1950s*. New York: Oxford University Press, 1998.

―――. *The Happiest Corpse I've Ever Seen: The Last 25 Years of the Broadway Musical*. New York: Palgrave Macmillan, 2004.

―――. *Make Believe: The Broadway Musical in the 1920s*. New York: Oxford University Press, 1997.

―――. *One More Kiss: The Broadway Musical in the 1970s*. New York: Palgrave MacMillan, 2003.

―――. *Open a New Window: The Broadway Musical in the 1960s*. New York: Palgrave, 2001.

―――. "Six Decades Later, Still the Great American Musical." *New York Times* (February 24, 2002): 1, 10.

―――. *Ziegfeld: The Man Who Invented Show Business*. New York: St. Martin's Press, 2008.

Morris, Mitchell. "*Cabaret*, America's *Weimar*, and Mythologies of the Gay Subject." *American Music* 22.1 (Spring, 2004): 145–57.

―――. *The Persistence of Sentiment: Essays on Pop Music in the '70s*. Berkeley: University of California Press (forthcoming).

Morris, Stephen Leigh. "John Doyle's *Sweeney Todd*; Who's Your Barber?" *LA Weekly* (March 17, 2008), http://www.laweekly.com/2008–03–20/stage/major-barber (accessed July 10, 2009).

Most, Andrea. *Making Americans: Jews and the Broadway Musical*. Cambridge, MA: Harvard University Press, 2004.

―――. " 'We Know We Belong to the Land': Jews and the American Musical Theater." Ph.D. dissertation, Brandeis University, 2001.

Motter, Charlotte Kay. *Theatre in High School: Planning, Teaching, Directing*. Lanham, MD: University Press of America, 1984.

Mueller, John. "Fred Astaire and the Integrated Musical." *Cinema Journal* 24.1 (Fall 1984): 28–40.

Nathan, George Jean. *The Popular Theatre*. New York: Alfred A. Knopf, 1918; revised 1923.

Nathan, George Jean. *The Theatre in the Fifties*. New York: Alfred A. Knopf, 1953.

National Thespian Society. "Membership Roll of the National Thespians." *High School Thespian* 1 (October 1929): 54.

―――. "National Thespian Roll." *High School Thespian* 10.5 (May/June 1939): 51.

Negrón-Muntaner, Frances. "Feeling Pretty: *West Side Story* and Puerto Rican Identity Discourses." *Social Text 63* 18.2 (2000): 83–106.

Ness, Sally Ann. "Dancing in the Field: Notes from Memory." In *Corporealities: Dancing Knowledge, Culture and Power*. Edited by Susan Leigh Foster. London: Routledge, 1995, pp. 129–54.

Nichols, Lewis. " 'Oklahoma!' a Musical Hailed as Delightful, Based on 'Green Grow the Lilacs,' Opens Here at the St. James Theatre." *New York Times* (April 1, 1943): 27.

Norris, Joe, Laura A. McCammon, and Carole S. Miller. *Learning to Teach Drama: A Case Narrative Approach*. Portsmouth, NH: Heinemann, 2000.

Odom, Leigh George. " 'The Black Crook' at Niblo's Garden." *Drama Review: TDR*: 26.1 (Spring 1982): 21–40.

Opelt, James. *Organizing and Managing the High School Theatre Program*. Boston: Allyn and Bacon, 1991.

Ostrow, Stuart. *A Producer's Broadway Journey*. Westport, CT: Praeger, 1999.

Overly, Jeff. "Instructor: Play Canceled Because of Gay Character." *Orange County Register* (February 13, 2009). http://articles.ocregister.com/2009-02-13/cities/24657324_1_gay-characters-gay-and-lesbian-students-drama-teacher, accessed May 10, 2011.

"The Ozdust Boutique Online." Araca Merchandise, http://www.wickedmerch.com (accessed September 13, 2008).

Page, Tim. "Broadway Song Trove Tops Original Hopes." *New York Times* (March 10, 1987): A-1.

Pareles, John. "What Is the Sound of Broadway? Hans Spialek Knows." *New York Times* (April 17, 1983): 2–4.

Parrent, Amy. "From 'The Beggar's Opera' to 'Sweeney Todd': The Art of the Broadway Orchestrator." *Music Educator's Journal* 66.9 (May 1980): 32–35.

Patterson, James T. *Grand Expectations: The United States, 1945–1974*. New York: Oxford University Press, 1996.

Patterson, Jim, Donna McKenna-Crook, and Melissa Swick. *Theatre in the Secondary Classroom: Methods and Strategies for the Beginning Teacher*. Portsmouth, NH: Heinemann, 2006.

Paulus, Diane. Interview with Matthew Small. *Talkin' Broadway Regional News* (April 13, 2009), http://www.talkinbroadway.com/regional/boston/boston128.html (accessed July 9, 2009).

Perkins, Patrick T. "'Hey! What's the Score?' Copyright in the Orchestrations of Broadway Musicals." *Columbia-VLA Journal of Law and the Arts* 16 (1991): 475–503.

Peyser, Joan. *The Memory of All That: The Life of George Gershwin*. New York: Billboard Books, 1998.

Peters, Brooks. "Making Your Garden Grow: Lillian Hellman and *Candide*." *Opera News* 65.1 (July 2000): 38.

Peterson, Bernard L., Jr. *A Century of Musicals in Black and White: An Encyclopedia of Musical Stage Works By, About, or Involving African Americans*. Westport, CT: Greenwood Press, 1993.

Pfister, Manfred. *The Theory and Analysis of Drama*. Translated by John Halliday. Cambridge: Cambridge University Press, 1988.

Pinsky Mark I. *The Gospel According to Disney: Faith, Trust and Pixie Dust*. Louisville, KY: Westminster John Knox Press, 2004.

Poggi, Jack. *Theater in America: The Impact of Economic Forces, 1870–1967*. Ithaca, NY: Cornell University Press, 1968.

Pollack, Howard. *George Gershwin: His Life and Work*. Berkeley: University of California Press, 2006.

Powrie, Phil, and Robynn Stilwell, eds. *Changing Tunes: The Use of Pre-existing Music in Film*. Aldershot, UK: Ashgate, 2006.

Prece, Paul, and William A. Everett. "The Megamusical and Beyond: The Creation, Internationalisation and Impact of a Genre." *The Cambridge Companion to the Musical*. Edited by William A. Everett and Paul R. Laird. Cambridge: Cambridge University Press, 2002, pp. 246–65.

Preston, Katherine K. "American Musical Theater before the Twentieth Century." In *Cambridge Companion to the Musical*. Edited by William A. Everett and Paul R. Laird. Cambridge: Cambridge University Press, 2002, pp. 3–28.

Prince, Hal. *Contradictions: Notes on Twenty-Six Years in the Theatre*. New York: Dodd, Mead, 1974.

Pullen, Kristen. *Actresses and Whores: On Stage and in Society*. Cambridge: Cambridge University Press, 2005.

Radloff, Bernhard. "Text." In *Encyclopedia of Contemporary Literary Theory: Approaches, Scholars, Terms*. Edited by Irena R. Makaryk. Toronto: University of Toronto Press, 1993, pp. 639–41.

Radway, Janice. "On the Gender of the Middlebrow Consumer and the Threat of the Culturally Fraudulent Female." *South Atlantic Quarterly* 93.4 (Fall 1994): 871–93.

———. *Reading the Romance: Women, Patriarchy and Popular Culture*. Chapel Hill: University of North Carolina Press. 1984.

———. "The Scandal of the Middlebrow: The Book-of-the-Month Club, Class Fracture, and Cultural Authority." *South Atlantic Quarterly* 89.4 (Fall 1990): 703–36.

Rappel, William J., and John R. Winnie. *Community Theatre Handbook*. Iowa City, IA: Institute of Public Affairs, 1961.

Ray, Celeste, ed. *Southern Heritage on Display: Public Ritual and Ethnic Diversity within Southern Regionalism*. Tuscaloosa: University of Alabama Press, 2002.

Reid, Louis R. "Composing While You Wait." *Dramatic Mirror* (June 2, 1917): 5.

Rich, Frank. "Catching That Fading Sound of Razzmatazz." *New York Times* (October 10, 1993): 2–34.

Rich, Frank, and Lisa Aronson. *The Theatre Art of Boris Aronson*. New York: Alfred A. Knopf, 1987.

Ries, Frank W. D. "Albertina Rasch: The Broadway Career." *Dance Chronicle* 6.2 (1983): 95–137.

———. "Sammy Lee: The Broadway Career." *Dance Chronicle* 9.1 (1986): 1–95.

Riis, Jacob A. *How the Other Half Lives: Studies among the Tenements of New York*. New York, 1890; reprinted New York: Kessinger, 2004. Online copy at www.authentichistory .com/1865–1897/progressive/riis/index.html (accessed November 4, 2010).

Riis, Thomas. *Just before Jazz: Black Musical Theater in New York, 1890–1915*. Washington, DC: Smithsonian Institution, 1989.

———. *More Than Just Minstrel Shows: The Rise of Black Musical Theatre at the Turn of the Century*. New York: Institute for Studies in American Music, 1992.

Riis, Thomas L., and Ann Sears. "The Successors of Rodgers and Hammerstein from the 1940s to the 1960s." In *The Cambridge Guide to the Musical*. Edited by William A. Everett and Paul R. Laird. Cambridge: Cambridge University Press, 2002, pp. 137–66.

Robertson, Campbell. "Tweens Love Broadway, but Can't Save It Alone." *New York Times* (October 2, 2007): late edition.

Rodgers, Richard. "How to Write Music in No Easy Lessons: A Self Interview." *Theatre Arts* (October 1939): 741–46; reprinted in Block, Geoffrey, ed. *The Richard Rodgers Reader*, 261–65. New York: Oxford University Press, 2002.

———. *Musical Stages: An Autobiography*. New York: Random House, 1975; reprinted New York: Da Capo Press, 1995, 2000, 2002 ("Updated Edition").

Rodgers, Richard, and Oscar Hammerstein II. *Oklahoma!*. New York: Williamson Music, 1943.

———. "Rodgers, Hammerstein Reply to Lee Newton on 'Show Boat.'" *Daily Worker* (25 October 1948): 13.

Rogin, Michael. *Blackface, White Noise: Jewish Immigrants in the Hollywood Melting Pot*. Berkeley: University of California Press, 1996.

———. "New Deal Blackface." In *Hollywood Musicals: The Film Reader*. Edited by Steven Cohan. London: Routledge, 2002, pp. 175–82.

Rojek, Chris. *Frank Sinatra*. Cambridge, MA: Polity, 2004.

Roost, Alisa. "Before *Oklahoma!*: A Reappraisal of Musical Theatre during the 1930s."
    Journal of American Drama and Theatre 16.1 (Winter 2004): 1–35.

Rosenberg, Bernard, and Ernest Harburg. *The Broadway Musical; Collaboration in
    Commerce and Art*. New York: New York University Press, 1993.

Rosenthal, Jean, and Lael Wertenbaker. *The Magic of Light: The Craft and Career of Jean
    Rosenthal, Pioneer in Lighting for the Modern Stage*. Boston: Little, Brown, 1972.

Rothrock, Carson. "Our Own Junior High School Musical." *English Journal* 61.8 (November
    1972): 1244–46.

Rourke, Constance. *American Humor: A Study of the National Character*. Garden City, NY:
    Doubleday, 1953 (originally published 1931).

Rozmaryn, Sharona. "Producing a High School Production of Agatha Christie's *Ten Little
    Indians*: A Case Study." Master's Thesis, University of Maryland, 1994.

Rubin, Martin. *Showstoppers: Busby Berkeley and the Tradition of Spectacle*. New York:
    Columbia University Press, 1993.

Runyon, Damon. *Guys and Dolls and Other Stories*. London: Penguin, 1956.

Russo, Vito. *The Celluloid Closet; Homosexuality in the Movies*. Rev. ed. New York: Harper
    and Row, 1987 (original version 1981).

Sandoval-Sanchez, Alberto. *José, Can You See? Latinos on and Off Broadway*. Madison:
    University of Wisconsin Press, 1999.

Sanjek, Russell. *Pennies from Heaven: The American Popular Music Business in the Twentieth
    Century*. Updated by David Sanjek. New York: Da Capo Press, 1996 (originally
    published 1988).

Sarris, Andrew. *"You Ain't Heard Nothin' Yet": The American Talking Film; History and
    Memory, 1927–1949*. New York: Oxford University Press, 1998.

Sartre, Jean-Paul. *What Is Literature?* Translated by Bernard Frechtman. London:
    Routledge, 2001.

Savran, David. *Highbrow/Lowdown: Theater, Jazz, and the Making of the New Middle Class*.
    Ann Arbor: University of Michigan Press, 2009.

———. "Middlebrow Anxiety." In his *A Queer Sort of Materialism: Recontextualizing
    American Theater*. Ann Arbor: University of Michigan Press, 2003.

———. *A Queer Sort of Materialism: Recontextualizing American Theater*. Ann Arbor:
    University of Michigan Press, 2003.

———. "Toward a Historiography of the Popular." *Theatre Survey* 45.2 (November 2004):
    211–17.

Sayler, Oliver Martin. *Our American Theatre*. New York: Brentano's, 1923.

Scherer, Barrymore Laurence. "Benjamin's Ragtime Band Captures the Real Cohan."
    Wall Street Journal (July 2, 2008): D-7.

Schiavi, Michael R. "Opening Ancestral Windows: Post-Stonewall Men and Musical
    Theatre." *New England Theatre Journal* 13 (2002): 77–98.

Schonberg, Harold C. "Stage View: The Surrender of Broadway to Amplified Sound."
    New York Times (March 15, 1981): 2–1.

Schwartz, Charles. *Cole Porter: A Biography*. New York: Dial Press, 1977.

Schwartz, Stephen. *Godspell*. Milwaukee, WI: Hal Leonard, 1971.

———. *Wicked*. Unpublished score, 2004.

Sculatti, Gene. *100 Best Selling Albums of the 60s*. New York: Barnes and Noble Books, 2004.

Sears, Ann. "The Coming of the Musical Play." In *The Cambridge Companion to the
    Musical*. Edited by William A. Everett and Paul R. Laird. Cambridge: Cambridge
    University Press, 2002, pp. 120–36.

Secrest, Meryle. *Stephen Sondheim: A Life*. New York: Alfred A. Knopf, 1998.

Shapiro, Henry D. "How Region Changed Its Meaning and Appalachia Changed Its Standing in the Twentieth Century." In *Bridging Southern Cultures: An Interdisciplinary Approach*. Edited by John Lowe. Baton Rouge: Louisiana State University Press, 2005.

Shepherd, John. *Tin Pan Alley*. London: Routledge and Kegan Paul, 1982.

Shimer, Genevieve, and Kate van Winkle. *The Playford Ball: 103 Early Country Dances*. Chicago: A Cappella Books and the Country Dance and Song Society, 1990.

Show Business: The Road to Broadway. Directed by Dori Berinstein, 2007. Liberation Entertainment DVD release, 2007.

Siegel, Marcia B. "Bridging the Critical Distance." In *The Routledge Dance Studies Reader*. Edited by Alexandra Carter. London: Routledge, 1998, pp. 91–97.

Silverman, Kaja. *The Acoustic Mirror: The Female Voice in Psychoanalysis and Cinema*. Bloomington: Indiana University Press, 1988.

Simon, Lucy, and Marsha Norman. *The Secret Garden*. Miami, FL: Warner Brothers Publications, 1991.

Simon, Robert. "Jerome Kern." *Modern Music* 6.2 (January–February 1929): 20–25.

Simonson, Robert. "John Doyle's Malicious Musicians: A Chat with the Director." *New York Sun* (October 31, 2005): Arts and Letters, 10.

Simond, Ike. *Old Slack's Reminiscence and Pocket History of the Colored Profession from 1865 to 1891*. [1891] Reprint edition. Bowling Green, OH: Popular Press, 1974.

Singer, Barry. *Ever After: The Last Years of Musical Theater and Beyond*. New York: ApplauseTheatre and Cinema Books, 2004.

Smith, Cecil, and Glenn Litton. *Musical Comedy in America*. New York: Theatre Arts Books, 1950 and 1981.

Smith, Ronn. *American Set Design 2*. New York: Theatre Communications Group, 1991.

Snelson, John. *Andrew Lloyd Webber*. New Haven: Yale University Press, 2004.

Sontag, Susan. "Notes on Camp." In her *Against Interpretation and Other Essays*. New York: Dell, 1966 (originally published in *Partisan Review* 31.4 [Fall 1964]).

Spewack, Samuel, and Bella Spewack. "Introduction: How to Write a Musical Comedy: An Esoteric Analysis of a New Art Form." In *Kiss Me, Kate*. New York: Knopf, 1953, pp. vii–xix.

Stacey, Jackie. *Star Gazing: Hollywood Cinema and Female Spectatorship*. London: Routledge, 1994.

Staiger, Janet. "Seeing Stars." In *Stardom: Industry of Desire*. Edited by Christine Gledhill. London: Routledge, 1991, pp. 3–16.

Stanfield, Peter. "From the Vulgar to the Refined: American Vernacular and Blackface Minstrelsy in *Show Boat*." In *Musicals: Hollywood and Beyond*. Edited by Bill Marshall and Robynn Stilwell. Exeter: Intellect, 2000, pp. 147–56.

Stearns, Marshall, and Jean Stearns. *Jazz Dance*. New York: Macmillan, 1968.

Stern, Lawrence. *School and Community Theater Management: A Handbook for Survival*. Boston: Allyn and Bacon, 1979.

Sternfeld, Jessica. *The Megamusical*. Bloomington: Indiana University Press, 2006.

———. "The Megamusical: Revolution on Broadway in the 1970s and 80s." Ph.D. dissertation, Princeton University, 2002.

Stevens, Gary, and Alan George. *The Longest Line: Broadway's Most Singular Sensation, A Chorus Line*. New York: Applause Books, 1995.

Steyn, Mark. *Broadway Babies Say Goodnight: Musicals Then and Now*. New York: Routledge, 1999.

Stilwell, Robynn J. "It May Look Like a Living Room…: The Musical Number and the Sitcom," *Echo* 5.1 (Spring 2003). http://www.humnet.ucla.edu/echo/volume5-issue1/stilwell/stilwell1.html, accessed May 10, 2011.

———. "Music of the Youth Revolution: Rock through the 1960s." In *The Cambridge History of Twentieth-Century Music*. Edited by Nicholas Cook and Anthony Pople. Cambridge: Cambridge University Press, 2004, pp. 418–52.

Stone, Lawrence. "The Revival of Narrative: Reflections on a New Old History." *Past and Present* 85 (November 1979): 3–24.

Stratyner, Barbara. *Ned Wayburn and the Dance Routine: From Vaudeville to the Ziegfeld Follies*. Studies in Dance History No. 13. Madison: University of Wisconsin Press for the Society of Dance Scholars, 1996.

Strouse, Charles, and Lee Adams. *Bye Bye Birdie*. New York: Strada Music, 1960.

Subotnik, Rose Rosengard. "Shoddy Equipment for Living? Deconstructing the Tin Pan Alley Song." *Musicological Identities: Essays in Honor of Susan McClary*. Edited by Steven Baur, Raymond Knapp, and Jacqueline Warwick. Aldershot, UK: Ashgate, 2008, pp. 205–18.

Suskin, Steven. *More Opening Nights on Broadway: A Critical Quotebook of the Musical Theatre 1965 through 1981*. New York: Schirmer, 1997.

———. *Opening Night on Broadway: A Critical Quotebook of the Golden Era of the Musical Theatre*, Oklahoma! *(1943) to* Fiddler on the Roof *(1964)*. New York: Schirmer Books, 1990.

———. *The Sound of Broadway Music: A Book of Orchestrators and Orchestrations*. New York: Oxford University Press, 2009.

Swados, Elizabeth. *At Play: Teaching Teenagers Theater*. New York: Faber and Faber, 2006.

Swain, Joseph P. *The Broadway Musical: A Critical and Musical Survey*. 2nd ed. Lanham, MD: Scarecrow Press, 2002.

Swayne, Steven. "Hearing Sondheim's Voices." Ph.D. dissertation, University of California, Berkeley, 1999.

———. *How Sondheim Found His Sound*. Ann Arbor: University of Michigan Press, 2008.

Symonds, Dominic. "The Corporeality of Musical Expression: 'The Grain of the Voice' and the Actor-Musician." *Studies in Musical Theatre* 1.2 (2007): 167–81.

Taitte, W. L. "Tarts of Gold." *Texas Monthly* (June 1978): 132.

Taruskin, Richard. *Text and Act: Essays on Music and Performance*. New York: Oxford University Press, 1995.

Taylor, John Russell, and Arthur Jackson. *The Hollywood Musical*. New York: McGraw-Hill, 1971.

Thomas, Frank, and Frank Johnston. *Disney Animation: The Illusion of Life*. New York: Abbeville Press, 1981.

Tinkcom, Matthew. "'Working Like a Homosexual': Camp Visual Codes and the Labor of Gay Subjects in the MGM Freed Unit." In *Hollywood Musicals: The Film Reader*. Edited by Steven Cohan. London: Routledge, 2002, pp. 115–28.

Toll, Robert C. *Blacking Up: The Minstrel Show in Nineteenth-Century America*. New York: Oxford University Press, 1974.

Tomassini, Anthony. "Pipe Down! We Can Hardly Hear You." *New York Times* (January 1, 2006): 2–1.

Toohey, John L. *A History of the Pulitzer Prize Plays*. New York: Citadel Press, 1967.

Treitler, Leo. "The Present as History." *Perspectives of New Music* 7.2 (Spring–Summer 1969): 1–58.

Tucker, Mark, ed. "RD Darell Criticism in the *Phonograph Monthly Review* (1927–1931)." *The Duke Ellington Reader*. New York: Oxford University Press, 1995.

Tucker, Sophie. *Some of These Days: The Autobiography of Sophie Tucker*. Garden City, NY: Doubleday, Doran, 1945.

U.S. Department of Education. "No Child Left Behind Act." 2001. http://www.ed.gov/policy/elsec/leg/esea02/index.html (accessed September 11, 2009).

Vaill, Amanda. *Somewhere: The Life of Jerome Robbins*. New York: Broadway Books, 2006.

van de Water, Manon and Annie Giannini. "Gay and Lesbian Theatre for Young People, or The Representation of 'Troubled Youth'" in *We Will Be Citizens: New Essays on Gay and Lesbian Theatre*. Edited by James Fisher. Jefferson, NC: McFarland, 2008, pp. 103–22.

Verley, Joy. *An Essential Manual for High-School Theater Directors: How to Structure and Organize a Youth Theater Program*. Portsmouth, NH: Smith and Kraus, 2001.

Vogel, Frederick G. *Hollywood Musicals Nominated for Best Picture*. Edited by Mary Vogel. Jefferson, NC: McFarland, 2003.

Wald, Elijah. *How the Beatles Destroyed Rock'n' Roll: An Alternative History of American Popular Music*. New York: Oxford University Press, 2009.

Walker, Alexander. *Stardom: The Hollywood Phenomenon*. London: Michael Joseph, 1970.

Walker, Don. "Music Goes 'Round: A Gentleman Who Arranges Theatre Tunes Tells How He Works." *New York Times* (April 12, 1942): X-1.

———. "Who Says 'Arranger'?" *Theatre Arts* 34.11 (November 1950): 53–54.

Wall, Carey. "There's No Business Like Show Business: A Speculative Reading of the Broadway Musical." In *Approaches to the American Musical*. Edited by Robert Lawson-Peebles. Exeter: University of Exeter Press, 1996, pp. 24–43.

Walsh, David, and Len Platt. *Musical Theater and American Culture*. Westport, CT: Greenwood, 2003.

Walsh, Michael. *Andrew Lloyd Webber: His Life and Works*. Updated and enlarged ed. New York: HarperCollins, 1989.

Wayburn, Ned. *The Art of Stage Dancing: The Story of a Beautiful and Profitable Profession*. New York: Belvedere, 1980.

Weber, Bruce. "Renewing the Lease on the Innocence of Youth" *New York Times* (August 18, 2000): E2.

Weber, William. "Beyond Zeitgeist: Recent Work in Music History." *Journal of Modern History* 66.2 (June 1994): 321–25.

Wells, Paul. *Understanding Animation*. London: Routledge, 1998.

Whedon, Joss. "Liner Notes." *Buffy the Vampire Slayer: Once More, with Feeling, Original Cast Album*. Rounder Records 1166190582, 2002.

White Christmas. Directed by Michael Curtiz. Choreographed by Robert Alton. Los Angeles: Paramount Pictures, 1954. DVD release, 2007.

White, Hayden. *Metahistory: The Historical Imagination in Nineteenth-Century Europe*. Baltimore: Johns Hopkins University Press, 1973.

Whiteley, Nigel. "Toward a Throw-Away Culture: Consumerism, 'Style Obsolesence' and Cultural Theory in the 1950s and 1960s." *Oxford Art Journal* 10.2 "The 60s" (1987): 3–27.

Whittaker, Jim. *Cosmic Light: The Birth of a Cult Classic*. Altoona, PA: Acme Books, 1998.

Wilder, Alec. *American Popular Song: The Great Innovators, 1900–1950*. Edited by James T. Maher. New York: Oxford University Press, 1990 (originally published 1972).

Wilk, Max. *Oh! The Story of Oklahoma!: A Celebration of America's Most Loved Musical*. New York: Applause, 2002, 1993.

Willett, Ralph. "From Gold Diggers to Bar Girls: A Selective History of the American Movie Musical." In *Approaches to the American Musical*. Edited by Robert Lawson-Peebles. Exeter: University of Exeter Press, 1996, pp. 44–54.

Willson, Meredith. *The Music Man*. New York: Frank Music, and Rinimer, 1958.

Wilson, Carl. *Let's Talk about Love: A Journey to the End of Taste*. New York: Continuum International, 2007.

Wind, Herbert Warren. "Profiles: Another Opening, Another Show." *New Yorker* (17 November 1951): 46–73.

Winer, Laurie. "Theater; Orchestrators Are Tired of Playing Second Fiddle." *New York Times* (July 29, 1990): 2–5.

Wolf, Stacy. *Changed for Good: A Feminist History of the Broadway Musical*. New York: Oxford University Press, 2011.

———. "'Defying Gravity': Queer Conventions in the Musical *Wicked*." *Theatre Journal* 60.1 (2007): 1–21.

———. "In Defense of Pleasure: Musical Theatre History in the Liberal Arts [A Manifesto]." *Theatre Topics* 17.1 (March 2007): 51–60.

———. *A Problem Like Maria: Gender and Sexuality in the American Musical*. Ann Arbor: University of Michigan Press, 2002.

———. "'Something Better than This': *Sweet Charity* and the Feminist Utopia of Broadway Musicals." *Modern Drama* 47.2 (Summer 2004): 309–32.

———. "'We'll Always Be Bosom Buddies': Female Duets and the Queering of Broadway Musical Theatre." *GLQ: A Journal of Lesbian and Gay Studies* 12.3 (2006): 351–76.

———. "*Wicked* Divas, Musical Theater, and Internet Girl Fans." *Camera Obscura 65* 22.2 (2007): 39–71.

Woll, Allen L. *Black Musical Theatre: From* Coontown *to* Dreamgirls. Baton Rouge: Louisiana State University Press, 1989.

———. *The Hollywood Musical Goes to War*. Chicago: Nelson-Hall, 1983.

Wollman, Elizabeth L. *Hard Times: The Adult Musical in New York City*. New York: Oxford University Press, forthcoming.

———. *The Theater Will Rock: A History of the Rock Musical, from Hair to Hedwig*. Ann Arbor: University of Michigan Press, 2006.

Womack, Kenneth, and Todd F. Davis. *Reading the Beatles: Cultural Studies, Literary Criticism, and the Fab Four*. Albany: State University of New York Press, 2006.

Wood, Graham. "Distant Cousin or Fraternal Twin? Analytical Approaches to the Film Musical." In *The Cambridge Companion to the Musical*. Edited by William A. Everett and Paul R. Laird. Cambridge: Cambridge University Press, 2002, pp. 212–30.

"Working in the Theatre." Online seminars. The American Theatre Wing. http://americantheatrewing.org/wit (accessed September 8, 2009).

Yeston, Maury. "The Lullaby of Broadway." *New York Times* (February 28, 2003): A-25.

Young, John Wray. *Community Theatre: A Manual for Success*. New York: Samuel French, 1971.

Zadan, Craig. *Sondheim & Co.* 2nd ed. New York: Perennial Library, 1989.

Ziegfeld, Richard, and Paulette Ziegfeld. *The Ziegfeld Touch: The Life and Times of Florenz Ziegfeld, Jr*. New York: Harry N. Abrams 1993.

Zipes, Jack. "Breaking the Disney Spell." In *From Mouse to Mermaid: The Politics of Film, Gender and Culture*. Edited by Elizabeth Bell, Lynda Haas, and Laura Sells. Bloomington: Indiana University Press, 1995.

———. *Happily Ever After: Fairy Tales, Children and the Culture Industry*. New York: Routledge, 1997.

INDEX

. . . .

Note: Page numbers in *italics* indicate photographs.

CPSIA information can be obtained at www.ICGtesting.com
Printed in the USA
BVOW060301120313

315307BV00005B/12/P